A Guide to the Leasehol
Housing and Urban Develop

A Guide to the Leasehold Reform, Housing and Urban Development Act 1993

Paul Matthews, LLB, BCL, Solicitor
Visiting Senior Lecturer, King's College, London

Denzil Millichap, LLB, LLM
Member of the Planning and Environmental Law Unit
of Linklaters & Paines

Butterworths
London, Dublin, Edinburgh
1993

United Kingdom	Butterworth & Co (Publishers) Ltd, 88 Kingsway, LONDON WC2B 6AB and 4 Hill Street, EDINBURGH EH2 3JZ
Australia	Butterworths, SYDNEY, MELBOURNE, BRISBANE, ADELAIDE, PERTH, CANBERRA and HOBART
Belgium	Butterworth & Co (Publishers) Ltd, BRUSSELS
Canada	Butterworth Canada Ltd, TORONTO and VANCOUVER
Ireland	Butterworth (Ireland) Ltd, DUBLIN
Malaysia	Malayan Law Journal Sdn Bhd, KUALA LUMPUR
New Zealand	Butterworths of New Zealand Ltd, WELLINGTON and AUCKLAND
Puerto Rico	Equity de Puerto Rico, Inc, HATO REY
Singapore	Butterworths Asia, SINGAPORE
USA	Butterworth Legal Publishers, AUSTIN, Texas; BOSTON, Massachusetts; CLEARWATER, Florida (D & S Publishers); ORFORD, New Hampshire (Equity Publishing); ST PAUL, Minnesota; and SEATTLE, Washington

The right of Paul Matthews and Denzil Millichap to be identified as the authors of this book has been asserted.

A CIP catalogue record for this book is available from the British Library.

ISBN 0 406 02650 5

Typeset by Doublestruck Limited, London
Printed and bound in Great Britain by Latimer Trend & Company Ltd, Plymouth

Preface

'Why so large cost, having so short a lease
Dost thou upon thy fading mansion spend?'

William Shakespeare, Sonnet 146

Answer: Because I can *enfranchise*. If anything encapsulates the motivation behind the Leasehold Reform, Housing and Urban Development Act 1993, it is this couplet from one of Shakespeare's more morbid sonnets. The assumption is that the best use of residential property will be made if long term control of it lies in the hands of those who live there. Hence the right to buy, the right of first refusal, and leasehold enfranchisement, amongst other things. In the public sector, as in the private, every encouragement is offered to residents to put their own money in place of the public's, and to give them more say over their own homes. Even in the planning sector it is clear that the objective is not more public money, but better use of that currently available.

The 1993 Act is really three Acts in one. First, it extends leasehold enfranchisement principles from houses to flats, and gives further rights to private sector residential leaseholders generally. Secondly, it makes significant changes to public sector housing law, that strange junction where landlord and tenant, social welfare and local government finance all meet in an ungodly jumble. Thirdly, it streamlines existing urban regeneration procedures in the planning and development fields by introducing a new central government body, the Urban Regeneration Agency.

In this book we have attempted to provide a guide to all three parts. As with all new law, we cannot describe how it will work in practice. In order to assist the reader, therefore, we have referred copiously to earlier legislation on which provisions of this Act are based. Case law, particularly that prompting legislative change, has also been noted where appropriate. Furthermore, since the House of Lords in *Pepper v Hart* [1993] 1 All ER 42 removed the blinkers that formerly prevented lawyers from looking at Parliamentary materials as an aid to construction, we have given detailed references to the debates. For this purpose we have looked at all the relevant reports in *Hansard* and the Committees, an immensely distressing exercise which we would not wish to inflict on anyone else.

Our thanks are due to a number of people who have helped in the production of this work. Julie-Ann Cole typed most of the book at a time of great pressure of other work. Heather Prior carried out basic research and collated materials in relation to Chapter 12. Peter Robson was kind enough to comment on a draft of Chapter 11, and prevented the perpetration of a number of errors. We are also grateful to editorial staff at Butterworths who have worked so hard to make this book happen so soon after Royal Assent.

The first-named author was responsible for Chapters 1 to 11, and the second-named for Chapter 12. The time constraints under which we have worked mean that some areas of the new law have not been covered as fully as we would have liked. We ask our readers to excuse such imperfections, and hope that they do not think of this book as Lord Westbury LC thought of title deeds, namely 'difficult to read, disgusting to touch, and impossible to understand'.

Paul Matthews
Denzil Millichap
9 August 1993

Contents

Table of statutes

References in this Tables to *Statutes* are to Halsbury's Statutes of England (Fourth Edition) showing the volume and page at which the annotated text of an Act may be found.

Table of cases

1 Introduction

GENERAL

1.1 Everyone in the property and housing law fields has heard of the new Leasehold Reform, Housing and Urban Development Act, which received Royal Assent on 20 July 1993. In places politically controversial (even amongst the Government's own supporters), wide-ranging and enormously complicated, this Act seems set to change the face of long leasehold residential property even more radically than the Leasehold Reform Act 1967 did more than a quarter of a century ago. It marks another stage in the Government's attempts to 'privatise' and 'individualise' housing stock, encouraging residents to take more responsibility for their homes, and diminishing the importance of both private and public landlords. At the same time, the state is to intervene in certain urban situations where the present authorities have been unable or unwilling (for whatever reasons) to take steps to revive the area.

1.2 Property lawyers and other professionals (such as surveyors, local government officers, and so on) need a guide to the new complexities. It is the purpose of this book to fulfil those needs, as well to provide a reference work for the future. After a general introduction to the Act in this chapter, Chapters 2–8 cover Part I of the Act, Chapters 9–11 cover Part II, and Chapter 12 covers Part III. The Appendix contains the full text of the Act, each section being cross-referenced for easy reference to its discussion in the relevant chapter.

PART I

Collective enfranchisement

1.3 The most significant reform made by this Act is the new right of collective enfranchisement for private sector tenants holding under long leases, enabling them through nominees to buy the (collective) freeholds of their blocks. This goes much further than Part III of the Landlord and Tenant Act 1987 (which only conferred a right of first refusal), and may be compared with the position in the public sector, where properties subject to secure tenancies may be transferred wholesale to the private sector pursuant to Part IV of the Housing Act 1988. Much of the scheme of collective enfranchisement is drawn from the procedures enacted in the Leasehold Reform Act 1967 and also in the 1988 Act. Chapter 2 discusses the qualifications and conditions for collective enfranchisement in detail, and Chapter 3 sets out the procedure to be followed.

Individual enfranchisement

1.4   Where collective enfranchisement for some reason does not apply, an individual long leaseholder in the private sector may be able to extend his lease by a further 90 years, for a market consideration. This new leasehold right is dealt with in Chapter 4.

Leasehold Reform Act 1967

1.5   The most politically controversial provisions of this Act are not a self-contained code, but are in fact merely amendments to the Leasehold Reform Act 1967. They remove rateable and other value limits previously imposed under the 1967 Act. As a result, the most valuable houses are for the first time brought within the 'individual enfranchisement' rights of the 1967 Act, and leaseholders are enabled to acquire the freeholds of their houses (but not to extend their leases). Certain other amendments to the 1967 Act (including negativing an anti-avoidance scheme) are also made. This is explained in Chapter 5.

Estate management schemes

1.6   In order to mitigate any damage to large estates that might result from their fragmentation, current landlords will be able to apply for an order to enable them to retain powers of management in respect of properties they own in an area, even if they are then individually or collectively enfranchised. A scheme having similar objects formed part of the 1967 Act, but this new scheme is cast in a quite different form. It is the subject of Chapter 6.

Management audits

1.7   Residential long leaseholders, on the other hand, are enabled to require an audit of the landlord's management, to ensure that his management obligations are being discharged in an efficient and effective manner, and that service charges are being equally well applied. Chapter 7 deals with this.

Other private sector matters

1.8   Various other matters connected with private sector residential leases are discussed in Chapter 8. These include the provisions of the Act bringing more tenants within the scope of Part III of the Landlord and Tenant Act 1987 (right of first refusal), enabling the Secretary of State to approve codes of practice for residential property management, and conferring jurisdiction on leasehold valuation tribunals in relation to Crown land.

PART II

1.9   Significant reforms are also made by this Act to public sector housing law, in Part II. The most important of these reforms is the new 'right to acquire on rent to mortgage terms', permitting tenants to buy their homes in a completely new way.

This effectively replaces the unsatisfactory concept of the 'shared ownership lease' (which was in fact nothing of the kind), the right to defer completion and the right to a mortgage. Chapter 9 discusses this new right. Chapter 10 deals with other reforms of public sector housing law, including a new right to repair, the delegation by housing authorities of their housing management functions, and new arrangements for the disposal of local authority housing. Chapter 11 deals with the reforms so far as they relate to Scotland.

PART III

1.10   Part III of the Act seeks to streamline various initiatives aimed principally at the regeneration of derelict urban land. The provisions set up the Urban Regeneration Agency: its powers are largely modelled on those given to Urban Development Corporations under legislation from 1980. In addition to utilising compulsory purchase (and other land-acquisition powers) the Agency will also help new businesses by providing grant-aid as it takes over responsibility for the Derelict Land Grant and City Grant regimes currently operated by the Department of the Environment. The function of English Estates (arranging for the supply of commercial and industrial sites in certain inner city areas) is also given to the Agency. In areas designated by the Secretary of State for the Environment, the Agency will be able to exercise certain planning and highway functions. No extra funding is going to be made available: however, if private sector proposals are promoted with vigour and innovative funding there could be considerable activity in both urban and non-urban locations as the remit of the Agency is not limited to urban areas. It is a 'roving' regeneration and development agency whose potential impact is very considerable. Part III of the Act is covered in Chapter 12.

NOTICES

1.11   Many of the procedures set out in Part I of the Act depend on notices and counternotices being served by one party on another. Certain general provisions are made in respect of such notices, whichever procedure they form part of. Thus such notices *must* be in writing, and may be sent by post: s 99(1). The Secretary of State *may* make regulations to prescribe the form of notices under Part I, as well as the particulars which they must contain: s 99(6).

1.12   In relation to collective enfranchisement (Chapters 2–3) and the right to a new lease (Chapter 4) the Act goes further. Those procedures require landlords and tenants to specify addresses for service in England and Wales. Section 99(2) states that service at such address is valid, and moreover allows a new address to be substituted for the old one. The tenant may also serve his immediate landlord at any address furnished to him under the Landlord and Tenant Act 1987, s 48 (but this section does not apply to all landlords). If the landlord ought to have furnished such an address but has not, the tenant may serve notices on the landlord at the address stated in any rent demand, under s 47 of the 1987 Act: s 99(3). These service procedures apply also to legal proceedings under the collective enfranchisement and new lease provisions: s 99(4).

1.13   A notice given by a tenant or tenants under the collective enfranchisement or new lease procedures must be signed by or on behalf of the tenant or tenants in respect of whom it is given, *unless* it is the tenant's initial notice (under s 13 or s 42) when it must be signed personally by such tenant or tenants: s 99(5).

REGULATIONS

1.14   The Secretary of State has power to make orders or regulations under various provisions in Part I of the Act. With one exception, such orders and regulations are made by him subject to annulment, ie the negative resolution of *either* House of Parliament: s 100(2). The one exception is the power to make regulations prescribing the form and particulars of notices, which are not subject to any parliamentary procedure: s 100(2). The power to make regulations is exerciseable so as to make different provision for different cases or areas, and can include procedural, incidental, supplementary and transitional provisions: s 100(1).

COURTS AND TRIBUNALS

The county court

1.15   As is usual in legislation dealing with landlord and tenant matters, the jurisdiction conferred on the court by Part I of the Act is conferred almost exclusively on the county court: s 90(1). But the jurisdiction of the county court is extended to 'any question arising under or by virtue of' the provisions of Chapters I, II or VII of Part I, even if jurisdiction is not otherwise conferred on it by s 90(1), as long as it is not a question falling within the jurisdiction of a leasehold valuation tribunal under s 91: s 90(2). The High Court has jurisdiction in relation to matters in Part I only when they are joined with other proceedings otherwise within the jurisdiction of the High Court: s 90(3). Conversely, the county court hearing proceedings within its jurisdiction under Part I of this Act has jurisdiction over other proceedings joined with them, even though it would otherwise not have such jurisdiction: s 90(4).

1.16   Where a provision of Chapter I or II imposes a requirement on a person, but this is not complied with by him, then any person interested may apply to the county court for an order requiring him to make good the default within a specified time: s 92(1). But the intended applicant must have given notice to the intended respondent at least 14 days previously, requiring him to make good the default: s 92(2).

Leasehold valuation tribunals[1]

1.17   Where there are disputes about the valuation of property or interests in property, or the terms on which the property should be acquired or leased, Part I of this Act confers jurisdiction to deal with such disputes upon 'leasehold valuation tribunals'. In fact, there is no such animal.[2] What *do* exist are rent assessment committees, constituted under the Rent Act 1977, Sch 10. These are specialist tribunals comprising lawyers, valuers and others. They deal with rent references under the Rent Act 1977, Part IV (protected tenancies) and the Housing Act 1988,

Part I (assured tenancies). When rent tribunals under the Rent Act 1977, Part V (restricted contracts) were abolished in 1980, their functions were transferred to rent assessment committees under the Housing Act 1980, s 72(2). In exercising such functions, a rent assessment committee is known as a rent tribunal: Housing Act 1980, s 72(3). The 1980 Act, by s 142, also transferred the valuation functions of the Lands Tribunal under the Leasehold Reform Act 1967, s 21, to rent assessment committees, but provided that in exercising such functions rent assessment committees should be known as leasehold valuation tribunals. Valuation functions under the Landlord and Tenant Act 1987, ss 13 (right of first refusal) and 31 (compulsory acquisition) were also conferred on rent assessment committees, again to be known, when exercising such functions, as leasehold valuation tribunals.

1 For parliamentary debates, see HC Standing Committee B, 26 November 1992, cols 320–324; HC, 9 February 1993, col 931; HL Committee, 22 March 1993, cols 152–153; HL Report, 20 May 1993, cols 1887–1888.
2 See the discussion in HC Standing Committee B, 26 November 1992, cols 292–294.

1.18   The 1993 Act, Part I, continues this process. The jurisdiction stated to be conferred on leasehold valuation tribunals is to be exercised by rent assessment committees constituted under the Rent Act 1977, Sch 10 (ss 91(1), 101(1)), and rent assessment committees when so acting are to be known as leasehold valuation tribunals: s 91(3). By s 91(2), the jurisdiction is not confined to the specific matters referred to in Part I, but also extends to disputes as to:

(a)   terms of acquisition in collective or individual enfranchisement cases;
(b)   terms of any leaseback arrangement in collective enfranchisement;
(c)   other payments to be made or costs to be paid (or a portion) in respect of either collective or individual enfranchisements.

1.19   Certain of the procedural provisions relating to rent assessment committees (sitting as leasehold valuation tribunals) under the Housing Act 1980, Sch 22, are applied to leasehold valuation tribunals under the 1993 Act (s 91(10)), but the form of and particulars to be contained in any application to a leasehold valuation tribunal may be prescribed by the Secretary of State: s 91(6). In proceedings relating to collective enfranchisement the participating tenants are not to be parties, as their interests are represented by the nominee purchaser (as to which see para 2.41): s 91(7). Costs incurred in relation to leasehold valuation tribunal proceedings are not recoverable by any party: s 91(8), and see also paras 3.86, 4.98.

Transfers between courts and leasehold valuation tribunals

1.20   A court faced with a question falling within the jurisdiction of a leasehold valuation tribunal under the collective or individual enfranchisment provisions *must* transfer the proceedings so far as they relate to that question to a leasehold valuation tribunal: s 91(4)(a). It can adjourn or dispose of the remainder of the proceedings as it thinks fit: s 91(4)(b). If the question is one relating to a matter to be decided by the court, then once the leasehold valuation tribunal has decided it, the court must give effect to that decision in its order: s 91(4). Power is conferred on the Secretary of State to make regulations for the procedure of leasehold valuation tribunals, and on the court rules committees to make rules of court, in each case in connection with such transfers: s 91(5).

'Becomes final'

1.21   There are frequent references in Part I to court orders or tribunal decisions 'becoming final'. If the order or decision is not appealed, then this occurs when the time for bringing an appeal has expired (s 101(9)(a)), even though it is usually possible with leave to bring an appeal out of time.[1] If an appeal (or a further appeal) is made and abandoned, or otherwise ceases to have effect, then the order or decision becomes final at that time: s 101(9)(b)(ii). If an appeal is made and fails (and any further appeals similarly) then the order or decision becomes final when the appeal is determined (if it is a final appeal) or when time for bringing any further appeal has expired (if it is not): s 101(9)(b)(i).

---

1   See *Hill & Redman*, **D** [952].

CROWN LAND

1.22   For this purpose, land is 'Crown land' if the Crown has an interest in it. 'Crown' includes the Crown Estates, the Duchies of Lancaster and Cornwall, and Government departments: s 94(11). Under the Leasehold Reform Act 1967 the immediate tenant or subtenant of the Crown has no right to obtain the freehold and has only a limited right to obtain an extended lease: para 8.6. Although a tenant or subtenant might or might not have a legal *right* to acquire the freehold or an extended lease, Crown practice has been *voluntarily* to permit freehold enfranchisement and extension of leases on the same basis as under the Act, unless special circumstances apply: para 8.6.

1.23   At the level of strict legal rights (as opposed to voluntary action by the Crown) the collective and individual enfranchisement provisions of this Act are restricted in their application to Crown land in the same way as are those in the Leasehold Reform Act 1967. Section 94(1)–(5) of the 1993 Act was based on s 33 of the 1967 Act, and makes similar provision. Thus, where the Crown has at any time been the tenant's immediate or superior landlord the tenant will have no right to enfranchise under this Act unless the Crown has ceased to have any such interest: s 94(1). The only exception to this is where the Crown is the superior landlord and consents to a new lease (under Chapter II of Part I) or the immediate landlord has a sufficient interest to grant such a lease without reference to the Crown: s 96(2). There are various special provisions relating to the powers of the Crown Estate Commissioners, the Duchy of Lancaster and the Duchy of Cornwall, corresponding to those in the Leasehold Reform Act 1967: s 94(3)–(5).

Leasehold valuation tribunal jurisdiction

1.24   As with the 1967 Act, the Crown by ministerial statement has voluntarily undertaken to abide by the collective individual enfranchisement provisions in the Act even though they do not strictly apply to most Crown properties: para 8.6. But the technical inapplicability of these provisions means that when a dispute arises between the parties which would have been referred to a leasehold valuation tribunal in the ordinary way, prima facie the tribunal has no jurisdiction to deal with it. The same problem arose in relation to the Leasehold Reform Act 1967 and it has now been solved (in this Act) by conferring jurisdiction on a rent assessment committee sitting as a leasehold valuation tribunal, by agreement of the parties: see para 8.7. For the collective and individual enfranchisement provisions of this Act, parallel provision is made by s 94(9), (10). Thus the Crown and the other parties involved may in essence *agree* to confer jurisdiction upon the tribunal to decide questions arising in connection with the acquisition of the freehold or the grant of a new lease.

Estate management schemes

1.25   As will be seen, provision is made by the 1993 Act, Part I, Chapter IV, to enable landlords and others to exercise certain management powers over estates despite enfranchisement. Special provision is made by s 94(6)–(8) of the Act for the case where the Crown is interested in the estate concerned. It enables the Crown to make the appropriate application to a leasehold valuation tribunal for an estate management order, even though the tenants acquiring the freeholds in the area do so under the voluntary scheme already referred to: s 94(7). However, not all the estate management scheme provisions in Part I, Chapter IV apply: s 94(8).

EXTENT OF THE ACT

England and Wales

1.26   Part I, Chapter I of Part II and Part III of the Act extend to England and Wales: s 188(4). If the Secretary of State does not by statutory instrument order otherwise, Part I of the Act will apply to the Scilly Isles in the same way as it does to the rest of England and Wales. But he has power by order to make Part I apply thereto with such exceptions, adaptations and modifications as he may direct: s 103.

Scotland

1.27   Chapter II of Part II (Scottish public sector housing law) applies to Scotland only: s 188(5). In addition, ss 174, 179 and 180 and Sch 17, para 8 (amendment of House of Commons Disqualification Act 1975) apply to Scotland as they do to England and Wales: s 188(6).

Northern Ireland

1.28   Only Sch 17, para 8 (amendment to House of Commons Disqualification Act 1975), Sch 21, para 3 (amendment to Parliamentary Commissioner Act 1967), and certain repeals extend to Northern Ireland: s 188(6)(b), (7).

COMMENCEMENT

1.29   Certain provisions came into force on the Royal Assent being given, ie 20 July 1993: ss 126–127, 135–140, 149–151, 181(1), (2), (4), 186, 188 and the repeal in the Local Government and Housing Act 1989, s 80(1): s 188(2). The remaining provisions, the bulk of the Act, come into force when so appointed by the Secretary of State by statutory instrument: s 188(2). In view of the need for various regulations and orders to be in place before the new rights and procedures can be made effective, this is considered unlikely to be before November 1993.

OTHER GENERAL PROVISIONS

1.30   There are the usual provisions relating to public expenditure (s 186), the various consequential amendments and repeals made by the Act (s 187; Schs 21, 22) and the short title to the Act: s 188(1).

INTERPRETATION

Defined terms

1.31   Because the three parts of this Act each deal with separate subject matter, it is more than usually difficult to use defined terms throughout. There are definition sections in various places, but it is not always easy to find the one that you need. For completeness, a list of the various definition sections is given here:

(i)   interpretation of Part I, Chapter I: s 38;
(ii) interpretation of Part I, Chapter II: s 62;
(iii) interpretation of Part I, Chapter V: s 84;
(iv) general interpretation of Part I: s 101;
(v)   interpretation of Part III: s 185.

An alphabetical table of defined terms has been included at the end of the book, to enable readers to find the required definition quickly.

Statutory precedent

1.32   Many of the provisions in Parts I and II of this Act are based on provisions in earlier statutes, such as the Landlord and Tenant Act 1954, the Leasehold Reform Act 1967, the Landlord and Tenant Act 1987, and the Housing Act 1988. The provisions in Part III are based upon legislation setting up urban development corporations, namely the Local Government Planning and Land Act 1980, Part XVI. In some cases particular words or phrases have been the subject of judicial decisions which may be helpful in construing the wording of the present Act. Accordingly, to assist the researcher, references are given in the text or footnote to 'predecessor' provisions where possible and appropriate.

Use of parliamentary materials

1.33   The recent decision of the House of Lords in *Pepper v Hart* [1993] 1 All ER 42, [1992] 3 WLR 1032 has completely changed the position regarding the use of parliamentary materials (and in particular records of debates) in the interpretation of statutes. The old rule was that reference to parliamentary material as an aid to statutory construction was not permissible: *Davis v Johnson* [1979] AC 264, [1978]

1 All ER 1132, HL; *Hadmore Productions Limited v Hamilton* [1983] 1 AC 191, [1982] 1 All ER 1042, HL.

1.34 Six out of seven law lords in *Pepper v Hart* held that reference to *certain* parliamentary material as an aid to construction was now to be permitted, where the legislation concerned was ambiguous or obscure, or the literal meaning led to absurdity. But the only material to which reference is henceforth to be allowed is *clear* statements by a minister, or other promoter of the Bill leading to the enactment in question, together with any other parliamentary material needed to understand such statements. It may be assumed that where a clause or other amendment is inserted in a Bill at the instance of another person (ie not the Government or promoter of the Bill) the clear statement concerned would have to be that of the promoter of the clause or amendment involved.

1.35 Lord Mackay of Clashfern LC dissented on the basis of the increased effort and cost involved, because:

> 'In practically every case it will be incumbent on those preparing the argument to examine the whole proceedings on the Bill in question in both Houses of Parliament' (at p 48).

The other law lords disagreed, considering that this would only be necessary in rare cases. Only time will tell who was right. To facilitate research, in this book references have been given to the parliamentary debates on the Bill, broken down by subject matter. Nearly every chapter of the book contains a footnote on the first page listing the debates relevant to the subject matter of that chapter.

1.36 A few points on parliamentary procedure, some general and some specific, can be made for the benefit of the intending researcher. First, as is commonly known, First Readings of Government Bills are purely formal and nothing is said about their content. Accordingly, no references are given to the First Reading in either House of Parliament. Second, Second Readings are concerned with the general principles of the Bill, rather than with detail. It is therefore unlikely that a helpful ministerial statement will be found on a point of detail in a Second Reading debate. Third, the most detailed discussion of proposed legislation takes place in committee. Although the debates on this Act at House of Lords committee stage are contained in House of Lords *Hansard* (because the committee was a committee of the whole House), the debates at House of Commons committee stage are not to be found in House of Commons *Hansard*, but in an entirely different series of reports altogether, because the committee stage of the Bill was entrusted to Standing Committee B. Not many libraries keep parliamentary debates anyway,[1] but, of those who do, few keep the reports of standing committee debates.[2] Fourth, it is a feature of this Act that a very significant number of amendments were made, and new clauses were added, at a late stage in its passage, in particular at the Report and Third Reading stages in the House of Lords. Indeed, in some cases amendments were then made (with Government assent) that ministers had opposed in the House of Commons or at early stages in the Lords.

---

1   In London, these include the libraries of the Law Society, University College London, the University of London (Senate House), the four Inns of Court, the Guildhall Library and Westminster Central Reference Library.
2   Of those libraries in the previous note, only Lincoln's Inn (from 1986–87), Senate House, Guildhall and Westminster Central Reference keep them.

2 The right to collective enfranchisement: concepts and qualifications

INTRODUCTION

The problems of leasehold tenure

2.1 The single most important change to English housing law wrought by the 1993 Act is the introduction of the right of long leaseholders of flats collectively to acquire the freehold from their landlords, so called 'collective enfranchisement'. The purpose of this change is to meet two perceived main problems with long leasehold tenure of flats. First, a lease is a wasting asset, and becomes increasingly difficult to mortgage, thus affecting the property market and population mobility. Second, not all landlords are good landlords. Some are difficult to contact, some fail to carry out repairing and other obligations, and some overcharge for services.[1] If the leaseholders acquire the freehold, they can grant themselves new leases (solving the first problem) and run their own management services (solving the second).

1 See HL 2R, 3 November 1992, col 152 per Michael Howard QC MP, Secretary of State for the Environment.

Partial solutions

2.2 Similar problems in relation to *houses* were addressed a generation ago in the Leasehold Reform Act 1967. Certain leaseholders of houses obtained the right to buy their freehold. But that Act did not apply to flats. Aspects of the second problem (poor landlords) have been addressed from time to time, and there are detailed legislative provisions concerning service charges,[1] the appointment of managers by the courts,[2] and even – but only in the most severe cases – the right of compulsory acquisition of the landlord's interest.[3] Apart from the case of the seriously defaulting landlord, the only step hitherto in the direction of addressing the first problem has been the introduction of a right of first refusal, ie when the landlord wishes to sell his interest, he must first offer it to his long leaseholders.[4]

1 Landlord and Tenant Act 1985, ss 18–30; *Hill & Redman*, **A** [3495]–[3518].
2 Landlord and Tenant Act 1987, Part II; *Hill & Redman*, **A** [2798].
3 Landlord and Tenant Act 1987, Part III; *Hill & Redman*, **A** [2800].
4 Landlord and Tenant Act 1987, Part I; *Hill & Redman*, **A** [2796].

The 1993 Act

2.3 But now the 1993 Act has gone further, and has boldly conferred a right of compulsory collective acquisition of the freehold upon long leaseholders of flats.

The principles of collective enfranchisement were hotly debated in Parliament,[1] some Conservatives criticising it as 'a Socialist measure', 'expropriation'[2] and 'private compulsory purchase',[3] and describing its provisions for compensating landlords as 'robbery'. The Opposition stated that it supported the principle of collective enfranchisement, but said that it did not go far enough.[4] They regarded the Bill as an irrelevance in not contributing to the construction of more homes, the rehousing of the homeless or a reduction in unemployment.[5] They therefore voted against the Bill on Second Reading. In addition, complaint was made from all sides that the Bill did not seek to tackle leasehold problems by introducing commonhold tenure.[6] (Unsuccessful attempts were in fact made during the passage of the Bill to introduce commonhold into it.)[7]

---

1 For debates see HC 2R, 3 November 1992, cols 152–154; HC Standing Committee B, 10 November 1992, cols 10–38, 12 November 1992, cols 39–76, 17 November 1992, cols 77–135; HC Report, 9 February 1993, cols 878–887, 926–927; HL 2R, 23 February 1993, cols 85–87; HL Committee, 9 March 1993, cols 930–1058, 15 March 1993 cols 1228–1246, 1255–1271; HL Report, 11 May 1993, cols 1185–1205, 1216–1251, 1252–1272, 18 May 1993, cols 1651–1655; HL 3R, 25 May 1993, cols 175–204; HC Lords Amendments, 14 June 1993, cols 645–662; HL Commons Reason, 8 July 1993, cols 1522–1528.
2 HC Report, 9 February 1993, cols 835 and 836 per Sir J Wiggin MP.
3 HC Report, 9 February 1993, col 868 per Roger Evans MP.
4 HC 2R, 3 November 1992, col 153 per Jerry Wiggin MP.
5 HC 2R, 3 November 1992, cols 164–174 per Jack Straw MP.
6 HC 2R, 3 November 1992, cols 155 and 200 (Nick Raynsford MP), 182 (Nigel Jones MP), 185 (Dudley Fishburn MP), 195 (George Howarth MP), 198 (John Butterfill MP), 207 (Matthew Carrington MP), 212 (Nigel Waterson MP), 213 (Glenda Jackson MP).
7 See eg HC Standing Committee B, 1 December 1992, cols 339–370.

THE RIGHT

2.4   The right to collective enfranchisement is conferred by this Act on 'qualifying tenants' of 'flats' contained in certain 'premises' at the 'relevant date': s 1(1). The right is to have the freehold of the 'premises' (in practice the block) transferred to the tenants' 'nominee purchaser' at a price determined under the Act : s 1(1)(a), (b). The tenants are also entitled to have the freehold of certain other property transferred with the block, ie 'appurtenant property' demised by a lease held by a qualifying tenant, and other property which such a tenant is entitled to use in common with occupiers of other premises: s 1(2), (3). This will include garages, gardens and communal areas, which need not be contained in the block itself.

2.5   However, the right to acquire other property used in common can be satisfied by the granting of equivalent permanent rights: s 1(4). Nor need the tenants necessarily seek to acquire the whole of the premises which under the Act they would be entitled to, provided that what they seek to acquire is itself capable of collective enfranchisement: s 1(5). The right to collective enfranchisement also entitles tenants to have acquired by their nominee purchaser most (though not all) leasehold interests in the block which are intermediate between their own leases of the flats and the ultimate freehold interest: s 2. But the owner of an interest extending to underlying minerals may require such minerals to be excepted from the acquisition, if proper provision is made for the support of the existing premises: s 1(6).[1] The right cannot be excluded or modified by agreement, nor can its exercise be agreed to be subject to the imposition of a penalty (s 93(1)),[2] though the court may approve a new lease under the individual enfranchisement provisions which does so: s 93(4).[3]

---

1   Based on Leasehold Reform Act 1967, s 2(6).
2   Based on ibid, s 23(1).
3   Based on ibid, s 23(4).

2.6   The purpose of this chapter is to set out the various concepts and defining terms employed in the legislation and then to discuss the qualifications required to exercise the right to collective enfranchisement. The following chapter will then deal with the procedure to be adopted in exercising the right.

PREMISES

2.7   Collective enfranchisement applies to whole buildings or parts of buildings, so it is important to be clear what are the 'premises' which will be acquired. There is a basic definition in s 3, but this is subject to exceptions for:

(a)   partly non-residential premises;
(b)   small premises with resident landlords;
(c)   property transferred for the public benefit;
(d)   Crown land;
(e)   National Trust property; and
(f)   cathedral property.

All of these will be dealt with later. In addition, there is the question of the acquisition of appurtenant property and other communal property.

Basic definition

2.8   There are three elements to the definition (s 3(1)):

(i)   a self-contained building or part of a building, the freehold of which is owned by the same person;
(ii)   containing two or more flats held by 'qualifying tenants' (as to which see para 2.15);
(iii) and in which at least two-thirds of the total flats are held by 'qualifying tenants'.

We must consider various aspects of these elements more closely.

2.9   'Building' is not defined, but it is used in the Leasehold Reform Act 1967 (where it is not defined either) and in other statutes, and there is considerable case law on its meaning.[1] This can be summarised by saying that a building is a man-made structure enclosing an area of land, of a reasonable size, and with some degree of permanence. Freehold is also not defined, but presumably means an estate in fee simple absolute in possession.[2] 'Self-contained' *is* defined, by s 3(2). The definition distinguishes a building from a part of a building. A *building* is self-contained if it is structurally detached. A *part of a building* is obviously not structurally detached. It is self-contained if:

(a)   it is vertically divided from the rest of the building, so that it could be redeveloped independently; and

(b)   services through pipes, cables, etc *either* are provided to that part independently of the rest *or* could be so provided without work involving significant interruption for the rest.

---

1   See *Hill & Redman*, **E** [501].
2   See *Hill & Redman*, **D** [1033].

2.10   The requirement that the freehold be owned by the same person is more problematic. Undoubtedly, if a 'self-contained' building or part of a building is divided between two freehold owners in such a way as not to make either part itself 'self-contained', the requirement is not satisfied. But what if the freehold is owned by A and B as joint tenants? It is clear that a reference in the legislation to 'the landlord' includes a reference to joint tenants together comprising the landlord: s 101(4). But here s 3(1)(a) refers to the 'same person', not 'the landlord'. The Interpretion Act 1978, s 6(c), provides that, unless the contrary intention appears, words in the singular include the plural.[1] Accordingly, if A and B as joint tenants own the freehold, that should satisfy s 3(1)(a).[2] 'Flat' is defined by s 101(1) as a separate set of premises forming part of a building, constructed or adapted for use as a dwelling and which (either wholly or to a material extent) overlays or underlies some other part of the building.

---

1   See eg *Baker v Lewis* [1947] KB 186, [1946] 2 All ER 592, CA.
2   The Minister in HC Committee C certainly thought so: HC Standing Committee B, 12 November 1992, cols 49–50.

Exclusion for non-residential premises

2.11   Premises including mixed residential and non-residential user (eg shops and flats together) are excluded if the proportion of non-residential user exceeds a certain threshold. This is where the internal floor area of the part or parts not occupied (or intended to be occupied) for residential purposes, and not comprised in the common parts, exceeds 10% of the internal floor area of the whole premises: s 4(1).[1] Thus a block of flats directly above a row of shops will probably be excluded unless there are more than nine floors of flats. For the purpose of computing the internal floor area of the whole premises, internal walls are ignored, but common parts are also disregarded: s 4(3). Parts of the premises used in conjunction with a particular flat (eg a garage or a storeroom) are treated as occupied, or intended to be occupied, for residential purposes: s 4(2).

---

1   Based on the Housing Act 1988, s 95(1).

Exclusion for small premises with resident landlords

2.12   Premises containing four 'units' or less are excluded if there is a 'resident landlord'. 'Unit' by s 38(1) means a separate set of premises either:

(a)   adapted or constructed for use as a dwelling (eg a flat); or

(b)   let, or intended for letting, on a business lease (eg a shop or an office).

'Premises with a resident landlord' is defined by s 10. There are three cumulative conditions to be satisfied: one negative, relating to the premises, and two positive, relating to the freehold owner of the premises. The negative condition is that the premises must *not* be or form part of 'a purpose-built block of flats': s 10(1)(a). This expression means a building which *as constructed* contained two or more flats: s 10(6).

2.13   The first positive condition is that *either* the freehold owner of the premises *or* 'an adult member of his family' currently occupies a unit in the premises as his only or principal home: s 10(1)(b)(i), (3). But a unit which is not a flat must actually be used as a dwelling: s 10(3). By s 10(5)[1] a person is an adult member of the freeholder's family if he or she is:

(a)   the freeholder's husband or wife (whatever age); or
(b)   the freeholder's, or freeholder's spouse's, mother or father; or
(c)   the freeholder's son, daughter, son-in-law, or daughter-in-law (aged 18 years or more).

For this purpose, references to son, daughter, son-in-law and daughter-in-law include references to stepson, stepdaughter and so on: s 10(5). 'Only or principal home' is not defined, but it occurs in other legislation, such as the Housing Act 1985, s 81[2] (the 'tenancy condition' for secure tenancies) and the Housing Act 1988, s 1(1)(b)[3] (condition for an assured tenancy).

1   Based on the Leasehold Reform Act 1967, s 18(3).
2   *Hill & Redman*, **D** [605].
3   *Hill & Redman*, **C** [2025].

2.14   The second positive condition is that *either*:

(a)   the freeholder (or an adult member of his family) has occupied the unit as his only or principal home for at least the last 12 months (s 10(1)(b)(ii)); *or*
(b)   the premises were 'premises with a resident landlord' immediately before the freeholder acquired the freehold, and since a date not more than 28 days later he (or an adult member of his family) has occupied the unit as his only or principal home: s 10(2).

For this purpose, where the freehold is held on trust, occupation by a person having an interest under the trust (ie a beneficiary) suffices, rather than occupation by the trustee: s 10(4).[1]

1   Based on the Leasehold Reform Act 1967, s 18(3).

QUALIFYING TENANT

2.15   With three exceptions, a 'qualifying tenant' is a tenant of the flat under a long lease at a low rent: s 5(1). The three exceptions (s 5(2)) are:

(a)   where the lease falls within the Landlord and Tenant Act 1954, Part II (a 'business tenancy');

(b)   where the lease was granted by a charitable housing trust in pursuance of its charitable purposes;

(c)   where the lease was made in breach of the terms of a superior lease, not being a long lease at a low rent, and the breach has not been waived.

2.16   It is not necessary, in order to be a qualifying tenant, that a person should be resident in the flat. There can be only one qualifying tenant in relation to a given flat at any one time (s 5(3)), although joint tenants can together constitute that qualifying tenant: s 5(4)(b). But if a tenant under an inferior lease of a flat is a qualifying tenant, then the tenant under any superior lease of the same flat cannot be: s 5(4)(a). A person cannot be a qualifying tenant of more than two flats in the same premises at the same time: s 5(5); cf s 39(4) (individual enfranchisement). If he *would* otherwise be a qualifying tenant of three or more, then *none* of those flats has a qualifying tenant: s 5(5). The prohibition cannot be evaded by using associated companies as 'stooge' tenants: s 5(6).

Long lease

2.17   'Long lease' is specifically defined by s 7. By s 7(1) it means any of five kinds of lease:

(a)   a lease for more than 21 years, whether or not terminable before expiry; this includes the case where a lease for 21 years or less has been renewed without premium so as to extend beyond 21 years: s 7(4);

(b)   a lease for a term fixed by law under a grant with a covenant or obligation for perpetual renewal (unless it is a sublease out of a lease which is *not* a 'long lease');

(c)   subject to an exception, a lease taking effect under the Law of Property Act 1925, s 149(6) (leases terminable after a death or marriage);

(d)   a lease granted pursuant to the right to buy or rent to mortgage schemes;

(e)   a shared ownership lease under Part V of the Housing Act 1985, where the tenant has acquired 100%.

2.18   The definition of (a) is very similar (though not identical) to that in the Housing Act 1985, s 115(1)(a)[1] (meaning of 'long tenancy' for purposes of secure tenancy legislation), though its ancestry goes back to the Leasehold Reform Act 1967, s 3(1)[2] (meaning of 'long tenancy' for purposes of the Leasehold Reform Act) and before that to the Landlord and Tenant Act 1954, s 2(4)[3] (meaning of 'long tenancy' for the purposes of the Landlord and Tenant Act 1954, Part I). The definitions of (b) and (d) are also based on those in the Housing Act 1985, s 115(1)(b), (c).[4] Definition (b) is referring to the term of 2,000 years or 2,000 less one day produced by the Law of Property Act 1922, s 145 and Sch 15, paras 1 and 5, for any case of a lease with a covenant for perpetual renewal.[5] The exception to definition (c) (see s 7(2)) is the case where:

(i)   the notice to terminate can be given at any time after death or marriage of the tenants; *and*

(ii)   the notice period is three months or less; *and*

(iii)   the tenant can neither assign (except by way of exchange under the Housing Act 1985, s 92) or sublet the whole.

In such a case the lease is not a 'long lease'.

1 See *Hill & Redman*, **D** [841]–[843].
2 See *Hill & Redman*, **E** [510]–[512].
3 See *Hill & Redman*, **E** [261]–[266].
4 *Hill & Redman*, **D** [841]–[843].
5 *Hill & Redman*, **A** [324]–[325].

2.19   The concept of a 'long lease' is extended to cover a number of other situations:

(a)   where a long lease at a low rent has come to an end but the tenant has become tenant under a new tenancy (whether express or by operation of law) of the same property or part: s 7(3);

(b)   any period during which the lease is or was continued under the Leasehold Property (Temporary Provisions) Act 1951, the Landlord and Tenant Act 1954, Part I, and the Local Government and Housing Act 1989, Sch 10: s 7(5);

(c)   where there are two or more separate leases existing between the same landlord and tenant between them covering the whole of one flat (and any 'appurtenant property' within s 1), but only one of the leases is a long lease; in this case they are treated as being one 'long lease' of the whole flat (and appurtenant property): s 7(6).

'At a low rent'

2.20   In order to exclude leases at a market rent from collective enfranchisement, a 'long lease' must be 'at a low rent' in order to qualify. The idea of such a test is not new, but is found in the Landlord and Tenant Act 1954, s 2(5)[1] and the Leasehold Reform Act 1967, s 4.[2] The test here adopted is different, however, and is materially identical to that inserted as the Leasehold Reform Act 1967, s 4A, by s 65 of this Act. Thus it incorporates the anti-avoidance provision now introduced for the Leasehold Reform Act, in that it looks at the rent payable *in the first year of the lease* and not subsequently.

26 *Hill & Redman*, **E** [261], [267].
27 *Hill & Redman*, **E** [517]–[523].

2.21   Thus, a lease of a flat (and any appurtenant property within s 1) is a lease at a low rent if during its first year (s 8(2)(a)) the rent payable did not exceed a certain figure. The figure depends on which of five categories the lease falls into. They are:

(i)   leases granted before 1 April 1963;

(ii)   leases granted between 1 April 1963 and 31 March 1990;

(iii) leases granted after 31 March 1990 pursuant to contracts made before 1 April 1990;

(iv)   other leases in Greater London;

(v)   other leases outside Greater London.

2.22   The corresponding figures are:

(i)   two-thirds of the 'letting value' (within s 4(1) of the Leasehold Reform Act 1967: s 8(3)) of the property;

(ii), (iii) two-thirds of the rateable value of the property on the commencement of the lease or (if later) the date on which the property first had a rateable value;

(iv) £1,000;

(v) £250.

Rateable value is to be determined in accordance with the Rent Act 1977, s 25(1), (2), (4):[1] s 8(2)(c). 'Rent' for this purpose means rent reserved as such, 'rent' for services, repairs, maintenance or insurance being disregarded: s 8(2)(d). Terms for providing for suspension of reduction or rent, or penal additions thereto are also disregarded: s 9(2)(e). A lease which is only a 'long lease' by virtue of s 7(4) (renewals taking the term over 21 years) is treated as entered into, and as having commenced, on the date of the last renewal: s 8(5). A 100% shared ownership lease is treated as commencing on the date when the tenant's 'share' reached 100%: s 8(6).

---

1   *Hill & Redman*, **C** [522]–[534].

'REVERSIONER' AND OTHER 'RELEVANT LANDLORDS'

2.23   The procedure for collective enfranchisement depends on identifying the parties between whom the negotiations and transaction must take place. We have seen who are the 'qualifying tenants'. Now we see whom they have to deal with. In principle, and subject to para 2.24, the 'reversioner' is the person who conducts the proceedings on behalf of himself and all the other 'relevant landlords'. If the proposed collective enfranchisement involves acquisition of the freehold and any other interests (including leasehold interests) of the freeholder, but no interest of anyone else, then the freeholder is the reversioner: s 9(1). In this case there will be no other 'relevant landlord'. But if interests of other persons (as well as those of the freeholder) are proposed to be acquired, then the freeholder and the owner of every leasehold interest proposed to be acquired is a 'relevant landlord'. In such a case the court may appoint another person (being a 'relevant landlord') to act as reversioner: Sch 1, paras 2–5. That person may either be someone agreed by all the 'relevant landlords' (Sch 1, para 2) or not (Sch 1, para 3): in the former case the court has no discretion; in the latter it has. The court may also remove a delaying or defaulting reversioner and appoint someone else: Sch 1, para 4.

Separate representation

2.24   The other relevant landlords may decide not to have their interests represented by the reversioner, and may individually give notice to both reversioner and nominee purchaser of their intention to deal directly with the nominee purchaser and to be separately represented in any legal proceedings: Sch 1, para 7(1). A relevant landlord may also require the reversioner to apply to a leasehold valuation tribunal for the tribunal to determine questions relating to the acquisition of any interest of his (Sch 1, para 7(3)), and may require the price payable for his interest to be paid to him instead of to the reversioner: Sch 1, para 7(4). The nominee purchaser also has limited rights to deal directly with particular relevant landlords: Sch 1, para 7(2).

2.25   All relevant landlords other than the reversioner, who have not notified their intention under Sch 1, para 7 to deal directly with the nominee purchaser or to be separately represented in legal proceedings, must assist the reversioner as he reasonably requires, including supplying information: Sch 1, para 8(1)(a). In particular, they must supply copies of notices received or given under the 'individual enfranchisement' (extended lease) provisions of the 1993 Act: Sch 4, para 3.

Change of landlord

2.26   The identity of the reversioner or other relevant landlord may change during the transaction. Suppose that, after the tenants' original notice under s 13 (para 3.11) has been given and registered (para 3.32), the freeholder or other relevant landlord disposes of his interest in the premises, or other property to be acquired, to a single acquirer without division. In such a case the new owner of the freehold or other interest steps into the shoes of the old. The new owner is treated as having taken all the steps which the old owner took, and as having received all the notices (or copy notices) which the old owner received: s 19(3). The same rules will apply again on any subsequent disposal while the tenants' initial notice remains in force: s 13(3). (But different rules will apply where the reversioner or other relevant landlord tries to divide his interest, or to create leases or subleases: see para 3.27.)

2.27   But suppose that, at the time the tenants' initial notice is served, the reversioner or other relevant landlord has contracted to sell his interest to a third party. In such a case, the parties may have expressly provided in their contract what is to happen (s 19(6)). Or the contractual doctrine of frustration[1] may apply. But otherwise, the 1993 Act provides that the operation of that contract is *suspended* so long as the tenant's notice continues in force: s 19(4). If a binding contract between nominee purchaser and reversioner and other relevant landlords is thereafter entered into, the contract with the third party is discharged to the extent that it relates to the disposal of the interest referred to: s 19(5).

---

1   See eg Chitty on Contracts, 25th edn, 1983, ch 23.

SPECIAL CATEGORIES OF LANDLORDS

2.28   A number of categories of landlords have special characteristics and must be specifically mentioned. These are mortgagees of a landlord's interest (or holders of debentures in a corporate landlord), landlords under disability, university or college landlords and ecclesiastical landlords.

Mortgagees and debenture holders

2.29   When a mortgagee of a landlord's interest goes into possession under the mortgage, the mortgagee is generally treated as the landlord for the purposes of collective enfranchisement (except in relation to s 35 and Sch 8: paras 3.96–3.98): Sch 2, para 2(1), (2).[1] Where a mortgagee has not gone into possession, but has appointed a receiver (or the court has done so), the landlord cannot make any application to the court under s 23 (landlord's intention to redevelop: see para 3.40) without the mortgagee's consent: Sch 2, para 2(3).[2] Moreover, the landlord can, if he wishes, require to be treated for collective enfranchisement purposes as if he *were* in possession: Sch 2, para 2(3). Notices under the collective enfranchisement procedure may be given to a mortgagee in possession or to a receiver appointed by a mortgagee or debenture holder or the court (the recipient being obliged to copy it to the others) or to trustees for debenture holders: Sch 2, para 2(4), (5).

1 Based on the Leasehold Reform Act 1967, s 25(1), (2).
2 Based on ibid, s 25(5).

Landlord under disability

2.30   Where the landlord is suffering from mental disorder and cannot deal with his property and affairs, the Court of Protection (or other authority under the Mental Health Act 1983, s 111(2)) may order that the landlord's receiver appointed under that Act (or under the Mental Health Act 1959), or another person authorised to do so, may take the landlord's place for collective enfranchisement purposes: Sch 2, para 4.[1]

1 Based on the Leasehold Reform Act 1967, s 26(2).

University or college landlords

2.31   There is no change to collective enfranchisement procedure merely because the landlord is a university or college to which the Universities and Colleges Estates Act 1925 applies. But sums payable to such a landlord as the price for acquiring an interest under collective enfranchisement are to be dealt with as if they were consideration on a sale effected under the 1925 Act: Sch 2, para 7(1).

Ecclesiastical landlords

2.32   For this purpose 'ecclesiastical landlord' includes both a capitular body[1] and (in relation to diocesan glebe land)[2] a diocesan board of finance: Sch 2, para 8(1). An ecclesiastical landlord needs the consent of the Church Commissioners to agree to the provisions of a conveyance under collective enfranchisement: Sch 2, para 8(2).[3] This does not apply where the court or leasehold valuation tribunal determines such provisions, but the Church Commissioners are nevertheless entitled to appear and be heard in any proceedings where the ecclesiastical landlord could appear and be heard: Sch 2, para 8(2).[4] There are various provisions as to the treatment of sums received under collective enfranchisement as the price for interests acquired and as to the potential applications of such sums: Sch 2, para 8(3), (4).[5]

1 Within the meaning of the Cathedrals Measure 1963.
2 Within the meaning of the Endowments and Glebe Measure 1976.
3 Based on the Leasehold Reform Act 1967, s 31(2).
4 Based on ibid.
5 Based on ibid, s 31(3), (4).

PARTICIPATING TENANTS

Categories

2.33   No one is forced to participate in the acquisition of the freehold. Not all qualifying tenants of specific premises may choose to join in the exercise of the right to collective enfranchisement. Some may be ineligible. Some may not know about it until it is too late (cf paras 3.18–3.19). Those who do not participate will ultimately change their landlord (ie to the nominee purchaser), but not their status as tenants. Those who do participate are known as participating tenants.

2.34   As at the date when the claim is first made, the participating tenants are those qualifying tenants by whom the initial notice is given: s 14(1)(a). Thereafter, the participating tenants will each fall into one of four categories:

(a)   qualifying tenants who were participating tenants from the beginning, and whose status has not changed since then: s 14(1)(b);

(b)   qualifying tenants who are assignees from participating tenants: s 14(2);

(c)   qualifying tenants who did not participate in making the original claim, but who are not assignees from participating tenants: s 14(3);

(d)   personal representatives of participating tenants: s 14(5).

Participating tenants by assignment

2.35   Qualifying tenants in category (b) are automatically entitled to become participating tenants if a binding contract has not by then been entered into: s 14(1). But they must notify the nominee purchaser of the assignment, electing 'whether or not' to become participating tenants, within 14 days of the assignment: s 14(2). 'Assignment' for this purpose includes an assent by personal representatives and an assignment by operation of law to a trustee in bankruptcy or to a mortgagee under the Law of Property Act 1925, s 89(2): s 14(10). If an assignee notifies the nominee purchaser within the 14–day period of his election to participate, he is treated as a participating tenant from the date of the assignment, for so long as he remains a qualifying tenant: s 14(4).

Other participating tenants

2.36   Qualifying tenants in category (c) are:

(i)   qualifying tenants at the time of the original exercise, but who were ineligible, or chose not to participate;

(ii)   tenants, but not qualifying tenants, at the time of the original exercise, who have now become qualifying tenants;

(iii)   qualifying tenants who are assignees from (i) or (ii).

2.37   Tenants in this category are not automatically entitled to become participating tenants. Assuming that a binding contract has not by then been entered into (s 14(11)) and that he is not then prohibited from participating (Sch 3, para 8) a qualifying tenant in this category may elect to participate only with the agreement of all the other participating tenants for the time being: s 14(3). If he obtains that agreement and does so elect, he must 'forthwith' notify the nominee purchaser (s 14(3)), and will be treated as a participating tenant from the date of the agreement with the other participating tenants, for so long as he remains a qualifying tenant: s 14(4).

Personal representatives

2.38   Turning to category (d), if there is by then no binding contract entered into, the personal representatives of a deceased participating tenant are obliged to notify the nominee purchaser of the death within 56 days of its happening, and to state their election whether or not to withdraw from participation in the claim to collective enfranchisement. If they do not state their intention to withdraw, they are treated as participating tenants from the date of the tenant's death, for so long as the lease is vested in them: s 14(5). If the lease is thereafter sold to a purchaser or vested in the beneficiary of the tenant's estate, then if the new tenant is a qualifying tenant he will automatically be entitled to elect to be a participating tenant in category (b).

Consequences of change in participating tenants

2.39   Where a person in categories (b), (c) or (d) becomes a participating tenant, any subsisting arrangements between nominee purchaser and participating tenants are automatically modified so as:

(i)   to substitute the new participating tenant for any tenant whom he has replaced; or
(ii)   if there is an assignment by a person who *remains* a qualifying tenant of a flat in the premises, to add the new participating tenant as a party to the arrangements: s 14(6).

The legislation does not deal expressly with the case where the new participating tenant is in category (c) but was not an assignee from a person who remains a qualifying tenant in the premises, eg where an original tenant did not participate in giving a s 13 notice but subsequently elected (and was agreed by the participating tenants) to become a participating tenant. Yet the arrangements between the participating tenants and the nominee purchaser must surely be modified in a similar way.

2.40   In the case of any change in the identity of the tenants, the nominee purchaser should receive a notification under these provisions. Within 28 days of receipt, he must give a notice to the reversioner and copy the notice to every other relevant landlord: s 14(7). The notice must give details relevant to the new participating tenant, including name and address, date of assignment or death (as the case may be) and identifying the flat in question: s 14(8), (9)(a). If the new tenant is becoming a participating tenant, then that tenant must personally sign the notice: s 14(9)(b).

NOMINEE PURCHASER

Status and functions

2.41   The function of the nominee purchaser is twofold. First, he acts for the participating tenants in conducting all the proceedings arising out of the claim to exercise collective enfranchisement. Second, *he* acquires the freehold and other interests in the premises or elsewhere, on behalf of the participating tenants: ss 15(1), 38(2). He is appointed by the participating tenants, and they can replace him: s 15(2), (3). The nominee purchaser can be an individual, a group of individuals, a corporate body (eg a limited company), a group of corporate bodies, or a mixture of individuals and corporate bodies. As between the nominee purchaser and the participating tenants, the terms on which the acquisition is made by the nominee purchaser are a matter for discussion and agreement. They may amount to a declaration of trust, or company articles of association or other shareholders' agreement, a mixture of these, or some other form of arrangement entirely.

Appointment and termination of appointment

2.42   The original nominee purchaser is the person nominated in the s 13 notice claiming to exercise collective enfranchisement: see para 3.15. But, before a binding contract is entered into with the reversioner and other relevant landlords (s 15(16)), the appointment can be terminated by notice from the participating tenants given to the nominee purchaser and to the reversioner of the premises: s 15(3), (4). The participating tenants must copy this notice to every relevant landlord: s 15(11). This must also *either* specify the name and address for service, of the new nominee purchaser, *or* state that a further notice giving such details (including the date of appointment) will be given within 28 days: s 15(5). If these provisions are not complied with, the appointment of a replacement nominee purchaser is invalid: s 15(5). (And if the further notice is not served within 28 days, the participating tenants' initial notice will be deemed withdrawn: see para 2.46.)

2.43   Similarly, before a binding contract is entered into with the reversioner and other relevant landlords (s 16(10)), the nominee purchaser may terminate his own appointment by a notice to each participating tenant and the reversioner, resigning 21 days after the date of the notice: s 16(1), (2). Or the nominee purchaser (being an individual) may die. In either case, the participating tenants then have 56 days to serve notice on the reversioner informing him of the resignation or the death, and giving him details of the new nominee purchaser and his address for service: s 16(3), (5). Failure to specify the name of the new nominee purchaser in this notice means that his appointment is invalid: s 16(3), (5).

2.44   Where two or more persons together constitute the nominee purchaser, then the rules for the termination of the appointment of (and for the appointment of a replacement for) one or more of them are exactly the same (s 15(3)), except that copies of any relevant notice must also be given to the remaining persons constituting the nominee purchaser: ss 15(1), 16(9). Moreover, if an appointment of one or more (but not all) terminates without an immediate replacement, the remainder will constitute the nominee purchaser for the time being: s 15(8).

Effects of termination

2.45   If the appointment of the nominee purchaser or one of the persons constituting the nominee purchaser terminates (including by resignation or death), anything done by or in relation to the nominee purchaser before such termination is treated as being done by or in relation to the nominee purchaser as subsequently constituted, thus ensuring the continuity of effect of those actions: ss 15(6), 16(4), (6). Furthermore, the person whose appointment so terminates is not liable for costs incurred thereafter in connection with the proposed acquisition: s 15(7), 16(4). (This does not apply where the person dies, however: cf s 16(6).) But he must on request of the nominee purchaser for the time being supply him, at an address in England and Wales, with all or any of the 'documents in his custody or control' relating to the acquisition. If he fails to do so without reasonable cause, or delays unreasonably in doing so, he is liable for any consequential costs incurred by the nominee purchaser or for which the nominee purchaser becomes liable (as to which see paras 3.86–3.87): ss 15(7), 16(4). (Again, this does not apply where the person concerned has died: cf s 16(6).)

Effects of interregnum

2.46   If the participating tenants give a notice terminating the nominee purchaser's appointment, but not immediately appointing a new nominee purchaser (see para 2.42), there will be a period during which there is no nominee purchaser. There will be a similar period if the nominee purchaser resigns or dies. During such period, all prescribed periods for giving notice or making an application which would otherwise expire during the interregnum are suspended: ss 15(9), 16(7). The 'interregnum' should be brought to an end by the participating tenants serving a further notice under s 15(5)(b), within 28 days, or under s 16(3), (5), within 56 days: see paras 2.42, 2.43. If that further notice is not so served, the initial notice claiming collective enfranchisement is deemed to be withdrawn: ss 15(10), 16(8).

RESIDENTIAL QUALIFICATION TO EXERCISE COLLECTIVE ENFRANCHISEMENT

2.47   We have looked at the various concepts and major defined terms used in the legislation. We thus have all the building blocks necessary to embark upon a discussion of the procedure for exercising the right to collective enfranchisement. But before that, it is necessary to note that, for a claim to collective enfranchisement to be valid, the notice so claiming must be given by a certain number of qualifying tenants of flats in particular premises. This number must not be less than two-thirds of the number of qualifying tenants in the premises, and not less than one-half the total number of flats: paras 3.11–3.12. But, in addition, at least half the tenants by whom the notice was given must satisfy the so called 'residence condition': s 13(2).

2.48   It will be recalled that the definition of qualifying tenant (para 2.15) does not require a person to be resident in the flat concerned. The question requiring some degree of residence was first raised at an early stage in House of Commons Committee,[1] but resisted by the Government as reducing the number of potential qualifying tenants, and hence tending to reduce the effectiveness of the collective enfranchisement legislation.[2] The question was revisited on House of Commons Report,[3] House of Lords Second Reading,[4] House of Lords Committee[5] and House of Lords Report.[6] Indeed, the House of Lords Minister, Lord Strathclyde, at one point said:

'I strongly believe that a residence qualification for collective enfranchisement in flats could not be fair . . . [and] would render unworkable this part of the Bill.'[7]

---

1   HC Committee, 17 November 1992, cols 96–97.
2   Ibid, cols 103–104.
3   HC Report, 9 February 1993, cols 834–851.
4   HL 2R, 23 February 1993, cols 102, 119, 129–130, 141, 174–175.
5   HL Committee, 9 March 1993, cols 930ff.
6   HL Report, 11 May 1993, cols 1185–1205, 1257–1263.
7   HL Committee, 9 March 1993, cols 954–955.

2.49   However, on House of Lords Report the Government unexpectedly accepted an amendment to the Bill which went some way towards imposing a residence requirement. Instead of requiring some degree of residence as a condition of being a 'qualifying tenant', the new provision requires only that half of the qualifying tenants involved in exercising the collective enfranchisement right should satisfy the residence condition.

The 'residence condition'

2.50   The 'residence condition' (s 6(2)) is that the tenant has occupied the flat (or part of it : s 7(3)(a)) as his only or principal home either:

(a)   for the last twelve months; or
(b)   for periods totalling three years in the last ten.

Use for other purposes as well is irrelevant: s 6(2). The phrase 'only or principal home' is not defined, though it has already been discussed: see para 2.13. The tenant's occupation does not have to have been by virtue of the lease concerned – or indeed any lease: s 6(3)(b). But occupation by a company or other 'artificial person', or the corporator of a corporation sole, is excluded: s 6(3). The phrase 'artificial person' is not defined, but presumably extends to foreign entities such as an *Anstalt* or an *établissement*, or a *Stiftung* or *fondation*. It is unclear whether it applies to trusts as such. The better view is that it does not, so long as the trustees concerned are natural persons (ie individuals) as opposed to legal persons (ie companies).

TRUSTS

2.51   This brings us to the position of trusts generally. Part I of the 1993 Act does not generally address the question whether the interests referred to, freehold or leasehold, are legal as opposed to equitable. If A holds the freehold on trust for B, must the qualifying tenants serve notice on B, or only on A? If tenant C holds the lease on trust for D, who is the qualifying tenant, C or D? If D is resident and C is not, then, if C is treated as the qualifying tenant, D's occupation will not satisfy the residence condition in s 6. Although in other statutes such as the Landlord and Tenant Act 1954 and the Leasehold Reform Act 1967 (from which some of the collective enfranchisement schemes provisions are drawn) specific provision has been made for trusts, whether of landlords' or tenants' interests, no such general provision has been made here.

2.52   Limited provision is made for trusts in relation to collective enfranchisement in s 10(4) (resident landlords), Sch 2, paras 3, 5 and 6. All of these deal with landlords' interests. Thus by s 10(4), if A holds the freehold for B, it is B's occupation that counts, and not A's: see para 2.14. Under Sch 2, para 3,[1] if A is 'custodian trustee' for B as 'managing trustee' (under the Public Trustee Act 1906, s 4), B is treated as the owner of the interest, except in relation to the execution of any document dealing with it. Sch 2, paras 5 and 6 deal with the applicability of certain statutory provisions concerning the sums paid by or payable to a landlord whose interest is held on trust for sale or settled and at settlement.

---

1   Based on the Leasehold Reform Act 1967, s 26(1).

2.53   More generally, specific provision is made for the case of both landlords' and tenants' interests being held by joint tenants: s 101(4). But if there is a joint tenancy, either of the freehold or of a lease, there will automatically be a trust (in fact a trust for sale): Law of Property Act 1925, s 36. Since the 1993 Act treats the joint tenants as together constituting 'the landlord' or 'the tenant' or 'the qualifying tenant' (as the case may be) it must be inferred that, subject to the exceptional cases mentioned, only legal owners are taken account of, and beneficiaries under trusts are ignored.

3 Collective enfranchisement: procedure[1]

PRELIMINARY ENQUIRIES

Freeholder and intermediate leaseholders

3.1   Before exercising the right to collective enfranchisement, the first thing that qualifying tenants need is information as to who owns the freehold of, and any intermediate leasehold interests in, the relevant premises. Thus, a qualifying tenant may give to his immediate landlord (or his agent for receiving rent) a notice requiring the name and address of a number of different persons, so far as known: s 11(1). These are:

(a)   the freeholder of the premises;

(b)   the freeholder of property outside the premises but which is let to the qualifying tenant or which he is entitled under the lease to use in common with others;

(c)   owners of leasehold interests in the premises: s 11(1), (2).

---

1   For parliamentary debates, see HC 2R, 3 November 1992, cols 152–154; HC Standing Committee B, 17 November 1992, cols 135–154, 19 November 1992, cols 155–190, 24 November 1992, cols 193–214; HC Report, 9 February 1993, cols 927–929; HL 2R, 23 February 1993, cols 87–87; HL Committee, 15 March 1993, cols 1271–1332, 22 March 1993, cols 9–78, 79–86; HL Report, 18 May 1993, cols 1655–1703; HL 3R, 25 May 1993, cols 204–209; HC Lords Amendments, 14 June 1993, cols 662–663; HL Commons Reason, 8 July 1993, cols 1528–1530.

3.2   If the qualifying tenant knows who the freeholder of the premises is, he may give him a similar notice requiring the name and address (so far as known) of:

(a)   every intermediate leaseholder of the premises;

(b)   every tenant or licensee of a unit in the premises; and

(c)   every tenant or licensee of common parts in the premises or property outside the premises which are *either* let to the qualifying tenant *or* which he is entitled under the lease to use in common with others: s 11(3).

The qualifying tenant may likewise require the freeholder or anyone in categories (a), (b) or (c) above to supply information relating to his own interest in the property, and (so far as known) the information relating to interests derived out of his own interest, so long as the information is reasonably required by the tenant in connection with the collective enfranchisement claim: s 11(4).

Documents

3.3   Where a qualifying tenant requires the supply of information about interests in the property under s 11(4), he also has rights in relation to certain documents in the custody or under the control of the recipient of the tenant's notice. By s 11(5),[1] these rights are:

(a) to be provided with a list of available documents;
(b) to inspect such documents; and
(c) to be provided with copies of them.

The documents concerned are those which the qualifying tenant reasonably requires to see in relation to the collective enfranchisement claim, and which a willing seller would make available to a willing buyer (at whatever stage in the transaction): s 11(6).[2] The word 'documents' means the same as it does in the Civil Evidence Act 1968, Part I: 1993 Act, s 11(9).[3] But the phrase 'in the custody or under the control' is not further explained.[4] Analogies from the law of documentary discovery may be helpful,[5] as rules of court[6] employ the phrase 'in the possession, custody or power'.

---

1 Based on Housing Act 1988, s 97(2).
2 Based on ibid, s 97(3).
3 As in Housing Act 1988, s 97(4).
4 See also the 1993 Act, s 84(2)(b); paras 7.20–7.21.
5 See Matthews and Malek, *Discovery*, 1992, paras 4.02–4.07, 4.32–4.47.
6 RSC Ord 24; CCR Ord 14.

Information about other applications

3.4 The qualifying tenant's notice under s 11(4) 'shall' require the recipient also to give the tenants certain information relating to:

(a) other claims to exercise collective enfranchisement of the premises which are still 'current'; and
(b) (so far as known) applications to the Treasury for designation or direction under the Inheritance Tax Act 1984:[1] s 12(1).

A claim is 'current' if the notice claiming collective enfranchisement has not been withdrawn, a binding contract entered into in pursuance of that notice remains in force, or where the court has ordered various interests to be vested in the nominee purchaser, but this has not yet happened: s 12(6). Although the legislation says that the 'notice . . . shall . . . require the recipient', it cannot be the case that a failure by the tenant to ask for this further information renders the whole notice invalid: the provision is directory rather than mandatory.[2]

---

1 See paras 3.73–3.74.
2 Cf *B v B* [1961] 2 All ER 396, [1961] 1 WLR 856; *Chelmsford RDC v Powell* [1963] 1 All ER 150, [1963] 1 WLR 123.

3.5 The recipient's obligation to supply information to the qualifying tenant about other claims to collective enfranchisement does not extend merely to claims already made. If any application to claim collective enfranchisement is made within the following six months, and the tenant requiring information under s 11(4) is not one of the qualifying tenants making the collective enfranchisement claim, the recipient has 28 days from the date of the application for collective enfranchisement to notify the tenant of its existence and of the identity of the nominee purchaser: s 12(4).

3.6   Moreover, if in response to a notice under s 11(4), the recipient has informed the tenant of a pending application to the Treasury for designation or a direction under the Inheritance Tax Act 1984, and within the following six months that application is granted, refused or withdrawn, the recipient must notify the tenant of this within 28 days: s 12(5).

Sanctions

3.7   What happens if the recipient of a notice under s 11 fails to comply with the Act's requirements? Unlike elsewhere in the Act,[1] there is no specific provision for application to the court for an order that the information be supplied. A general provision, applying to both collective and individual enfranchisement, empowers the court,[2] on an application made at least 14 days after a *further* notice has been served requiring the making good of an existing default, to order the respondent to make good the default within such time as the court may specify: s 92. But this is permissive only, and does not prevent application being made, after the expiry of the 28 days, for an injunction requiring compliance with the statutory obligations.[3] However, an easier solution in many cases today, if the title to the land is registered, is to apply to the Land Registry, where most or all of the same information will be available publicly within a few days, on payment of the usual fees.

---

1   Ss 46–50, 81(4)–(7).
2   The county court: para 1.15.
3   Cf *Ashby v Ebdon* [1985] Ch 394, [1984] 3 All ER 869.

PROCEDURE

General

3.8   Much of the procedure to be followed is contained in the 1993 Act and its schedules. In particular, provision is made for the form and mode of service for the many notices required: paras 1.11–1.13. The Secretary of State may supplement these provisions by way of regulations, in particular dealing with investigation of title, payments and discharge from performance on account of others' default: s 98(1), (2). But, subject to this, the procedure to be followed is 'as nearly as may be' to the case of a contract of sale freely negotiated between the parties: s 98(1).

3.9   Whereas the preliminary enquiries already described could be carried out by any individual tenant, the claim to exercise the right to collective enfranchisement is necessarily a collective act on behalf of many tenants. (For the same reason it is very different from claiming the right to a new lease, so called 'individual enfranchisement' under Chapter II of Part I of the Act.) Accordingly, tenants will have to be agreed amongst themselves on many things *apart from* their basic desire to acquire the freehold. That is not easy, particularly where tenants are absent from their flats, or differ in views or financial resources. Moreover, the scale and amount of information that must be provided to the reversioner (as to whom see para 2.23) on claiming to exercise the right, mean that professional advisers must be involved long before that step is taken. That is not only time-consuming, but costly – and we have not yet begun.

Valuation

3.10   In particular, before the initial notice can be served claiming collective enfranchisement, the qualifying tenants must obtain from a 'qualified surveyor' a valuation of the freehold in the premises, of the freehold of any other property to be acquired and of any intermediate leasehold interest to be acquired: s 13(6). For this purpose a surveyor is qualified if *both*:

(a)   he is a fellow or professional associate of the Royal Institute of Chartered Surveyors or the Institute of Surveyors, Valuers and Auctioneers, or if he satisfies other requirements prescribed by the Secretary of State; *and*

(b)   he is believed by the qualifying tenants to have the ability and experience to value the premises in question: s 13(7).

The valuation must be prepared on the basis of the valuation rules set out in Sch 6: see paras 3.75–3.85.

INITIAL NOTICE

3.11   The first real step – and the most important – in the procedure is for the qualifying tenants to serve their notice under s 13. The notice must be given to the reversioner of the premises by a minimum number of qualifying tenants, half of whom must then satisfy the residence condition under s 6: see para 2.47. The minimum number of qualifying tenants required for a valid notice is the greater of:

(i)   two-thirds of the number of qualifying tenants, and

(ii)   half of the flats,

in the premises: s 13(2).

3.12   Some examples may make this clearer. Suppose a block contains twelve flats. Half of twelve is six. So the minimum needed will be six. If there are twelve qualifying tenants, two-thirds of twelve is eight. Eight is greater than six, so eight must sign, of whom four must be resident. If there are ten or eleven qualifying tenants, two-thirds of ten or eleven (rounded up) is seven. Seven is greater than six, so seven must sign, of whom four (half, rounded up) must be resident. If there are nine qualifying tenants, two-thirds of nine is six, the same as half of twelve. So six must sign, and three of those must be resident. If there are fewer than nine qualifying tenants, two-thirds of their number will be less than six (ie half of twelve) so six will still have to sign, of whom three must be resident. If there are fewer than six qualifying tenants, there can be no collective enfranchisement.

Copies of initial notice

3.13   The qualifying tenants must copy their notice to every other person believed by them to be a 'relevant landlord' (see para 2.23) of the premises: Sch 3, para 12(1).[1] Details of such copying must be given in the initial notice itself: Sch 3, para 12(2). The reversioner receiving the initial notice or a relevant landlord receiving a copy must himself copy it to any other believed relevant landlord who is not stated, or otherwise known, to have received a copy: Sch 3, para 13(1), (2).[2] At the same time, he must add the further recipient's names to the details of the recipients given in the initial notice, and tell the qualifying tenants of this: Sch 3, para 13(3).

1   Paragraph 12 is based on the Leasehold Reform Act 1967, Sch 3, para 8.
2   Paragraph 13 is also based on the Leasehold Reform Act 1967, Sch 3, para 8.

3.14   If any person who, under the s 11 preliminary enquiry procedure (see paras 3.1–3.7), has previously notified his interest to any of the qualifying tenants giving the notice, does not receive a copy of the initial notice, that initial notice will cease to have effect once the counternotice period runs out: Sch 3, para 14(1). Any other failure to comply with Sch 3, paras 12 and 13, and any reasonable delay in so complying, renders a person liable to compensate other persons who suffer loss: Sch 3, para 14(2).[1] Where any person to be given a notice or copy notice cannot be found, or his identity ascertained, special procedures apply: paras 3.56–3.68.

1   Based on the Leasehold Reform Act 1967, Sch 3, para 8(3).

Content of initial notice

3.15   Section 13(3) requires that the initial notice must contain certain information:

(i)   details of the premises (and any other property) the freehold of which is to be acquired or over which rights are to be granted;
(ii)   details of any leasehold interests to be acquired;
(iii)   details of any flats or other units in the premises which are to be subject to mandatory leaseback (see para 3.88);
(iv)   a statement of grounds showing that the premises are within the collective enfranchisement provisions;
(v)   the proposed purchase price for (i) and (ii) above;
(vi)   the names and addresses of all the qualifying tenants in the premises (not just those who sign the notice) and details of their leases and residence qualification (if any);
(vii)   the identity of the nominee purchaser and his address for service in England and Wales;
(viii)   confirmation that a surveyor's valuation has been obtained, stating his name (s 13(6));
(ix)   a date by which the reversioner must serve his counternotice (which must be not less than two months later): s 13(5).

3.16   In addition, the notice must be accompanied by a plan showing the various properties detailed in (i) above. It is not necessary that the tenants should claim collective enfranchisement over the entirety of the property which they could so claim (s 1(5)), provided, of course, that the premises in respect of which the claim is actually made are none the less premises to which collective enfranchisement applies: see paras 2.7–2.14.

Prohibition on further notices

3.17   So long as the initial notice remains in force, and for 12 months after it is withdrawn (or deemed withdrawn) or an order under s 23(1) is obtained, no subsequent notice under these provisions may be given in relation to the same premises, or any part of them: s 13(8), (9). Nor (for the same period) can one be given in relation to other premises including the whole or any part of the original premises: s 13(10). A notice continues in force from the date of service ('the relevant date') until:

(a) a binding contract is entered into pursuant to that notice;

(b) an order is made to vest interests in the nominee purchaser; or

(c) the notice is (or is deemed to be) withdrawn, or is otherwise treated by the legislation as no longer of effect: s 13(11).

Informing other tenants

3.18 Note that there is no requirement that qualifying tenants intending to serve a s 13 notice should inform others. A provision to this effect was proposed, but not accepted, at House of Lords committee stage.[1] As we have seen, a qualifying tenant who could have participated (had he known) in the s 13 notice, but did not, has no right subsequently to join in without the consent of the existing participating tenants: para 2.37. Thus, qualifying tenants who were disliked might simply not be invited to participate, and instead of all being tenants of the original landlord, the minority could ultimately find themselves tenants of their erstwhile co-tenants, now landlord!

---

1 HL Committee, 15 March 1993, cols 1281–1286; see also cols 1303ff.

3.19 Moreover, in principle, there is nothing to prevent a *subsequent* acquisition under collective enfranchisement taking place some time after the first; if enough of the then majority were to side with the minority, the 'trap' could be sprung in reverse. In its efforts to provide long leaseholders a stick with which to beat the landlord, Parliament may in fact have given them a stick with which to beat each other.

Inadequate notice

3.20 What happens if a notice is purportedly given under s 13, but it does not comply with the requirements of that section? The section says that the notice 'must' contain certain details. The Act also provides that the notice is not invalid because of any inaccuracy in the details given, or because of any misdescription of property (and indeed there is an amendment procedure): Sch 3, para 15.[1] Nor is it invalid merely because one of the persons who gave the notice was not a qualifying tenant entitled to participate in giving the notice, or (contrary to what the notice says) does not satisfy the residence condition: Sch 3, para 16(1). (Of course, it will be invalid if, without the ineligible person, the ordinary requirements of s 13(2) are not met: Sch 3, para 16.) But the Act says nothing about the effect of failure to include necessary details at all. Indeed, in the case where supposed qualifying tenants sign the notice, but turn out not to be qualifying tenants, the Act specifically provides that (*if* it makes a difference to satisfying the numerical and residence thresholds) the notice is *deemed withdrawn*, rather than invalid in the first place: see para 3.31.

---

1 Based on the Leasehold Reform Act 1967, Sch 3, para 6(3).

INELIGIBILITY TO PARTICIPATE IN GIVING NOTICE

3.21   A number of qualifying tenants are specifically prevented from participating in the giving of a notice under s 13. These are:

(a)   a tenant who has given notice to terminate the lease: Sch 3, para 1(a);[1]

(b)   a tenant in relation to whose flat an agreement under the Local Government Housing Act 1989, Sch 10, para 17 subsists: Sch 3, para 1(b);[2]

(c)   a tenant who more than four months previously received notice to terminate the lease under the Landlord and Tenant Act 1954, s 4 or a notice under the Local Government and Housing Act 1989, Sch 10, para 4(1): Sch 3, para 2(1);[3]

(d)   a tenant who has been ordered by a court to give up possession of the flat: Sch 3, para 3(1);

(e)   a tenant who in relation to the whole or part of *his flat*[4] has received a notice to treat under compulsory purchase procedures or has thereafter entered into a contract with the public body concerned, and the notice or contract is still in force: Sch 3, para 4(1).[5]

---

1   Based on the Leasehold Reform Act 1967, Sch 3, para 1(1).
2   Ibid.
3   Based on Ibid, para 2(1).
4   For compulsory purchase procedures in relation to any part of the premises greater than the flat, see para 3.71.
5   Based on the Leasehold Reform Act 1967, s 5(6).

3.22   In addition, a tenant against whom proceedings to terminate his lease are pending must not participate in giving a s 13 notice without the leave of the court: Sch 3, para 3(2). The court must not give such leave unless satisfied that the sole or main reason for giving the notice is to avoid the consequences of the breach of covenant leading to the proceedings: Sch 3, para 3(3). But, if leave is granted, and the claim is made, it can proceed on the footing that the tenant's lease is subsisting despite the proceedings and any order thereafter made in them. If the claim is effective, the court can vary or set aside any order made in those proceedings: Sch 3, para 3(4).[1]

---

1   Based on the Leasehold Reform Act 1967, Sch 3, para 4(2).

THE EFFECTS OF GIVING A SECTION 13 NOTICE

Notices to terminate

3.23   If within the four months before giving the s 13 notice the landlord gave a qualifying tenant a notice to terminate the lease under the Landlord and Tenant Act 1954, s 4, or a notice under the Local Government and Housing Act 1989, Sch 10, para 4(1), that landlord's notice will cease to have effect when the s 13 notice is served: Sch 3, para 2(2).[1] It does not appear to be necessary that the qualifying tenant was one of those participating in the s 13 notice. What happens if subsequently the claim to collective enfranchisement is not 'effective', ie does not result in a binding contract being entered into between the parties, or a vesting order being made under ss 24(4)(a), (b), 25(6)(a), (b)? In such a case, the landlord may within one month of the claim to collective enfranchisement ceasing to be 'current' serve a further notice to terminate the lease under Landlord and Tenant Act 1954, s 4 or under the Local Government and Housing Act 1989, Sch 10, para 4(1): Sch 3, para 2(3).[2] Specific provision is made as to the termination date to be specified in such further notice: Sch 3, para 2(4), (5). For this purpose 'current' means that the s 13 notice continues to be in force or, if it is not a valid notice, until it is set aside or withdrawn: Sch 3, para 10(1)(d).

1   Based on the Leasehold Reform Act 1967, Sch 3, para 2(2).
2   Based on ibid, para 2(3).

3.24   So long as the claim to collective enfranchisement remains 'current' (see para 3.23), no notice to terminate the lease of the flat held by a participating tenant is of any effect, whether it is a tenant's notice, or a landlord's notice under the Landlord and Tenant Act 1954, s 4 or the Local Government and Housing Act 1989, Sch 10, para 4(1): Sch 3, para 5.[1] Nor can proceedings be brought to enforce a right of re-entry of forfeiture in relation to the lease of any flat held by a participating tenant, except with the leave of the court: Sch 3, para 7(1)(a).[2] Leave is only to be given if the court is satisfied that the sole or main reason for participating in making the claim was to avoid the consequences of the breach leading to the proposed proceedings; if leave is given, the tenant will cease to be a participating tenant.

1   Based on the Leasehold Reform Act 1967, Sch 3, paras 1(2), 2(2).
2   Based on ibid, Sch 3, para 4(1).

Termination in other ways

3.25   Similarly, Sch 3, para 6[1] provides that, so long as the claim remains current, and for three months thereafter, the lease of a flat held by a participating tenant cannot come to an end in any of the following ways:

(a)   by effluxion of time;
(b)   following a notice to quit given by the landlord;
(c)   by the termination of a superior lease.

1   Based on the Leasehold Reform Act 1967, Sch 3, para 3(1).

3.26   If the claim turns out not to be 'effective' (para 3.23), and a lease will otherwise be terminated before the end of the three months, it terminates at the end of those three months: Sch 3, para 6. But the lease can still terminate in any other way, even whilst the collective enfranchisement claim remains in force: Sch 3, para 6(2). Nor do these provisions affect the court's power to grant relief against forfeiture, or to grant relief under the Landlord and Tenant Act 1954, s 16(2) or Sch 5, para 9 (including as applied by the Local Government and Housing Act 1989, Sch 10): Sch 3, para 6(2), (3).

Prohibition on subdivision and subdemises

3.27   A final negative effect of a s 13 notice is the impact on third parties who subsequently deal with the reversioner or other relevant landlords. Once the notice has been registered (see para 3.32), then so long as it continues in force the reversioner cannot divide his interest in the premises or in any other property to be acquired, and neither he nor any other relevant landlord may create any leasehold interest which would itself have been liable to be acquired: s 19(1). Any transaction is void to the extent that it attempts to have the prohibited effect: s 19(1). Dispositions by a reversioner or relevant landlord of his *entire* interests to a single acquirer without division are not void, but are dealt with in a different way: para 2.26. There are also provisions dealing with the case where at the time of the initial notice there already exists a valid contract by the reversioner or relevant landlord to dispose of his entire interest to a single acquirer without division: see para 2.27.

Right of access

3.28   Once he has received the notice (or a copy) under s 13, a reversioner or other relevant landlord, and their agents, will have a right of access to every part of the premises and any other freehold property to be acquired, in which the reversioner or other relevant landlord has a freehold or leasehold interest, to enable him to obtain a valuation of his interest: s 17(1). A similar right of access is given to the nominee purchaser and his agents, where such access is reasonably required in connection with any matter arising out of the notice: s 17(2). Such rights of access are exercisable at any reasonable time, on giving at least ten days' notice to the occupier or (if unoccupied) to the person entitled to occupy: s 17(3).

Disclosure of side-agreements

3.29   The nominee purchaser is supposed to be a vehicle for the participating tenants to acquire the freehold in the premises. Collective enfranchisement was not intended as a means of benefiting non-participating tenants, or indeed third parties. Such side effects are dealt with by s 18. The fear that prompted this section was that qualifying tenants might agree to make a s 13 claim using the smallest possible number of qualifying tenants, as this would reduce the 'marriage value' element of the price (para 3.78) to a minimum, whilst having side-agreements with the other qualifying tenants, allowing them to participate after acquisition.[1] As will be seen, the section as drafted extends much wider than that.

---

1 HL Committee, 15 March 1993, cols 1314–1323.

3.30   Thus, if at any time after service of the s 13 notice, and before the 'valuation date' (see para 3.75), a person who is not a participating tenant has a contractual right to obtain any interest in the premises from the nominee purchaser (other than a security interest: s 18(4)), the existence of that contract must be disclosed to the reversioner as soon as possible after the s 13 notice is served or (if later) after the contract is made: s 18(1)(a). Similarly, if the nominee purchaser is a company and at any time during the same period a person who is not a participating tenant holds a share in that company, the existence of the shareholding must be likewise disclosed: s 18(1)(b). The sanction for non-disclosure before determination of the price payable by the nominee purchaser is that the nominee purchaser *and* the participating tenants are jointly and severally liable to pay to the reversioner or other relevant landlord the difference between the price actually determined and the price that would have been determined if disclosure had been made: s 18(2).

Deduction of title

3.31 The reversioner also has the right, within 21 days of the service of the s 13 notice, to require the nominee purchaser to deduce the title to the lease of any of the qualifying tenants giving the notice: s 20(1). The nominee purchaser has 21 days within which to comply: s 20(2). The consequences of failure to comply depend on whether it would have made any difference if the qualifying tenant had not been one of those giving the notice. If, without the qualifying tenant in question (and without any other qualifying tenant in respect of whom a similar failure has occured), the s 13 notice would not have satisfied the number and residence thresholds in s 13(2)(b) (see para 2.47), the notice is deemed withdrawn at the end of the 21-day period: s 20(3). Curiously, there is no similar entitlement for a reversioner to require the nominee purchaser to deduce the title to the lease for any tenant who *subsequently* becomes a participating tenant under s 14(3) (para 2.37).

Registration of initial notice

3.32 Although the collective enfranchisement provisions effectively confer on qualifying tenants a form of option to purchase the freehold, the lease of a qualifying tenant does not thereby become registrable under the Land Charges Act 1972. Nor is the right of a qualifying tenant under this Act an overriding interest under the Land Registration Act 1925: s 97(1).[1] But, on the other hand, a notice given under s 13 *is* registrable under the Land Charges Act 1972 or the Land Registration Act 1925 (as appropriate) as if it were an estate contract: s 97(1).[2] Similarly, court orders made under s 26(1) of this Act (where the landlord cannot be ascertained or found) are also registrable, as are applications for such orders: s 97(2). And for the purposes of the Land Registration Act 1925, s 57(1), applicants for such orders are treated as persons interested in the land in question: s 97(3).

1 Based on the Leasehold Reform Act 1967, s 5(5).
2 Based on ibid, s 5(5).

REVERSIONER'S COUNTERNOTICE

3.33 The next step in the procedure is for the reversioner to serve a counternotice by the date specified in the tenant's s 13 notice, which will be at least two months from the date of that notice: s 21(1).[1] By s 21(2), the counternotice must elect for one of three things:

(a) admit the participating tenants' entitlement to collective enfranchisement in relation to the specified premises;
(b) deny that entitlement, for reasons stated;
(c) *in addition* to either (a) or (b), state the appropriate landlord's intention to apply to the court for an order that collective enfranchisement be not exercisable, on grounds of intended redevelopment (such applications are dealt with in paras 3.40–3.43).

1 Section 21 is based on the Leasehold Reform Act 1967, Sch 3, para 7.

3.34   The counternotice must give an address in England and Wales for services of notices on the reversioner: s 21(6). It must also inform the nominee purchaser of any claim made to an extended lease ('individual enfranchisement') under s 42, and any counternotice served in response: Sch 4, para 1. Indeed, while the s 13 notice continues to be in force, or any binding contract pursuant to that notice remains in force, or interests remain to be vested under an order of the court, the reversioner is under a *continuing* duty, after serving his counternotice, to inform the nominee purchaser of any such claim to an extended lease and any notice subsequently withdrawing such notice: Sch 4, para 2. If the reversioner fails to serve a counternotice at all, the tenants' remedy is to apply to the court: para 3.45.

Admitting the entitlement

3.35   Where the counternotice admits the tenant's entitlement to collective enfranchisement, it must go on to state which of the proposals (eg purchase price, other property to be acquired) are accepted and which are not, and, in the case of rejected proposals, what the reversioner proposes instead: s 21(3)(a). In particular, where the tenants' claim extends to property used in common (under s 1(3)(a)) and the reversioner counterproposes the grant of equivalent rights under s 1(4), these must be fully specified: s 21(3)(b).

3.36   Whether or not the reversioner accepts the tenants' proposals, there are other matters with which he must deal in his counternotice. First, if he wishes to put forward what are called 'additional leaseback proposals', he must set these out too: s 21(3)(a). These are proposals for the leasing back to the reversioner of certain flats or units in the premises in accordance with s 36 and Sch 9 (see paras 3.88–3.93): s 21(7). Second, the reversioner can require the nominee purchaser to acquire any reversioner's or other relevant landlord's interest in *any* property which (in the event of the acquisition going ahead) would for all practical purposes cease to be of use and benefit to him, or would cease to be reasonably manageable or maintainable by him: s 21(4). In this case, the reversioner must state these interests in the counternotice: s 21(3)(c). The nominee purchaser or his agent will then have the right of access to such property for valuation purposes: s 21(5).

Denying entitlement

3.37   Where the counternotice does not admit the tenant's entitlement to collective enfranchisement, the nominee purchaser may, within two months from receiving the counternotice, apply to the court for a declaration as to the participating tenants' entitlement on the date of service of the original s 13 notice: s 22(1)(a), (2). Although the marginal note to the section reads 'Proceedings relating to validity of initial notice', the court appears not to be concerned with whether the *notice* itself was valid, but with the logically prior question whether the participating tenants were *entitled* to serve a notice. The court procedure here does not appear to be predicated on a valid original notice having 'been given in accordance with s 13' (as is the procedure under s 25, for example).

3.38   Thus, if the court is satisfied that the participating tenants *were* so entitled, then the court *must* so declare: s 22(1)(b). (The words are 'shall by order make a declaration', which is tautologous.) In most cases the court must also declare that the reversioner's counternotice (if any) is of no effect, and require the reversioner to give a further counternotice (giving much the same information as the original) by a specified date: s 22(3), (5). But these further requirements do not apply if the counternotice had stated the reversioner's intention to apply to the court for an order that collective enfranchisement be not exercisable on grounds of proposed redevelopment, and either such an application to court is pending or the time for making it has not yet expired: s 22(4). (As to such applications, see paras 3.40–3.43.)

3.39 If, on the other hand, the court is not satisfied that the participating tenants were entitled to exercise collective enfranchisement on the date their notice was served, then the court will dismiss the application, and their notice will cease to have effect when the court order 'becomes final' (as to which see para 1.21): s 22(6).

Landlord's intention to redevelop

3.40 Here, the reversioner in his counternotice may or may not admit the tenant's right, but he states the intention of an 'appropriate landlord' to seek an order from the court preventing collective enfranchisement being exercised, on the grounds that that landlord intends to redevelop the whole or a substantial part of the premises. For this purpose 'appropriate landlord' means the reversioner or any other relevant landlord, or any two or more of them acting together: s 23(10). The appropriate landlord must make his application within two months from the date of the counternotice being given, although if the counternotice did not admit the tenant's entitlement in principle, he cannot proceed with the application until any order declaring that the tenants were entitled to exercise collective enfranchisement has 'become final': s 23(3).

3.41 If no application is made within the two-month period, or one is made which is subsequently withdrawn, the reversioner must give a second counternotice to the nominee purchaser within two months of the end of the first two month period or the withdrawal of the application, as appropriate: s 23(6), (7). This counternotice must give the same information as the original counternotice (except a statement admitting or denying the tenants' right or stating an intention to redevelop): s 23(9). But the requirement for a second counternotice does not apply if the nominee purchaser has applied for a declaration under s 22 that the participating tenants were entitled to exercise the right to collective enfranchisement: s 23(8). This is because, if the application succeeds, the reversioner will already have been required under s 21(3)(b) to give a second counternotice.

Facts to consider

3.42 On the application the court has to consider whether:

(a)   two-thirds of the long leases of flats in the specified premises are due to terminate within five years of the date of the original notice;
(b)   the applicant intends after such termination to demolish, reconstruct or carry out substantial building work on all or a substantial part of the premises;[1] and
(c)   he cannot reasonably do this without obtaining possession of the flats concerned.

If the court is satisfied of all three matters, it may (not must) declare that collective enfranchisement is not exercisable in relation to the premises: s 23(1), (2).

1   The statutory words are taken from the Landlord and Tenant Act 1954, s 12(1)(a), and the Leasehold Reform Act 1967, s 17(1).

3.43   But if, on the other hand, the court dismisses the application, then it must also:

(i)   declare the reversioner's counternotice to be of no effect;

(ii)   require the reversioner to give a further counternotice by a specified date.

As before, the second counternotice must give the same information (except for admission or denial of the tenant's right or stating an intention to redevelop) as in the original counternotice: s 23(9).

Dispute as to terms

3.44   Where the reversioner's counternotice admits the tenant's entitlement to collective enfranchisement, or the reversioner's or other landlord's challenge to the right (or to its exercise) has been unsuccessful, and he has served a new counternotice, either the original or the new counternotice may dispute some of the terms of acquisition: see paras 3.35, 3.38, 3.41, 3.43. 'Terms of acquisition' includes the interests to be acquired, the extent of the property concerned, the purchase price, apportionment or other matters in connection with severance of a reversionary interest, and the provisions in any conveyance: s 24(8). If any of these remains in dispute at the end of two months after the counternotice in question was given, either nominee purchaser or reversioner may apply to a leasehold valuation tribunal to determine the dispute: s 24(1). The application must be made within six months of the service of the counternotice concerned: s 24(2). The tribunal is expressly given power to determine that the property in which any interest is to be acquired should be less extensive than that specified in the s 13 notice: s 91(9).

FAILURE TO GIVE COUNTERNOTICE

3.45   The collective enfranchisement procedure depends on the reversioner responding to the tenant's claim. If the system is to work effectively, there has to be some sanction for a failure by the reversioner to serve a counternotice (or a further counternotice, if so required). The legislation could have achieved this by treating the reversioner as having admitted everything put forward by the tenants, or at any rate preventing him from opposing that. Although simple and certain, this might have produced negative effects for the reversioner (and any other relevant landlords) disproportionate to the default involved. Accordingly, a slower and less effective – but probably fairer – sanction has been adopted.

3.46   The procedure applies where an initial notice has been given in accordance with s 13, but the reversioner has failed to give his counternotice in time (para 3.33), or is treated as having so failed, or has failed to give a further counternotice where required to do so (see paras 3.38, 3.41, 3.43). In such cases, the nominee purchaser may, within six months from the expiry of the period for service of the counter-notice in question, apply to the court for an order determining the terms of the acquisition 'in accordance with the proposals contained in the initial notice': s 25(1), (4). But, if Sch 9, Part II (see para 3.89) is applicable, those terms will also include provision for leaseback, under s 36, of flats or other units in the premises: s 25(2).

3.47   It is clear that the court has no discretion as to the terms, but must accept those proposed in the initial notice. But before the court may make the order sought, it must first be satisfied that, on the date of giving the initial notice, the participating tenants were entitled to exercise collective enfranchisement in relation to the premises, and that any applicable requirements of Sch 3, Part II (see para 3.13) as to giving copies of the notice were complied with: s 25(3).

FAILURE TO ENTER BINDING CONTRACT

3.48   Under the terms of the Leasehold Reform Act 1967 and the extended long lease ('individual enfranchisement') provisions of this Act, the valid service of the initial notice itself creates a ultimate obligation to convey the freehold or grant a new lease. But the collective enfranchisement provisions are different. Instead, the legislation assumes that, after resolving all disputes as to terms, the nominee purchaser and the reversioner will enter a binding contract for the sale of the freehold and other interests to the nominee purchaser. This device means that the statute does not need to provide what happens in case of breach of contract, or the position vis-à-vis third parties – in default of express provision, the general law of contract will apply. But it *does* mean that the statute has to provide for the case where the parties, for whatever reason, do not enter a binding contract.

3.49   There are two situations that must be considered. The first is the case of the reversioner who participates in the process. He serves counternotices, perhaps makes applications to the court or disputes terms before the leasehold valuation tribunal, but ultimately the terms of acquisition are agreed[1] or determined. What he does *not* do is sign up. The other case is that of the reversioner who refuses to participate. He does not serve counternotices, and is in effect dragged along by court and tribunal orders. (The case of the reversioner who cannot be identified, or, if identified, cannot be located, is quite different, and is dealt with later: see paras 3.56–3.68.)

1   This means agreed subject to contract: s 38(4).

3.50   In either of the two cases mentioned, the parties have a certain amount of time (the 'appropriate period') after the terms have been agreed or determined in which to enter the contract. Once that 'appropriate period' has elapsed, either nominee purchaser or reversioner has two months within which to apply to the court for an order appropriate to the circumstances: ss 24(3), 25(5). The appropriate order may be one for the interests to be acquired to be vested in the nominee purchaser, whether on the terms already agreed or determined, or on those terms modified in some way, or it may be one deeming the tenant's initial notice to have been withdrawn at the end of the appropriate period: ss 24(4), 25(6).

3.51   The period of time that must elapse before an application may be made (ie the 'appropriate period') depends on whether the terms of acquisition were agreed by the parties or resolved by the leasehold valuation tribunal or the court. If the parties agree them, it is two months from the date on which final agreement[1] was reached: s 24(6)(a). But if the leasehold valuation tribunal or the court determines them, then it is the period stipulated by the leasehold valuation tribunal or the court or, if no period is stipulated, two months from the date on which the determination or order became final: ss 24(6)(b), 25(8).

---

1   See previous note.

3.52   Where the court makes an order for interests 'to be vested in' the nominee purchaser under s 24(4)(a) or (b) or s 25(6)(a) or (b) (called a 'vesting order'), the provisions of Sch 5 apply. These make it clear that the vesting order does not itself operate to vest any interest in the nominee purchaser. Instead, on the nominee purchaser paying into court the 'appropriate sum', a person designated by the court will execute a conveyance in a form approved by a leasehold valuation tribunal and containing approved provisions to give effect to the proposed terms of acquisition: Sch 5, para 2. The 'appropriate sum' is the aggregate of:

(a)   the price payable in accordance with Sch 6 (see paras 3.75–3.85); and
(b)   any amount or estimated amounts due at the time from tenants to their landlord: Sch 5, para 3.

Payment of the appropriate sum into court satisfies any claims against the nominee purchaser or the participating tenants (and their estates) in respect of the price payable. Finally, it should be noted that a 'vesting order' ceases to have effect if before the conveyance is executed any acquiring authority for compulsory purchase purposes (see s 30) serves notice to treat: Sch 5, para 5(3).

WITHDRAWAL FROM ACQUISITION

3.53   An individual participating tenant cannot withdraw from the acquisition on his own, although in certain circumstances he can of course cease to be a participating tenant: cf paras 2.33–2.40. But at any time before a binding contract is entered into, the participating tenants may *collectively* withdraw from the acquisition by giving a notice under s 28, withdrawing their initial notice under s 13. If they do so, there is a potential costs sanction. A notice under s 28 must be given to the nominee purchaser, the reversioner, and every other relevant landlord known or believed to have elected to deal independently with the nominee purchaser, rather than through the reversioner: s 28(2). A notice given to other relevant landlords must state that they are recipients: s 28(2). This is so that the nominee purchaser can copy the notice he receives to any relevant landlord who has elected to deal independently, but is not stated in the notice to have received one: s 28(3).

Deemed withdrawal

3.54   In addition to express withdrawal of the s 13 notice, there are a number of situations in which that notice is deemed to be withdrawn, usually as a form of sanction for non-compliance with time limits. These situations are as follows:

(a)   where a reversioner denies the entitlement to collective enfranchisement, and the nominee purchaser does not apply to the court for a declaration of entitlement within two months of the counternotice, or an application is made but subsequently withdrawn: s 29(1);

(b)   where the reversioner admits entitlement to collective enfranchisement but there remains a dispute as to terms, and no application to the leasehold valuation tribunal is made within six months of the counternotice: s 29(2)(a);

(c)   where the terms are agreed or determined, but no binding contract is entered into and no application is made to the court within two months of the end of the 'appropriate period' (see para 3.51): s 29(2)(b), (4);

(d)   where the reversioner fails to give a counternotice (or further counternotice), but the nominee purchaser does not apply to the court for an order determining the terms within six months of the date by which the counternotice should have been given: s 29(3);

(e)   where the further notice under s 15(5)(b) or s 16(5) relating to the nominee purchaser is not served in time: s 29(5)(a), (b);

(f)   where the nominee purchaser does not comply with the reversioner's require-ment under s 20 for evidence of a tenant's right to participate: s 29(5)(c);

(g)   where the court so orders under s 24(4)(c) or s 25(6)(c), by reason of the nominee purchaser's failure to enter a binding contract: s 29(5)(d), (e).

Costs sanction

3.55   If the participating tenants do withdraw (or are deemed to withdraw) from the acquisition, the reversioner and relevant landlords are entitled to be paid the costs they have incurred in pursuance of the initial notice up to the time of receipt of the notice of withdrawal, and for which the nominee purchaser would have been liable if the acquisition had been completed: ss 28(4), (7), 29(6). The liability to pay these costs is not only that of the participating tenants who gave the notice of withdrawal but (with one exception) also of every other person who is not now but has in the past been a participating tenant: s 28(4). The exception is for a participating tenant who assigns his lease to another person who becomes a participating tenant by virtue of s 14(4) (para 2.37): s 28(5). The liability for costs in all cases of *actual* withdrawal and in cases of deemed withdrawal (e) above is joint and several (s 28(6)(a)), and then the nominee purchaser is not liable for any costs under s 33: s 28(6)(b).

WHERE THE LANDLORD CANNOT BE FOUND

3.56   As has been seen, the collective enfranchisement procedure is based on service of the tenants' notice on the reversioner: para 3.11. As with the right to an extended lease ('individual enfranchisement'), therefore, a separate procedure is needed to deal with the case where the identity of the reversioner or of *all* the relevant landlords cannot be ascertained, or, though ascertained, he or they cannot be found. In such a case at least two-thirds of the qualifying tenants in particular premises may apply to the court for an order under which the nominee purchaser or other person is granted a conveyance of the required interests: ss 26(1),[1] 27(1).

---

1   Based on the Leasehold Reform Act 1967, s 27(1).

3.57   This procedure does not, however, apply where at least one of the relevant landlords can be found, but one or more of the other persons on whom a copy of the qualifying tenants' notice should be served cannot be ascertained or found. In such a case the court has power simply to dispense with the need to give a copy to that person: s 26(2). (If the missing person is the freeholder, then the court may also make an order appointing another relevant landlord to be the reversioner: s 26(3).) Thereafter, if any notice given to claim the right to collective enfranchisement contains a statement of the effect of the order, the requirements of the legislation in relation to serving the missing person will be satisfied: s 26(7), (8).

3.58   Since the application in either case is ex hypothesi concerned with a missing person, the court has a kind of interlocutory power, before making any order on the application, to require the tenants to take such steps as the court thinks appropriate to try to trace the missing person: s 26(5).[1] This may involve advertising or other methods of bringing the existence of the qualifying tenants' claim to his attention: s 26(5).[2]

1   Based on the Leasehold Reform Act 1967, s 27(2).
2   Ibid.

The vesting order

3.59   Under the missing landlord procedure, the order of the court is known as a 'vesting order': s 26(1). This is misleading, because it suggests that the order itself vests the required interests in the nominee purchasers. It does not. All it does is to take the place of:

(a)   service of the tenants' notice on the reversioner; and
(b)   admission in principle of the tenants' right to enfranchise.

In particular, there is no nominee purchaser because there has been no notice under s 13. The terms of the acquisition are left to be determined by a further application to a leasehold valuation tribunal: s 27(1). Once that is done, the person appointed by the applicants, and specified in the order as transferee, pays the necessary sums into court, and only then is a conveyance executed in favour of the transferee, by the person designated by the court. This vests the interests expressed to be conveyed in the transferee: s 27(3).[1] The transferee will probably be the person or persons who, if a section 13 notice had been served, would have been designated as nominee purchaser.

1   Based on the Leasehold Reform Act 1967, s 27(3).

3.60   The essentially preliminary nature of the vesting order is also shown by the provision that an application for a vesting order may be withdrawn at any time before the conveyance is executed: ie even though a vesting order has by then actually been made: s 26(6). In practice, if the order has been made, but the tenants wish to withdraw, they will just do nothing further, ie in particular they will not apply to the leasehold valuation tribunal. It is also difficult to see what the court would do if an application were made to withdraw an application after an order had been made on that application. Similarly if, before the conveyance is executed, the missing person 'is traced', then no further 'proceedings' may be taken with the view to that conveyance being executed: s 26(5). This will include any part of the proceedings remaining before the vesting order is made, but also the application to the leasehold valuation tribunal to determine the terms of the acquisition.

3.61 There is no definition or elucidation of the word 'traced', nor is it clear what degree of certainty is required that it is indeed the person sought who has been found, and not someone else. Does it mean merely that an address has come to light? Or that the person has actually been seen? Does it matter that it happens accidentally, rather than as a result of deliberate searching? And to whose knowledge must the information come? Presumably it must come to the knowledge of the tenants. There is no express requirement for the tenants to inform the court, much less the person himself, that the missing person has been traced.

3.62 This vagueness is very unhelpful, because once the missing person 'is traced', in principle the parties are stated to be in the same legal position as if the applicants had served a s 13 notice: s 26(5)(a).[1] The unfairness of this situation to the traced person (since he will probably not know anything about it) is tempered, though not cured, by the court's power in such a case to give directions as to the steps to be taken for giving effect to the party's rights and obligations (s 26(5)(b)),[2] and obviously these may include notifying him of what is going on. Moreover, if the applicants merely do not proceed with an application to the court – or if the court has already made a 'vesting order' – the court will have no reason to invoke its powers.

---

1 Based on the Leasehold Reform Act 1967, s 27(2)(a).
2 Based on ibid, s 27(2)(b).

3.63 The general rule – that on the missing person being traced the parties are in the same position as if the s 13 notice had been served – does not apply if the application for a vesting order is withdrawn (s 26(6)),[1] unless some step has by then been taken (whether by the applicants or otherwise) to give effect to that general legal position. In that exceptional case, the application may only be withdrawn with the consent of every person owning an interest which the applicants seek to have vested in them, or of the court: s 26(6). The court must not give leave unless it is just to do so because of matters learnt by the applicants from tracing the missing person: s 26(6). All in all, the consequences of 'tracing' the missing person are poorly conceived, badly drafted and needlessly complex.

---

1 Based on the Leasehold Reform Act 1967, s 27(7).

3.64 Where the court is faced with an application for a vesting order, it must not make the order unless it is satisfied by the applicants of three things:

(i) the identity of the owner of the freehold of, or of another interest in, the premises cannot be ascertained, or (if ascertained) he cannot be found: s 26(1);

(ii) on the date of making the application, the premises concerned were premises to which the collective enfranchisement provisions applied: s 26(4)(a);

(iii) on that date there was nothing in the legislation to prevent the applicant giving a valid notice under s 13 in relation to those premises: s 26(4)(b).

Application to leasehold valuation tribunal

3.65   Once the vesting order has been made, an application will be made to a leasehold valuation tribunal to determine the terms of the acquisition. Since the leasehold valuation tribunal normally has no jurisdiction until a notice and counternotice have been served (see para 3.44) and since the effect of the vesting order is to put the qualifying tenants in the same position as if notice had been given (s 27(1)), it seems that a vesting order must be made before the leasehold valuation tribunal can consider the matter. The leasehold valuation tribunal is specifically given power to determine that the vesting order made by the court should have effect in respect of property less (but not more) extensive than that specified in the application to the court: s 27(2). In particular, it seems (although the drafting could be clearer) that the underlying minerals must be excluded: s 27(4).[1] Moreover, the leasehold valuation tribunal is to assume in every case that the missing person has no interest in any other property than that which is to be the subject of the conveyance, and any minerals underlying that property: s 27(4).

1   Based on the Leasehold Reform Act 1967, s 27(4).

Engrossment and payment

3.66   After the leasehold valuation tribunal has determined the terms of the acquisition, the conveyance can be drawn up. The leasehold valuation tribunal will have determined the amounts to be paid into court (in aggregate called 'the appropriate sum') and these are:

(a)   the price that would be payable under Sch 6 (see para 3.75) in respect of the missing person's interest; and

(b)   amounts or estimated amounts due from the tenants to the missing person under the leases (or any collateral agreement) at the time of execution of the conveyance, ie arrears of ground rent, service charge and so on: s 27(5).

3.67   In (b) the statute refers to sums 'due to the transferor from any tenants of his'. But in these provisions 'the transferor' may not be the tenant's immediate landlord, but a person further up the landlord and tenant chain: see para 2.5. In such a case the only 'tenants of his' will be higher up the chain than the participating tenants. Yet the participating tenants have to pay these sums.

3.68   Once the conveyance has been executed, payment into court of the 'appropriate sum' satisfies any claims against applicants for the vesting order in respect of the amounts in (a) above: s 27(6).[1] Nothing is said as to (b), so it must be supposed that the immediate landlord's claim against the tenant for sums due under the old lease and any collateral agreement remains unsatisfied. Another curiosity is that the Act makes no provision for the missing person, if and when he turns up, to withdraw the money from court. Presumably he must apply to the court for an order for payment out, and must prove that he is indeed the person concerned before he can obtain such an order.

1   Based on the Leasehold Reform Act 1967, s 27(6).

INTERACTION WITH OTHER PROCEEDINGS

3.69   Particular problems could arise when the collective enfranchisement procedure is under way and then another statutory procedure concerning the property is activated, or vice versa. One obvious example is an application being made for lease extension (individual enfranchisement), under Part I, Chapter II of this Act. Another is the commencement of compulsory acquisition procedures. The legislation makes specific provision for both situations.

Claims for lease extension

3.70   The basic rule is that the collective enfranchisement procedure takes priority over the lease extension procedure. Thus, if a claim to collective enfranchisement is made whilst a claim to a new lease is 'current', the tenant's notice claiming a new lease is suspended until the claim to collective enfranchisement comes to an end: s 54(2).[1] Similarly, if a claim to a new lease is made whilst a claim to collective enfranchisement is 'current', the tenant's notice claiming a new lease does not take effect but is suspended for so long as the claim to collective enfranchisement remains current: s 54(1). See further on this paras 4.103–4.108.

---

1   Cf the Leasehold Reform Act 1967, s 5(8).

Compulsory acquisition procedures

3.71   There are three cases to consider. The first is where the participating tenants give notice under s 13 to exercise collective enfranchisement and subsequently compulsory acquisition procedures are commenced in relation to the premises concerned (or part of them). The second is where compulsory acquisition procedures are already under way in relation to the premises concerned when the tenants serve their s 13 notice. The third case is similar to the second, but the compulsory purchase procedure relates, not to the 'premises', but either to other property outside the premises, or to intermediate leasehold interests in the premises.

3.72   In the second case the tenant's notice never takes effect: s 30(1).[1] In the third case the s 13 notice 'shall not specify' the outside property or intermediate leasehold interest: s 30(3). This is rather cryptic, particularly since (in relation to intermediate leaseholds) it overlaps with s 30(1). In the first case the s 13 notice ceases to have effect if, before a binding contract is entered into, a 'notice to treat' is served: s 30(4).[2] But since the tenant's notice in that case was already served by then, the compensation payable in respect of any person's interest in the premises is to be determined on the basis of the value of such interest as affected by the notice: s 30(6).[3] If the notice to treat is not served until after a binding contract has been entered into, but before completion, then (without prejudice to the doctrine of frustration of contracts) the parties are discharged from further performance: s 30(5).[4] There are no provisions for revival of the procedure if the compulsory acquisition does not proceed.

---

1   Based on the Leasehold Reform Act 1967, s 5(6).

---

2 Ibid.
3 Ibid.
4 Based on ibid, s 5(7).

PROPERTY TRANSFERRED FOR PUBLIC BENEFIT

3.73   In some circumstances, land or buildings may be designated by the Treasury as a property of outstanding scenic, historic, architectural or scientific interest: Inheritance Tax Act 1984, s 31(1)(b), (c), (d). If on a transfer an undertaking is then given by the transferee to preserve and maintain it, and to allow the public reasonable access, that transfer of the property will not give rise to a charge to inheritance tax: Inheritance Tax Act 1984, s 30(1). During the passage of the Bill the House of Lords voted in favour of a provision preventing collective or individual enfranchisement in cases of property to which these provisions applied.[1] The Government brought forward[2] a differently worded provision to similar effect – though restricted to collective enfranchisement alone – and this now forms s 31 of this Act. (A similar provision was added by s 68 of this Act to the Leasehold Reform Act 1967: see para 5.15.)

1 HL Report, 11 May 1993, cols 1240–1251.
2 HL 3R, 25 May 1993, cols 186–187, 207–209.

3.74   Section 31 applies not only when a Treasury designation has been made under the Inheritance Tax Act 1984, s 31(1)(b), (c) or (d), but also in circumstances closely associated with such a designation, in particular where an application for designation is pending: the Leasehold Reform, Housing and Urban Development Act 1993, s 31(2)(b), (d). The section operates in two ways. First, it causes the s 13 notice to be of no effect if at that time the above conditions are satisfied: s 31(1). Second, it causes a s 13 notice already served to *cease* to be of effect if those conditions *subsequently* are satisfied: s 31(4). In the latter case, the nominee purchaser will not be liable for any costs under s 33 (see para 3.86), but the person claiming that s 31 applies is liable both to the qualifying tenants and to the nominee purchaser for their reasonable costs: s 31(5). A person claiming that the conditions were satisfied must supply the nominee purchaser with evidence in support of that claim. Failure to do so renders him liable for any costs reasonably incurred by the nominee purchaser in consequence of that failure: s 31(6).

THE PRICE

3.75   The price to be paid by the nominee purchaser for the freehold and other interests to be acquired under collective enfranchisement is determined in accordance with Sch 6 of the Act: s 32(1). The procedure can be compared with that under the Leasehold Reform Act 1967, s 9.[1] Unlike that procedure, the date as at which the valuation is to be calculated is not the date of making the initial claim,[2] but the date when all the terms of acquisition (save amounts to be paid) have been agreed or determined: Sch 6, para 1(1). The rules for determining the price for different kinds of interest are set out in separate parts of the Schedule. Thus, the freehold of the specified premises is dealt with in Part II, intermediate leasehold interests in Part III, and other interests in Part IV. Parts V and VI of the Schedule deal with interests which have negative values (ie are burdensome rather than beneficial).

1 See *Hill & Redman*, **E** [581]–[589].
2 See the Leasehold Reform Act 1967, s 37(1)(d).

Freehold of specified premises

3.76 According to Sch 6, para 2, the price payable for the freehold interest in the specified premises is the aggregate of three elements:

(a) the value of the freeholder's interest in the premises;
(b) the freeholder's share of the 'marriage value';
(c) any compensation payable to the freeholder in respect of losses suffered in respect of other properties.

If the aggregate of these three is negative, the price payable is nil.

Value of freeholder's interest

3.77 This is the amount which the interest might be expected to realise if sold by a willing vendor on an open market basis, and on certain assumptions: Sch 6, para 3(1).[1] These assumptions are:

(a) that the vendor is selling an estate in fee simple subject to certain leases;
(b) that the 1993 Act confers no right to enfranchise (except in relation to a claim to extend a lease by a non-participating tenant);
(c) that the tenant's improvements are disregarded;
(d) that the vendor is selling on the terms of the conveyance to be made under this Act.

But other assumptions may also be made: para 3(2). Any defaults in title must also be taken account of in the value: para 3(3).[2] There are also certain anti-avoidance provisions involving the creation of overriding leases, corresponding to the provision made by the Leasehold Reform Act 1979[3] in relation to enfranchisement under the 1967 Act: para 3(5).

1 Based on the Leasehold Reform Act 1967, s 9(1).
2 Based on ibid, s 9(2).
3 See *Hill & Redman*, **E** [1081]–[1083].

Freeholder's share of marriage value

3.78 'Marriage value' is a well known valuation concept. Two assets may be worth a total of $£X$ in separate hands, but $£(X+Y)$ in the same hands. The marriage value is the difference, $£(X+Y) - £X$, ie $£Y$. In the context of landlord and tenant law, the Secretary of State for the Environment explained it thus:[1]

'Marriage value is the difference between the aggregate of the values of the freehold and leasehold interests before and after enfranchisement. In other words, it represents the increase in value when the freehold and the leasehold come under the same control. It is how the market puts a monetary value on the tenant's special interest in acquiring the property and it reflects the fact that the former tenant of the house gains an unencumbered freehold, and the fact that the tenants collectively in a block of flats can grant themselves new leases for little or no premium.'[2]

---

1   See HC Report, 9 February 1993, cols 874.
2   As to 'marriage value' under the Leasehold Reform Act 1967, see *Hill & Redman*, **E** [583]–[584].

3.79   The marriage value is accordingly defined for collective enfranchisement purposes as the increase in aggregate value of the freehold and intermediate leasehold interests in the premises, considered as under the participating tenants' control, compared with the aggregate value of these interests in the hands of their owners before collective enfranchisement: para 4(2). But it is an increase in value attributable to the participating tenants' ability to grant themselves new leases, which, if the nominee purchaser were buying the interests on the open market, he would have to agree to share with the sellers in order to agree the price: para 4(2)(a), (b). The freehold and other intermediate leasehold interests are to be valued on the basis set out in Sch 6, para 3 (see para 3.77): para 4(3), (4). It should be noted that the marriage value 'released' by the acquisition (and hence taken into account here) is only that relating to the flats of *participating* tenants. Hence the need for s 18, which has already been discussed (see paras 3.29–3.30).

3.80   The freeholder's share of the marriage value is that agreed by the reversioner and the nominee purchaser, or determined by the leasehold valuation tribunal as the share that would be awarded by a 'open market agreement' but it must not be less than 50%: Sch 6, para 4(1). This seems unduly advantageous to the freeholder, since it means that he can get more, but cannot get less, than the tenant. In practice, leasehold valuation tribunals have in the past awarded marriage value to both parties equally, on the basis that 'it takes two to tango'. The 50% 'floor' was the subject of fierce debate in Parliament. Some Conservatives argued for a 100% share for the landlord, whereas Opposition members sought to remove the floor altogether.[1] It should be noted that the freeholder will have to share his part of the marriage value with intermediate landlords in some circumstances: Sch 6, para 9.

---

1   See HC Report, 9 February 1993, cols 858–878; HL Committee, 22 March 1993, cols 9–28, 45–56.

Compensation for other freeholder losses

3.81   The freeholder is also entitled to receive payment, in such amount as is reasonable, to compensate him for loss or damage to other property interests. This covers the diminution in value of the freeholder's interest in other property resulting from the acquisition of his interest in the specified premises, and any other loss or compensation payable in respect of damage to his other property interests (including development value): para 5.

Intermediate leasehold interests

3.82   Each intermediate leasehold interest must be separately valued and paid for: para 6(1). The total price in each case is the aggregate of the value of the interest (under para 7) plus any compensation for other losses (under para 8). If the aggregate is negative, then the price is nil: para 6(2). In valuing the interest itself, in many cases the method of calculation of the value will be identical to that in relation to the interest of the freeholder: para 7(1).

3.83   But there is a complex formula to be applied in the case where the intermediate leaseholder's interest is a very small value.[1] This is where the 'profit rent' (difference between rents payable and receivable) is £5 per annum or less, and the future interest in possession (between the end of the inferior lease and the end of the intermediate lease) will be less than one month in duration: para 7(2)–(10). The compensation payable to an intermediate leaseholder is calculated in the same way as for a freeholder: para 8. Intermediate leaseholders are also entitled to part of the freeholder's share of the marriage value in some circumstances: para 9.

---

1   Based on the Leasehold Reform Act 1967, Sch 1, para 7A.

Other interests to be acquired

3.84   Other interests, such as the freeholder's interest in property outside the premises, and interest in property used in common with others, must also be valued and paid for. The total price in each case will be the aggregate of the value of the interest (under para 11) plus any compensation for other losses (under para 13) plus – in the case of freeholds – a proportion of marriage value (under para 12): para 10(1). Freeholds are valued as in Sch 6, para 3 (see para 3.77), and leaseholds likewise, unless they are of very small value, when they are valued as in para 7(2)–(10) (see para 3.83). Marriage value for freeholds is determined as under para 4: para 12(1). If leasehold interests are being acquired in the same property, the freeholder will have to share his proportion of marriage value with leaseholders in some cases: para 12(2), (3). Compensation for other losses is calculated as under para 5: para 13.

Interests with negative values

3.85   Some leases have a negative value, eg where the rent payable to the landlord is greater than the rent receivable from subleases, or where the economic costs of the tenant's obligations under the lease and sublease are greater than the benefits. The Government took the view that if an interest had a negative value, the owner need not pay the nominee purchaser for taking it off his hands. Instead, the value would be nil. Advantage could be taken of that rule, by creating pairs of leases, one (positive value) above the other (negative value), so that the negative value was in effect ignored, and only the positive value taken into account – thus artificially inflating the price of enfranchisement. Parts V and VI are highly technical and are designed to prevent artificial schemes of that sort, whilst not interfering with what may be termed 'naturally occurring' negative value leasehold interests.[1]

1   See HL Committee, 15 March 1993, cols 1330–1332.

COSTS OF ACQUISITION OF REVERSIONER AND OTHER RELEVANT LANDLORDS

3.86   In general, the nominee purchaser is liable for the reasonable costs incurred by the reversioner or any other relevant landlord, 'of and incidental to' certain matters in connection with the acquisition: s 33(1).[1] These matters are:

(a)   any investigation reasonably undertaken of questions arising out of the s 13 notice (eg whether the relevant landlord's interest is liable to be acquired at all);

(b)   deducing, evidencing and verifying the title to the landlord's interests;

(c)   making out and furnishing abstracts and copies for the nominee purchaser;

(d)   any valuation of any interest in the specified premises or any other property;

(e)   the conveyance.

But they do not include costs incurred in connection with leasehold valuation tribunal proceedings (s 33(5)), which are not recoverable: see para 1.19. Costs incurred in connection with court proceedings are not within (a)–(e) above anyway, but will be dealt with under the usual litigation costs rules.

1   Based on the Leasehold Reform Act 1967, s 9(4).

3.87   There are three exceptions to the general rule stated above. The first exception is that costs are excluded if on a voluntary transaction an undertaking by the grantee of the new lease to pay such costs would be void:[1] s 33(1). The second and third exceptions are where the tenant's notice ceases to have effect because the landlord establishes his intention to redevelop, or the land is to be compulsorily acquired: s 33(4). For this purpose, 'reasonable' refers to costs for services which 'might reasonably be expected to have been incurred' in a voluntary transaction: s 33(2). Two or more persons liable for the same costs are jointly and severally liable for them: s 33(7).

1   See *Hill & Redman*, **A** [842]–[847].

LEASEBACK

3.88   In certain circumstances where collective enfranchisement is being exercised by the participating tenants, the nominee purchaser is, or can be obliged, on taking a conveyance in the freehold, to grant a leaseback to the freeholder of a particular flat or other unit: s 36 and Sch 9.[1] The main reason for so doing is that there is a (public sector) periodical tenant or a business tenant in occupation and the leaseback will ensure that the freeholder continues to be that tenant's landlord. Another reason will be where the freeholder is resident in the flat in question.

1   Cf the leaseback provisions in the Housing Act 1988, s 100 and the Housing (Change of Landlord) Regulations 1989.

Secure tenancies and housing association tenancies

3.89   Where at the time of the acquisition a flat in the specified premises was let on a secure tenancy (under the Housing Act 1985, s 79) and the freeholder (and any intermediate landlord) is a public sector landlord, the nominee purchaser 'shall grant' to the freeholder a lease of the flat under those provisions: Sch 9, para 2. Similarly, where a flat in the premises is let by a housing association 'as freeholder' on a non-secure tenancy to a tenant who is not a qualifying tenant, the nominee purchaser 'shall grant' to the housing association a lease of the flat: Sch 9, para 3. The general principle is that no one can be forced to accept a legal estate against his will.[1] But here the words of the statute are imperative ('shall grant'), and the cross-heading for this part of the Schedule is 'MANDATORY LEASEBACK'. This compares with Part III, which contains a notice procedure for the landlord to require a leaseback if he wishes, and the cross-heading of which is 'RIGHT OF FREEHOLDER TO REQUIRE LEASEBACK OF CERTAIN UNITS'. Accordingly, it appears that the freeholder has no choice in the matter, but must accept the lease. The lease must conform with Sch 9, Part IV, except to the extent that the parties agree or a leasehold valuation tribunal determines to be reasonable in the circumstances: para 4.

---

1   See eg *Thompson v Leach* (1697) 1 Ld Raym 313.

3.90   The position of the secure tenant under the tenancy is not affected by the acquisition of the freehold and the leaseback arrangement; the secure tenancy continues without interruption: Sch 10, para 2(2). For the succession purposes of the secure tenancy legislation, a person granting a new tenancy of a flat (after a leaseback) who was a 'successor' before the leaseback is treated as a successor in relation to the new tenancy: Sch 10, para 2(3). Similar, but more complex, provision is made for the purposes of determining whether the right to buy is not exercisable in relation to the new tenancy by reason of the applicability of two exceptions to the right to buy: Sch 10, para 2(4), (5).

Non-qualifying tenants and resident landlords

3.91   Where a flat or other unit in the premises is not subject to mandatory leaseback (see para 3.89) but is let to a person who is not a qualifying tenant of it, the freeholder may by notice *require* the nominee purchaser to grant him a lease of it: Sch 9, para 5. Similarly, if the freeholder is a qualifying tenant of a flat or other unit, and his occupation renders the whole premises 'premises with a resident landlord' (ee paras 2.12–2.14), then the same notice procedure applies to enable the freeholder to require a leaseback: Sch 9, para 6. In such a case the lease of the flat or other unit is deemed to be surrendered on the grant of the lease: para 6(2)(b). Strictly speaking, there cannot be a qualifying tenant of a unit other than a flat, but for these purposes the tests in ss 5, 7 and 8 of the Act apply: para 6(3). The new lease must conform with Sch 9, Part IV, except to the extent that the parties agree or a leasehold valuation tribunal determines to be reasonable in the circumstances: para 7.

Terms of the lease

3.92   Schedule 9, Part IV sets out the basic provisions of the leaseback.[1] The lease will be for 999 years at a 'peppercorn', ie nominal, rent: para 8. Generally, there will be no exclusion of the Law of Property Act 1925, s 62: para 9. There will be provisions for rights of support, light and air, passage of water, gas and other fuels, drainage, and rights relating to cables, and other easements, including rights of way: paras 10, 11. Lessor's covenants will include repair of structure and exterior, maintenance of services, insurance and rebuilding or reinstatement: para 14. The only lessee's covenant expressly provided for will be one for keeping the interior in good repair: para 15. There will also be service charge provisions: para 16. The lease may not prohibit assignment or subletting, except assignment or subletting of business premises without the lessor's consent (not to be unreasonably withheld): para 17. Nor may there be any provision for termination, except forfeiture for breach of any term: para 18.

---

1   Cf the Housing (Change of Landlord) Regulations 1989, Sch 4.

Relationship with mortgages

3.93   A lease granted under these provisions takes effect 'immediately after' the acquisition of the freehold by the nominee purchaser: s 36(2). It is not made clear what happens if the freehold is acquired by the nominee purchaser with the aid of a loan secured by a mortgage, expressed to take effect simultaneously with the acquisition of the freehold. The proper analysis of the acquisition and leaseback is not that the freeholder has transferred the reversion only, with a partial interest remaining in the freeholder, but that there is a disposition of the *whole* freehold with an immediate grant back: *Nichols v IRC* [1975] 2 All ER 120, [1975] 1 WLR 534, CA. In this situation, does the mortgage take priority over the lease, or vice versa? Certainly the valuation provisions of Sch 6 assume that the mortgage does not take priority, because the freeholder is not paid for that part of his interest attributable to the leaseback of the flat (even though in fact it has not by then occurred): Sch 6, para 3(4). The assumption must be that the order of priority will be:

(i)   lease pursuant to leaseback;
(ii)   any new mortgage of the freehold;
(iii) freehold.

One other point to make clear is that, where the flat or other unit to be leased back to the freeholder is already subject to a lease, the leaseback is a lease of the freehold *reversion*: s 36(3).

COMPLETION OF THE ACQUISITION

3.94   The conveyance to the nominee purchaser may consist of freeholds only, or mixed freeholds and leaseholds. In relation to the freeholds, the conveyance must grant the nominee purchaser an estate in fee simple absolute (although the statute does not say 'in possession'[1]) subject only to encumbrances agreed or determined under the collective enfranchisement provisions: s 34(1). In relation to the leaseholds, it must simply dispose of those interests to the nominee purchaser: s 34(2). It will have effect under the Law of Property Act 1925, s 2(1) to overreach encumbrances capable of being overreached (s 34(3)),[2] but not burdens originating in tenure and the like:[3] s 34(5).[4] Rentcharges capable of being overreached *will* be overreached (s 34(4)), but the conveyance will be made subject to others: s 34(6)[4] to (8). The terms of the conveyance will conform to Sch 7 to the Act, except so far as agreed between the nominee purchaser and the transferor of the given interest (*not* necessarily the reversioner): s 34(9). It will also contain a statement that it is a conveyance executed for the purposes of Part I, Chapter I of the Act. This statement must comply with prescribed Land Registry requirements: s 34(10).

---

1 Cf *Hill & Redman*, **D** [1033].
2 Based on the Leasehold Reform Act 1967, s 8(4).
3 Ie on the enfranchisement of copyhold land under the Law of Property Act 1922, Sch 12, para 6.
4 Based on the Leasehold Reform Act 1967, s 8(3).
5 Based on ibid, s 8(4).

Terms of conveyance

3.95 The provisions of Sch 7 (contents of conveyances) mostly relate to conveyances of freehold interests. The only paragraph applicable to leasehold interests (as also to freehold) is para 2,[1] which provides that in general the effects of the Law of Property Act 1925, ss 62 and 63, shall not be restricted, and that the transferor (whether of a freehold or leasehold interest) is only obliged to transfer what he has or could get, and gives no covenant for title wider than that implied by the Law of Property Act 1925, s 76(1)(f), in the case of a trustee or mortgagee. Other provisions in that Schedule cover rights of support, light and air, passage of water, gas or other fuel, drainage and rights relating to cables (para 3), rights of way (para 4) and restrictive covenants (para 5).

---

1 Based on the Leasehold Reform Act 1967, s 10(1).

Discharge of existing mortgages

3.96 Certain existing mortgages, charges or liens (other than the vendor's lien) will be automatically discharged, and any term of years by way of security extinguished, on the execution of the conveyance: s 35(1).[1] In such cases it is not even necessary for the mortgagee, chargee or lienee to be a party (s 35(1)), although of course he can be: Sch 8, para 5(2).[2] This exceptional treatment applies to mortgages, charges and liens on the interest(s) acquired under collective enfranchisement which are intended to secure payment of money or performance of any other obligation, *and* would not be overreached apart from those provisions: s 35(2). The nominee purchaser and reversioner can, however, agree that the interest in question should be acquired *subject* to the mortgage, charge or lien, and in that case there will be no discharge: s 35(3).

---

1 Based on the Leasehold Reform Act 1967, s 12(1).
2 Based on ibid, s 12(7).

3.97 But the exceptional treatment given by s 35 comes with strings attached. The *nominee purchaser* is under a duty to apply the price otherwise payable for the interest which is subject to the mortgage, charge or lien in or towards the redemption of that mortgage, charge or lien: Sch 8, para 2.[1] (Though this does not normally apply to a debenture holder's charge: para 2(3)[2].) There are specific rules excluding the consolidation of mortgages, charges and liens (para 3(1)),[3] and for three months' notice to be given of the intended discharge, whatever the terms of the security may say: para 3(2).[4]

1   Based on the Leasehold Reform Act 1967, s 12(2).
2   Based on ibid, s 12(5).
3   Based on ibid, s 12(3).
4   Based on ibid, s 12(4).

3.98   In case of difficulty in ascertaining the amount payable, or in making a payment, in respect of a mortgage, charge or lien, the nominee purchaser may make payments into court: para 4.[1] Indeed, the landlord, or a security holder, may require him to do so: para 4(3). Naturally, discharge of the security in this fashion does not prejudice any right or remedy for enforcement of the obligations so secured: para 5(1).[2]

1   Based on the Leasehold Reform Act 1967, s 13(1).
2   Based on ibid, s 12(6).

Vendor's lien

3.99   A person whose interest in property is being acquired under the collective enfranchisement provisions has a vendor's lien. By s 32(2)[1] this extends not just to the price payable, but also to:

(a)   amounts due to him from tenants of the premises (or any part);
(b)   amounts due to him under s 18(2) (compensation for loss flowing from non-disclosure of side agreements);
(c)   costs due to him under s 33.

However, para (a) does not cover amounts due from tenants of premises to be comprised in a leaseback agreement: s 32(3).

1   Based on the Leasehold Reform Act 1967, s 9(5).

ACQUISITION OF INTERESTS FROM LOCAL AUTHORITIES

3.100   Certain public sector landlords and acquirers from them are obliged to obtain ministerial consent or carry out consultation before making certain disposals of their land. Section 37 and Sch 10, para 1 of this Act disapply some of these provisions in relation to disposals by such persons of freehold or leasehold interests under the collective enfranchisement procedure. The provisions concerned are:

(a)   the Housing Act 1985, ss 42 and 43 (local authorities);
(b)   the Housing Act 1988, s 133 (acquirers from local authorities);
(c)   the Housing Associations Act 1985, ss 9(1), (1A) (housing associations);
(d)   the Housing Act 1988, s 79(1)(2) (housing action trusts);

(e)   the Housing Act 1988, s 81 (acquirers from housing action trusts);
(f)   the Housing Act 1988, s 105(1) (acquirers from certain public sector landlords).

4 Individual right to a new lease

INTRODUCTION

4.1 As already noted (para 2.1), leasehold tenure has two main problems. First, a lease is a wasting asset. Second, the relationship between landlord and tenant may work well, or it may work badly. In order to combat both problems, the Leasehold Reform Act 1967 introduced the right for leaseholders of some residential houses to buy the freehold. Nothing was done by that Act in relation to leases of flats. We have seen that the 1993 Act now gives certain flat leaseholders the right collectively to buy the freehold of their block, again in order to solve the problem of the wasting asset (because the leaseholders can grant themselves new leases) and the problem of the bad landlord (because the leaseholders control the management).

4.2 But some leaseholders of flats are excluded from the right of collective enfranchisement. Others may not wish to exercise it, or may fail to persuade sufficient leaseholders in their block to do so. To deal at least with the wasting asset problem, although not that of poor management, the 1993 Act confers on certain tenants of flats the right to require a new long lease, in substitution for existing leases. Unlike the right to collective enfranchisement, this is an *individual* right, exercisable on a 'flat by flat' basis. As with the provisions dealing with the right to collective enfranchisement, the legislation conferring this new right is also complex. Unfortunately, many of the obscurities in the drafting were left unilluminated by the legislative debates.[1]

---

1   See HC 2R, 3 November 1992, col 154; HC Standing Committee B, 24 November 1992, cols 214–258; HC Report, 9 February 1993, col 929; HL 2R, 23 February 1993, col 87; HL Committee, 22 March 1993, cols 86–109; HL Report, 18 May 1993, cols 1703-1707; HL 3R, 25 May 1993, cols 209–212; HC Lords' Amendments, 14 June 1993, col 663.

THE RIGHT

4.3   The right conferred by this Act is to obtain a new lease for a period equivalent to the unexpired term of the old lease plus 90 years, at a 'peppercorn' rent, but on payment of a market value premium, *in substitution for* the existing lease: s 56(1). 'Peppercorn' is not defined, but presumably means 'nominal'.[1] If the new lease is not granted by the immediate landlord, then other sums may be payable to intermediate landlords: s 56(2). The terms of the new lease are dealt with later (paras 4.49–4.53); broadly speaking, they are to be the same as those of the old lease: s 57. But the landlord may require underlying minerals comprised in the old lease to be excluded in the new, if proper provision is made for support of the existing premises: s 39(7).[2] The right to a new lease can be exercised more than once in respect of the same flat (s 59(1)), subject to certain landlords' objections, such as the intention to redevelop, dealt with later (paras 4.44–4.45). The right cannot by agreement be excluded or modified or made exercisable only in circumstances leading to the imposition of a penalty on the tenant (s 93(1)), though in limited circumstances the court may approve a new lease under these provisions which does so: s 93(4).

1 Cf *Hill & Redman*, **A** [1457] n 11.
2 Based on the Leasehold Reform Act 1967, s 2(6).

WHO QUALIFIES FOR THE RIGHT?

4.4   The right to a new lease is conferred only on certain tenants. These are tenants who satisfy two conditions on the day that notice is given to the landlord to exercise the right. (This day is called 'the relevant date' in the legislation: s 39(8).) The two conditions are:

(a)   the tenant must be a 'qualifying tenant of the flat', and this is (broadly speaking) the same personal qualification for a tenant to be a 'qualifying tenant' in relation to the right to collective enfranchisement;
(b)   the tenant must have a residence qualification of at least three years in the last ten.

4.5   There was originally a third, negative, condition included in the Bill, ie that the right to collective enfranchisement was not exercisable in relation to the building, or part of building, containing the flat. Attempts at both House of Commons committee stage and House of Lords committee stage to remove this condition were debated at length, but rejected, the Government on the first occasion saying that:

> 'the amendment would be disastrous. It would undermine the whole concept of encouraging qualifying tenants to move towards leasehold enfranchisement.'[1]

The condition remained in the Bill until the Third Reading in the House of Lords, when, in one of those parliamentary episodes so frustrating to legal authors, it was deleted by a Government amendment, without any debate whatever, and without a division being called.[2]

1 HC Standing Committee B, 24 November 1992, col 239, per Mr Tony Baldry (Under-Secretary of State for the Environment); see also HL Committee, 22 March 1993, cols 86–101.
2 HL 3R, 25 May 1993, col 209.

'Qualifying tenant of the flat'

4.6   Each of the two remaining conditions must be considered in more detail. First, the tenant must be a 'qualifying tenant of the flat': s 39(2)(a). This condition has two parts. The expression 'qualifying tenant' is to be construed by reference to ss 5 (except sub-ss (5) and (6)), 7 and 8 of the Act. Accordingly, it is to mean almost the same as it does for the purpose of collective enfranchisement (paras 2.15–2.22). In particular, a flat held by a tenant under two or more separate leases from the same landlord is treated for the purposes of the right to a new lease as if there were a single lease of the flat: s 7(6).

4.7   Thus, in general, a qualifying tenant is a tenant under a long lease (as defined by s 7), at a low rent (as defined by s 8). But excluded are leases falling within the Landlord and Tenant Act 1954, Part II, leases granted by charitable housing trusts in pursuance of their charitable purposes and certain leases granted in breach of the terms of a superior lease. National Trust property is also excluded (s 95), as is property within the precinct of an Anglican cathedral: s 96. Crown leases are in a special position, which was considered in Chapter 1: para 1.22. We should note that a person may be a qualifying tenant of more than one flat at a time (s 39(4)), although the residence qualification may prevent individual enfranchisement of more than one flat at the same time. (The position for collective enfranchisement is different: para 2.16.)

4.8   The word 'flat' basically means the same as for the right to collective enfranchisement, ie separate premises forming part of a building, constructed or adapted for use as a dwelling, and all or part of which is above or below another part of the building (s 101(1)). However, for the purpose of individual enfranchisement, this definition is modified in an unnecessarily complex way. First, 'flat' is *generally* extended to include any garage, outhouse, garden, yard and appurtenances belonging to or usually enjoyed with the flat and let to the tenant on the application date: s 62(2). Second, in considering under s 9 whether the lease of the flat is a lease at a low rent, it is *this* extended definition of 'flat' which applies, rather than the modified (but less extended) definition provided in s 8(7): s 62(4). But third, this extension of the definition does *not* apply for the purposes of s 47 (landlord's intention to redevelop premises containing flat) or s 55(1) (compulsory purchase of flat), or any other provision referring to the premises 'containing' the flat, for which the ordinary definition applies: s 62(3).

Residence qualification

4.9   As the Bill was originally drafted, it contained no residential qualification for the exercise of the individual right to a new lease. At House of Lords committee stage a Government-proposed amendment was accepted, to introduce the present residential requirement.[1] One speaker described it as 'the result of a deal reached in another place [ie the House of Commons] between the Government and the big estates'.[2] The requirement is that the tenant should have occupied the flat 'as his only or principal home' *either* for the last three years *or* for periods amounting to three years in the last ten: s 39(2)(b).[3] Use for other purposes as well does not affect the matter.

---

1   HL Committee, 22 March 1993, cols 101–106.
2   Ibid, col 104, per Lord Coleraine.
3   Based on the Leasehold Reform Act 1967, s 1(1)(b).

4.10   The phrase 'only or principal home' is not defined, but it occurs in other legislation, such as the Housing Act 1985, s 81 (the 'tenancy condition' for secure tenancies)[1] and the Housing Act 1988, s 1(1)(b) (condition for an assured tenancy).[2] It is not clear what 'the last three years' adds to 'periods amounting to three years in the last ten', since residence for the last three years will always amount to three years in the last ten. What *is* clear is that occupation need only have been of *part* of the flat to qualify (s 39(5)(a)), and it need not have been by virtue of the lease now sought to be renewed, or indeed any lease: s 39(5)(b). Joint tenants can of course together constitute the potential 'qualifying tenant' (s 101(4)), and in such a case the residence qualification need only be satisfied in respect of one of them: s 39(6).

---

1   See *Hill & Redman*, **D** [605].
2   See ibid, **C** [2025].

WHO GRANTS THE NEW LEASE?

4.11   In many cases the qualifying tenant's immediate landlord is the freeholder, or has a sufficient leasehold interest to grant a new lease of 90 years. But the legislation provides for the situation where this is not the case. Section 40(1) defines 'the landlord' for the purposes of granting the new lease as the person having an interest in the flat which satisfies three cumulative conditions. This need not be the immediate landlord at all. The definition is based on that in the Landlord and Tenant Act 1954, s 44 ('landlord' for business tenancy purposes), where a similar problem arises.[1]

---

1   See *Hill & Redman*, **B** [644].

4.12   The first two conditions are simple:

(a)   it is an interest in reversion superior to the tenant's lease; and
(b)   it is an interest long enough in duration to have the new lease granted out of it, ie it is a freehold or a sufficiently long leasehold.

But it is possible for more than one interest in the same flat to satisfy both of these conditions at the same time. For example, where freeholder A demises to B for 999 years, B subdemises to C for 125 years, and C sub-subdemises to D (actually in possession) for 30 years, then (for the moment), the interests of A, B and C all satisfy both conditions. So there is a third condition:

(c)   the interest must not itself be superior to an interest which meets the first two conditions.

4.13   The effect of these words is to exclude the interests of A and B in our example, and leave only that of C. So C would be the 'landlord'. But once C's sublease has less than 90 years left to run, then only the interests of A and B will satisfy the first two conditions, and condition (c) will exclude A's interest, to leave only B's. Accordingly, in such a case B would be 'the landlord' for the purposes of granting a new lease. In general terms we can see that 'the landlord' is the lowest person in the landlord chain capable of granting the new lease. In the business tenancy legislation, this person is usually referred to as 'the competent landlord'.[1] The 1993 Act uses the same expression for the purposes of s 40 and Sch 11, which makes specific provision for the procedure to obtain a new lease where the 'competent' landlord is not the immediate landlord: see paras 4.86–4.88.

---

1 Landlord and Tenant Act 1954, Sch 6, para 1.

PRELIMINARY ENQUIRIES

4.14 The fact that different procedures are involved, as well as the fact that the initial notice must be served on the 'competent landlord', means that a tenant needs to know at the outset who that person is. Thus, before the exercise is embarked upon, the qualifying tenant may by notice ask his immediate landlord, or anyone receiving rent on his behalf:

(a) whether the immediate landlord owns the freehold, and
(b) if not, who does, who holds any intermediate leases, and how long they are, as well as the extent of the premises to which they relate: s 41(1), (2).

As elsewhere in the 1993 Act, freehold is not defined. We must assume that this means to refer to an estate in fee simple absolute in possession.[1]

---

1 See *Hill & Redman*, **D** [1033].

4.15 As to (b), the immediate landlord (or his agent) is of course only obliged to reply to the extent of his knowledge: s 41(1). Curiously, if the notice is given to the person receiving the rent, rather than to the landlord himself, that person is under no obligation *either* to pass the notice to the landlord *or* to ask the landlord for the information requested, although the landlord may have it. If the tenant knows the identity of the freehold owner (whether as a result of the notice procedure or otherwise) he may ask the freehold owner for similar details of the intermediate leaseholders and their leases, so far as he knows them: s 41(3)(a). If he knows the identity of any of the intermediate leaseholders, he may ask them for similar details of their own leases, and, so far as they are aware of them, the identities of the freeholder and any other intermediate leaseholders (and details of *their* leases): s 43(3)(b).

4.16 Where a notice is given seeking information under these provisions, it must also require the recipient to give details of any claim made to exercise the right to collective enfranchisement in respect of the premises containing the tenant's flat and which is still 'current': s 41(4). For this purpose, a claim is 'current' if the notice claiming to exercise the collective right has not been withdrawn, a binding contract entered into pursuant to that notice is still in force, or where the court has ordered various interests to be vested in the nominee purchaser but this has not yet happened: s 41(5)(b). Although the legislation says that the 'notice . . . shall . . . require the recipient', it cannot be the case that a failure by the tenant to ask for this further information renders the whole notice invalid: the provision is directory rather than mandatory.[1]

---

1 Cf *B v B* [1961] 2 All ER 396, [1961] 1 WLR 856; *Chelmsford RDC v Powell* [1963] 1 All ER 150, [1963] 1 WLR 123.

Sanctions

4.17   The recipient of a notice under s 41 seeking information has 28 days to supply the information (if he has it) to the qualifying tenant: s 41(6). An incentive to do so is that a copy of the tenant's notice claiming a new lease must then be served on that person: para 4.22. But, unlike elsewhere in this Act,[1] no specific provision is made for applications to the court, in case of failure to supply, for an order that it be supplied. The 'court' is the county court: para 1.15. A general provision, applying to both collective and individual enfranchisement, empowers the court, on an application made at least 14 days after a *further* notice has been served requiring the making good of an *existing* default, to order the respondent to make good the default within such time as the court may specify: s 92. However, this general provision is permissive only, and does not prevent application being made, at any time after the 28-day period has expired, for an injunction requiring the recipient to comply with his statutory obligations.[2] But it will be borne in mind that, where the premises concerned are registered land, most or all of the same information will in any case be available publicly from the Land Registry, on payment of the usual fees, within a few days.

1   Eg ss 46–50, 81(4)–(7).
2   Cf *Ashby v Ebdon* [1985] Ch 394, [1984] 3 All ER 869.

TRUSTS

4.18   A question not generally addressed by the legislation is whether the freehold and leasehold interests referred to are *legal* as opposed to *equitable*. Suppose A holds the freehold on trust for B. Must tenant C serve notice on B, or only on A? If tenant C holds the lease on trust for D, does D's occupation count to satisfy the residence requirement? The existence of a trust may be as much of an encumbrance on the landlord's title as a mortgage. The draftsman has expressly dealt with the latter (paras 4.65–4.68) but has made only limited provision for the former. This is curious, because both the Leasehold Reform Act 1967 and the Landlord and Tenant Act 1954, Part II (on which many of the provisions of the present scheme are modelled) deal expressly with trusts, both of the landlord's interest and of the tenant's interest.[1]

1   Leasehold Reform Act 1967, s 6; Landlord and Tenant Act 1954, s 41.

4.19   The limited provision made in individual enfranchisement cases for trusts is contained in Sch 2, paras 3, 5 and 6, and Sch 11, para 10(3), dealing exclusively with landlord's interests. Where in our example A is a 'custodian trustee' for B (as managing trustee) under the Public Trustee Act 1906, s 4, then the landlord's interest is deemed to be vested in B rather than in A, except as regards the execution of any instrument dealing with that interest: Sch 2, para 3. In all other cases of A's being a trustee for B, it seems that A is to be treated as the landlord, and B is ignored. Schedule 2, paras 5 and 6 simply provide that where the landlord's interest is held on trust for sale or on a settlement under the Settled Land Act 1925, certain statutory provisions apply to the compensation which a landlord may have to pay in some circumstances, and that where that interest is held on trust for sale the payment *received* by the landlord is treated as the proceeds of sale. Sch 11, para 10(3) deals with a very modest conveyancing point (para 4.88). Subject to that, trusts are ignored, and only legal interests are taken into account in operating the individual enfranchisement procedure. This may bear hardly on the beneficiaries of both landlord and tenant trusts in many cases.

OTHER CASES

4.20   Certain other special cases are also dealt with by Sch 2, namely where the landlord is a university or college to which the University and College Estates Act 1925 applies, an ecclesiastical landlord (as defined) or is a landlord under mental disability, or there is a mortgagee in possession of a landlord's interest. These cases have been dealt with in relation to collective enfranchisement (paras 2.28–2.32) and the position is similar for individual enfranchisement.

PROCEDURE

4.21   As a general point it should be observed that the general structure and many of the detailed provisions to be followed are contained in the sections of the Act or in its Schedules. In particular, there are provisions relating to the form and mode of service of the many notices that are required: see para 1.11. But the Secretary of State has power to make further detailed provision by way of regulations, in particular dealing with the investigation of title, with payments and with discharge from performance of obligations where the failure to perform is caused by some other person: s 98. Subject to such express provision, the procedure to be followed is to be 'as nearly as may be' to the case of a contract of lease freely negotiated between the parties: s 98(1).

The tenant's initial notice

4.22   A qualifying tenant claims to exercise the right to a new lease by giving a notice to 'the landlord' (as established under paras 4.11–4.13), and to any person party to his lease *other than* the immediate landlord: s 42(1), (2). The tenant's notice is treated as given to 'the landlord' if it is given to any of the intermediate landlords instead (Sch 11, para 1), although the tenant must give copies to all the landlords of whom he is aware anyway: Sch 11, para 2. Every recipient must copy in all the other landlords of whom he is aware who have not already received a copy, and must inform the tenant if he knows who the competent landlord is: Sch 11, para 3. If any person who has notified the tenant under s 41 (paras 4.14–4.15) of his interest does not receive a copy of the tenant's notice, that notice will cease to have effect once the counternotice period runs out: Sch 11, para 4. Where the person to be served cannot be found or his identity ascertained special procedures apply: paras 4.73–4.85.

4.23   Section 42(3) requires that the notice must give details of:

(i)   the tenant;
(ii)   the flat;

(iii)   the existing lease (including details showing that it is a 'lease at a low rent');
(iv)   the periods of residence satisfying the residential requirement;
(v)   the premium and other amounts payable on the grant of the new lease;
(vi)   the terms to be contained in that lease;
(vii) the professional agent acting for the tenant (and a service address in England and Wales);
(viii) the date (not less than two months later: s 42(5)) by which the landlord must respond.

4.24   So long as this initial notice remains in force, and for 12 months after it ceases to be so, no subsequent notice under these provisions may be given in relation to the same flat: s 42(6), (7). This means that a purchaser of a flat in respect of which a notice has been given within the twelve months before purchase must be sure to take an assignment of the benefit of the notice together with a lease, or a hiatus will occur before a new notice can be served. A notice continues in force from the date of service (ie 'the relevant date') until the new lease is granted, the new notice is withdrawn (or deemed to be withdrawn), or is otherwise treated by the legislation as ceasing to have effect: s 42(8). However, the operation of the tenant's notice can be *suspended* in some cases, and this will be dealt with later: see para 4.103.

4.25   What is the effect of a notice purportedly given under s 42, but which does not comply with its requirements? The section says that the notice 'must' contain certain details. The Act says that the notice is not invalid because of any inaccuracy in the details given or any misdescription of property (and indeed an amendment procedure is laid down): Sch 12, para 9. But the Act is silent as to the effect of failure to include necessary details at all. Moreover, as we shall see later, the landlord's means of complaining about the form of the notice are limited: para 4.42.

4.26   A tenant's notice is of no effect if it is given:

(a)   after the tenant has given notice to terminate the lease (Sch 12, para 1);
(b)   whilst an agreement under the Local Government and Housing Act 1989, Sch 10, para 17, subsists (Sch 12, para 1);
(c)   after an order has been made for possession of the flat (Sch 12, para 3(1));
(d)   (except with the landlord's written consent) more than two months after the landlord has given notice to terminate the lease under the Landlord and Tenant Act 1954, s 4, or the Local Government and Housing Act 1989, Sch 10, para 4(1) (Sch 12, para 2(1), (2)).

4.27   On the other hand, if the tenant serves his notice under s 42 within the two months mentioned in (d) above, the *landlord's* notice to terminate ceases to have effect: Sch 12, para 2(3). There are special provisions dealing with the case where the tenant's claim to a new lease turns out not to be effective, no lease being granted, and the landlord re-serves his notice to terminate under the statutory provisions mentioned: Sch 12, para 2(4)–(6). 'Effective' for this purpose means resulting in the granting of a new lease: Sch 12, para 8(1)(b).

4.28   If proceedings for re-entry or forfeiture are pending, but no possession order has yet been made, the tenant 'shall not give' a section 42 notice unless the court gives leave: Sch 12, para 3(2). The court must not give such leave unless satisfied that the sole or main reason for giving the notice is to avoid the consequences of the breach of covenant which has led to the proceedings: Sch 12, para 3(3). But if leave is granted and the claim is made, it can proceed notwithstanding the pending proceedings, and, if the claim is effective, the court can vary or set aside any order made in those proceedings: Sch 12, para 3(4).

THE EFFECTS OF GIVING NOTICE

Positive effects

4.29   The general effect of a valid notice being given under s 42 is stated to be equivalent to that of a contract for a new lease between landlord and tenant: s 43(1).[1] The reference to 'landlord' includes intermediate and ultimate landlords in relation to their own separate interests: s 43(5), (6). Presumably, the reference to a contract is to an *enforceable* contract.[2] Certainly, in the case of default by either party in respect of their obligations the rights and remedies are the same as if it were a case of breach of contract: s 43(4).[3] This is reinforced by s 58(1),[4] which provides that, once a qualifying tenant having the statutory right to a new lease *gives notice* of his claim in accordance with s 42, 'then except as provided by this Chapter the landlord shall be bound to grant to the tenant', and the tenant 'shall be bound to accept' the new lease.

---

1   Based on the Leasehold Reform Act 1967, s 5(1).
2   Cf the Law of Property (Miscellaneous Provisions) Act 1989, s 2.
3   Based on the Leasehold Reform Act 1967, s 5(3).
4   Based on ibid, ss 8(1), 14(1).

4.30   Thus the tenant is thereafter a tenant in equity for 90 years and more under the doctrine of *Walsh v Lonsdale*,[1] and the landlord's and tenant's rights and obligations are in principle transmissible and enforceable in the same way. In particular, a notice under s 44 is registrable under the Land Charges Act 1972 or the Land Registration Act 1925 in the same way as if it were an estate contract: s 97(1).[2] However, the *Walsh v Lonsdale* rights and obligations of the tenant are transmissible only with the existing lease itself: s 43(3).[3] If the lease is assigned without the benefit of the notice, it is automatically withdrawn: s 43(3).[4]

---

1   (1882) 21 Ch D 9, CA; see *Hill & Redman*, **A** [514].
2   Based on the Leasehold Reform Act 1967, s 5(5).
3   Based on ibid, s 5(2).
4   Ibid.

4.31   A second positive effect of a notice under s 42 is that the landlord and his agents have a right of access to the flat for the purpose of obtaining the valuation: s 44(1). The right is exercisable 'at any reasonable time' on giving not less than three days' notice to the tenant: s 44(2). Like all other notices in this procedure, the notice must be in writing and may be sent by post: s 99(1).

Negative effects

4.32   Whilst a tenant's notice under s 42 remains in force, no notice terminating the lease can be given, either by tenant or landlord, under the Landlord and Tenant Act

1954 or the Local Government and Housing Act 1989, Sch 10, para 4(1): Sch 12, para 4. Nor can proceedings be brought to enforce a right of re-entry or forfeiture, except with the leave of the court, which is only to be given if the court is satisfied that the sole or main reason for giving the notice was to avoid the consequences of the breach leading to the proposed proceedings; if leave *is* given, the notice ceases to have effect: Sch 12, para 6. Similarly, whilst a tenant's notice remains in force, and for three months thereafter, the lease of the flat cannot come to an end in any of the following ways:

(a)   by effluxion of time;
(b)   following a notice to quit given by the immediate landlord; or
(c)   by the termination of a superior lease.

4.33   If the claim turns out not to be effective, and a lease would otherwise have terminated before the end of the three months, it terminates at the end of those three months: Sch 12, para 5(1). Subject to the foregoing, the tenant's lease can be terminated in any other way, even whilst the tenant's notice remains in force: Sch 12, para 5(2). These provisions do not affect the court's power to grant relief against forfeiture, or to grant relief under the Landlord and Tenant Act 1954, s 16(2): Sch 12, paras 5(2), 7.

LANDLORD'S COUNTERNOTICE

4.34   The next step in the procedure is for the landlord to reply formally to the tenant's notice. By the date specified in the tenant's notice (see para 4.23), the landlord must serve a counternotice: s 45(1). By s 45(2), this must do one of three things:

(a)   admit the tenant's right to a new lease in principle;
(b)   deny that right, for reasons stated;
(c)   *in addition* to either (a) or (b), state the landlord's[1] intention to apply to the court for an order that any right to a new lease be not exercisable, on grounds of intended redevelopment (such applications are dealt with in paras 4.44–4.47 below).

If the landlord is acting on behalf of other landlords, the counternotice must specify them: Sch 11, para 5. It must also give an address in England and Wales for service of notices on the landlord: s 45(4). If the landlord fails to serve a counternotice at all, then the tenant's remedy is to apply to the court: para 4.55.

---

1   'Landlord' here exceptionally includes intermediate landlords: Sch 11, para 9(2).

Admitting the right

4.35   Where the counternotice admits in principle the tenant's right to a new lease, it must go on to state which of the tenant's proposals (premium payable, terms of lease, etc) are accepted and which are not, and in the case of rejected proposals, what the landlord proposes instead: s 45(3). The landlord must take care in admitting the right in principle in his counternotice, because he will be bound by the admission in relation to the tenant's being a 'qualifying tenant' and satisfying the residential qualification, unless he can show he was induced to make the admission by misrepresentation or concealment of material facts: s 45(5). But the admission does not conclude the question whether the particulars of the flat given by the tenant are correct: s 45(5).

4.36   The landlord's counternotice may not only accept the tenant's right to a new lease, but may accept all of his stated proposals. In that case there is unlikely to be any reason why the matter should not speedily proceed to the grant of the new lease. But the tenant retains the right until grant to withdraw from the transaction by serving a notice of withdrawal on 'the landlord', every other intermediate landlord, and any 'third party' (as defined by s 62(1)): s 52(1), (2). However, the tenant will still be liable for the recipient's costs down to the time when the notice of withdrawal is given: s 52(3). (Costs are dealt with later: paras 4.98–4.99.)

Disputes

4.37   In other cases, however, the landlord's counternotice may lead to a dispute between the parties. But it must be recalled that it is not *agreement* finally reached between the parties that gives rise to the landlord's obligation to grant a new lease, but (subject to certain statutory provisions) service of a valid notice (see para 4.29). Thus any dispute is really about whether or not there already *is* an obligation to grant a lease, and on what terms, and not about whether there should be an obligation in the future.

4.38   There can be three kinds of true dispute. The first is where the landlord does not admit the right of the tenant to a new lease. The second is where the landlord challenges the exercise of the tenant's right on the basis that the landlord intends to redevelop the premises concerned. The third is where the terms of acquisition are not or cannot be agreed.

4.39   There are two other cases of difficulty, though really they are cases of landlord 'refusal' rather than 'dispute'. One is where the landlord refuses to serve a counternotice (or, having given the first one, refuses to give a subsequent counternotice when he is obliged so to do). The other is where the tenant's right is accepted or established, and all the terms of acquisition likewise, but the landlord fails to make the grant (of course, the tenant may be at fault here too). In all of these cases, 'refusal' as well as 'dispute', application may be made to the court or to a leasehold valuation tribunal to decide what is to be done. The court and leasehold valuation tribunals were dealt with in Chapter 1: paras 1.15–1.21. We will deal with the procedures involved in chronological order.

DISPUTE AS TO TENANT'S RIGHT

4.40   Where the landlord's counternotice does not admit the tenant's right to a new lease, the landlord may within two months from the date of giving the counternotice apply to the court to determine the question of that right: s 46(1)(a), (2). If no application is made within the two-month period, or one is made but subsequently withdrawn, then the position is treated as if the landlord had simply failed to give a counternotice at all. It will then be up to the tenant to apply for an order determining the terms of acquisition: see para 4.56 below. Accordingly, a heel-dragging landlord gains two months by serving a counternotice not admitting the tenant's right, rather than by not serving a counternotice at all.

Successful landlord

4.41   If the landlord does make his application within the two months, and it is not withdrawn, what the court must decide is whether, at the date of serving his original notice, the tenant had the right to acquire a new lease of his flat: s 46(1)(b). If the court is satisfied that the tenant at that date had no such right, then it must make a declaration to that effect: s 46(1). (The actual words are 'shall by order make a declaration', which is tautologous.) The tenant's notice will cease to have effect on the order 'becoming final' (para 1.21): s 46(3). This means that, despite the fact that the marginal note to s 46 reads 'Proceedings relating to validity of tenant's notice', the court is not at all concerned with whether the tenant *has* served a proper notice, but with the logically prior question whether the tenant was *entitled* to serve a proper notice.

4.42   Once the court reaches the conclusion that he was so entitled, it seemingly has no power to consider the form of the notice that was in fact given, but instead must dismiss the landlord's application: s 46(3), (4) ('If, however . . .'). This is odd, because the legislation (in particular ss 43(1), 56(1)) otherwise assumes that the tenant will only be entitled to compel the landlord to grant him a new lease if (a) the right was conferred on him (the substantive question), *and* (b) he has properly claimed to exercise that right by giving a notice which complies with s 42 (the procedural question). It is true that s 46 assumes that the tenant's original notice was valid (see eg sub-s (3)), but it is notable that the court procedure is not predicated on a notice having 'been given in accordance with section 42' (as is s 49, for example).

Successful tenant

4.43   Where the court does dismiss the landlord's application, there are two possibilities. If the landlord's counternotice stated his intention to redevelop the relevant premises, and his application to the court for an appropriate order is pending – or has not been made but still could be (see para 4.44), then the court will do nothing further on this occasion: s 46(5). But in any other case, in addition to dismissing the landlord's application, the court by s 46(4) *must*:

(a)   declare the landlord's counternotice to be of no effect; and
(b)   require the landlord to give a further counternotice by the date specified in the order. This second counternotice must state the landlord's acceptance of, or counterproposals to, the tenant's proposals set out in his original notice: s 46(6).

LANDLORD'S INTENTION TO REDEVELOP

4.44   Here the landlord in his counternotice may or may not admit the tenant's right, but he states his intention to seek an order from the court preventing any right from being exercised, on the grounds that he (or an intermediate landlord:

Sch 11, para 9(2)) intends to redevelop the premises containing the flat. He (or the intermediate landlord) must make such an application within two months of his giving his counternotice, although if his counternotice does not admit the tenant's right in principle, he cannot *proceed* with this application until any order dismissing his earlier application concerning the tenant's right has 'become final' (as to which see para 1.21): s 47(3).

4.45   If the landlord makes no application within the two-month limit or he makes one which is subsequently withdrawn, the landlord must give a second counternotice to the tenant within two months of the end of the first two-month period or of the withdrawal of the application, as appropriate: s 47(5), (6). The counternotice must state the landlord's acceptance of, or counterproposals to, the tenant's proposals set out in his original notice: s 47(8). (This requirement for a second counternotice does not apply if the landlord has applied for a declaration under s 46 that the tenant has no right to a lease: s 47(7). This is because, if that application was dismissed, the landlord will have already been required under s 46(4) to give a second counternotice.)

Facts to consider

4.46   On the application the court has to consider whether:

(a)   the tenant's lease is due to terminate within five years of the relevant date;
(b)   the landlord intends after such termination to demolish, reconstruct or carry out substantial building work on all or a substantial part of the premises containing the flat, for redevelopment purposes; and
(c)   the landlord cannot reasonably carry out his intention without obtaining possession of the flat.

If the court is satisfied of all three matters, it may (not must) declare that the right to a new lease is not exercisable: s 47(1), (2).

4.47   But if on the other hand the court dismisses the application, then it must also:

(i)   declare the landlord's counternotice to be of no effect; and
(ii)   require the landlord to give a further counternotice by the date specified in the order.

As before, the second counternotice must state the landlord's acceptance of, or counterproposals to, the tenant's proposals set out in his original notice: s 47(8).

DISPUTE AS TO TERMS

4.48   Where the landlord's counternotice admits the tenant's right to a new lease, or the landlord's challenge to that right or its exercise has been overruled by the court, and he has served a new counternotice, either the original or the new counternotice may dispute some of the terms of the acquisition: see paras 4.34, 4.43, 4.45, 4.47. 'Terms of acquisition' includes the terms of the lease, the premium or other amounts to be paid, and all the other terms on which the tenant is to acquire the lease: s 48(7). No doubt the parties will negotiate to attempt to resolve the outstanding points, but if anything remains in dispute two months after the counternotice in question was given, either landlord or tenant may apply to a leasehold valuation tribunal to determine the dispute: s 48(1). The application must be made within six months of the service of the counternotice in question: s 48(2). The tribunal is expressly given power to determine that the property of which a lease is to be granted should be less extensive than that specified in the tenant's notice: s 91(9).

TERMS OF THE LEASE

4.49   We have already seen that the new lease when granted is to last for a term comprising the unexpired term of the old lease plus 90 years, and is to be at a peppercorn rent: para 4.3. With certain limited exceptions, the remaining terms of the lease will be the same as those of the old lease, modified as necessary or appropriate to take account of certain circumstances: s 57(1).[1] These circumstances are:

(a)   the omission from the new lease of any property included in the old: s 57(1)(a);
(b)   alterations made to the property since the old lease was granted: s 57(1)(b);
(c)   any differences in, and the combined effect of, two or more separate leases which for present purposes (see para 4.6) together comprise the old lease: s 57(1)(c).

---

1   Based on the Leasehold Reform Act 1967, s 15(1).

4.50   In addition, s 57(6) provides that either party may require that, for the purposes of the new lease, a term of the old may be excluded or modified in so far as:

(a)   it is necessary to remedy a 'defect' in the old lease; or
(b)   it would be unreasonable not to do so in view of 'changes' since the old lease was granted affecting the suitability of the old lease's provisions.

What all this means is impossible to guess at. None of the critical words, such as 'defect' or 'changes', is defined. But the new lease will not contain any carryover from the old lease which confers a right of renewal, option to purchase or right of pre-emption, or creates a break clause: s 57(4).[1] Renewals and termination of the lease to be granted are governed exclusively by statutory provisions: paras 4.89, 4.100.

---

1   Based on the Leasehold Reform Act 1967, s 15(5).

Collateral agreements

4.51   Where there was any agreement 'collateral' to the old lease, provision must be made, either in the terms of the new lease or in another collateral agreement, for the original collateral agreement to be continued, with any necessary adaptations: s 57(3).[1] No definition or explanation of 'collateral' is given in the Act, and in particular there is nothing to restrict it to an agreement between the same parties as the old lease. Indeed, it is specifically provided that any third party to a 'collateral' agreement must be a party to the new collateral agreement and 'shall . . . join in its execution': s 57(9)(b). Not every agreement relating to the flat can be described as 'collateral' to the lease of that flat, but no guidance is given as to where the line must be drawn.

---

1 Based on the Leasehold Reform Act 1967, s 15(4).

Service charges

4.52 Notwithstanding the peppercorn rent, the new lease may require payments to be made (as rent or otherwise) by tenant to landlord in respect of the provision for services, repairs, maintenance or insurance: s 57(2)(a).[1] If the old lease contains such provisions then the new one will do so as well: s 57(1). But if the old lease did not contain such provisions, then the new one must make 'just' provision for the tenant to pay sums to the landlord 'related to' (but, be it noted, not necessarily 'covering') the cost to the landlord in respect of these matters: s 57(2)(b)(i).[2] Moreover, the provision must make such liability enforceable in the same way as rent, ie by distress, re-entry, 'or otherwise': s 57(2)(b)(ii).[3] Finally, on the question of rent, if the new lease is granted after the 'term date' (ie the expiry date: s 101(1)) of the old lease, then a sum will be added to the initial rent payable under the new to cover the period between the term date and the new grant: s 57(5).[4]

---

1 Based on the Leasehold Reform Act 1967, s 15(3).
2 Ibid.
3 Ibid.
4 Based on ibid, s 15(6).

Mandatory terms

4.53 The foregoing provisions relating to the terms of the lease are not mandatory, in the sense that the parties may agree to disapply any or all of them: s 57(6),[1] (9). But there are a few provisions in the lease which apparently it is not open to the parties to agree to omit or modify. One is that there must be a provision 'in accordance with s 59(3)', ie that no lease carved out of the new lease can itself confer the right to a new lease under these provisions: s 57(7)(a).[2] Another is that the new lease must reserve to the immediate landlord for the time being the right to obtain possession in accordance with s 61 (termination for redevelopment (see para 4.89): s 57(7)(b).[3] It is difficult to see why the landlord and the tenant should not be entitled, if they wish, to agree to the contrary in relation to either matter. Lastly, the lease must contain a statement that it is granted under s 57, and the statement must comply with land registration rules: s 57(11).

---

1 Based on the Leasehold Reform Act 1967, s 15(7).
2 Based on ibid, s 15(8).
3 Ibid.

POSITION OF THIRD PARTIES

4.54 A person who is a third party to the old lease or to a collateral agreement must be made a party to the new lease (or new collateral agreement) and must execute it: s 57(9). This much is clear. What is not so clear is what is to happen if the third party was performing some function in the context of the old landlord and tenant relationship and it is 'necessary or expedient' to provide for the continued performance of that function in the future. On the one hand, s 57(9) says that nothing in section 57 requires the third party to discharge any function after the term date of the old lease. On the other hand, s 57(10) says that where it is so 'necessary or expedient' then the new lease or agreement (to which of course the third party *must* be a party: s 57(9)) 'shall make provision for that function to be discharged after that date (whether by the third party or by some other person)'. The only resolution of this seeming opposition is to say that the third party must join in the lease or agreement, but cannot be required against his will to perform his old function, or indeed any other. And if he will not do so, then 'some other person' must be found to do so. Why a third party should be obliged to enter a lease or agreement but cannot be obliged to do anything under it is not explained.

FAILURE TO GIVE COUNTERNOTICE

4.55   The acquisition procedure normally depends on the landlord responding to the claim made by the tenant. Therefore, if the system is to work effectively, there has to be some sanction for a failure by the landlord to serve a counternotice, or a further counternotice when required to do so. One way of dealing with this would have been to treat the landlord as thereby admitting everything put forward by the tenant, or at any rate debarring him from opposing what the tenant said. That would have been simple and certain, but it might have produced negative effects for the landlord disproportionate to his default. Instead the legislation has opted for a much slower and less effective sanction – though perhaps fairer.

4.56   The procedure applies where a tenant has given a notice in accordance with s 42, but the landlord has failed to give his counternotice in time (para 4.34), or is treated as having so failed (para 4.40), or has failed to give a further counternotice where required to do so (paras 4.43, 4.45, 4.47). In such a case, the tenant may within six months from the expiry of the period for service of the counternotice in question apply to the court for an order determining the terms of the acquisition 'in accordance with the proposals contained in the tenant's notice': s 49(1), (3). It is clear that the court has no discretion as to the terms, but must accept the tenant's proposals. And after all, unlike the leasehold valuation tribunal (to which disputes as to terms are referred for determination: para 4.48) the court does not have the relevant expertise to decide such questions. The reason why *the court* has to 'rubber stamp' the tenant's proposals is that, before it can make the order sought, it must first be satisfied that on the date of giving the original notice the tenant had the right to acquire a new lease of his flat, and that he complied with any applicable requirements in Sch 11, Part I as to the giving of copies of his original notice: s 49(2).

THE GRANT OF THE NEW LEASE

Payments by the tenant

4.57   The terms of the lease, including its duration and service charges payable under it, have been dealt with: paras 4.49–4.53. Assuming that the tenant is entitled under the Act to a new lease, and has followed the statutory procedure, the landlord will be obliged to grant the new lease on having *paid* to him the premium as under Sch 13 (see paras 4.92–4.97), and having *tendered* to him certain other sums, so far as ascertained: s 56(1)(b), (3).[1] These further sums are:

(a)   sums payable by the tenant by way of, or recoverable as, rent in respect of the flat up to the date of tender: s 56(3)(a);

(b)   the landlord's and others' costs of the new lease under s 60 (see paras 4.98–4.99): s 56(3)(b);

(c)   any other sums payable by the tenant to the landlord, any immediate or intermediate landlord, and any third party to the lease, in respect of the old lease: s 56(3)(c).

Where any of these sums is not fully ascertained, tender is made by offering 'reasonable security' for them: s 56(3).[2]

---

1   Based on the Leasehold Reform Act 1967, s 14(3).
2   Ibid.

4.58   Some of the sums referred to may be sums to which the landlord is not ultimately entitled. For example, the landlord may not be the immediate landlord under the old lease, and sums may be paid to the landlord in respect of rent and service charge properly due to the immediate landlord. It is specifically provided that any sums in (a), (b) or (c) above due to others which are 'tendered' to the landlord 'shall be payable' to the person properly entitled by the landlord: s 56(4). This is poor drafting: 'tendered' only means 'offered to', and not necessarily received by, the person to whom it is tendered. Yet the 'tenderee' is still obliged to pay to someone else. Moreover, except where Sch 11, para 7(2) applies, there is no express provision that payment to the landlord discharges the tenant's obligations to any third party, although this is probably implied.

4.59   Payments under Sch 13 in respect of buying out the interests of intermediate landlords are not covered by s 56(4), but by Sch 11, para 7(2) (to which s 56(4) is expressly made subject in any event). That paragraph enables an intermediate landlord to notify the landlord and the tenant that payment for his interest shall be paid by the tenant to the intermediate landlord or his agent. But if he fails to give such notice, or to implement the arrangements notified, then the landlord is by statute authorised to receive payment for him, and the landlord's receipt is a discharge for the tenant.

Consent and consultation

4.60   Certain statutory provisions require that a consent be obtained or consultation take place before a long lease can be granted. However, some of these provisions are specifically disapplied for the purposes of granting a lease under this Chapter: s 56(6), (7). The provisions disapplied are listed in Sch 10, para 1(2)(a), (b), (d).

Covenants against subdemises

4.61   The grant of a new lease is specifically provided not to be a breach of any covenant against subdemises contained in a superior lease; nor will it 'trigger' any other unpleasant consequences such as determining the superior lease automatically: s 56(5). However, the width of the drafting may cause difficulty. It prevents *any* provision in a lease 'relating to a subdemise by the tenant under the lease' from having effect 'with reference to' the granting of the new lease. Thus an intermediate landlord who grants a new lease under s 56 need not inform his own landlord of that fact, if his lease would otherwise oblige him to do so. Yet, conversely, this provision has no effect in a case where it might be very necessary, eg where a landlord has a charged premises to a bank on a valuation based on a 'fag end' residential lease being the only encumbrance, and has covenanted not to grant any further lease. Granting the new lease may well be a breach of that covenant to the bank. The exact position will depend on whether, on its true construction, the landlord's covenant covers compulsory new leases.

Covenants for title and landlord's liability

4.62   When the new lease is granted, there will be no landlord's covenant for title beyond that implied by the general law (see Law of Property Act 1925, ss 76–77), unless the landlord voluntarily chooses to give one: s 57(8).[1] Moreover, the landlord is entitled, in entering any covenant in the lease, to limit his personal liability to 'breaches of that covenant for which he is responsible': s 57(8).[2] This is ambiguous. At one level it is trite, since a person is only ever liable for breaches for which he is responsible, thus equating 'liable' and 'responsible'. But it probably means that a landlord may limit his liability to breaches committed whilst he remains landlord, so that once he has assigned his interest he has no liability in respect of breaches of covenant committed thereafter.

---

1   Based on the Leasehold Reform Act 1967, s 15(9).
2   Ibid.

Supply of counterpart

4.63   Where the landlord's interest is mortgaged, charged or subject to a lien, by virtue of which the security holder is entitled to possession of the documents of title relating to that interest, the landlord must within one month of the grant of the new lease deliver to the security holder a counterpart of the lease duly executed by the tenant: s 58(3).[1] (The reference to 'a' counterpart is mysterious, because normally there is only one.) If the landlord fails to do this, the mortgagee may treat the failure to supply as contractual, as if there were a stipulation to that effect in the mortgage: s 58(6)(a). In practice, however, the mortgagee will only know about the lease and be able to take any action if the landlord complies with his obligation and sends him the counterpart!

---

1   Based on the Leasehold Reform Act 1967, s 14(5).

EFFECT OF GRANT ON SUBSISTING MORTGAGES

4.64   An important question, where a new lease is granted, is the relationship between that lease and:

(a)   a mortgage or charge on the landlord's interest; and/or

(b)   a mortgage or charge on the old lease.

These two fact situations are both dealt with to some extent by the legislation.

Mortgage of landlord's interest

4.65   Where there is a mortgage, charge or lien (all called 'mortgage' in the Act: s 62(1)) on the landlord's interest, the *general* law requires a distinction to be drawn between leases granted before and leases granted after the creation of the security interest. The former are free of the security interest: the latter are subject to it unless *either*:

(a)   the landlord retains the power to grant leases binding on the mortgagee (for example Law of Property Act 1925, s 99; but this is invariably excluded by the mortgage deed); *or*

(b)   the mortgagee consents to the lease being free of the mortgage.

4.66   In most cases of leases granted under this Act, that general law will continue to apply. There is a cryptic provision in s 93(5), (7), which appears to empower the court to approve a lease which is binding on a prior mortgage, but only if the old lease was granted before the commencement of Chapter II. Apart from this, the Act concerns itself only with the comparatively rare case where the old lease (on the basis of which the new lease is to be granted) was granted after the mortgage was created *and* was not authorised by the mortgagee – and hence is not otherwise binding on him. In such a case, subject to an exception which we will consider in a moment, the new lease granted under this Act is *not* subject to the mortgage, and the mortgagee is treated as having consented to its creation: s 58(1).[1]

---

1   Based on the Leasehold Reform Act 1967, s 14(4).

4.67   But the scope of this special rule is drastically cut down by s 58(2). This provides that the special rule will not apply where the old lease was granted after the coming into force of this Chapter of the Act and would not otherwise be binding on the mortgagee. In other words, the special rule is transitional, and applies only to new leases derived from pre-commencement old leases.

4.68   Where the special rule does not apply it may bear hardly on the tenant. His new lease is subject to the mortgage on the landlord's interest. To mitigate this, in such a case the landlord is by statute obliged to do what is 'necessary' to prevent the lease being 'defeated' by the mortgagee: s 58(7).[1] This is difficult to make sense of. The obvious thing for him to do is to persuade the mortgagee to agree to postpone his mortgage to the new lease, but the mortgagee will not agree: why should he? Another possibility is for the landlord to pay off the mortgage, but the premium for the lease may represent only a fraction of the amount secured by the mortgage. And in any case s 58(7) elliptically states that the landlord is not obliged to acquire a better title than he has – which is what paying off the mortgage would be, on any rational construction of the word 'better'. Nevertheless, Sch 11, para 11 seems to assume that paying off *part* of the debt secured by the mortgage – ie that proportion that can be said to be attributable to the flat – is what will be necessary.

---

1   Based on the Leasehold Reform Act 1967, s 14(7).

Mortgage of old lease

4.69   Where the old lease was subject to a mortgage the new lease becomes likewise subject, and the terms of the mortgage apply to it as they applied to the old lease: s 58(4). A person entitled to possession of documents of title relating to the old lease is similarly entitled to such documents relating to the new lease. In particular, the tenant must within one month of receiving the new lease back from the Land Registry deliver it to such person: s 58(5).[1] Failure so to deliver entails the same consequences, under s 58(6), as where the landlord fails to deliver the counterpart new lease to *his* mortgagee: see para 4.63.

---

44 Based on the Leasehold Reform Act 1967, s 14(6).

FAILURE TO ENTER INTO NEW LEASE

4.70   Lastly, there is the problem of failure to enter into the new lease. The tenant's right has been admitted (or any challenge has been defeated), all the terms of acquisition have been agreed or determined by a leasehold valuation tribunal – but the lease has still not been granted: s 48(3). Or the landlord failed to serve a counternotice, and the tenant has obtained an order of the court determining the terms – but the new lease again has still not been granted: s 49(4). The fact that the new lease still has not been granted may be the fault of either landlord or tenant, or of both.

4.71   If one of them is ready to go ahead, but the other is not, what can he do? Once a certain period of time has elapsed, he has two months within which to apply to the court for an order that the other party carry out his obligations under the transaction, and the court may make such order as it thinks fit: ss 48(3), (5), 49(4), (6). This order may provide for the tenant's notice to be deemed withdrawn as from the end of the 'waiting time': ss 48(4), 49(5).

4.72   The period of time that must elapse before an application may be made (called 'the appropriate period') depends on whether the terms of acquisition were agreed by the parties or resolved by the leasehold valuation tribunal or the court. If the parties agree them, the appropriate period is two months from the date on which final agreement was reached: s 48(6)(a). If the leasehold valuation tribunal or the court resolved them, it is the period stipulated by the leasehold valuation tribunal in its determination or by the court in its order, or, if none was fixed, two months from the date on which the determination or order became final: ss 48(6)(b), 49(7).

WHERE THE LANDLORD CANNOT BE FOUND

4.73   As has been seen, the lease extension procedure is based on service of the tenant's notice on the landlord: para 4.29. As with the right to collective enfranchisement, therefore, a separate procedure is needed to deal with the case where the identity of the landlord cannot be ascertained, or, though ascertained, he cannot be found. In such a case the tenant may apply to the court for an order under which the tenant is granted a new lease in substitution for his old one: ss 50(1),[1] 51(1).

---

1   Based on the Leasehold Reform Act 1967, s 27(1).

4.74   This procedure does not, however, apply where the *landlord* can be found, but one of the *other* persons on whom a copy of the tenant's notice should be served cannot be ascertained or found. In such a case, the court has power simply to dispense with the need to give a copy to that person: s 50(2). Thereafter, if any tenant's notice given to claim the right to a new lease contains a statement of the effect of the order, the requirements of the legislation in relation to serving the missing person will be satisfied: s 50(6), (7).

4.75   Since the application in either case is ex hypothesi concerned with a missing person, the court has a kind of interlocutory power, before making any order on the application, to require the tenant to take such steps as it thinks appropriate to try to trace the missing landlord or other person: s 50(4).[1] This may involve advertising or other methods of bringing the proceedings or the tenant's claim to his attention: s 50(4).[2]

---

1   Based on the Leasehold Reform Act 1967, s 27(2).
2   Ibid.

The vesting order

4.76   Under the missing landlord procedure, the order of the court is known as a 'vesting order': s 50(1). This is misleading, because it suggests that the order itself vests the new lease in the tenant. It does not. All it does is to take the place of:

(a)   service of the tenant's notice on the landlord; and
(b)   admission in principle of the tenant's right to a new lease.

The terms of the acquisition are left to be determined by a further application to a leasehold valuation tribunal: s 51(1). Once that is done, the tenant pays the necessary sums into court, and only then is a new lease executed in favour of the tenant, by the person designated by the court. This vests the lease in the tenant: s 51(3).[1]

---

1   Based on the Leasehold Reform Act 1967, s 27(3).

4.77   The essentially preliminary nature of the vesting order is also shown by the provision that an *application* for a vesting order may be withdrawn by the tenant at any time *before the lease is executed*, ie even though a vesting order has by then actually been made: s 50(5). In practice, if the order has been made, but the tenant wishes to withdraw, he will just do nothing further, ie in particular will not apply to the leasehold valuation tribunal. It is also very difficult to see what the court would do if an application were made to withdraw an application after an order had been made. Similarly, if, *before the lease is executed*, the missing landlord 'is traced', then no further 'proceedings' may be taken with a view to that lease being executed: s 50(4). This will include any part of the proceedings remaining before the vesting order is made, but also the application to the leasehold valuation tribunal to determine the terms of the acquisition.

4.78   There is no definition or elucidation of the word 'traced'. Nor is it clear what degree of certainty is required that it is indeed the landlord who has been found, and not someone else. Does it mean merely that an address has come to light? Or that the landlord has actually been seen? Does it matter that it happens accidentally, rather than as a result of deliberate searching? And to whose knowledge must the information come? Presumably it must come to the knowledge of the tenant. There is no express requirement for the tenant to inform the court, much less the landlord himself, that the landlord has been traced.

4.79   This vagueness is very unhelpful, because, once the landlord 'is traced', in principle the landlord and tenant are stated to be in the same legal position as if the tenant had served a s 44 notice on the landlord: s 50(4)(a). The unfairness to the landlord of this situation (since he will probably not know anything about it) is tempered, though not cured, by the court's power in such a case to give directions as to the steps to be taken for giving effect to the parties' rights and obligations (s 50(4)(b)), and obviously these may include notifying the landlord of what is going on. Moreover, if the tenant merely does not go on with his application to the court – or if the court has already *made* a 'vesting order' – the court will have no reason to invoke its powers.

4.80   But the general rule, that on the landlord being traced the parties are in the same position as if the tenant had served a notice on the landlord, does not apply if the tenant withdraws his application for a vesting order (s 50(5)[1]), *unless* some step has by then been taken (whether by landlord or tenant) to give effect to that general legal position. In that exceptional case, the tenant may only withdraw his application with the consent of the landlord or of the court: s 50(5). The court must not give leave unless it is just to do so because of matters learnt by the tenant from tracing the landlord: s 50(5). All in all, the consequences of 'tracing' the missing landlord are poorly conceived, badly drafted and needlessly complex.

---

1   Based on the Leasehold Reform Act 1967, s 27(7).

4.81   Where the court is faced with an application for a vesting order, it must not make the order unless it is satisfied by the tenant of three things:

(i)   the landlord's identity cannot be ascertained, or he cannot be found: s 50(1)(b);
(ii)   on the date of making the application, the tenant had the right to a new lease: s 50(3)(a);
(iii)   on that date there was nothing in the legislation to prevent him giving a valid notice under s 42: s 50(3)(b).

Application to leasehold valuation tribunal

4.82   Once the vesting order has been made, the tenant will apply to a leasehold valuation tribunal to determine the terms of the acquisition. Since the leasehold valuation tribunal normally has no jurisdiction until a notice and counternotice have been served (para 4.48), and since the effect of the vesting order is to put the tenant in the same position as if notice had been given (s 51(1)), it seems that a vesting order must be made before the leasehold valuation tribunal can consider the matter. The leasehold valuation tribunal is specifically given power to determine that the vesting order made by the court should have effect in respect of property less (but not more) extensive than that specified in the tenant's application to the court: s 51(2). In particular, it seems (although the drafting could be clearer) that the underlying minerals must be excluded: s 51(4).[1] Moreover, the leasehold valuation tribunal is to assume in every case that the landlord has no interest in any other property than that which is to be the subject of the new lease and any minerals underlying that property: s 51(4).

1   Based on the Leasehold Reform Act 1967, s 27(4).

Engrossment and payment

4.83   After the leasehold valuation tribunal has determined the terms of the acquisition by the tenant, the new lease can be drawn up. The leasehold valuation tribunal will have determined the amounts to be paid (in aggregate called 'the appropriate sum') by the tenant and these are:

(a)   the premium payable under Sch 13 (see para 4.92) for the grant of the new lease;

(b)   any other amounts payable under Sch 13 to buy out intermediate landlords;

(c)   amounts due from the tenant to the landlord under the tenant's old lease (or any collateral agreement) at the time of entering into the new, ie arrears of ground rent, service charge and so on: s 51(5).

4.84   Curiously, in (c) the statute refers to sums 'due to the landlord from the tenant'. We have seen that in these provisions 'the landlord' may not be the tenant's immediate landlord, but a person further up the landlord and tenant chain: see para 4.11. Yet it is very unlikely that a tenant will owe sums to a landlord other than his immediate landlord. This point only arises in relation to missing landlords; the equivalent statutory provision dealing with participating landlords is cast in quite different terms: see para 4.57.

4.85   Once the lease has been granted, payment into court of the 'appropriate sum' satisfies any claims against the tenant in respect of the amounts in (a) and (b) above: s 51(6).[1] Nothing is said as to (c), so it must be supposed that the immediate landlord's claim against the tenant for sums due under the old lease and any collateral agreement remains unsatisfied. Another curiosity is that the Act makes no provision for the missing landlord, if and when he turns up, to withdraw the money from court. Presumably the landlord must apply to the court for an order for payment out, and must prove that he is indeed the landlord concerned before he can obtain such an order.

1   Based on the Leasehold Reform Act 1967, s 27(6).

PROCEDURE WHERE THE COMPETENT LANDLORD IS NOT THE IMMEDIATE LANDLORD

4.86   Throughout the procedure, it is 'the landlord' who takes all the necessary steps and deals with the tenant. But we have seen (para 4.11) that he may not be the immediate landlord. In such a case the landlord acts as agent for all the landlords concerned: s 40(2). Schedule 11 contains provisions regulating the relationship between the various landlords. Thus, generally, the acts of the competent landlord (ie 'the landlord' as defined) will bind the intermediate landlords: Sch 11, para 6. Where the various landlords cannot agree how the competent landlord should act, any of them can apply to the court for directions: Sch 11, para 6(1). Similarly, application can be made for directions where one of the landlords cannot be found or his identity ascertained: Sch 11, para 6(3). As long as the competent landlord acts in good faith and with reasonable care, he will not be liable to the other landlords for loss caused by his acts or omissions: Sch 11, para 6(4).

4.87   Schedule 11, para 7 allows the other landlords to give the competent landlord notice:

(a)   to be separately represented in legal proceedings, or
(b)   individually to receive any payments due to them under Sch 13 in respect of their interests.

However, they are under a general obligation to co-operate with the competent landlord in dealing with the transaction, and to contribute fairly to irrecoverable costs and expenses: Sch 11, para 8. There appears to be no provision for them to contribute to a 'float' pending reimbursement by the tenant of costs and expenses recoverable from him (as to these see paras 4.98–4.99). But the competent landlord cannot bind the other landlords in relation to applications to the court to defeat the tenant's exercise of the right on grounds of intended redevelopment (see paras 4.44–4.47). Such applications must be made by individual landlords on their own behalf: Sch 11, para 9.

4.88   The conveyancing procedure is also affected. All subsisting intermediate leases are deemed surrendered just before the new lease was granted and then regranted thereafter, except where any intermediate lease was vested in the tenant or in a trustee for him, in which case there is a deemed surrender but no deemed regrant: Sch 11, para 10. Sections 57(2) (para 4.52) and 59(3) (para 4.53) also apply taking account of the landlord and tenant chain.

LANDLORD'S RIGHT TO TERMINATE

4.89   In limited circumstances a new lease granted under the Act may be terminated by a court order on redevelopment grounds. If this happens the tenant will be entitled to compensation. An application to the court for such an order can only be made by the landlord during one of two periods: s 61(2). The first is the period of 12 months beginning with the date on which the old lease would have terminated had it run its full course. The second is the period of the last five years of the new lease, or (if the new lease is not the first lease of the flat to be granted under the Act) what would have been the last five years of the previous 'new' lease, had there not been a further new lease granted in the meantime: s 61(3).

4.90   Before the court may make an order terminating the lease, s 61(1) requires that it must be satisfied both:

(a)   of the landlord's intention, for redevelopment purposes, to demolish or reconstruct or carry out substantial construction works on the whole or a substantial part of the premises containing the flat; and

(b)   of the reasonable need to obtain possession of the flat in order to carry out the works.

Those requirements stem originally from the Landlord and Tenant Act 1954, s 30(1)(f) (opposition by landlord to new business tenancy on grounds of intended redevelopment).[1] They also appear in the Housing Act 1985, Sch 2, Ground 10 (ground for possession in secure tenancy)[2] and the Housing Act 1988, Sch 2, Ground 6 (ground for possession in assured tenancy).[3] If the court upholds the landlord's contention, and makes the order, the new lease will come to an end, and compensation will be payable, computed under Sch 14, paras 5 and 6: s 61(4).

---

1   See *Hill & Redman*, **B** [514], and also the Leasehold Reform Act 1967, s 17.
2   See *Hill & Redman*, **D** [1440].
3   See ibid, **C** [2250].

4.91   Schedule 14 also makes detailed provision for the date on which the new lease terminates (para 2), for dealing with immediate or derivative subleases (para 3), for jurisdiction for possession proceedings (para 4), for dealing with deductions from, and the application of, the compensation (para 7), for the effect of delay or bad faith in making an application (para 8), and for dealing with the situations where the tenant is a trustee for sale (para 9), a university or college (para 10) or an ecclesiastical body (paras 11 and 12).

CALCULATION OF PREMIUM PAYABLE FOR NEW LEASE

4.92   The calculation of the premium payable by the tenant to the landlord for the new lease, and of the other amounts payable by the tenant to intermediate landlords, are governed by Sch 13. The procedure can be compared with that under the Leasehold Reform Act 1967.[1] Unlike that procedure, the date as at which the valuation is to be calculated is not the date of making the initial claim,[2] but the date when all the terms of acquisition (save amounts to be paid) have been agreed or determined: Sch 13, para 1. According to Sch 13, para 2, the premium payable to the landlord is the aggregate of three elements:

(a)   the diminution in value of the landlord's interest in the flat;
(b)   the landlord's share of the 'marriage value';
(c)   any compensation payable to the landlord in respect of losses suffered in respect of *other* property.

---

1   See *Hill & Redman*, **E** [581]–[589].
2   See the Leasehold Reform Act 1967, s 37(1)(d).

Diminution in value

4.93   This is the difference between the values of the landlord's interest before and after the grant of the new lease: Sch 13, para 3(1). The values are calculated on an open market basis, disregarding certain factors: para 3(2). A curiosity is that where the landlord owns the freehold reversion in the block, the valuation is on the basis that the landlord is selling the freehold interest *in the flat*. A separately sold freehold flat in the middle of a block otherwise retained by the landlord would be of little interest on the open market (particularly if on an upper floor), because of the difficulty of enforcing positive covenants against others. Any defects in title must be taken account of in the value: para 3(5).[1] There are also certain anti-avoidance provisions involving the creation of overriding leases, corresponding to the provision made by the Leasehold Reform Act 1979[2] in relation to enfranchisement under the 1967 Act: para 3(6).

1 Based on the Leasehold Reform Act 1967, s 9(2).
2 See *Hill & Redman*, **E** [1081]–[1083].

Share of marriage value

4.94 'Marriage value' is a well known valuation concept. Two assets may be worth a total of $£X$ in separate hands, but $£(X+Y)$ in the same hands. The marriage value is the difference, $£(X+Y) - £X$, ie $£Y$. It has already been discussed, in relation to collective enfranchisement (paras 3.78–3.79). Here, however, it is not quite the case that two assets end up in the same hands; instead the tenant's asset is vastly increased in size and value, and the landlord's asset is similarly decreased. But the principle is the same. If the tenant gets another 90 years' worth from the landlord, and at effectively no rent, the tenant's interest becomes very nearly worth a freehold, and the landlord's interest becomes worth practically nothing. (Of course there may be exceptional factors in any particular case which alter that position.)

4.95 The marriage value is accordingly defined as the *difference* between:

(a) the aggregate values of the interests of all parties (including any intermediate landlords) *before* the grant of the new lease, and
(b) the aggregate values of such interests after the grant.[1]

Where the interest of either landlord or tenant before the grant was very small (eg the old lease had just been granted *or* was about to run out) then the difference between the two aggregates is virtually nothing, and there is no – or nearly no – marriage value. But where the interests of landlord and tenant before the grant are about equal in value (ie where there are about 20 to 30 years left to run on the lease) then the difference between the two aggregates – and hence the marriage value – will be at its greatest.

1 At an earlier stage, item (b) consisted solely of the value of the tenant's interest after the grant. Notwithstanding that the Minister thought this was 'fair both to landlord and to tenant' (HC Standing Committee B, 24 November 1992, col 254), this was subsequently changed to the present text, though without any explanation or debate.

4.96 The landlord's share of the marriage value is that agreed by the parties or determined by a leasehold valuation tribunal as the share that would be awarded by an 'open market' agreement, but it must not be less than 50%: Sch 13, para 4(1). This seems unduly advantageous to the landlord, since it means he can get more, but cannot get less, than the tenant. In practice, leasehold valuation tribunals have in the past awarded marriage value to both parties equally, on the basis that 'it takes two to tango'.[1] The 50% 'floor' was the subject of fierce debate in Parliament.

Some Conservatives argued for 100% for the landlord, whereas opposition members sought to remove the floor altogether.[2] It should be noted that the landlord will have to share his part of the marriage value with intermediate landlords in some circumstances: Sch 13, para 10.

---

1   See eg *Norfolk v Masters, Fellows and Scholars of Trinity College Cambridge* (1976) 32 P & CR 147; *Lloyd-Jones v Church Comrs* [1983] RVR 89; see also HL Committee, 22 March 1993, col 127, per Lord Strathclyde.
2   See para 3.80.

Compensation for other landlord losses

4.97   Intermediate landlords may also be entitled to receive payment from the tenant in respect of their interests. The amount of this payment is the aggregate of the diminution in value of the intermediate landlord's interest and any compensation payable in respect of damage to other property interests: para 6. The diminution in value of an intermediate landlord's interest is the difference in its value before and after the new lease is granted: para 7. In many cases the method of calculation of the value will be identical to that in relation to the interest of the competent landlord: para 8(1). But there is a complex formula to be applied in the case where the intermediate landlord's interest is of very small value. This is where the 'profit rent' (difference between rents payable and receivable) is £5 per annum or less, and the future interest in possession (between the end of the inferior lease and the end of the intermediate lease) will be less than one month in duration: para 8(2)–(9). The compensation payable to an intermediate landlord is calculated in the same way as the competent landlord: para 9. Intermediate landlords are also entitled to share part of the landlord's share of the marriage value in some circumstances: para 10.

COSTS OF LANDLORDS AND THIRD PARTIES

4.98   Costs incurred by landlords and third parties to leases in a lease renewal are in general to be paid by the tenant. Section 60(1),[1] (3) provides that, with three exceptions, these costs are the reasonable costs incurred by such landlords and third parties after the s 42 notice is given and until either the notice is withdrawn (or deemed withdrawn) or the new lease is granted. They cover:

(a)   any investigation reasonably undertaken of the tenant's right;
(b)   any valuation of the tenant's flat for Sch 13 purposes;
(c)   the grant of the new lease.

But they do not include costs incurred in connection with leasehold valuation tribunal proceedings (s 60(5)), which are not recoverable: para 1.19. Costs incurred in connection with court proceedings are not within (a)–(c) above anyway, but will be dealt with under the usual litigation costs rules.[2]

---

1   Based on the Leasehold Reform Act 1967, ss 9(4), 14(2).
2   See the County Court Rules 1981, Ord 38.

4.99 The first exception to the general rule above is that costs are excluded if on a voluntary transaction an undertaking by the grantee of the new lease to pay such costs would be void. The second and third exceptions are where the tenant's notice ceases to have effect because the landlord establishes his intention to redevelop, or the land is to be compulsorily acquired: s 60(4). For this purpose, 'reasonable' refers to costs for services which 'might reasonably be expected to have been incurred' in a voluntary transaction: s 60(2).

FURTHER RENEWALS

4.100 Subject to the possible operation of s 93(4) of the Act (para 4.3), the lease of a particular flat may be renewed more than once under these provisions: s 59(1). Indeed, there seems to be nothing to prevent a new s 42 notice being given the day after the first new lease is granted. Since each renewal is for a term adding 90 years to the current unexpired term, a series of renewals could build up a very long lease at a peppercorn rent which (in theory at least) could then be converted to a freehold of the flat under the Law of Property Act 1925, s 153.[1] The attraction of s 153 is that if a leasehold is converted to a freehold thereunder, the leasehold covenants are retained, but run with and against the freehold: Law of Property Act 1925, s 153(8).

---

1 See *Hill & Redman*, **A** [3430], and *Taylor*, (1958) 22 Conv (NS) 101.

Lack of security of tenure

4.101 Although the tenant may be able to renew the lease indefinitely, however, all other statutory security of tenure is removed from the lease when it expires: s 59(2)(a). So far as concerns subleases derived from the new lease, none of the Landlord and Tenant Act 1954, s 1, the Landlord and Tenant Act 1954, Part II, or the Local Government and Housing Act 1989, Sch 10 applies (s 59(2)(b)), and neither may any person retain possession under such sublease by virtue of the Rent Act 1977, Part VII, the Rent (Agriculture) Act 1976 or the Housing Act 1988, Part I. There are provisions requiring an actual or prospective grantor of a sublease to inform the other party of the fact that the lease is one granted or to be granted under this Act: s 59(4).[1] Lastly, no sublease derived from a lease renewal granted under the Act can itself qualify for renewal: s 59(3).[2]

---

1 Based on the Leasehold Reform Act 1967, s 16(6).
2 Based on ibid, s 16(4).

INTERACTION WITH OTHER PROCEEDINGS

4.102 Particular problems could arise where the lease renewal procedure is under way and then another statutory procedure concerning the property is activated. One obvious example is an application being made for collective enfranchisement, under Part I, Chapter I of this Act. Another is the commencement of compulsory acquisition procedures. The legislation makes specific provision for both situations.

Claims for collective enfranchisement

4.103   The general rule is that if a claim to collective enfranchisement is made whilst a claim to a new lease is 'current',[1] the tenant's notice claiming a new lease is suspended until the claim to collective enfranchisement comes to an end: s 54(2). Similarly, if a claim to a new lease is made whilst a claim to collective enfranchisement is 'current',[2] the tenant's notice claiming a new lease does not take effect but is suspended for so long as the claim to collective enfranchisement remains current: s 54(1). In either case the landlord must inform the tenant of the suspension and various details of the claim to collective enfranchisement: s 54(3).

---

1   Seemingly not defined, but see note 2 below.
2   Defined by the 1993 Act, s 54(11)(b).

Reactivation of tenant's claim

4.104   If the claim to collective enfranchisement for any reason 'ceases to be current', the tenant's claim to a new lease will be reactivated. It is necessary to distinguish the two cases (a) where the tenant's claim is made first and the collective claim second, and (b) where the collective claim was made first and the tenant's claim second. In the latter case the tenant's claim is suspended from the outset. Then from the moment that the collective claim ceases to be current (which the landlord must tell the tenant of: s 54(8)), the tenant's claim springs into life. The only modification to the procedure is that, for the date specified in the tenant's notice of the date by which the landlord must serve his counternotice (para 4.23), the statute substitutes such date as will give the landlord exactly the same period to respond from the date of revival of the tenant's claim as he would have had from the date of service of the original notice: s 54(4).

4.105   The former case, where the tenant's claim is made first, and only subsequently interrupted by the collective claim, is more difficult. The tenant's claim may have advanced a long way down the track, or only a very little way, before it is suspended. The legislation divides these cases into two groups, and treats each group differently.

4.106   The first group comprises cases where before the suspension it was for the *landlord* to take the next step, ie:

(a)   the landlord was due to serve his original counternotice;
(b)   the landlord, having denied the tenant's right or stated his intention to oppose its exercise on grounds of intention to redevelop, was due to apply to the court for the relevant order;
(c)   the landlord, having failed in his challenge to the tenant's right or its exercise, was due to serve a *further* counternotice: s 54(6).

4.107   In such cases the time period during which the landlord must take the next step *starts again* from the date when the collective claim ceases to be current: s 54(5). Because the landlord is intimately involved in the collective claim, he will be aware of this. The tenant may not be aware, so the landlord must inform the tenant (s 54(8)), unless the tenant has previously informed the landlord that he is so aware: s 54(9).

4.108   The second group of cases includes all other cases, being mostly those where before the suspension it was for the *tenant* to take the next step. As already mentioned, the tenant may not know that the collective claim has ceased to be current, and the landlord must so inform the tenant, unless the tenant has already so informed the landlord: s 54(8), (9). As before, the time period for taking the next step starts again, but only from the date of the landlord's notice to the tenant under s 54(8), or a tenant's notice to the landlord under s 54(7).

Compulsory acquisition procedures

4.109   There are two cases to consider. The first is where the tenant gives notice under s 42 to claim a new lease and subsequently compulsory acquisition procedures are commenced in relation to the flat concerned. The second is where compulsory acquisition procedures are already under way when the tenant serves his s 42 notice. In the second case the tenant's notice never takes effect: s 55(1).[1] In the first case the tenant's notice ceases to have effect on the date when the 'notice to treat' is served: s 55(2).[2] But, since the tenant's notice in that case was already served by then, the compensation payable in respect of any person's interest in the flat is to be determined on the basis of the value of such interest as affected by the notice (see paras 4.29–4.30): s 55(3).[3] There are no provisions for revival of the procedure if the compulsory acquisition does not proceed.

---

1   Based on the Leasehold Reform Act 1967, s 5(6)(a).
2   Based on ibid, s 5(6)(b).
3   Based on ibid, s 5(6).

5 Extension of the Leasehold Reform Act 1967

INTRODUCTION

5.1 Chapter III of Part I of the 1993 Act is the shortest of the Act's Chapters, with six sections and one Schedule. But it created the most political controversy during the Bill's passage through Parliament.[1] The angry reactions of large estate owners such as the Duke of Westminster and the Earl of Cadogan gave extra prominence to the enactment of the present provisions, which in the context of the other significant changes made by this Act was disproportionate.

---

1 For the debates, see: HC 2R, 3 November 1992, cols 154–155; HC Standing Committee B, 24 and 25 November 1992, cols 258–271; HC Report, 9 February 1993, cols 822–834, 858–878, 903–922, 931; HL 2R, 23 February 1993, col 87; HL Committee, 22 March 1993, cols 109–128; HL Report, 18 May 1993, cols 1707-1713; HL 3R, 25 May 1993, cols 211–212; HC Lords Amendments, 14 June 1993, cols 663–682.

5.2 The major purpose of these provisions is to enable leaseholders whose properties were previously excluded by financial limits from the Leasehold Reform Act to take advantage of that Act. The opportunity has also been taken to make certain general amendments to the Leasehold Reform Act enfranchisement scheme, including negativing one landlord scheme to avoid the Act (s 64), altering the calculation of the price to be paid for enfranchisement by those now brought into the Act (s 66), and creating two new exceptions to the right to enfranchise under the Act (ss 67 and 68). Consequently, none of the six sections stands alone: they all operate to amend the 1967 Act.

EXTENDED RIGHT TO ENFRANCHISE

5.3 The extension of the right to enfranchise to leaseholders previously excluded by financial limits could have been achieved by simply removing those limits. However, the Government's desire to tilt the balance back towards landlords from tenants in the politically sensitive question of purchase price and other landlord compensation would have been more difficult to achieve. Accordingly, a new section has been inserted into the Leasehold Reform Act providing for fresh rights to enfranchise where the tenant would otherwise be prevented by financial criteria from doing so. It is the provisions of *this* section (and the section designed to negative so called 'Prince of Wales' clauses) which are then subjected to the price and compensation amendments which the Government desired to make.

Rateable values

5.4   Where the only matter preventing enfranchisement has been that the rateable value (or its post-1990 equivalent) of the property was too high, a new s 1A(1), inserted by s 63 of the 1993 Act, provides that the tenant shall now have the right to enfranchise as if the rateable value limit were not exceeded. In other words, every tenant who fell outside the rateable value limits now has a separate right to enfranchise under s 1A(1), if he satisfies the other conditions.

Low rent

5.5   Where the problem was that the tenancy concerned was not a tenancy 'at a low rent' as defined by the 1967 Act, s 4, a new s 1A(2) (also inserted by s 63) now provides an additional test of 'low rent'. This is set out in the new s 4A[1] in the 1967 Act, inserted by s 65 of the 1993 Act. It does not mean that the 'low rent' test has now been abolished, but it does mean that many tenants whose ground rents have been deliberately set so as to prevent them qualifying under the Leasehold Reform Act will now be able to qualify under s 1A(2). Obviously, a tenant who fell on the wrong side of both rateable value and low rent limits may now satisfy the latter under s 1A(2) and then qualify under s 1A(1). Both new rights are retrospective in the sense that they apply to persons whose leases were granted before the commencement of the 1993 Act.

---

1   This is in substance identical to the 1993 Act, s 8 (test for collective enfranchisement): para 2.20.

5.6   The new s 4A(1) provides that a tenancy *is* a tenancy at a low rent if *during its first year* (s 4A(1)(a)) the rent payable did not exceed a certain figure. The certain figure depends on which of five categories the tenancy in question falls into. These categories are:

(1)   tenancies entered into before 1 April 1963;
(2)   tenancies entered into between 1 April 1963 and 31 March 1990;
(3)   tenancies entered into after 31 March 1990 in pursuance of contracts made before 1 April 1990;
(4)   other tenancies in Greater London;
(5)   other tenancies outside Greater London.

5.7   The corresponding figures are:

(1)   two-thirds of the 'letting' value (within s 4(1) of the 1967 Act) of the property;
(2),(3) two-thirds of the rateable value of the property on the commencement of the tenancy or (if later) the date on which the property first had a rateable value;
(4)   £1,000;
(5)   £250.

For the purposes of s 4A(1), the provisions of s 4(1)(b), (c) of the 1967 Act (meaning of 'rent' and disregards therefrom) apply as they do for s 4(1) itself: s 4A(2)(c). The figures in (iv) and (v) are subject to amendment by ministerial order: s 4A(3).

'PRINCE OF WALES' CLAUSES

5.8   Before 1980 a common means of seeking to avoid the enfranchisement provisions of the Leasehold Reform Act was to grant a tenancy terminable by notice after a death or a marriage - typically the death of the last survivor of those descendants of King George V living at the date of the grant. Sometimes the clause simply specified the Prince of Wales as the life concerned. The effect of this was to prevent the lease qualifying as a 'long tenancy' within s 3(1) of the 1967 Act.

5.9   The Housing Act 1980, s 141 prospectively amended the 1967 Act so that such devices would not work in future leases, although 'Prince of Wales' clauses in leases then existing would still have effect to keep their leases outside the right to enfranchise. The Government has now accepted that even pre-1980 leases which contained such clauses should be subject to enfranchisement.[1] Accordingly, s 64(1) of the 1993 Act inserts a new s 1B into the 1967 Act to achieve this end, and this effectively negatives proviso (a) to s 3(1) of that Act. Section 64(2) makes consequential changes.

---

1   See HL Report, 9 February 1993, cols 832–834.

PRICE PAYABLE ON ENFRANCHISEMENT

5.10   The price payable on enfranchisement by the tenant under the 1967 Act as originally enacted was silent as to whether to take 'marriage value'[1] into account, ie the fact that the sitting tenant would pay more than any third party to acquire the freehold. In *Custins v Hearts of Oak Building Society* [1969] RVR 58 and *Haw v Peek* [1969] CLY 2042 the Lands Tribunal held that it nevertheless *should* be taken into account. Parliament responded with the Housing Act 1969, s 82, which inserted words into s 9(1) designed to reverse the effect of these decisions. Marriage value was thereafter ignored in calculating the price to be paid by the tenant.

---

1   For this concept, see paras 3.78–3.79.

5.11   The Housing Act 1974, s 118(4) added a new s 9(1A), containing an entirely new method of valuing those properties brought by the 1974 Act within the enfranchisement provisions of the 1967 Act for the first time. The absence in s 9(1A) of the extra words inserted in s 9(1) by the 1969 Act was held by the Lands Tribunal in *Norfolk v Masters, Fellows and Scholars of Trinity College Cambridge* (1976) 32 P & CR 147 to mean that marriage value had to be taken into account in valuing under s 9(1A).[1]

---

1   See *Hill & Redman*, **E** [584].

5.12   Properties enfranchised under the 1993 rights (ie under new ss 1A and 1B of the 1967 Act) are to be valued on the basis of s 9(1A), rather than s 9(1): s 66(1), inserting a new s 9(1C). Thus marriage value *will* be taken into account if appropriate. But it is specifically provided that, where it is taken into account, not more than 50% of the marriage value is to go to the tenant: s 9(1C)(a). Moreover, the landlord whose tenant enfranchises under s 1A or 1B is also to be entitled, in an appropriate case, to compensation for the diminution in value of any other of his property caused by the tenant's acquisition (so-called 'severance'), and indeed any other loss he suffers referable to ownership of property: ss 9(1C)(b), 9A(1), (2). These losses will include development value: s 9A(3), (4). Where the tenant's acquisition takes place under s 1A or s 1B the term 'price' in the 1967 Act will bear an extended meaning, including the compensation payable under s 9A: s 9A(5). It should be noted that s 9 (as amended) is reprinted in Sch 14 to the 1993 Act.

EXCEPTIONS TO ENFRANCHISEMENT

Charitable housing trusts

5.13   Intensive lobbying and parliamentary debate (particularly at committee stage in the House of Lords) in favour of an exemption *generally* for charitable trusts led the Government, at a very late stage in the Bill's progress,[1] to put forward a limited provision dealing with charitable housing trusts. Section 67 is the result. It amends the Leasehold Reform Act 1967, so as to exclude from the right to enfranchise cases where the tenant's immediate landlord is a charitable housing trust (*not* simply a charity in the general sense), and the house is part of the housing accommodation provided by the trust as part of its charitable purposes: s 67(2).

---

1   HL Report, 18 May 1993, cols 1711–1712.

5.14   But the exclusion is not retrospective, and operates in two quite distinct ways. In relation to tenants of charitable housing trusts who are otherwise brought into the Leasehold Reform Act by the new ss 1A and 1B, they are excluded from the beginning, whenever their tenancies were granted: s 67(3). But in relation to all other tenants of charitable housing trusts, only those tenants whose tenancies were granted after the commencement of this Chapter of the 1993 Act are to be excluded: s 67(3). In other words, any tenant who before the commencement of these provisions had, or was acquiring, the right to enfranchise, will *not* be excluded by this amendment.

Property transferred for public benefit

5.15   In certain circumstances, land or buildings may be designated by the Treasury as property of outstanding scenic, historic, architectural or scientific interest: Inheritance Tax Act 1984, s 31(1)(b), (c), (d). If on a transfer an undertaking is then given by the transferee to preserve and maintain it, and to allow the public reasonable access, that transfer of the property will not give rise to a charge to inheritance tax: Inheritance Tax Act 1984, s 30(1). It was felt, during the passage of the Bill,[1] that the Leasehold Reform Act should not apply to such property, particularly given that enfranchisement under the Act would lead to an inheritance tax charge on the landlord. Accordingly, s 68 of the 1993 Act inserts a new s 32A into the 1967 Act designed to prevent acquisition by the tenant of the freehold in circumstances associated with the above process. (Similar provision is made in relation to collective enfranchisement by the 1993 Act, s 31.)

1   See HL Committee, 9 March 1993, cols 1050–1054, HL Report, 11 May 1993, cols 1240–1250; HL 3R 25 May 1993, cols 212–213.

5.16   As with the provision relating to charitable housing trusts, the new section only operates in relation to (a) tenancies granted after the commencement of Chapter III of Part I of the 1993 Act, and (b) tenancies qualifying only under ss 1A and 1B (whenever granted): s 32A(1). It applies not only when a Treasury designation has been made under the Inheritance Tax Act 1984, s 31(1)(b), (c) or (d), but also in circumstances closely associated with such a designation, in particular where an application for designation is pending: s 32A(2), (3). The section operates by causing the tenant's initial notice under the 1967 Act to be of no effect if at that time the above conditions are satisfied, or, if he first serves his notice and then the conditions later become satisfied, to cease then to be of effect: s 32A(1), (4). The person claiming that the conditions are satisfied must supply the tenant with evidence in support of his claim: s 32A(6).

6 Estate management schemes

6.1 When the Leasehold Reform Act 1967 was passed there was concern that wholesale enfranchisement would damage or destroy the character of estates held by one landlord, whose leasehold powers to manage such estates in the interests of all would be removed by tenants purchasing their individual freeholds. To meet such concern s 19 of the 1967 Act was enacted. The same fear prompted the inclusion of Part I, Chapter IV (ss 69–75) in the 1993 Act. The new system borrows some features from the old, but is otherwise quite distinct. Unfortunately, it was not much debated in Parliament.[1] Special provisions apply where the Crown is interested in the estate concerned: para 1.25.

---

1 HC 2R: 3 November 1992, col 155; HC Standing Committee B: 26 November 1992, cols 271–286; HL 2R: 23 February 1993, col 87; HL Committee: 22 March 1993, cols 128-143; HL Report: 18 May 1993, cols 1713-1732; HL 3R : 25 May 1993, cols 213-215.

WHAT IS AN ESTATE MANAGEMENT SCHEME?

6.2 An estate management scheme is a scheme to enable a landlord (or a third party) to retain powers of management in respect of, and rights against, houses and premises, primarily those which he may be required to sell under ss 1A or 1B of the 1967 Act or the collective enfranchisement provisions of the 1993 Act. However, it may extend to property where the landlord's interest is disposed of otherwise than under those provisions: s 69(6). For the purposes of the 1993 Act, it is a scheme approved by a leasehold valuation tribunal for an area occupied directly or indirectly under leases held under one landlord (apart from unoccupied property, and property occupied by the landlord or his licensees), which is designed to achieve these objects: s 69(1). It may at first sight look like a perpetuation of the landlord/tenant relationship, but the Government's intention was avowedly not to undermine the object of enfranchisement.[1]

---

1 HL Deb, 18 May 1993, cols 1713–1714, per Lord Strathclyde.

Content of Scheme

6.3 The scheme may make different provision for different areas covered by it, and it will include provision for varying or terminating its provisions in stated circumstances: s 69(2).[1] It may in particular make provision:

91

(a)   regulating the redevelopment, use or appearance of property (s 69(3)(a));
(b)   empowering the landlord to maintain, repair or renew such property (s 69(3)(b));
(c)   imposing obligations to maintain, repair or renew (or pay for the costs of such work actually carried out)[2] on those 'from time to time occupying *or interested in*'[3] such property (s 69(3)(c));
(d)   permitting inspection of the property (s 69(3)(d)).[4]

It may also enable a charge[5] to be imposed on the property to recover sums due to the landlord, and where this occurs the landlord will be in the position of a mortgagee by deed under the general law having powers of sale and leasing and of appointing a receiver:[6] s 69(3).[7] But the provisions of the scheme may include anything ancillary to the matters referred to in s 69(3).[8] However, it should not contain provisions dictating how property owners should dispose of their interests.[9]

1   Based on the 1967 Act, s 19(6).
2   An attempt to extend this provision to cover costs *to be incurred*, and thus authorise sinking funds, was defeated on House of Lords Report: HL Deb, 18 May 1993, cols 1716–1722.
3   This phrase is not defined.
4   For the general contents of a scheme approved by the High Court under the 1967 Act, see *Re Copes Hill Estate, Wimbledon* (1971) 219 EG 1604.
5   The scheme could provide for this to be postponed to a building society charge under the 1967 Act: *Re Abbots Park Estate* (No 2) [1972] 3 All ER 148, [1972] 1 WLR 1597.
6   See in particular the Law of Property Act 1925, s 101(1)(iii).
7   Based on the 1967 Act, s 19(8).
8   *Re Abbots Park Estate* [1972] 2 All ER 177, [1972] 1 WLR 598; cf *Re Sherwood Close (Barnes) Management Co Ltd* [1972] Ch 208, [1971] 3 All ER 1293.
9   HL Deb, 22 March 1993, col 133, per Lord Strathclyde.

The landlord

6.4   Prima facie, the person to enforce such a scheme is the landlord, and the scheme must identify who this is: s 69(4)(a). The scheme is not affected if the landlord transfers his interest in the property: s 69(4).[1] But the scheme must[2] also permit the landlord separately to transfer his rights or powers under the scheme to a local authority or other body (s 69(4)(b)), and such a transfer may be made conditional on the leasehold valuation tribunal's approval or indeed on any other circumstance: s 69(5). Where such a separate transfer is made then, for the purposes of the estate management scheme legislation, the transferee is treated as if it were the landlord: s 69(7).[3]

1   Based on the 1967 Act, s 19(7).
2   See HL Deb, 18 May 1993, col 1723.
3   Based on the 1967 Act, s 19(7).

TIME LIMITS FOR MAKING APPLICATIONS

6.5   Estate management schemes are intended to be created as soon as possible after the legislation comes into force, ideally before tenants begin to exercise their rights under this Act.[1] Thus the general rule is that an application to a leasehold valuation tribunal for approval of an estate management scheme must be made within two years of the relevant provisions of the Act coming into force: s 70(1). However, there are two main exceptions to this general time limit.

---

1   See HL Deb, 18 May 1993, col 1728.

Secretary of State's consent

6.6   The first exception to the general time limit is where the Secretary of State gives consent for the application to be made out of time. He may only do this (a) if he is satisfied that the proposed application could not have been made before the expiry of the two-year period, or (b) if he is satisfied that, if an application had been made, the Tribunal would probably have dismissed it, but because of a change in circumstances the application would probably now be granted: s 72(2)(a), (3). In addition, the Secretary of State must also be satisfied that adequate notice of the request for consent (and its purpose) has been given to persons interested: s 72(2)(b). A request to the Secretary of State for consent must be in writing, and comply with prescribed formalities (s 72(4)), and the procedure for considering it may also be prescribed: s 72(5). If the Secretary of State gives consent, the application must be made within six months thereafter: s 72(1).

Applications within conservation areas

6.7   The second exception relates to applications made by certain public bodies for approval of schemes within conservation areas.[1] It only applies when no scheme has yet been approved for all or any part of the area concerned, there is no outstanding application for approval, no consent has been granted within the last six months by the Secretary of State to make an application out of time and no application to the Secretary of State for his consent is pending: s 73(2). Moreover, the leasehold valuation tribunal must be satisfied that an application for approval by landlords within the two-year period *could* have been approved: s 73(1). In such a case, either

(a)   the local planning authority[2] for the scheme area; or
(b)   two or more authorities covering that area, acting with or without the Historic Buildings and Monuments Commission for England; or
(c)   the Commission by itself;[3]

has a limited period in which to apply to the leasehold valuation tribunal for approval of the scheme: s 73(1), (5).

---

1   Within the meaning of the Planning (Listed Buildings and Conservation Areas) Act 1990.
2   Again within the meaning of the Planning (Listed Buildings and Conservation Areas) Act 1990.
3   If the land is wholly in England and it has consulted all relevant local planning authorities.

6.8   However, the period is quite short, and is best seen as a 'window' rather than as a mere extension of time. This is because the application period *begins* in the future, and does not simply extend the original period. There are in fact four such 'windows'. Two of these are straightforward:

(1)   if no application has been made to the leasehold valuation tribunal, then it is the period of six months from the expiry of the original two-year period (s 73(3)(a));

(2)   if any application *has* been made to the leasehold valuation tribunal, then it is a period of six months from the date on which the application last to be withdrawn or dismissed is so withdrawn or dismissed (s 73(3)(b)).

The other two windows are more complex: if, during the period of either of the above windows, a request is made to the Secretary of State for consent to apply out of time, then an application can be made under these provisions during the period of:

(3)   six months from the date when the request is withdrawn or refused (s 73(3)(i));

(4)   twelve months from the date on which it is granted (s 73(3)(ii)).

Notice of application

6.9   Before considering any application made to it, the leasehold valuation tribunal must be satisfied that adequate notice (by advertisement or otherwise) has been given to persons interested: s 70(4). Where the area in respect of which the application is made is wholly or partly in a conservation area, these persons include local planning authorities and (if the whole area is in England) the Historic Buildings and Monuments Commission for England: s 70(5). The notice given must inform both of the fact of the application and of the provisions intended to be made by it, and also must invite representations about the application to the tribunal within a reasonable time: s 70(4). The tribunal must give persons making such representations the opportunity to appear and be heard at the time the application is considered: s 70(6).

WHO MAY APPLY?

6.10   An application to the tribunal to approve a scheme is normally made by the landlord concerned (s 70(1)) but there are exceptions to this. First, certain public bodies may in some circumstances make an application (see para 6.7). Second, two or more landlords of neighbouring areas may make a joint application. In this case, in order for approval to be given, it must appear to the tribunal that a scheme could have been approved for the combined areas if they were covered by a single landlord, and also that the applicants are willing to co-operate in the management of a property and the administration of the scheme: s 71(1).[1] A third exception is that a body representing the interests of tenants and tenant purchasers in a given area may apply, either alone or jointly with the landlord or landlords concerned, provided that the scheme could have been approved if the landlord had applied *and* that the representative body is otherwise suitable: s 71(3).[2] In this last case the tribunal may permit an application originally commenced by one applicant to be continued by another: s 71(3).

---

1   Based on the Leasehold Reform Act 1967, s 19(12).
2   Based on ibid, s 19(13).

CONSIDERATION BY THE TRIBUNAL

6.11 Where an application is made to the leasehold valuation tribunal, it must consider various matters, including the past development and present character of the area, architectural or historical considerations, and also neighbouring areas.[1] But it must have regard primarily to the benefits likely to result from the scheme to the area as a whole, and to the extent to which it is reasonable to impose obligations on those acquiring their landlord's interests: s 70(3).[2] The tribunal must not approve the scheme unless satisfied that it is in the general interest that the landlord should retain the powers and rights conferred by the scheme, in order to maintain standards and amenity and regulate redevelopment: s 70(2).

---

1 See eg *Eton College v Nassar* [1991] 2 EGLR 271; Lord Strathclyde in HL Deb, 18 May 1993, col 1714, referred to his anxiety 'to ensure that proper consideration should be given to heritage matters', but the legislation does not explicitly refer to this.
2 Based on the Leasehold Reform Act 1967, s 19(3).

6.12 Where an application is made otherwise than by the landlord, the scheme can be modified to reflect this fact. Thus, where the application is made by public bodies under s 73(1), the rights or powers that might have been conferred on the landlord may be conferred on the applicant(s): s 73(4). Similarly, where a representative body is involved, the scheme may confer 'landlord's' rights and powers upon it, and enable it to participate in the administration of a scheme and the management of the property concerned: s 73(4).[1] In this case, however, the tribunal may impose terms as to compensation of the landlord and otherwise: s 71(4).

---

1 Based on the Leasehold Reform Act 1967, s 19(13).

THE TRIBUNAL'S DECISION

6.13 On an application for approval, the tribunal can do one of two things: it can approve the scheme or it can dismiss the application. The test for approval of a scheme by the tribunal is twofold. First, the scheme (with any modifications proposed or agreed to by the applicant) must appear to the tribunal to be 'fair and practicable'. Second, it must not appear to the tribunal to give the landlord a degree of control 'out of proportion to' *either* that which he previously exercised *or* that which is necessary for the scheme's purposes: s 70(7).[1] It will be noted that the phrase is 'out of proportion to' and not 'greater than'.

---

1 Based on the Leasehold Reform Act 1967, s 19(5).

Dismissing the application

6.14 However, if this dual test is not met, the tribunal cannot without more simply dismiss the application. The tribunal may come to the conclusion that, taking everything into account, *no* scheme can be approved for the area in question under that application, and may make a declaration to that effect: s 70(9).[1] In such a case it may dismiss the application: s 70(10)(a). If it will not so declare, the tribunal must in effect attempt to persuade the applicant to modify the scheme to something more suitable. Only if the tribunal is of the opinion that the applicant will not agree to a suitable scheme or is not proceeding with due despatch may the tribunal then dismiss the application: s 70(10)(b).[2]

---

1   Based on the Leasehold Reform Act 1967, s 19(4)(b).
2   Section 72(10) is based on ibid, s 19(5).

EFFECT OF TRIBUNAL'S APPROVAL

6.15   An estate management scheme approved by the tribunal is a local land charge and is registrable as such (s 70(11), (12)),[1] although the provisions for compensation in the event of non-registration in the Local Land Charges Act 1975 do not apply: s 70(13).[2] Once the scheme is registered, any individual acquisition under the Leasehold Reform Act 1967 or collective enfranchisement under the 1993 Act will take effect subject to its provisions and the price will be adjusted accordingly: s 70(12)(b), (c).

---

1   Based on the Leasehold Reform Act 1967, s 19(10).
2   Based on ibid, s 19(10A).

The 'originating authority'

6.16   Where the application was made by the landlord, he is treated as the 'originating authority' in respect of the local land charge for the purposes of the Local Land Charges Act 1975 (s 70(11)),[1] and the provisions of the scheme are enforceable against the property concerned by him as if the persons occupying or interest in such property had covenanted directly with him to be bound by those provisions: s 70(12)(a). Where the application was made by a representative body then these statutory provisions may be modified by the scheme to enable that body to play its full role in the administration of the scheme and the management of the property (s 71(5)).

---

1   Based on the Leasehold Reform Act 1967, s 19(10).

6.17   Where the application was made by a local planning authority and/or the Historic Buildings and Monuments Commission, then that authority or the Commission (as the case may be) will be treated as the 'originating authority' for local land charge purposes. It will also be treated as the person entitled to enforce the provisions of the scheme against the properties concerned (s 73(8)(a)), although not in relation to any property outside the planning authority's own authority area: s 73(9). However, in that case, the price of subsequent acquisitions by tenants from the landlord will *not* be adjusted to take account of the existence of the scheme: s 73(8)(b), (10).

PENDING APPLICATIONS AND CLAIMS TO ENFRANCHISE

6.18   A particular problem is the interaction of the tribunal procedure (including requests to the Secretary of State to apply out of time) with a claim to acquire the freehold under ss 1A or 1B of the 1967 Act or a claim to collective enfranchisement under this Act. Complex provision is made for this situation by s 74. Whether the claim to enfranchise is made before the application for approval of an estate management scheme (or request for consent to apply), or vice versa, the position on the happening of the second of those two events is the same.

Individual enfranchisement

6.19   In the case of an individual enfranchisement claim, the landlord need do nothing further for the present in relation to that claim, except that which appears to him to be reasonable in the circumstances. If the tenant's original notice preceded the tribunal application or request for the Secretary of State's consent, then the tenant may, but need not, withdraw it: s 74(2).[1] The incentive to withdraw it is that the tenant will not then be liable for costs incurred by the landlord in pursuance of the original notice (as he otherwise would be): s 74(4). If the tenant does not withdraw his notice, then the individual enfranchisement procedure will revive once the tribunal application is itself withdrawn or the tribunal's decision dismissing the application becomes final (as to which see para 1.21) or (if it is the case of a request for the Secretary of State's consent) once the request for consent is withdrawn or refused, or six months after the request for the Secretary of State's request is granted, and no application to the tribunal has been made in reliance on such consent: s 74(5), (6). Revival of the claim procedure is of course without prejudice to anything properly done in pursuance of the suspension: s 74(7).

---

1   Based on the Leasehold Reform Act 1967, s 19(14).

Collective enfranchisement

6.20   In the case of a claim to collective enfranchisement, once again the notice making the claim may be withdrawn (s 74(3)(a)), and once more the incentive to do so is being discharged from liability to pay the reversioner's costs incurred in pursuance of the notice: s 74(4). But if there is no withdrawal, the reversioner must, if he has not already done so, give the nominee purchaser (as to which term see para 2.41) a counternotice under s 21 (see para 3.33). Apart from that step, and any proceedings designed to establish the validity of the original notice claiming the right to collective enfranchisement or to defeat the claim by establishing the landlord's intention to redevelop, no further proceedings may be brought or counternotice given under Chapter 1 of the Act, and no further steps taken towards determining the terms of the proposed enfranchisement, except those which appear to the reversioner to be reasonable in the circumstances: s 74(3).

6.21   As with the claim to an individual enfranchisement (see para 6.19), the claim to collective enfranchisement will revive in circumstances where the tribunal application is withdrawn or finally dismissed, or once the request for the Secretary of State's consent is withdrawn or refused, or six months have expired since it was granted without any application having been made to the tribunal: s 74(5), (6). Again, revival is without prejudice to anything properly done during the suspension: s 74(7). But, assuming no notice of withdrawal was given, and that before the revival *either* the reversioner admitted the nominee purchaser's rights to collective enfranchisement under s 21(2)(a) *or* the reversioner would have been obliged (were it not for the tribunal application or request for the Secretary of State's consent) to serve a second counternotice under s 23(6) (as to which see para 3.41) then upon revival the reversioner is obliged to give a further counternotice to the nominee purchaser within two months thereafter: s 74(8). The further counternotice is designed to pick up the threads of the suspended claim to collective enfranchisement, and must comply with certain of the provisions of the Act applying to an original counternotice: s 75(9).

VARIATION OF 1967 ACT SCHEMES

6.22   Finally, the Act modifies the variation procedures of certain existing estate management schemes under the 1967 Act. Section 75(1) provides that a scheme under the 1967 Act which includes power to vary with the approval of the High Court shall have effect as if the reference to the High Court was a reference to the leasehold valuation tribunal, and as if any consequential modifications were then made. However, leasehold valuation tribunal bears a special meaning for this purpose: ie a rent assessment committee within the Housing Act 1980, s 142(2) (s 75(5)), and not, as elsewhere in this part of the Act, a rent assessment committee constituted under the Rent Act 1977, Sch 10: see ss 91(1), 101(1). (See also paras 1.17–1.19.) Variation of a scheme under the 1967 Act may be made to extend the scheme to the properties brought within the 1967 Act for the first time by this Act (s 75(2)), and further variations are possible: s 75(3). An application to a leasehold valuation tribunal under s 75 must comply with the requirements prescribed by the Secretary of State: s 75(4).

7 Management audits

INTRODUCTION

7.1 Over the years, residential tenants have been given considerable rights against their landlords in respect of services which they provide, and the charges which they make for such provision. The Landlord and Tenant Act 1985, ss 18–30B (as amended) and the Landlord and Tenant Act 1987, Part V, are the current sources of such rights.[1] The 1993 Act, in Part I, Ch V, takes the process further by establishing a new right of residential tenants to carry out a 'management audit' of the let property. This is designed to establish the degree to which the landlord's management obligations are being effectively and efficiently discharged, and the service charge moneys are being efficiently and effectively applied: s 78(1).

---

1   See *Hill & Redman*, **A** [3495]–[3518.3].

7.2 The new right does not apply to all tenants, nor to all properties. It applies only to 'qualifying tenants' and to 'relevant premises and any appurtenant property'. Generally the right is exercisable by at least two-thirds of the qualifying tenants in the relevant premises: s 76(2)(b). But where the relevant premises contain only one or two qualifying tenants, then one qualifying tenant may exercise the right on his own: s 76(2)(a), (5). Once the right has been exercised, 12 months must elapse before any of the same qualifying tenants may require another audit: s 85(5). The drafting of the various provisions is tortuous, and unfortunately this part of the Act was not much considered during Parliamentary debates.[1] We shall begin by considering the three basic concepts used in the legislation.

---

1   HL Committee, 22 March 1993, cols 143–145; HL 3R, 25 May 1993, cols 215–216.

CONCEPTS USED IN THE LEGISLATION

Qualifying tenant

7.3 For a person to be a qualifying tenant, a number of conditions must be met:

(a) the tenancy involved must be of a dwelling (s 77(1)), ie a building or part of a building occupied or intended to be occupied as a separate dwelling (s 101(1));

(b) the tenancy must be a 'long lease' (s 77(1)(a), referring to s 77(2)), but not a 'business lease' (s 77(1)(a)), ie not a tenancy within the Landlord and Tenant Act 1954, Part II (s 101(1));

(c)   service charge (as defined by the Landlord and Tenant Act 1985, s 18(1)) must be payable under the tenancy (s 77(1)(b));

(d)   the tenancy must *not* be 'superior' to any other tenancy of the same dwelling meeting the previous conditions (s 77(4)(a)), ie must not have carved out of it any sub-tenancy which itself qualifies.

7.4   Two or more joint tenants of a tenancy satisfying these conditions together constitute the qualifying tenant (s 77(4)(b)), though any one of them may give the 'trigger' notice initiating the audit procedure: s 77(6). A person can be a 'qualifying tenant' in relation to more than one dwelling at the same time: s 77(5). 'Dwelling' is not defined, though case law has built up on its use in other landlord and tenant legislation.[1] There is nothing to require a qualifying tenant to be an individual as opposed to a corporate body.

1   See *Hill & Redman*, **C** [308], [310], [2023]; **D** [593].

Relevant premises

7.5   'Relevant premises' has three elements. First, you look for the 'building' containing the dwellings let to the qualifying tenants: s 76(3)(a)(i), (6)(a)(i). 'Building' is not defined, although it has been extensively discussed in cases on the use of the word in earlier legislation.[1] Second, you look to see in respect of how much of *that* building the qualifying tenants are obliged to pay common service charge contributions to discharge or help discharge the costs of management functions: s 76(3)(a), (6)(a). 'Common service charge contributions' are contributions by two or more tenants to the same costs: s 76(8). Thus, for example, in the case of a mixed office and residential block where all the residents are qualifying tenants, and the service charges paid by the qualifying tenants met the management function costs of the residential part of the building, only that residential part would count for this purpose. Third, you look to see if there are any *other* buildings in respect of which the same qualifying tenants similarly pay service charges – for example other blocks of residential accommodation managed together as a single unit – and you apply the same test to such other buildings: s 76(3)(a)(ii), (6)(a)(ii).

1   See *Hill & Redman*, **A** [3540.2]; **C** [396]; **D** [414]; **E** [501].

7.6   Thus, that part of the original building for the management functions of which the qualifying tenants pay service charges, and the part of any other buildings for which they similarly pay, together constitute the 'relevant premises': s 76(3)(a), (6)(a). In the case of a single block of flats where the tenants pay service charges for the upkeep of the block, the relevant premises will be that block. If there are several blocks of mixed business and residential user and the tenants pay service charges into a 'pool' for the upkeep of the residential parts of *all* the blocks, then the relevant premises will be the residential parts of all the blocks.

Appurtenant property

7.7   But 'relevant premises' is not the end of the story. There may be outbuildings, garages or gardens which are not in the 'building(s)' but the costs of management of which are met by qualifying tenants' service charges. Such property, although not 'relevant premises', is called 'appurtenant property': s 76(3)(b), (6)(b). A management audit under these provisions is carried out in relation to the relevant premises *and* any appurtenant property.

THE AUDITOR

7.8   Only an 'auditor' can carry out a management audit: s 78(3). There are three qualifications, one positive and two negative. First, he must be either a qualified accountant (within the Housing Act 1985, s 28(1)), a qualified surveyor (within s 78(6) of the 1993 Act), or satisfy requirements prescribed by the Secretary of State: s 78(4)(a), (6). Second, he must not be disqualified from acting within the meaning of the Housing Act 1985, s 28(1):[1] s 78(4)(b). Third, he must not be a tenant, qualifying or otherwise, of any part of the relevant premises: s 78(4)(b).

---

1   See s 28(4) of that Act: bodies corporate and certain persons connected with the landlord.

7.9   The auditor is appointed by the person or persons requiring the management audit, ie by two-thirds of the qualifying tenants in the normal case, and by one qualifying tenant where there are only one or two qualifying tenants in the relevant premises: s 78(3)(b). The Act is silent on the auditor's costs, and therefore these will be the subject of agreement between appointor(s) and appointee. There is no statutory mechanism for recovering these costs from the landlord, even if the audit reveals maladministration. The auditor may appoint persons to assist him in carrying out the audit (s 78(5)), and, as we shall see, such assistants may carry out some of the functions and exercise some of the rights conferred by the statute upon the auditor.

AUDIT PROCEDURE

The initial notice

7.10   The first step is for the qualifying tenant(s) to appoint the auditor, and to sign the notice to the landlord exercising the right to an audit: ss 81(1)(b), 80(2)(b). Section 80(3) requires this notice to contain:

(a)   the full names of the qualifying tenants requiring the audit and the addresses of the dwellings of which they are qualifying tenants;
(b)   the auditor's name and address;
(c)   details of the documents which the auditor requires production or inspection of under his powers in that behalf (see para 7.13);
(d)   the date of any inspection of the property proposed by the auditor (see para 7.12).

7.11   The auditor so appointed then gives the tenants' notice to the landlord or to the person who receives rent on his behalf (who must then forward it to the landlord): s 80(3), (5). As already noted, a management audit cannot be required by any qualifying tenant(s) within 12 months of a previous management audit notice having been served on behalf of the same qualifying tenant(s): s 83(5).

Inspection of property

7.12 To make the audit effective, the auditor needs access to information. This is given by s 79. First of all, the auditor, or his assistant under s 78(5), may inspect the common parts of the relevant premises or any appurtenant property: s 79(4). He must give notice of his intention to do so in the notice to the landlord exercising the right to an audit (see para 7.6) and the date proposed must be between one and two months from the date of giving the notice: s 80(4). Within one month the landlord must either approve the date or propose another date, which must be within the two months from the date of the original notice given by the auditor: s 81(1)(c). If no inspection has been carried out after two months from the date of the original notice, the court on the application of the auditor (made within four months of that date: s 81(7)) may order an inspection to be carried out on a date specified on that order: s 81(6).

Supply of information

7.13 Second, and more important, the auditor or his assistant may require the landlord to supply him with the service charge costs summary available to tenants under the Landlord and Tenant Act 1985, s 21(1), and to give him reasonable facilities for inspecting or copying the supporting documentation: s 79(2)(a). In addition, he may require reasonable facilities for the inspection and copying of any other 'documents the sight of which is reasonably required' by him for the audit's purposes: s 79(2)(b), (c). This may extend to documents in the custody or control of a superior landlord: para 7.20. He may require such facilities not only from the *landlord* in the notice under para 7.6: s 79(3)(a), but also from a 'relevant person', ie a person:

(a)   responsible for discharging the landlord's management functions; or
(b)   responsible for applying the service charges; or
(c)   entitled to enforce payment of the service charges.

7.14 In this case the right is exercised by the auditor or his assistant giving a notice to the 'relevant person' at the same time, so far as practicable, as the notice to the landlord under para 7.10: s 79(3)(b). A person who subsequently ceases to be a relevant person will, however, remain under a duty to discharge the obligations of a relevant person to the extent that he remains in a position to do so: s 83(4). In all cases, supply of documents and facilities for copying of documents may be made on payment of a reasonable charge to be determined by the supplier: s 79(5)(b). However, facilities for simple inspection of documents must be given free of charge (s 79(5)(a)), although that does not preclude the landlord from treating the cost of providing such facilities as part of his own management costs: s 79(6).

Time limits and sanctions

7.15 The landlord must supply the service charge costs summary and give the supporting documentation facilities within one month of the initial auditor's notice: s 81(1)(a). In the case of other documents, the landlord or relevant person must, within one month from the initial notice, *either* allow inspection or copying, *or* state grounds for objecting to so doing: s 81(1)(b), (3). Initially, there is no sanction for failure to comply with these time limits. But once two, but not more than four, months from the initial notice have elapsed, then the auditor may apply to the court for an order requiring the landlord or relevant person to comply with the requirement within a stated period: s 81(4), (7).

7.16   The court must not make an order unless satisfied that the documents concerned fall within the prescribed categories, ie the service charges, costs summary under the Landlord and Tenant Act 1985, s 21(1), and 'documents the sight of which is reasonably required . . . for the purpose of carrying out the audit':[1] s 81(5). But there is no requirement that, if so satisfied, the court must make the order. In other words, there is a discretion. Before making any such application to the court the sensible auditor will obviously seek an indemnity from the qualifying tenants who appointed him. The complexity of the procedure, coupled with the delays inherent in using the county court, mean that a determined filibuster may prevent relevant documents being disclosed for many months, which is hardly satisfactory.

---

1   See s 79(2)(b).

Confidentiality

7.17   One objection that landlords and others may make to disclosure is that of confidentiality. Some of the documents concerned may be highly sensitive, commercially and otherwise, particularly in mixed residential and commercial developments, where high values are involved. There is no provision for the court to order disclosure subject to blanking out irrelevant or particularly confidential sections. It is also a question whether documents disclosed pursuant to these provisions or a court order are held subject to an implied obligation of confidence: can the auditor show them to the tenants? Can the tenants publish the information or otherwise make use of it?

7.18   Consistent with general principle,[1] it is submitted that, since the information concerned is extorted from the landlord or relevant person by legal compulsion, and there is no express relaxation on the purposes for which use of it may be made, that information is held confidentially by the auditor for the purposes of that audit and any tenants' action based on the audit's result. It may be shown to tenants, but only for the same purposes (and they will be subject to the same obligation[2]). It must not be used for other audits for other tenants or for any collateral purpose, such as press publication.[3]

---

1   See *Marcel v Metropolitan Police Comr* [1992] Ch 225 at 236-237, 256, 260, 262; *Re Barlow Clowes Gilt Managers Ltd* [1992] Ch 208 at 217.
2   Cf *Distillers Co (Biochemicals) Ltd v Times Newspapers Ltd* [1975] QB 613 at 619, 621.
3   Ibid, at 625.

THE POSITION OF A SUPERIOR LANDLORD

7.19   The legislation expressly provides for the case where information is required of a landlord for a management audit, but some or all of the information is in the hands of a superior landlord. The position is different depending on the type of information sought. First, suppose the auditor has required the landlord to supply a service charge costs summary under s 79(2)(a).[1] If any information 'necessary' for complying with the notice is in the 'possession' of a superior landlord, the landlord must make a written request for that information to his own landlord; if *that* person is not the superior landlord concerned, then he must make a similar request to his own landlord, and so on: s 82(1)(a). The superior landlord must comply with the request within one month of its being made: s 82(1)(b). The landlord who received the auditor's notice must then comply with that notice (so far as concerned the summary) within the original one month time limit, or such further time 'as is reasonable': s 82(1)(c).

---

1   See para 7.13.

7.20   The second case is where the auditor requires to inspect or copy specified documents (whether the documents supporting the service charge cost summary or otherwise) but the documents concerned are 'in the custody or under the control' of a superior landlord. In this case the landlord must, on receiving the auditor's notice, inform him as soon as possible of the name and address of the superior landlord. The auditor may then give a notice directly to the superior landlord requiring him to afford the auditor the inspection or copying facilities required: s 82(2). The superior landlord is in the same position, with regard to objections to production, and possible applications to the court for an order requiring inspection or copying facilities, as was the original landlord: s 82(3).

7.21   It is unclear why the legislation in the first case refers to information 'in the possession' of a superior landlord but in the second case refers to documents 'in the custody or under the control' of a superior landlord.[1] None of these terms is defined. A similar phrase, 'in the possession, custody or power', is employed in the context of documentary discovery in rules of court,[2] and cases on these words may provide some assistance.[3]

---

1   Cf the 1993 Act, s 11(6): para 3.03.
2   RSC Ord 24; CCR Ord 14.
3   See Matthews and Malek, *Discovery*, 1992, paras 4.32–4.47.

ASSIGNMENT BY THE LANDLORD

7.22   A problem will arise if, after a landlord has been required to provide documents or facilities for a management audit, but before he has completely complied with his obligations, he disposes of all or part of his interest as landlord in the dwellings owned by the qualifying tenants. The position is that, to the extent that the original landlord remains in a position to discharge any or all of his remaining obligations, he must still do so: s 83(2). To the extent that the landlord's assignee is in a position to discharge any of these obligations, then that assignee must do so: s 83(1). To the extent that it is appropriate, the rules previously outlined have effect as if any reference to the landlord were instead a reference to the assignee (s 83(3)(a)), although the time limits for compliance will run from the date of disposal rather than from the date of the original notice: s 83(3)(b).

7.23   The provisions may bear hardly upon an assignee. First, because to the extent that *neither* the original landlord *nor* his assignee is in a position to discharge the requirements of the audit procedure, it appears from the drafting that the obligation falls on the assignee *exclusively*: s 83(2) ('but otherwise . . . '). Second, there is no provision in the legislation for the landlord to inform the assignee that the audit procedure has been commenced, nor for any 'repeat' notice to be served upon the assignee. No doubt conveyancers will now add a further question to the list of standard preliminary enquiries before contract, asking whether any notices have been received under these provisions, and appropriate warranties will be sought in the contract itself.

THE POINT OF IT ALL

7.24   The management audit is a means for tenants to find out how effectively and efficiently the landlord is discharging his management functions and applying service charges which he levies. But the legislation does not provide any sanction against him in case inefficiency or maladministration is discovered. The use to which the tenants put the results of the audit is a matter for them under the general law. One use is in resisting landlords' claims to service charges in future, on the grounds that they are unreasonable or are based on costs which ought not to be taken into account.[1] They may also be used by the tenants as part or all of the basis for deciding to seek collectively to enfranchise under this Act,[2] to exercise the right of first refusal,[3] to apply to the court for the appointment of a manager[4] or compulsorily to acquire the landlord's interest.[5]

---

1   See the Landlord and Tenant Act 1985, ss 18–30.
2   See Chapters 2–3.
3   Landlord and Tenant Act 1985, Part I.
4   Ibid, Part II.
5   Ibid, Part III.

8 Miscellaneous changes to residential landlord and tenant law

8.1 The 1993 Act makes a number of miscellaneous amendments to residential landlord and tenant law, and these are contained in Chapter VI of Part I. They relate to such disparate topics as:

(a) compulsory acquisition of the landlord's interest under the Landlord and Tenant Act 1987, Part III (s 85);
(b) variation of leases under the Landlord and Tenant Act 1987, Part IV (s 86);
(c) codes of practice for management of residential property (s 87);
(d) jurisdiction of leasehold valuation tribunals in relation to enfranchisement of Crown land (s 88);
(e) discrimination against residents with mental disorders (s 89).

These provisions were not much debated in Parliament.[1]

---

1 HC Standing Committee B, 26 November 1992, cols 286–320; HL Committee, 22 March 1993, cols 145–154; HL Report, 20 May 1993, cols 1860–1887, 1892–1896; HL 3R, 25 May 1993, cols 216–217.

COMPULSORY ACQUISITION OF THE LANDLORD'S INTEREST

8.2 Under the Landlord and Tenant Act 1987, Part III[1] 'qualifying tenants' (ie long leaseholders) of residential property may apply to the court in certain circumstances for an order enabling them compulsorily to purchase the landlord's interest. These are, generally, circumstances where the landlord has fallen down on his obligations to repair, maintain, ensure or manage the premises, or where there has been a manager appointed by the court under Part II of the Act for the last three years.[2]

---

1 See *Hill & Redman*, **A** [3572]–[3586.4].
2 See the Landlord and Tenant Act 1987, s 29.

8.3 The 1993 Act makes three amendments to this scheme. First, instead of there being a requirement (in order to invoke the court's jurisdiction) that a certain proportion[1] of the flats concerned be let *on long leases*, it will now be required that not less than two-thirds of the flats in the building are held by 'qualifying tenants' (who basically must have long leases): s 85(2). Second, the proportion of qualifying tenants in the building needed to invoke the court's jurisdiction is raised from one-half to two-thirds: s 85(3). Third, if the application is based on a failure by the landlord to look after the building, then it is no longer to be necessary, for an order

106

to be made, that the appointment of a manager under Part II of the Act should be an inadequate remedy: s 85(4).

---

1   100% for 1–3 flats, 75–89% for 4–9 flats, 90% for 10 + flats.

VARIATION OF LEASES

8.4   The Landlord and Tenant Act 1987, Part IV introduced a procedure under which the court may vary the terms of a long lease of a flat on the application of one party, and even though the other party does not consent. This procedure only applies where the lease fails to make satisfactory provision for any of certain matters, in particular maintenance, repair and insurance of the building, or the flat concerned, or the computation of service charges payable under the lease. In relation to this last point, the court has hitherto only had power to vary the provisions relating to computation of service charges if the amounts payable by all the tenants together would *exceed* the whole of the landlord's expenditure (see s 35(4)(c) of the 1987 Act). But the 1993 Act, by a provision added only at House of Lords Report stage, now gives the court power to vary also if the aggregate of all the tenant's payments would be *less* than the landlord's expenditure: s 86.

CODES OF PRACTICE

8.5   Codes of practice are very much in vogue. The 1993 Act, s 87 empowers the Secretary of State to approve one or more codes of practice for management of residential property, and to approve any amendments thereto. But he cannot do so unless satisfied that the code (or amendments) will be brought to the attention of those likely to be affected by them: s 87(2). Codes may cover the discharge of management functions, dispute resolution, competitive tendering, and trusts of service charges, amongst other things: s 87(6). Failure to comply with the provision of a code is not in itself actionable, but such a provision may be taken into account if relevant to any question arising in proceedings: s 87(7).[1] Unlike other provisions in Part I of the 1993 Act, s 87 applies just as much to residential property let on licences to occupy as it does to property let on leases: s 87(9).

---

1   Based on the Employment Act 1980, s 3(8), and see also the Road Traffic Act 1988, s 38(7) (Highway Code).

JURISDICTION OF LEASEHOLD VALUATION TRIBUNALS IN RELATION TO ENFRANCHISEMENT OF CROWN LAND

8.6   Under the Leasehold Reform Act 1967 neither the immediate tenant of the Crown nor his own subtenant has any right to obtain the freehold (s 33(1)), although in certain circumstances he can obtain an extended lease: s 33(4). A subtenant also in some circumstances has a right to an extended lease from his immediate landlord, even though his landlord is the tenant of the Crown: s 33(1)(a), (b). But although a tenant may not have a legal *right* to acquire the freehold or an extended lease, by reason of a Crown interest in the land, the Crown practice has been *voluntarily* to permit enfranchisement and extension of leases on like terms and subject to like procedure as that contained in the Act unless special circumstances apply. This was originally confirmed by a ministerial statement in 1967,[1] and was reconfirmed (albeit in slightly different and more complex terms) by a statement made in November 1992.[2]

1   HC Written Answers, 31 May 1967, col 42.
2   HC Written Answers, 2 November 1992, cols 19–20.

8.7   But if in the *voluntary* procedure disputes arise between the parties, on price or other terms of the transaction, no tribunal has hitherto had any jurisdiction to resolve such a dispute. The purpose of s 88 is to supply that jurisdiction. It is made clear that the jurisdiction is conferred on a rent assessment committee (sitting as a leasehold valuation tribunal) by the parties' agreement: s 88(2)(c). The Secretary of State has power to prescribe the form of application to a leasehold valuation tribunal (s 93), and some of the provisions relating to leasehold valuation tribunals constituted for the purposes of the 1967 Act also apply to tribunals constituted under this section: s 88(4).

DISCRIMINATION AGAINST RESIDENTS WITH MENTAL DISORDERS

8.8   Some leases and tenancy agreements impose restrictions on the occupation of the premises by persons with mental disorders. During the Committee[1] and Report[2] stages in the House of Lords, attempts were made unsuccessfully to persuade the Government to accept a new clause designed to render such restrictions void. The strength of feeling in the House of Lords, however, led the Government to introduce its own clause, now s 89 of the Act, on Third Reading.[3] This avoids any provision in a lease of any property including a dwelling (house or flat) which imposes any restrictions on (a) the occupation of the dwelling by persons with mental disorders, or (b) the provision for them of accommodation within the dwelling. But the new provision does not apply to agreements made before s 91 comes into force, nor does it apply to licence agreements.

1   HL Deb, 22 March 1993, cols 153–154.
2   HL Deb, 20 May 1993, cols 1892–1896.
3   HL Deb, 25 May 1993, cols 216–217.

9 The right to acquire on rent to mortgage terms[1]

RIGHTS ANCILLARY TO THE RIGHT TO BUY

9.1 The introduction of the right to buy by the Housing Act 1980[2] produced its own problems. One was what to do about secure tenants who wished to buy but could not obtain appropriate finance, usually because of insufficient income. The legislation therefore included a further right, ie the right to a mortgage,[3] under which the landlord authority would be the lender of last resort if no private sector lender was willing to make funds available to the tenant. In case the tenant did not meet the financial criteria set out for the right to a mortgage, the legislation also included the right, for a tenant who had claimed the right to buy, to defer completion for up to two years,[4] thus freezing the price but allowing for an improvement in financial circumstances. Subsequently, and as an alternative to deferring completion, the Government introduced the so-called right to a shared ownership lease[5] (which legally speaking was nothing of the kind).[6]

---

1 For Parliamentary Debates, see HC 2R, 3 November 1992, cols 155–157; HC Standing Committee B, 1 December 1992, cols 414–430, 3 December 1992, cols 432–450; HC 3R, 10 February 1993, col 1026; HL 2R, 23 February 1993, cols 87–88; HL Committee, 29 March 1993 cols 612–635; HL Report, 20 May 1993, cols 1905–1910.
2 Section 1; later Housing Act 1985, s 118; see *Hill & Redman*, **D** [852]–[860].
3 Housing Act 1985, s 132; *Hill & Redman*, **D** [975]–[982].
4 Housing Act 1985, s 142; *Hill & Redman*, **D** [1052]–[1061].
5 Originally in the Housing and Building Control Act 1984, s 12; later the Housing Act 1985, (old) s 143; *Hill & Redman*, **D** [1062].
6 *Hill & Redman*, **D** [1063].

9.2 These ancillary rights were considered necessary to enable tenants with lower financial resources to exercise the right to buy. Although they have been used, they have not been used as much as the Government anticipated – particularly the right to a shared ownership lease. Accordingly, all three rights are to be abolished[1] by the 1993 Act (s 107), and replaced by an entirely new scheme, the right to acquire on rent to mortgage terms: s 108, substituting a new s 143 into the Housing Act 1985. The new s 143 is accompanied by new ss 143A, 143B, 144, 146, 147, 148, 149, 150, 151, 151A in the 1985 Act. Section 145 disappears completely. Sections 144, 146–151 are substitutions for the old sections. Partial substitutions are made in ss 152, 153, 155 and 156 of the 1985 Act. Accordingly, references hereafter in this chapter to sections of the Housing Act 1985 are references to the *new* sections, as inserted or substituted by the 1993 Act, rather than to the old sections, unless the contrary is stated.

---

1 Although the abolition of the *right* to a mortgage does not affect local authorities' *powers* to grant them.

The 'rent to mortgage' concept[1]

9.3   The concept of rent to mortgage is simple. Operating it is of course more difficult. The tenant's existing rent payments are turned into mortgage repayments, supporting a capital sum borrowed and paid over to the landlord. The tenant in essence buys his home for what he can afford to pay. The *difference* between what he pays and what he would pay to buy under the right to buy is left outstanding as a liability (secured by a charge) only to be paid on the subsequent disposal of the property or on the death of the last member of the tenant's family to live there. Of course, voluntary payments to reduce or clear this liability can be made at any time. We shall deal with rent to mortgage and its various procedures in more detail, but it is worth noting that many of the provisions are based on equivalent steps in the right to buy procedure, and to facilitate understanding and proper instruction reference to the earlier provisions is made where appropriate.

1   'Pilot' schemes were previously monitored in Basildon, Milton Keynes and Wales: HC Standing Committee B, 1 December 1992, col 421; 3 December 1992, cols 432–438.

THE 'RENT TO MORTGAGE' RIGHT

9.4   The right to acquire on rent to mortgage terms ('rent to mortgage' for short) is conferred on a secure tenant whose right to buy has been established and whose notice claiming to exercise it remains in force: Housing Act 1985, s 143(1). Where two or more persons jointly have the right to buy, the same applies to rent to mortgage: Housing Act 1985, s 143(3).[1] But rent to mortgage cannot be exercised if the tenant would be precluded (under s 121 of the 1985 Act) from exercising the right to buy: Housing Act 1985, s 143(2). Nor can it be exercised if the tenant has claimed or been found entitled to housing benefit at any time from 12 months before claiming rent to mortgage up to the day when a conveyance or grant is executed under rent to mortgage: Housing Act 1985, s 143A, inserted by 1993 Act, s 108. Similarly, rent to mortgage cannot be exercised if the tenant's financial resources are too high: Housing Act 1985, s 143B, inserted by 1993 Act s 108. The calculation involved in s 143B is complex and depends on various formulae. This is considered below.

1   Based on Housing Act 1985, s 118(2); *Hill & Redman*, **D** [852].

Financial threshold

9.5   The exclusion of tenants from rent to mortgage for financial reasons depends on two separate matters: the first is a calculation of the tenant's ability to finance a purchase; the second is setting a financial threshold for the property in question, above which the tenant ought to purchase outright rather than use rent to mortgage. The second matter is easy. The threshold (called the 'maximum initial payment') is fixed at 80% of the price which the tenant would pay for his home if he exercised the right to buy: s 143B(2). This will take into account the tenant's discount.

9.6 The first matter, the tenant's ability to finance a purchase, is more complicated. It does not depend on the tenant's actual resources, but on what he is currently paying as rent. The thinking is that, if he can pay his current rent, he can make mortgage payments of the same or less. (In recent times, the fall in interest rates, coupled with standstills, or even increases, in public sector housing rents, has meant that the gap between mortgage payments and rents for similar properties has narrowed, and, in some cases, has been eliminated.) If the tenant were to exercise rent to mortgage, he would have to raise and pay his landlord a certain capital sum by reference to the rent he was then paying. This is the 'minimum initial payment'. If this exceeds the threshold for the particular property, ie the maximum initial payment, then the tenant is not allowed to go for rent to mortgage. He can only exercise the right to buy.

MINIMUM INITIAL PAYMENT

Stages 1 and 2

9.7 Calculating the minimum initial payment is messy. If the property is a house there are three stages. If it is a flat there are four. The first stage in each case is to capitalise the existing rent (calculated monthly), on the basis that it forms the amount of monthly mortgage instalments, net of tax, for a 25-year repayment mortgage at the standard national interest rate declared by the Secretary of State under Housing Act 1985, Sch 16, para 2: s 143B(6), (7). The capital sum that could be borrowed on that basis is not, however, the minimum initial payment (although it is under the parallel Scottish system: para 11.7). The second stage is that the Secretary of State declares a multiplier of his own choosing[1] (s 143B(3), (4)), and divides it into the capital sum produced above. The resulting figure is known as the 'relevant amount': s 143B(6),(8)). The idea is apparently to produce a 'relevant amount' equivalent to the periodical sum which would finance a mortgage giving maximum tax relief (ie £30,000). At current interest rates, this is about £45 per week.[2]

---

1 See HC Standing Committee B, 1 December 1992, cols 426–428; HL Committee, 29 March 1993, cols 618–619, 622–623.
2 See HL Committee, 29 March 1993, col 618.

Stages 3 and 4

9.8 The third stage consists of working through two alternative mathematical formulae. The first alternative applies if the current *weekly* rent does not exceed the 'relevant amount'. In that case the minimum initial payment for houses is simply the weekly rent multiplied by the Secretary of State's multiplier: s 143B(3). The second alternative applies if the current weekly rent *does exceed* the 'relevant amount'. In that case the minimum initial payment for houses is the aggregate of:

(a)   the maximum home loan on which tax relief is available – currently £30,000; and
(b)   the sum of the excess of weekly rent over the 'relevant amount' multiplied by the Secretary of State's multiplier: s 143B(4).

In other words, where the weekly rent is less than the 'relevant amount', the rent is roughly capitalised as it is; where the weekly rent is more, it is the tax relief limit *plus* the roughly capitalised rent excess. The fourth stage only applies to flats. The minimum initial payment for a flat is 80% of what it would be if the property were a house (s 143B(5)), so that 20% must be deducted from the figure produced at the third stage.[1]

---

1   This is to reflect the fact that flat buyers have less flexibility over repairs and maintenance than house buyers: HC Standing Committee B, 1 December 1992, col 427.

PROCEDURE

Tenant's notice

9.9   A secure tenant claims to exercise rent to mortgage by written notice to the landlord: Housing Act 1985, s 144(1), substituted by the 1993 Act, s 109. Such notice puts an end to any notices to complete served by the landlord under the right to buy procedure: s 144(3). But the rent to mortgage notice can itself be withdrawn by the tenant (s 144(2)), and then the tenant may complete the original right to buy procedure: s 144(4).

Landlord's counternotice

9.10   As soon as practicable after service of the tenant's notice under the Housing Act 1985, s 144, the landlord must by written notice to the tenant *either* admit the tenant's right to rent to mortgage *or* deny it, with reasons: Housing Act 1985, s 146(1), substituted by the 1993 Act, s 110. If he admits it, then, by the Housing Act 1985, s 146(1), (2), the landlord must also give the tenant certain information:

(a)   the applicable 'relevant amount' and multipliers;
(b)   the minimum initial payment;
(c)   the proportion that the minimum initial payment bears to the right to buy price;
(d)   the landlord's so-called 'share' (para 9.13);
(e)   the amount of 'initial discount' (para 9.13);
(f)   the provisions required in the conveyance or grant and mortgage under s 151B.

Tenant's election

9.11   The Housing Act 1985, s 146A(1), (2) (inserted by the 1993 Act, s 111) requires the tenant, within 12 weeks of the landlord's counternotice, by written notice to the landlord to elect to do one of three things:

(i)   to pursue rent to mortgage;
(ii)   to withdraw the rent to mortgage application and pursue right to buy;
(iii)   to withdraw the rent to mortgage application and also to withdraw from right to buy.

(A comparable election procedure has now been introduced for ordinary right to buy cases: see para 10.02.) If the tenant chooses to pursue rent to mortgage, he must also state the amount of the initial payment he will make: s 146A(1)(a). This must not be less than the minimum initial payment (para 9.08), nor more than the maximum initial payment (para 9.05), and may be varied by further written notice to the landlord: s 146A(3).

Default notice

9.12   If the tenant fails to make any election under s 146A within the 12-twelve week period, the landlord can serve a written default notice on the tenant requiring him to do so within 28 days: Housing Act 1985, s 146B(1), inserted by the 1993 Act, s 111. The 28-day period can be extended by the landlord (s 146B(2)), or automatically if circumstances render it unreasonable to expect the tenant to comply in time: s 146B(3). The landlord's notice must inform the tenant that non-compliance with the default notice will cause the application for rent to mortgage to be automatically withdrawn: s 146B(1), (4).

Landlord's share and initial discount

9.13   But the tenant may serve notice electing to pursue rent to mortgage and state his proposed initial payment, or having done so he may subsequently notify a variation of that proposed payment. In either case the landlord must respond with a written notice informing the tenant of the 'landlord's share' and the amount of initial discount of the assumption of the tenant's proposed payment: Housing Act 1985, s 147, substituted by the 1993 Act, s 112. The computations of the 'landlord's share' and the 'initial discount' again involve the use of formulae: s 148, substituted by the 1993 Act, s 113. Put simply, the 'landlord's share' is that proportion of the value of the property attributable to the part of the usual right to buy price which is not covered by the tenant's initial payment. The initial discount is the same proportion of the normal right to buy discount as the tenant's initial payment is of the normal right to buy price. Similarly, if, on a normal right to buy, the tenant would be obliged to repay any discount previously obtained by him, the proportion of the previous discount recoverable on a rent to mortgage transaction is that same proportion.

Change of landlord

9.14   In principle the tenant is not affected if, after having claimed to exercise rent to mortgage, the landlord transfers his interest to a third party. The parties are in the same position as if the third party had been landlord when the tenant's rent to mortgage notice was given, and as if the third party had done everything which the landlord did: Housing Act 1985, s 149(1),[1] substituted by the 1993 Act, s 114. But if the circumstances after the transfer differ materially from those before (eg third party's interest differs from that of landlord, or an exception to the right to buy becomes or ceases to be applicable), all parties must do whatever is needed to put themselves in the same position as they would have been in if the landlord had originally been in the same circumstances as the third party now is: s 149(2).[2]

---

1   Based on the Housing Act 1985, s 137(1); *Hill & Redman,* **D** [1014].
2   Based on the Housing Act 1985, s 137(2); *Hill & Redman,* **D** [1015].

Completion

9.15   Once the tenant has established his right to rent to mortgage and all matters relating to the grant (including the mortgage securing redemption of the so-called 'landlord's share': para 9.21), the landlord is under a duty to complete the transaction, by conveying an estate in fee simple[1] if it is a house, or by granting a long lease if it is a flat: Housing Act 1985, s 150(1),[2] substituted by the 1993 Act, s 115. The landlord's obligation is enforceable by injunction: s 150(3).[3] But the landlord is not obliged to complete so long as any rent or other payment is wholly or partly outstanding for more than four weeks: s 150(2).[4] The form of the freehold conveyance or of the long lease is essentially the same as under the right to buy procedure, ie in each case it must comply with the relevant provisions of the Housing Act 1985, Sch 6: s 151(1),[5] substituted by the 1993 Act, s 116. It must also comply with the provisions of the new Sch 6A (inserted by the 1993 Act, s 117(2)), dealing with the redemption of the landlord's share: s 151A. In particular, this will require a covenant for such redemption in certain circumstances, such as a subsequent disposal or the death of certain persons: para 9.16. The tenant's secure tenancy will come to an end on the grant, any subtenancy being governed by the Law of Property Act 1925, s 139: s 151(2).[6]

---

1   See *Hill & Redman*, **D** [1033].
2   Based on the Housing Act 1985, s 138(1); *Hill & Redman*, **D** [1022].
3   Ibid, s 138(3); *Hill & Redman*, **D** [1025].
4   Ibid, s 137(2); *Hill & Redman*, **D** [1024].
5   Ibid, s 139(1); *Hill & Redman*, **D** [1032]–[1033].
6   Ibid, s 139(2); *Hill & Redman*, **D** [1034].

REDEMPTION OF 'LANDLORD'S SHARE'

General

9.16   Reference has been made to the landlord's 'share', which is essentially defined as the proportion of the value of the property not covered by the tenant's initial payment: para 9.13. But it seems clear that this does not mean that landlord and tenant on completion become co-owners.[1] Instead, there is an inchoate liability on the tenant to pay to the landlord in the future a sum of money calculated only once the liability has crystallised. This will *in fact* be the same proportion of the *then* value of the property, less a discount in some cases: para 9.17. So the overall effect in financial terms is similar to co-ownership, but the tenant/purchaser remains sole owner, at least until the liability to pay attaches. (We may note that the position under the equivalent Scottish provisions is both clearer and simpler: para 11.8.)

---

1   Cf *Hill & Redman*, **D** [1063], discussing shared–ownership leases.

9.17   The tenant's liability is created by a covenant, required by the Housing Act 1985, Sch 6A, inserted by s 117(2) of and Sch 16 to the 1993 Act. The covenant is to make a 'final' payment to 'redeem' the landlord's share immediately after *either*:

(a)   making a 'relevant disposal' (not being an 'excluded disposal'); *or*

(b)   the expiry of one year from a 'relevant death': Sch 6A, para 1.[1]

The value of the landlord's share for redemption purposes is the percentage share which he has before redemption, multiplied by the value of the property at the time of redemption: Sch 6A, para 3. Where the payer is or includes the tenant–purchaser, a 'qualifying spouse' or a 'qualifying resident', the amount of the redemption payment is the then value of the landlord's share less a final discount of 20%: Sch 6A, para 4(1). However, there is no 'final discount' if the final payment is made by anyone else or by a 'qualifying resident' more than two years[2] after the tenant or a qualifying spouse has ceased to have beneficial interest in the property: Sch 6A, para 4(2), (3). Nor may the final discount reduce the total purchase price below the right to buy price at the time or, aggregated with other discounts, exceed the maximum prescribed discount under the right to buy: Sch 6A, para 5(1), (2).

1   Based on the Housing Act 1985, s 155(1); *Hill & Redman*, **D** [1135].
2   Between one and two years the final discount is reduced to 10%: Sch 6A, para 5(3).

Definitions

9.18   For these purposes 'relevant disposal' means what it does elsewhere in the Housing Act 1985, ie a further conveyance of the freehold or an assignment of the lease, or the grant of a lease for more than 21 years (unless at a rack rent): Housing Act 1985, s 159.[1] But 'excluded disposal' is not the 'exempted disposal' found elsewhere.[2] For present purposes, Sch 6A para 1(2) defines it to cover only:

(a)   transfers between spouses;
(b)   transmission by will or on intestacy;
(c)   disposal pursuant to court order on divorce or family provision.

'Relevant death' is the death of the last person in the group comprising the tenant, any 'qualifying spouse' (para 12(2), (4)) and any 'qualifying resident' (para 12(3), (4)): Sch 6A, para 1(3), (4). Broadly, it refers to the time when the family unit has disappeared from the property, and it will be inherited by other persons who did not live there. (Again, the equivalent Scottish provisions are much simpler: para 11.11.)

1   See *Hill & Redman*, **D** [1172]–[1174].
2   Though based on it: Housing Act 1985, s 160; *Hill & Redman*, **D** [1181]–[1184].

Power to redeem

9.19   In addition to the covenant to redeem in the above circumstances, the conveyance or grant must permit the tenant–purchaser (at no cost to himself: Sch 6A, para 10), to redeem the landlord's share, either wholly (Sch 6A, para 2) or partly, though in the latter case subject to a minimum payment of 10% of the property's value at the time: Sch 6A, para 6. In the former case the payment is a 'final' payment; in the latter it is an 'interim' payment. Following an interim payment the landlord's reduced share can be calculated by the use of another formula (Sch 6A, para 7) but the principles are the same as previously employed: para 9.13. Provision is also made for the calculation of an 'interim discount' Sch 6A, para 7), but no provision is made for deducting this from any payment to be made. It will be included in the aggregate of all discounts, which must not exceed a prescribed figure: Sch 6A, para 5(2).

Value of the property

9.20   For the purposes of these provisions, the value of the property at a given time is the value agreed by the parties, or determined by an independent valuer appointed pursuant to the provisions of the conveyance or grant: Housing Act 1985, Sch 6A, paras 8(1),12(1). The cost of an independent valuer must be borne by the tenant or his successors: Sch 6A, para 9. The valuation is to be the open market price, on the assumption that the vendor discharges all mortgages (including those securing the redemption of the 'landlord's share' and the repayment of discount on early disposal): para 8(3). However, tenant's improvements and failures to repair, and burdens created by the tenant, must be disregarded: para 8(4). Special provisions apply where at the valuation date the property has been destroyed or damaged by an insurable peril but has not been fully rebuilt or reinstated: para 8(5), (6).

Mortgage to secure redemption

9.21   The tenant–purchaser's liability to redeem the 'landlord's share' must be secured by a mortgage having priority immediately after that securing the loan (from an approved lender) enabling him to buy the property: Housing Act 1985, s 151B(1), (2), inserted by the 1993 Act, s 118. Approved lenders are the Housing Corporation, building societies, banks and trustees savings banks, insurance companies, friendly societies and other bodies specified by order under the Housing Act 1985, s 156: s 151B(5). Advances by approved lenders for *other* purposes than buying the property, even if 'tacked' to their original mortgage, only take priority over the mortgage to secure redemption if the landlord gives written consent: s 151B(3). But the landlord must consent if the purpose of the loan is an 'approved purpose', ie to redeem the landlord's interest, to pay the cost of works or service charge in respect of the property, or to discharge other prior mortgages or costs and interests connected therewith: s 151B(6). The landlord may also in writing postpone the mortgage to secure redemption to any other mortgage not having priority to its mortgage, but which secures a loan to the tenant by an approved lender, and must do so if the loan is for an approved purpose: s 151B(4). The mortgage to secure redemption must contain (or not contain, as the case may be) provisions prescribed by the Secretary of State (s 151B(8)), but otherwise will contain provisions agreed between the parties or determined by the county court to be reasonably required by either party: s 151B(9).

CONSEQUENTIAL AMENDMENTS TO RIGHT TO BUY PROCEDURE

9.22   A number of amendments to the right to buy procedure have been made consequential on the introduction of rent to mortgage. These amendments affect two main areas: landlord's notices to complete, and repayment of discount on early disposal.

Landlord's notices to complete

9.23   There are three changes. First, the Housing Act 1985, s 152(3) is replaced, so that the landlord's first notice to complete cannot be served earlier than 12 months from the landlord's counternotice under s 146, instead of three years after the tenant claimed the right to buy or nine months after the landlord gave notice of the mortgage terms: s 119(1). Second, the definition of 'relevant matters' is altered: s 119(2). Third, a reference in s 153(4) to the right to a shared ownership lease is changed to the right to rent to mortgage: s 119(3). The overall effect is to make the 'notice to complete' procedure applicable *only* to rent to mortgage cases.

Repayment of discount

9.24   Here there are four main changes. First, the Housing Act 1985, s 155(3) is replaced, so that it deals with the case of an early disposal after a conveyance or grant has been made in pursuance of rent to mortgage, whether or not the landlord's share has been redeemed by the date of such disposal: s 120(1). Second, the Housing Act 1985, s 155(3A)(b) is replaced by a provision referring to the minimum initial payment under rent to mortgage rather than to the tenant's initial sum under a shared ownership lease: s 120(2). Third, the Housing Act 1985, s 156(2) is replaced by three subsections, (2), (2A) and (2B): s 120(3). They redraw the provisions governing the priority of the charge to secure the liability to repay discount, to take account of the fact that s 151B in rent to mortgage cases has created a new statutory mortgage. Fourth, a new s 155(4A), (4B) is inserted by s 120(4), to provide a definition of 'approved purposes' (similar, but not identical, to that in s 151B(6)) for the purposes of this section.

10 Other amendments to public sector housing law in England and Wales

10.1 The opportunity has been taken in this Act to make a number of other amendments to public sector housing law, in particular to the general right to buy procedure (the rent to mortgage scheme having been dealt with in Chapter 9), housing action trusts, housing welfare services, management agreements, disposals of housing stock by local authorities and housing associations, and defective housing. There are also changes to the right to repair, a new right to compensation for tenants' improvements, and an extended right to information from local authority landlords. Some of these changes were hotly debated in Parliament.[1]

---

1 For debates, see: HC 2R, 3 November 1992, cols 157–160; HC Standing Committee B, 1 December 1992, cols 371–414, 8 December 1992, cols 475–530, 537–552, 562–579, 581–586, 10 December 1992, cols 587–662, 15 December 1992, cols 663–716, 21 January 1993, cols 923–952, 26 January 1993, cols 955–987; HC Report, 10 February 1993, cols 937–952; HL 2R, 23 February 1993, col 88; HL Committee, 29 March 1993, cols 598–612, 638–661, 674–712; HL Report, 20 May 1993, cols 1901–1905, 1910–1912, 1926–1927, 1928–1935; HL 3R, 25 March 1993, cols 224–232; HC Lords Amendments, 14 June 1993, cols 682–701.

THE RIGHT TO BUY

Election procedure

10.2 In future, the new s 125D of the Housing Act 1985 (inserted by the 1993 Act, s 105(1)) will require the secure tenant exercising the right to buy, within 12 weeks of the landlord admitting the right to buy or (if later) the determination of the property's value by the district valuer, to serve notice on the landlord electing to do one of the following:

(a) pursue the right to buy;
(b) withdraw his claim;
(c) pursue rent to mortgage.

(A comparable procedure has been introduced as part of the rent to mortgage scheme itself: para 9.11.)

10.3 If the tenant fails to make any election under s 125D within the 12-week period, the landlord can serve a written default notice on the tenant, requiring him to do so within 28 days: Housing Act 1985, s 125E(1), inserted by the 1993 Act, s 105(1). The 28-day period can be extended either by the landlord (s 125E(2)), or automatically if circumstances render it unreasonable to expect the tenant to comply in time: s 125E(3). The landlord's notice must inform the tenant that non-compliance with the default notice will cause the application for the right to buy to be automatically withdrawn: s 125E(4).

10.4 A consequential amendment has been made to the Housing Act s 125, by the 1993 Act, s 104. In future, s 125(5) will require the landlord to inform the tenant of the election procedure and its consequences, and of the rent to mortgage scheme, as well as of the other matters relevant to the right to buy scheme.

---

1 See *Hill & Redman*, **D** [903].

Exceptions to right to buy

10.5 Amendments are made by the 1993 Act, s 106, to the Housing Act 1985, Sch 5, paras 10(1) (groups of dwelling houses for persons of pensionable age) and 11 (individual dwelling houses for persons of pensionable age).[1] These amendments do not apply, however, to any case where the tenant's notice claiming the right to buy was served before s 106 came into force: s 106(3). For this purpose, reservice under the Housing Act 1985 (s 177) does not count: s 106(4). The phrase 'persons of pensionable age' occurs twice in para 10(1). It has been replaced by 'elderly persons' in the first place and by 'persons aged 60 or more' in the second: s 106(1).

---

1 See *Hill & Redman*, **D** [1461].

10.6 Paragraph 11 is recast in a different form: s 106(2). As before, the exception to the right to buy applies only to properties first let before 1 January 1990. It covers the case where the dwelling house is particularly suitable for occupation by elderly persons, and was let for such occupation. If the tenant wishes to challenge the landlord's view that a particular property falls within the exception, he must do so by applying to the Secretary of State (who will decide) within 56 days of the landlord's counternotice under the Housing Act 1985, s 124, or else the landlord's view will prevail: para 11(4), (5). The county court has no jurisdiction in the matter: para 11(3).

Repairs

10.7 The Housing Act 1985, s 96[1] (under which the Secretary of State made regulations empowering tenants to carry out their own repairs and deduct the cost from rent) is replaced by a new s 96, by the 1993 Act, s 121. This empowers the Secretary of State to make regulations entitling secure tenants of *local housing authorities* to have 'qualifying repairs' carried out in their homes at the landlord's expense: s 96(1). The 1993 Act gives some idea of the kind of scheme which the Government had in mind, by providing (s 96(2)) that these regulations may, but not must, include provision:

(a) for tenants to apply to landlords for repairs to be done, and for landlords to issue repair notices specifying the repair, the contractor to carry it out, and a completion date;

(b) for the landlord to issue a further repair notice to a contractor specified by the tenant, if the first contractor does not perform before the due date; and

(c)   for compensation to be payable by the landlord to the tenant, if repairs are not carried out within a certain period.

---

1   See *Hill & Redman*, **D** [722].

10.8   Procedurally, the regulations may require landlords to inform tenants of the scheme, to maintain lists of contractors, to send copies of all repair notices to tenants; they may confer jurisdiction on the county court, and enable any compensation payable to tenants to be set off against sums owed by them to the landlords: s 96(3). A 'qualifying repair' for this purpose is a repair of a description prescribed by the regulations which the landlord is obliged by an express or implied dwelling house repairing covenant to carry out: s 96(6).

COMPENSATION FOR IMPROVEMENTS

10.9   This is entirely new. The 1993 Act, s 122, inserts two new sections into the Housing Act 1985, namely s 99A (right to compensation) and 99B (persons qualifying). Although the persons qualifying are set out in the primary legislation, the details of the right itself are to be the subject of regulations which the Secretary of State may (not must) make. But the power to make regulations is only exercisable in relation to a restricted class of case, ie those which satisfy three conditions:

(i)   a secure tenant has made an 'improvement', for work having begun before the commencement of s 122 of the 1993 Act;

(ii)   the landlord or its predecessor (being a local authority) consented in writing (or is treated as having consented) to the improvement;

(iii)   the tenancy has now come to an end, *or* ceased to be secure *or* (in some case) been assigned, and at that time the landlord is a local authority and the tenancy is a secure tenancy: s 99A(1), (8).

10.10   The regulations may restrict compensation to prescribed categories of improvement: s 99A(3)(a). 'Improvement' is defined by the Housing Act 1985, s 97(2)[1] to mean any alteration in, or addition to, a dwelling-house (or its fixtures and fittings), including the erection of an aerial and carrying out external decoration. The regulations may restrict compensation even if the improvement otherwise qualifies (s 99A(3)(b), (c)) and may prescribe maxima (s 99A(4)) and minima payable: s 99A(3)(d). The regulations may also make procedural, incidental, supplementary and transitional provisional provisions: s 99A(5).

---

1   See *Hill & Redman*, **D** [725].

'Qualifying person'

10.11   This expression is defined by the Housing Act 1985, s 99B, inserted by the 1993 Act, s 122. It covers a number of categories of person:

(a)   the tenant (or one of several joint tenants) at the time the tenancy ended, ceased to be secure, or (in some cases) was assigned: s 99B(1)(a);

(b)   the tenant (or one of several joint tenants) who made the improvement in question: s 99B(2)(a);

(c)   a person who became a joint tenant with (b) above: s 99B(2)(b);

(d)   a person who succeeds to the tenancy on the death of (b) above (s 99B(2)(c)), but not in the circumstances set out in s 99B(3);

(e)   an assignee of (b) above who would have been qualified to succeed him: s 99B(2)(d);

(f)   an assignee of (b) above pursuant to an order under the Matrimonial Causes Act 1973, s 24: s 99B(2)(e);

(g)   a transferee from (b) above under the Matrimonial Homes Act 1983, Sch 1, para 2: s 99B(2)(f).

If there is more than one qualifying person in relation to an improvement, but one of them cannot be found, compensation may be paid to the other(s), but the missing person is entitled to recover his share from the recipient(s): s 99B(4).

RIGHT TO INFORMATION

10.12   A landlord who lets on secure tenancies is already obliged to provide certain information to his tenants: see the Housing Act 1985, s 104.[6] This information includes information on the express terms of secure tenancies, on the right to buy, and on the landlord's repairing obligations. The 1993 Act, s 123, extends that obligation by adding a new s 104(3) to the 1985 Act. This requires a *local authority* landlord to supply each of its *secure* tenants, within 12 months of publication by it, and thereafter annually, with a copy of its statutory information on the right to buy and on the landlord's repairing obligations.

---

6   See *Hill & Redman*, **D** [775].

DISPOSALS BY HOUSING ACTION TRUSTS

10.13   Housing action trusts were created by the Housing Act 1988, Part III.[7] They are bodies corporate, nominated by the Secretary of State to take over housing, planning and public health functions of selected areas in England and Wales. Land, including housing stock, may be transferred to a housing action trust from a local housing authority: Housing Act 1988, s 74.[8] A housing action trust may also dispose of land in certain ways: Housing Act 1988, s 79.[9] The 1993 Act makes a number of changes to the rules governing disposals of land by a housing action trust.

---

7   See *Hill & Redman*, **D** [1629]–[1704].
8   Ibid, **D** [1642].
9   Ibid, **D** [1646].

Changes to old rules

10.14   Previously, a disposal of a house subject to a secure tenancy to a local housing authority or local authority was subject to special rules in s 84 of the 1988 Act.[1] For the purposes of these rules, 'house' includes a flat: Housing Act 1988, s 92(1)(b).[2] Now, by s 124(1) of the 1993 Act (amending s 79(2)(b) of the 1988 Act), such a disposal is no longer subject to such rules. A consequential change is made to s 84(1) by s 124(2) of the 1993 Act. However, the consultation requirements of s 84(7) (which have to be complied with before the Secretary of State will consent to a disposal) still apply to disposals of houses let on secure tenancies by a local housing authority or local authority: 1993 Act, s 124(3), amending s 84(7).

1   See *Hill & Redman*, **D** [1681].
2   Ibid, **D** [1703].

10.15   Second, a situation can arise where a house held by a housing action trust is the subject of two potentially inconsistent procedures, namely:

(a)   intended disposal of it by the housing action trust; and
(b)   attempted purchase (under the Housing Act 1988, Part IV)[12] of the block containing the 'house'.

In this case, which procedure takes priority depends on which of two events first takes place:

(i)   service of a notice under s 84(2) by the housing action trust wishing to dispose of the house; and
(ii)   service of an application under s 96 by the intended purchaser of the block.

If (i) occurs first then any application under s 96 made subsequently is deemed to exclude the building containing the house: 1993 Act, s 124(4). If (ii) occurs first then any notice subsequently served under s 84(2) is deemed to exclude a reference to the house: 1993 Act, s 124(5).

12 See *Hill & Redman*, **D** [1705]–[1813].

New rules

10.16   The main change is to introduce a new right for secure tenants of a housing action trust wishing to dispose of their dwelling houses to become tenants of the local housing authority: s 84A, inserted by the 1993 Act, s 125(5). But s 84A only comes into play in certain circumstances. Under s 84(2), (3) (as substituted by 1993 Act, s 125(1)) a housing action trust wishing to dispose of properties let on secure tenancies must notify the local housing authority, who must reply as to the consequences for the tenants if they should become tenants of that authority.

10.17   That reply is given to the tenants in question under s 84(4)(d), (e) (substituted by the 1993 Act, s 125(2)), and the tenants may make representations under s 84(4)(f), for example that they wish to become tenants of the authority. If the tenant of a house, or the majority of tenants of a block of flats who make representations under s 84(4)(f), makes or make representations that he or they wish to become tenant(s) of the authority, then the Secretary of State must transfer the house or block of flats from the housing action trust to the authority, together with other property enjoyed therewith: s 84A(1), (2), (3). The transfer can be on appropriate financial terms: s 84A(4), (5).

HOUSING WELFARE SERVICES

10.18   In *R v Ealing London Borough, ex p Lewis* (1992) 90 LGR 571, the Court of Appeal held that local authority costs of operating a homeless persons unit, the housing advisory service and sheltered housing service could not be debited to the Housing Revenue Account. Sections 126–128 of the 1993 Act are designed to reverse that decision retrospectively.

10.19   A new section 11A is inserted into the Housing Act 1985 by the 1993 Act, s 126. This expressly empowers local housing authorities to provide (and charge for) welfare services to or for persons for whom their housing accommodation is provided: s 11A(1), (2). But these services will not include repair, maintenance, supervision or management of houses or other property: s 11A(3). These powers are granted without prejudice to those contained in the Local Government Act 1972, s 137 (powers to incur expenditure for purposes not otherwise authorised).

10.20   The Local Government and Housing Act 1989, Sch 4, is amended by the 1993 Act, s 127 so as to enable income derived from charges for welfare services to be credited to the Housing Revenue Account, and to enable expenditure on such services to be debited to that account. It is made clear by the 1993 Act, ss 126 and 127 that these provisions are deemed always to have effect. The Secretary of State is also given power to repeal these new provisions: s 128.

MANAGEMENT AGREEMENTS

10.21   The Housing Act 1985, s 27[1] permits a local housing authority to delegate its management functions to other bodies, usually housing co-operatives. The 1993 Act makes various amendments to these provisions. The management agreement must now contain provisions prescribed by the Secretary of State (s 27(3), amended by the 1993 Act, s 129(1)), and the Secretary of State's approval under s 27(5) (as substituted by the 1993 Act, s 129(2)) may be given generally or particularly, and conditionally or unconditionally. The Secretary of State also now has power to exclude certain management functions from the scope of s 27 (new s 27(6), inserted by the 1993 Act, s 129(3)).

10.22   Before seeking the Secretary of State's approval for a housing management agreement, the authority must consult the tenants: Housing Act, s 27A.[2] Previously, the effect of s 27A was that if a majority of the tenants were against the agreement, the Secretary of State could not approve it. But s 27A has now been replaced by a substitute (1993 Act, s 130), which contains no such restriction. Consultation must still take place, and (if the agreement is made) tenants must be consulted from time to time, particularly on standards achieved, but they can no longer prevent the Secretary of State from approving the agreement. Moreover, so far as secure tenants are concerned, the provisions of new s 27A *replace* those in the Housing Act 1985, s 105[3] (consultation on matters of housing management): s 27A(5).

---

1   See *Hill & Redman*, **D** [474].
2   See *Hill & Redman*, **D** [482].
3   Ibid, **D** [782].

10.23   The provisions of s 27A can be modified by regulations made by the Secretary of State as he thinks necessary or expedient in relation to a local housing authority's proposal to invite tenders under the Local Government Act 1988, s 7 (compulsory competitive tendering), *if* the proposal would necessarily involve entering into a housing management agreement: s 27AA, inserted by the 1993 Act, s 131.

10.24   Under the Housing Act 1985, s 27C, a qualifying tenants' association could require a local housing authority to consider entering a management agreement or disposing of housing stock to it. If the tenants' proposal was rejected, the authority had to give reasons. A new section, s 27AB, is inserted into the Housing Act 1985 by the 1993 Act, s 132(1), replacing s 27C[16] (which is repealed: s 132(2)), and takes matters even further. The new provision empowers the Secretary of State to make regulations which can (inter alia) require authorities to enter management agreements with 'tenant management organisations'. The regulations may also require authorities to provide or finance accommodation, facilities and training, and arrange feasibility studies and tenant ballots: s 27AB(2). Moreover, they may provide for the management agreement to be in a particular form and to contain particular terms (s 27AB(3)), and may make procedural, incidental, supplementary and transitional provisions: s 27AB(4).

---

16 See *Hill & Redman*, **D** [492].

10.25   A local housing authority cannot enter a housing management agreement with a tenant management organisation except under the regulations, and these regulations will effectively replace the provisions of ss 27A and 105 (consultation) and the Local Government Act 1988, s 33 (restrictions on contracts with local authority companies). 'Tenant management organisation' is to be defined by the regulations: s 27AB(8).

VOLUNTARY DISPOSALS

Local authorities

10.26   In addition to the right to buy, under which secure tenants can require their landlords to transfer the freehold or grant a long lease of their homes to them, there is a parallel system of *voluntary* disposals by public sector landlords to tenants: Housing Act 1985, s 32–44.[1] This system contains provision for discounts from the purchase price and consequently a provision for a charge to secure repayment of discount in certain circumstances: s 36.[2] The introduction of the rent to mortgage scheme, with its provision for 'redemption' of the so-called 'landlord's share', secured by a charge on the property, resulted in a redrawing of the priorities of the various charges that may now subsist on a particular property: para 9.24. The 1993 Act, s 133 amends the Housing Act 1985, s 36 so as to provide for charges to have similar priority if there is a voluntary disposal.

---

1   See *Hill & Redman*, **D** [498]–[554].
2   Ibid, **D** [515].

Housing associations

10.27   Voluntary disposal by housing associations do not fall under the Housing Act 1985, s 32–44, but under the Housing Assocations Act 1985, s 8–12 and Sch 2.[1] The changes made by the 1993 Act, s 133 to the Housing Act 1985, s 36 are mirrored by those made by the 1993 Act, s 134 to the Housing Associations Act 1985, Sch 2, para 2[2] (liability to repay discount is a charge on premises). Thus the order of priorities, and the method of changing that order, is to be the same for right to buy, rent to mortgage, and voluntary disposals by both housing associations and other public sector landlords.

1   See *Hill & Redman*, **D** [1515]–[1534], [1551]–[1500].
2   Ibid, **D** [1551].

Programmes for disposals

10.28   Large-scale disposal of local authority housing stock usually generates substantial costs to the Exchequer, particularly in the form of housing benefit which becomes payable. The 1993 Act, s 135 introduces a new system of limiting disposals by local authorities of their housing stock. Essentially, a local authority cannot dispose of 500 or more dwelling houses *to the same person* in a five-year period unless the Secretary of State has included the intended further disposals in a disposals programme for that year: s 135(1)–(3). The Secretary of State has power to vary both the numerical and the time limits: s 135(1)(b), (2)(b).

10.29   Local authorities must apply to the Secretary of State for disposals to be included (either specifically or generically: s 135(4)) in the programme for that year: s 135(5). In considering which disposals to include in the programme, the Secretary of State is required to have regard for a predetermined ceiling on increases in public expenditure brought about by the disposals: s 135(6). In considering individual disposals, he can have regard also to the tenants' own views and various other matters: s 135(7). Of course, inclusion of a particular disposal in the programme does not do away with the need for the Secretary of State's consent where that need otherwise exists: s 135(9).

Levy

10.30   In order to mitigate the increase in public expenditure resulting from voluntary transfers, s 136 imposes a tax (called a 'levy') on the net proceeds of the voluntary transfer. Broadly, an authority will be liable to pay the levy when it has disposed of 500 or more properties to any one purchaser over five years: s 136(1)–(3). The levy is at the rate of 20% (variable by the Secretary of State) on the sum produced by deducting the debts referrable to the housing being transferred from the actual or notional capital receipts in respect of that housing. However, the calculation of the debt figure is not spelt out: it is left as 'such amount as may be calculated in accordance with such formula as the Secretary of State may determine': s 136(3). The Secretary of State has power to determine all the necessary administrative arrangements in connection with the new tax: s 136(5). Payments of 'levy' are to be treated by authorities as expenditure for capital purposes (s 136(7)), and must be paid into the Consolidated Fund: s 136(10).

Transitional provisions

10.31   Obviously, local authorities must plan ahead. But until the Act was passed, nothing could legally be done. This would have an impact on short-term planning, ie for the next financial year. Accordingly, s 137 (which, like ss 135 and 136, came into force on Royal Assent) enables authorities planning to dispose of housing stock to 'hit the ground running'. In effect, s 137 retrospectively validates any disposals programme prepared *before* Royal Assent. The section was introduced at House of Commons committee stage in January 1993, and the Secretary of State in fact sought applications from authorities early in 1993 for inclusion in the first disposals programme.

DEFECTIVE HOUSING

10.32   The Housing Act 1985, s 569 provided for central Government to contribute towards certain expenses of local government in dealing with defective housing. In particular, it provided for annual payments over 20 years. The Local Government and Housing Act 1989, s 157 amended that provision in relation (inter alia) to central Government contributions paid *after* 31 March 1990 in respect of expenses incurred *before* 1 April 1990. Now the 1993 Act, s 138, amends s 157 of the 1989 Act, so that it has effect in relation to s 569 of the 1985 Act in relation *instead* to central Government contribution paid *after* 31 March 1990 in respect of the expenditure incurred *between* 1 April 1989 and 31 March 1990. In other words, it now provides a backstop in time (ie 1 April 1989) for the expenditure which can be affected by s 157 of the 1989 Act.

10.33   But local authority expenditure before 1 April 1989 can still be covered, by an entirely new provision in the 1993 Act, s 139. This applies to expenditure within the 1985 Act, s 569(1) to which the central Government had not by 1 January 1993 made any contribution within s 569(2). In such a case annual payments made after 31 December 1993 by central Government are calculated and paid in accordance with the 1993 Act, s 139(2)–(7).

HOUSING REVENUE ACCOUNT SUBSIDY

10.34   Under s 80(1) of the Local Government and Housing Act 1989, the Secretary of State is required to determine formally to calculate housing revenue account subsidy by 25 December in any year for the following year. But before he can do this he must consult local government on the proposed determination. This cannot, in practice, happen until after the Government's spending plans have been announced in a given year. The new 'unified' Budget, combining tax-raising and Government spending in a single statement, will in future take place in late November. This will not leave sufficient time for consultation before the 25 December deadline. The Opposition sought to impose a new deadline of 11 January, but the Government's view won the day,[1] and accordingly the 1993 Act, s 140 simply deletes the 25 December requirement from s 80(1) of the 1989 Act.

1   HL Committee, 29 March 1993, cols 710–712.

11 Amendments to Scottish housing law

INTRODUCTION

11.1   The English lawyer who writes about Scottish law does so at his peril. It is not simply that the rules are often very different; the jurisprudential basis and hence the fundamental principles are different too – even when the detailed rules produce the same result. Moreover, although the Scottish is numerically a small legal profession, there is a significant literature, even on modern topics such as public sector housing law.[1]

---

1   See the *Stair Memorial Encyclopedia*, vol 11, 1990; Himsworth, *Public Sector Housing Law in Scotland*, 3rd edn, 1989.

11.2   The reasons for dealing with the Scottish law provisions of the 1993 Act in this book are:

(1)   rightly or wrongly, the Government included the Scottish provisions in the 1993 Act, and the book is intended as a guide to the *whole* Act;

(2)   the Scottish provisions form only a small proportion of the provisions of the Act, 17 sections out of 190, and no Schedules out of 22; a separate book on the Scottish aspects will be unviable, and ex hypothesi no existing book deals with them;

(3)   the Scottish provisions parallel the changes (or at any rate some of them) made by this Act to English public sector housing law: for comparative purposes it makes sense to have the same person dealing with both;

(4)   public housing law, like social security, employment and tax law, amongst others, are instruments of social policy of the Government of the UK as a whole, and hence are not intended to have different effects north and south of the border. It is not like the 'lawyer's law' of contract, tort/delict, property and succession, even though some of these matters are involved as the legal framework for implementing the 'social' legal subject.

11.3   The first and second reasons show why this book deals with the Scottish provisions at all; the third and fourth explain why no Scottish lawyer has dealt with them. Scottish readers are nevertheless asked to pardon any inadequacies in what follows. During the passage of the bill through Parliament,[2] Scottish MPs (and one Scottish Lord) were quick to take offence at these provisions not being dealt with in a separate bill under the special arrangements for exclusively Scottish legislation.[3] It is hoped that Scottish readers of this book will not feel similarly aggrieved.

---

2   For debates, see HL 2R, 3 November 1992, cols 159–160; HC Standing Committee B, 3 December 1992, cols 450–474, 8 December 1992, cols 530–537, 552–562, 579–581; 15 December 1992,

cols 716–740; HC Report, 9 February 1993, cols 933–935, 951–952; HL 2R, 23 February 1993, cols
88–89, 103–107; HL Committee, 29 March 1993, cols 635–646; HL Report, 20 May 1993, cols 1912–
1915, 1935–1938.
3   HC 2R, 3 November 1992, col 159; HC Standing Committee B, 8 December 1992, col 553 (cf 559),
15 December 1992, col 717; HL 2R, 23 February 1993, cols 103–104.

RENT TO LOAN

General

11.4   The 1993 Act has modified the existing right of secure tenants to purchase
their house by enabling it to be exercised through the so-called 'rent to loan' scheme
(hereafter 'rent to loan'). This is directly comparable to (though much simpler than)
the rent to mortgage scheme introduced for secure tenants in England and Wales,
discussed in Chapter 9. The 1993 Act, by ss 141 and 142, inserts five new sections
into the Housing (Scotland) Act 1987 (in this chapter referred to as 'HSA 1987') as
ss 62A, 73A, 73B, 73C and 73D. Finally, s 143 of the 1993 Act makes a number of
related amendments to HSA. The introduction of rent to loan follows the
monitoring of a pilot project among tenants of Scottish Homes and new town
development corporations.[1]

1   See HL Committee, 3 December 1992, cols 451–469.

11.5   By s 62A(1), the rent to loan scheme is available to every tenant who has the
right to purchase a house under HSA 1987, s 61, *except*:

(a)   where the house is designated defective;
(b)   where the tenants are claiming, or determined to be entitled to, housing
      benefit in the period beginning 12 months before applying to purchase and
      ending when the contract of sale is constituted: HSA 1987 s 62A(2).

Initial capital payment

11.6   The scheme splits the purchase price into two elements: the initial capital
payment ('ICP') and the deferred financial commitment ('DFC'): HSA 1987,
s 73A(1). The tenant will be entitled to ownership of the house in exchange for the
ICP, and the conditions in the offer under HSA 1987, s 63(2) must reflect this:
s 73A(3). The ICP will be discounted in the same way as the price under standard
right to purchase is discounted, but the applicable percentage discount (in HSA
1987, s 62(3)) is reduced by 15 (or such figure as the Secretary of State may specify)
in each case for purchase under rent to loan: s 73A(2).

11.7   The ICP is determined by the tenant, but must not be less than the capitalised
value of 90% of the then weekly rent at a statutory rate of interest over a period of
25 years (or until the applicant reaches pensionable age, if this is sooner, though
subject to a minimum of ten years): HSA 1987, s 73B. In other words, the tenant
turns his rent into mortgage repayments and obtains a capital sum with which he
buys his house.

Deferred financial commitment

11.8   DFC is a liability to pay further money to the landlord–seller on the subsequent sale of the house by the tenant–purchaser, or on his death (although there are exceptions to this: see para 11.11). The exact amount will not be known until the liability crystallises. It is found in this way:

(1)   deduct ICP from discounted purchase price under s 62(1);
(2)   express the balance as a percentage of market value under s 62(2);
(3)   reduce the percentage by seven (as a further discount) and any percentage representing voluntary interim payments;
(4)   generally speaking the DFC is that percentage of the resale value of the house;
(5)   in the rare case where s 73D(5) applies, add the further sum under s 73D(6).

'Resale value' is broadly open market value at the time for which the value is required (s 73C(8)(a)), *disregarding* works adding value to the house, or failure by the purchaser to keep the house in repair (s 73C(9)), but *including* building insurance moneys not applied in rebuilding or reinstating a destroyed or damaged house: s 73C(10).

11.9   DFC must be secured by a standard security over the house: HSA 1987, s 73A(4). This will have priority over the standard security securing liability to repay discount under s 72(1), but will rank immediately after any standard security granted as security of a loan from a recognised lender (under HSA 1987, s 222) to buy or improve the house: s 73C(7). It will similarly rank after any other standard security if the original seller consents: s 73C(7).

11.10   The tenant–purchaser may make voluntary interim payments (within certain statutory limits: s 73D(3)) to reduce the DFC: s 73C(4). The advantage of doing so is *not* saving interest, for no interest accrues on the DFC: s 73C(2). Instead, it is that amounts paid are turned into percentages of the *original* market value under s 62(2) and credited against the percentage represented by the DFC. Thus, in a time of rising property prices, voluntary interim payments will go further to pay off the DFC than a final payment on resale. DFC *must* be paid as soon as possible after destruction of or damage to the house by a peril usually insured against, *unless* the house is rebuilt or reinstated: s 73C(5), (6).

11.11   Subject to limited exceptions, any remaining DFC must be paid to the original seller of the house on sale or other disposal of the house, or on the death of the purchaser: s 73C(3)(a). But the rule does not apply where:

(a)   the sale or disposal is to the purchaser's spouse or cohabitee, for whom the house is then the only principal home; or
(b)   on the purchaser's death the house passes by succession to someone who has lived there as his only or principal home for the last 12 months; or
(c)   on a joint purchaser's death the house was the only or principal home of one or more surviving joint purchasers.

In any of such cases, s 73D(2) provides that the DFC is payable on:

(i)   the disposal of the house by the new (or surviving) owner in (a), (b) or (c); or
(ii)   the death of such person (or, if more than one, the last of them for whom it was the only or principal home both on becoming such person and at his death).

Other amendments

11.12   In future, a tenant seeking to exercise a right to purchase under HSA 1987, s 61 must include in his s 63(1) notice to the landlord a statement whether he wishes to proceed to purchase by way of rent to loan: s 143(2)(a), amending HSA 1987, s 63(1). If the tenant says that he does, then the landlord's notice in reply under s 63(2) will have to include certain extra information relating to the rent to loan scheme: s 143(2)(b), amending HSA 1987, s 63(2). A new section 63(3) is also inserted (by s 143(2)(c)). This requires the landlord to amend his offer to sell, recalculating the DFC, if the tenant tells the landlord of his intention to make an ICP larger than the minimum. Where the tenant proceeds under the rent to loan scheme, the 'fixed price option' under s 67 will not apply: HSA 1987, s 67(4) (inserted by s 143(3)).

11.13   Minor amendments are made to HSA 1987, s 71 (reference to Lands Tribunal) by s 143(4), to reflect the fact that offers to sell may need to be amended where the rent to loan scheme is invoked. Definitions are inserted into HSA 1987, s 82 (interpretation of HSA 1987, Part III), by s 143(5), of the expressions 'rent to loan purchaser' and 'rent to loan scheme'. Lastly, HSA 1987, s 214 (power of local authority to make advances for the purpose of increasing housing accommodation) is *extended* to apply to a DFC (s 143(6)), whereas HSA 1987, s 216 (house loans to tenants exercising right to purchase) is *restricted* so as not to cover cases of purchase by way of rent to loan: s 143(7).

ABATEMENT OF PRICE IN RIGHT TO PURCHASE

11.14   In order to provide a modest form of compensation to tenants whose difficulty in exercising the right to purchase is attributable to landlord delay, and also to provide a modest sanction against such landlords, s 144 introduces three new sections into HSA 1987, ss 66A, 66B and 66C. The first of these deals with delay before the contract of sale, the second deals with delay after the contract of sale, and the third contains provisions supplemental to both. In each case, the compensation for the tenant and the sanction for the landlord is that the rent paid by the tenant during the period of delay is deducted from the price otherwise to be paid by the tenant–purchaser: ss 66A(2), 66B(3). Periods of delay from both sections can be aggregated to reduce the price: (s 66C(1)), and, if the total period of delay taking into account is 12 months or more, the reduction in price is increased by 50% (variable by the Secretary of State): s 66C(2). There is a consequential amendment, by s 145, to HSA 1987, s 72, to backdate the three-year 'discount repayment' period (which normally starts on the contract being concluded between landlord and tenant) so as to include a period of delay counted under s 66A(1).

RIGHT TO HAVE REPAIRS CARRIED OUT

11.15   The potential 'right to repair' scheme under HSA 1987, s 60, under which tenants could carry out repairs and deduct the cost from their rent, but which was never in fact brought into effect, is replaced by a new scheme. Section 146 of the 1993 Act substitutes a new HSA 1987, s 60, paralleling the provision made to the equivalent law in England and Wales: paras 10.07–10.08. The new s 60(1) empowers the Secretary of State to make regulations entitling secure tenants of prescribed landlords to have 'qualifying repairs' carried out to their houses. The regulations must prescribe the maximum payment in respect of a single repair and the maximum time within which to complete it: s 60(2).

11.16   The 1993 Act gives an idea of the kind of scheme envisaged, because the regulations *may* provide (inter alia):

(1)   for landlords to maintain lists of contractors and to inform tenants of this;
(2)   for landlords, on the application of tenants, to issue works orders to 'the usual contractor' stating the time for completion;
(3)   in the case of contractor failure to complete in time, for tenants to be compensated and to have the right to instruct another listed contractor instead, at the landlord's expense.

For this purpose, a 'qualifying repair' is one so prescribed in the regulations, and 'usual contractor' means the landlord's direct services or organisation or the contractor to whom the landlord has contracted all its repairs: HSA 1987, s 60(7).

COMPENSATION FOR IMPROVEMENTS

11.17   As with the equivalent provisions for England and Wales (paras 10.09–10.10) this is entirely new. The 1993 Act, s 147, inserts a new HSA 1987, s 58A. Unlike the English provision (which empowers the Secretary of State to make regulations conferring a right to compensation), s 58A(2) itself confers upon 'qualifying persons' (ie certain tenants of certain public sector landlords) the right to compensation for 'qualifying improvement works'. This compensation is to be paid on the termination of the tenancy (or circumstances which will lead to that under HSA 1987, s 46(1)), a change of landlord or an assignment of the tenancy to a new tenant.

11.18   But a number of conditions must be satisfied:

(1)   the landlord was one of those specified in HSA 1987, s 61(2)(a)(i)–(iv);
(2)   the landlord consented to the works;
(3)   the work was of a kind prescribed as 'improvement work' by the Secretary of State and was begun before the commencement of the 1993 Act, s 147;
(4)   compensation has not been paid under HSA 1987, s 58 (reimbursement of cost of work done by secured tenant).

The regulations may also prescribe other requirements, positive or negative, or limitations on compensation, as well as procedural, incidental, supplementary and transitional provisions.

11.19   A 'qualifying person' is a person who, at the time compensation is payable, is the tenant of one of the specified landlords, and:

(a)   carried out the work; or
(b)   is a tenant of a joint tenancy existing when the work was done; or
(c)   succeeded to the tenancy under s 52 on the death of a tenant who did the work, and the tenancy did not cease to be secure on that succession: s 58A(1)(b).

If there is more than one such person, and one of them is missing, the compensation may be claimed by and paid to the other(s), but without prejudice to the missing person's entitlement to recover his share from such other(s): s 58A(5).

RIGHT TO INFORMATION

11.20   A new section is inserted in HSA, s 75A, by the 1993 Act, s 148. It requires certain public sector landlords to supply each of its secure tenants annually with information about the right to purchase. The information must be in the form considered by the landlord best suited to explain that right simply and appropriately.

HOUSING WELFARE SERVICES

11.21   Various provisions have been inserted into HSA 1987 by the 1993 Act on this subject, paralleling the provisions applicable to England and Wales: paras 10.18–10.20. The new s 5A, inserted by the 1993 Act, s 149, empowers local authorities to provide welfare services to or for persons for whom their housing accommodation is provided: s 5A(1). These services will not, however, include repair, maintenance, supervision or management of houses or other property: s 5A(4). The authority may charge for the welfare services (s 5A(2)), and may attribute income from and expenditure on such services for housing revenue account (HSA 1987, Sch 15, para 4A, inserted by the 1993 Act, s 150), but need not do so: s 5A(3). The 1993 Act makes clear that these provisions are deemed always to have been part of the HSA 1987. The Secretary of State is given power wholly or partly to repeal these provisions: HSA 1987, s 5B, inserted by the 1993 Act, s 151.

MANAGEMENT AGREEMENTS WITH HOUSING CO-OPERATIVES

11.22   New s 22A (inserted into the HSA 1987 by the 1993 Act, s 152) entitles certain housing co-operatives (within HSA 1987, s 22(1)) to require the local authority to enter a housing management agreement (s 22A(2)), and thus effectively take over the authority's management functions under HSA 1987, s 17(1) in relation to particular housing stock. But the local authority must first be satisfied that the applicant housing co-operative is:

(a)   approved by the Secretary of State;
(b)   able to perform the functions competently and efficiently; and
(c)   is representative of the tenants of the houses: s 22A(3).

If a local authority is not satisfied of (b) or (c), or if the parties cannot agree the terms of the agreement, the housing co-operative may appeal to the Secretary of State (s 22A(4), (6)) who may (if he takes a different view) require the local authority to enter into the agreement, or determine the terms, as the case may be: s 22A(5), (6). All such agreements must be approved by the Secretary of State, either generally or specifically: s 22A(7).

STANDARDS AND PERFORMANCE IN HOUSING MANAGEMENT

11.23   New provisions are inserted into the HSA 1987 concerning standards and performances in housing management by the 1993 Act, s 153. There are two main aspects: the publication of information, and the preparation of plans. First, a local authority must annually publish certain information about:

(a)   the standard of housing management undertaken to be provided by the authority;
(b)   past performance of the authority;
(c)   the authority's future intentions in this respect; and
(d)   any other matters specified.

11.24   The information concerned is both:

(i)   that prescribed by the Secretary of State: s 17A(1)(a); and
(ii)   that considered appropriate by the authority: s 17A(1)(b), (c).

But, before publication, an authority must consult its tenants (s 17A(2)), although the Secretary of State may direct it to consult tenants representing less than the whole of their district or area: s 17A(3). The authority must at the time of publication send a copy to the Secretary of State. If he considers it unsatisfactory, he may direct the authority to publish the information in a specified manner: s 17B.

11.25   The Secretary of State may also give the local authority three months' notice to prepare and submit to him a housing management plan for their housing stock: s 17C.

ALLOCATION OF HOUSING

11.26   Two main changes are made by the 1993 Act to the rules regarding allocation of housing. First, HSA 1987, s 20 has a new subsection (3) added (by s 154) to provide for an elected member of a local authority to be excluded from housing allocation decisions where *either* the particular house is situated, *or* the applicant for that house resides, in the electoral division or ward for which that member sits.

11.27   The other main change is that the 1993 Act, s 155(1), substitutes a new HSA 1987, s 21(1), the effect of which is to require local authorities for the first time *to make* and publish rules governing the allocation of housing, instead of (as previously) just to publish any such rules they might have. That, however, remains the position so far as Scottish Homes and the development corporations are concerned. A modest amendment to HSA 1987, s 19(3), consequential on the change made to s 21(1), is made by the 1993 Act, s 155(2).

DEFECTIVE DWELLINGS

11.28 The HSA 1987, s 299 deals with the jurisdiction of the Sheriff to deal with questions arising out of Part XIV (defective dwellings). The 1993 Act, s 156, adds two new subsections to this section. Subsection (4) provides a measure of damages for a failure by public sector authority to inform a person acquiring a defective dwelling of the defect: this is the difference between the vacant possession market value of the defective house and the vacant possession market value that the house would have without the defect. However, this provision only applies to legal proceedings begun before 1 December 1994, whenever the damages were awarded. Subsection (5) makes it clear that the failure to inform, which is the basis of the claim, may have occurred either before or after the coming into force of the 1993 Act, s 156.

OTHER AMENDMENTS

11.29 The 1993 Act by s 157 makes a number of other amendments to the HSA 1987. An amendment to s 17(1) (by section 157(1)) is consequential on the provisions relating to housing management agreements (para 11.23). An amendment to s 62(3)(b) (by s 157(3)(a)) deletes the requirement for occupation for earning discount to be continuous, and an amendment to s 61(10)(b)(i), (ii) (by s 157(2)) is consequential upon that. A new section 62(3A) (inserted by s 157(3)(b)) requires that any previous discount(s) given to the 'appropriate person' should be deducted from the discount to be given on the occasion of the present purchase, and s 157(3)(c) substitutes a new definition of appropriate persons for that contained in s 62(4). Finally, HSA 1987, s 248 (repairs grants) is amended so as to exclude s 240(2)(c) and thus enable grants to be made for works intended to reduce exposure to radon gas: s 157(4).

12 Development of urban and other areas: the Urban Regeneration Agency

INTRODUCTION

12.1 Part III of the 1993 Act contains provisions for the establishment of the Urban Regeneration Agency ('the Agency'). The Agency will take over two existing strategies for dealing with inner city dereliction: the first comprises the Derelict Land Grant and City Grant regimes operated by the Department of the Environment and the second is English Estates (arranging for the supply of commercial and industrial sites in certain inner city areas). In addition to these strategies it will have a site assembly function – hence there are powers to acquire land. These functions are then augmented by powers which are similar to those in the Local Government, Planning and Land Act 1980 ('the 1980 Act'), relating to Urban Development Corporations ('UDCs'). The Agency will therefore have four basic functions (exercised individually or in concert as the situation demands):

(a) giving assistance (primarily financial through grant-aid etc) to private sector-led initiatives;
(b) providing commercial and industrial sites for businesses;
(c) assembling land; and
(d) taking over planning and certain highway functions in areas designated under powers granted to the Secretary of State where problems of dereliction etc warrant a longer-term and more intensive involvement of the Agency.

It is this last role (using the 1980 Act framework for UDCs) which is probably going to have the highest visibility. It is a role which can be carried out on almost any area of land in England. Indeed, the Government intends that the Agency operates as a 'roving' UDC. It can then facilitate regeneration by using its range of planning and highway powers that can be given to it by the Secretary of State when designating an area under the 1993 Act: the other three roles can also play their parts in providing a comprehensive package of powers allowing the private, public and voluntary sectors in the designated area to stimulate physical development.

12.2 In carrying out its functions, the Agency will have to 'have regard to' guidance issued by the Secretary of State for the Environment; it is also required to follow directions given by him. The Agency is interested primarily in economic regeneration and so facilitating co-operation between the private sector and the public sector (eg local authorities) will be one of its chief tasks. Prior to the introduction of the legislation and during the passage of the legislation through Parliament a certain amount of criticism was made of the Agency in relation to its underlying philosophy (very little different from that of the UDCs). It was argued forcefully that the provision of social infrastructure and social regeneration was not given appropriate emphasis in the legislation. The 1993 Act emerged without any substantial modifications in this respect and so economic regeneration (primarily by way of bringing land into productive use for the private sector) will be uppermost in the approach taken by the Agency. However, in respect of the Agency's grant-making powers it should be noted that the provision of various forms of social infrastructure is now reflected in amended City Grant provisions (see para 12.44).

THE AGENCY'S STATUTORY AIMS

Regeneration and development

12.3   There are two aims which the Agency is set by the legislation. The first ('the main object') is to 'secure the regeneration of land': s 159(1). This is identical to the sole objective of UDCs in the 1980 Act. In adapting the UDC model to the needs of the Agency the Government has added a second (subsidiary) aim. This is the object of 'securing the development of land': s 159(3). This second aim is not restricted to areas of dereliction: however, it is likely that the Agency will be concerned primarily with the regeneration aim. Comments in the Consultation Paper (issued in July 1992 by the Department of the Environment) are relevant here: in para 8 of the Consultation Paper it was stated that the Agency will 'identify urban dereliction in England and draw up a prioritised programme for reclamation and development'.

Social aspects of regeneration

12.4   There are statutory references to social infrastructure and the environment (see paras 12.38 and 12.39 on the latter): however, these references constitute examples of the types of physical development that can achieve the aims of regeneration and development. Neither of the two statutory aims is phrased in terms that put social infrastructure at the forefront of the Agency's mandate. Since the other types of regeneration and development listed in s 159(4) are capable of achieving the two aims of the Agency this infers that social and environmental objectives are not of principal interest to the Agency (and any guidance or directions issued by the Secretary of State). This legislative focus was the subject of considerable criticism during the consultation exercise (initiated by the Consultation Paper) and in Parliament: at the forefront of such remarks was often the criticism made of UDCs as regards their record on social infrastructure and social and environmental regeneration.

Which land can be regenerated?

12.5   The main regeneration objective of the Agency is centred on specified categories of land. Section 159(2) describes these categories and they are:

(a)   vacant or unused land;
(b)   urban land which is under-used or ineffectively used;
(c)   land which is contaminated, derelict, neglected or unsightly; and
(d)   land which is likely to become derelict, neglected or unsightly by reason of actual or apprehended collapse of the surface (eg as a result of mining).

Having taken these categories as a starting point the Agency must then determine (having regard to guidance and any relevant directions) which land within these categories is 'suitable for regeneration': s 159(1). So private sector initiatives will need to target these categories *and* satisfy criteria contained in guidance and (if appropriate) directions. In practice the 'prioritised programme' noted in para 12.3 may be the effective starting point in determining those areas where the Agency intends to concentrate its attention.

Rural and urban land

12.6   It should be noted that land to be regenerated need not (apart from the second category of under-used urban land) be urban in nature. (There is, of course, the definitional problem of what is meant by 'urban'.) Rural areas can therefore find their way onto the list for Agency action. (Though it should be noted that in rural areas the Rural Development Commission remains in control of the provision of commercial and industrial sites: the role of English Estates in such areas is one of agent for the Commission and the leading role of the Commission in this respect is to be retained after the Agency is established: Consultation Paper, para 7.) A similar breadth (covering both urban and non-urban land) is also apparent in the provisions relating to designation of areas as either urban regeneration areas or urban development areas (see paras 12.30 and 12.31).

English Estates

12.7   The role of English Estates in providing commercial and industrial sites for business in urban areas will continue (under the umbrella of the Agency): s 184 provides for the dissolution of the English Industrial Estates Corporation and the transfer of its property, rights and liabilities to the Agency.

Which land can be developed?

12.8   The second (subsidiary) aim of the Agency is to secure the 'development' of land: s 159(3). Here there are no specified categories of land: however, in determining which land is 'suitable for development' the Agency will not only have regard to guidance (and any directions) from the Secretary of State; it must also have the consent of the Secretary of State. The 'opinion' of the Secretary of State (see also s 170(1), para 12.30) will no doubt be important in this respect.

The means for achieving regeneration and development

12.9   Regeneration and development are rather generalised concepts. The legislation does provide key examples of what, in physical terms, is comprehended by these concepts: s 159(4). These examples are expressed as the 'means' by which the two statutory objectives can be achieved. These means indicate the parameters for regeneration and development. The four (principal) approaches to achieving the two statutory aims of the Agency are:

(a)   securing that land and buildings are brought into effective use;
(b)   developing, or encouraging the development of, existing and new industry and commerce;

(c)   creating an attractive and safe environment;
(d)   facilitating the provision of housing and providing, or facilitating the provision of, social and recreational facilities.

As noted earlier (see para 12.2) the environmental and social infrastructure aims of the Agency are not given particular prominence. The fact that they come third and fourth in the list of 'means' (although of no legal significance) may be reflected in the content of schemes approved by the Agency: they may well play more subsidiary roles to the first two 'means' – securing the effective use of land and the development of industry and commerce. This could depend, however, on the particular circumstances of the case: if an area requires significant investment in social infrastructure and the creation of a good environment then a scheme for regenerating that area may well have to include significant elements of this kind in order to get private sector investment. Social and environmental concerns can be important factors, therefore, in determining the marketability of premises and so enter the equation in this manner.

Increased flexibility in the language

12.10   The language is broadly similar to that found in s 136(2) of the 1980 Act. It reflects the 'enabling' role which the Government sees as most appropriate for the Agency. The Consultation Paper suggested (para 10) that the Agency should:

'. . . operate wherever possible as an enabling body. It would aim to promote development with the private sector and would work closely with local authorities, the voluntary sector and other bodies involved in urban renewal.'

A non-exhaustive list of means

12.11   The statutory language states that the s 159 aims of the Agency are to be achieved 'in particular' by the four 'means' discussed above. The quoted phrase seems to indicate that the list is not exhaustive and so other 'means' could be used to achieve the Agency's regeneration and development aims. One example could be the provision of appropriate transport infrastructure – this can be an essential element in regenerating an area by encouraging commercial and industrial development: the example of London Docklands illustrates the point well. Physical development which does not fall within the four categories established by s 159(4) would not therefore be outside the scope of the legislation – as long as it constituted a means for achieving the aims of regeneration or development.

GENERAL POWERS OF THE AGENCY

12.12   There are general-purpose powers given to the Agency in addition to specific powers which arise where the Secretary of State has made a designation order (see paras 12.30ff on this) or where the powers to acquire land are being exercised (see paras 12.19ff). Most of the general-purpose powers given to the Agency are set out in s 160(1); they are very extensive. Those listed in s 160(1)(a)–(f) are almost identical to the list of powers given to UDCs in s 136(3) of the 1980 Act. The Agency can therefore acquire, reclaim, improve, etc land; it can carry out development; it can provide means of access, services or other facilities for land; it can seek to ensure the provision of water and other utilities and it can carry on 'any business or undertaking for the purposes of its objects'. By virtue of s 160(1)(g)–(k) the Agency may also:

(a)   form or acquire interests in bodies corporate (with the consent of the Secretary of State);

(b)   act with other persons, whether in partnership or otherwise;

(c)   give financial assistance to other persons;

(d)   act as agent for other persons; and

(e)   provide advisory or other services or facilities.

A general-purpose power is also (as with the UDCs) given to the Agency to do 'anything necessary or expedient for the purposes of its objects or for purposes incidental to those purposes': s 160(1)(l). Since those objects are the regeneration and development aims then the breadth of the powers given to the Agency is wide indeed. Furthermore, since it has a remit over non-urban land and can secure the 'development' of almost any land the Agency (subject to financial restraints, see para 12.16, and appropriate consents etc from the Secretary of State) has a national remit. Indeed, it has the capacity to be not only a 'roving' UDC but also a 'roving' local planning authority for practically any area of land within England by virtue of the powers that could be granted to it by the Secretary of State when designating regeneration or development areas under s 170 of the 1993 Act (see para 12.30). These powers thus emphasise the very considerable discretion given to the Agency (subject of course to the control exercised by the Secretary of State by way of guidance and directions) in dealing with a range of situations that are perceived to merit its intervention. Any company or person involved in a transaction with the Agency cannot use a failure by the Agency to observe its objects or the contravention of any direction given under s 167(2) as a basis for invalidating that transaction: s 168.

Financial assistance

12.13   A central aspect of the Agency's facilitating role in helping the regeneration of urban areas is the provision of financial assistance. Such assistance must be for 'qualifying expenditure' and will be given on such 'terms and conditions as the Agency, with the consent of the Secretary of State, considers appropriate'. Section 164(2)(a)–(f) states that expenditure incurred in connection with the following constitutes 'qualifying expenditure':

–   the acquisition of land; the reclamation, improvement or refurbishment of land;

–   the development and redevelopment of land; the equipment or fitting out of land;

–   the provision of means of access, services or other facilities for land; and

–   the carrying out of environmental improvements.

The forms of such assistance comprise grants, loans, guarantees and outright expenditure for the benefit of the person assisted: s 164(3)(a)–(d). The provision of grant aid will be by way of a unified grant regime which will replace the existing grants to be transferred to the Agency (see para 12.44): this unified grant system is also to include the proposed Property Development Grant of English Estates (to be introduced when the property market has recovered sufficiently). Financial assistance will be given on such terms and conditions as the Agency 'considers appropriate': s 164(1)(b). Section 164(5) indicates that the terms and conditions on which financial assistance may be given may include provision as to the circumstances in which the assistance must be repaid or otherwise made good to the Agency: it may also include provision as to the circumstances in which the Agency is entitled to recover the proceeds of any disposal of land in respect of which assistance was provided. Section 164(6) imposes a general requirement that any person receiving such assistance shall comply with the terms and conditions on which it is given and gives an express power to the Agency to enforce compliance with such terms and conditions. Parent company guarantees, bonds, etc and various other mechanisms found in ordinary commercial transactions can therefore be employed where the Agency considers their use 'appropriate'.

12.14   The Agency is not allowed, in giving such assistance, to 'purchase loan or share capital in a company': s 164(3). During the passage of the legislation it was argued that this contradicted the general power of the Agency to 'form or acquire interests in bodies corporate'.[1] The explanation appears to be that the former provision is to prevent the Agency 'bailing out' companies that are in financial difficulty while the latter allows it to be involved in the setting up of companies that are specifically designed for the regeneration or development aims of the Agency in a particular area.[2]

---

1 HC Deb, 14 January 1993, Standing Committee B, col 856 per D Henderson.
2 HC Deb, 14 January 1993, Standing Committee B, cols 856 and 857 per J Redwood.

CONSTITUTION AND FINANCE

12.15   Section 158(2) and Sch 17 deal with membership and staffing of the Agency. The minimum number of members (all appointed by the Secretary of State) is six: of these one is appointed Chairman, another Deputy Chairman. The daily administration of the Agency is under the control of a Chief Executive – appointed by the Agency with the consent of the Secretary of State. Terms and conditions of employment, pension arrangements and other aspects of employment of staff are also subject to approval by the Secretary of State (and the Treasury). The provisions of Sch 17 set out a reasonably standard framework as regards membership, remuneration, proceedings, etc for the Agency.

Local input

12.16   The constitution of the Agency has been criticised in that it makes no provision for a regional structure.[1] Attempts were made to have a regional input at the decision-making level but the Government was reluctant to have regional committees as this would be cumbersome.[2] However, the Opposition contended that great expense would be incurred in gathering local knowledge and information: information which a local committee would already have. The legislation does not rule out the possibility of links being established with local expertise. Paragraph 4 of Sch 17 does permit flexibility as regards the exercise of functions by committees, sub-committees and officers: so where the Agency (and, no doubt, the Secretary of State) considers it appropriate such committees (since they can include persons who are not members of the Agency (ibid, para 5(4)) can be used to establish links with those who have local experience thus encouraging a flow of information and expertise from the periphery.

1   HC Deb, 14 January 1993, Standing Committee B, col 823, per D Henderson.
2   HC Deb, 14 January 1993, Standing Committee B, col 825, per J Redwood.

Confidential discussions

12.17   There is no provision in the legislation requiring that public access be given to meetings etc on a basis similar to that which applies to local authorities. Such provisions were promoted by the Opposition: however, the Government argued that there was a need to balance openness with the necessity for the Agency to maintain commercial confidentiality and therefore it was not possible to make a general presumption in favour of public access.[1]

1   HL Deb, 19 April 1993, Committee, col 1315, per Viscount Goschen.

Finance

12.18   The finances of the Agency are covered in Sch 18. The Agency may borrow up to £200 million (or up to £300 million if the Secretary of State so specifies by statutory instrument): Sch 18, para 7(1). The budget for the Agency in 1993–1994 is to be approximately £264 million; this will rise to around £300 million for 1995–96 – which will include proceeds from the sale of assets from English Estates.[1] The Agency is required to submit a yearly report to the Secretary of State – this is to include its audited accounts for the preceding financial year: Sch 18, para 12. The report will then be laid before each House of Parliament by the Secretary of State: Sch 18, para 12(2).

1   HC Deb, 12 January 1993, Standing Committee B, col 789 per J Redwood.

LAND-ASSEMBLY POWERS

12.19   The importance of land assembly is the reason why the Agency is given powers to acquire land. The Consultation Paper (para 15) indicated that guidance from the Secretary of State would ensure that the Agency 'developed land and managed estates itself only as a last resort'. This again points to the 'enabling' role of the Agency. The Agency has powers to acquire land by agreement and by compulsory purchase order (the consent of the Secretary of State is required for compulsory acquisition): s 162(1). In the case of publicly-owned land the Secretary of State is empowered to make vesting orders transferring such land to the Agency (see para 12.19).

Compulsory purchase

12.20   The provisions of s 162 and Sch 20 deal with the compulsory acquisition of land and follow closely those in the 1980 Act. The Agency will employ the standard compulsory purchase procedures and the normal safeguards will apply: all its proposals will be advertised and all those with an interest in the land will have a right to object.

Acquisition by vesting order

12.21   These provisions in s 161 follow closely s 141 of the 1980 Act. The Secretary of State can thus transfer land held by 'a local authority, statutory undertakers or other public body' to the Agency. The definition of 'statutory undertakers' is widely drawn in s 161(7) and the Secretary of State can increase the scope of the category by statutory instrument. It was argued during debate that the Agency should have to demonstrate an absolute need for the transfer.[1] The Government rejected this, arguing that, although acquisition by agreement was intended to be the norm, it was necessary to have such a vesting order procedure so that land held in diverse or reluctant ownership could be assembled for a major development project. The Consultation Paper suggested that the vesting powers would be used primarily where vacant public sector land was not being used. The powers would only be used where the 'wider local economy is damaged by the lack of activity on the site and the public body holding the land is making insufficient progress with bringing it back into use' (para 18).

---

1 HC Deb, 14 January 1993, Standing Committee B, col 846 per D Henderson.

The Agency's relationship with local government

12.22   Clearly, the Agency is a mechanism by which central Government can seek to secure physical regeneration and development of urban and non–urban areas by exercising wide discretionary powers under the general direction of the Secretary of State. He has a number of functions (fiscal, supervisory, etc) which mean that the approach taken by the Agency in achieving its statutory objectives will be very closely controlled by central Government. The role of guidance (see para 12.26) will be a crucial element in setting the parameters for the Agency: where general or particular issues warrant more specific control then the power to issue directions will no doubt be used. Although the legal status of guidance is not 'binding' in the sense that directions are, it is unlikely that officers of the Agency will easily take decisions that are not covered or are in conflict with such guidance. The private sector and public sector bodies having dealings with the Agency may be able to persuade officers of the Agency to take a more flexible view of such guidance. This may involve noting the general objectives etc of the Agency and so they may secure regeneration by means other than those envisaged in the Secretary of State's guidance notes. When exercising planning powers in the light of the development plan (especially if adopted by the local planning authority shortly before designation of a regeneration or development area) the Agency may have to be careful with the exercise of development control functions which could result in a decision that is contrary to that plan (see paras 12.35ff on the exercise of planning functions).

Power to enter and survey land

12.23   Section 163 grants powers similar to those in other enactments which authorise entry onto land in order to survey it or estimate its value. One particular feature of interest is that the power to survey 'shall be construed as including power to search and bore for the purpose of ascertaining the nature of the subsoil or the presence of minerals in it': s 163(2). The 'nature' of the subsoil and the reference to boring indicates that the potential for contamination of land being surveyed is a specific concern: this is hardly surprising given the regeneration aim of the Agency and its use of power under the derelict land grant system to deal with land whose condition requires 'treatment' before it can be brought into beneficial use. This particular power is but one reminder of the problems that contaminated land will pose in the activities of the Agency and indicates one of the main issues it will address in meeting its brief.

12.24   Admission can be demanded as of right, when required, if 28 days' notice of the intended entry has been given to the occupier by the Agency: s 163(3)(b). Wilful obstruction of any person acting in exercise of the powers under s 163 is a summary offence, punishable by a fine not exceeding level 2 on the standard scale: s 163(4). The person using the powers to survey land is under an obligation not to divulge any information obtained by him relating to any manufacturing process or trade secret and contravention of this obligation may result in an unlimited fine or a custodial sentence of up to two years: s 163(7). Compensation may also be claimed from the Agency by any person with an interest in the land where the use of powers under s 163 results in damage to that land: s 163(8). If the person surveying the land has had to demand admission as of right by giving 28 days' notice of intended entry, he will also have to give notice of his intention to carry out any works proposed for boring into the soil: s 163(10). This requirement is not that clear: it may mean that the surveyor need only mention that he intends to make boreholes in various unspecified places: on a stricter interpretation it may mean that he will have to give a clear indication of where such boring will actually take place and the dimensions of the borehole. Such specificity will, however, be difficult until he has made an initial survey to judge the most appropriate locations for carrying out such works. If the land is held by statutory undertakers and they object to the proposed works, on the ground that the execution of the works will be seriously detrimental to the carrying out of their undertaking, then the authority of the appropriate minister is required for the carrying out of any such works: s 163(11).

SECRETARY OF STATE'S CONSENT, GUIDANCE AND DIRECTIONS

Consent

12.25   In numerous provisions the Secretary of State's consent is required. Section 166 indicates that such consent may be conditional or unconditional and may be given in relation to a particular situation or a category of situations: s 166(a) and (b). Such consent may also be revoked or varied by notice – except where it relates to something done or agreed to be done by the Agency: s 166(c). Contractual arrangements entered into by the Agency on the basis of an earlier consent cannot therefore be overridden by a revocation or variation of that consent.

Guidance

12.26   Section 167(1) requires that the Agency 'shall have regard to guidance' given by the Secretary of State in deciding:

(a)   which land is suitable for regeneration or development;
(b)   which of its functions it is to exercise for securing the regeneration or development of land; and
(c)   how it is to exercise such functions.

The power given to the Secretary of State to issue guidance to the Agency is therefore implicit in this provision.

Content of guidance

12.27   During debate on the Bill it was argued that the Secretary of State's guidance could be crucial to the Agency's success and therefore there should be an opportunity to discuss this guidance publicly. It was also suggested that the guidance should reflect a statutory requirement that highlighted the need for environmentally sustainable development. In defence of the section as drafted, the Government said that the draft of the 'central core' of guidance would be available in a single document. This would cover the whole range of the Agency's work leaving the Agency free to establish its own specific priorities. There will be three key themes to the core guidance. These are that the Agency:

(a)   should operate wherever possible through partnerships and should develop close links with local authorities;
(b)   must operate within the planning framework; and
(c)   should always be aware of the environmental implications of its activities.[1]

The core guidance will be published in draft (for consultation) before the Agency is established. This will then form the basis for more detailed guidance.

---

1   HL Deb, 20 May 1993, Report Stage, col 1953, per Lord Strathclyde.

Directions

12.28   The power to make directions (which can either restrict the Agency in the exercise of its functions or require the exercise of such functions in any manner so specified) is set out in s 167(2) and (3). Such directions may be of particular or general application and may be varied or revoked by subsequent directions.

REGENERATION/DEVELOPMENT AREAS

12.29   The strategies of providing financial assistance, acquiring land and providing industrial and commercial sites may not be sufficient to secure the regeneration or development of particularly derelict areas. Where there is severe and widespread dereliction a longer-term commitment by the Agency may be required. Such a situation is also likely to require the use of more extensive powers (relating to planning controls and highway matters) which are only available if the Secretary of State uses powers under s 170 to designate such an area. Such a designation can then also include provisions relating to planning and highway matters (see paras 12.35ff on the Agency as planning authority). This is the fourth role of the Agency and it bears comparison in particular with the similar powers given to UDCs in their attempts to 'secure regeneration'.

The designation power

12.30   Section 170(1) provides that a designation order can be made in respect of two categories of land in England, namely:

(a)   any 'urban area'; and
(b)   any area 'which in the opinion of the Secretary of State, is suitable for urban development'.

The existence of the second category underlines the comments made earlier (see para 12.12 regarding the Agency's 'roving' planning authority status) that the Agency has a wide-ranging remit: indeed, it might be more appropriate to refer to the Agency as the 'Urbanisation Agency' as its main aim is to 're-urbanise' those areas whose previous urban uses have left them derelict, under-used, etc while its subsidiary aim is to urbanise land which is not yet urban in character. (This interpretation arises from bringing together the criteria in s 170(1) regarding land which can be designated under the 1993 Act and the statement in s 159(2) and (3) regarding the two aims of the Agency.) In either case a designation order can be made in respect of such land arises if 'it appears to' the Secretary of State that either of the following are appropriate:

(a)   that all or any of the planning powers covered by s 167 should be exercised by the Agency in respect of the area of land (in whole or in part); or
(b)   that the powers under ss 172 and 173 (relating to the adoption of streets and making of traffic regulation orders) should be made available to the Agency.

In such cases designation of the area can proceed using the powers in s 170. The order can include provision for any or all of ss 171, 172 and 173 to be applied to that area: s 170(1).

12.31   The legislation seems to indicate that a designated area must *either* be an urban area (where there is dereliction etc) requiring regeneration *or* a non-urban area that can be developed so that it becomes urbanised. (This distinction approximates to the two aims of the whole regime – the regeneration aim and the development aim.) As regards the latter type of area (non-urbanised land which is suitable for urbanisation) the undefined terms and the subjectively-phrased powers given to the Secretary of State mean that the Agency will be able to operate (subject to Secretary of State approval) in a very wide range of situations. Technically, however, it would seem to be beyond the scope of the legislation to designate (as a single area) land which is in fact a mixture of the two types of area – derelict urban land and non-urban land. This is a clear possibility where a derelict urban area borders a rural area. However, the co-ordinated designation (as two designated areas sharing a common boundary) of such contiguous areas would get around this slight difficulty.

Consultation duty

12.32 Prior to using the designation power, the Secretary of State is required to consult with every local authority who may have land included in the proposed designated area: s 170(3).

The concept of consultation

12.33 The courts have examined the concept of 'consultation'. To fulfil the requirements of the 1993 Act as regards any duty to consult (such as with designation of areas under s 170) the Secretary of State's procedures will have to satisfy the general criteria set out by the courts. In *R v Secretary of State for Social Services, ex p Association of Metropolitan Authorities* [1986] 1 All ER 164 at p 167 it was stated that:

> '. . . in any context the essence of consultation is the communication of a genuine invitation to give advice and a genuine consideration of that advice. In my view it must go without saying that to achieve consultation, sufficient information must be supplied by the consulting to the consulted party to enable it to tender helpful advice. Sufficient time must be given by the consulting to the consulted party to enable it to do that and sufficient time must be available for such advice to be considered by the consulting parties. Sufficient, in that context, does not mean ample, but at least enough to enable the relevant purpose to be fulfilled.'

The sufficiency of both information and time will thus be central to the adequacy of the consultation process: however, the courts are unlikely to interfere unless there is a blatant instance of a failure to consult such that the designation is affected by *Wednesbury* unreasonableness.[1] Naturally, the Secretary of State is not obliged to follow the 'advice' given during the consultation process – he must merely give 'genuine consideration' to such advice.

---

1   *Associated Provincial Picture Houses v Wednesbury Corpn* [1948] 1 KB 223, [1947] 2 All ER 680, CA.

Amendment of a designated area's boundaries

12.34 Section 170(5) applies s 14 of the Interpretation Act 1978 such that the power to amend the designation order includes the power to amend the boundaries of any designated area. This provision allows for parts of an area to be de-designated when regeneration/development has been completed in those parts. There are parallels with the provisions of s 179 dealing with amendment (also achieving an incremental de-designation) of UDC boundaries (see para 12.48).

The Agency as local planning authority

12.35 One of the principal effects of designation can be to invest the Agency with a wide range of planning powers under the planning legislation. This can be achieved by provisions in the order made by the Secretary of State – as envisaged by s 171. This section follows closely s 149 of the 1980 Act and allows the Agency to exercise the relevant planning functions for all or any part of an urban regeneration area or development area designated by the relevant order. The range of planning powers covered is considerable and covers both hazardous substances control as well as listed building and conservation area control. Although plan-making functions under Part II of the Town and Country Planning Act 1990 ('TCPA 1990') are not included in the powers that can be vested in the Agency the various provisions relating to the development control and enforcement functions are covered.

12.36   These provisions relating to planning powers were resisted during its passage through both Houses of Parliament. Confirmation was given that the Agency would only undertake work in the context of national and local land use policy.[1] Such constraints affect (in any event) all local planning authorities: the principal impact on decision-making arising from an adopted development plan for the area will not be changed by reason of the identity of the local planning authority. Section 54A of the TCPA 1990 and its 'presumption in favour of proposals that are in accordance with the development plan' will still operate.[2] However, where an area is designated under the 1993 Act provisions then the very fact of designation will be particularly relevant to decision-making under the planning Acts: the fact of designation, as the following suggests, may be the starting point for 'overriding' what the development plan may say about a particular site.

1   HC Deb, 14 January 1993, Standing Committee B, col 865 per J Redwood.
2   See the Secretary of State for the Environment's guidance on this presumption in Planning Policy Guidance Note No 1, para 25.

12.37   The statutory aim of regeneration will be of particular importance when it comes to assessing if there are 'other material considerations' that indicate that the planning application should *not* be handled in accordance with the policy in the adopted development plan for the area – as envisaged by s 54A of the TCPA 1990. Designation of an area for regeneration or development under the 1993 Act may indicate that an application for permission should be treated in a manner that is at variance with the adopted development plan: this is acceptable if the proposed development has a bearing on the regeneration aim of the designation. The statutory objective of regeneration could serve to justify a grant of permission that is at variance with plan policy: it could also justify a refusal of permission in contradiction of plan policy. In the former case an industrial/commercial development may be important in terms of economic regeneration of the designated area – even though the adopted local plan may have envisaged (for example) a housing use for the land concerned. In the latter case an application for a use which could prejudice inward investment (eg because of fears about its polluting or contaminating impact) might be refused even if the application was for a site which had been designated for such a development in the adopted development plan.[1] The fact of designation as a regeneration area may therefore mean that development plan policy is subordinated to the 1993 Act objectives of (economic) regeneration.

1   See, for example, the ministerial decision refusing planning permission for an incinerator in Howdon, North Tyneside (2 November 1992, APP/K9530/A/89/145489) which assessed the impact on the confidence of investors in a nearby regeneration site (in a UDC). It was decided that, if permission were to be granted, there would be a detrimental impact on such inward investment into the UDC as a result of the perceived risk of air pollution etc. This detriment was unacceptable and so the potential impact of such perceived risk justified refusal.

Planning functions and environmental concerns

12.38   Concern was also expressed that the legislation had been drafted without giving due regard to the environment. Amendments were tabled requiring the Agency to have as its main objective the aim of securing environmentally sustainable development.[1]

1   HL Deb, 19 April 1993, Committee, col 1282, per Lord Norrie.

12.39   To counter this the Government said that it was committed to ensuring that environmental considerations are taken into account at all levels of decision-making and that the Agency would be expected to consider environmental effects in developing its general programmes. The Government also said that the Agency's corporate plans would be submitted to the Secretary of State and in considering them he would seek to assure himself that the Agency had examined the environmental impacts of each part of its programme. It was also emphasised that the Agency would already be subject to s 11 of the Countryside Act 1968 in that it should have regard to the desirability of conserving the natural beauty and amenity of the countryside in the exercise of its functions.[1]

1   HL Deb, 19 April 1993, Committee, col 1289, per Lord Strathclyde.

Highway powers

12.40   In addition to affecting the allocation of planning powers, the designation of an area can also involve the Agency being given powers relating to the adoption and connection of private streets and the making of traffic regulation orders. Section 178 also makes amendments to provisions of the Highways Act 1980 which introduce similar powers for UDCs in urban development areas.

Connection of private streets

12.41   The Agency is given powers to serve a 'connection notice' on the local highway authority requiring it to connect a private street to an existing highway: s 165(1). A connection notice must specify the private street and the existing highway, the works which appear to be necessary to make the connection and the period within which those works should be carried out: s 165(2). There is a duty to consult the local highway authority about the proposed contents of the notice before serving such a connection notice: s 165(3). By virtue of s 165(4) the local highway authority may appeal against the notice within two months of service of the notice – the appeal is determined by the Secretary of State after considering any representations made to him by the Agency and the local highway authority: s 165(5). The Secretary of State may set aside or confirm a connection notice and is given powers of modification in that respect: ibid. When a connection notice becomes effective, the local highway authority is required to carry out the works specified in the notice within such period as may be so specified and may recover from the Agency the expenses reasonably incurred by them in doing so: s 161(7). The Agency has default powers to carry out those works or complete them if the local highway authority does not carry out the works specified in the connection notice within the period so stated: s 165(8).

Adoption of private streets

12.42   Section 172 allows the Agency to set in train a process which results in the street works authority (see the Highways Act 1980, s 203(3)) being required to adopt a private street in a designated area where that street has had street works executed upon it. The procedure involves the Secretary of State: his confirmation of the 'adoption notice' is required: s 172(4). His power to impose conditions upon the confirmation of the adoption notice requiring the street works authority to adopt the private street may involve financial payments from the Agency: s 172(4)(a).

Traffic regulation orders for private streets

12.43   The possibility of a local authority, *qua* traffic authority under the Road Traffic Regulation Act 1984 ('1984 Act'), not co-operating with the Agency is covered by the provisions of s 173. This section allows the Secretary of State (in relation to a designated area) to make road traffic regulation orders under s 1 or s 6 of the 1984 Act upon submission by the Agency that such an order should be made: s 173(1). This power applies only to private streets.

CITY GRANT AND DERELICT LAND GRANT

12.44   Section 175 enables the Secretary of State to hand over grant-aid powers (Derelict Land Grant and City Grant) to the Agency. The Agency may thus be appointed as agent for such financial assistance as is covered by s 1 of the Derelict Land Act 1982 and (in relation to England only) ss 27–29 of the Housing and Planning Act 1986 (City Grant). The criteria relating to each of the grant-aid powers are mirrored in almost identical terms in provisions of the 1993 Act dealing with the statutory aims of the Agency in s 159 (see paras 12.3ff). Changes to the criteria for City Grants have been made by s 174 (amending s 27 of the Housing and Planning Act 1986): the changes introduce language used elsewhere in the 1993 Act as regards the objects of the Agency and the means for achieving those objects. The grant-making powers under the amended s 27 also reflect an increased concern for the provision of social infrastructure (more so than the unamended City Grant powers): the criteria now (in addition to housing and social facilities) also address the provision of recreational, training and educational facilities and also health services for people who live in the area that is being regenerated.

12.45   The Agency will administer such financial assistance as has been committed before the Agency takes over the grant-making powers. The guidance issued by the Department of Environment (in the form, for example, of the Derelict Land Grant Aid policy – DLGA1) is to be replaced by similar guidance from the Agency relating to its grant-making powers. The Government is not proposing to make any significant increase in the funding available for grant aid when handing over responsibility for their administration to the Agency. When the Agency is in being, the Government envisages that grant-aid will be allocated under a unified grant system – leading to the disappearance of the terms 'City Grant' and 'Derelict Land Grant'.[1]

---

1   HC Deb, 14 January 1993, Standing Committee B, cols 869 and 870 per J Redwood.

URBAN DEVELOPMENT CORPORATIONS

12.46 Some changes were introduced into the UDC regime established under the 1980 Act. These serve to link the UDC regime with the framework established by the 1993 Act and, for example, allow the Agency to have a role in the winding-up of UDCs.

UDCs as agents of the agency

12.47 Section 177 empowers the Agency to appoint an existing UDC as agent. This enables a UDC to operate outside its area on land which can conveniently be regenerated in tandem with the activities of the UDC rather than having the Agency directly involved. An amendment was proposed to allow the relevant local authority to act as an agent for the Agency: this was defeated by the Government as it was felt to be unnecessary, given that the legislation provides for the Agency to enter into agreements with local authorities to support projects.[1] It was also emphasised that City Challenge teams would not act as local agents for the Agency.

---

1 HC Deb, 14 January 1993, Standing Committee B, col 871 per Redwood.

Adjustment of UDC areas

12.48 The Secretary of State is given order-making powers under amendments made to s 134 of the 1980 Act to alter the boundaries of any urban development area: s 179. The purpose of this section is to allow for the incremental de-designation of the areas administered by UDCs by the alteration of the boundaries of such areas. The provision means that parts of the area subject to the UDC's jurisdiction can be transferred back to the control of the local authority: normally this would be after negotiation with the local authority.

Consultation

12.49 By virtue of a new s 134(3B) of the 1980 Act the Secretary of State is obliged to consult (see para 12.33 on this term) the local authority into whose jurisdiction the land to be excluded by such an order will return: s 179. The local authority concerned can use the consultation process and the parliamentary process (see the new s 134(5) of the 1980 Act inserted by s 179(5) of the 1993 Act) to make their views known about any appropriate arrangements for resources etc.

Winding up of UDCs – amendments

12.50 Section 180 supplements the arrangements in the 1980 Act as regards the winding up of UDCs. A new s 165A(1) is introduced into the 1980 Act: s 180. This provision allows for a wider power for the transfer of property etc from a UDC to the Secretary of State than was previously given by s 165(3) of the 1980 Act – repealed by s 180(2) of the 1993. The repealed section only covered transfers of liabilities to the Secretary of State. The new power means that the Secretary of State has order-making powers to transfer to himself any 'property, rights or liabilities' which are vested in a UDC. Such an order cannot affect the proposed transfer of such interests where they are already covered by an agreement made under s 165 of the 1980 Act (and approved by the Secretary of State and the Treasury). Such an agreement can be made between the UDC and the Agency (as a result of amendments carried out by s 180(1)). Such agreements will probably be more commonly used than the Secretary of State's order-making powers. The degree of control exercised over UDCs and the Agency by the Secretary of State make such agreements rather more attractive in terms of administrative efficiency. The Agency (acting under the guidance and direction of the Secretary of State) can therefore decide what will happen to property and land accumulated by UDCs that has come to it by way of such agreements.

NOTICES

12.51   Section 183 sets out relatively standard provisions relating to the service of notices on individuals, bodies corporate and partnerships.

Leasehold Reform, Housing and Urban Development Act 1993

Leasehold Reform, Housing and Urban Development Act 1993

(1993 c 28)

ARRANGEMENT OF SECTIONS

PART I
LANDLORD AND TENANT

CHAPTER I
COLLECTIVE ENFRANCHISEMENT IN CASE OF TENANTS OF FLATS

CHAPTER IV
ESTATE MANAGEMENT SCHEMES IN CONNECTION WITH ENFRANCHISMENT

CHAPTER V
TENANTS RIGHT TO MANAGEMENT AUDIT

CHAPTER VI
MISCELLANEOUS

Compulsory acquisition of landlord's interest

Variation of leases

Codes of practice

*Jurisdiction of leasehold valuation tribunals in relation to
enfranchisement etc of Crown land*

Provision of accommodation for persons with mental disorders

CHAPTER VII
GENERAL

PART II
PUBLIC SECTOR HOUSING

CHAPTER I
ENGLAND AND WALES

Right to buy

Abolition of certain ancillary rights

Right to acquire on rent to mortgage terms

Other rights of secure tenants

Housing welfare services

PART IV
SUPPLEMENTAL

SCHEDULES:

An Act to confer rights to collective enfranchisement and lease renewal on tenants of flats; to make further provision with respect to enfranchisement by tenants of houses; to make provision for auditing the management, by landlords or other persons, of residential property and for the approval of codes of practice relating thereto; to amend Parts III and IV of the Landlord and Tenant Act 1987; to confer jurisdiction on leasehold valuation tribunals as respects Crown land; to make provision for rendering void agreements preventing the occupation of leasehold property by persons with mental disorders; to amend Parts II, IV and V of the Housing Act 1985, Schedule 2 to the Housing Associations Act 1985, Parts I and III and sections 248 and 299 of the Housing (Scotland) Act 1987, Part III of the Housing Act 1988, and Part VI of the Local Government and Housing Act 1989; to make provision with respect to certain disposals requiring consent under Part II of the Housing Act 1985, including provision for the payment of a levy; to alter the basis of certain contributions by the Secretary of State under section 569 of that Act; to establish and confer functions on a body to replace the English Industrial Estates Corporation and to be known as the Urban Regeneration Agency; to provide for the designation of certain urban and other areas and to make provision as to the effect of such designation; to amend section 23 of the Land Compensation Act 1961, section 98 of the Local Government, Planning and Land Act 1980 and section 27 of the Housing and Planning Act 1986; to make further provision with respect to urban development corporations and urban development areas; and for connected purposes.

[20 July 1993]

PART I
LANDLORD AND TENANT

CHAPTER I
COLLECTIVE ENFRANCHISEMENT IN CASE OF TENANTS OF FLATS

Preliminary

1 The right to collective enfranchisement

(1) This Chapter has effect for the purpose of conferring on qualifying tenants of flats contained in premises to which this Chapter applies on the relevant date the right, exercisable subject to and in accordance with this Chapter, to have the freehold of those premises acquired on their behalf—

(a) by a person or persons appointed by them for the purpose, and

(b) at a price determined in accordance with this Chapter;

and that right is referred to in this Chapter as "the right to collective enfranchisement".

(2) Where the right to collective enfranchisement is exercised in relation to any such premises ("the relevant premises")—

(a) the qualifying tenants by whom the right is exercised shall be entitled, subject to and in accordance with this Chapter, to have acquired, in like manner, the freehold of any property which is not comprised in the relevant premises but to which this paragraph applies by virtue of subsection (3); and

(b) section 2 has effect with respect to the acquisition of leasehold interests to which paragraph (a) or (b) of subsection (1) of that section applies.

(3) Subsection (2)(a) applies to any property if the freehold of it is owned by the person who owns the freehold of the relevant premises and at the relevant date either—

(a) it is appurtenant property which is demised by the lease held by a qualifying tenant of a flat contained in the relevant premises; or

(b) it is property which any such tenant is entitled under the terms of the lease of his flat to use in common with the occupiers of other premises (whether those premises are contained in the relevant premises or not).

(4) The right of acquisition in respect of the freehold of any such property as is mentioned in subsection (3)(b) shall, however, be taken to be satisfied with respect to that property if, on the acquisition of the relevant premises in pursuance of this Chapter, either—

(a) there are granted by the freeholder—
    (i) over that property, or
    (ii) over any other property,
such permanent rights as will ensure that thereafter the occupier of the flat referred to in that provision has as nearly as may be the same rights as those enjoyed in relation to that property on the relevant date by the qualifying tenant under the terms of his lease; or

(b) there is acquired from the freeholder the freehold of any other property over which any such permanent rights may be granted.

(5) A claim by qualifying tenants to exercise the right to collective enfranchisement may be made in relation to any premises to which this Chapter applies despite the fact that those premises are less extensive than the entirety of the premises in relation to which those tenants are entitled to exercise that right.

(6) Any right or obligation under this Chapter to acquire any interest in property shall not extend to underlying minerals in which that interest subsists if—

(a) the owner of the interest requires the minerals to be excepted, and

(b) proper provision is made for the support of the property as it is enjoyed on the relevant date.

(7) In this section—

"appurtenant property", in relation to a flat, means any garage, outhouse, garden, yard or appurtenances belonging to, or usually enjoyed with, the flat;

"the freeholder" means the person who owns the freehold of the relevant premises;

"the relevant premises" means any such premises as are referred to in subsection (2).

(8) In this Chapter "the relevant date", in relation to any claim to exercise the right to collective enfranchisement, means the date on which notice of the claim is given under section 13.

Definitions For "qualifying tenant", see s 5; for "flat", see s 101(1); for "lease", see s 101(1), (2); for "the right to collective enfranchisement", see sub-s (1) above; for "the relevant premises", see sub-ss (2), (7) above; for "appurtenant property" and "the freeholder", see sub-s (7) above; for "the relevant date", see sub-s (8) above.
References See paras 2.4, 2.5 ff.

---

2   Acquisition of leasehold interests

(1) Where the right to collective enfranchisement is exercised in relation to any premises to which this Chapter applies ("the relevant premises"), then, subject to and in accordance with this Chapter—

    (a)   there shall be acquired on behalf of the qualifying tenants by whom the right is exercised every interest to which this paragraph applies by virtue of subsection (2); and

    (b)   those tenants shall be entitled to have acquired on their behalf any interest to which this paragraph applies by virtue of subsection (3);

and any interest so acquired on behalf of those tenants shall be acquired in the manner mentioned in paragraphs (a) and (b) of section 1(1).

(2) Paragraph (a) of subsection (1) above applies to the interest of the tenant under any lease which is superior to the lease held by a qualifying tenant of a flat contained in the relevant premises.

(3) Paragraph (b) of subsection (1) above applies to the interest of the tenant under any lease (not falling within subsection (2) above) under which the demised premises consist of or include—

    (a)   any common parts of the relevant premises, or

    (b)   any property falling within section 1(2)(a) which is to be acquired by virtue of that provision,

where the acquisition of that interest is reasonably necessary for the proper management or maintenance of those common parts, or (as the case may be) that property, on behalf of the tenants by whom the right to collective enfranchisement is exercised.

(4) Where the demised premises under any lease falling within subsection (2) or (3) include any premises other than—

    (a)   a flat contained in the relevant premises which is held by a qualifying tenant,

    (b)   any common parts of those premises, or

    (c)   any such property as is mentioned in subsection (3)(b),

the obligation or (as the case may be) right under subsection (1) above to acquire the interest of the tenant under the lease shall not extend to his interest under the lease in any such other premises.

(5) Where the qualifying tenant of a flat is a public sector landlord and the flat is let under a secure tenancy, then if—

    (a)   the condition specified in subsection (6) is satisfied, and

    (b)   the lease of the qualifying tenant is directly derived out of a lease under which the tenant is a public sector landlord,

the interest of that public sector landlord as tenant under that lease shall not be liable to be acquired by virtue of subsection (1) to the extent that it is an interest in the flat or in any appurtenant property; and the interest of a public sector landlord as tenant under any lease out of which the qualifying tenant's lease is indirectly derived shall, to the like extent, not be liable to be so acquired (so long as the tenant under every lease intermediate between that lease and the qualifying tenant's lease is a public sector landlord).

(6) The condition referred to in subsection (5)(a) is that either—

    (a)   the qualifying tenant is the immediate landlord under the secure tenancy, or

    (b)   he is the landlord under a lease which is superior to the secure tenancy and the tenant under that lease, and the tenant under every lease (if any) intermediate between it and the secure tenancy, is also a public sector landlord;

and in subsection (5) "appurtenant property" has the same meaning as in section 1.

(7) In this section "the relevant premises" means any such premises as are referred to in subsection (1).

3   Premises to which this Chapter applies

(1) Subject to section 4, this Chapter applies to any premises if—

(a)   they consist of a self-contained building or part of a building and the freehold of the whole of the building or of that part of the building is owned by the same person;

(b)   they contain two or more flats held by qualifying tenants; and

(c)   the total number of flats held by such tenants is not less than two thirds of the total number of flats contained in the premises.

(2) For the purposes of this section a building is a self-contained building if it is structurally detached, and a part of a building is a self-contained part of a building if—

(a)   it constitutes a vertical division of the building and the structure of the building is such that that part could be redeveloped independently of the remainder of the building; and

(b)   the relevant services provided for occupiers of that part either—

(i)   are provided independently of the relevant services provided for occupiers of the remainder of the building, or

(ii)   could be so provided without involving the carrying out of any works likely to result in a significant interruption in the provision of any such services for occupiers of the remainder of the building;

and for this purpose "relevant services" means services provided by means of pipes, cables or other fixed installations.

4   Premises excluded from right

(1) This Chapter does not apply to premises falling within section 3(1) if—

(a)   any part or parts of the premises is or are neither—

(i)   occupied, or intended to be occupied, for residential purposes, nor

(ii)   comprised in any common parts of the premises; and

(b)   the internal floor area of that part or of those parts (taken together) exceeds 10 per cent of the internal floor area of the premises (taken as a whole).

(2) Where in the case of any such premises any part of the premises (such as, for example, a garage, parking space or storage area) is used, or intended for use, in conjunction with a particular dwelling contained in the premises (and accordingly is not comprised in any common parts of the premises), it shall be taken to be occupied, or intended to be occupied, for residential purposes.

(3) For the purpose of determining the internal floor area of a building or of any part of a building, the floor or floors of the building or part shall be taken to extend

(without interruption) throughout the whole of the interior of the building or part, except that the area of any common parts of the building or part shall be disregarded.

(4) This Chapter does not apply to premises falling within section 3(1) if the premises are premises with a resident landlord and do not contain more than four units.

Definitions For "premises with a resident landlord", see s 10; for "common parts" and "dwelling", see s 101(1).
References See para 2.11 ff.

5 Qualifying tenants

(1) Subject to the following provisions of this section, a person is a qualifying tenant of a flat for the purposes of this Chapter if he is tenant of the flat under a long lease at a low rent.

(2) Subsection (1) does not apply where—
  (a) the lease is a business lease; or
  (b) the immediate landlord under the lease is a charitable housing trust and the flat forms part of the housing accommodation provided by it in the pursuit of its charitable purposes; or
  (c) the lease was granted by sub-demise out of a superior lease other than a long lease at a low rent, the grant was made in breach of the terms of the superior lease, and there has been no waiver of the breach by the superior landlord;
and in paragraph (b) "charitable housing trust" means a housing trust within the meaning of the Housing Act 1985 which is a charity within the meaning of the Charities Act 1993.

(3) No flat shall have more than one qualifying tenant at any one time.

(4) Accordingly—
  (a) where a flat is for the time being let under two or more leases to which subsection (1) applies, any tenant under any of those leases which is superior to that held by any other such tenant shall not be a qualifying tenant of the flat for the purposes of this Chapter; and
  (b) where a flat is for the time being let to joint tenants under a lease to which subsection (1) applies, the joint tenants shall (subject to paragraph (a) and subsection (5)) be regarded for the purposes of this Chapter as jointly constituting the qualifying tenant of the flat.

(5) Where apart from this subsection—
  (a) a person would be regarded for the purposes of this Chapter as being (or as being among those constituting) the qualifying tenant of a flat contained in any particular premises consisting of the whole or part of a building, but
  (b) that person would also be regarded for those purposes as being (or as being among those constituting) the qualifying tenant of each of two or more other flats contained in those premises,
then, whether that person is tenant of the flats referred to in paragraphs (a) and (b) under a single lease or otherwise, there shall be taken for those purposes to be no qualifying tenant of any of those flats.

(6) For the purposes of subsection (5) in its application to a body corporate any flat let to an associated company (whether alone or jointly with any other person or persons) shall be treated as if it were so let to that body; and for this purpose "associated company" means another body corporate which is (within the meaning of section 736 of the Companies Act 1985) that body's holding company, a subsidiary of that body or another subsidiary of that body's holding company.

Definitions   For "long lease", see s 7; for "lease at a low rent", see s 8; for "business lease" and "flat", see s 101(1); for "lease" and related expressions, see s 101(1), (2) (and note also s 101(3)); for "charitable housing trust", see sub-s (2) above; for "associated company", see sub-s (6) above.
References   See paras 2.15, 2.16 ff.

6   Qualifying tenants satisfying residence condition

(1) For the purposes of this Chapter a qualifying tenant of a flat satisfies the residence condition at any time when the condition specified in subsection (2) is satisfied with respect to him.

(2) That condition is that the tenant has occupied the flat as his only or principal home—
  (a)   for the last twelve months, or
  (b)   for periods amounting to three years in the last ten years,
whether or not he has used it also for other purposes.

(3) For the purposes of subsection (2)—
  (a)   any reference to the tenant's flat includes a reference to part of it; and
  (b)   it is immaterial whether at any particular time the tenant's occupation was in right of the lease by virtue of which he is a qualifying tenant or in right of some other lease or otherwise;
but any occupation by a company or other artificial person, or (where the tenant is a corporation sole) by the corporator, shall not be regarded as occupation for the purposes of that subsection.

(4) In the case of a lease held by joint tenants—
  (a)   the condition specified in subsection (2) need only be satisfied with respect to one of the joint tenants; and
  (b)   subsection (3) shall apply accordingly (the reference to the lease by virtue of which the tenant is a qualifying tenant being read for this purpose as a reference to the lease by virtue of which the joint tenants are a qualifying tenant).

Definitions   For "qualifying tenant", see s 5; for "flat", see s 101(1); for "lease" and related expressions (including "tenant"), see s 101(1), (2).
References   See para 2.50 ff.

7   Meaning of "long lease"

(1) In this Chapter "long lease" means (subject to the following provisions of this section)—
  (a)   a lease granted for a term of years certain exceeding 21 years, whether or not it is (or may become) terminable before the end of that term by notice given by or to the tenant or by re-entry, forfeiture or otherwise;
  (b)   a lease for a term fixed by law under a grant with a covenant or obligation for perpetual renewal (other than a lease by sub-demise from

one which is not a long lease) or a lease taking effect under section 149(6) of the Law of Property Act 1925 (leases terminable after a death or marriage);

(c) a lease granted in pursuance of the right to buy conferred by Part V of the Housing Act 1985 or in pursuance of the right to acquire on rent to mortgage terms conferred by that Part of that Act; or

(d) a shared ownership lease, whether granted in pursuance of that Part of that Act or otherwise, where the tenant's total share is 100 per cent.

(2) A lease terminable by notice after a death or marriage is not to be treated as a long lease for the purposes of this Chapter if—

(a) the notice is capable of being given at any time after the death or marriage of the tenant;

(b) the length of the notice is not more than three months; and

(c) the terms of the lease preclude both—

(i) its assignment otherwise than by virtue of section 92 of the Housing Act 1985 (assignments by way of exchange), and

(ii) the sub-letting of the whole of the premises comprised in it.

(3) Where the tenant of any property under a long lease at a low rent, on the coming to an end of that lease, becomes or has become tenant of the property or part of it under any subsequent tenancy (whether by express grant or by implication of law), then that tenancy shall be deemed for the purposes of this Chapter (including any further application of this subsection) to be a long lease irrespective of its terms.

(4) Where—

(a) a lease is or has been granted for a term of years certain not exceeding 21 years, but with a covenant or obligation for renewal without payment of a premium (but not for perpetual renewal), and

(b) the lease is or has been renewed on one or more occasions so as to bring to more than 21 years the total of the terms granted (including any interval between the end of a lease and the grant of a renewal),

this Chapter shall apply as if the term originally granted had been one exceeding 21 years.

(5) References in this Chapter to a long lease include—

(a) any period during which the lease is or was continued under Part I of the Landlord and Tenant Act 1954 or under Schedule 10 to the Local Government and Housing Act 1989;

(b) any period during which the lease was continued under the Leasehold Property (Temporary Provisions) Act 1951.

(6) Where in the case of a flat there are at any time two or more separate leases, with the same landlord and the same tenant, and—

(a) the property comprised in one of those leases consists of either the flat or a part of it (in either case with or without any appurtenant property), and

(b) the property comprised in every other lease consists of either a part of the flat (with or without any appurtenant property) or appurtenant property only,

then in relation to the property comprised in such of those leases as are long leases, this Chapter shall apply as it would if at that time—

(i) there were a single lease of that property, and

(ii) that lease were a long lease;

but this subsection has effect subject to the operation of subsections (3) to (5) in relation to any of the separate leases.

(7) In this section—

"appurtenant property" has the same meaning as in section 1;

"shared ownership lease" means a lease—

(a) granted on payment of a premium calculated by reference to a percentage of the value of the demised premises or the cost of providing them, or

(b) under which the tenant (or his personal representatives) will or may be entitled to a sum calculated by reference, directly or indirectly, to the value of those premises; and

"total share", in relation to the interest of a tenant under a shared ownership lease, means his initial share plus any additional share or shares in the demised premises which he has acquired.

Definitions   For "lease at a low rent", see s 8; for "interest", see s 101(1); for "lease" and related expressions, see s 101(1), (2); for "shared ownership lease" and "total share", see sub-s (7) above.
References   See paras 2.17–2.19 ff.

8   Leases at a low rent

(1) For the purposes of this Chapter a lease of a flat is a lease at a low rent if either no rent was payable under it in respect of the flat during the initial year or the aggregate amount of rent so payable during that year did not exceed the following amount, namely—

(a) where the lease was entered into before 1st April 1963, two-thirds of the letting value of the flat (on the same terms) on the date of the commencement of the lease;

(b) where—

(i) the lease was entered into either on or after 1st April 1963 but before 1st April 1990, or on or after 1st April 1990 in pursuance of a contract made before that date, and

(ii) the flat had a rateable value at the date of the commencement of the lease or else at any time before 1st April 1990,

two-thirds of the rateable value of the flat on the appropriate date; or

(c) in any other case, £1,000 if the flat is in Greater London or £250 if elsewhere.

(2) For the purposes of subsection (1)—

(a) "the initial year", in relation to any lease, means the period of one year beginning with the date of the commencement of the lease;

(b) "the appropriate date" means the date of the commencement of the lease or, if the flat in question did not have a rateable value on that date, the date on which the flat first had a rateable value;

(c) section 25(1), (2) and (4) of the Rent Act 1977 (rateable value etc) shall apply, with any necessary modifications, for the purpose of determining the amount of the rateable value of a flat on a particular date;

(d) "rent" means rent reserved as such, and there shall be disregarded any part of the rent expressed to be payable in consideration of services to be provided, or of repairs, maintenance or insurance to be effected by the landlord, or to be payable in respect of the cost thereof to the landlord under the lease or a superior landlord; and

(e) there shall be disregarded any term of the lease providing for suspension or reduction of rent in the event of damage to property demised, or for any penal addition to the rent in the event of a contravention of or non-compliance with the terms of the lease or an agreement collateral thereto.

(3) In subsection (1)(a) above the reference to letting value shall be construed in like manner as, under the law of England and Wales, the reference to letting value is to be construed where it appears in the proviso to section 4(1) of the Leasehold Reform Act 1967 (meaning of "low rent").

(4) Accordingly, in determining the letting value of a flat at any time for the purposes of subsection (1)(a) above, regard shall be had to whether, and (if so) in what amount, a premium might then have been lawfully demanded as the whole or part of the consideration for the letting.

(5) Where, by virtue of section 7(4), a lease which has been renewed on one or more occasions is to be treated as a long lease for the purposes of this Chapter, then for the purpose of determining under this section whether it is for those purposes a long lease at a low rent—

(a) the lease shall be deemed to have been entered into on the date of the last renewal of the lease; and

(b) that date shall be deemed to be the date of the commencement of the lease.

(6) Subsection (2)(a) above shall have effect in relation to any shared ownership lease falling within section 7(1)(d) as if the reference to the date of commencement of the lease were a reference to the date on which the tenant's total share became 100 per cent; and section 7(7) shall apply for the interpretation of this subsection.

(7) In this section any reference to a flat let under a lease includes a reference to any appurtenant property (within the meaning of section 1) which on the relevant date is let with the flat to the tenant under the lease.

Definitions   For "flat", see s 101(1) (and note also sub-s (7) above); for "lease", see s 101(1), (2); for "shared ownership lease", by virtue of sub-s (6) above, see s 7(7); for "the appropriate date", "the initial year" and "rent", see sub-s (2) above; for "letting value", see sub-s (3) above.
References   See paras 2.20–2.22 ff.

---

9   The reversioner and other relevant landlords for the purpose of this Chapter

(1) Where, in connection with any claim to exercise the right to collective enfranchisement in relation to any premises, it is not proposed to acquire any interests other than—

(a) the freehold of the premises, or

(b) any other interests of the person who owns the freehold of the premises,

that person shall be the reversioner in respect of the premises for the purposes of this Chapter.

(2) Where, in connection with any such claim, it is proposed to acquire interests of persons other than the person who owns the freehold of the premises to which the claim relates, then—

(a) the reversioner in respect of the premises shall for the purposes of this Chapter be the person identified as such by Part I of Schedule 1 to this Act; and

(b) the person who owns the freehold of the premises, and every person who owns any leasehold interest which it is proposed to acquire under or by virtue of section 2(1)(a) or (b), shall be a relevant landlord for those purposes.

(3) Subject to the provisions of Part II of Schedule 1, the reversioner in respect of any premises shall, in a case to which subsection (2) applies, conduct on behalf of all the relevant landlords all proceedings arising out of any notice given with respect to the premises under section 13 (whether the proceedings are for resisting or giving effect to the claim in question).

(4) Schedule 2 (which makes provision with respect to certain special categories of landlords) has effect for the purposes of this Chapter.

Definitions   For "the right to collective enfranchisement", see s 1(1); for "interest", see s 101(1).
References   See para 2.23 ff.

---

10   Premises with a resident landlord

(1) For the purposes of this Chapter any premises falling within section 3(1) are at any time premises with a resident landlord if—
- (a)   the premises are not, and do not form part of, a purpose-built block of flats; and
- (b)   the freeholder, or an adult member of the freeholder's family—
  - (i)   at that time occupies a flat contained in the premises as his only or principal home, and
  - (ii)   has so occupied such a flat throughout a period of not less than twelve months ending with that time.

(2) Where any premises falling within section 3(1) would at any time ("the relevant time") be premises with a resident landlord but for the fact that subsection (1)(b)(ii) above does not apply, the premises shall nevertheless be treated for the purposes of this Chapter as being at that time premises with a resident landlord if—
- (a)   immediately before the date when the freeholder acquired his interest in the premises the premises were (or, had this Chapter then been in force, would have been) such premises for the purposes of this Chapter; and
- (b)   the freeholder, or an adult member of the freeholder's family—
  - (i)   entered into occupation of a flat contained in the premises within the period of 28 days beginning with that date, and
  - (ii)   has occupied such a flat as his only or principal home throughout the period beginning with the time when he so entered into occupation and ending with the relevant time.

(3) In paragraph (b) of each of subsections (1) and (2) any reference to a flat includes a reference to a unit (other than a flat) which is used as a dwelling.

(4) Where the freehold interest in any premises is held on trust, subsections (1) and (2) shall apply as if, in paragraph (b) of each of those subsections, any reference to the freeholder were instead a reference to a person having an interest under the trust (whether or not also a trustee).

(5) For the purposes of this section a person is an adult member of another's family if that person is—
- (a)   the other's wife or husband; or
- (b)   a son or daughter or a son-in-law or daughter-in-law of the other, or of the other's wife or husband, who has attained the age of 18; or

(c) the father or mother of the other, or of the other's wife or husband;
and in paragraph (b) any reference to a person's son or daughter includes a reference
to any stepson or stepdaughter of that person, and "son-in-law" and "daughter-in-
law" shall be construed accordingly.

(6) In this section—
"the freeholder", in relation to any premises, means the person who owns the
freehold of the premises;
"purpose-built block of flats" means a building which as constructed
contained two or more flats.

Definitions For "dwelling", "flat" and "interest", see s 101(1); for "the relevant time", see sub-s (2)
above; as to "adult member of ... family", see sub-s (5) above; for "the freeholder" and "purpose-built
block of flats", see sub-s (6) above.
References See paras 2.12–2.14 ff.

Preliminary inquiries by tenants

11 Right of qualifying tenant to obtain information about superior interests etc

(1) A qualifying tenant of a flat may give—
(a) to his immediate landlord, or
(b) to any person receiving rent on behalf of his immediate landlord,
a notice requiring the recipient to give the tenant (so far as known to the recipient)
the name and address of the person who owns the freehold of the relevant premises
and the name and address of every other person who has an interest to which
subsection (2) applies.

(2) In relation to a qualifying tenant of a flat, this subsection applies to the
following interests, namely—
(a) the freehold of any property not contained in the relevant premises—
(i) which is demised by the lease held by the tenant, or
(ii) which the tenant is entitled under the terms of his lease to use in
common with other persons; and
(b) any leasehold interest in the relevant premises or in any such property
which is superior to that of the tenant's immediate landlord.

(3) Any qualifying tenant of a flat may give to the person who owns the
freehold of the relevant premises a notice requiring him to give the tenant (so far as
known to him) the name and address of every person, apart from the tenant, who
is—
(a) a tenant of the whole of the relevant premises, or
(b) a tenant or licensee of any separate set or sets of premises contained in the
relevant premises, or
(c) a tenant or licensee of the whole or any part of any common parts so
contained or of any property not so contained—
(i) which is demised by the lease held by a qualifying tenant of a flat
contained in the relevant premises, or
(ii) which any such qualifying tenant is entitled under the terms of his
lease to use in common with other persons.

(4) Any such qualifying tenant may also give
(a) to the person who owns the freehold of the relevant premises, or

(b) to any person falling within subsection (3)(a), (b) or (c),

a notice requiring him to give the tenant—

    (i) such information relating to his interest in the relevant premises or (as the case may be) in any such property as is mentioned in subsection (3)(c), or

    (ii) (so far as known to him) such information relating to any interest derived (whether directly or indirectly) out of that interest,

as is specified in the notice, where the information is reasonably required by the tenant in connection with the making of a claim to exercise the right to collective enfranchisement in relation to the whole or part of the relevant premises.

(5) Where a notice is given by a qualifying tenant under subsection (4), the following rights shall be exercisable by him in relation to the recipient of the notice, namely—

    (a) a right, on giving reasonable notice, to be provided with a list of documents to which subsection (6) applies;

    (b) a right to inspect, at any reasonable time and on giving reasonable notice, any documents to which that subsection applies; and

    (c) a right, on payment of a reasonable fee, to be provided with a copy of any documents which are contained in any list provided under paragraph (a) or have been inspected under paragraph (b).

(6) This subsection applies to any document in the custody or under the control of the recipient of the notice under subsection 4—

    (a) sight of which is reasonably required by the qualifying tenant in connection with the making of such a claim as is mentioned in that subsection; and

    (b) which, on a proposed sale by a willing seller to a willing buyer of the recipient's interest in the relevant premises or (as the case may be) in any such property as is mentioned in subsection (3)(c), the seller would be expected to make available to the buyer (whether at or before contract or completion).

(7) Any person who—

    (a) is required by a notice under any of subsections (1) to (4) to give any information to a qualifying tenant, or

    (b) is required by a qualifying tenant under subsection (5) to supply any list of documents, to permit the inspection of any documents or to supply a copy of any documents,

shall comply with that requirement within the period of 28 days beginning with the date of the giving of the notice referred to in paragraph (a) or (as the case may be) with the date of the making of the requirement referred to in paragraph (b).

(8) Where—

    (a) a person has received a notice under subsection (4), and

    (b) within the period of six months beginning with the date of receipt of the notice, he—

        (i) disposes of any interest (whether legal or equitable) in the relevant premises otherwise than by the creation of an interest by way of security for a loan, or

        (ii) acquires any such interest (otherwise than by way of security for a loan),

then (unless that disposal or acquisition has already been notified to the qualifying tenant in accordance with subsection (7)) he shall notify the qualifying tenant of that disposal or acquisition within the period of 28 days beginning with the date when it occurred.

(9) In this section—

"document" has the same meaning as in Part I of the Civil Evidence Act 1968;

"the relevant premises", in relation to any qualifying tenant of a flat, means—

(a) if the person who owns the freehold interest in the flat owns the freehold of the whole of the building in which the flat is contained, that building, or

(b) if that person owns the freehold of part only of that building, that part of that building;

and any reference to an interest in the relevant premises includes an interest in part of those premises.

Definitions   For "the right to collective enfranchisement", see s 1(1); for "qualifying tenant", see s 5; for "common parts", "disposal", "flat" and "interest", see s 101(1); for "lease" and related expressions, see s 101(1), (2); for "document" and "the relevant premises", see sub-s (9).
References   See paras 3.1–3.7 ff.

12 Right of qualifying tenant to obtain information about other matters

(1) Any notice given by a qualifying tenant under section 11(4) shall, in addition to any other requirement imposed in accordance with that provision, require the recipient to give the tenant—

(a) the information specified in subsection (2) below; and

(b) (so far as known to the recipient) the information specified in subsection (3) below.

(2) The information referred to in subsection (1)(a) is—

(a) whether the recipient has received in respect of any premises containing the tenant's flat—

(i) a notice under section 13 in the case of which the relevant claim is still current, or

(ii) a copy of such a notice; and

(b) if so, the date on which the notice under section 13 was given and the name and address of the nominee purchaser for the time being appointed for the purposes of section 15 in relation to that claim.

(3) The information referred to in subsection (1)(b) is—

(a) whether the tenant's flat is comprised in any property in the case of which any of paragraphs (a) to (d) of section 31(2) is applicable; and

(b) if paragraph (b) or (d) of that provision is applicable, the date of the application in question.

(4) Where—

(a) within the period of six months beginning with the date of receipt of a notice given by a tenant under section 11(4), the recipient of the notice receives in respect of any premises containing the tenant's flat—

(i) a notice under section 13, or

(ii) a copy of such a notice, and

(b) the tenant is not one of the qualifying tenants by whom the notice under section 13 is given,

the recipient shall, within the period of 28 days beginning with the date of receipt of the notice under section 13 or (as the case may be) the copy, notify the tenant of the date on which the notice was given and of the name and address of the nominee purchaser for the time being appointed for the purposes of section 15 in relation to the relevant claim.

(5) Where—

(a) the recipient of a notice given by a tenant under section 11(4) has, in accordance with subsection (1) above, informed the tenant of any such application as is referred to in subsection (3)(b) above; and

(b) within the period of six months beginning with the date of receipt of the notice, the application is either granted or refused by the Commissioners of Inland Revenue or is withdrawn by the applicant,

the recipient shall, within the period of 28 days beginning with the date of the granting, refusal or withdrawal of the application, notify the tenant that it has been granted, refused or withdrawn.

(6) In this section "the relevant claim", in relation to a notice under section 13, means the claim in respect of which that notice is given; and for the purposes of subsection (2) above any such claim is current if—

(a) that notice continues in force in accordance with section 13(11), or

(b) a binding contract entered into in pursuance of that notice remains in force, or

(c) where an order has been made under section 24(4)(a) or (b) or 25(6)(a) or (b) with respect to any such premises as are referred to in subsection (2)(a) above, any interests which by virtue of the order fall to be vested in the nominee purchaser have yet to be so vested.

Definitions   For "qualifying tenant", see s 5; for "the nominee purchaser", see s 15; for "flat" and "interest", see s 101(1); for "tenant", see s 101(2); for "the relevant claim", see sub-s (6) above.
References   See para 3.4 ff.

The initial notice

13 Notice by qualifying tenants of claim to exercise right

(1) A claim to exercise the right to collective enfranchisement with respect to any premises is made by the giving of notice of the claim under this section.

(2) A notice given under this section ("the initial notice")—

(a) must be given to the reversioner in respect of those premises; and

(b) must be given by a number of qualifying tenants of flats contained in the premises as at the relevant date which—

(i) is not less than two-thirds of the total number of such tenants, and

(ii) is not less than one-half of the total number of flats so contained;

and not less than one-half of the qualifying tenants by whom the notice is given must satisfy the residence condition.

(3) The initial notice must—

(a) specify and be accompanied by a plan showing—

(i) the premises of which the freehold is proposed to be acquired by virtue of section 1(1),

(ii) any property of which the freehold is proposed to be acquired by virtue of section 1(2)(a), and

(iii) any property of the person who owns the freehold of the specified premises over which it is proposed that rights (specified in the notice) should be granted by him in connection with the acquisition of the freehold of the specified premises or of any such property so far as falling within section 1(3)(a);

(b) contain a statement of the grounds on which it is claimed that the specified premises are, on the relevant date, premises to which this Chapter applies;

(c) specify—
  (i) any leasehold interest proposed to be acquired under or by virtue of section 2(1)(a) or (b), and
  (ii) any flats or other units contained in the specified premises in relation to which it is considered that any of the requirements in Part II of Schedule 9 to this Act are applicable;

(d) specify the proposed purchase price for each of the following, namely—
  (i) the freehold interest in the specified premises,
  (ii) the freehold interest in any property specified under paragraph (a)(ii), and
  (iii) any leasehold interest specified under paragraph (c)(i);

(e) state the full names of all the qualifying tenants of flats contained in the specified premises and the addresses of their flats, and contain the following particulars in relation to each of those tenants, namely—
  (i) such particulars of his lease as are sufficient to identify it, including the date on which the lease was entered into, the term for which it was granted and the date of the commencement of the term,
  (ii) such further particulars as are necessary to show that the lease is a lease at a low rent, and
  (iii) if it is claimed that he satisfies the residence condition, particulars of the period or periods falling within the preceding ten years for which he has occupied the whole or part of his flat as his only or principal home;

(f) state the full name or names of the person or persons appointed as the nominee purchaser for the purposes of section 15, and an address in England and Wales at which notices may be given to that person or those persons under this Chapter; and

(g) specify the date by which the reversioner must respond to the notice by giving a counter-notice under section 21.

(4) In a case where the tenant's lease is held by joint tenants, subsection (3)(e)(iii) shall have effect as if any reference to the tenant were a reference to any joint tenant by virtue of whose occupation of the flat in question it is claimed that the residence condition is satisfied.

(5) The date specified in the initial notice in pursuance of subsection (3)(g) must be a date falling not less than two months after the relevant date.

(6) A notice shall not be given under this section with respect to any premises unless the qualifying tenants by whom it is given have obtained a valuation prepared by a qualified surveyor in respect of—

(a) the freehold interest in the specified premises,
(b) the freehold interest in any property specified under subsection (3)(a)(ii), and
(c) any leasehold interest specified under subsection (3)(c)(i),

and any such notice must contain a statement confirming that they have done so and state the name of the surveyor in question.

(7) For the purposes of subsection (6) a person is a qualified surveyor if—

    (a) he is a fellow or professional associate of the Royal Institution of Chartered Surveyors or of the Incorporated Society of Valuers and Auctioneers or satisfies such other requirement or requirements as may be prescribed by regulations made by the Secretary of State; and

    (b) he is reasonably believed by the qualifying tenants to have ability in, and experience of, the valuation of premises of the particular kind, and in the particular area, in question;

and any valuation prepared for the purposes of that subsection must be prepared in conformity with the provisions of Schedule 6 so far as relating to the determination of the price payable under this Chapter for the interest in question.

(8) Where any premises have been specified in a notice under this section, no subsequent notice which specifies the whole or part of those premises may be given under this section so long as the earlier notice continues in force.

(9) Where any premises have been specified in a notice under this section and—

    (a) that notice has been withdrawn, or is deemed to have been withdrawn, under or by virtue of any provision of this Chapter or under section 74(3), or

    (b) in response to that notice, an order has been applied for and obtained under section 23(1),

no subsequent notice which specifies the whole or part of those premises may be given under this section within the period of twelve months beginning with the date of the withdrawal or deemed withdrawal of the earlier notice or with the time when the order under section 23(1) becomes final (as the case may be).

(10) In subsections (8) and (9) any reference to a notice which specifies the whole or part of any premises includes a reference to a notice which specifies any premises which contain the whole or part of those premises; and in those subsections and this "specifies" means specifies under subsection (3)(a)(i).

(11) Where a notice is given in accordance with this section, then for the purposes of this Chapter the notice continues in force as from the relevant date—

    (a) until a binding contract is entered into in pursuance of the notice, or an order is made under section 24(4)(a) or (b) or 25(6)(a) or (b) providing for the vesting of interests in the nominee purchaser;

    (b) if the notice is withdrawn or deemed to have been withdrawn under or by virtue of any provision of this Chapter or under section 74(3), until the date of the withdrawal or deemed withdrawal, or

    (c) until such other time as the notice ceases to have effect by virtue of any provision of this Chapter.

(12) In this Chapter "the specified premises", in relation to a claim made under this Chapter, means—

    (a) the premises specified in the initial notice under subsection (3)(a)(i), or

    (b) if it is subsequently agreed or determined under this Chapter that any less extensive premises should be acquired in pursuance of the notice in satisfaction of the claim, those premises;

and similarly references to any property or interest specified in the initial notice under subsection (3)(a)(ii) or (c)(i) shall, if it is subsequently agreed or determined under this Chapter that any less extensive property or interest should be acquired in pursuance of the notice, be read as references to that property or interest.

(13) Schedule 3 to this Act (which contains restrictions on participating in the exercise of the right to collective enfranchisement, and makes further provision in connection with the giving of notices under this section) shall have effect.

Definitions   For "the right to collective enfranchisement", see s 1(1); for "the relevant date", see s 1(8); for "qualifying tenant", see s 5; for "lease at a low rent", see s 8; for "the reversioner", see s 9; for "the nominee purchaser", see s 15; for "flat" and "interest", see s 101(1); for "lease" and related expressions, see s 101(1), (2); for "the initial notice", see sub-s (2) above; as to "qualified surveyor", see sub-s (7) above; for "specifies", see sub-s (10) above; for "the specified premises", sub-s (12) above. **References**   See paras 2.47–2.49, 3.10–3.32 ff.

Participating tenants and nominee purchaser

14 The participating tenants

(1) In relation to any claim to exercise the right to collective enfranchisement, the participating tenants are (subject to the provisions of this section and Part I of Schedule 3) the following persons, namely—

    (a) in relation to the relevant date, the qualifying tenants by whom the initial notice is given; and

    (b) in relation to any time falling after that date, such of those qualifying tenants as for the time being remain qualifying tenants of flats contained in the specified premises.

(2) Where the lease by virtue of which a participating tenant is a qualifying tenant of his flat is assigned to another person, the assignee of the lease shall, within the period of 14 days beginning with the date of the assignment, notify the nominee purchaser—

    (a) of the assignment, and

    (b) as to whether or not the assignee is electing to participate in the proposed acquisition.

(3) Where a qualifying tenant of a flat contained in the specified premises—

    (a) is not one of the persons by whom the initial notice was given, and

    (b) is not such an assignee of the lease of a participating tenant as is mentioned in subsection (2),

then (subject to paragraph 8 of Schedule 3) he may elect to participate in the proposed acquisition, but only with the agreement of all the persons who are for the time being participating tenants; and, if he does so elect, he shall notify the nominee purchaser forthwith of his election.

(4) Where a person notifies the nominee purchaser under subsection (2) or (3) of his election to participate in the proposed acquisition, he shall be regarded as a participating tenant for the purposes of this Chapter—

    (a) as from the date of the assignment or agreement referred to in that subsection; and

    (b) so long as he remains a qualifying tenant of a flat contained in the specified premises.

(5) Where a participating tenant dies, his personal representatives shall, within the period of 56 days beginning with the date of death, notify the nominee purchaser—

(a) of the death of the tenant, and

(b) as to whether or not the personal representatives are electing to withdraw from participation in the proposed acquisition;

and, unless the personal representatives of a participating tenant so notify the nominee purchaser that they are electing to withdraw from participation in that acquisition, they shall be regarded as a participating tenant for the purposes of this Chapter—

(i) as from the date of the death of the tenant, and

(ii) so long as his lease remains vested in them.

(6) Where in accordance with subsection (4) or (5) any assignee or personal representatives of a participating tenant ("the tenant") is or are to be regarded as a participating tenant for the purposes of this Chapter, any arrangements made between the nominee purchaser and the participating tenants and having effect immediately before the date of the assignment or (as the case may be) the date of death shall have effect as from that date—

(a) with such modifications as are necessary for substituting the assignee or (as the case may be) the personal representatives as a party to the arrangements in the place of the tenant; or

(b) in the case of an assignment by a person who remains a qualifying tenant of a flat contained in the specified premises, with such modifications as are necessary for adding the assignee as a party to the arrangements.

(7) Where the nominee purchaser receives a notification under subsection (2), (3) or (5), he shall, within the period of 28 days beginning with the date of receipt of the notification—

(a) give a notice under subsection (8) to the reversioner in respect of the specified premises, and

(b) give a copy of that notice to every other relevant landlord.

(8) A notice under this subsection is a notice stating—

(a) in the case of a notification under subsection (2)—

(i) the date of the assignment and the name and address of the assignee,

(ii) that the assignee has or (as the case may be) has not become a participating tenant in accordance with subsection (4), and

(iii) if he has become a participating tenant (otherwise than in a case to which subsection (6)(b) applies), that he has become such a tenant in place of his assignor;

(b) in the case of a notification under subsection (3), the name and address of the person who has become a participating tenant in accordance with subsection (4); and

(c) in the case of a notification under subsection (5)—

(i) the date of death of the deceased tenant,

(ii) the names and addresses of the personal representatives of the tenant, and

(iii) that in accordance with that subsection those persons are or (as the case may be) are not to be regarded as a participating tenant.

(9) Every notice under subsection (8)—

(a) shall identify the flat with respect to which it is given; and

(b) if it states that any person or persons is or are to be regarded as a participating tenant, shall be signed by the person or persons in question.

(10) In this section references to assignment include an assent by personal representatives and assignment by operation of law, where the assignment is—

    (a) to a trustee in bankruptcy, or

    (b) to a mortgagee under section 89(2) of the Law of Property Act 1925 (foreclosure of leasehold mortgage),

and references to an assignee shall be construed accordingly.

(11) Nothing in this section has effect for requiring or authorising anything to be done at any time after a binding contract is entered into in pursuance of the initial notice.

Definitions   For "the right to collective enfranchisement", see s 1(1); for "the relevant date", see s 1(8); for "qualifying tenant", see s 5; for "the initial notice", see s 13 ; for "the specified premises", see s 13(12); for "the nominee purchaser", see s 15; for "flat", see s 101(1); for "lease" and related expressions, see s 101(1), (2); as to "assignment", see sub-s (10) above.

References   See paras 2.33–2.40 ff.

---

15 The nominee purchaser: appointment and replacement

(1) The nominee purchaser shall conduct on behalf of the participating tenants all proceedings arising out of the initial notice, with a view to the eventual acquisition by him, on their behalf, of such freehold and other interests as fall to be so acquired under a contract entered into in pursuance of that notice.

(2) In relation to any claim to exercise the right to collective enfranchisement with respect to any premises, the nominee purchaser shall be such person or persons as may for the time being be appointed for the purposes of this section by the participating tenants; and in the first instance the nominee purchaser shall be the person or persons specified in the initial notice in pursuance of section 13(3)(f).

(3) The appointment of any person as the nominee purchaser, or as one of the persons constituting the nominee purchaser, may be terminated by the participating tenants by the giving of a notice stating that that person's appointment is to terminate on the date on which the notice is given.

(4) Any such notice must be given—

    (a) to the person whose appointment is being terminated, and

    (b) to the reversioner in respect of the specified premises.

(5) Any such notice must in addition either—

    (a) specify the name or names of the person or persons constituting the nominee purchaser as from the date of the giving of the notice, and an address in England and Wales at which notices may be given to that person or those persons under this Chapter; or

    (b) state that the following particulars will be contained in a further notice given to the reversioner within the period of 28 days beginning with that date, namely—

        (i) the name of the person or persons for the time being constituting the nominee purchaser,

        (ii) if falling after that date, the date of appointment of that person or of each of those persons, and

        (iii) an address in England and Wales at which notices may be given to that person or those persons under this Chapter;

and the appointment of any person by way of replacement for the person whose appointment is being terminated shall not be valid unless his name is specified, or is one of those specified, under paragraph (a) or (b).

(6) Where the appointment of any person is terminated in accordance with this section, anything done by or in relation to the nominee purchaser before the date of termination of that person's appointment shall be treated, so far as necessary for the purpose of continuing its effect, as having been done by or in relation to the nominee purchaser as constituted on or after that date.

(7) Where the appointment of any person is so terminated, he shall not be liable under section 33 for any costs incurred in connection with the proposed acquisition under this Chapter at any time after the date of termination of his appointment; but if—

(a) at any such time he is requested by the nominee purchaser for the time being to supply to the nominee purchaser, at an address in England and Wales specified in the request, all or any documents in his custody or under his control that relate to that acquisition, and

(b) he fails without reasonable cause to comply with any such request or is guilty of any unreasonable delay in complying with it,

he shall be liable for any costs which are incurred by the nominee purchaser, or for which the nominee purchaser is liable under section 33, in consequence of the failure.

(8) Where—

(a) two or more persons together constitute the nominee purchaser, and

(b) the appointment of any (but not both or all) of them is terminated in accordance with this section without any person being appointed by way of immediate replacement,

the person or persons remaining shall for the time being constitute the nominee purchaser.

(9) Where—

(a) a notice given under subsection (3) contains such a statement as is mentioned in subsection (5)(b), and

(b) as a result of the termination of the appointment in question there is no nominee purchaser for the time being,

the running of any period which—

(i) is prescribed by or under this Part for the giving of any other notice or the making of any application, and

(ii) would otherwise expire during the period beginning with the date of the giving of the notice under subsection (3) and ending with the date when the particulars specified in subsection (5)(b) are notified to the reversioner,

shall (subject to subsection (10)) be suspended throughout the period mentioned in paragraph (ii).

(10) If—

(a) the circumstances are as mentioned in subsection (9)(a) and (b), but

(b) the particulars specified in subsection (5)(b) are not notified to the reversioner within the period of 28 days specified in that provision,

the initial notice shall be deemed to have been withdrawn at the end of that period.

(11) A copy of any notice given under subsection (3) or (5)(b) shall be given by the participating tenants to every relevant landlord (other than the reversioner) to whom the initial notice or a copy of it was given in accordance with section 13 and Part II of Schedule 3; and, where a notice under subsection (3) terminates the

appointment of a person who is one of two or more persons together constituting the nominee purchaser, a copy of the notice shall also be so given to every other person included among those persons.

(12) Nothing in this section applies in relation to the termination of the appointment of the nominee purchaser (or of any of the persons constituting the nominee purchaser) at any time after a binding contract is entered into in pursuance of the initial notice; and in this Chapter references to the nominee purchaser, so far as referring to anything done by or in relation to the nominee purchaser at any time falling after such a contract is so entered into, are references to the person or persons constituting the nominee purchaser at the time when the contract is entered into or such other person as is for the time being the purchaser under the contract.

Definitions   For "the right to collective enfranchisement", see s 1(1); for "relevant landlord" and "the reversioner", see s 9; for "the initial notice", see s 13; for "the specified premises", see s 13(12); for "the participating tenants", see s 14.
References   See paras 2.41, 2.42, 2.44–2.46 ff.

16   The nominee purchaser: retirement or death

(1) The appointment of any person as the nominee purchaser, or as one of the persons constituting the nominee purchaser, may be terminated by that person by the giving of a notice stating that he is resigning his appointment with effect from 21 days after the date of the notice.

(2) Any such notice must be given—
    (a)   to each of the participating tenants; and
    (b)   to the reversioner in respect of the specified premises.

(3) Where the participating tenants have received any such notice, they shall, within the period of 56 days beginning with the date of the notice, give to the reversioner a notice informing him of the resignation and containing the following particulars, namely—
    (a)   the name or names of the person or persons for the time being constituting the nominee purchaser,
    (b)   if falling after that date, the date of appointment of that person or of each of those persons, and
    (c)   an address in England and Wales at which notices may be given to that person or those persons under this Chapter;
and the appointment of any person by way of replacement for the person resigning his appointment shall not be valid unless his name is specified, or is one of those specified, under paragraph (a).

(4) Subsections (6) to (8) of section 15 shall have effect in connection with a person's resignation of his appointment in accordance with this section as they have effect in connection with the termination of a person's appointment in accordance with that section.

(5) Where the person, or one of the persons, constituting the nominee purchaser dies, the participating tenants shall, within the period of 56 days beginning with the date of death, give to the reversioner a notice informing him of the death and containing the following particulars, namely—
    (a)   the name or names of the person or persons for the time being constituting the nominee purchaser,
    (b)   if falling after that date, the date of appointment of that person or of each

and the appointment of any person by way of replacement for the person who has died shall not be valid unless his name is specified, or is one of those specified, under paragraph (a).

(6) Subsections (6) and (8) of section 15 shall have effect in connection with the death of any such person as they have effect in connection with the termination of a person's appointment in accordance with that section.

(7) If—

    (a) the participating tenants are required to give a notice under subsection (3) or (5), and

    (b) as a result of the resignation or death referred to in that subsection there is no nominee purchaser for the time being,

the running of any period which—

    (i) is prescribed by or under this Part for the giving of any other notice or the making of any application, and

    (ii) would otherwise expire during the period beginning with the relevant date and ending with the date when the particulars specified in that subsection are notified to the reversioner,

shall (subject to subsection (8)) be suspended throughout the period mentioned in paragraph (ii); and for this purpose "the relevant date" means the date of the notice of resignation under subsection (1) or the date of death (as the case may be).

(8) If—

    (a) the circumstances are as mentioned in subsection (7)(a) and (b), but

    (b) the participating tenants fail to give a notice under subsection (3) or (as the case may be) subsection (5) within the period of 56 days specified in that subsection,

the initial notice shall be deemed to have been withdrawn at the end of that period.

(9) Where a notice under subsection (1) is given by a person who is one of two or more persons together constituting the nominee purchaser, a copy of the notice shall be given by him to every other person included among those persons; and a copy of any notice given under subsection (3) or (5) shall be given by the participating tenants to every relevant landlord (other than the reversioner) to whom the initial notice or a copy of it was given in accordance with section 13 and Part II of Schedule 3.

(10) Nothing in this section applies in relation to the resignation or death of the nominee purchaser (or any of the persons together constituting the nominee purchaser) at any time after a binding contract is entered into in pursuance of the initial notice.

Definitions   For "the reversioner", see s 9; for "the initial notice", see s 13; for "the specified premises", see s 13(12); for "the participating tenants", see s 14; for "the nominee purchaser", see s 15; for "the relevant date", see sub-s (7) above.
References   See paras 2.43–2.46 ff.

Procedure following giving of initial notice

17 Access by relevant landlords for valuation purposes

(1) Once the initial notice or a copy of it has been given in accordance with section 13 or Part II of Schedule 3 to the reversioner or to any other relevant landlord, that person and any person authorised to act on his behalf shall, in the case of—

(a) any part of the specified premises, or

(b) any part of any property specified in the notice under section 13(3)(a)(ii), in which he has a freehold or leasehold interest which is included in the proposed acquisition by the nominee purchaser, have a right of access thereto for the purpose of enabling him to obtain a valuation of that interest in connection with the notice.

(2) Once the initial notice has been given in accordance with section 13, the nominee purchaser and any person authorised to act on his behalf shall have a right of access to—

(a) any part of the specified premises, or

(b) any part of any property specified in the notice under section 13(3)(a)(ii), where such access is reasonably required by the nominee purchaser in connection with any matter arising out of the notice.

(3) A right of access conferred by this section shall be exercisable at any reasonable time and on giving not less than 10 days' notice to the occupier of any premises to which access is sought (or, if those premises are unoccupied, to the person entitled to occupy them).

Definitions For "relevant landlord" and "the reversioner", see s 9; for "the initial notice", see s 13; for "the specified premises", see s 13(12); for "the nominee purchaser", see s 15; as to "proposed acquisition by the nominee purchaser", see s 38(2); as to an interest of a relevant landlord in the specified premises, see s 38(3); for "interest", see s 101(1).
References See para 3.28 ff.

---

18 Duty of nominee purchaser to disclose existence of agreements affecting specified premises etc

(1) If at any time during the period beginning with the relevant date and ending with the valuation date for the purposes of Schedule 6—

(a) there subsists between the nominee purchaser and a person other than a participating tenant any agreement (of whatever nature) providing for the disposal of a relevant interest, or

(b) if the nominee purchaser is a company, any person other than a participating tenant holds any share in that company by virtue of which a relevant interest may be acquired,

the existence of that agreement or shareholding shall be notified to the reversioner by the nominee purchaser as soon as possible after the agreement or shareholding is made or established or, if in existence on the relevant date, as soon as possible after that date.

(2) If—

(a) the nominee purchaser is required to give any notification under subsection (1) but fails to do so before the price payable to the reversioner or any other relevant landlord in respect of the acquisition of any interest of his by the nominee purchaser is determined for the purposes of Schedule 6, and

(b) it may reasonably be assumed that, had the nominee purchaser given the notification, it would have resulted in the price so determined being increased by an amount referable to the existence of any agreement or shareholding falling within subsection (1)(a) or (b),

the nominee purchaser and the participating tenants shall be jointly and severally liable to pay the amount to the reversioner or (as the case may be) the other relevant landlord.

(3) In subsection (1) "relevant interest" means any interest in, or in any part of the specified premises or any property specified in the initial notice under section 13(3)(a)(ii).

(4) Paragraph (a) of subsection (1) does not, however, apply to an agreement if the only disposal of such an interest for which it provides is one consisting in the creation of an interest by way of security for a loan.

Definitions   For "relevant landlord" and "the reversioner", see s 9; for "the initial notice", see s 13; for "the specified premises", see s 13(12); for "participating tenants", see s 14; for "the nominee purchaser", see s 15; for "disposal" and "interest", see s 101(1); for "relevant interest", see sub-s (3) above.
References   See paras 3.29, 3.30 ff.

19   Effect of initial notice as respects subsequent transactions by freeholder etc

(1) Where the initial notice has been registered in accordance with section 97(1), then so long as it continues in force—

   (a) the person who owns the freehold of the specified premises shall not—

      (i) make any disposal severing his interest in those premises or in any property specified in the notice under section 13(3)(a)(ii), or

      (ii) grant out of that interest any lease under which, if it had been granted before the relevant date, the interest of the tenant would to any extent have been liable on that date to acquisition by virtue of section 2(1)(a) or (b); and

   (b) no other relevant landlord shall grant out of his interest in the specified premises or in any property so specified any such lease as is mentioned in paragraph (a)(ii);

and any transaction shall be void to the extent that it purports to effect any such disposal or any such grant of a lease as is mentioned in paragraph (a) or (b).

(2) Where the initial notice has been so registered and at any time when it continues in force—

   (a) the person who owns the freehold of the specified premises disposes of his interest in those premises or in any property specified in the notice under section 13(3)(a)(ii), or

   (b) any other relevant landlord disposes of any interest of his specified in the notice under section 13(3)(c)(i),

subsection (3) below shall apply in relation to that disposal.

(3) Where this subsection applies in relation to any such disposal as is mentioned in subsection (2)(a) or (b), all parties shall for the purposes of this Chapter be in the same position as if the person acquiring the interest under the disposal—

   (a) had become its owner before the initial notice was given (and was accordingly a relevant landlord in place of the person making the disposal), and

   (b) had been given any notice or copy of a notice given under this Chapter to that person, and

   (c) had taken all steps which that person had taken;

and, if any subsequent disposal of that interest takes place at any time when the initial notice continues in force, this subsection shall apply in relation to that disposal as if any reference to the person making the disposal included any predecessor in title of his.

(4) Where immediately before the relevant date there is in force a binding contract relating to the disposal to any extent—

(a) by the person who owns the freehold of the specified premises, or

(b) by any other relevant landlord,

of any interest of his falling within subsection (2)(a) or (b), then, so long as the initial notice continues in force, the operation of the contract shall be suspended so far as it relates to any such disposal.

(5) Where—

(a) the operation of a contract has been suspended under subsection (4) ("the suspended contract"), and

(b) a binding contract is entered into in pursuance of the initial notice,

then (without prejudice to the general law as to the frustration of contracts) the person referred to in paragraph (a) or (b) of that subsection shall, together with all other persons, be discharged from the further performance of the suspended contract so far as it relates to any such disposal as is mentioned in subsection (4).

(6) In subsections (4) and (5) any reference to a contract (except in the context of such a contract as is mentioned in subsection (5)(b)) includes a contract made in pursuance of an order of any court; but those subsections do not apply to any contract providing for the eventuality of a notice being given under section 13 in relation to the whole or part of the property in which any such interest as is referred to in subsection (4) subsists.

Definitions   For "the relevant date", see s 1(8); for "relevant landlord", see s 9; for "the initial notice", see s 13; for "the specified premises", see s 13(12); for "disposal" and "interest", see s 101(1); for "lease" and related expressions, see s 101(1), (2); for "the suspended contract", see sub-s (5) above.
References   See paras 2.26, 2.27, 3.27 ff.

---

20 Right of reversioner to require evidence of tenant's right to participate

(1) The reversioner in respect of the specified premises may, within the period of 21 days beginning with the relevant date, give the nominee purchaser a notice requiring him, in the case of any person by whom the initial notice was given, to deduce the title of that person to the lease by virtue of which it is claimed that he is a qualifying tenant of a flat contained in the specified premises.

(2) The nominee purchaser shall comply with any such requirement within the period of 21 days beginning with the date of the giving of the notice.

(3) Where—

(a) the nominee purchaser fails to comply with a requirement under subsection (1) in the case of any person within the period mentioned in subsection (2), and

(b) the initial notice would not have been given in accordance with section 13(2)(b) if—

(i) that person, and

(ii) any other person in the case of whom a like failure by the nominee purchaser has occurred,

had been neither included among the persons who gave the notice nor included among the qualifying tenants of the flats referred to in that provision,

the initial notice shall be deemed to have been withdrawn at the end of that period.

Definitions For "the relevant date", see s 1(8); for "qualifying tenant", see s 5; for "the reversioner", see s 9; for "the initial notice", see s 13; for "the specified premises", see s 13(12); for "the nominee purchaser", see s 15; for "flat", see s 101(1); for "lease" and related expressions, see s 101(1), (2).
References See para 3.31 ff.

21 Reversioner's counter-notice

(1) The reversioner in respect of the specified premises shall give a counter-notice under this section to the nominee purchaser by the date specified in the initial notice in pursuance of section 13(3)(g).

(2) The counter-notice must comply with one of the following requirements, namely—

(a) state that the reversioner admits that the participating tenants were on the relevant date entitled to exercise the right to collective enfranchisement in relation to the specified premises;

(b) state that, for such reasons as are specified in the counter-notice, the reversioner does not admit that the participating tenants were so entitled;

(c) contain such a statement as is mentioned in paragraph (a) or (b) above but state that an application for an order under subsection (1) of section 23 is to be made by such appropriate landlord (within the meaning of that section) as is specified in the counter-notice, on the grounds that he intends to redevelop the whole or a substantial part of the specified premises.

(3) If the counter-notice complies with the requirement set out in subsection (2)(a), it must in addition—

(a) state which (if any) of the proposals contained in the initial notice are accepted by the reversioner and which (if any) of those proposals are not so accepted, and specify—

(i) in relation to any proposal which is not so accepted, the reversioner's counter-proposal, and

(ii) any additional leaseback proposals by the reversioner;

(b) if (in a case where any property specified in the initial notice under section 13(3)(a)(ii) is property falling within section 1(3)(b)) any such counter-proposal relates to the grant of rights or the disposal of any freehold interest in pursuance of section 1(4), specify—

(i) the nature of those rights and the property over which it is proposed to grant them, or

(ii) the property in respect of which it is proposed to dispose of any such interest,

as the case may be;

(c) state which interests (if any) the nominee purchaser is to be required to acquire in accordance with subsection (4) below;

(d) state which rights (if any) the person who owns the freehold of the specified premises, or any other relevant landlord, desires to retain—

(i) over any property in which he has any interest which is included in the proposed acquisition by the nominee purchaser, or

(ii) over any property in which he has any interest which the nominee purchaser is to be required to acquire in accordance with subsection (4) below,

on the grounds that the rights are necessary for the proper management or maintenance of property in which he is to retain a freehold or leasehold interest; and

(e) include a description of any provisions which the reversioner or any other relevant landlord considers should be included in any conveyance to the nominee purchaser in accordance with section 34 and Schedule 7.

(4) The nominee purchaser may be required to acquire on behalf of the participating tenants the interest in any property of the person who owns the freehold of the specified premises or of any other relevant landlord, if the property—

(a) would for all practical purposes cease to be of use and benefit to him, or

(b) would cease to be capable of being reasonably managed or maintained by him,

in the event of his interest in the specified premises or (as the case may be) in any other property being acquired by the nominee purchaser under this Chapter.

(5) Where a counter-notice specifies any interest in pursuance of subsection (3)(c), the nominee purchaser or any person authorised to act on his behalf shall, in the case of any part of the property in which that interest subsists, have a right of access thereto for the purpose of enabling the nominee purchaser to obtain, in connection with the proposed acquisition by him, a valuation of that interest; and subsection (3) of section 17 shall apply in relation to the exercise of that right as it applies in relation to the exercise of a right of access conferred by that section.

(6) Every counter-notice must specify an address in England and Wales at which notices may be given to the reversioner under this Chapter.

(7) The reference in subsection (3)(a)(ii) to additional leaseback proposals is a reference to proposals which relate to the leasing back, in accordance with section 36 and Schedule 9, of flats or other units contained in the specified premises and which are made either—

(a) in respect of flats or other units in relation to which Part II of that Schedule is applicable but which were not specified in the initial notice under section 13(3)(c)(ii), or

(b) in respect of flats or other units in relation to which Part III of that Schedule is applicable.

(8) Schedule 4 (which imposes requirements as to the furnishing of information by the reversioner about the exercise of rights under Chapter II with respect to flats contained in the specified premises) shall have effect.

Definitions For "the right to collective enfranchisement", see s 1(1); for "the relevant date", see s 1(8); for "relevant landlord" and "the reversioner", see s 9; for "the initial notice", see s 13; for "the specified premises", see s 13(12); for "the participating tenants", see s 14; for "the nominee purchaser", see s 15; for "the appropriate landlord", by virtue of sub-s (2) above, see s 23(10); for "conveyance" and "unit", see s 38(1); as to "proposed acquisition by the nominee purchaser", see s 38(2); as to an interest of a relevant landlord in the specified premises, see s 38(3); for "disposal", "flat" and "interest", see s 101(1).
References See paras 3.33–3.36 ff.

Applications to court or leasehold valuation tribunal

22 Proceedings relating to validity of initial notice

(1) Where—

(a) the reversioner in respect of the specified premises has given the nominee purchaser a counter-notice under section 21 which (whether it complies with the requirement set out in subsection (2)(b) or (c) of that section) contains such a statement as is mentioned in subsection (2)(b) of that section, but

(b) the court is satisfied, on an application made by the nominee purchaser, that the participating tenants were on the relevant date entitled to exercise the right to collective enfranchisement in relation to the specified premises,

the court shall by order make a declaration to that effect.

(2) Any application for an order under subsection (1) must be made not later than the end of the period of two months beginning with the date of the giving of the counter-notice to the nominee purchaser.

(3) If on any such application the court makes an order under subsection (1), then (subject to subsection (4)) the court shall make an order—

(a) declaring that the reversioner's counter-notice shall be of no effect, and

(b) requiring the reversioner to give a further counter-notice to the nominee purchaser by such date as is specified in the order.

(4) Subsection (3) shall not apply if—

(a) the counter-notice complies with the requirement set out in section 21(2)(c), and

(b) either—

(i) an application for an order under section 23(1) is pending, or

(ii) the period specified in section 23(3) as the period for the making of such an application has not expired.

(5) Subsections (3) to (5) of section 21 shall apply to any further counter-notice required to be given by the reversioner under subsection (3) above as if it were a counter-notice under that section complying with the requirement set out in subsection (2)(a) of that section.

(6) If an application by the nominee purchaser for an order under subsection (1) is dismissed by the court, the initial notice shall cease to have effect at the time when the order dismissing the application becomes final.

Definitions For "the right to collective enfranchisement", see s 1(1); for "the relevant date", see s 1(8); for "the reversioner", see s 9; for "the specified premises", see s 13(12); for "the participating tenants", see s 14; for "the nominee purchaser", see s 15; for "unit", see s 38(1); for "the court", "flat" and "interest", see s 101(1).
References See paras 3.37–3.39 ff.

23 Tenants' claim liable to be defeated where landlord intends to redevelop

(1) Where the reversioner in respect of the specified premises has given a counter-notice under section 21 which complies with the requirement set out in subsection (2)(c) of that section, the court may, on the application of any appropriate landlord, by order declare that the right to collective enfranchisement shall not be exercisable in relation to those premises by reason of that landlord's intention to redevelop the whole or a substantial part of the premises.

(2) The court shall not make an order under subsection (1) unless it is satisfied—

(a) that not less than two-thirds of all the long leases on which flats contained in the specified premises are held are due to terminate within the period of five years beginning with the relevant date; and

(b) that for the purposes of redevelopment the applicant intends, once the leases in question have so terminated—

      (i)   to demolish or reconstruct, or

      (ii) to carry out substantial works of construction on,

   the whole or a substantial part of the specified premises; and

  (c)   that he could not reasonably do so without obtaining possession of the flats demised by those leases.

(3) Any application for an order under subsection (1) must be made within the period of two months beginning with the date of the giving of the counter-notice to the nominee purchaser; but, where the counter-notice is one falling within section 22(1)(a), such an application shall not be proceeded with until such time (if any) as an order under section 22(1) becomes final.

(4) Where an order under subsection (1) is made by the court, the initial notice shall cease to have effect on the order becoming final.

(5) Where an application for an order under subsection (1) is dismissed by the court, the court shall make an order—

  (a)   declaring that the reversioner's counter-notice shall be of no effect, and

  (b)   requiring the reversioner to give a further counter-notice to the nominee purchaser by such date as is specified in the order.

(6) Where—

  (a)   the reversioner has given such a counter-notice as is mentioned in subsection (1), but

  (b)   either—

      (i)   no application for an order under that subsection is made within the period referred to in subsection (3), or

      (ii) such an application is so made but is subsequently withdrawn,

then (subject to subsection (8)), the reversioner shall give a further counter-notice to the nominee purchaser within the period of two months beginning with the appropriate date.

(7) In subsection (6) "the appropriate date" means—

  (a)   if subsection (6)(b)(i) applies, the date immediately following the end of the period referred to in subsection (3); and

  (b)   if subsection (6)(b)(ii) applies, the date of withdrawal of the application.

(8) Subsection (6) shall not apply if any application has been made by the nominee purchaser under section 22(1).

(9) Subsections (3) to (5) of section 21 shall apply to any further counter-notice required to be given by the reversioner under subsection (5) or (6) above as if it were a counter-notice under that section complying with the requirement set out in subsection (2)(a) of that section.

(10) In this section "appropriate landlord", in relation to the specified premises, means—

  (a)   the reversioner or any other relevant landlord; or

  (b)   any two or more persons falling within paragraph (a) who are acting together.

Definitions   For "the right to collective enfranchisement", see s 1(1); for "long lease", see s 7; for "relevant landlord" and "the reversioner", see s 9; for "the initial notice", see s 13; for "the specified premises", see s 13(12); for "the nominee purchaser", see s 15; for "the court" and "flat", see s 101(1); for "lease" and related expressions, see s 101(1), (2).
References   See paras 3.40–3.43 ff.

24 Applications where terms in dispute or failure to enter contract

(1) Where the reversioner in respect of the specified premises has given the nominee purchaser—

    (a) a counter-notice under section 21 complying with the requirement set out in subsection (2)(a) of that section, or

    (b) a further counter-notice required by or by virtue of section 22(3) or section 23(5) or (6),

but any of the terms of acquisition remain in dispute at the end of the period of two months beginning with the date on which the counter-notice or further counter-notice was so given, a leasehold valuation tribunal may, on the application of either the nominee purchaser or the reversioner, determine the matters in dispute.

(2) Any application under subsection (1) must be made not later than the end of the period of six months beginning with the date on which the counter-notice or further counter-notice was given to the nominee purchaser.

(3) Where—

    (a) the reversioner has given the nominee purchaser such a counter-notice or further counter-notice as is mentioned in subsection (1)(a) or (b), and

    (b) all of the terms of acquisition have been either agreed between the parties or determined by a leasehold valuation tribunal under subsection (1),

but a binding contract incorporating those terms has not been entered into by the end of the appropriate period specified in subsection (6), the court may, on the application of either the nominee purchaser or the reversioner, make such order under subsection (4) as it thinks fit.

(4) The court may under this subsection make an order—

    (a) providing for the interests to be acquired by the nominee purchaser to be vested in him on the terms referred to in subsection (3);

    (b) providing for those interests to be vested in him on those terms, but subject to such modifications as—

        (i) may have been determined by a leasehold valuation tribunal, on the application of either the nominee purchaser or the reversioner, to be required by reason of any change in circumstances since the time when the terms were agreed or determined as mentioned in that subsection, and

        (ii) are specified in the order; or

    (c) providing for the initial notice to be deemed to have been withdrawn at the end of the appropriate period specified in subsection (6);

and Schedule 5 shall have effect in relation to any such order as is mentioned in paragraph (a) or (b) above.

(5) Any application for an order under subsection (4) must be made not later than the end of the period of two months beginning immediately after the end of the appropriate period specified in subsection (6).

(6) For the purposes of this section the appropriate period is—

    (a) where all of the terms of acquisition have been agreed between the parties, the period of two months beginning with the date when those terms were finally so agreed;

    (b) where all or any of those terms have been determined by a leasehold valuation tribunal under subsection (1)—

        (i) the period of two months beginning with the date when the decision of the tribunal under that subsection becomes final, or

(ii) such other period as may have been fixed by the tribunal when making its determination.

(7) In this section "the parties" means the nominee purchaser and the reversioner and any relevant landlord who has given to those persons a notice for the purposes of paragraph 7(1)(a) of Schedule 1.

(8) In this Chapter "the terms of acquisition", in relation to a claim made under this Chapter, means the terms of the proposed acquisition by the nominee purchaser, whether relating to—

(a) the interests to be acquired,

(b) the extent of the property to which those interests relate or the rights to be granted over any property,

(c) the amounts payable as the purchase price for such interests,

(d) the apportionment of conditions or other matters in connection with the severance of any reversionary interest, or

(e) the provisions to be contained in any conveyance,

or otherwise, and includes any such terms in respect of any interest to be acquired in pursuance of section 1(4) or 21(4).

Definitions   For "relevant landlord" and "the reversioner", see s 9; for "the initial notice", see s 13; for "the specified premises", see s 13(12); for "the nominee purchaser", see s 15; for "conveyance", see s 38(1); for "the court" and "interest", see s 101(1); as to "the appropriate period", see sub-s (6) above; for "the parties", see sub-s (7) above; for "the terms of acquisition", see sub-s (8) above.
References   See paras 3.44, 3.48–3.52 ff.

---

25 Applications where reversioner fails to give counter-notice or further counter-notice

(1) Where the initial notice has been given in accordance with section 13 but—

(a) the reversioner has failed to give the nominee purchaser a counter-notice in accordance with section 21(1), or

(b) if required to give the nominee purchaser a further counter-notice by or by virtue of section 22(3) or section 23(5) or (6), the reversioner has failed to comply with that requirement,

the court may, on the application of the nominee purchaser, make an order determining the terms on which he is to acquire, in accordance with the proposals contained in the initial notice, such interests and rights as are specified in it under section 13(3).

(2) The terms determined by the court under subsection (1) shall, if Part II of Schedule 9 is applicable, include terms which provide for the leasing back, in accordance with section 36 and that Part of that Schedule, of flats or other units contained in the specified premises.

(3) The court shall not make any order on an application made by virtue of paragraph (a) of subsection (1) unless it is satisfied—

(a) that the participating tenants were on the relevant date entitled to exercise the right to collective enfranchisement in relation to the specified premises; and

(b) if applicable, that the requirements of Part II of Schedule 3 were complied with as respects the giving of copies of the initial notice.

(4) Any application for an order under subsection (1) must be made not later than the end of the period of six months beginning with the date by which the

counter-notice or further counter-notice referred to in that subsection was to be given to the nominee purchaser.

(5) Where—
  (a) the terms of acquisition have been determined by an order of the court under subsection (1), but
  (b) a binding contract incorporating those terms has not been entered into by the end of the appropriate period specified in subsection (8),

the court may, on the application of either the nominee purchaser or the reversioner, make such order under subsection (6) as it thinks fit.

(6) The court may under this subsection make an order—
  (a) providing for the interests to be acquired by the nominee purchaser to be vested in him on the terms referred to in subsection (5);
  (b) providing for those interests to be vested in him on those terms, but subject to such modifications as—
      (i) may have been determined by a leasehold valuation tribunal, on the application of either the nominee purchaser or the reversioner, to be required by reason of any change in circumstances since the time when the terms were determined as mentioned in that subsection, and
      (ii) are specified in the order; or
  (c) providing for the initial notice to be deemed to have been withdrawn at the end of the appropriate-period specified in subsection (8);

and Schedule 5 shall have effect in relation to any such order as is mentioned in paragraph (a) or (b) above.

(7) Any application for an order under subsection (6) must be made not later than the end of the period of two months beginning immediately after the end of the appropriate period specified in subsection (8).

(8) For the purposes of this section the appropriate period is—
  (a) the period of two months beginning with the date when the order of the court under subsection (1) becomes final, or
  (b) such other period as may have been fixed by the court when making that order.

Definitions   For "the right to collective enfranchisement", see s 1(1); for "the relevant date", see s 1(8); for "the reversioner", see s 9; for "the initial notice", sees 13; for "the specified premises", see s 13(12); for "the nominee purchaser", see s 15; for "the terms of acquisition", see s 24(8); for "the court", "flat" and "interest", see s 101(1).
References   See paras 3.45–3.52 ff.

26   Applications where relevant landlord cannot be found

(1) Where not less than two-thirds of the qualifying tenants of flats contained in any premises to which this Chapter applies desire to make a claim to exercise the right to collective enfranchisement in relation to those premises but—
  (a) (in a case to which section 9(1) applies) the person who owns the freehold of the premises cannot be found or his identity cannot be ascertained, or
  (b) (in a case to which section 9(2) applies) each of the relevant landlords is someone who cannot be found or whose identity cannot be ascertained,

the court may, on the application of the qualifying tenants in question, make a vesting order under this subsection—

(i) with respect to any interests of that person (whether in those premises or in any other property) which are liable to acquisition on behalf of those tenants by virtue of section 1(1) or (2)(a) or section 2(1), or

(ii) with respect to any interests of those landlords which are so liable to acquisition by virtue of any of those provisions,

as the case may be.

(2) Where in a case to which section 9(2) applies—

(a) not less than two-thirds of the qualifying tenants of flats contained in any premises to which this Chapter applies desire to make a claim to exercise the right to collective enfranchisement in relation to those premises, and

(b) paragraph (b) of subsection (1) does not apply, but

(c) a notice of that claim or (as the case may be) a copy of such a notice cannot be given in accordance with section 13 or Part II of Schedule 3 to any person to whom it would otherwise be required to be so given because he cannot be found or his identity cannot be ascertained,

the court may, on the application of the qualifying tenants in question, make an order dispensing with the need to give such a notice or (as the case may be) a copy of such a notice to that person.

(3) If that person is the person who owns the freehold of the premises, then on the application of those tenants, the court may, in connection with an order under subsection (2), make an order appointing any other relevant landlord to be the reversioner in respect of the premises in place of that person; and if it does so references in this Chapter to the reversioner shall apply accordingly.

(4) The court shall not make an order on any application under subsection (1) or (2) unless it is satisfied—

(a) that on the date of the making of the application the premises to which the application relates were premises to which this Chapter applies; and

(b) that on that date the applicants would not have been precluded by any provision of this Chapter from giving a valid notice under section 13 with respect to those premises.

(5) Before making any such order the court may require the applicants to take such further steps by way of advertisement or otherwise as the court thinks proper for the purpose of tracing the person or persons in question; and if, after an application is made for a vesting order under subsection (1) and before any interest is vested in pursuance of the application, the person or (as the case may be) any of the persons referred to in paragraph (a) or (b) of that subsection is traced, then no further proceedings shall be taken with a view to any interest being so vested, but (subject to subsection (6))—

(a) the rights and obligations of all parties shall be determined as if the applicants had, at the date of the application, duly given notice under section 13 of their claim to exercise the right to collective enfranchisement in relation to the premises to which the application relates; and

(b) the court may give such directions as the court thinks fit as to the steps to be taken for giving effect to those rights and obligations, including directions modifying or dispensing with any of the requirements of this Chapter or of regulations made under this Part.

(6) An application for a vesting order under subsection (1) may be withdrawn at any time before execution of a conveyance under section 27(3) and, after it is withdrawn, subsection (5)(a) above shall not apply; but where any step is taken

(whether by the applicants or otherwise) for the purpose of giving effect to subsection (5)(a) in the case of any application, the application shall not afterwards be withdrawn except—

(a) with the consent of every person who is the owner of any interest the vesting of which is sought by the applicants, or

(b) by leave of the court,

and the court shall not give leave unless it appears to the court just to do so by reason of matters coming to the knowledge of the applicants in consequence of the tracing of any such person.

(7) Where an order has been made under subsection (2) dispensing with the need to give a notice under section 13, or a copy of such a notice, to a particular person with respect to any particular premises, then if—

(a) a notice is subsequently given under that section with respect to those premises, and

(b) in reliance on the order, the notice or a copy of the notice is not to be given to that person,

the notice must contain a statement of the effect of the order.

(8) Where a notice under section 13 contains such a statement in accordance with subsection (7) above, then in determining for the purposes of any provision of this Chapter whether the requirements of section 13 or Part II of Schedule 3 have been complied with in relation to the notice, those requirements shall be deemed to have been complied with so far as relating to the giving of the notice or a copy of it to the person referred to in subsection (7) above.

(9) Rules of court shall make provision—

(a) for requiring notice of any application under subsection (3) to be served by the persons making the application on any person who the applicants know or have reason to believe is a relevant landlord; and

(b) for enabling persons served with any such notice to be joined as parties to the proceedings.

Definitions   For "the right to collective enfranchisement", see s 1(1); for "the relevant date", see s 1(8); for "the reversioner", see s 9; for "the initial notice", sees 13; for "the specified premises", see s 13(12); for "the nominee purchaser", see s 15; for "the terms of acquisition", see s 24(8); for "the court", "flat" and "interest", see s 101(1).
References   See paras 3.56–3.64 ff.

---

27 Supplementary provisions relating to vesting orders under section 26(1)

(1) A vesting order under section 26(1) is an order providing for the vesting of any such interests as are referred to in paragraph (i) or (ii) of that provision—

(a) in such person or persons as may be appointed for the purpose by the applicants for the order, and

(b) on such terms as may be determined by a leasehold valuation tribunal to be appropriate with a view to the interests being vested in that person or those persons in like manner (so far as the circumstances permit) as if the applicants had, at the date of their application, given notice under section 13 of their claim to exercise the right to collective enfranchisement in relation to the premises with respect to which the order is made.

(2) If a leasehold valuation tribunal so determines in the case of a vesting order under section 26(1), the order shall have effect in relation to interests which are less extensive than those specified in the application on which the order was made.

(3) Where any interests are to be vested in any person or persons by virtue of a vesting order under section 26(1), then on his or their paying into court the appropriate sum in respect of each of those interests there shall be executed by such person as the court may designate a conveyance which—

(a) is in a form approved by a leasehold valuation tribunal, and

(b) contains such provisions as may be so approved for the purpose of giving effect so far as possible to the requirements of section 34 and Schedule 7;

and that conveyance shall be effective to vest in the person or persons to whom the conveyance is made the interests expressed to be conveyed, subject to and in accordance with the terms of the conveyance.

(4) In connection with the determination by a leasehold valuation tribunal of any question as to the interests to be conveyed by any such conveyance, or as to the rights with or subject to which they are to be conveyed, it shall be assumed (unless the contrary is shown) that any person whose interests are to be conveyed ("the transferor") has no interest in property other than those interests and, for the purpose of excepting them from the conveyance, any minerals underlying the property in question.

(5) The appropriate sum which in accordance with subsection (3) is to be paid into court in respect of any interest is the aggregate of—

(a) such amount as may be determined by a leasehold valuation tribunal to be the price which would be payable in respect of that interest in accordance with Schedule 6 if the interest were being acquired in pursuance of such a notice as is mentioned in subsection (1)(b); and

(b) any amounts or estimated amounts determined by such a tribunal as being, at the time of execution of the conveyance, due to the transferor from any tenants of his of premises comprised in the premises in which that interest subsists (whether due under or in respect of their leases or under or in respect of agreements collateral thereto).

(6) Where any interest is vested in any person or persons in accordance with this section, the payment into court of the appropriate sum in respect of that interest shall be taken to have satisfied any claims against the applicants for the vesting order under section 26(1), their personal representatives or assigns in respect of the price payable under this Chapter for the acquisition of that interest.

(7) Where any interest is so vested in any person or persons, section 32(5) shall apply in relation to his or their acquisition of that interest as it applies in relation to the acquisition of any interest by a nominee purchaser.

Definitions   For "the right to collective enfranchisement", see s 1(1); for "conveyance", see s 38(1); for "the court" and "interest", see s 101(1); as to "tenant", see s 101(1), (2); for "the transferor", see sub-s (4) above; as to "the appropriate sum", see sub-s (5) above.
References   See paras 3.59, 3.65–3.68 ff.

Termination of acquisition procedures

28   Withdrawal from acquisition by participating tenants

(1) At any time before a binding contract is entered into in pursuance of the initial notice, the participating tenants may withdraw that notice by the giving of a notice to that effect under this section ("a notice of withdrawal").

(2) A notice of withdrawal must be given—
  (a) to the nominee purchaser;
  (b) to the reversioner in respect of the specified premises; and
  (c) to every other relevant landlord who is known or believed by the participating tenants to have given to the nominee purchaser a notice under paragraph 7(1) or (4) of Schedule 1;

and, if by virtue of paragraph (c) a notice of withdrawal falls to be given to any person falling within that paragraph, it shall state that he is a recipient of the notice.

(3) The nominee purchaser shall, on receiving a notice of withdrawal, give a copy of it to every relevant landlord who—
  (a) has given to the nominee purchaser such a notice as is mentioned in subsection (2)(c); and
  (b) is not stated in the notice of withdrawal to be a recipient of it.

(4) Where a notice of withdrawal is given by the participating tenants under subsection (1)—
  (a) those persons, and
  (b) (subject to subsection (5)) every other person who is not a participating tenant for the time being but has at any time been such a tenant,
shall be liable—
  (i) to the reversioner, and
  (ii) to every other relevant landlord,
for all relevant costs incurred by him in pursuance of the initial notice down to the time when the notice of withdrawal or a copy of it is given to him in accordance with subsection (2) or (3).

(5) A person falling within paragraph (b) of subsection (4) shall not be liable for any costs by virtue of that subsection if—
  (a) the lease in respect of which he was a participating tenant has been assigned to another person; and
  (b) that other person has become a participating tenant in accordance with section 14(4);
and in paragraph (a) above the reference to an assignment shall be construed in accordance with section 14(10).

(6) Where any liability for costs arises under subsection (4)—
  (a) it shall be a joint and several liability of the persons concerned; and
  (b) the nominee purchaser shall not be liable for any costs under section 33.

(7) In subsection (4) "relevant costs", in relation to the reversioner or any other relevant landlord, means costs for which the nominee purchaser would (apart from subsection (6)) be liable to that person under section 33.

Definitions   For "relevant landlord" and "the reversioner", see s 9; for "the initial notice", see s 13; for "the specified premises", see s 13(12); for "the participating tenants", see s 14; for "the nominee purchaser", see s 15; for "lease" and related expressions (including "tenant"), see s 101(1), (2); for "a notice of withdrawal", see sub-s (1) above; for "relevant costs" in sub-s (4) above, see sub-s (7) above.
References   See paras 3.53, 3.55 ff.

---

29 Deemed withdrawal of initial notice

(1) Where, in a case falling within paragraph (a) of subsection (1) of section 22—

    (a) no application for an order under that subsection is made within the period specified in subsection (2) of that section, or

    (b) such an application is so made but is subsequently withdrawn, the initial notice shall be deemed to have been withdrawn—

        (i) (if paragraph (a) above applies) at the end of that period, or

        (ii) (if paragraph (b) above applies) on the date of the withdrawal of the application.

(2) Where—

    (a) in a case to which subsection (1) of section 24 applies, no application under that subsection is made within the period specified in subsection (2) of that section, or

    (b) in a case to which subsection (3) of that section applies, no application for an order under subsection (4) of that section is made within the period specified in subsection (5) of that section,

the initial notice shall be deemed to have been withdrawn at the end of the period referred to in paragraph (a) or (b) above (as the case may be).

(3) Where, in a case falling within paragraph (a) or (b) of subsection (1) of section 25, no application for an order under that subsection is made within the period specified in subsection (4) of that section, the initial notice shall be deemed to have been withdrawn at the end of that period.

(4) Where, in a case to which subsection (5) of section 25 applies, no application for an order under subsection (6) of that section is made within the period specified in subsection (7) of that section, the initial notice shall be deemed to have been withdrawn at the end of that period.

(5) The following provisions, namely—

    (a) section 15(10),

    (b) section 16(8),

    (c) section 20(3),

    (d) section 24(4)(c), and

    (e) section 25(6)(c),

also make provision for a notice under section 13 to be deemed to have been withdrawn at a particular time.

(6) Where the initial notice is deemed to have been withdrawn at any time by virtue of any provision of this Chapter, subsections (4) and (5) of section 28 shall apply for the purposes of this section in like manner as they apply where a notice of withdrawal is given under that section, but as if the reference in subsection (4) of that section to the time when a notice or copy is given as there mentioned were a reference to the time when the initial notice is so deemed to have been withdrawn.

(7) Where the initial notice is deemed to have been withdrawn by virtue of section 15(10) or 16(8)—

    (a) the liability for costs arising by virtue of subsection (6) above shall be a joint and several liability of the persons concerned; and

    (b) the nominee purchaser shall not be liable for any costs under section 33.

(8) In the provisions applied by subsection (6), "relevant costs", in relation to the reversioner or any other relevant landlord, means costs for which the nominee purchaser is, or would (apart from subsection (7)) be, liable to that person under section 33.

Definitions   For "relevant landlord" and "the reversioner", see s 9; for "the initial notice", see s 13; for "the nominee purchaser", see s 15; for "relevant costs" in the provisions applied by sub-s (6) above, see sub-s (8) above.
References   See para 3.54 ff.

30 Effect on initial notice or subsequent contract of institution of compulsory acquisition procedures

(1) A notice given under section 13 shall be of no effect if on the relevant date—

    (a) any acquiring authority has, with a view to the acquisition of the whole or part of the specified premises for any authorised purpose—

        (i) served notice to treat on any relevant person, or

        (ii) entered into a contract for the purchase of the interest of any such person in the premises or part of them, and

    (b) the notice to treat or contract remains in force.

(2) In subsection (1) "relevant person", in relation to the specified premises, means—

    (a) the person who owns the freehold of the premises; or

    (b) any other person who owns any leasehold interest in the premises which is specified in the initial notice under section 13(3)(c)(i).

(3) A notice given under section 13 shall not specify under subsection (3)(a)(ii) or (c)(i) of that section any property or leasehold interest in property if on the relevant date—

    (a) any acquiring authority has, with a view to the acquisition of the whole or part of the property for any authorised purpose—

        (i) served notice to treat on the person who owns the freehold of, or any such leasehold interest in, the property, or

        (ii) entered into a contract for the purchase of the interest of any such person in the property or part of it, and

    (b) the notice to treat or contract remains in force.

(4) A notice given under section 13 shall cease to have effect if before a binding contract is entered into in pursuance of the notice, any acquiring authority serves, with a view to the acquisition of the whole or part of the specified premises for any authorised purpose, notice to treat as mentioned in subsection (1)(a).

(5) Where any such authority so serves notice to treat at any time after a binding contract is entered into in pursuance of the notice given under section 13 but before completion of the acquisition by the nominee purchaser under this Chapter, then (without prejudice to the general law as to the frustration of contracts) the parties to the contract shall be discharged from the further performance of the contract.

(6) Where subsection (4) or (5) applies in relation to the initial notice or any contract entered into in pursuance of it, then on the occasion of the compulsory acquisition in question the compensation payable in respect of any interest in the specified premises (whether or not the one to which the relevant notice to treat relates) shall be determined on the basis of the value of the interest—

    (a) (if subsection (4) applies) subject to and with the benefit of the rights and obligations arising from the initial notice and affecting that interest; or

    (b) (if subsection (5) applies) subject to and with the benefit of the rights and obligations arising from the contract and affecting that interest.

(7) In this section—

(a) "acquiring authority", in relation to the specified premises or any other property, means any person or body of persons who has or have been, or could be, authorised to acquire the whole or part of those premises or that property compulsorily for any purpose; and

(b) "authorised purpose", in relation to any acquiring authority, means any such purpose.

Definitions For "the relevant date", see s 1(8); for "the initial notice", see s 13; for "the specified premises", see s 13(12); for "the nominee purchaser", see s 15; for "relevant person" in sub-s (1) above, see sub-s (2) above; for "acquiring authority" and "authorised purpose", see sub-s (7) above.
References See paras 3.71, 3.72 ff.

---

31 Effect on initial notice of designation for inheritance tax purposes and applications for designation

(1) A notice given under section 13 shall be of no effect if on the relevant date the whole or any part of—

(a) the specified premises, or

(b) any property specified in the notice under section 13(3)(a)(ii), is qualifying property.

(2) For the purposes of this section the whole or any part of the specified premises, or of any property specified as mentioned in subsection (1), is qualifying property if—

(a) it has been designated under section 31(1)(b), (c) or (d) of the Inheritance Tax Act 1984 (designation and undertakings relating to conditionally exempt transfers), whether with or without any other property, and no chargeable event has subsequently occurred with respect to it; or

(b) an application to the Board for it to be so designated is pending; or

(c) it is the property of a body not established or conducted for profit and a direction has been given in relation to it under section 26 of that Act (gifts for public benefit), whether with or without any other property; or

(d) an application to the Board for a direction to be so given in relation to it is pending.

(3) For the purposes of subsection (2) an application is pending as from the time when it is made to the Board until such time as it is either granted or refused by the Board or withdrawn by the applicant; and for this purpose an application shall not be regarded as made unless and until the applicant has submitted to the Board all such information in support of the application as is required by the Board.

(4) A notice given under section 13 shall cease to have effect if, before a binding contract is entered into in pursuance of the notice, the whole or any part of—

(a) the specified premises, or

(b) any property specified in the notice under section 13(3)(a)(ii), becomes qualifying property.

(5) Where a notice under section 13 ceases to have effect by virtue of subsection (4) above—

(a) the nominee purchaser shall not be liable for any costs under section 33; and

(b) the person who applied or is applying for designation or a direction shall be liable—

  (i) to the qualifying tenants by whom the notice was given for all reasonable costs incurred by them in the preparation and giving of the notice; and

  (ii) to the nominee purchaser for all reasonable costs incurred in pursuance of the notice by him or by any other person who has acted as the nominee purchaser.

(6) Where it is claimed that subsection (1) or (4) applies in relation to a notice under section 13, the person making the claim shall, at the time of making it, furnish the nominee purchaser with evidence in support of it; and if he fails to do so he shall be liable for any costs which are reasonably incurred by the nominee purchaser in consequence of the failure.

(7) In subsection (2)—

 (a) paragraphs (a) and (b) apply to designation under section 34(1)(a), (b) or (c) of the Finance Act 1975 or section 77(1)(b), (c) or (d) of the Finance Act 1976 as they apply to designation under section 31(1)(b), (c) or (d) of the Inheritance Tax Act 1984; and

 (b) paragraphs (c) and (d) apply to a direction under paragraph 13 of Schedule 6 to the Finance Act 1975 as they apply to a direction under section 26 of that Act of 1984.

(8) In this section—

"the Board" means the Commissioners of Inland Revenue;

"chargeable event" means—

 (a) any event which in accordance with any provision of Chapter II of Part II of the Inheritance Tax Act 1984 (exempt transfers) is a chargeable event, including any such provision as applied by section 78(3) of that Act (conditionally exempt occasions); or

 (b) any event which would have been a chargeable event in the circumstances mentioned in section 79(3) of that Act (exemption from ten-yearly charge).

Definitions For "the relevant date", see s 1(8); for "qualifying tenant", see s 5; for "the specified premises", see s 13(12); for "the nominee purchaser", see s 15; as to "qualifying property", see sub-s (2) above; as to "the Board" and "chargeable event", see sub-s (8) above.

References See paras 3.73, 3.74 ff.

Determination of price and costs of enfranchisement

32 Determination of price

(1) Schedule 6 to this Act (which relates to the determination of the price payable by the nominee purchaser in respect of each of the freehold and other interests to be acquired by him in pursuance of this Chapter) shall have effect.

(2) The lien of the owner of any such interest (as vendor) on the specified premises, or (as the case may be) on any other property, for the price payable shall extend—

 (a) to any amounts which, at the time of the conveyance of that interest, are due to him from any tenants of his of premises comprised in the premises in which that interest subsists (whether due under or in respect of their leases or under or in respect of agreements collateral thereto); and

 (b) to any amount payable to him by virtue of section 18(2); and

 (c) to any costs payable to him by virtue of section 33.

(3) Subsection (2)(a) does not apply in relation to amounts due to the owner of any such interest from tenants of any premises which are to be comprised in the premises demised by a lease granted in accordance with section 36 and Schedule 9.

(4) In subsection (2) the reference to the specified premises or any other property includes a reference to a part of those premises or that property.

(5) Despite the fact that in accordance with Schedule 6 no payment or only a nominal payment is payable by the nominee purchaser in respect of the acquisition by him of any interest he shall nevertheless be deemed for all purposes to be a purchaser of that interest for a valuable consideration in money or money's worth.

Definitions   For "the specified premises", see s 13(12); for "the nominee purchaser", see s 15; for "conveyance", see s 38(1); for "lease" and related expressions (including "tenant"), see s 101(1), (2).
References   See paras 3.75, 3.99 ff.

33   Costs of enfranchisement

(1) Where a notice is given under section 13, then (subject to the provisions of this section and sections 28(6), 29(7) and 31(5)) the nominee purchaser shall be liable, to the extent that they have been incurred in pursuance of the notice by the reversioner or by any other relevant landlord, for the reasonable costs of and incidental to any of the following matters, namely—
    (a)   any investigation reasonably undertaken—
        (i)   of the question whether any interest in the specified premises or other property is liable to acquisition in pursuance of the initial notice, or
        (ii)   of any other question arising out of that notice;
    (b)   deducing, evidencing and verifying the title to any such interest;
    (c)   making out and furnishing such abstracts and copies as the nominee purchaser may require;
    (d)   any valuation of any interest in the specified premises or other property;
    (e)   any conveyance of any such interest;
but this subsection shall not apply to any costs if on a sale made voluntarily a stipulation that they were to be borne by the purchaser would be void.

(2) For the purposes of subsection (1) any costs incurred by the reversioner or any other relevant landlord in respect of professional services rendered by any person shall only be regarded as reasonable if and to the extent that costs in respect of such services might reasonably be expected to have been incurred by him if the circumstances had been such that he was personally liable for all such costs.

(3) Where by virtue of any provision of this Chapter the initial notice ceases to have effect at any time, then (subject to subsection (4)) the nominee purchaser's liability under this section for costs incurred by any person shall be a liability for costs incurred by him down to that time.

(4) The nominee purchaser shall not be liable for any costs under this section if the initial notice ceases to have effect by virtue of section 23(4) or 30(4).

(5) The nominee purchaser shall not be liable under this section for any costs which a party to any proceedings under this Chapter before a leasehold valuation tribunal incurs in connection with the proceedings.

(6) In this section references to the nominee purchaser include references to any person whose appointment has terminated in accordance with section 15(3) or

16(1); but this section shall have effect in relation to such a person subject to section 15(7).

(7) Where by virtue of this section, or of this section and section 29(6) taken together, two or more persons are liable for any costs, they shall be jointly and severally liable for them.

Definitions   For "the reversioner" and "relevant landlord", see s 9; for "the initial notice", see s 13; for "the specified premises", see s 13(12); for "the nominee purchaser", see s 15; for "conveyance", see s 38(1); for "interest", see s 101(1).
References   See paras 3.86, 3.87 ff.

Completion of acquisition

34 Conveyance to nominee purchaser

(1) Any conveyance executed for the purposes of this Chapter, being a conveyance to the nominee purchaser of the freehold of the specified premises or of any other property, shall grant to the nominee purchaser an estate in fee simple absolute in those premises or that property, subject only to such incumbrances as may have been agreed or determined under this Chapter to be incumbrances subject to which that estate should be granted, having regard to the following provisions of this Chapter.

(2) Any such conveyance shall, where the nominee purchaser is to acquire any leasehold interest in the specified premises or (as the case may be) in the other property to which the conveyance relates, provide for the disposal to the nominee purchaser of any such interest.

(3) Any conveyance executed for the purposes of this Chapter shall have effect under section 2(1) of the Law of Property Act 1925 (conveyances overreaching certain equitable interests etc) to overreach any incumbrance capable of being overreached under section 2(1)—

   (a) as if, where the interest conveyed is settled land for the purposes of the Settled Land Act 1925, the conveyance were made under the powers of that Act, and

   (b) as if the requirements of section 2(1) as to payment of the capital money allowed any part of the purchase price paid or applied in accordance with section 35 below or Schedule 8 to this Act to be so paid or applied.

(4) For the purposes of this section "incumbrances" includes—

   (a) rentcharges, and

   (b) (subject to subsection (5)) personal liabilities attaching in respect of the ownership of land or an interest in land though not charged on that land or interest.

(5) Burdens originating in tenure, and burdens in respect of the upkeep or regulation for the benefit of any locality of any land, building, structure, works, ways or watercourse shall not be treated as incumbrances for the purposes of this section; but any conveyance executed for the purposes of this Chapter shall be made subject to any such burdens.

(6) A conveyance executed for the purposes of this Chapter shall not be made subject to any incumbrance capable of being overreached by the conveyance, but shall be made subject (where they are not capable of being overreached) to—

    (a) rentcharges redeemable under sections 8 to 10 of the Rentcharges Act 1977, and

    (b) those falling within paragraphs (c) and (d) of section 2(3) of that Act (estate rentcharges and rentcharges imposed under certain enactments),

except as otherwise provided by subsections (7) and (8) below.

(7) Where any land is to be conveyed to the nominee purchaser by a conveyance executed for the purposes of this Chapter, subsection (6) shall not preclude the person who owns the freehold interest in the land from releasing, or procuring the release of, the land from any rentcharge.

(8) The conveyance of any such land ("the relevant land") may, with the agreement of the nominee purchaser (which shall not be unreasonably withheld), provide in accordance with section 190(1) of the Law of Property Act 1925 (charging of rentcharges on land without rent owner's consent) that a rentcharge—

    (a) shall be charged exclusively on other land affected by it in exoneration of the relevant land, or

    (b) shall be apportioned between other land affected by it and the relevant land.

(9) Except to the extent that any departure is agreed to by the nominee purchaser and the person whose interest is to be conveyed, any conveyance executed for the purposes of this Chapter shall—

    (a) as respects the conveyance of any freehold interest, conform with the provisions of Schedule 7, and

    (b) as respects the conveyance of any leasehold interest, conform with the provisions of paragraph 2 of that Schedule (any reference in that paragraph to the freeholder being read as a reference to the person whose leasehold interest is to be conveyed).

(10) Any such conveyance shall in addition contain a statement that it is a conveyance executed for the purposes of this Chapter; and any such statement shall comply with such requirements as may be prescribed by rules made in pursuance of section 144 of the Land Registration Act 1925 (power to make general rules).

Definitions   For "the specified premises", see s 13(12); for "the nominee purchaser", see s 15; for "conveyance", see s 38(1); for "disposal" and "interest", see s 101(1); for "incumbrances", see sub-s (4) above; for "the relevant land", see sub-s (8) above.
References   See paras 3.73, 3.74 ff.

---

35 Discharge of existing mortgages on transfer to nominee purchaser

(1) Subject to the provisions of Schedule 8, where any interest is acquired by the nominee purchaser in pursuance of this Chapter, the conveyance by virtue of which it is so acquired shall, as regards any mortgage to which this section applies, be effective by virtue of this section—

    (a) to discharge the interest from the mortgage, and from the operation of any order made by a court for the enforcement of the mortgage, and

    (b) to extinguish any term of years created for the purposes of the mortgage,

and shall do so without the persons entitled to or interested in the mortgage or in any such order or term of years becoming parties to or executing the conveyance.

(2) Subject to subsections (3) and (4), this section applies to any mortgage of the interest so acquired (however created or arising) which—

    (a) is a mortgage to secure the payment of money or the performance of any other obligation by the person from whom the interest is so acquired or any other person; and

    (b) is not a mortgage which would be overreached apart from this section.

(3) This section shall not apply to any such mortgage if it has been agreed between the nominee purchaser and the reversioner or (as the case may be) any other relevant landlord that the interest in question should be acquired subject to the mortgage.

(4) In this section and Schedule 8 "mortgage" includes a charge or lien; but neither this section nor that Schedule applies to a rentcharge.

Definitions   For "relevant landlord" and "the reversioner", see s 9; for "the nominee purchaser", see s 15; for "conveyance", see s 38(1); for "interest", see s 101(1); for "mortgage", see sub-s (4) above.
References   See para 3.96 ff.

36 Nominee purchaser required to grant leases back to former freeholder in certain circumstances

(1) In connection with the acquisition by him of the freehold of the specified premises, the nominee purchaser shall grant to the person from whom the freehold is acquired such leases of flats or other units contained in those premises as are required to be so granted by virtue of Part II or III of Schedule 9.

(2) Any such lease shall be granted so as to take effect immediately after the acquisition by the nominee purchaser of the freehold of the specified premises.

(3) Where any flat or other unit demised under any such lease ("the relevant lease") is at the time of that acquisition subject to any existing lease, the relevant lease shall take effect as a lease of the freehold reversion in respect of the flat or other unit.

(4) Part IV of Schedule 9 has effect with respect to the terms of a lease granted in pursuance of Part II or III of that Schedule.

Definitions   For "the specified premises", see s 13(12); for "the nominee purchaser", see s 15; for "unit", see s 38(1); for "flat", see s 101(1); for "lease" and related expressions, see s 101(1), (2).
References   See paras 3.88, 3.93 ff.

37 Acquisition of interests from local authorities etc

Schedule 10 to this Act (which makes provision with respect to the acquisition of interests from local authorities etc in pursuance of this Chapter) shall have effect.

References   See para 3.100 ff.

Supplemental

38 Interpretation of Chapter I

(1) In this Chapter (unless the context otherwise requires)—
    "conveyance" includes assignment, transfer and surrender, and related expressions shall be construed accordingly;
    "the initial notice" means the notice given under section 13;
    "the nominee purchaser" shall be construed in accordance with section 15;

"the participating tenants" shall be construed in accordance with section 14;

"premises with a resident landlord" shall be construed in accordance with section 10;

"public sector landlord" means any of the persons listed in section 171(2) of the Housing Act 1985;

"qualifying tenant" shall be construed in accordance with section 5;

"the relevant date" has the meaning given by section 1(8);

"relevant landlord" and "the reversioner" shall be construed in accordance with section 9;

"the right to collective enfranchisement" means the right specified in section 1(1);

"secure tenancy" has the meaning given by section 79 of the Housing Act 1985;

"the specified premises" shall be construed in accordance with section 13(12);

"the terms of acquisition" has the meaning given by section 24(8);

"unit" means—

    (a) a flat;

    (b) any other separate set of premises which is constructed or adapted for use for the purposes of a dwelling; or

    (c) a separate set of premises let, or intended for letting, on a business lease.

(2) Any reference in this Chapter (however expressed) to the acquisition or proposed acquisition by the nominee purchaser is a reference to the acquisition or proposed acquisition by the nominee purchaser, on behalf of the participating tenants, of such freehold and other interests as fall to be so acquired under a contract entered into in pursuance of the initial notice.

(3) Any reference in this Chapter to the interest of a relevant landlord in the specified premises is a reference to the interest in those premises by virtue of which he is, in accordance with section 9(2)(b), a relevant landlord.

(4) Any reference in this Chapter to agreement in relation to all or any of the terms of acquisition is a reference to agreement subject to contract.

Definitions   For "business lease", "dwelling", "flat" and "interest", see s 101(1).
References   See para 2.12 ff.

CHAPTER II

INDIVIDUAL RIGHT OF TENANT OF FLAT TO ACQUIRE NEW LEASE

Preliminary

39 Right of qualifying tenant of flat to acquire new lease

(1) This Chapter has effect for the purpose of conferring on a tenant of a flat, in the circumstances mentioned in subsection (2), the right, exercisable subject to and in accordance with this Chapter, to acquire a new lease of the flat on payment of a premium determined in accordance with this Chapter.

(2) Those circumstances are that on the relevant date for the purposes of this Chapter—

    (a) the tenant is a qualifying tenant of the flat; and

    (b) the tenant has occupied the flat as his only or principal home—

(i) for the last three years, or

(ii) for periods amounting to three years in the last ten years,

whether or not he has used it also for other purposes.

(3) The following provisions, namely—

(a) section 5 (with the omission of subsections (5) and (6)),

(b) section 7, and

(c) section 8,

shall apply for the purposes of this Chapter as they apply for the purposes of Chapter I; and references in this Chapter to a qualifying tenant of a flat shall accordingly be construed by reference to those provisions.

(4) For the purposes of this Chapter a person can be (or be among those constituting) the qualifying tenant of each of two or more flats at the same time, whether he is tenant of those flats under one lease or under two or more separate leases.

(5) For the purposes of subsection (2)(b) above—

(a) any reference to the tenant's flat includes a reference to part of it; and

(b) it is immaterial whether at any particular time the tenant's occupation was in right of the lease by virtue of which he is a qualifying tenant or in right of some other lease or otherwise;

but any occupation by a company or other artificial person, or (where the tenant is a corporation sole) by the corporator, shall not be regarded as occupation for the purposes of that provision.

(6) In the case of a lease held by joint tenants—

(a) the condition in subsection (2)(b) need only be satisfied with respect to one of the joint tenants; and

(b) subsection (5) shall apply accordingly (the reference to the lease by virtue of which the tenant is a qualifying tenant being read for this purpose as a reference to the lease by virtue of which the joint tenants are a qualifying tenant).

(7) The right conferred by this Chapter on a tenant to acquire a new lease shall not extend to underlying minerals comprised in his existing lease if—

(a) the landlord requires the minerals to be excepted, and

(b) proper provision is made for the support of the premises demised by that existing lease as they are enjoyed on the relevant date.

(8) In this Chapter "the relevant date", in relation to a claim by a tenant under this Chapter, means the date on which notice of the claim is given to the landlord under section 42.

Definitions For "qualifying tenant", see s 39(3); for "flat" and "interest", see s 101(1)(and note also as to "flat", s 62(2)–(4)); for "lease" and related expressions (including "tenant"), see s 101(1), (2); for "the landlord", see sub-s (1) above; for "the competent landlord", "other landlord", "the tenant" and "the tenant's lease", see sub-s (4) above.
References See paras 4.4–4.10 ff.

---

40 The landlord for the purposes of this Chapter

(1) In this Chapter "the landlord", in relation to the lease held by a qualifying tenant of a flat, means the person who is the owner of that interest in the flat which for the time being fulfils the following conditions, namely—

(a) it is an interest in reversion expectant (whether immediately or not) on the termination of the tenant's lease, and

(b) it is either a freehold interest or a leasehold interest whose duration is such as to enable that person to grant a new lease of that flat in accordance with this Chapter,

and is not itself expectant (whether immediately or not) on an interest which fulfils those conditions.

(2) Where in accordance with subsection (1) the immediate landlord under the lease of a qualifying tenant of a flat is not the landlord in relation to that lease for the purposes of this Chapter, the person who for those purposes is the landlord in relation to it shall conduct on behalf of all the other landlords all proceedings arising out of any notice given by the tenant with respect to the flat under section 42 (whether the proceedings are for resisting or giving effect to the claim in question).

(3) Subsection (2) has effect subject to the provisions of Schedule 11 to this Act (which makes provision in relation to the operation of this Chapter in cases to which that subsection applies).

(4) In this section and that Schedule—
(a) "the tenant" means any such qualifying tenant as is referred to in subsection (2) and "the tenant's lease" means the lease by virtue of which he is a qualifying tenant;
(b) "the competent landlord" means the person who, in relation to the tenant's lease, is the landlord (as defined by subsection (1)) for the purposes of this Chapter;
(c) "other landlord" means any person (other than the tenant or a trustee for him) in whom there is vested a concurrent tenancy intermediate between the interest of the competent landlord and the tenant's lease.

(5) Schedule 2 (which makes provision with respect to certain special categories of landlords) has effect for the purposes of this Chapter.

Definitions For "qualifying tenant", see s 39(3); for "flat" and "interest", see s 101(1) (and note also as to "flat", s 62(2)–(4)); for "lease" and related expressions (including "tenant"), see s 101(1), (2); for "the landlord", see sub-s (1) above; for "the competent landlord", "other landlord", "the tenant" and "the tenant's lease", see sub-s (4) above.
References See paras 4.11–4.13 ff.

Preliminary inquiries by qualifying tenant

41 Right of qualifying tenant to obtain information about superior interests etc

(1) A qualifying tenant of a flat may give—
(a) to his immediate landlord, or
(b) to any person receiving rent on behalf of his immediate landlord,
a notice requiring the recipient to state whether the immediate landlord is the owner of the freehold interest in the flat and, if not, to give the tenant such information as is mentioned in subsection (2) (so far as known to the recipient).

(2) That information is—
(a) the name and address of the person who owns the freehold interest in the flat;
(b) the duration of the leasehold interest in the flat of the tenant's immediate landlord and the extent of the premises in which it subsists; and

    (c) the name and address of every person who has a leasehold interest in the flat which is superior to that of the tenant's immediate landlord, the duration of any such interest and the extent of the premises in which it subsists.

(3) If the immediate landlord of any such qualifying tenant is not the owner of the freehold interest in the flat, the tenant may also—

    (a) give to the person who is the owner of that interest a notice requiring him to give the tenant such information as is mentioned in paragraph (c) of subsection (2) (so far as known to that person);

    (b) give to any person falling within that paragraph a notice requiring him to give the tenant—

        (i) particulars of the duration of his leasehold interest in the flat and the extent of the premises in which it subsists, and

        (ii) (so far as known to him) such information as is mentioned in paragraph (a) of that subsection and, as regards any other person falling within paragraph (c) of that subsection, such information as is mentioned in that paragraph.

(4) Any notice given by a qualifying tenant under this section shall, in addition to any other requirement imposed in accordance with subsections (1) to (3), require the recipient to state—

    (a) whether he has received in respect of any premises containing the tenant's flat—

        (i) a notice under section 13 in the case of which the relevant claim under Chapter I is still current, or

        (ii) a copy of such a notice; and

    (b) if so, the date on which the notice under section 13 was given and the name and address of the nominee purchaser for the time being appointed for the purposes of section 15 in relation to that claim.

(5) For the purposes of subsection (4)—

    (a) "the relevant claim under Chapter I", in relation to a notice under section 13, means the claim in respect of which that notice is given; and

    (b) any such claim is current if—

        (i) that notice continues in force in accordance with section 13(11), or

        (ii) a binding contract entered into in pursuance of that notice remains in force, or

        (iii) where an order has been made under section 24(4)(a) or (b) or 25(6)(a) or (b) with respect to any such premises as are referred to in subsection (4)(a) above, any interests which by virtue of the order fall to be vested in the nominee purchaser for the purposes of Chapter I have yet to be so vested.

(6) Any person who is required to give any information by virtue of a notice under this section shall give that information to the qualifying tenant within the period of 28 days beginning with the date of the giving of the notice.

Definitions   For "qualifying tenant", see s 39(3); for "the nominee purchaser", see s 15; for "flat" and "interest", see s 101(1) (and note also as to "flat", s 62(2)–(4)); as to "tenant", see s 101(2); for "the relevant claim under Chapter I", see sub-s (5) above.
References   See paras 4.14–4.17 ff.

The tenant's notice

42 Notice by qualifying tenant of claim to exercise right

(1) A claim by a qualifying tenant of a flat to exercise the right to acquire a new lease of the flat is made by the giving of notice of the claim under this section.

(2) A notice given by a tenant under this section ("the tenant's notice") must be given—

    (a) to the landlord, and

    (b) to any third party to the tenant's lease.

(3) The tenant's notice must—

    (a) state the full name of the tenant and the address of the flat in respect of which he claims a new lease under this Chapter;

    (b) contain the following particulars, namely—

        (i) sufficient particulars of that flat to identify the property to which the claim extends,

        (ii) such particulars of the tenant's lease as are sufficient to identify it, including the date on which the lease was entered into, the term for which it was granted and the date of the commencement of the term,

        (iii) such further particulars as are necessary to show that the tenant's lease is, in accordance with section 8 (as that section applies in accordance with section 39(3)), a lease at a low rent, and

        (iv) particulars of the period or periods falling within the preceding ten years for which the tenant has occupied the whole or part of the flat as his only or principal home;

    (c) specify the premium which the tenant proposes to pay in respect of the grant of a new lease under this Chapter and, where any other amount will be payable by him in accordance with any provision of Schedule 13, the amount which he proposes to pay in accordance with that provision;

    (d) specify the terms which the tenant proposes should be contained in any such lease;

    (e) state the name of the person (if any) appointed by the tenant to act for him in connection with his claim, and an address in England and Wales at which notices may be given to any such person under this Chapter; and

    (f) specify the date by which the landlord must respond to the notice by giving a counter-notice under section 45.

(4) If the tenant's lease is held by joint tenants, the reference to the tenant in subsection (3)(b)(iv) shall be read as a reference to any joint tenant with respect to whom it is claimed that the condition in section 39(2)(b) is satisfied.

(5) The date specified in the tenant's notice in pursuance of subsection (3)(f) must be a date falling not less than two months after the date of the giving of the notice.

(6) Where a notice under this section has been given with respect to any flat, no subsequent notice may be given under this section with respect to the flat so long as the earlier notice continues in force.

(7) Where a notice under this section has been given with respect to a flat and—

    (a) that notice has been withdrawn, or is deemed to have been withdrawn, under or by virtue of any provision of this Chapter, or

    (b) in response to that notice, an order has been applied for and obtained under section 47(1), no subsequent notice may be given under this section with respect to the flat within the period of twelve months beginning with the date of the withdrawal or deemed withdrawal of the earlier notice or with the time when the order under section 47(1) becomes final (as the case may be).

(8) Where a notice is given in accordance with this section, then for the purposes of this Chapter the notice continues in force as from the relevant date—

(a) until a new lease is granted in pursuance of the notice;

(b) if the notice is withdrawn, or is deemed to have been withdrawn, under or by virtue of any provision of this Chapter, until the date of the withdrawal or deemed withdrawal; or

(c) until such other time as the notice ceases to have effect by virtue of any provision of this Chapter;

but this subsection has effect subject to section 54.

(9) Schedule 12 (which contains restrictions on terminating a tenant's lease where he has given a notice under this section and makes other provision in connection with the giving of notices under this section) shall have effect.

Definitions For "qualifying tenant", see s 39(3); for "the relevant date", see s 39(8); for "the landlord", see s 40(1); for "third party", see s 62(1); for "flat", see s 101(1) (and note also s 62(2)–(4)); for "lease" and related expressions, see s 101(1), (2); for "the tenant's notice", see sub-s (2) above.
References See paras 4.22–4.28 ff.

43 General provisions as respects effect of tenant's notice

(1) Where a notice has been given under section 42 with respect to any flat, the rights and obligations of the landlord and the tenant arising from the notice shall enure for the benefit of and be enforceable against them, their personal representatives and assigns to the like extent (but no further) as rights and obligations arising under a contract for leasing freely entered into between the landlord and the tenant.

(2) Accordingly, in relation to matters arising out of any such notice, references in this Chapter to the landlord and the tenant shall, in so far as the context permits, include their respective personal representatives and assigns.

(3) Notwithstanding anything in subsection (1), the rights and obligations of the tenant shall be assignable with, but shall not be capable of subsisting apart from, the lease of the entire flat; and, if the tenant's lease is assigned without the benefit of the notice, the notice shall accordingly be deemed to have been withdrawn by the tenant as at the date of the assignment.

(4) In the event of any default by the landlord or the tenant in carrying out the obligations arising from the tenant's notice, the other of them shall have the like rights and remedies as in the case of a contract freely entered into.

(5) In a case to which section 40(2) applies, the rights and obligations of the landlord arising out of the tenant's notice shall, so far as their interests are affected, be rights and obligations respectively of the competent landlord and of each of the other landlords, and references to the landlord in subsections (1) and (2) above shall apply accordingly.

(6) In subsection (5) "competent landlord" and "other landlord" have the meaning given by section 40(4); and subsection (5) has effect without prejudice to the operation of section 40(2) or Schedule 11.

Definitions   For "the landlord", see s 40(1); for "the tenant's notice", see s 42; for "flat", see s 101(1) (and note also s 62(2)–(4)); as to "tenant" and "leasing", see s 101(2); for "competent landlord" and "other landlord" in sub-s (5) above, see sub-s (6) above.
References   See paras 4.29, 4.30 ff.

Procedure following giving of tenant's notice

44   Access by landlords for valuation purposes

(1) Once the tenant's notice or a copy of it has been given in accordance with section 42 or Part I of Schedule 11—

    (a) to the landlord for the purposes of this Chapter, or

    (b) to any other landlord (as defined by section 40(4)),

that landlord and any person authorised to act on his behalf shall have a right of access to the flat to which the notice relates for the purpose of enabling that landlord to obtain, in connection with the notice, a valuation of his interest in the flat.

(2) That right shall be exercisable at any reasonable time and on giving not less than 3 days' notice to the tenant.

Definitions   For "the landlord", see s 40(1); for "the tenant's notice", see s 42; for "flat", see s 101(1) (and note also s 62(2)–(4)); as to "tenant", see s 101(2).
References   See paras 4.31 ff.

45   Landlord's counter-notice

(1) The landlord shall give a counter-notice under this section to the tenant by the date specified in the tenant's notice in pursuance of section 42(3)(f).

(2) The counter-notice must comply with one of the following requirements—

    (a) state that the landlord admits that the tenant had on the relevant date the right to acquire a new lease of his flat;

    (b) state that, for such reasons as are specified in the counter-notice, the landlord does not admit that the tenant had such a right on that date;

    (c) contain such a statement as is mentioned in paragraph (a) or (b) above but state that the landlord intends to make an application for an order under section 47(1) on the grounds that he intends to redevelop any premises in which the flat is contained.

(3) If the counter-notice complies with the requirement set out in subsection (2)(a), it must in addition—

    (a) state which (if any) of the proposals contained in the tenant's notice are accepted by the landlord and which (if any) of those proposals are not so accepted; and

    (b) specify, in relation to each proposal which is not accepted, the landlord's counter-proposal.

(4) The counter-notice must specify an address in England and Wales at which notices may be given to the landlord under this Chapter.

(5) Where the counter-notice admits the tenant's right to acquire a new lease of his flat, the admission shall be binding on the landlord as to the matters mentioned in section 39(2)(a) and (b), unless the landlord shows that he was induced to make the admission by misrepresentation or the concealment of material facts; but the admission shall not conclude any question whether the particulars of the flat stated in the tenant's notice in pursuance of section 42(3)(b)(i) are correct.

Definitions   For "the relevant date", see s 39(8); for "the landlord", see s 40(1); for "the tenant's notice", see s 42; for "flat" see s 101(1) (and note also s 62(2)–(4)); for "lease" and related expressions (including "tenant"), see s 101(1), (2).
References   See paras 4.34, 4.35 ff.

Applications to court or leasehold valuation tribunal

46   Proceedings relating to validity of tenant's notice

(1) Where—

    (a)   the landlord has given the tenant a counter-notice under section 45 which (whether it complies with the requirement set out in subsection (2)(b) or (c) of that section) contains such a statement as is mentioned in subsection (2)(b) of that section, and

    (b)   the court is satisfied, on an application made by the landlord, that on the relevant date the tenant had no right under this Chapter to acquire a new lease of his flat,

the court shall by order make a declaration to that effect.

(2) Any application for an order under subsection (1) must be made not later than the end of the period of two months beginning with the date of the giving of the counter-notice to the tenant; and if, in a case falling within paragraph (a) of that subsection, either—

    (a)   no application for such an order is made by the landlord within that period, or

    (b)   such an application is so made but is subsequently withdrawn,

section 49 shall apply as if the landlord had not given the counter-notice.

(3) If on any such application the court makes such a declaration as is mentioned in subsection (1), the tenant's notice shall cease to have effect on the order becoming final.

(4) If, however, any such application is dismissed by the court, then (subject to subsection (5)) the court shall make an order—

    (a)   declaring that the landlord's counter-notice shall be of no effect, and

    (b)   requiring the landlord to give a further counter-notice to the tenant by such date as is specified in the order.

(5) Subsection (4) shall not apply if—

    (a)   the counter-notice complies with the requirement set out in section 45(2)(c), and

    (b)   either—

        (i)   an application for an order under section 47(1) is pending, or

        (ii)   the period specified in section 47(3) as the period for the making of such an application has not expired.

(6) Subsection (3) of section 45 shall apply to any further counter-notice required to be given by the landlord under subsection (4) above as if it were a counter-notice under that section complying with the requirement set out in subsection (2)(a) of that section.

Definitions   For "the relevant date", see s 39(8); for "the landlord", see s 40(1); for "the court", see s 101(1); as to "tenant", see s 101(2).
References   See paras 4.40–4.43 ff.

47 Application to defeat tenant's claim where landlord intends to redevelop

(1) Where the landlord has given the tenant a counter-notice under section 45 which complies with the requirement set out in subsection (2)(c) of that section, the court may, on the application of the landlord, by order declare that the right to acquire a new lease shall not be exercisable by the tenant by reason of the landlord's intention to redevelop any premises in which the tenant's flat is contained; and on such an order becoming final the tenant's notice shall cease to have effect.

(2) The court shall not make an order under subsection (1) unless it is satisfied—

    (a) that the tenant's lease of his flat is due to terminate within the period of five years beginning with the relevant date; and

    (b) that for the purposes of redevelopment the landlord intends, once the lease has so terminated—

        (i) to demolish or reconstruct, or

        (ii) to carry out substantial works of construction on,

    the whole or a substantial part of any premises in which the flat is contained; and

    (c) that he could not reasonably do so without obtaining possession of the flat.

(3) Any application for an order under subsection (1) must be made within the period of two months beginning with the date of the giving of the counter-notice to the tenant; but, where the counter-notice is one falling within section 46(1)(a), such an application shall not be proceeded with until such time (if any) as any order dismissing an application under section 46(1) becomes final.

(4) Where an application for an order under subsection (1) is dismissed by the court, the court shall make an order—

    (a) declaring that the landlord's counter-notice shall be of no effect, and

    (b) requiring the landlord to give a further counter-notice to the tenant by such date as is specified in the order.

(5) Where—

    (a) the landlord has given such a counter-notice as is mentioned in subsection (1), but

    (b) either—

        (i) no application for an order under that subsection is made within the period referred to in subsection (3), or

        (ii) such an application is so made but is subsequently withdrawn,

then (subject to subsection (7)), the landlord shall give a further counter-notice to the tenant within the period of two months beginning with the appropriate date.

(6) In subsection (5) "the appropriate date" means—

    (a) if subsection (5)(b)(i) applies, the date immediately following the end of the period referred to in subsection (3); and

    (b) if subsection (5)(b)(ii) applies, the date of withdrawal of the application.

(7) Subsection (5) shall not apply if any application has been made by the landlord for an order under section 46(1).

(8) Subsection (3) of section 45 shall apply to any further counter-notice required to be given by the landlord under subsection (4) or (5) above as if it were a counter-notice under that section complying with the requirement set out in subsection (2)(a) of that section.

Definitions For "the relevant date", see s 39(8); for "the landlord", see s 40(1); for "the tenant's notice", see s 42; for "the court" and "flat", see s 101(1) (and note also as to "flat", s 62(3), (4)); for "lease" and related expressions (including "tenant"), see s 101(1), (2); for "the appropriate date" in sub-s (5) above, see sub-s (6) above.
References See paras 4.44–4.47 ff.

48 Applications where terms in dispute or failure to enter into new lease

(1) Where the landlord has given the tenant—

    (a) a counter-notice under section 45 which complies with the requirement set out in subsection (2)(a) of that section, or

    (b) a further counter-notice required by or by virtue of section 46(4) or section 47(4) or (5),

but any of the terms of acquisition remain in dispute at the end of the period of two months beginning with the date when the counter-notice or further counter-notice was so given, a leasehold valuation tribunal may, on the application of either the tenant or the landlord, determine the matters in dispute.

(2) Any application under subsection (1) must be made not later than the end of the period of six months beginning with the date on which the counter-notice or further counter-notice was given to the tenant.

(3) Where—

    (a) the landlord has given the tenant such a counter-notice or further counter-notice as is mentioned in subsection (1)(a) or (b), and

    (b) all the terms of acquisition have been either agreed between those persons or determined by a leasehold valuation tribunal under subsection (1),

but a new lease has not been entered into in pursuance of the tenant's notice by the end of the appropriate period specified in subsection (6), the court may, on the application of either the tenant or the landlord, make such order as it thinks fit with respect to the performance or discharge of any obligations arising out of that notice.

(4) Any such order may provide for the tenant's notice to be deemed to have been withdrawn at the end of the appropriate period specified in subsection (6).

(5) Any application for an order under subsection (3) must be made not later than the end of the period of two months beginning immediately after the end of the appropriate period specified in subsection (6).

(6) For the purposes of this section the appropriate period is—

    (a) where all of the terms of acquisition have been agreed between the tenant and the landlord, the period of two months beginning with the date when those terms were finally so agreed; or

    (b) where all or any of those terms have been determined by a leasehold valuation tribunal under subsection (1)—

        (i) the period of two months beginning with the date when the decision of the tribunal under subsection (1) becomes final, or

        (ii) such other period as may have been fixed by the tribunal when making its determination.

(7) In this Chapter "the terms of acquisition", in relation to a claim by a tenant under this Chapter, means the terms on which the tenant is to acquire a new lease of his flat, whether they relate to the terms to be contained in the lease or to the premium or any other amount payable by virtue of Schedule 13 in connection with the grant of the lease, or otherwise.

Definitions   For "the landlord", see s 40(1); for "the tenant's notice", see s 42; for "the court", see s 101(1); for "lease" and related expressions (including "tenant"), see s 101(1), (2); as to "the appropriate period", see sub-s (6) above; for "the terms of acquisition", see sub-s (7) above.
References   See paras 4.48, 4.70–4.72 ff.

49   Applications where landlord fails to give counter-notice or further counter-notice

(1) Where the tenant's notice has been given in accordance with section 42 but—

   (a) the landlord has failed to give the tenant a counter-notice in accordance with section 45(1), or

   (b) if required to give a further counter-notice to the tenant by or by virtue of section 46(4) or section 47(4) or (5), the landlord has failed to comply with that requirement,

the court may, on the application of the tenant, make an order determining, in accordance with the proposals contained in the tenant's notice, the terms of acquisition.

(2) The court shall not make such an order on an application made by virtue of paragraph (a) of subsection (1) unless it is satisfied—

   (a) that on the relevant date the tenant had the right to acquire a new lease of his flat; and

   (b) if applicable, that the requirements of Part I of Schedule 11 were complied with as respects the giving of copies of the tenant's notice.

(3) Any application for an order under subsection (1) must be made not later than the end of the period of six months beginning with the date by which the counter-notice or further counter-notice referred to in that subsection was required to be given.

(4) Where—

   (a) the terms of acquisition have been determined by an order of the court under this section, but

   (b) a new lease has not been entered into in pursuance of the tenant's notice by the end of the appropriate period specified in subsection (7),

the court may, on the application of either the tenant or the landlord, make such order as it thinks fit with respect to the performance or discharge of any obligations arising out of that notice.

(5) Any such order may provide for the tenant's notice to be deemed to have been withdrawn at the end of the appropriate period specified in subsection (7).

(6) Any application for an order under subsection (4) must be made not later than the end of the period of two months beginning immediately after the end of the appropriate period specified in subsection.

(7) For the purposes of this section the appropriate period is—

   (a) the period of two months beginning with the date when the order of the court under subsection (1) becomes final, or

   (b) such other period as may have been fixed by the court when making that order.

Definitions   For "the relevant date", see s 39(8); for "the landlord", see s 40(1); for "the tenant's notice", see s 42; for "the terms of acquisition", see s 48(7); for "the court" and "flat", see s 101(1) (and note also as to "flat", s 62(2)–(4)); for "lease" and related expressions (including "tenant"), see s 101(1), (2).
References   See paras 4.55, 4.56, 4.71, 4.72 ff.

50 Applications where landlord cannot be found

(1) Where—
- (a) a qualifying tenant of a flat desires to make a claim to exercise the right to acquire a new lease of his flat, but
- (b) the landlord cannot be found or his identity cannot be ascertained,

the court may, on the application of the tenant, make a vesting order under this subsection.

(2) Where—
- (a) a qualifying tenant of a flat desires to make such a claim as is mentioned in subsection (1), and
- (b) paragraph (b) of that subsection does not apply, but
- (c) a copy of a notice of that claim cannot be given in accordance with Part I of Schedule 11 to any person to whom it would otherwise be required to be so given because that person cannot be found or his identity cannot be ascertained,

the court may, on the application of the tenant, make an order dispensing with the need to give a copy of such a notice to that person.

(3) The court shall not make an order on any application under subsection (1) or (2) unless it is satisfied—
- (a) that on the date of the making of the application the tenant had the right to acquire a new lease of his flat; and
- (b) that on that date he would not have been precluded by any provision of this Chapter from giving a valid notice under section 42 with respect to his flat.

(4) Before making any such order the court may require the tenant to take such further steps by way of advertisement or otherwise as the court thinks proper for the purpose of tracing the person in question; and if, after an application is made for a vesting order under subsection (1) and before any lease is executed in pursuance of the application, the landlord is traced, then no further proceedings shall be taken with a view to a lease being so executed, but (subject to subsection (5))—
- (a) the rights and obligations of all parties shall be determined as if the tenant had, at the date of the application, duly given notice under section 42 of his claim to exercise the right to acquire a new lease of his flat; and
- (b) the court may give such directions as the court thinks fit as to the steps to be taken for giving effect to those rights and obligations, including directions modifying or dispensing with any of the requirements of this Chapter or of regulations made under this Part.

(5) An application for a vesting order under subsection (1) may be withdrawn at any time before execution of a lease under section 51(3) and, after it is withdrawn, subsection (4)(a) above shall not apply; but where any step is taken (whether by the landlord or the tenant) for the purpose of giving effect to subsection (4)(a) in the case of any application, the application shall not afterwards be withdrawn except—
- (a) with the consent of the landlord, or
- (b) by leave of the court,

and the court shall not give leave unless it appears to the court just to do so by reason of matters coming to the knowledge of the tenant in consequence of the tracing of the landlord.

(6) Where an order has been made under subsection (2) dispensing with the need to give a copy of a notice under section 42 to a particular person with respect to any flat, then if—

(a) a notice is subsequently given under that section with respect to that flat, and

(b) in reliance on the order, a copy of the notice is not to be given to that person,

the notice must contain a statement of the effect of the order.

(7) Where a notice under section 42 contains such a statement in accordance with subsection (6) above, then in determining for the purposes of any provision of this Chapter whether the requirements of Part I of Schedule 11 have been complied with in relation to the notice, those requirements shall be deemed to have been complied with so far as relating to the giving of a copy of the notice to the person referred to in subsection (6) above.

Definitions   For "qualifying tenant", see s 39(3); for "the landlord", see s 40(1); for "the court" and "flat", see s 101(1) (and note also as to "flat", s 62(2)–(4)); for "lease" and related expressions, see s 101(1), (2).
References   See paras 4.73–4.81 ff.

51   Supplementary provisions relating to vesting orders under section 50(1)

(1) A vesting order under section 50(1) is an order providing for the surrender of the tenant's lease of his flat and for the granting to him of a new lease of it on such terms as may be determined by a leasehold valuation tribunal to be appropriate with a view to the lease being granted to him in like manner (so far as the circumstances permit) as if he had, at the date of his application, given notice under section 42 of his claim to exercise the right to acquire a new lease of his flat.

(2) If a leasehold valuation tribunal so determines in the case of a testing order under section 50(1), the order shall have effect in relation to property which is less extensive than that specified in the application on which the order was made.

(3) Where any lease is to be granted to a tenant by virtue of a vesting order under section 50(1), then on his paying into court the appropriate sum there shall be executed by such person as the court may designate a lease which—

(a) is in a form approved by a leasehold valuation tribunal, and

(b) contains such provisions as may be so approved for the purpose of giving effect so far as possible to section 56(1) and section 57 (as that section applies in accordance with subsections (7) and (8) below);

and that lease shall be effective to vest in the person to whom it is granted the property expressed to be demised by it, subject to and in accordance with the terms of the lease.

(4) In connection with the determination by a leasehold valuation tribunal of any question as to the property to be demised by any such lease, or as to the rights with or subject to which it is to be demised, it shall be assumed (unless the contrary is shown) that the landlord has no interest in property other than the property to be demised and, for the purpose of excepting them from the lease, any minerals underlying that property.

(5) The appropriate sum to be paid into court in accordance with subsection (3) is the aggregate of—

(a) such amount as may be determined by a leasehold valuation tribunal to be the premium which is payable under Schedule 13 in respect of the grant of the new lease;

    (b) such other amount or amounts (if any) as may be determined by such a tribunal to be payable by virtue of that Schedule in connection with the grant of that lease; and

    (c) any amounts or estimated amounts determined by such a tribunal as being, at the time of execution of that lease, due to the landlord from the tenant (whether due under or in respect of the tenant's lease of his flat or under or in respect of an agreement collateral thereto).

(6) Where any lease is granted to a person in accordance with this section, the payment into court of the appropriate sum shall be taken to have satisfied any claims against the tenant, his personal representatives or assigns in respect of the premium and any other amounts payable as mentioned in subsection (5)(a) and (b).

(7) Subject to subsection (8), the following provisions, namely—

    (a) sections 57 to 59, and

    (b) section 61 and Schedule 14,

shall, so far as capable of applying to a lease granted in accordance with this section, apply to such a lease as they apply to a lease granted under section 56; and subsections (6) and (7) of that section shall apply in relation to a lease granted in accordance with this section as they apply in relation to a lease granted under that section.

(8) In its application to a lease granted in accordance with this section—

    (a) section 57 shall have effect as if—

        (i) any reference to the relevant date were a reference to the date of the application under section 50(1) in pursuance of which the vesting order under that provision was made, and

        (ii) in subsection (5) the reference to section 56(3)(a) were a reference to subsection (5)(c) above; and

    (b) section 58 shall have effect as if—

        (i) in subsection (3) the second reference to the landlord were a reference to the person designated under subsection (3) above, and

        (ii) subsections (6)(a) and (7) were omitted.

Definitions   For "the relevant date", see s 39(8); for "the landlord", see s 40(1); for "flat", see s 101(1) (and note also s 62(2)–(4)); for "lease" and related expressions (including "tenant"), see s 101(1), (2); as to "the appropriate sum", see sub-s (5).
References   See paras 4.76, 4.82–4.85 ff.

Termination or suspension of acquisition procedures

52 Withdrawal by tenant from acquisition of new lease

(1) At any time before a new lease is entered into in pursuance of the tenant's notice, the tenant may withdraw that notice by the giving of a notice to that effect under this section ("a notice of withdrawal").

(2) A notice of withdrawal must be given—

    (a) to the landlord for the purposes of this Chapter;

    (b) to every other landlord (as defined by section 40(4)); and

    (c) to any third party to the tenant's lease.

(3) Where a notice of withdrawal is given by the tenant to any person in accordance with subsection (2), the tenant's liability under section 60 for costs incurred by that person shall be a liability for costs incurred by him down to the time when the notice is given to him.

Definitions For "the landlord", see s 40(1); for "the tenant's notice", see s 42; for "third party", see s 62(1); for "lease" and related expressions (including "tenant"), see s 101(1), (2); for "a notice of withdrawal", see sub-s (1) above.
References See para 4.36 ff.

53 Deemed withdrawal of tenant's notice

(1) Where—

   (a) in a case to which subsection (1) of section 48 applies, no application under that subsection is made within the period specified in subsection (2) of that section, or

   (b) in a case to which subsection (3) of that section applies, no application for an order under that subsection is made within the period specified in subsection (5) of that section,

the tenant's notice shall be deemed to have been withdrawn at the end of the period referred to in paragraph (a) or (b) above (as the case may be).

(2) Where, in a case falling within paragraph (a) or (b) of subsection (1) of section 49, no application for an order under that subsection is made within the period specified in subsection (3) of that section, the tenant's notice shall be deemed to have been withdrawn at the end of that period.

(3) Where, in a case to which subsection (4) of section 49 applies, no application for an order under that subsection is made within the period specified in subsection (6) of that section, the tenant's notice shall be deemed to have been withdrawn at the end of that period.

(4) The following provisions, namely—

   (a) section 43(3),

   (b) section 48(4), and

   (c) section 49(5),

also make provision for a notice under section 42 to be deemed to have been withdrawn at a particular time.

54 Suspension of tenant's notice during currency of claim under Chapter I

(1) If, at the time when the tenant's notice is given—

   (a) a notice has been given under section 13 with respect to any premises containing the tenant's flat, and

   (b) the relevant claim under Chapter I is still current,

the operation of the tenant's notice shall be suspended during the currency of that claim; and so long as it is so suspended no further notice shall be given, and no application shall be made, under this Chapter with a view to resisting or giving effect to the tenant's claim.

(2) If, at any time when the tenant's notice continues in force, a notice is given under section 13 with respect to any premises containing the tenant's flat, then, as from the date which is the relevant date for the purposes of Chapter I in relation to that notice under section 13, the operation of the tenant's notice shall be suspended during the currency of the relevant claim under Chapter I; and so long as it is so suspended no further notice shall be given, and no application shall be made or proceeded with, under this Chapter with a view to resisting or giving effect to the tenant's claim.

(3) Where the operation of the tenant's notice is suspended by virtue of subsection (1) or (2), the landlord shall give the tenant a notice informing him of its suspension—

(a) (if it is suspended by virtue of subsection (1)) not later than the date specified in the tenant's notice in pursuance of section 42(3)(f); or

(b) (if it is suspended by virtue of subsection (2)) as soon as possible after the date referred to in that subsection;

and any such notice shall in addition inform the tenant of the date on which the notice under section 13 was given and of the name and address of the nominee purchaser for the time being appointed for the purposes of section 15 in relation to the relevant claim under Chapter I.

(4) Where—

(a) the operation of the tenant's notice is suspended by virtue of subsection (1), and

(b) as a result of the relevant claim under Chapter I ceasing to be current, the operation of the tenant's notice subsequently ceases to be so suspended and the tenant's notice thereupon continues in force in accordance with section 42(8),

then, as from the date when that claim ceases to be current ("the termination date"), this Chapter shall apply as if there were substituted for the date specified in the tenant's notice in pursuance of section 42(3)(f) such date as results in the period of time intervening between the termination date and that date being equal to the period of time intervening between the relevant date and the date originally so specified.

(5) Where—

(a) the operation of the tenant's notice is suspended by virtue of subsection (2), and

(b) its suspension began in circumstances falling within subsection (6), and

(c) as a result of the relevant claim under Chapter I ceasing to be current, the operation of the tenant's notice subsequently ceases to be so suspended and the tenant's notice thereupon continues in force in accordance with section 42(8),

any relevant period shall be deemed to have begun on the date when that claim ceases to be current.

(6) The circumstances referred to in subsection (5)(b) are that the suspension of the operation of the tenant's notice began—

(a) before the date specified in the tenant's notice in pursuance of section 42(3)(f) and before the landlord had given the tenant a counter-notice under section 45; or

(b) after the landlord had given the tenant a counter-notice under section 45 complying with the requirement set out in subsection (2)(b) or (c) of that section but—

(i) before any application had been made for an order under section 46(1) or 47(1), and

(ii) before the period for making any such application had expired; or

(c) after an order had been made under section 46(4) or 47(4) but—

(i) before the landlord had given the tenant a further counter-notice in accordance with the order, and

(ii) before the period for giving any such counter-notice had expired.

(7) Where—

    (a) the operation of the tenant's notice is suspended by virtue of subsection (2), and

    (b) its suspension began otherwise than in circumstances falling within subsection (6), and

    (c) as a result of the relevant claim under Chapter I ceasing to be current, the operation of the tenant's notice subsequently ceases to be so suspended and the tenant's notice thereupon continues in force in accordance with section 42(8),

any relevant period shall be deemed to have begun on the date on which the tenant is given a notice under subsection (8) below or, if earlier, the date on which the tenant gives the landlord a notice informing him of the circumstances by virtue of which the operation of the tenant's notice has ceased to be suspended.

(8) Where subsection (4), (5) or (7) applies, the landlord shall, as soon as possible after becoming aware of the circumstances by virtue of which the operation of the tenant's notice has ceased to be suspended as mentioned in that subsection, give the tenant a notice informing him that, as from the date when the relevant claim under Chapter I ceased to be current, the operation of his notice is no longer suspended.

(9) Subsection (8) shall not, however, require the landlord to give any such notice if he has received a notice from the tenant under subsection (7).

(10) In subsections (5) and (7) "relevant period" means any period which—

    (a) is prescribed by or under this Part for the giving of any notice, or the making of any application, in connection with the tenant's notice; and

    (b) was current at the time when the suspension of the operation of the tenant's notice began.

(11) For the purposes of this section—

    (a) "the relevant claim under Chapter I", in relation to a notice under section 13, means the claim in respect of which that notice is given; and

    (b) any such claim is current if—

        (i) that notice continues in force in accordance with section 13(11), or

        (ii) a binding contract entered into in pursuance of that notice remains in force, or

        (iii) where an order has been made under section 24(4)(a) or (b) or 25(6)(a) or (b) with respect to any such premises as are referred to in subsection (1) or (2) above (as the case may be), any interests which by virtue of the order fall to be vested in the nominee purchaser for the purposes of Chapter I have yet to be so vested.

Definitions   For "the relevant date", see s 39(8); for "the landlord", see s 40(1); for "the tenant's notice", see s 42; for "flat", see s 101(1) (and note also s 62(2)–(4)); as to "tenant", see s 101(2); for "the termination date", see sub-s (4) above; for "relevant period" in sub-ss (5), (7) above, see sub-s (10) above; for "the relevant claim under Chapter I", see sub-s (11) above.
References   See paras 3.70, 4.103–4.108 ff.

---

55 Effect on tenant's notice of institution of compulsory acquisition procedures

(1) A notice given by a tenant under section 42 shall be of no effect if on the relevant date—

    (a) any person or body of persons who has or have been, or could be, authorised to acquire the whole or part of the tenant's flat compulsorily for any purpose has or have, with a view to its acquisition for that purpose—

    (i)   served notice to treat on the landlord or the tenant, or

    (ii) entered into a contract for the purchase of the interest of either of them in the flat or part of it, and

  (b) the notice to treat or contract remains in force.

(2) A notice given by a tenant under section 42 shall cease to have effect if, before a new lease is entered into in pursuance of it, any such person or body of persons as is mentioned in subsection (1) serves or serve notice to treat as mentioned in that subsection.

(3) Where subsection (2) applies in relation to a notice given by a tenant under section 42, then on the occasion of the compulsory acquisition in question the compensation payable in respect of any interest in the tenant's flat (whether or not the one to which the relevant notice to treat relates) shall be determined on the basis of the value of the interest subject to and with the benefit of the rights and obligations arising from the tenant's notice and affecting that interest.

Definitions   For "the relevant date", see s 39(8); for "the landlord", see s 40(1); for "flat" and "interest", see s 101(1) (note also as to "flat", s 62(2)–(4)); as to "tenant", see s 101(2).
References   See para 4.109 ff.

Grant of new lease

56 Obligation to grant new lease

(1) Where a qualifying tenant of a flat has under this Chapter a right to acquire a new lease of the flat and gives notice of his claim in accordance with section 42, then except as provided by this Chapter the landlord shall be bound to grant to the tenant, and the tenant shall be bound to accept—

  (a) in substitution for the existing lease, and

  (b) on payment of the premium payable under Schedule 13 in respect of the grant,

a new lease of the flat at a peppercorn rent for a term expiring 90 years after the term date of the existing lease.

(2) In addition to any such premium there shall be payable by the tenant in connection with the grant of any such new lease such amounts to the owners of any intermediate leasehold interests (within the meaning of Schedule 13) as are so payable by virtue of that Schedule.

(3) A tenant shall not be entitled to require the execution of any such new lease otherwise than on tendering to the landlord, in addition to the amount of any such premium and any other amounts payable by virtue of Schedule 13, the amount so far as ascertained—

  (a) of any sums payable by him by way of rent or recoverable from him as rent in respect of the flat up to the date of tender;

  (b) of any sums for which at that date the tenant is liable under section 60 in respect of costs incurred by any relevant person (within the meaning of that section); and

  (c) of any other sums due and payable by him to any such person under or in respect of the existing lease;

and, if the amount of any such sums is not or may not be fully ascertained, on offering reasonable security for the payment of such amount as may afterwards be found to be payable in respect of them.

(4) To the extent that any amount tendered to the landlord in accordance with subsection (3) is an amount due to a person other than the landlord, that amount shall be payable to that person by the landlord; and that subsection has effect subject to paragraph 7(2) of Schedule 11.

(5) No provision of any lease prohibiting, restricting or otherwise relating to a sub-demise by the tenant under the lease shall have effect with reference to the granting of any lease under this section.

(6) It is hereby declared that nothing in any of the provisions specified in paragraph 1(2) of Schedule 10 (which impose requirements as to consent or consultation or other restrictions in relation to disposals falling within those provisions) applies to the granting of any lease under this section.

(7) For the purposes of subsection (6), paragraph 1(2) of Schedule 10 has effect as if the reference to section 79(2) of the Housing Act 1988 (which is not relevant in the context of subsection (6)) were omitted.

Definitions   For "qualifying tenant", see s 39(3); for "the landlord", see s 40(1); for "the existing lease", see s 62(1); for "flat" and "the term date", see s 101(1) (and note also as to "flat", s 62(2)–(4)); for "lease" and related expressions (including "tenant"), see s 101(1), (2).
References   See paras 4.3, 4.57–4.61 ff.

---

57   Terms on which new lease is to be granted

(1) Subject to the provisions of this Chapter (and in particular to the provisions as to rent and duration contained in section 56(1)), the new lease to be granted to a tenant under section 56 shall be a lease on the same terms as those of the existing lease, as they apply on the relevant date, but with such modifications as may be required or appropriate to take account—

    (a)   of the omission from the new lease of property included in the existing lease but not comprised in the flat;

    (b)   of alterations made to the property demised since the grant of the existing lease; or

    (c)   in a case where the existing lease derives (in accordance with section 7(6) as it applies in accordance with section 39(3)) from more than one separate leases, of their combined effect and of the differences (if any) in their terms.

(2) Where during the continuance of the new lease the landlord will be under any obligation for the provision of services, or for repairs, maintenance or insurance—

    (a)   the new lease may require payments to be made by the tenant (whether as rent or otherwise) in consideration of those matters or in respect of the cost thereof to the landlord; and

    (b)   (if the terms of the existing lease do not include any provision for the making of any such payments by the tenant or include provision only for the payment of a fixed amount) the terms of the new lease shall make, as from the term date of the existing lease, such provision as may be just—

        (i)   for the making by the tenant of payments related to the cost from time to time to the landlord, and

    (ii) for the tenant's liability to make those payments to be enforceable by distress, re-entry or otherwise in like manner as if it were a liability for payment of rent.

(3) Subject to subsection (4), provision shall be made by the terms of the new lease or by an agreement collateral thereto for the continuance, with any suitable adaptations, of any agreement collateral to the existing lease.

(4) For the purposes of subsections (1) and (3) there shall be excluded from the new lease any term of the existing lease or of any agreement collateral thereto in so far as that term—

    (a) provides for or relates to the renewal of the lease,

    (b) confers any option to purchase or right of pre-emption in relation to the flat demised by the existing lease, or

    (c) provides for the termination of the existing lease before its term date otherwise than in the event of a breach of its terms;

and there shall be made in the terms of the new lease or any agreement collateral thereto such modifications as may be required or appropriate to take account of the exclusion of any such term.

(5) Where the new lease is granted after the term date of the existing lease, then on the grant of the new lease there shall be payable by the tenant to the landlord, as an addition to the rent payable under the existing lease, any amount by which, for the period since the term date or the relevant date (whichever is the later), the sums payable to the landlord in respect of the flat (after making any necessary apportionment) for the matters referred to in subsection (2) fall short in total of the sums that would have been payable for such matters under the new lease if it had been granted on that date; and section 56(3)(a) shall apply accordingly.

(6) Subsections (1) to (5) shall have effect subject to any agreement between the landlord and tenant as to the terms of the new lease or an agreement collateral thereto; and either of them may require that for the purposes of the new lease any term of the existing lease shall be excluded or modified in so far as—

    (a) it is necessary to do so in order to remedy a defect in the existing lease; or

    (b) it would be unreasonable in the circumstances to include, or include without modification, the term in question in view of changes occurring since the date of commencement of the existing lease which affect the suitability on the relevant date of the provisions of that lease.

(7) The terms of the new lease shall—

    (a) make provision in accordance with section 59(3); and

    (b) reserve to the person who is for the time being the tenant's immediate landlord the right to obtain possession of the flat in question in accordance with section 61.

(8) In granting the new lease the landlord shall not be bound to enter into any covenant for title beyond that implied from the grant, and a person entering into any covenant required of him as landlord shall be entitled to limit his personal liability to breaches of that covenant for which he is responsible.

(9) Where any person—

    (a) is a third party to the existing lease, or

    (b) (not being the landlord or tenant) is a party to any agreement collateral thereto, then (subject to any agreement between him and the landlord and the tenant) he shall be made a party to the new lease or (as the case may be) to an agreement collateral thereto, and shall accordingly join in its execution; but nothing in this section has effect so as to require the new lease or (as the case may be) any such collateral agreement to provide for him to discharge any function at any time after the term date of the existing lease.

(10) Where—
  (a) any such person ("the third party") is in accordance with subsection (9) to discharge any function down to the term date of the existing lease, but
  (b) it is necessary or expedient in connection with the proper enjoyment by the tenant of the property demised by the new lease for provision to be made for the continued discharge of that function after that date,
the new lease or an agreement collateral thereto shall make provision for that function to be discharged after that date (whether by the third party or by some other person).

(11) The new lease shall contain a statement that it is a lease granted under section 56; and any such statement shall comply with such requirements as may be prescribed by rules made in pursuance of section 144 of the Land Registration Act 1925 (power to make general rules).

Definitions   For "the relevant date", see s 39(8); for "the landlord", see s 40(1); for "the existing lease" and "third party", see s 62(1) (and note also as to "the third party" sub-s (10)); for "flat" and "the term date", see s 101(1) (and note also as to "flat" s 62(2)–(4)); for "lease" and related expressions (including "tenant"), see s 101(1), (2).
References   See paras 4.49–4.54, 4.62 ff.

---

58   Grant of new lease where interest of landlord or tenant is subject to a mortgage

(1) Subject to subsection (2), a qualifying tenant shall be entitled to be granted a new lease under section 56 despite the fact that the grant of the existing lease was subsequent to the creation of a mortgage on the landlord's interest and not authorised as against the persons interested in the mortgage; and a lease granted under that section—
  (a) shall be deemed to be authorised as against the persons interested in any mortgage on the landlord's interest (however created or arising), and
  (b) shall be binding on those persons.

(2) A lease granted under section 56 shall not, by virtue of subsection (1) above, be binding on the persons interested in any such mortgage if the existing lease—
  (a) is granted after the commencement of this Chapter, and
  (b) being granted subsequent to the creation of the mortgage, would not, apart from that subsection, be binding on the persons interested in the mortgage.

(3) Where—
  (a) a lease is granted under section 56, and
  (b) any person having a mortgage on the landlord's interest is thereby entitled to possession of the documents of title relating to that interest,
the landlord shall, within one month of the execution of the lease, deliver to that person a counterpart of it duly executed by the tenant.

(4) Where the existing lease is, immediately before its surrender on the grant of a lease under section 56, subject to any mortgage, the new lease shall take effect subject to the mortgage in substitution for the existing lease; and the terms of the mortgage, as set out in the instrument creating or evidencing it, shall accordingly apply in relation to the new lease in like manner as they applied in relation to the existing lease.

(5) Where—
(a) a lease granted under section 56 takes effect subject to any such subsisting mortgage on the existing lease, and
(b) at the time of execution of the new lease the person having the mortgage is thereby entitled to possession of the documents of title relating to the existing lease,

he shall be similarly entitled to possession of the documents of title relating to the new lease; and the tenant shall deliver the new lease to him within one month of the date on which the lease is received from Her Majesty's Land Registry following its registration.

(6) Where—
(a) the landlord fails to deliver a counterpart of the new lease in accordance with subsection (3), or
(b) the tenant fails to deliver the new lease in accordance with subsection (5),

the instrument creating or evidencing the mortgage in question shall apply as if the obligation to deliver a counterpart or (as the case may be) deliver the lease were included in the terms of the mortgage as set out in that instrument.

(7) A landlord granting a lease under section 56 shall be bound to take such steps as may be necessary to secure that the lease is not liable in accordance with subsection (2) to be defeated by persons interested in a mortgage on his interest; but a landlord is not obliged, in order to grant a lease for the purposes of that section, to acquire a better title than he has or could require to be vested in him.

Definitions   For "qualifying tenant", see s 39(3); for "the landlord", see s 40(1); for "the existing lease" and "mortgage", see s 62(1); for "interest", see s 101(1); for "lease" and related expressions (including "tenant"), see s 101(1), (2).
References   See paras 4.63, 4.65–4.69 ff.

---

59   Further renewal, but no security of tenure, after grant of new lease

(1) The right to acquire a new lease under this Chapter may be exercised in relation to a lease of a flat despite the fact that the lease is itself a lease granted under section 56; and the provisions of this Chapter shall, with any necessary modifications, apply for the purposes of or in connection with any claim to exercise that right in relation to a lease so granted as they apply for the purposes of or in connection with any claim to exercise that right in relation to a lease which has not been so granted.

(2) Where a lease has been granted under section 56—
(a) none of the statutory provisions relating to security of tenure for tenants shall apply to the lease;
(b) after the term date of the lease none of the following provisions, namely—
(i) section 1 of the Landlord and Tenant Act 1954 or Schedule 10 to the Local Government and Housing Act 1989 (which make

provision for security of tenure on the ending of long residential tenancies), or

    (ii) Part II of that Act of 1954 (business tenancies),

shall apply to any sub-lease directly or indirectly derived out of the lease; and

    (c) after that date no person shall be entitled by virtue of any such sub-lease to retain possession under—

        (i) Part VII of the Rent Act 1977 (security of tenure for protected tenancies etc) or any enactment applying or extending that Part of that Act,

        (ii) the Rent (Agriculture) Act 1976, or

        (iii) Part I of the Housing Act 1988 (assured tenancies etc).

(3) Where a lease has been granted under section 56, no long lease created immediately or derivatively by way of sub-demise under the lease shall confer on the sub-tenant, as against the tenant's landlord, any right under this Chapter to acquire a new lease (and for this purpose "long lease" shall be construed in accordance with section 7).

(4) Any person who—

    (a) grants a sub-lease to which subsection (2)(b) and (c) will apply, or

    (b) negotiates with a view to the grant of such a sub-lease by him or by a person for whom he is acting as agent,

shall inform the other party that the sub-lease is to be derived out of a lease granted under section 56, unless either he knows that the other party is aware of it or he himself is unaware of it.

(5) Where any lease contains a statement to the effect that it is a lease granted under section 56, the statement shall be conclusive for the purposes of subsections (2) to (4) in favour of any person who is not a party to the lease, unless the statement appears from the lease to be untrue.

Definitions   For "flat" and "term date", see s 101(1) (and note also as to "flat", s 62(2)–(4)); for "lease" and related expressions (including "tenant"), see s 101(1), (2); as to "long lease", see sub-s (3) above. **References**   See paras 4.100, 4.101 ff.

Costs incurred in connection with new lease

60   Costs incurred in connection with new lease to be paid by tenant

(1) Where a notice is given under section 42, then (subject to the provisions of this section) the tenant by whom it is given shall be liable, to the extent that they have been incurred by any relevant person in pursuance of the notice, for the reasonable costs of and incidental to any of the following matters, namely—

    (a) any investigation reasonably undertaken of the tenant's right to a new lease;

    (b) any valuation of the tenant's flat obtained for the purpose of fixing the premium or any other amount payable by virtue of Schedule 13 in connection with the grant of a new lease under section 56;

    (c) the grant of a new lease under that section;

but this subsection shall not apply to any costs if on a sale made voluntarily a stipulation that they were to be borne by the purchaser would be void.

(2) For the purposes of subsection (1) any costs incurred by a relevant person in respect of professional services rendered by any person shall only be regarded as reasonable if and to the extent that costs in respect of such services might reasonably be expected to have been incurred by him if the circumstances had been such that he was personally liable for all such costs.

(3) Where by virtue of any provision of this Chapter the tenant's notice ceases to have effect, or is deemed to have been withdrawn, at any time, then (subject to subsection (4)) the tenant's liability under this section for costs incurred by any person shall be a liability for costs incurred by him down to that time.

(4) A tenant shall not be liable for any costs under this section if the tenant's notice ceases to have effect by virtue of section 47(1) or 55(2).

(5) A tenant shall not be liable under this section for any costs which a party to any proceedings under this Chapter before a leasehold valuation tribunal incurs in connection with the proceedings.

(6) In this section "relevant person", in relation to a claim by a tenant under this Chapter, means the landlord for the purposes of this Chapter, any other landlord (as defined by section 40(4)) or any third party to the tenant's lease.

Definitions   For "the landlord", see s 40(1); for "the tenant's notice", see s 42; for "third party", see s 62(1); for "flat", see s 101(1) (and note also s 62(2)–(4)); for "lease" and related expressions (including "tenant"), see s 101(1), (2); for "relevant person", see sub-s (6) above.
References   See paras 4.98, 4.99 ff.

Landlord's right to terminate new lease

61   Landlord's right to terminate new lease on grounds of redevelopment

(1) Where a lease of a flat ("the new lease") has been granted under section 56 but the court is satisfied, on an application made by the landlord—
   (a)   that for the purposes of redevelopment the landlord intends—
      (i)   to demolish or reconstruct, or
      (ii)   to carry out substantial works of construction on,
      the whole or a substantial part of any premises in which the flat is contained, and
   (b)   that he could not reasonably do so without obtaining possession of the flat,
the court shall by order declare that the landlord is entitled as against the tenant to obtain possession of the flat and the tenant is entitled to be paid compensation by the landlord for the loss of the flat.

(2) An application for an order under this section may be made—
   (a)   at any time during the period of 12 months ending with the term date of the lease in relation to which the right to acquire a new lease was exercised; and
   (b)   at any time during the period of five years ending with the term date of the new lease.

(3) Where the new lease is not the first lease to be granted under section 56 in respect of a flat, subsection (2) shall apply as if paragraph (b) included a reference to the term date of any previous lease granted under that section in respect of the flat, but paragraph (a) shall be taken to be referring to the term date of the lease in relation to which the right to acquire a new lease was first exercised.

(4) Where an order is made under this section, the new lease shall determine, and compensation shall become payable, in accordance with Schedule 14 to this Act; and the provisions of that Schedule shall have effect as regards the measure of compensation payable by virtue of any such order and the effects of any such order where there are sub-leases, and as regards other matters relating to orders and applications under this section.

(5) Except in subsection (1)(a) or (b), any reference in this section to the flat held by the tenant under the new lease includes any premises let with the flat under that lease.

Definitions For "the landlord", see s 40(1); for "the court", "flat" and "term date", see s 101(1) (and note also as to "flat", sub-s (5) above and s 62(2)–(4)); for "lease" and related expressions (including "tenant"), see s 101(1), (2); for "the new lease", see sub-s (1) above.
References See paras 4.89, 4.90 ff.

Supplemental

62 Interpretation of Chapter II

(1) In this Chapter—

"the existing lease", in relation to a claim by a tenant under this Chapter, means the lease in relation to which the claim is made;

"the landlord", in relation to such a claim, has the meaning given by section 40(1);

"mortgage" includes a charge or lien;

"qualifying tenant" shall be construed in accordance with section 39(3);

"the relevant date" (unless the context otherwise requires) has the meaning given by section 39(8);

"the tenant's notice" means the notice given under section 42;

"the terms of acquisition" shall be construed in accordance with section 48(7);

"third party", in relation to a lease, means any person who is a party to the lease apart from the tenant under the lease and his immediate landlord.

(2) Subject to subsection (3), references in this Chapter to a flat, in relation to a claim by a tenant under this Chapter, include any garage, outhouse, garden, yard and appurtenances belonging to, or usually enjoyed with, the flat and let to the tenant with the flat on the relevant date (or, in a case where an application is made under section 50(1), on the date of the making of the application).

(3) Subsection (2) does not apply—

(a) to any reference to a flat in section 47 or 55(1); or

(b) to any reference to a flat (not falling within paragraph (a) above) which occurs in the context of a reference to any premises containing the flat.

(4) In the application of section 8 for the purposes of this Chapter (in accordance with section 39(3)) references to a flat shall be construed in accordance with subsection (2) above, instead of in accordance with subsection (7) of section 8.

Definitions For "flat", see s 101(1); for "lease" and related expressions (including "landlord" and "tenant"), see s 101(1), (2); for "the relevant date", see sub-s (1) above.
References See para 4.65 ff.

CHAPTER III
ENFRANCHISEMENT UNDER LEASEHOLD REFORM ACT 1967

Extension of right to enfranchise

63 Extension of right to enfranchise to houses whose value or rent exceeds applicable limit

After section 1 of the Leasehold Reform Act 1967 there shall be inserted—

"1A Right to enfranchisement only in case of houses whose value or rent exceeds applicable limit under s 1 or 4

(1) Where subsection (1) of section 1 above would apply in the case of the tenant of a house but for the fact that the applicable financial limit specified in subsection (1)(a)(i) or (ii) or (as the case may be) subsection (5) or (6) of that section is exceeded, this Part of this Act shall have effect to confer on the tenant the same right to acquire the freehold of the house and premises as would be conferred by subsection (1) of that section if that limit were not exceeded.

(2) Where a tenancy of any property is not a tenancy at a low rent in accordance with section 4(1) below but is a tenancy falling within section 4A(1) below, the tenancy shall nevertheless be treated as a tenancy at a low rent for the purposes of this Part of this Act so far as it has effect for conferring on any person a right to acquire the freehold of a house and premises.".

Definitions For "house" and "house and premises", see the Leasehold Reform Act 1967, s 2; for "low rent", see s 4 of that Act; as to "tenant", see s 5(1) of that Act; for 'tenancy", see s 37(1) of that Act.
References See para 5.4 ff.

64 Tenancies terminable after death or marriage

(1) The following section shall be inserted in the Leasehold Reform Act 1967 after the section 1A inserted by section 63 above—

"1B Right of enfranchisement only in case of certain tenancies terminable after death or marriage

Where a tenancy granted so as to become terminable by notice after a death or marriage—
    (a) is (apart from this section) a long tenancy in accordance with section 3(1) below, but
    (b) was granted before 18th April 1980 or in pursuance of a contract entered into before that date,
then (notwithstanding section 3(1)) the tenancy shall be a long tenancy for the purposes of this Part of this Act only so far as this Part has effect for conferring on any person a right to acquire the freehold of a house and premises.".

(2) In section 3(1) of that Act (meaning of "long tenancy")—
    (a) after "and includes" there shall be inserted "both a tenancy taking effect under section 149(6) of the Law of Property Act 1925 (leases terminable after a death or marriage) and"; and
    (b) in the proviso (which prevents certain categories of tenancies terminable after death or marriage being long tenancies), for the words from "if either" onwards there shall be substituted "if—

    (a) the notice is capable of being given at any time after the death or marriage of the tenant;

    (b) the length of the notice is not more than three months; and

    (c) the terms of the tenancy preclude both—

        (i) its assignment otherwise than by virtue of section 92 of the Housing Act 1985 (assignments by way of exchange), and

        (ii) the sub-letting of the whole of the premises comprised in it."

Definitions For "house" and "house and premises", see the Leasehold Reform Act 1967, s 2; for "long tenancy", see s 3 of that Act; as to "tenant", see s 5(1) of that Act; for 'tenancy", see s 37(1) of that Act.

References See paras 5.7–5.9 ff.

65 Additional "low rent" test

After section 4 of the Leasehold Reform Act 1967 there shall be inserted—

"4A Alternative rent limits for purposes of section 1A(2)

(1) For the purposes of section 1A(2) above a tenancy of any property falls within this subsection if either no rent was payable under it in respect of the property during the initial year or the aggregate amount of rent so payable during that year did not exceed the following amount, namely—

    (a) where the tenancy was entered into before 1st April 1963, two-thirds of the letting value of the property (on the same terms) on the date of the commencement of the tenancy;

    (b) where—

        (i) the tenancy was entered into either on or after 1st April 1963 but before 1st April 1990, or on or after 1st April 1990 in pursuance of a contract made before that date, and

        (ii) the property had a rateable value at the date of the commencement of the tenancy or else at any time before 1st April 1990,

    two-thirds of the rateable value of the property on the relevant date; or

    (c) in any other case, £1,000 if the property is in Greater London or £250 if elsewhere.

(2) For the purposes of subsection (1) above—

    (a) "the initial year", in relation to any tenancy, means the period of one year beginning with the date of the commencement of the tenancy;

    (b) "the relevant date" means the date of the commencement of the tenancy or, if the property did not have a rateable value on that date, the date on which it first had a rateable value; and

    (c) paragraphs (b) and (c) of section 4(1) above shall apply as they apply for the purposes of section 4(1);

and it is hereby declared that in subsection (1) above the reference to the letting value of any property is to be construed in like manner as the reference in similar terms which appears in the proviso to section 4(1) above.

(3) Section 1(7) above applies to any amount referred to in subsection (1)(c) above as it applies to the amount referred to in subsection (1)(a)(ii) of that section."

Definitions   For "tenancy", see the Leasehold Reform Act 1967, s 37(1); for "the initial year", "letting value" and "the relevant date", see s 4A(2) of that Act, as inserted above.
References   See para 5.5 ff.

66   Price payable by tenant on enfranchisement by virtue of section 63 or 64

(1) In section 9 of the Leasehold Reform Act 1967 (purchase price and costs of enfranchisement, etc), after subsection (1B) there shall be inserted—

"(1C) Notwithstanding subsection (1) above, the price payable for a house and premises where the right to acquire the freehold arises by virtue of any one or more of the provisions of sections 1A and 1B above shall be determined in accordance with subsection (1A) above; but in any such case—

(a) if in determining the price so payable there falls to be taken into account any marriage value arising by virtue of the coalescence of the freehold and leasehold interests, the share of the marriage value to which the tenant is to be regarded as being entitled shall not exceed one-half of it; and

(b) section 9A below has effect for determining whether any additional amount is payable by way of compensation under that section;

and in a case where the provision (or one of the provisions) by virtue of which the right to acquire the freehold arises is section 1A(1) above, subsection (1A) above shall apply with the omission of the assumption set out in paragraph (b) of that subsection."

(2) Section 9 of that Act, as amended by this section and with the omission of repealed provisions, is set out in Schedule 15 to this Act.

(3) After section 9 of that Act there shall be inserted—

"9A   Compensation payable in cases where right to enfranchisement arises by virtue of section 1A or 1B

(1) If, in a case where the right to acquire the freehold of a house and premises arises by virtue of any one or more of the provisions of sections 1A and 1B above, the landlord will suffer any loss or damage to which this section applies, there shall be payable to him such amount as is reasonable to compensate him for that loss or damage.

(2) This section applies to—

(a) any diminution in value of any interest of the landlord in other property resulting from the acquisition of his interest in the house and premises; and

(b) any other loss or damage which results therefrom to the extent that it is referable to his ownership of any interest in other property.

(3) Without prejudice to the generality of paragraph (b) of subsection (2) above, the kinds of loss falling within that paragraph include loss of development value in relation to the house and premises to the extent that it is referable as mentioned in that paragraph.

(4) In subsection (3) above "development value", in relation to the house and premises, means any increase in the value of the landlord's interest in the house and premises which is attributable to the possibility of demolishing, reconstructing, or carrying out substantial works of construction on, the whole or a substantial part of the house and premises.

(5) In relation to any case falling within subsection (1) above—

    (a) any reference (however expressed)—

        (i) in section 8 or 9(3) or (5) above, or

        (ii) in any of the following provisions of this Act,

    to the price payable under section 9 above shall be construed as including a reference to any amount payable to the landlord under this section; and

    (b) for the purpose of determining any such separate price as is mentioned in paragraph 7(1)(b) of Schedule 1 to this Act, this section shall accordingly apply (with any necessary modifications) to each of the superior interests in question."

Definitions   For "tenancy", see the Leasehold Reform Act 1967, s 37(1); for "the initial year", "letting value" and "the relevant date", see s 4A(2) of that Act, as inserted above.
References   See paras 5.10–5.12 ff.

Exceptions to right to enfranchise

67 Exclusion of right to enfranchise in case of houses let by charitable housing trusts

(1) Section 1 of the Leasehold Reform Act 1967 (tenants entitled to enfranchisement or extension) shall be amended as follows.

(2) In subsection (3) (excepted cases) there shall be added at the end—

"or, in the case of any right to which subsection (3A) below applies, at any time when the tenant's immediate landlord is a charitable housing trust and the house forms part of the housing accommodation provided by the trust in the pursuit of its charitable purposes."

(3) After subsection (3) there shall be inserted—

"(3A) For the purposes of subsection (3) above this subsection applies as follows—

    (a) where the tenancy was created after the commencement of Chapter III of Part I of the Leasehold Reform, Housing and Urban Development Act 1993, this subsection applies to any right to acquire the freehold of the house and premises; but

    (b) where the tenancy was created before that commencement, this subsection applies only to any such right exercisable by virtue of any one or more of the provisions of sections 1A and 1B below;

and in that subsection "charitable housing trust" means a housing trust within the meaning of the Housing Act 1985 which is a charity within the meaning of the Charities Act 1993."

Definitions   For "house" and "house and premises", see the Leasehold Reform Act 1967, s 2; as to "landlord" and "tenant", see s 5(1) of that Act; for "tenancy", see s 37(1)(f) of that Act; for "charitable housing trust", see s 1(3A) of that Act, as inserted above.
References   See paras 5.13, 5.14 ff.

68 Exclusion of right in case of property transferred for public benefit etc

After section 32 of the Leasehold Reform Act 1967 there shall be inserted—

"32A Property transferred for public benefit etc

(1) A notice of a person's desire to have the freehold of a house and premises under this Part shall be of no effect if at the relevant time the whole or any part of the house and premises is qualifying property and either—

    (a) the tenancy was created after the commencement of Chapter III of Part I of the Leasehold Reform, Housing and Urban Development Act 1993; or

    (b) (where the tenancy was created before that commencement) the tenant would not be entitled to have the freehold if either or both of sections 1A and 1B above were not in force.

(2) For the purposes of this section the whole or any part of the house and premises is qualifying property if—

    (a) it has been designated under section 31(1)(b), (c) or (d) of the Inheritance Tax Act 1984 (designation and undertakings relating to conditionally exempt transfers), whether with or without any other property, and no chargeable event has subsequently occurred with respect to it; or

    (b) an application to the Board for it to be so designated is pending; or

    (c) it is the property of a body not established or conducted for profit and a direction has been given in relation to it under section 26 of that Act (gifts for public benefit), whether with or without any other property; or

    (d) an application to the Board for a direction to be so given in relation to it is pending.

(3) For the purposes of subsection (2) above an application is pending as from the time when it is made to the Board until such time as it is either granted or refused by the Board or withdrawn by the applicant; and for this purpose an application shall not be regarded as made unless and until the applicant has submitted to the Board all such information in support of the application as is required by the Board.

(4) A notice of a person's desire to have the freehold of a house and premises under this Part shall cease to have effect if—

    (a) before completion of the conveyance in pursuance of the tenant's notice, the whole or any part of the house and premises becomes qualifying property; and

    (b) the condition set out in subsection (1)(a) or (as the case may be) subsection (1)(b) above is satisfied.

(5) Where a tenant's notice ceases to have effect by virtue of subsection (4) above—

    (a) section 9(4) above shall not apply to require the tenant to make any payment to the landlord in respect of costs incurred by reason of the notice; and

    (b) the person who applied or is applying for designation or a direction shall be liable to the tenant for all reasonable costs incurred by the tenant in connection with his claim to acquire the freehold of the house and premises.

(6) Where it is claimed that subsection (1) or (4) above applies in relation to a tenant's notice, the person making the claim shall, at the time of making it, furnish the tenant with evidence in support of it; and if he fails to do so he

shall be liable for any costs which are reasonably incurred by the tenant in consequence of the failure.

(7) In subsection (2) above—

(a) paragraphs (a) and (b) apply to designation under section 34(1)(a), (b) or (c) of the Finance Act 1975 or section 77(1)(b), (c) or (d) of the Finance Act 1976 as they apply to designation under section 31(1)(b), (c) or (d) of the Inheritance Tax Act 1984; and

(b) paragraphs (c) and (d) apply to a direction under paragraph 13 of Schedule 6 to the Finance Act 1975 as they apply to a direction under section 26 of that Act of 1984.

(8) In this section—

"the Board" means the Commissioners of Inland Revenue;

"chargeable event" means—

(a) any event which in accordance with any provision of Chapter II of Part II of the Inheritance Tax Act 1984 (exempt transfers) is a chargeable event, including any such provision as applied by section 78(3) of that Act (conditionally exempt occasions); or

(b) any event which would have been a chargeable event in the circumstances mentioned in section 79(3) of that Act (exemption from ten-yearly charge)."

Definitions   For "house" and "house and premises", see the Leasehold Reform Act 1967, s 2; as to "tenant", see s 5(1) of that Act; for "tenancy", see s 37(1)(f) of that Act; as to "qualifying property", see s 32A(2) of that Act, as inserted above; for "the board" and "chargeable event", see s 32A(8) of that Act, as so inserted.
References   See paras 5.15, 5.16 ff.

CHAPTER IV
ESTATE MANAGEMENT SCHEMES IN CONNECTION WITH ENFRANCHISEMENT

69   Estate management schemes

(1) For the purposes of this Chapter an estate management scheme is a scheme which (subject to sections 71 and 73) is approved by a leasehold valuation tribunal under section 70 for an area occupied directly or indirectly under leases held from one landlord (apart from property occupied by him or his licensees or for the time being unoccupied) and which is designed to secure that in the event of tenants—

(a) acquiring the landlord's interest in their house and premises ("the house") under Part I of the Leasehold Reform Act 1967 by virtue of any one or more of the provisions of sections 1A and 1B of that Act (as inserted by sections 63 and 64 above), or

(b) acquiring the landlord's interest in any premises ("the premises") in accordance with Chapter I of this Part of this Act,

the landlord will—

(i) retain powers of management in respect of the house or premises, and

(ii) have rights against the house or premises in respect of the benefits arising from the exercise elsewhere of his powers of management.

(2) An estate management scheme may make different provision for different parts of the area of the scheme, and shall include provision for terminating or varying all or any of the provisions of the scheme, or excluding part of the area, if a

change of circumstances makes it appropriate, or for enabling it to be done by or with the approval of a leasehold valuation tribunal.

(3) Without prejudice to any other provision of this section, an estate management scheme may provide for all or any of the following matters—

    (a) for regulating the redevelopment, use or appearance of property in which tenants have acquired the landlord's interest as mentioned in subsection (1)(a) or (b);

    (b) for empowering the landlord for the time being to carry out works of maintenance, repair, renewal or replacement in relation to any such property or carry out work to remedy a failure in respect of any such property to comply with the scheme, or for making the operation of any provisions of the scheme conditional on his doing so or on the provision or maintenance by him of services, facilities or amenities of any description;

    (c) for imposing on persons from time to time occupying or interested in any such property obligations in respect of the carrying out of works of maintenance, repair, renewal or replacement in relation to the property or property used or enjoyed by them in common with others, or in respect of costs incurred by the landlord for the time being on any matter referred to in this paragraph or in paragraph (b) above;

    (d) for the inspection from time to time of any such property on behalf of the landlord for the time being, and for the recovery by him of sums due to him under the scheme in respect of any such property by means of a charge on the property;

and the landlord for the time being shall have, for the enforcement of any charge imposed under the scheme, the same powers and remedies under the Law of Property Act 1925 and otherwise as if he were a mortgagee by deed having powers of sale and leasing and of appointing a receiver.

(4) Except as provided by the scheme, the operation of an estate management scheme shall not be affected by any disposition or devolution of the landlord's interest in the property within the area of the scheme or in parts of that property; but the scheme—

    (a) shall include provision for identifying the person who is for the purposes of the scheme to be treated as the landlord for the time being; and

    (b) shall also include provision for transferring, or allowing the landlord for the time being to transfer, all or any of the powers and rights conferred by the scheme on the landlord for the time being to a local authority or other body, including a body constituted for the purpose.

(5) Without prejudice to the generality of paragraph (b) of subsection (4), an estate management scheme may provide for the operation of any provision for transfer included in the scheme in accordance with that paragraph to be dependent—

    (a) on a determination of a leasehold valuation tribunal effecting or approving the transfer;

    (b) on such other circumstances as the scheme may provide.

(6) An estate management scheme may extend to property in which the landlord's interest is disposed of otherwise than as mentioned in subsection (1)(a) or (b) (whether residential property or not), so as to make that property, or allow it to be made, subject to any such provision as is or might be made by the scheme for property in which tenants acquire the landlord's interest as mentioned in either of those provisions.

(7) In this Chapter references to the landlord for the time being shall have effect, in relation to powers and rights transferred to a local authority or other body as contemplated by subsection (4)(b) above, as references to that authority or body.

Definitions   For "interest", see s 101(1); for "lease" and related expressions (including "landlord" and "tenant"), see s 101(1), (2) (and note also as to "landlord for the time being", sub-s (7) above); for "the house" and "the premises", see sub-s (1) above.
References   See paras 6.2–6.4 ff.

70 Approval by leasehold valuation tribunal of estate management scheme

(1) A leasehold valuation tribunal may, on an application made by a landlord for the approval of a scheme submitted by him to the tribunal, approve the scheme as an estate management scheme for such area falling within section 69(1) as is specified in the scheme; but any such application must (subject to section 72) be made within the period of two years beginning with the date of the coming into force of this section.

(2) A leasehold valuation tribunal shall not approve a scheme as an estate management scheme for any area unless it is satisfied that, in order to maintain adequate standards of appearance and amenity and regulate redevelopment within the area in the event of tenants acquiring the interest of the landlord in any property as mentioned in section 69(1)(a) or (b), it is in the general interest that the landlord should retain such powers of management and have such rights falling within section 69(1)(i) and (ii) as are conferred by the scheme.

(3) In considering whether to approve a scheme as an estate management scheme for any area, a leasehold valuation tribunal shall have regard primarily to—
  (a) the benefit likely to result from the scheme to the area as a whole (including houses or premises likely to be acquired from the landlord as mentioned in section 69(1)(a) or (b)); and
  (b) the extent to which it is reasonable to impose, for the benefit of the area, obligations on tenants so acquiring the interest of their landlord;
but the tribunal shall also have regard to the past development and present character of the area and to architectural or historical considerations, to neighbouring areas and to the circumstances generally.

(4) A leasehold valuation tribunal shall not consider any application for it to approve a scheme unless it is satisfied that the applicant has, by advertisement or otherwise, given adequate notice to persons interested—
  (a) informing them of the application for approval of the scheme and the provision intended to be made by the scheme, and
  (b) inviting them to make representations to the tribunal about the application within a time which appears to the tribunal to be reasonable.

(5) In subsection (4) "persons interested" includes, in particular, in relation to any application for the approval of a scheme for any area ("the scheme area") within a conservation area—
  (a) each local planning authority within whose area any part of the scheme area falls, and
  (b) if the whole of the scheme area is in England, the Historic Buildings and Monuments Commission for England.

(6) Where representations about an application are made under subsection (4)(b), the tribunal shall afford to the persons making those representations an opportunity to appear and be heard by the tribunal at the time when the application is considered by it.

(7) Subject to the preceding provisions of this section, a leasehold valuation tribunal shall, after considering the application, approve the scheme in question either—

    (a) as originally submitted, or

    (b) with any relevant modifications proposed or agreed to by the applicant,

if the scheme (with those modifications, if any) appears to the tribunal—

    (i) to be fair and practicable, and

    (ii) not to give the landlord a degree of control out of proportion to that previously exercised by him or to that required for the purposes of the scheme.

(8) In subsection (7) "relevant modifications" means modifications relating to the extent of the area to which the scheme is to apply or to the provisions contained in it.

(9) If, having regard to—

    (a) the matters mentioned in subsection (3), and

    (b) the provision which it is practicable to make by a scheme,

the tribunal thinks it proper to do so, the tribunal may declare that no scheme can be approved for the area in question in pursuance of the application.

(10) A leasehold valuation tribunal shall not dismiss an application for the approval of a scheme unless—

    (a) it makes such a declaration as is mentioned in subsection (9); or

    (b) in the opinion of the tribunal the applicant is unwilling to agree to a suitable scheme or is not proceeding in the matter with due despatch.

(11) A scheme approved under this section as an estate management scheme for an area shall be a local land charge, notwithstanding section 2(a) or (b) of the Local Land Charges Act 1975 (matters which are not local land charges), and for the purposes of that Act the landlord for that area shall be treated as the originating authority as respects any such charge.

(12) Where such a scheme is registered in the appropriate local land charges register—

    (a) the provisions of the scheme relating to property of any description shall so far as they respectively affect the persons from time to time occupying or interested in that property be enforceable by the landlord for the time being against them, as if each of them had covenanted with the landlord for the time being to be bound by the scheme; and

    (b) in relation to any acquisition such as is mentioned in section 69(1)(a) above, section 10 of the Leasehold Reform Act 1967 (rights to be conveyed on enfranchisement) shall have effect subject to the provisions of the scheme, and the price payable under section 9 of that Act shall be adjusted so far as is appropriate (if at all); and

    (c) in relation to any acquisition such as is mentioned in section 69(1)(b) above, section 34 of, and Schedule 7 to, this Act shall have effect subject to the provisions of the scheme, and any price payable under Schedule 6 to this Act shall be adjusted so far as is appropriate (if at all).

(13) Section 10 of the Local Land Charges Act 1975 (compensation for non-registration etc) shall not apply to schemes which, by virtue of subsection (11) above, are local land charges.

(14) In this section and in section 73 "conservation area" and "local planning authority" have the same meaning as in the Planning (Listed Buildings and Conservation Areas) Act 1990; and in connection with the latter expression—

    (a)   the expression "the planning Acts" in the Town and Country Planning Act 1990 shall be treated as including this Act; and

    (b)   paragraphs 4 and 5 of Schedule 4 to the Planning (Listed Buildings and Conservation Areas) Act 1990 (further provisions as to exercise of functions by different authorities) shall apply in relation to functions under or by virtue of this section or section 73 of this Act as they apply in relation to functions under section 69 of that Act.

Definitions   For "estate management scheme", see s 69; for "interest", see s 101(1); as to "landlord" and "tenant", see s 101(2); for "persons interested" in sub-s (4) above, see sub-s (5) above; for "relevant modifications" in sub-s (7) above, see sub-s (8) above; for "conservation area", "local planning authority" and "the planning Acts", see sub-s (14) above.
References   See paras 6.5, 6.9, 6.10, 6.13–6.16 ff.

71 Applications by two or more landlords or by representative bodies

(1) Where, on a joint application made by two or more persons as landlords of neighbouring areas, it appears to a leasehold valuation tribunal—

    (a)   that a scheme could in accordance with subsections (1) and (2) of section 70 be approved as an estate management scheme for those areas, treated as a unit, if the interests of those persons were held by a single person, and

    (b)   that the applicants are willing to be bound by the scheme to co-operate in the management of their property in those areas and in the administration of the scheme,

the tribunal may (subject to the provisions of section 70 and subsection (2) below) approve the scheme under that section as an estate management scheme for those areas as a whole.

(2) Any such scheme shall be made subject to conditions (enforceable in such manner as may be provided by the scheme) for securing that the landlords and their successors co-operate as mentioned in subsection (1)(b) above.

(3) Where it appears to a leasehold valuation tribunal—

    (a)   that a scheme could, on the application of any landlord or landlords, be approved under section 70 as an estate management scheme for any area or areas, and

    (b)   that any body of persons—

        (i)   is so constituted as to be capable of representing for the purposes of the scheme the persons occupying or interested in property in the area or areas (other than the landlord or landlords or his or their licensees), or such of them as are or may become entitled to acquire their landlord's interest as mentioned in section 69(1)(a) or (b), and

        (ii)   is otherwise suitable,

an application for the approval of the scheme under section 70 may be made to the tribunal by the representative body alone or by the landlord or landlords alone or by both jointly and, by leave of the tribunal, may be proceeded with by the representative body or by the landlord or landlords despite the fact that the body or landlord or landlords in question did not make the application.

(4) Without prejudice to section 69(4)(b), any such scheme may with the consent of the landlord or landlords, or on such terms as to compensation or otherwise as appear to the tribunal to be just—

(a) confer on the representative body any such rights or powers under the scheme as might be conferred on the landlord or landlords for the time being, or

(b) enable the representative body to participate in the administration of the scheme or in the management by the landlord or landlords of his or their property in the area or areas.

(5) Where any such scheme confers any rights or powers on the representative body in accordance with subsection (4) above, section 70(11) and (12)(a) shall have effect with such modifications (if any) as are provided for in the scheme.

Definitions For "estate management scheme", see s 69; for "interest", see s 101(1); as to "landlord", see s 101(2).
References See paras 6.10–6.12, 6.16 ff.

---

72 Applications after expiry of two-year period

(1) An application for the approval of a scheme for an area under section 70 (including an application in accordance with section 71(1) or (3)) may be made after the expiry of the period mentioned in subsection (1) of that section if the Secretary of State has, not more than six months previously, consented to the making of such an application for that area or for an area within which that area falls.

(2) The Secretary of State may give consent under subsection (1) to the making of an application ("the proposed application") only where he is satisfied—

(a) that either or both of the conditions mentioned in subsection (3) apply; and

(b) that adequate notice has been given to persons interested informing them of the request for consent and the purpose of the request.

(3) The conditions referred to in subsection (2)(a) are—

(a) that the proposed application could not have been made before the expiry of the period mentioned in section 70(1); and

(b) that—

(i) any application for the approval under section 70 of a scheme for the area, or part of the area, to which the proposed application relates would probably have been dismissed under section 70(10)(a) had it been made before the expiry of that period; but

(ii) because of a change in any of the circumstances required to be considered under section 70(3) the proposed application would, if made following the giving of consent by the Secretary of State, probably be granted.

(4) A request for consent under subsection (1) must be in writing and must comply with such requirements (if any) as to the form of, or the particulars to be contained in, any such request as the Secretary of State may by regulations prescribe.

(5) The procedure for considering a request for consent under subsection (1) shall be such as may be prescribed by regulations made by the Secretary of State.

References See para 6.6 ff.

---

73 Applications by certain public bodies

(1) Where it appears to a leasehold valuation tribunal after the expiry of the period mentioned in section 70(1) that a scheme could, on the application of any landlord or landlords within that period, have been approved under section 70 as an estate management scheme for any area or areas within a conservation area, an application for the approval of the scheme under that section may, subject to subsections (2) and (3) below, be made to the tribunal by one or more bodies constituting the relevant authority for the purposes of this section.

(2) An application under subsection (1) may only be made if—

  (a) no scheme has been approved under section 70 for the whole or any part of the area or areas to which the application relates ("the scheme area"); and

  (b) any application which has been made in accordance with section 70(1), 71(1) or 71(3) for the approval of a scheme for the whole or any part of the scheme area has been withdrawn or dismissed; and

  (c) no request for consent under section 72(1) which relates to the whole or any part of the scheme area is pending or has been granted within the last six months.

(3) An application under subsection (1) above must be made within the period of six months beginning—

  (a) with the date on which the period mentioned in section 70(1) expires, or

  (b) if any application has been made as mentioned in subsection (2)(b) above, with the date (or, as the case may be, the latest date) on which any such application is withdrawn or dismissed,

whichever is the later; but if at any time during that period of six months a request of a kind mentioned in subsection (2)(c) above is pending or granted, an application under subsection (1) above may, subject to subsection (2) above, be made within the period of—

  (i) six months beginning with the date on which the request is withdrawn or refused, or

  (ii) twelve months beginning with the date on which the request is granted,

as the case may be.

(4) A scheme approved on an application under subsection (1) may confer on the applicant or applicants any such rights or powers under the scheme as might have been conferred on the landlord or landlords for the time being.

(5) For the purposes of this section the relevant authority for the scheme area is—

  (a) where that area falls wholly within the area of a local planning authority—

    (i) that authority; or

    (ii) subject to subsection (6), that authority acting jointly with the Historic Buildings and Monuments Commission for England ("the Commission"); or

    (iii) subject to subsection (6), the Commission; or

  (b) in any other case—

    (i) all of the local planning authorities within each of whose areas any part of the scheme area falls, acting jointly; or

    (ii) subject to subsection (6), one or more of those authorities acting jointly with the Commission; or

    (iii) subject to subsection (6), the Commission.

(6) The Commission may make, or join in the making of, an application under subsection (1) only if—

    (a) the whole of the scheme area is in England; and

    (b) they have consulted any local planning authority within whose area the whole or any part of the scheme area falls.

(7) Where a scheme is approved on an application under subsection (1) by two or more bodies acting jointly, the scheme shall, if the tribunal considers it appropriate, be made subject to conditions (enforceable in such manner as may be provided by the scheme) for securing that those bodies co-operate in the administration of the scheme.

(8) Where a scheme is approved on an application under subsection (1)—

    (a) section 70(11) and (12)(a) shall (subject to subsection (9) below) have effect as if any reference to the landlord, or the landlord for the time being, for the area for which an estate management scheme has been approved were a reference to the applicant or applicants; and

    (b) section 70(12)(b) and (c) shall each have effect with the omission of so much of that provision as relates to the adjustment of any such price as is there mentioned.

(9) A scheme so approved shall not be enforceable by a local planning authority in relation to any property falling outside the authority's area; and in the case of a scheme approved on a joint application made by one or more local planning authorities and the Commission, the scheme may provide for any of its provisions to be enforceable in relation to property falling within the area of a local planning authority either by the authority alone, or by the Commission alone, or by the authority and the Commission acting jointly, as the scheme may provide.

(10) For the purposes of—

    (a) section 9(1A) of the Leasehold Reform Act 1967 (purchase price on enfranchisement) as it applies in relation to any acquisition such as is mentioned in section 69(1)(a) above, and

    (b) paragraph 3 of Schedule 6 to this Act as it applies in relation to any acquisition such as is mentioned in section 69(1)(b) above (including that paragraph as it applies by virtue of paragraph 7 or 11 of that Schedule),

it shall be assumed that any scheme approved under subsection (1) and relating to the property in question had not been so approved, and accordingly any application for such a scheme to be approved, and the possibility of such an application being made, shall be disregarded.

(11) Section 70(14) applies for the purposes of this section.

Definitions   For "estate management scheme", see s 69; for "conservation area" and "local planning authority", see s 70(14); as to "landlord", see s 101(2) (and note as to "landlord for the time being", s 69(7)); for "the scheme area", see sub-s (2) above; for "the Commission", see sub-s (5)(a)(ii) above.
References   See paras 6.7, 6.8, 6.12, 6.17 ff.

---

74 Effect of application for approval on claim to acquire freehold

(1) Subject to subsections (5) and (6), this subsection applies where—

    (a) an application ("the scheme application") is made for the approval of a scheme as an estate management scheme for any area or a request ("the request for consent") is made for consent under section 72(1) in relation to any area, and

  (b) whether before or after the making of the application or request—

      (i) the tenant of a house in that area gives notice of his desire to have the freehold under Part I of the Leasehold Reform Act 1967, being entitled to do so by virtue only of either or both of the sections of that Act referred to in section 69(1)(a) above, or

     (ii) a notice is given under section 13 above in respect of any premises in the area.

(2) Where subsection (1) applies by virtue of paragraph (b)(i) of that subsection, then—

  (a) no further steps need be taken towards the execution of a conveyance to give effect to section 10 of the 1967 Act beyond those which appear to the landlord to be reasonable in the circumstances; and

  (b) if the notice referred to in subsection (1)(b)(i) ("the tenant's notice") was given before the making of the scheme application or the request for consent, that notice may be withdrawn by a further notice given by the tenant to the landlord.

(3) Where subsection (1) applies by virtue of paragraph (b)(ii) of that subsection, then—

  (a) if the notice referred to in that provision ("the initial notice") was given before the making of the scheme application or the request for consent, the notice may be withdrawn by a further notice given by the nominee purchaser to the reversioner;

  (b) unless the initial notice is so withdrawn, the reversioner shall, if he has not already given the nominee purchaser a counter-notice under section 21, give him by the date referred to in subsection (1) of that section a counter-notice which complies with one of the requirements set out in subsection (2) of that section (but in relation to which subsection (3) of that section need not be complied with); and

  (c) no proceedings shall be brought under Chapter I in pursuance of the initial notice otherwise than under section 22 or 23, and, if the court under either of those sections makes an order requiring the reversioner to give a further counter-notice to the nominee purchaser, the date by which it is to be given shall be such date as falls two months after subsection (1) above ceases to apply;

but no other counter-notice need be given under Chapter I, and (subject to the preceding provisions of this subsection) no further steps need be taken towards the final determination (whether by agreement or otherwise) of the terms of the proposed acquisition by the nominee purchaser beyond those which appear to the reversioner to be reasonable in the circumstances.

(4) If the tenant's notice or the initial notice is withdrawn in accordance with subsection (2) or (3) above, section 9(4) of the 1967 Act or (as the case may be) section 33 above shall not have effect to require the payment of any costs incurred in pursuance of that notice.

(5) Where the scheme application is withdrawn or dismissed, subsection (1) does not apply at any time falling after—

  (a) the date of the withdrawal of the application, or

  (b) the date when the decision of the tribunal dismissing the application becomes final, as the case may be; and subsection (1) does not apply at any time falling after the date on which a scheme is approved for the area referred to in that subsection, or for any part of it, in pursuance of the scheme application.

(6) Where the request for consent is withdrawn or refused, subsection (1) does not apply at any time falling after the date on which the request is withdrawn or refused, as the case may be; and where the request is granted, subsection (1) does not apply at any time falling more than six months after the date on which it is granted (unless that subsection applies by virtue of an application made in reliance on the consent).

(7) Where, in accordance with subsection (5) or (6), subsection (1) ceases to apply as from a particular date, it shall do so without prejudice to—

(a) the effect of anything done before that date in pursuance of subsection (2) or (3); or

(b) the operation of any provision of this Part, or of regulations made under it, in relation to anything so done.

(8) If, however, no notice of withdrawal has been given in accordance with subsection (3) before the date when subsection (1) so ceases to apply and before that date either—

(a) the reversioner has given the nominee purchaser a counter-notice under section 21 complying with the requirement set out in subsection (2)(a) of that section, or

(b) section 23(6) would (but for subsection (3) above) have applied to require the reversioner to give a further counter-notice to the nominee purchaser,

the reversioner shall give a further counter-notice to the nominee purchaser within the period of two months beginning with the date when subsection (1) ceases to apply.

(9) Subsections (3) to (5) of section 21 shall apply to any further counter-notice required to be given by the reversioner under subsection (8) above as if it were a counter-notice under that section complying with the requirement set out in subsection (2)(a) of that section; and sections 24 and 25 shall apply in relation to any such counter-notice as they apply in relation to one required by section 22(3).

(10) In this section—

"the 1967 Act" means the Leasehold Reform Act 1967; and

"the nominee purchaser" and "the reversioner" have the same meaning as in Chapter I of this Part of this Act;

and references to the approval of a scheme for any area include references to the approval of a scheme for two or more areas in accordance with section 71 or 73 above.

Definitions   For "estate management scheme", see s 69; as to "landlord" and "tenant", see s 101(2); for "the scheme application" and "the request for consent", see sub-s (1) above; for "the tenant's notice", see sub-s (2) above; for "the initial notice", by virtue of sub-s (3)(a) above, see s 13; for "the reversioner", by virtue of sub-s (10) above, see s 9; for "the nominee purchaser", by virtue of sub-s (10) above, see s 15.
References   See paras 6.18–6.21 ff.

---

75   Variation of existing schemes

(1) Where a scheme under section 19 of the Leasehold Reform Act 1967 (estate management schemes in connection with enfranchisement under that Act) includes,

in pursuance of subsection (6) of that section, provision for enabling the termination or variation of the scheme, or the exclusion of part of the area of the scheme, by or with the approval of the High Court, that provision shall have effect—

   (a) as if any reference to the High Court were a reference to a leasehold valuation tribunal, and

   (b) with such modifications (if any) as are necessary in consequence of paragraph (a).

(2) A scheme under that section may be varied by or with the approval of a leasehold valuation tribunal for the purpose of, or in connection with, extending the scheme to property within the area of the scheme in which the landlord's interest may be acquired as mentioned in section 69(1)(a) above.

(3) Where any such scheme has been varied in accordance with subsection (2) above, section 19 of that Act shall apply as if the variation had been effected under provisions included in the scheme in pursuance of subsection (6) of that section (and accordingly the scheme may be further varied under provisions so included).

(4) Any application made under or by virtue of this section to a leasehold valuation tribunal shall comply with such requirements (if any) as to the form of, or the particulars to be contained in, any such application as the Secretary of State may by regulations prescribe.

(5) In this section any reference to a leasehold valuation tribunal is a reference to such a rent assessment committee as is mentioned in section 142(2) of the Housing Act 1980 (leasehold valuation tribunals).

Definitions   For "interest", see s 101(1); as to "landlord", see s 101(2); for "leasehold valuation tribunal", see sub-s (5) above.
References   See para 6.22 ff.

CHAPTER V
TENANTS' RIGHT TO MANAGEMENT AUDIT

76 Right to audit management by landlord

(1) This Chapter has effect to confer on two or more qualifying tenants of dwellings held on leases from the same landlord the right, exercisable subject to and in accordance with this Chapter, to have an audit carried out on their behalf which relates to the management of the relevant premises and any appurtenant property by or on behalf of the landlord.

(2) That right shall be exercisable—

   (a) where the relevant premises consist of or include two dwellings let to qualifying tenants of the same landlord, by either or both of those tenants; and

   (b) where the relevant premises consist of or include three or more dwellings let to qualifying tenants of the same landlord, by not less than two-thirds of those tenants;

and in this Chapter the dwellings let to those qualifying tenants are referred to as "the constituent dwellings".

(3) In relation to an audit on behalf of two or more qualifying tenants—

   (a) "the relevant premises" means so much of—

      (i) the building or buildings containing the dwellings let to those tenants, and

(ii) any other building or buildings,

as constitutes premises in relation to which management functions are discharged in respect of the costs of which common service charge contributions are payable under the leases of those qualifying tenants; and

(b) "appurtenant property" means so much of any property not contained in the relevant premises as constitutes property in relation to which any such management functions are discharged.

(4) This Chapter also has effect to confer on a single qualifying tenant of a dwelling the right, exercisable subject to and in accordance with this Chapter, to have an audit carried out on his behalf which relates to the management of the relevant premises and any appurtenant property by or on behalf of the landlord.

(5) That right shall be exercisable by a single qualifying tenant of a dwelling where the relevant premises contain no other dwelling let to a qualifying tenant apart from that let to him.

(6) In relation to an audit on behalf of a single qualifying tenant—

(a) "the relevant premises" means so much of—

(i) the building containing the dwelling let to him, and

(ii) any other building or buildings,

as constitutes premises in relation to which management functions are discharged in respect of the costs of which a service charge is payable under his lease (whether as a common service charge contribution or otherwise); and

(b) "appurtenant property" means so much of any property not contained in the relevant premises as constitutes property in relation to which any such management functions are discharged.

(7) The provisions of sections 78 to 83 shall, with any necessary modifications, have effect in relation to an audit on behalf of a single qualifying tenant as they have effect in relation to an audit on behalf of two or more qualifying tenants.

(8) For the purposes of this section common service charge contributions are payable by two or more persons under their leases if they may be required under the terms of those leases to contribute to the same costs by the payment of service charges.

Definitions   For "qualifying tenant", see s 77; for "landlord", "management functions" and "service charge", see s 84 (and note also as to "landlord", s 101(2)); for "dwelling", see s 101(1); for "lease" and related expressions (including "tenant"), see s 101(1), (2); for "the constituent dwellings", see sub-s (2) above; for "appurtenant property" and "the relevant premises", see sub-ss (3), (6) above; as to "common service charge contributions", see sub-s (8) above.

References   See paras 7.2, 7.5–7.7 ff.

---

77 Qualifying tenants

(1) Subject to the following provisions of this section, a tenant is a qualifying tenant of a dwelling for the purposes of this Chapter if—

(a) he is a tenant of the dwelling under a long lease other than a business lease; and

(b) any service charge is payable under the lease.

(2) For the purposes of subsection (1) a lease is a long lease if—

(a) it is a lease falling within any of paragraphs (a) to (c) of subsection (1) of section 7; or

(b) it is a shared ownership lease (within the meaning of that section), whether granted in pursuance of Part V of the Housing Act 1985 or otherwise and whatever the share of the tenant under it.

(3) No dwelling shall have more than one qualifying tenant at any one time.

(4) Accordingly—

(a) where a dwelling is for the time being let under two or more leases falling within subsection (1), any tenant under any of those leases which is superior to that held by any other such tenant shall not be a qualifying tenant of the dwelling for the purposes of this Chapter; and

(b) where a dwelling is for the time being let to joint tenants under a lease falling within subsection (1), the joint tenants shall (subject to paragraph (a)) be regarded for the purposes of this Chapter as jointly constituting the qualifying tenant of the dwelling.

(5) A person can, however, be (or be among those constituting) the qualifying tenant of each of two or more dwellings at the same time, whether he is tenant of those dwellings under one lease or under two or more separate leases.

(6) Where two or more persons constitute the qualifying tenant of a dwelling in accordance with subsection (4)(b), any one or more of those persons may sign a notice under section 80 on behalf of both or all of them.

Definitions   For "service charge", see s 84; for "business lease" and "dwelling", see s 101(1); for "lease" and related expressions (including "tenant"); see s 101(1), (2); as to "long lease" and "shared ownership lease", see sub-s (2) above.
References   See paras 7.3, 7.4 ff.

---

78 Management audits

(1) The audit referred to in section 76(1) is an audit carried out for the purpose of ascertaining—

(a) the extent to which the obligations of the landlord which—

(i) are owed to the qualifying tenants of the constituent dwellings, and

(ii) involve the discharge of management functions in relation to the relevant premises or any appurtenant property,

are being discharged in an efficient and effective manner; and

(b) the extent to which sums payable by those tenants by way of service charges are being applied in an efficient and effective manner;

and in this Chapter any such audit is referred to as a "management audit".

(2) In determining whether any such obligations as are mentioned in subsection (1)(a) are being discharged in an efficient and effective manner, regard shall be had to any applicable provisions of any code of practice for the time being approved by the Secretary of State under section 87.

(3) A management audit shall be carried out by a person who—

(a) is qualified for appointment by virtue of subsection (4); and

(b) is appointed—

(i) in the circumstances mentioned in section 76(2)(a), by either or both of the qualifying tenants of the constituent dwellings, or

(ii) in the circumstances mentioned in section 76(2)(b), by not less than two-thirds of the qualifying tenants of the constituent dwellings;

and in this Chapter any such person is referred to as "the auditor".

(4) A person is qualified for appointment for the purposes of subsection (3) above if—

(a) he has the necessary qualification (within the meaning of subsection (1) of section 28 of the 1985 Act (meaning of "qualified accountant")) or is a qualified surveyor;

(b) he is not disqualified from acting (within the meaning of that subsection); and

(c) he is not a tenant of any premises contained in the relevant premises.

(5) For the purposes of subsection (4)(a) above a person is a qualified surveyor if he is a fellow or professional associate of the Royal Institution of Chartered Surveyors or of the Incorporated Society of Valuers and Auctioneers or satisfies such other requirement or requirements as may be prescribed by regulations made by the Secretary of State.

(6) The auditor may appoint such persons to assist him in carrying out the audit as he thinks fit.

Definitions   For "the constituent dwellings", see s 76(2); for "appurtenant property" and "the relevant premises", see s 76(3), (6); for "qualifying tenant", see s 77; for "landlord", "management functions" and "service charge", see s 84 (and note also as to "landlord", s 101(2)); for "dwelling", see s 101(1); for "management audit", see sub-s (1) above; for "the auditor", see sub-s (3) above; as to "a qualified surveyor", see sub-s (5) above.

References   See paras 7.8, 7.9 ff.

---

79   Rights exercisable in connection with management audits

(1) Where the qualifying tenants of any dwellings exercise under section 80 their right to have a management audit carried out on their behalf, the rights conferred on the auditor by subsection (2) below shall be exercisable by him in connection with the audit.

(2) The rights conferred on the auditor by this subsection are—

(a) a right to require the landlord—

(i) to supply him with such a summary as is referred to in section 21(1) of the 1985 Act (request for summary of relevant costs) in connection with any service charges payable by the qualifying tenants of the constituent dwellings, and

(ii) to afford him reasonable facilities for inspecting, or taking copies of or extracts from, the accounts, receipts and other documents supporting any such summary;

(b) a right to require the landlord or any relevant person to afford him reasonable facilities for inspecting any other documents sight of which is reasonably required by him for the purpose of carrying out the audit; and

(c) a right to require the landlord or any relevant person to afford him reasonable facilities for taking copies of or extracts from any documents falling within paragraph (b).

(3) The rights conferred on the auditor by subsection (2) shall be exercisable by him—

(a) in relation to the landlord, by means of a notice under section 80; and

(b) in relation to any relevant person, by means of a notice given to that person at (so far as is reasonably practicable) the same time as a notice under section 80 is given to the landlord;

and, where a notice is given to any relevant person in accordance with paragraph (b) above, a copy of that notice shall be given to the landlord by the auditor.

(4) The auditor shall also be entitled, on giving notice in accordance with section 80, to carry out an inspection of any common parts comprised in the relevant premises or any appurtenant property.

(5) The landlord or (as the case may be) any relevant person shall—
- (a) where facilities for the inspection of any documents are required under subsection (2)(a)(ii) or (b), make those facilities available free of charge;
- (b) where any documents are required to be supplied under subsection (2)(a)(i) or facilities for the taking of copies or extracts are required under subsection (2)(a)(ii) or (c), be entitled to supply those documents or (as the case may be) make those facilities available on payment of such reasonable charge as he may determine.

(6) The requirement imposed on the landlord by subsection (5)(a) to make any facilities available free of charge shall not be construed as precluding the landlord from treating as part of his costs of management any costs incurred by him in connection with making those facilities so available.

(7) In this Chapter "relevant person" means a person (other than the landlord) who—
- (a) is charged with responsibility—
  - (i) for the discharge of any such obligations as are mentioned in section 78(1)(a), or
  - (ii) for the application of any such service charges as are mentioned in section 78(1)(b); or
- (b) has a right to enforce payment of any such service charges.

(8) In this Chapter references to the auditor in the context of—
- (a) being afforded any such facilities as are mentioned in subsection (2), or
- (b) the carrying out of any inspection under subsection (4),

shall be read as including a person appointed by the auditor under section 78(6).

Definitions For "the constituent dwellings", see s 76(2); for "appurtenant property" and "the relevant premises", see s 76(3), (6); for "qualifying tenant", see s 77; for "management audit", see s 78(1); for "the auditor", see s 78(3), (6); for "landlord" and "service charge" see s 84; for "common parts" and "dwelling", see s 101(1); for "relevant person", see sub-s (7) above.
References See paras 7.12–7.14 ff.

---

80 Exercise of right to have a management audit

(1) The right of any qualifying tenants to have a management audit carried out on their behalf shall be exercisable by the giving of a notice under this section.

(2) A notice given under this section—
- (a) must be given to the landlord by the auditor, and
- (b) must be signed by each of the tenants on whose behalf it is given.

(3) Any such notice must—
- (a) state the full name of each of those tenants and the address of the dwelling of which he is a qualifying tenant;
- (b) state the name and address of the auditor;
- (c) specify any documents or description of documents—

      (i)   which the landlord is required to supply to the auditor under section 79(2)(a)(i), or

      (ii) in respect of which he is required to afford the auditor facilities for inspection or for taking copies or extracts under any other provision of section 79(2); and

  (d) if the auditor proposes to carry out an inspection under section 79(4), state the date on which he proposes to carry out the inspection.

(4) The date specified under subsection (3)(d) must be a date falling not less than one month nor more than two months after the date of the giving of the notice.

(5) A notice is duly given under this section to the landlord of any qualifying tenants if it is given to a person who receives on behalf of the landlord the rent payable by any such tenants; and a person to whom such a notice is so given shall forward it as soon as may be to the landlord.

Definitions   For "qualifying tenant", see s 77; for "management audit", see s 78(1); for "the auditor", see s 78(3), (6); for "landlord", see s 84 (and note also s 101(2)); for "dwelling", see s 101(1).
References   See paras 7.10–7.12 ff.

---

81 Procedure following giving of notice under section 80

(1) Where the landlord is given a notice under section 80, then within the period of one month beginning with the date of the giving of the notice, he shall—

  (a) supply the auditor with any document specified under subsection (3)(c)(i) of that section, and afford him, in respect of any document falling within section 79(2)(a)(ii), any facilities specified in relation to it under subsection (3)(c)(ii) of section 80;

  (b) in the case of every other document or description of documents specified in the notice under subsection (3)(c)(ii) of that section, either—

      (i)   afford the auditor facilities for inspection or (as the case may be) taking copies or extracts in respect of that document or those documents, or

      (ii) give the auditor a notice stating that he objects to doing so for such reasons as are specified in the notice; and

  (c) if a date is specified in the notice under subsection (3)(d) of that section, either approve the date or propose another date for the carrying out of an inspection under section 79(4).

(2) Any date proposed by the landlord under subsection (1)(c) must be a date falling not later than the end of the period of two months beginning with the date of the giving of the notice under section 80.

(3) Where a relevant person is given a notice under section 79 requiring him to afford the auditor facilities for inspection or taking copies or extracts in respect of any documents or description of documents specified in the notice, then within the period of one month beginning with the date of the giving of the notice, he shall, in the case of every such document or description of documents, either—

  (a) afford the auditor the facilities required by him; or

  (b) give the auditor a notice stating that he objects to doing so for such reasons as are specified in the notice.

(4) If by the end of the period of two months beginning with—

  (a) the date of the giving of the notice under section 80, or

(b) the date of the giving of such a notice under section 79 as is mentioned in subsection (3) above,

the landlord or (as the case may be) a relevant person has failed to comply with any requirement of the notice, the court may, on the application of the auditor, make an order requiring the landlord or (as the case may be) the relevant person to comply with that requirement within such period as is specified in the order.

(5) The court shall not make an order under subsection (4) in respect of any document or documents unless it is satisfied that the document or documents falls or fall within paragraph (a) or (b) of section 79(2).

(6) If by the end of the period of two months specified in subsection (2) no inspection under section 79(4) has been carried out by the auditor, the court may, on the application of the auditor, make an order providing for such an inspection to be carried out on such date as is specified in the order.

(7) Any application for an order under subsection (4) or (6) must be made before the end of the period of four months beginning with—

(a) in the case of an application made in connection with a notice given under section 80, the date of the giving of that notice; or

(b) in the case of an application made in connection with such a notice under section 79 as is mentioned in subsection (3) above, the date of the giving of that notice.

Definitions For "the auditor", see s 78(3), (6); for "relevant person", see s 79(7); for "landlord", see s 84 (and note also s 101(2)); for "the court", see s 101(1).
References See paras 7.15, 7.16 ff.

---

82 Requirement relating to information etc held by superior landlord

(1) Where the landlord is required by a notice under section 80 to supply any summary falling within section 79(2)(a), and any information necessary for complying with the notice so far as relating to any such summary is in the possession of a superior landlord—

(a) the landlord shall make a written request for the relevant information to the person who is his landlord (and so on, if that person is himself not the superior landlord);

(b) the superior landlord shall comply with that request within the period of one month beginning with the date of the making of the request; and

(c) the landlord who received the notice shall then comply with it so far as relating to any such summary within the time allowed by section 81(1) or such further time, if any, as is reasonable.

(2) Where—

(a) the landlord is required by a notice under section 80 to afford the auditor facilities for inspection or taking copies or extracts in respect of any documents or description of documents specified in the notice, and

(b) any of the documents in question is in the custody or under the control of a superior landlord,

the landlord shall on receiving the notice inform the auditor as soon as may be of that fact and of the name and address of the superior landlord, and the auditor may then give the superior landlord a notice requiring him to afford the facilities in question in respect of the document.

(3) Subsections (3) to (5) and (7) of section 81 shall, with any necessary modifications, have effect in relation to a notice given to a superior landlord under subsection (2) above as they have effect in relation to any such notice given to a relevant person as is mentioned in subsection (3) of that section.

References   See paras 7.19–7.21 ff.

83 Supplementary provisions

(1) Where—
- (a) a notice has been given to a landlord under section 80, and
- (b) at a time when any obligations arising out of the notice remain to be discharged by him—
    - (i) he disposes of the whole or part of his interest as landlord of the qualifying tenants of the constituent dwellings, and
    - (ii) the person acquiring any such interest of the landlord is in a position to discharge any of those obligations to any extent,

that person shall be responsible for discharging those obligations to that extent, as if he had been given the notice under that section.

(2) If the landlord is, despite any such disposal, still in a position to discharge those obligations to the extent referred to in subsection (1), he shall remain responsible for so discharging them; but otherwise the person referred to in that subsection shall be responsible for so discharging them to the exclusion of the landlord.

(3) Where a person is so responsible for discharging any such obligations (whether with the landlord or otherwise)
- (a) references to the landlord in section 81 shall be read as including, or as, references to that person to such extent as is appropriate to reflect his responsibility for discharging those obligations; but
- (b) in connection with the discharge of any such obligations by that person, that section shall apply as if any reference to the date of the giving of the notice under section 80 were a reference to the date of the disposal referred to in subsection (1).

(4) Where—
- (a) a notice has been given to a relevant person under section 79, and
- (b) at a time when any obligations arising out of the notice remain to be discharged by him, he ceases to be a relevant person, but
- (c) he is, despite ceasing to be a relevant person, still in a position to discharge those obligations to any extent,

he shall nevertheless remain responsible for discharging those obligations to that extent; and section 81 shall accordingly continue to apply to him as if he were still a relevant person.

(5) Where—
- (a) a notice has been given to a landlord under section 80, or
- (b) a notice has been given to a relevant person under section 79,

then during the period of twelve months beginning with the date of that notice, no subsequent such notice may be given to the landlord or (as the case may be) that person on behalf of any persons who, in relation to the earlier notice, were qualifying tenants of the constituent dwellings.

Definitions For "the constituent dwellings", see s 76(2); for "qualifying tenant", see s 77; for "relevant person", see s 79(7); for "landlord", see s 84; for "disposal", "dwelling" and "interest", see s 101(1).
References See paras 7.11, 7.14, 7.22, 7.23 ff.

84 Interpretation of Chapter V

In this Chapter—

"the 1985 Act" means the Landlord and Tenant Act 1985;

"appurtenant property" shall be construed in accordance with section 76(3) or (6);

"the auditor", in relation to a management audit, means such a person as is mentioned in section 78(3);

"the constituent dwellings" means the dwellings referred to in section 76(2)(a) or (b) (as the case may be);

"landlord" means immediate landlord;

"management audit" means such an audit as is mentioned in section 78(1);

"management functions" includes functions with respect to the provision of services or the repair, maintenance or insurance of property;

"relevant person" has the meaning given by section 79(7);

"the relevant premises" shall be construed in accordance with section 76(3) or (6);

"service charge" has the meaning given by section 18(1) of the 1985 Act.

CHAPTER VI
MISCELLANEOUS

Compulsory acquisition of landlord's interest

85 Amendment of Part III of Landlord and Tenant Act 1987

(1) Part III of the Landlord and Tenant Act 1987 (compulsory acquisition by tenants of their landlord's interest) shall be amended as follows.

(2) In section 25 (compulsory acquisition of landlord's interest by qualifying tenants)—

(a) for subsection (2)(c) there shall be substituted –

"(c) the total number of flats held by such tenants is not less than two-thirds of the total number of flats contained in the premises.";

and

(b) subsection (3) shall be omitted.

(3) In section 27(4) (meaning of requisite majority in relation to qualifying tenants), for "more than 50 per cent" there shall be substituted "not less than two-thirds".

(4) In section 29(2) (conditions for making acquisition orders), the words from "and (c)" onwards shall be omitted.

Definitions For "tenant", see the Landlord and Tenant Act 1987, s 59(1), (2); for "flat", see s 60(1) of that Act.
References See paras 8.2, 8.3 ff.

Variation of leases

86 Variation of leases under Part IV of Landlord and Tenant Act 1987

In section 35(4) of the Landlord and Tenant Act 1987 (variation of lease on grounds that it fails to make satisfactory provision with respect to the computation of a service charge), in paragraph (c), for "exceed" there shall be substituted "either exceed or be less than".

References   See para 8.4 ff.

Codes of practice

87 Approval by Secretary of State of codes of management practice

(1) The Secretary of State may, if he considers it appropriate to do so, by order—

    (a) approve any code of practice—

        (i) which appears to him to be designed to promote desirable practices in relation to any matter or matters directly or indirectly concerned with the management of residential property by relevant persons; and

        (ii) which has been submitted to him for his approval;

    (b) approve any modifications of any such code which have been so submitted; or

    (c) withdraw his approval for any such code or modifications.

(2) The Secretary of State shall not approve any such code or any modifications of any such code unless he is satisfied that arrangements have been made for the text of the code or the modifications to be published in such manner as he considers appropriate for bringing the provisions of the code or the modifications to the notice of those likely to be affected by them (which, in the case of modifications of a code, may include publication of a text of the code incorporating the modifications).

(3) The power of the Secretary of State under this section to approve a code of practice which has been submitted to him for his approval includes power to approve a part of any such code; and references in this section to a code of practice may accordingly be read as including a reference to a part of a code of practice.

(4) At any one time there may be two or more codes of practice for the time being approved under this section.

(5) A code of practice approved under this section may make different provision with respect to different cases or descriptions of cases, including different provision for different areas.

(6) Without prejudice to the generality of subsections (1) and (5)—

    (a) a code of practice approved under this section may, in relation to any such matter as is referred to in subsection (1), make provision in respect of relevant persons who are under an obligation to discharge any function in connection with that matter as well as in respect of relevant persons who are not under such an obligation; and

    (b) any such code may make provision with respect to—

        (i) the resolution of disputes with respect to residential property between relevant persons and the tenants of such property;

        (ii) competitive tendering for works in connection with such property; and

      (iii) the administration of trusts in respect of amounts paid by tenants by way of service charges.

(7) A failure on the part of any person to comply with any provision of a code of practice for the time being approved under this section shall not of itself render him liable to any proceedings; but in any proceedings before a court or tribunal—

    (a) any code of practice approved under this section shall be admissible in evidence; and

    (b) any provision of any such code which appears to the court or tribunal to be relevant to any question arising in the proceedings shall be taken into account in determining that question.

(8) For the purposes of this section—

    (a) "relevant person" means any landlord of residential property or any person who discharges management functions in respect of such property, and for this purpose "management functions" includes functions with respect to the provision of services or the repair, maintenance or insurance of such property;

    (b) "residential property" means any building or part of a building which consists of one or more dwellings let on leases, but references to residential property include—

      (i) any garage, outhouse, garden, yard and appurtenances belonging to or usually enjoyed with such dwellings,

      (ii) any common parts of any such building or part, and

      (iii) any common facilities which are not within any such building or part; and

    (c) "service charge" means an amount payable by a tenant of a dwelling as part of or in addition to the rent—

      (i) which is payable, directly or indirectly, for services, repairs, maintenance or insurance or any relevant person's costs of management, and

      (ii) the whole or part of which varies or may vary according to the costs or estimated costs incurred or to be incurred by any relevant person in connection with the matters mentioned in sub-paragraph (i).

(9) This section applies in relation to dwellings let on licences to occupy as it applies in relation to dwellings let on leases, and references in this section to landlords and tenants of residential property accordingly include references to licensors and licensees of such property.

Definitions For "common parts" and "dwelling", see s 101(1); for "lease" and related expressions (including "landlord" and "tenant"), see s 101(1), (2); for "management functions", "relevant person", "residential property" and "service charge", see sub-s (8) above.

References See para 8.5 ff.

Jurisdiction of leasehold valuation tribunals in relation to enfranchisement etc of Crown land

88 Jurisdiction of leasehold valuation tribunals in relation to enfranchisement etc of Crown land

(1) This section applies where any tenant under a lease from the Crown is proceeding with a view to acquiring the freehold or an extended lease of a house and premises in circumstances in which, but for the existence of any Crown interest in the land subject to the lease, he would be entitled to acquire the freehold or such an extended lease under Part I of the Leasehold Reform Act 1967.

(2) Where—
(a) this section applies in accordance with subsection (1), and
(b) any question arises in connection with the acquisition of the freehold or an extended lease of the house and premises which is such that, if the tenant were proceeding as mentioned in that subsection in pursuance of a claim made under Part I of that Act, a leasehold valuation tribunal constituted for the purposes of that Part of that Act would have jurisdiction to determine it in proceedings under that Part, and
(c) it is agreed between—
    (i) the appropriate authority and the tenant, and
    (ii) all other persons (if any) whose interests would fall to be represented in proceedings brought under that Part for the determination of that question by such a tribunal,
that that question should be determined by such a tribunal,
a rent assessment committee constituted for the purposes of this section shall have jurisdiction to determine that question.

(3) A rent assessment committee shall, when constituted for the purposes of this section, be known as a leasehold valuation tribunal.

(4) Paragraphs 1 to 3 of Schedule 22 to the Housing Act 1980 (provisions relating to leasehold valuation tribunals constituted for the purposes of Part I of the Leasehold Reform Act 1967) shall apply to a leasehold valuation tribunal constituted for the purposes of this section.

(5) Any application made to such a leasehold valuation tribunal must comply with such requirements (if any) as to the form of, or the particulars to be contained in, any such application as the Secretary of State may by regulations prescribe.

(6) For the purposes of this section "lease from the Crown" means a lease of land in which there is, or has during the subsistence of the lease been, a Crown interest superior to the lease; and "Crown interest" and "the appropriate authority" in relation to a Crown interest mean respectively—
(a) an interest comprised in the Crown Estate, and the Crown Estate Commissioners;
(b) an interest belonging to Her Majesty in right of the Duchy of Lancaster, and the Chancellor of the Duchy;
(c) an interest belonging to the Duchy of Cornwall, and such person as the Duke of Cornwall or the possessor for the time being of the Duchy appoints;
(d) any other interest belonging to a government department or held on behalf of Her Majesty for the purposes of a government department, and the Minister in charge of that department.

(7) In this section any reference to a leasehold valuation tribunal constituted for the purposes of Part I of the Leasehold Reform Act 1967 is a reference to such a rent assessment committee as is mentioned in section 142(2) of the Housing Act 1980 (leasehold valuation tribunals).

Definitions For "interest", see s 101(1); for "lease" and related expressions (including "tenant"), see s 101(1), (2); for "the appropriate authority", "Crown interest" and "lease from the Crown", see sub-s (6) above; as to "leasehold valuation tribunal constituted for the purposes of Part I of the Leasehold Reform Act 1967", see sub-s (7) above.
References See paras 8.6, 8.7 ff.

Provision of accommodation for persons with mental disorders

89 Avoidance of provisions preventing occupation of leasehold property by persons with mental disorders

(1) Any agreement relating to a lease of any property which comprises or includes a dwelling (whether contained in the instrument creating the lease or not and whether made before the creation of the lease or not) shall be void in so far as it would otherwise have the effect of prohibiting or imposing any restriction on—

    (a) the occupation of the dwelling, or of any part of the dwelling, by persons with mental disorders (within the meaning of the Mental Health Act 1983), or

    (b) the provision of accommodation within the dwelling for such persons.

(2) Subsection (1) applies to any agreement made after the coming into force of this section.

Definitions   For "dwelling", see s 101(1); for "lease" see s 101(1), (2).
References   See para 8.8 ff.

CHAPTER VII
GENERAL

90 Jurisdiction of county courts

(1) Any jurisdiction expressed to be conferred on the court by this Part shall be exercised by a county court.

(2) There shall also be brought in a county court any proceedings for determining any question arising under or by virtue of any provision of Chapter I or II or this Chapter which is not a question falling within its jurisdiction by virtue of subsection (1) or one falling within the jurisdiction of a leasehold valuation tribunal by virtue of section 91.

(3) Where, however, there are brought in the High Court any proceedings which, apart from this subsection, are proceedings within the jurisdiction of the High Court, the High Court shall have jurisdiction to hear and determine any proceedings joined with those proceedings which are proceedings within the jurisdiction of a county court by virtue of subsection (1) or (2).

(4) Where any proceedings are brought in a county court by virtue of subsection (1) or (2), the court shall have jurisdiction to hear and determine any other proceedings joined with those proceedings, despite the fact that, apart from this subsection, those other proceedings would be outside the court's jurisdiction.

References   See para 1.15 ff.

91 Jurisdiction of leasehold valuation tribunals

(1) Any jurisdiction expressed to be conferred on a leasehold valuation tribunal by the provisions of this Part (except section 75 or 88) shall be exercised by a rent assessment committee constituted for the purposes of this section; and any question arising in relation to any of the matters specified in subsection (2) shall, in default of agreement, be determined by such a rent assessment committee.

(2) Those matters are—
- (a) the terms of acquisition relating to—
  - (i) any interest which is to be acquired by a nominee purchaser in pursuance of Chapter I, or
  - (ii) any new lease which is to be granted to a tenant in pursuance of Chapter II,

  including in particular any matter which needs to be determined for the purposes of any provision of Schedule 6 or 13;
- (b) the terms of any lease which is to be granted in accordance with section 36 and Schedule 9;
- (c) the amount of any payment falling to be made by virtue of section 18(2);
- (d) the amount of any costs payable by any person or persons by virtue of any provision of Chapter I or II and, in the case of costs to which section 33(1) or 60(1) applies, the liability of any person or persons by virtue of any such provision to pay any such costs; and
- (e) the apportionment between two or more persons of any amount (whether of costs or otherwise) payable by virtue of any such provision.

(3) A rent assessment committee shall, when constituted for the purposes of this section, be known as a leasehold valuation tribunal; and in the following provisions of this section references to a leasehold valuation tribunal are (unless the context otherwise requires) references to such a committee.

(4) Where in any proceedings before a court there falls for determination any question falling within the jurisdiction of a leasehold valuation tribunal by virtue of Chapter I or II or this section, the court—
- (a) shall by order transfer to such a tribunal so much of the proceedings as relate to the determination of that question; and
- (b) may then dispose of all or any remaining proceedings, or adjourn the disposal of all or any such proceedings pending the determination of that question by the tribunal, as it thinks fit;

and accordingly once that question has been so determined the court shall, if it is a question relating to any matter falling to be determined by the court, give effect to the determination in an order of the court.

(5) Without prejudice to the generality of any other statutory provision—
- (a) the power to make regulations under section 74(1)(b) of the Rent Act 1977 (procedure of rent assessment committees) shall extend to prescribing the procedure to be followed consequent on a transfer under subsection (4) above; and
- (b) rules of court may prescribe the procedure to be followed in connection with such a transfer.

(6) Any application made to a leasehold valuation tribunal under or by virtue of this Part must comply with such requirements (if any) as to the form of, or the particulars to be contained in, any such application as the Secretary of State may by regulations prescribe.

(7) In any proceedings before a leasehold valuation tribunal which relate to any claim made under Chapter I, the interests of the participating tenants shall be represented by the nominee purchaser, and accordingly the parties to any such proceedings shall not include those tenants.

(8) No costs which a party to any proceedings under or by virtue of this Part before a leasehold valuation tribunal incurs in connection with the proceedings shall

be recoverable by order of any court (whether in consequence of a transfer under subsection (4) or otherwise).

(9) A leasehold valuation tribunal may, when determining the property in which any interest is to be acquired in pursuance of a notice under section 13 or 42, specify in its determination property which is less extensive than that specified in that notice.

(10) Paragraphs 1 to 3 and 7 of Schedule 22 to the Housing Act 1980 (provisions relating to leasehold valuation tribunals constituted for the purposes of Part I of the Leasehold Reform Act 1967) shall apply to a leasehold valuation tribunal constituted for the purposes of this section; but—

(a) in relation to any proceedings which relate to a claim made under Chapter I of this Part of this Act, paragraph 7 of that Schedule shall apply as if the nominee purchaser were included among the persons on whom a notice is authorised to be served under that paragraph; and

(b) in relation to any proceedings on an application for a scheme to be approved by a tribunal under section 70, paragraph 2(a) of that Schedule shall apply as if any person appearing before the tribunal in accordance with subsection (6) of that section were a party to the proceedings.

(11) In this section—

"the nominee purchaser" and "the participating tenants" have the same meaning as in Chapter I;

"the terms of acquisition" shall be construed in accordance with section 24(8) or section 48(7), as appropriate;

and the reference in subsection (10) to a leasehold valuation tribunal constituted for the purposes of Part I of the Leasehold Reform Act 1967 shall be construed in accordance with section 88(7) above.

Definitions   For "the participating tenants", by virtue of sub-s (11), see s 14; for "the nominee purchaser", by virtue of that subsection; see s 15; for "interest", see s 101(1); for "lease" and related expressions (including "tenant"), see s 101(1), (2); for "the terms of acquisition", see sub-s (11) above. **References**   See paras 1.18–1.20, 3.44, 4.48 ff.

---

92 Enforcement of obligations under Chapters I and II

(1) The court may, on the application of any person interested, make an order requiring any person who has failed to comply with any requirement imposed on him under or by virtue of any provision of Chapter I or II to make good the default within such time as is specified in the order.

(2) An application shall not be made under subsection (1) unless—

(a) a notice has been previously given to the person in question requiring him to make good the default, and

(b) more than 14 days have elapsed since the date of the giving of that notice without his having done so.

References   See para 1.16 ff.

---

93 Agreements excluding or modifying rights of tenant under Chapter I and II

(1) Except as provided by this section, any agreement relating to a lease (whether contained in the instrument creating the lease or not and whether made before the creation of the lease or not) shall be void in so far as it—

(a) purports to exclude or modify—

(i)   any entitlement to participate in the making of a claim to exercise the right to collective enfranchisement under Chapter I,

(ii) any right to acquire a new lease under Chapter II, or

(iii) any right to compensation under section 61; or

(b) provides for the termination or surrender of the lease in the event of the tenant becoming a participating tenant for the purposes of Chapter I or giving a notice under section 42; or

(c) provides for the imposition of any penalty or disability on the tenant in that event.

(2) Subsection (1) shall not be taken to preclude a tenant from surrendering his lease, and shall not—

(a) invalidate any agreement for the acquisition on behalf of a tenant of an interest superior to his lease, or for the acquisition by a tenant of a new lease, on terms different from those provided by Chapters I and II; or

(b) where a tenant has become a participating tenant for the purposes of Chapter I or has given a notice under section 42, invalidate—

(i)   any agreement that the notice given under section 13 or (as the case may be) section 42 shall cease to have effect, or

(ii) any provision of such an agreement excluding or restricting for a period not exceeding three years any such entitlement or right as is mentioned in subsection (1)(a)(i) or (ii); or

(c) where a tenant's right to compensation under section 61 has accrued, invalidate any agreement as to the amount of the compensation.

(3) Where—

(a) a tenant having the right to acquire a new lease under Chapter II—

(i)   has entered into an agreement for the surrender of his lease without the prior approval of the court, or

(ii) has entered into an agreement for the grant of a new lease without any of the terms of acquisition (within the meaning of that Chapter) having been determined by a leasehold valuation tribunal under that Chapter, or

(b) a tenant has been granted a new lease under Chapter II or by virtue of subsection (4) below and, on his landlord claiming possession for the purposes of redevelopment, enters into an agreement without the prior approval of the court for the surrender of the lease,

then on the application of the tenant a county court, or any court in which proceedings are brought on the agreement, may, if in its opinion the tenant is not adequately recompensed under the agreement for his rights under Chapter II, set aside or vary the agreement and give such other relief as appears to it to be just having regard to the situation and conduct of the parties.

(4) Where a tenant has the right to acquire a new lease under Chapter II, there may with the approval of the court be granted to him in satisfaction of that right a new lease on such terms as may be approved by the court, which may include terms excluding or modifying—

(a) any entitlement to participate in the making of a claim to exercise the right to collective enfranchisement under Chapter I, or

(b) any right to acquire a further lease under Chapter II.

(5) Subject to the provisions specified in subsection (6) and to subsection (7), a lease may be granted by virtue of subsection (4), and shall if so granted be binding on persons entitled to any interest in or charge on the landlord's estate—

(a) despite the fact that, apart from this subsection, it would not be authorised against any such persons, and

(b) despite any statutory or other restrictions on the landlord's powers of leasing.

(6) The provisions referred to in subsection (5) are—

(a) section 36 of the Charities Act 1993 (restrictions on disposition of charity land); and

(b) paragraph 8(2)(c) of Schedule 2 to this Act.

(7) Where the existing lease of the tenant is granted after the commencement of Chapter II and, the grant being subsequent to the creation of a charge on the landlord's estate, the existing lease is not binding on the persons interested in the charge, a lease granted by virtue of subsection (4) shall not be binding on those persons.

(8) Where a lease is granted by virtue of subsection (4), then except in so far as provision is made to the contrary by the terms of the lease, the following provisions shall apply in relation to the lease as they apply in relation to a lease granted under section 56, namely—

(a) section 58(3), (5) and (6);

(b) section 59(2) to (5); and

(c) section 61 and Schedule 14;

and subsections (5) to (7) of section 56 shall apply in relation to the lease as they apply in relation to a lease granted under that section.

Definitions   For "the existing lease", see s 62(1); for "the court" and "interest", see s 101(1); for "lease" and related expressions (including "landlord" and "tenant"), see s 101(1), (2).
References   See paras 2.5, 4.3 ff.

94   Crown land

(1) Subject to subsection (2), Chapters I and II shall apply to a lease from the Crown if (and only if) there has ceased to be a Crown interest in the land subject to it.

(2) Where a tenant under a lease from the Crown would, but for the existence of any Crown interest, be entitled to acquire a new lease under Chapter II, then if—

(a) that Crown interest is superior to the interest of the person who for the purposes of Chapter II is the landlord in relation to the lease, and

(b) either—

(i) that landlord is entitled to grant such a new lease without the concurrence of the appropriate authority, or

(ii) the appropriate authority notifies that landlord that, as regards any Crown interest affected, the authority will concur in granting such a new lease,

subsection (1) shall apply as if there had ceased to be any Crown interest in the land subject to the lease, and Chapter II shall apply accordingly.

(3) The restriction imposed by section 3(2) of the Crown Estate Act 1961 (general provisions as to management) on the term for which a lease may be granted by the Crown Estate Commissioners shall not apply where—

(a) the lease is granted by way of renewal of a long lease at a low rent, and

(b) it appears to the Crown Estate Commissioners that, but for the existence of any Crown interest, there would be a right to acquire a new lease under Chapter II of this Part of this Act.

(4) Where, in the case of land belonging—
  (a) to Her Majesty in right of the Duchy of Lancaster, or
  (b) to the Duchy of Cornwall,
it appears to the appropriate authority that a tenant under a long lease at a low rent would, but for the existence of any Crown interest, be entitled to acquire a new lease under Chapter II, then a lease corresponding to that to which the tenant would be so entitled may be granted to take effect wholly or partly out of the Crown interest by the same person and with the same formalities as in the case of any other lease of such land.

(5) In the case of land belonging to the Duchy of Cornwall, the purposes authorised by section 8 of the Duchy of Cornwall Management Act 1863 for the advancement of parts of such gross sums as are there mentioned shall include the payment to tenants under leases from the Crown of sums corresponding to those which, but for the existence of any Crown interest, would be payable by way of compensation under section 61 above.

(6) The appropriate authority in relation to any area occupied under leases from the Crown may make an application for the approval under section 70 of a scheme for that area which is designed to secure that, in the event of tenants under those leases acquiring freehold interests in such circumstances as are mentioned in subsection (7) below, the authority will—
  (a) retain powers of management in respect of the premises in which any such freehold interests are acquired, and
  (b) have rights against any such premises in respect of the benefits arising from the exercise elsewhere of the authority's powers of management.

(7) The circumstances mentioned in subsection (6) are circumstances in which, but for the existence of any Crown interest, the tenants acquiring any such freehold interests would be entitled to acquire them as mentioned in section 69(1)(a) or (b).

(8) Subject to any necessary modifications—
  (a) subsections (2) to (7) of section 69 shall apply in relation to any such scheme as is mentioned in subsection (6) above as they apply in relation to an estate management scheme; and
  (b) section 70 shall apply in relation to the approval of such a scheme as it applies in relation to the approval of a scheme as an estate management scheme.

(9) Subsection (10) applies where—
  (a) any tenants under leases from the Crown are proceeding with a view to acquiring the freehold of any premises in circumstances in which, but for the existence of any Crown interest, they would be entitled to acquire the freehold under Chapter I, or
  (b) any tenant under a lease from the Crown is proceeding with a view to acquiring a new lease of his flat in circumstances in which, but for the existence of any Crown interest, he would be entitled to acquire such a lease under Chapter II.

(10) Where—
  (a) this subsection applies in accordance with subsection (9), and
  (b) any question arises in connection with the acquisition of the freehold of those premises or any such new lease which is such that, if the tenants or tenant were proceeding as mentioned in that subsection in pursuance of a claim made under Chapter I or (as the case may be) Chapter II, a

leasehold valuation tribunal would have jurisdiction to determine it in proceedings under that Chapter, and

(c) it is agreed between—
  (i) the appropriate authority and the tenants or tenant, and
  (ii) all other persons (if any) whose interests would fall to be represented in proceedings brought under that Chapter for the determination of that question by a leasehold valuation tribunal,

that that question should be determined by such a tribunal,

a leasehold valuation tribunal shall have jurisdiction to determine that question; and references in this subsection to a leasehold valuation tribunal are to such a tribunal constituted for the purposes of section 91.

(11) For the purposes of this section "lease from the Crown" means a lease of land in which there is, or has during the subsistence of the lease been, a Crown interest superior to the lease; and "Crown interest" and "the appropriate authority" in relation to a Crown interest mean respectively—

(a) an interest comprised in the Crown Estate, and the Crown Estate Commissioners;

(b) an interest belonging to Her Majesty in right of the Duchy of Lancaster, and the Chancellor of the Duchy;

(c) an interest belonging to the Duchy of Cornwall, and such person as the Duke of Cornwall or the possessor for the time being of the Duchy appoints;

(d) any other interest belonging to a government department or held on behalf of Her Majesty for the purposes of a government department, and the Minister in charge of that department.

(12) For the purposes of this section "long lease at a low rent" shall be construed in accordance with sections 7 and 8.

Definitions For "interest" and "flat", see s 101(1); for "lease" and related expressions (including "landlord" and "tenant"), see s 101(1), (2); for "the appropriate authority", "Crown interest" and "lease from the Crown", see sub-s (11) above; and as to "long lease at a low rent", see sub-s (12) above.
References See paras 1.22–1.25 ff.

95 Saving for National Trust

Chapters I and II shall not prejudice the operation of section 21 of the National Trust Act 1907, and accordingly there shall be no right under Chapter I or II to acquire any interest in or new lease of any property if an interest in the property is under that section vested inalienably in the National Trust for Places of Historic Interest or Natural Beauty.

Definitions For "interest", see s 101(1); for "lease", see s 101(1), (2).
References See para 4.7 ff.

96 Property within cathedral precinct

There shall be no right under Chapter I or II to acquire any interest in or lease of any property which for the purposes of the Care of Cathedrals Measure 1990 is within the precinct of a cathedral church.

Definitions For "interest", see s 101(1); for "lease", see s 101(1), (2).
References See para 4.7 ff.

97 Registration of notices, applications and orders under Chapters I and II

(1) No lease shall be registrable under the Land Charges Act 1972 or be taken to be an estate contract within the meaning of that Act by reason of any rights or obligations of the tenant or landlord which may arise under Chapter I or II, and any right of a tenant arising from a notice given under section 13 or 42 shall not be an overriding interest within the meaning of the Land Registration Act 1925; but a notice given under section 13 or 42 shall be registrable under the Land Charges Act 1972, or may be the subject of a notice or caution under the Land Registration Act 1925, as if it were an estate contract.

(2) The Land Charges Act 1972 and the Land Registration Act 1925—

(a) shall apply in relation to an order made under section 26(1) or 50(1) as they apply in relation to an order affecting land which is made by the court for the purpose of enforcing a judgment or recognisance; and

(b) shall apply in relation to an application for such an order as they apply in relation to other pending land actions.

(3) The persons applying for such an order in respect of any premises shall be treated for the purposes of section 57 of the Land Registration Act 1925 (inhibitions) as persons interested in relation to any registered land containing the whole or part of those premises.

Definitions For "the court", see s 101(1); for "lease" and related expressions (including "landlord" and "tenant"), see s 101(1), (2).
References See paras 3.32, 4.30 ff.

98 Power to prescribe procedure under Chapters I and II

(1) Where a claim to exercise the right to collective enfranchisement under Chapter I is made by the giving of a notice under section 13, or a claim to exercise the right to acquire a new lease under Chapter II is made by the giving of a notice under section 42, then except as otherwise provided by Chapter I or (as the case may be) Chapter II—

(a) the procedure for giving effect to the notice, and

(b) the rights and obligations of all parties in relation to the investigation of title and other matters arising in giving effect to the notice,

shall be such as may be prescribed by regulations made by the Secretary of State and, subject to or in the absence of provision made by any such regulations, shall be as nearly as may be the same as in the case of a contract of sale or leasing freely negotiated between the parties.

(2) Regulations under this section may, in particular, make provision—

(a) for a person to be discharged from performing any obligations arising out of a notice under section 13 or 42 by reason of the default or delay of some other person;

(b) for the payment of a deposit—

(i) by a nominee purchaser (within the meaning of Chapter I) on exchange of contracts, or

(ii) by a tenant who has given a notice under section 42; and

(c) with respect to the following matters, namely—

(i) the person with whom any such deposit is to be lodged and the capacity in which any such person is to, hold it, and

(ii) the circumstances in which the whole or part of any such deposit is to be returned or forfeited.

Definitions   For "the nominee purchaser", see s 15; as to "tenant", see s 101(2).
References   See paras 3.8, 4.21 ff.

99 Notices

(1) Any notice required or authorised to be given under this Part—
  (a) shall be in writing; and
  (b) may be sent by post.

(2) Where in accordance with Chapter I or II an address in England and Wales is specified as an address at which notices may be given to any person or persons under that Chapter—
  (a) any notice required or authorised to be given to that person or those persons under that Chapter may (without prejudice to the operation of subsection (3)) be given to him or them at the address so specified; but
  (b) if a new address in England and Wales is so specified in substitution for that address by the giving of a notice to that effect, any notice so required or authorised to be given may be given to him or them at that new address instead.

(3) Where a tenant is required or authorised to give any notice under Chapter I or II to a person who
  (a) is the tenant's immediate landlord, and
  (b) is such a landlord in respect of premises to which Part VI of the Landlord and Tenant Act 1987 (information to be furnished to tenants) applies,
the tenant may, unless he has been subsequently notified by the landlord of a different address in England and Wales for the purposes of this section, give the notice to the landlord—
  (i) at the address last furnished to the tenant as the landlord's address for service in accordance with section 48 of that Act (notification of address for service of notices on landlord); or
  (ii) if no such address has been furnished, at the address last furnished to the tenant as the landlord's address in accordance with section 47 of that Act (landlord's name and address to be contained in demands for rent).

(4) Subsections (2) and (3) apply to notices in proceedings under Chapter I or II as they apply to notices required or authorised to be given under that Chapter.

(5) Any notice which is given under Chapter I or II by any tenants or tenant must—
  (a) if it is a notice given under section 13 or 42, be signed by each of the tenants, or (as the case may be) by the tenant, by whom it is given; and
  (b) in any other case, be signed by or on behalf of each of the tenants, or (as the case may be) by or on behalf of the tenant, by whom it is given.

(6) The Secretary of State may by regulations prescribe—
  (a) the form of any notice required or authorised to be given under this Part; and
  (b) the particulars which any such notice must contain (whether in addition to, or in substitution for, any particulars required by virtue of any provision of this Part).

References   See paras 1.11–1.13 ff.

100 Orders and regulations

(1) Any power of the Secretary of State to make orders or regulations under this Part—

    (a) may be so exercised as to make different provision for different cases or descriptions of cases, including different provision for different areas; and

    (b) includes power to make such procedural, incidental, supplementary and transitional provision as may appear to the Secretary of State necessary or expedient.

(2) Any power of the Secretary of State to make orders or regulations under this Part shall be exercisable by statutory instrument which (except in the case of regulations making only such provision as is mentioned in section 99(6)) shall be subject to annulment in pursuance of a resolution of either House of Parliament.

References   See para 1.14 ff.

101 General interpretation of Part I

(1) In this Part—

    "business lease" means a tenancy to which Part II of the Landlord and Tenant Act 1954 applies;

    "common parts", in relation to any building or part of a building, includes the structure and exterior of that building or part and any common facilities within it;

    "the court" (unless the context otherwise requires) means, by virtue of section 90(1), a county court;

    "disposal" means a disposal whether by the creation or the transfer of an interest, and includes the surrender of a lease and the grant of an option or right of pre-emption, and "acquisition" shall be construed accordingly (as shall expressions related to either of these expressions);

    "dwelling" means any building or part of a building occupied or intended to be occupied as a separate dwelling;

    "flat" means a separate set of premises (whether or not on the same floor)—

        (a) which forms part of a building, and

        (b) which is constructed or adapted for use for the purposes of a dwelling, and

        (c) either the whole or a material part of which lies above or below some other part of the building;

    "interest" includes estate;

    "lease" and "tenancy", and related expressions, shall be construed in accordance with subsection (2);

    "rent assessment committee" means a rent assessment committee constituted under Schedule 10 to the Rent Act 1977;

    "the term date", in relation to a lease granted for a term of years certain, means (subject to subsection (6)) the date of expiry of that term, and, in relation to a tenancy to which any of the provisions of section 102 applies, shall be construed in accordance with those provisions.

(2) In this Part "lease" and "tenancy" have the same meaning, and both expressions include (where the context so permits)—

    (a) a sub-lease or sub-tenancy, and

(b) an agreement for a lease or tenancy (or for a sub-lease or sub-tenancy), but do not include a tenancy at will or at sufferance; and the expressions "landlord" and "tenant", and references to letting, to the grant of a lease or to covenants or the terms of a lease, shall be construed accordingly.

(3) In this Part any reference (however expressed) to the lease held by a qualifying tenant of a flat is a reference to a lease held by him under which the demised premises consist of or include the flat (whether with or without one or more other flats).

(4) Where two or more persons jointly constitute either the landlord or the tenant or qualifying tenant in relation to a lease of a flat, any reference in this Part to the landlord or to the tenant or qualifying tenant is (unless the context otherwise requires) a reference to both or all of the persons who jointly constitute the landlord or the tenant or qualifying tenant, as the case may require.

(5) Any reference in this Part to the date of the commencement of a lease is a reference to the date of the commencement of the term of the lease.

(6) In the case of a lease which derives (in accordance with section 7(6)) from more than one separate leases, references in this Part to the date of the commencement of the lease or to the term date shall, if the terms of the separate leases commenced at different dates or those leases have different term dates, have effect as references to the date of the commencement, or (as the case may be) to the term date, of the lease comprising the flat in question (or the earliest date of commencement or earliest term date of the leases comprising it).

(7) For the purposes of this Part property is let with other property if the properties are let either under the same lease or under leases which, in accordance with section 7(6), are treated as a single lease.

(8) For the purposes of this Part any lease which is reversionary on another lease shall be treated as if it were a concurrent lease intermediate between that other lease and any interest superior to that other lease.

(9) For the purposes of this Part an order of a court or a decision of a leasehold valuation tribunal is to be treated as becoming final—
    (a) if not appealed against, on the expiry of the time for bringing an appeal; or
    (b) if appealed against and not set aside in consequence of the appeal, at the time when the appeal and any further appeal is disposed of—
        (i) by the determination of it and the expiry of the time for bringing a further appeal (if any), or
        (ii) by its being abandoned or otherwise ceasing to have effect.

References   See paras 1.21, 2.10, 2.53, 7.3 ff.

102 Term date and other matters relating to periodical tenancies

(1) Where either of the following provisions (which relate to continuation tenancies) applies to a tenancy, namely—
    (a) section 19(2) of the Landlord and Tenant Act 1954 ("the 1954 Act"), or
    (b) paragraph 16(2) of Schedule 10 to the Local Government and Housing Act 1989 ("the 1989 Act"),
the tenancy shall be treated for the relevant purposes of this Part as granted to expire—
    (i) on the date which is the term date for the purposes of the 1954 Act (namely, the first date after the commencement of the 1954 Act on

which, apart from the 1954 Act, the tenancy could have been brought to an end by a notice to quit given by the landlord under the tenancy), or
  (ii) on the date which is the term date for the purposes of Schedule 10 to the 1989 Act (namely, the first date after the commencement of Schedule 10 to the 1989 Act on which, apart from that Schedule, the tenancy could have been brought to an end by such a notice to quit),

as the case may be.

(2) Subject to subsection (1), where under section 7(3) a tenancy created or arising as a tenancy from year to year or other periodical tenancy is to be treated as a long lease, then for the relevant purposes of this Part, the term date of that tenancy shall be taken to be the date (if any) on which the tenancy is to terminate by virtue of a notice to quit given by the landlord under the tenancy before the relevant date for those purposes, or else the earliest date on which it could as at that date (in accordance with its terms and apart from any enactment) be brought to an end by such a notice to quit.

(3) Subject to subsection (1), in the case of a tenancy granted to continue as a periodical tenancy after the expiry of a term of years certain, or to continue as a periodical tenancy if not terminated at the expiry of such a term, any question whether the tenancy is at any time to be treated for the relevant purposes of this Part as a long lease, and (if so) with what term date, shall be determined as it would be if there had been two tenancies, as follows—
  (a) one granted to expire at the earliest time (at or after the expiry of that term of years certain) at which the tenancy could (in accordance with its terms and apart from any enactment) be brought to an end by a notice to quit given by the landlord under the tenancy; and
  (b) the other granted to commence at the expiry of the first (and not being one to which subsection (1) applies).

(4) In this section "the relevant purposes of this Part" means the purposes of Chapter I or, to the extent that section 7 has effect for the purposes of Chapter II in accordance with section 39(3), the purposes of that Chapter.

Definitions For "lease" and related expressions (including "landlord" and "tenancy"), see s 101(1), (2); for "the relevant purposes of this Part", see sub-s (4) above.

---

103 Application of Part I to Isles of Scilly
This Part applies to the Isles of Scilly subject to such exceptions, adaptations and modifications as the Secretary of State may by order direct.

References See para 1.26 ff.

PART II
PUBLIC SECTOR HOUSING

CHAPTER I
ENGLAND AND WALES

Right to buy

104 Landlord's notice of purchase price and other matters
For subsection (5) of section 125 (landlord's notice of purchase price and other matters) of the Housing Act 1985 (in this Chapter referred to as "the 1985 Act") there shall be substituted the following subsection—

"(5) The notice shall also inform the tenant of—

    (a) the effect of sections 125D and 125E(1) and (4) (tenant's notice of intention, landlord's notice in default and effect of failure to comply),

    (b) his right under section 128 to have the value of the dwelling-house at the relevant time determined or re-determined by the district valuer,

    (c) the effect of section 136(2) (change of tenant after service of notice under section 125),

    (d) the effect of sections 140 and 141(1), (2) and (4) (landlord's notices to complete and effect of failure to comply),

    (e) the effect of the provisions of this Part relating to the right to acquire on rent to mortgage terms, and

    (f) the relevant amount and multipliers for the time being declared by the Secretary of State for the purposes of section 143B."

Definitions For "relevant time", see the Housing Act 1985, s 122(2); for "right to acquire on rent to mortgage terms", see s 143 of that Act, as substituted by s 108; for "dwelling-house", see ss 183, 184 of that Act, as amended, in the case of s 184, by s 187(1), Sch 21, para 24; for "tenant", see s 621(3) of that Act; for "district valuer", see s 622 of that Act.
References See para 10.4 ff.

105 Tenant's notice of intention etc

(1) After section 125C of the 1985 Act there shall be inserted the following sections—

"125D Tenant's notice of intention

(1) Where a notice under section 125 has been served on a secure tenant, he shall within the period specified in subsection (2) either—

    (a) serve a written notice on the landlord stating either that he intends to pursue his claim to exercise the right to buy or that he withdraws that claim, or

    (b) serve a notice under section 144 claiming to exercise the right to acquire on rent to mortgage terms.

(2) The period for serving a notice under subsection (1) is the period of twelve weeks beginning with whichever of the following is the later—

    (a) the service of the notice under section 125, and

    (b) where the tenant exercises his right to have the value of the dwelling-house determined or re-determined by the district valuer, the service of the notice under section 128(5) stating the effect of the determination or re-determination.

125E Landlord's notice in default

(1) The landlord may, at any time after the end of the period specified in section 125D(2) or, as the case may require, section 136(2), serve on the tenant a written notice—

    (a) requiring him, if he has failed to serve the notice required by section 125D(1), to serve that notice within 28 days, and

    (b) informing him of the effect of this subsection and subsection (4).

(2) At any time before the end of the period mentioned in subsection (1)(a) (or that period as previously extended) the landlord may by written notice served on the tenant extend it (or further extend it).

(3) If at any time before the end of that period (or that period as extended under subsection (2)) the circumstances are such that it would not be reasonable to expect the tenant to comply with a notice under this section, that period (or that period as so extended) shall by virtue of this subsection be extended (or further extended) until 28 days after the time when those circumstances no longer obtain.

(4) If the tenant does not comply with a notice under this section, the notice claiming to exercise the right to buy shall be deemed to be withdrawn at the end of that period (or, as the case may require, that period as extended under subsection (2) or (3))."

(2) For subsections (2) to (5) of section 136 of the 1985 Act (change of tenant after notice claiming to exercise the right to buy) there shall be substituted the following subsection—

"(2) If a notice under section 125 (landlord's notice of purchase price and other matters) has been served on the former tenant, then, whether or not the former tenant has served a notice under subsection (1) of section 125D (tenant's notice of intention), the new tenant shall serve a notice under that subsection within the period of twelve weeks beginning with whichever of the following is the later—

(a) his becoming the secure tenant, and

(b) where the right to have the value of the dwelling-house determined or re-determined by the district valuer is or has been exercised by him or the former tenant, the service of the notice under section 128(5) stating the effect of the determination or re-determination."

Definitions   For "secure tenant", see the Housing Act 1985, ss 79, 185; for "right to buy", see s 118(1) of that Act; for "the former tenant" and "the new tenant", see s 136(1) of that Act; for "right to acquire on rent to mortgage terms", see s 143 of that Act, as substituted by s 108; for "dwelling-house", see ss 183, 184 of that Act, as amended, in the case of s 184, by s 187(1), Sch 21, para 24; for "landlord", see s 621 of that Act; for "district valuer", see s 622 of that Act.
References   See para 10.2 ff.

106 Exceptions to the right to buy

(1) In paragraph 10(1) (groups of dwelling-houses for persons of pensionable age) of Schedule 5 to the 1985 Act (exceptions to the right to buy)—

(a) for the words "persons of pensionable age", in the first place where they occur, there shall be substituted the words "elderly persons"; and

(b) for those words, in the second place where they occur, there shall be substituted the words "persons aged 60 or more".

(2) For paragraph 11 (individual dwelling-houses for persons of pensionable age) of that Schedule there shall be substituted the following paragraph—

"11.—(1) The right to buy does not arise if the dwelling-house—

(a) is particularly suitable, having regard to its location, size, design, heating system and other features, for occupation by elderly persons, and

(b) was let to the tenant or a predecessor in title of his for occupation by a person who was aged 60 or more (whether the tenant or predecessor or another person).

(2) In determining whether a dwelling is particularly suitable, no regard shall be had to the presence of any feature provided by the tenant or a predecessor in title of his.

(3) Notwithstanding anything in section 181 (jurisdiction of county court), any question arising under this paragraph shall be determined as follows.

(4) If an application for the purpose is made by the tenant to the Secretary of State before the end of the period of 56 days beginning with the service of the landlord's notice under section 124, the question shall be determined by the Secretary of State.

(5) If no such application is so made, the question shall be deemed to have been determined in favour of the landlord.

(6) This paragraph does not apply unless the dwelling-house concerned was first let before 1st January 1990."

(3) Subsections (1) and (2) do not apply in any case where the tenant's notice claiming to exercise the right to buy was served before the day on which this section comes into force.

(4) For the purposes of subsection (3), no account shall be taken of any steps taken under section 177 of the 1985 Act (amendment or withdrawal and re-service of notice to correct mistakes).

Definitions For "right to buy", see the Housing Act 1985, s 118(1); for "dwelling-house", see ss 183, 184 of that Act, as amended, in the case of s 184, by s 187(1), Sch 21, para 24; for "landlord" and "tenant", see s 621 of that Act.
References See paras 10.5, 10.6 ff.

Abolition of certain ancillary rights

107 Abolition of right to a mortgage, right to defer completion and right to be granted a shared ownership lease

The following rights ancillary to the right to buy are hereby abolished, namely—

(a) the right to a mortgage conferred by sections 132 to 135 of the 1985 Act;

(b) the right to defer completion conferred by section 142 of that Act; and

(c) the right to be granted a shared ownership lease conferred by sections 143 to 151 of that Act.

References See para 9.2 ff.

Right to acquire on rent to mortgage terms

108 Right to acquire on rent to mortgage terms

For section 143 of the 1985 Act there shall be substituted the following sections—

"Right to acquire on rent to mortgage terms

143 Right to acquire on rent to mortgage terms

(1) Subject to subsection (2) and sections 143A and 143B, where—

(a) a secure tenant has claimed to exercise the right to buy, and

(b) his right to buy has been established and his notice claiming to exercise it remains in force,

he also has the right to acquire on rent to mortgage terms in accordance with the following provisions of this Part.

(2) The right to acquire on rent to mortgage terms cannot be exercised if the exercise of the right to buy is precluded by section 121 (circumstances in which right to buy cannot be exercised).

(3) Where the right to buy belongs to two or more persons jointly, the right to acquire on rent to mortgage terms also belongs to them jointly.

143A Right excluded by entitlement housing benefit

(1) The right to acquire on rent to mortgage to terms cannot be exercised if—

(a) it has been determined that the tenant is or was entitled to housing benefit in respect of any part of the relevant period, or

(b) a claim for housing benefit in respect of any part of that period has been made (or is treated as having been made) by or on behalf of the tenant and has not been determined or withdrawn.

(2) In this section "the relevant period" means the period—

(a) beginning twelve months before the day on which the tenant claims to exercise the right to acquire on rent to mortgage terms, and

(b) ending with the day on which the conveyance or grant is executed in pursuance of that right.

143B Right excluded if minimum initial payment exceeds maximum initial payment

(1) The right to acquire on rent to mortgage terms cannot be exercised if the minimum initial payment in respect of the dwelling-house exceeds the maximum initial payment in respect of it.

(2) The maximum initial payment in respect of a dwelling-house is 80 per cent of the price which would be payable if the tenant were exercising the right to buy.

(3) Where, in the case of a dwelling-house which is a house, the weekly rent at the relevant time did not exceed the relevant amount, the minimum initial payment shall be determined by the formula—

$$P = R \times M$$

where—

P = the minimum initial payment;

R = the amount of the weekly rent at the relevant time;

M = the multiplier which at that time was for the time being declared by the Secretary of State for the purposes of this subsection.

(4) Where, in the case of a dwelling-house which is a house, the weekly rent at the relevant time exceeded the relevant amount, the minimum initial payment shall be determined by the formula—

$$P = Q + (E \times M)$$

275

where—
- P = the minimum initial payment;
- Q = the qualifying maximum for the year of assessment which included the relevant time;
- E = the amount by which the weekly rent at that time exceeded the relevant amount;
- M = the multiplier which at that time was for the time being declared by the Secretary of State for the purposes of this subsection.

(5) The minimum initial payment in respect of a dwelling-house which is a flat is 80 per cent of the amount which would be the minimum initial payment in respect of the dwelling-house if it were a house.

(6) The relevant amount and multipliers for the time being declared for the purposes of this section shall be such that, in the case of a dwelling-house which is a house, they will produce a minimum initial payment equal to the capital sum which, in the opinion of the Secretary of State, could be raised on a 25 year repayment mortgage in the case of which the net amount of the monthly mortgage payments was equal to the rent at the relevant time calculated on a monthly basis.

(7) For the purposes of subsection (6) the Secretary of State shall assume—
- (a) that the interest rate applicable throughout the 25 year term were the standard national rate for the time being declared by the Secretary of State under paragraph 2 of Schedule 16 (local authority mortgage interest rates); and
- (b) that the monthly mortgage payments represented payments of capital and interest only.

(8) In this section—
"net amount", in relation to monthly mortgage payments, means the amount of such payments after deduction of tax under section 369 of the Income and Corporation Taxes Act 1988 (mortgage interest payable under deduction of tax);
"qualifying maximum" means the qualifying maximum defined in section 367(5) of that Act (limit on relief for interest on certain loans);
"relevant amount" means the amount which at the relevant time was for the time being declared by the Secretary of State for the purposes of this section;
"relevant time" means the time of the service of the landlord's notice under section 146 (landlord's notice admitting or denying right);
"rent" means rent payable under the secure tenancy, but excluding any element which is expressed to be payable for services, repairs, maintenance or insurance or the landlord's costs of management."

Definitions For "secure tenancy" and "secure tenant", see the Housing Act 1985, ss 79, 185; for "right to buy", see s 118(1) of that Act; for "flat" and "house", see s 183 of that Act; for "dwelling-house", see ss 183, 184 of that Act, as amended, in the case of s 184, by s 187(1), Sch 21, para 24 post; for "landlord" and "tenant", see s 621 of that Act; for "right to acquire on rent to mortgage terms", see s 143 of that Act, as substituted above; for "minimum initial payment" and "maximum initial payment", see s 143B of that Act, as so substituted; for "the relevant period" in s 143A of that Act, as inserted above, see sub-s (2) thereof, as so inserted; as to "net amount", "qualifying maximum", "relevant amount", "relevant time" and "rent" in s 143B of that Act, as so inserted, see sub-s (8) thereof, as so inserted.
References See paras 9.2–9.8 ff.

---

109 Tenant's notice claiming right

For sections 144 and 145 of the 1985 Act there shall be substituted the following section—

"144 Tenant's notice claiming right

(1) A secure tenant claims to exercise the right to acquire on rent to mortgage terms by written notice to that effect served on the landlord.

(2) The notice may be withdrawn at any time by notice in writing served on the landlord.

(3) On the service of a notice under this section, any notice served by the landlord under section 140 or 141 (landlord's notices to complete purchase in pursuance of right to buy) shall be deemed to have been withdrawn; and no such notice may be served by the landlord whilst a notice under this section remains in force.

(4) Where a notice under this section is withdrawn, the tenant may complete the transaction in accordance with the provisions of this Part relating to the right to buy."

Definitions   For "secure tenant", see the Housing Act 1985, ss 79, 185; for "right to buy", see s 118(1) of that Act; for "right to acquire on rent to mortgage terms", see s 143 of that Act, as substituted by s 108; for "landlord" and "tenant", see s 621 of that Act.
References   See para 9.9 ff.

110 Landlord's notice admitting or denying right

For section 146 of the 1985 Act there shall be substituted the following section—

146 Landlord's notice admitting or denying right

(1) Where a notice under section 144 (notice claiming to exercise the right to acquire on rent to mortgage terms) has been served by the tenant, the landlord shall, unless the notice is withdrawn, serve on the tenant as soon as practicable a written notice either—
- (a) admitting the tenant's right and informing him of the matters mentioned in subsection (2), or
- (b) denying it and stating the reasons why, in the opinion of the landlord, the tenant does not have the right to acquire on rent to mortgage terms.

(2) The matters are—
- (a) the relevant amount and multipliers for the time being declared by the Secretary of State for the purposes of section 143B;
- (b) the amount of the minimum initial payment;
- (c) the proportion which that amount bears to the price which would be payable if the tenant exercised the right to buy;
- (d) the landlord's share on the assumption that the tenant makes the minimum initial payment;
- (e) the amount of the initial discount on that assumption; and
- (f) the provisions which, in the landlord's opinion, should be contained in the conveyance or grant and the mortgage required by section 151B (mortgage for securing redemption of landlord's share)."

Definitions   For "right to buy", see the Housing Act 1985, s 118(1); for "right to acquire on rent to mortgage terms", see s 143 of that Act, as substituted by s 108; for "minimum initial payment", see s 143B of that Act, as so substituted; for "landlord's share", see ss 148, 151A of, Sch 6A, para 7 to, that Act, as substituted and inserted by ss 113, 117; for "landlord" and "tenant", see s 621 of that Act.
References   See para 9.10 ff.

111 Tenant's notice of intention etc

After section 146 of the 1985 Act there shall be inserted the following sections—

"146A Tenant's notice of intention

(1) Where a notice under section 146 has been served on a secure tenant, he shall within the period specified in subsection (2) serve a written notice on the landlord stating either—

    (a) that he intends to pursue his claim to exercise the right to acquire on rent to mortgage terms and the amount of the initial payment which he proposes to make, or

    (b) that he withdraws that claim and intends to pursue his claim to exercise the right to buy, or

    (c) that he withdraws both of those claims.

(2) The period for serving a notice under subsection (1) is the period of twelve weeks beginning with the service of the notice under section 146.

(3) The amount stated in a notice under subsection (1)(a)—

    (a) shall not be less than the minimum initial payment and not more than the maximum initial payment, and

    (b) may be varied at any time by notice in writing served on the landlord.

146B Landlord's notice in default

(1) The landlord may, at any time after the end of the period specified in section 146A(2), serve on the tenant a written notice—

    (a) requiring him, if he has failed to serve the notice required by section 146A(1), to serve that notice within 28 days, and

    (b) informing him of the effect of this subsection and subsection (4).

(2) At any time before the end of the period mentioned in subsection (1)(a) (or that period as previously extended) the landlord may by written notice served on the tenant extend it (or further extend it).

(3) If at any time before the end of that period (or that period as extended under subsection (2)) the circumstances are such that it would not be reasonable to expect the tenant to comply with a notice under this section, that period (or that period as so extended) shall by virtue of this subsection be extended (or further extended) until 28 days after the time when those circumstances no longer obtain.

(4) If the tenant does not comply with a notice under this section the notice claiming to exercise the right to acquire on rent to mortgage terms shall be deemed to be withdrawn at the end of that period (or, as the case may require, that period as extended under subsection (2) or (3))."

Definitions   For "secure tenant", see the Housing Act 1985, ss 79, 185; for "right to buy", see s 118(1) of that Act; for "right to acquire on rent to mortgage terms", see s 143 of that Act, as substituted by s 108; for "initial payment", "minimum initial payment" and "maximum initial payment", see s 143B of that Act, as so substituted; for "landlord" and "tenant", see s 621 of that Act.
References   See paras 9.11, 9.12 ff.

112 Notice of landlord's share and initial discount

For section 147 of the 1985 Act there shall be substituted the following section—

"147 Notice of landlord's share and initial discount

(1) Where a secure tenant has served—

    (a)   a notice under section 146A(1)(a) stating that he intends to pursue his claim to exercise the right to acquire on rent to mortgage terms, and the amount of the initial payment which he proposes to make, or

    (b)   a notice under section 146A(3)(b) varying the amount stated in a notice under section 146A(1)(a),

the landlord shall, as soon as practicable, serve on the tenant a written notice complying with this section.

(2) The notice shall state—

    (a)   the landlord's share on the assumption that the amount of the tenant's initial payment is that stated in the notice under section 146A(1)(a) or, as the case may be, section 146A(3)(b), and

    (b)   the amount of the initial discount on that assumption,

determined in each case in accordance with section 148."

Definitions   For "secure tenant", see the Housing Act 1985, ss 79, 185, Vol 21; for "right to acquire on rent to mortgage terms", see s 143 of that Act, as substituted by s 108; for "initial payment", see s 143B of that Act, as so substituted; for "landlord" and "tenant", see s 621 of that Act.
References   See para 9.13 ff.

113 Determination of landlord's share, initial discount etc

For section 148 of the 1985 Act there shall be substituted the following section—

"148 Determination of landlord's share, initial discount etc

The landlord's share shall be determined by the formula—

$$S = \frac{P - IP}{P} \times 100$$

the amount of the initial discount shall be determined by the formula—

$$ID = \frac{IP}{P} \times D$$

and the amount of any previous discount which will be recovered by virtue of the transaction shall be determined by the formula—

$$RD = \frac{IP}{P} \times PD$$

where—

    S = the landlord's share expressed as a percentage;

P = the price which would be payable if the tenant were exercising the right to buy;

IP = the amount of the tenant's initial payment (but disregarding any reduction in pursuance of section 153B(3));

ID = the amount of the initial discount;

D = the amount of the discount which would be applicable if the tenant were exercising the right to buy;

RD = the amount of any previous discount which will be recovered by virtue of the transaction;

PD = the amount of any previous discount which would be recovered if the tenant were exercising the right to buy."

Definitions For "right to buy", see the Housing Act 1985, s 118(1); for "initial payment", see s 143B of, and Sch 6A, para 6 to, that Act, as substituted and inserted respectively by s 108 and s 117(2) (Sch 6A is set out in Sch 16); for "landlord" and "tenant", see s 621 of that Act.
References See para 9.13 ff.

114 Change of landlord after notice claiming right

For section 149 of the 1985 Act there shall be substituted the following section—

"149 Change of landlord after notice claiming right

(1) Where the interest of the landlord in the dwelling-house passes from the landlord to another body after a secure tenant has given a notice claiming to exercise the right to acquire on rent to mortgage terms, all parties shall subject to subsection (2) be in the same position as if the other body—

(a) had become the landlord before the notice was given, and

(b) had been given that notice and any further notice given by the tenant to the landlord, and

(c) had taken all steps which the landlord had taken.

(2) If the circumstances after the disposal differ in any material respect, as for example where—

(a) the interest of the disponee in the dwelling-house after the disposal differs from that of the disponor before the disposal, or

(b) any of the provisions of Schedule 5 (exceptions to the right to buy) becomes or ceases to be applicable,

all those concerned shall, as soon as practicable after the disposal, take all such steps (whether by way of amending or withdrawing and re-serving any notice or extending any period or otherwise) as may be requisite for the purpose of securing that all parties are, as nearly as may be, in the same position as they would have been if those circumstances had obtained before the disposal."

Definitions For "secure tenant", see the Housing Act 1985, ss 79, 185; for "right to acquire on rent to mortgage terms", see s 143 of that Act, as substituted by s 108; for "dwelling-house", see ss 183, 184 of that Act, as amended, in the case of s 184, by s 187(1), Sch 21, para 24; for "landlord" and "tenant", see s 621 of that Act.
References See para 9.14 ff.

115 Duty of landlord to convey freehold or grant lease

For section 150 of the 1985 Act there shall be substituted the following section—

"150 Duty of landlord to convey freehold or grant lease

(1) Where a secure tenant has claimed to exercise the right to acquire on rent to mortgage terms and that right has been established, then, as soon as all matters relating to the grant and to securing the redemption of the landlord's share have been agreed or determined, the landlord shall make to the tenant—

(a) if the dwelling-house is a house and the landlord owns the freehold, a grant of the dwelling-house for an estate in fee simple absolute, or

(b) if the landlord does not own the freehold or if the dwelling-house is a flat (whether or not the landlord owns the freehold), a grant of a lease of the dwelling-house,

in accordance with the following provisions of this Part.

(2) If the tenant has failed to pay the rent or any other payment due from him as a tenant for a period of four weeks after it has been lawfully demanded from him, the landlord is not bound to comply with subsection (1) while the whole or part of that payment remains outstanding.

(3) The duty imposed on the landlord by subsection (1) is enforceable by injunction."

Definitions   For "secure tenant", see the Housing Act 1985, ss 79, 185; for "right to acquire on rent to mortgage terms", see s 143 of that Act, as substituted by s 108; for "landlord's share", see s 148 of that Act, as substituted by s 113, and Sch 6A, para 7 to that Act, as inserted by s 117(2) (Sch 6A is set out in Sch 16); for "flat" and "house", see s 183 of that Act; for "dwelling-house", see ss 183, 184 of that Act, as amended, in the case of s 184, by s 187(1), Sch 21, para 24; for "landlord" and "tenant", see s 621 of that Act.
References   See para 9.15 ff.

---

116 Terms and effect of conveyance or grant: general

(1) For section 151 of the 1985 Act there shall be substituted the following section—

"151 Terms and effect of conveyance or grant: general

(1) A conveyance of the freehold executed in pursuance of the right to acquire on rent to mortgage terms shall conform with Parts I and II of Schedule 6; a grant of a lease so executed shall conform with Parts I and III of that Schedule; and Part IV of that Schedule applies to such a conveyance or lease as it applies to a conveyance or lease executed in pursuance of the right to buy.

(2) The secure tenancy comes to an end on the grant to the tenant of an estate in fee simple, or of a lease, in pursuance of the right to acquire on rent to mortgage terms; and if there is then a sub-tenancy section 139 of the Law of Property Act 1925 (effect of extinguishment of reversion) applies as on a merger or surrender."

(2) In Part III of Schedule 6 to the 1985 Act (terms of lease granted in pursuance of right to buy or right to acquire on rent to mortgage terms), after paragraph 16D there shall be inserted the following paragraph—

"16E.—(1) Where a lease of a flat granted in pursuance of the right to acquire on rent to mortgage terms requires the tenant to pay—

(a) service charges in respect of repairs (including works for the making good of structural defects), or

(b) improvement contributions,

his liability in respect of costs incurred at any time before the final payment is made is restricted as follows.

(2) He is not required to pay any more than the amount determined by the formula—

$$M = P \times \frac{100 - S}{100}$$

where—

> M = the maximum amount which he is required to pay;
> P = the amount which, but for this paragraph, he would be required to pay;
> S = the landlord's share at the time expressed as a percentage."

Definitions   For "secure tenancy", see the Housing Act 1985, ss 79, 185; for "right to acquire on rent to mortgage terms", see s 143 of that Act, as substituted by s 108; for "flat", see s 183 of that Act; for "improvement" and "improvement contribution", see s 187 of that Act; for "landlord", "lease", "tenancy" and "tenant", see s 621 of that Act; for "service charge", see s 621A of that Act; for "final payment", see Sch 6A, para 1 to that Act, as inserted by s 117(2) and as set out in Sch 16.
References   See para 9.15 ff.

---

117 Redemption of landlord's share

(1) After section 151 of the 1985 Act there shall be inserted the following section—

"151A Redemption of landlord's share

Schedule 6A (which makes provision for the redemption of the landlord's share) shall have effect; and a conveyance of the freehold or a grant of a lease executed in pursuance of the right to acquire on rent to mortgage terms shall conform with that Schedule."

(2) After Schedule 6 to the 1985 Act there shall be inserted as Schedule 6A the Schedule set out in Schedule 16 to this Act.

Definitions   For "right to acquire on rent to mortgage terms", see the Housing Act 1985, s 143, as substituted by s 108; for "landlord" and "lease", see s 621 of that Act.
References   See paras 9.15–9.20 ff.

---

118 Mortgage for securing redemption of landlord's share

After section 151A of the 1985 Act there shall be inserted the following section—

"151B Mortgage for securing redemption of landlord's share

(1) The liability that may arise under the covenant required by paragraph 1 of Schedule 6A (covenant for the redemption of the landlord's share in the circumstances there mentioned) shall be secured by a mortgage.

(2) Subject to subsections (3) and (4), the mortgage shall have priority immediately after any legal charge securing an amount advanced to the secure tenant by an approved lending institution for the purpose of enabling him to exercise the right to acquire on rent to mortgage terms.

(3) The following, namely—

(a) any advance which is made otherwise than for the purpose mentioned in subsection (2) and is secured by a legal charge having priority to the mortgage, and

(b) any further advance which is so secured,

shall rank in priority to the mortgage if, and only if, the landlord by written notice served on the institution concerned gives its consent; and the landlord shall so give its consent if the purpose of the advance or further advance is an approved purpose.

(4) The landlord may at any time by written notice served on an approved lending institution postpone the mortgage to any advance or further advance which—

(a) is made to the tenant by that institution, and

(b) is secured by a legal charge not having priority to the mortgage;

and the landlord shall serve such a notice if the purpose of the advance or further advance is an approved purpose.

(5) The approved lending institutions for the purposes of this section are—

the Corporation,

a building society,

a bank,

a trustee savings bank,

an insurance company,

a friendly society,

and any body specified, or of a class or description specified, in an order made under section 156.

(6) The approved purposes for the purposes of this section are—

(a) to enable the tenant to make an interim or final payment,

(b) to enable the tenant to defray, or to defray on his behalf, any of the following—

(i) the cost of any works to the dwelling-house,

(ii) any service charge payable in respect of the dwelling-house for works, whether or not to the dwelling-house, and

(iii) any service charge or other amount payable in respect of the dwelling-house for insurance, whether or not of the dwelling-house, and

(c) to enable the tenant to discharge, or to discharge on his behalf, any of the following—

(i) so much as is still outstanding of any advance or further advance which ranks in priority to the mortgage,

(ii) any arrears of interest on such an advance or further advance, and

(iii) any costs and expenses incurred in enforcing payment of any such interest, or repayment (in whole or in part) of any such advance or further advance.

(7) Where different parts of an advance or further advance are made for different purposes, each of those parts shall be regarded as a separate advance or further advance for the purposes of this section.

(8) The Secretary of State may by order prescribe—

(a) matters for which the deed by which the mortgage is effected must make provision, and

(b) terms which must, or must not, be contained in that deed,

but only in relation to deeds executed after the order comes into force.

(9) The deed by which the mortgage is effected may contain such other provisions as may be—

(a) agreed between the mortgagor and the mortgagee, or

(b) determined by the county court to be reasonably required by the mortgagor or the mortgagee.

(10) An order under this section—

(a) may make different provision with respect to different cases or descriptions of case, including different provision for different areas, and

(b) shall be made by statutory instrument which shall be subject to annulment in pursuance of a resolution of either House of Parliament."

Definitions For "the corporation", see the Housing Act 1985, s 6A; for "secure tenant", see ss 79, 185 of that Act; for "right to acquire on rent to mortgage terms", see s 143 of that Act, as substituted by s 108; for "interim payment", see s 143B of that Act, as so substituted, and Sch 6A, para 6 to that Act, as inserted by s 117(2) and as set out in Sch 16; for "landlord's share", see s 148 of that Act, as substituted by s 113, and Sch 6A, para 7 to that Act, as inserted by s 117(2) and as set out in Sch 16; for "dwelling-house", see ss 183, 184 of that Act, as amended, in the case of s 184, by s 187(1), Sch 21, para 24; for "final payment", see Sch 6A, para 1 to that Act, as inserted by s 117(2) and as set out in Sch 16; for "landlord" and "tenant", see s 621 of that Act; for "service charge", see s 621A of that Act; for "bank", "building society", "friendly society", "insurance company" and "trustee savings bank", see s 622 of that Act; as to "approved lending institution", see sub-s (5) above.
References See para 9.21 ff.

119 Landlord's notices to complete

(1) For subsection (3) of section 152 of the 1985 Act (landlord's first notice to complete) there shall be substituted the following section—

"(3) A notice under this section shall not be served earlier than twelve months after the service of the notice under section 146 (landlord's notice admitting or denying right)."

(2) In subsection (5) of that section, for the words "the amount to be left outstanding or advanced on the security of the dwelling-house" there shall be substituted the words "securing the redemption of the landlord's share".

(3) In subsection (4) of section 153 of the 1985 Act (landlord's second notice to complete), for the words "the right to be granted a shared ownership lease" there shall be substituted the words "the right to acquire on rent to mortgage terms".

Definitions For "right to acquire on rent to mortgage terms", see the Housing Act 1985, s 143, as substituted by s 108; for "landlord's share", see s 148 of that Act, as substituted by s 113, and Sch 6A, para 7 to that Act, as inserted by s 117(2) and as set out in Sch 16.
References See para 9.23 ff.

120 Repayment of discount on early disposal

(1) For subsection (3) of section 155 of the 1985 Act (repayment of discount on early disposal) there shall be substituted the following subsection—

"(3) In the case of a conveyance or grant in pursuance of the right to acquire on rent to mortgage terms, the covenant shall be to pay to the landlord on demand, if within the period of three years commencing with the making of the initial payment there is a relevant disposal which is not an exempted disposal (but if there is more than one such disposal, then only on the first of them), the discount (if any) to which the tenant was entitled on the making of—

    (a) the initial payment,

    (b) any interim payment made before the disposal, or

    (c) the final payment if so made,

reduced, in each case, by one-third for each complete year which has elapsed after the making of the initial payment and before the disposal."

(2) In subsection (3A) of that section, for paragraph (b) there shall be substituted the following paragraph –

    "(b) any reference in subsection (3) (other than paragraph (a) thereof) to the making of the initial payment shall be construed as a reference to the date which precedes that payment by the period referred to in paragraph (a) of this subsection."

(3) For subsection (2) of section 156 of the 1985 Act (liability to repay discount is a charge on the premises) there shall be substituted the following subsections—

    "(2) Subject to subsections (2A) and (2B), the charge has priority as follows—

        (a) if it secures the liability that may arise under the covenant required by section 155(2), immediately after any legal charge securing an amount advanced to the secure tenant by an approved lending institution for the purpose of enabling him to exercise the right to buy;

        (b) if it secures the liability that may arise under the covenant required by section 155(3), immediately after the mortgage—

            (i) which is required by section 151B (mortgage for securing redemption of landlord's share), and

            (ii) which, by virtue of subsection (2) of that section, has priority immediately after any legal charge securing an amount advanced to the secure tenant by an approved lending institution for the purpose of enabling him to exercise the right to acquire on rent to mortgage terms.

    (2A) The following, namely—

        (a) any advance which is made otherwise than for the purpose mentioned in paragraph (a) or (b) of subsection (2) and is secured by a legal charge having priority to the charge taking effect by virtue of this section, and

        (b) any further advance which is so secured,

shall rank in priority to that charge if, and only if, the landlord by written notice served on the institution concerned gives its consent; and the landlord shall so give its consent if the purpose of the advance or further advance is an approved purpose.

    (2B) The landlord may at any time by written notice served on an approved lending institution postpone the charge taking effect by virtue of this section to any advance or further advance which—

        (a) is made to the tenant by that institution, and

        (b) is secured by a legal charge not having priority to that charge;

and the landlord shall serve such a notice if the purpose of the advance or further advance is an approved purpose."

(4) After subsection (4) of that section there shall be inserted the following subsections—

"(4A) The approved purposes for the purposes of this section are—
    (a)   to enable the tenant to make an interim or final payment,
    (b)   to enable the tenant to defray, or to defray on his behalf, any of the following—
        (i)   the cost of any works to the dwelling-house,
        (ii) any service charge payable in respect of the dwelling-house for works, whether or not to the dwelling-house, and
        (iii) any service charge or other amount payable in respect of the dwelling-house for insurance, whether or not of the dwelling-house, and
    (c)   to enable the tenant to discharge, or to discharge on his behalf, any of the following—
        (i)   so much as is still outstanding of any advance or further advance which ranks in priority to the charge taking effect by virtue of this section,
        (ii) any arrears of interest on such an advance or further advance, and
        (iii) any costs and expenses incurred in enforcing payment of any such interest, or repayment (in whole or in part) of any such advance or further advance.

(4B) Where different parts of an advance or further advance are made for different purposes, each of those parts shall be regarded as a separate advance or further advance for the purposes of this section."

Definitions   For "secure tenant", see the Housing Act 1985, ss 79, 185; for "right to buy", see s 118(1) of that Act; for "right to acquire on rent to mortgage terms", see s 143 of that Act, as substituted by s 108; for "initial payment" and "interim payment", see s 143B of that Act, as so substituted, and Sch 6A, para 6 to that Act, as inserted by s 117(2) and as set out in Sch 16; for "relevant disposal", see ss 159, 163(1) of that Act (and see also s 452(3) thereof); for "exempted disposal", see s 160 of that Act; for "dwelling-house", see ss 183, 184 of that Act, as amended, in the case of s 184, by s 187(1), Sch 21, para 24; for "final payment", see Sch 6A, para 1 to that Act, as inserted by s 117(2) and as set out in Sch 16; for "landlord" and "tenant", see s 621 of that Act; for "service charge", see s 621A of that Act; for "approved lending institutions" in s 156 of that Act, see sub-s (4) thereof; and for an "approved lending institution" in relation to the advancing of money for the purpose of enabling a tenant to exercise the right to acquire on rent to mortgage terms, see s 151B(5) of that Act, as inserted by s 118; as to "the approved purposes" for the purposes of s 156 of that Act, see sub-s (4A) thereof, as inserted by sub-s (4) above.
References   See para 9.24 ff.

Other rights of secure tenants

121 Right to have repairs carried out

For section 96 of the 1985 Act there shall be substituted the following section—

"96 Right to have repairs carried out

(1) The Secretary of State may make regulations for entitling secure tenants whose landlords are local housing authorities, subject to and in accordance with the regulations, to have qualifying repairs carried out, at their landlords' expense, to the dwelling-houses of which they are such tenants.

(2) The regulations may make all or any of the following provisions, namely—

    (a) provision that, where a secure tenant makes an application to his landlord for a qualifying repair to be carried out, the landlord shall issue a repair notice—

        (i) specifying the nature of the repair, the listed contractor by whom the repair is to be carried out and the last day of any prescribed period; and

        (ii) containing such other particulars as may be prescribed;

    (b) provision that, if the contractor specified in a repair notice fails to carry out the repair within a prescribed period, the landlord shall issue a further repair notice specifying such other listed contractor as the tenant may require; and

    (c) provision that, if the contractor specified in a repair notice fails to carry out the repair within a prescribed period, the landlord shall pay to the tenant such sum by way of compensation as may be determined by or under the regulations.

(3) The regulations may also make such procedural, incidental, supplementary and transitional provisions as may appear to the Secretary of State necessary or expedient, and may in particular—

    (a) require a landlord to take such steps as may be prescribed to make its secure tenants aware of the provisions of the regulations;

    (b) require a landlord to maintain a list of contractors who are prepared to carry out repairs for which it is responsible under the regulations;

    (c) provide that, where a landlord issues a repair notice, it shall give to the tenant a copy of the notice and the prescribed particulars of at least two other listed contractors who are competent to carry out the repair;

    (d) provide for questions arising under the regulations to be determined by the county court; and

    (e) enable the landlord to set off against any compensation payable under the regulations any sums owed to it by the tenant.

(4) Nothing in subsection (2) or (3) shall be taken as prejudicing the generality of subsection (1).

(5) Regulations under this section—

    (a) may make different provision with respect to different cases or descriptions of case, including different provision for different areas, and

    (b) shall be made by statutory instrument which shall be subject to annulment in pursuance of a resolution of either House of Parliament.

(6) In this section—

    "listed contractor", in relation to a landlord, means any contractor (which may include the landlord) who is specified in the landlord's list of contractors;

    "qualifying repair", in relation to a dwelling-house, means any repair of a prescribed description which the landlord is obliged by a repairing covenant to carry out;

    "repairing covenant", in relation to a dwelling-house, means a covenant, whether express or implied, obliging the landlord to keep in repair the dwelling-house or any part of the dwelling- house;

and for the purposes of this subsection a prescribed description may be framed by reference to any circumstances whatever."

Definitions   For "local housing authority", see the Housing Act 1985, ss 1, 2(2); for "dwelling house", see s 112 of that Act; for "secure tenant", see s 79 of that Act; for "landlord" and "tenant", see s 621 of that Act; for "listed contractor", "qualifying repair" and "repairing covenant", in s 96 of that Act, as substituted above, see sub-s (6) thereof, as so substituted.
References   See paras 10.7, 10.8 ff.

---

122 Right to compensation for improvements

After section 99 of the 1985 Act there shall be inserted the following sections—

"99A Right to compensation for improvements

(1) The powers conferred by this section shall be exercisable as respects cases where a secure tenant has made an improvement and—

    (a) the work on the improvement was begun not earlier than the commencement of section 122 of the Leasehold Reform, Housing and Urban Development Act 1993,

    (b) the landlord, or a predecessor in title of the landlord (being a local authority), has given its written consent to the improvement or is to be treated as having given its consent, and

    (c) at the time when the tenancy comes to an end the landlord is a local authority and the tenancy is a secure tenancy.

(2) The Secretary of State may make regulations for entitling the qualifying person or persons (within the meaning given by section 99B)—

    (a) at the time when the tenancy comes to an end, and

    (b) subject to and in accordance with the regulations,

to be paid compensation by the landlord in respect of the improvement.

(3) The regulations may provide that compensation shall be not payable if—

    (a) the improvement is not of a prescribed description,

    (b) the tenancy comes to an end in prescribed circumstances,

    (c) compensation has been paid under section 100 in respect of the improvement, or

    (d) the amount of any compensation which would otherwise be payable is less than a prescribed amount;

and for the purposes of this subsection a prescribed description may be framed by reference to any circumstances whatever.

(4) The regulations may provide that the amount of any compensation payable shall not exceed a prescribed amount but, subject to that, shall be determined by the landlord, or calculated, in such manner, and taking into account such matters, as may be prescribed.

(5) The regulations may also make such procedural, incidental, supplementary and transitional provisions as may appear to the Secretary of State necessary or expedient, and may in particular—

    (a) provide for the manner in which and the period within which claims for compensation under the regulations are to be made, and for the procedure to be followed in determining such claims,

    (b) prescribe the form of any document required to be used for the purposes of or in connection with such claims,

    (c) provide for questions arising under the regulations to be determined by the district valuer or the county court, and

    (d) enable the landlord to set off against any compensation payable under the regulations any sums owed to it by the qualifying person or persons.

(6) Nothing in subsections (3) to (5) shall be taken as prejudicing the generality of subsection (2).

(7) Regulations under this section—

    (a) may make different provision with respect to different cases or descriptions of case, including different provision for different areas, and

    (b) shall be made by statutory instrument which (except in the case of regulations making only such provision as is mentioned in subsection (5)(b)) shall be subject to annulment in pursuance of a resolution of either House of Parliament.

(8) For the purposes of this section and section 99B, a tenancy shall be treated as coming to an end if—

    (a) it ceases to be a secure tenancy by reason of the landlord condition no longer being satisfied, or

    (b) it is assigned, with the consent of the landlord—

        (i) to another secure tenant who satisfies the condition in subsection (2) of section 92 (assignments by way of exchange), or

        (ii) to an assured tenant who satisfies the conditions in subsection (2A) of that section.

99B Persons qualifying for compensation

(1) A person is a qualifying person for the purposes of section 99A(2) if—

    (a) he is, at the time when the tenancy comes to an end, the tenant or, in the case of a joint tenancy at that time, one of the tenants, and

    (b) he is a person to whom subsection (2) applies.

(2) This subsection applies to—

    (a) the improving tenant;

    (b) a person who became a tenant jointly with the improving tenant;

    (c) a person in whom the tenancy was vested, or to whom the tenancy was disposed of, under section 89 (succession to periodic tenancy) or section 90 (devolution of term certain) on the death of the improving tenant or in the course of the administration of his estate;

    (d) a person to whom the tenancy was assigned by the improving tenant and who would have been qualified to succeed him if he had died immediately before the assignment;

    (e) a person to whom the tenancy was assigned by the improving tenant in pursuance of an order made under section 24 of the Matrimonial Causes Act 1973 (property adjustment orders in connection with matrimonial proceedings);

    (f) a spouse or former spouse of the improving tenant to whom the tenancy has been transferred by an order under paragraph 2 of Schedule 1 to the Matrimonial Homes Act 1983.

(3) Subsection (2)(c) does not apply in any case where the tenancy ceased to be a secure tenancy by virtue of section 89(3) or, as the case may be, section 90(3).

(4) Where, in the case of two or more qualifying persons, one of them ("the missing person") cannot be found—

   (a) a claim under regulations made under section 99A may be made by, and compensation under those regulations may be paid to, the other qualifying person or persons; but

   (b) the missing person shall be entitled to recover his share of any compensation so paid from that person or those persons.

(5) In this section "the improving tenant" means—

   (a) the tenant by whom the improvement mentioned in section 99A(1) was made, or

   (b) in the case of a joint tenancy at the time when the improvement was made, any of the tenants at that time."

Definitions   For "local authority", see the Housing Act 1985, s 4(e); for "improvement", see s 97(2) of that Act; for "dwelling-house", see s 112 of that Act; for "secure tenancy" and "secure tenant", see s 79 of that Act; for "landlord", "tenancy" and "tenant", see s 621 of that Act; for "district valuer", see s 622 of that Act; for "the missing person", see s 99B(4) of that Act, as inserted above; for "the improving tenant", see s 99B(5) of that Act, as so inserted; as to a tenancy coming to an end, see s 99A(8) of that Act, as inserted above.
References   See paras 10.9–10.11 ff.

123 Right to information

After subsection (2) of section 104 of the 1985 Act (provision of information about tenancies) there shall be inserted the following subsection—

   "(3) A local authority which is the landlord under a secure tenancy shall supply the tenant, at least once in every relevant year, with a copy of such information relating to the provisions mentioned in subsection (1)(b) and (c) as was last published by it; and in this subsection "relevant year" means any period of twelve months beginning with an anniversary of the date of such publication."

Definitions   For "local authority", see the Housing Act 1985, s 4(e); for "secure tenancy", see s 79 of that Act; for "landlord" and "tenant", see s 621 of that Act.
References   See para 10.12 ff.

124 Existing rights with respect to disposals by housing action trusts

(1) In subsection (2)(b) of section 79 of the Housing Act 1988 (disposals by housing action trusts), the words "in accordance with section 84 below" shall be omitted.

(2) For subsection (1) of section 84 of that Act (provisions applicable to disposals of dwelling-houses let on secure tenancies) there shall be substituted the following subsection—

   "(1) The provisions of this section apply in any case where—
      (a) a housing action trust proposes to make a disposal of one or more houses let on secure tenancies which would result in a person who,

before the disposal, is a secure tenant of the trust becoming, after the disposal, the tenant of another person, and

    (b) that other person is not a local housing authority or other local authority."

(3) In subsection (7) of that section—

    (a) after the words "a disposal to which this section applies," there shall be inserted the words "or a disposal which would be such a disposal if subsection (1)(b) above were omitted,"; and

    (b) after the words "such further consultation" there shall be inserted the words "or, as the case may be, such consultation.

(4) Where—

    (a) a house held by a housing action trust is specified in a notice served by the trust under section 84(2) of the Housing Act 1988, and

    (b) the building containing the house is specified in an application subsequently made to the trust under section 96 of that Act (application to exercise right conferred by Part IV),

that Part shall apply as if the building containing the house, and any other property reasonably required for occupation with that building, had not been specified in the application.

(5) Where—

    (a) a building containing a house held by a housing action trust is specified in an application made to the trust under section 96 of the Housing Act 1988, and

    (b) the house is specified in a notice subsequently served by the trust under subsection (2) of section 84 of that Act,

that section shall apply as if the house had not been specified in the notice.

(6) In this section "house" has the same meaning as in Part III of the Housing Act 1988.

Definitions For "house", "local housing authority", and "secure tenant", see the Housing Act 1988, s 92(1).
References See para 10.14, 10.15 ff.

---

125 New rights with respect to such disposals

(1) For subsections (2) and (3) of section 84 of the Housing Act 1988 (disposal by housing action trusts of dwelling-houses let on secure tenancies) there shall be substituted the following subsections—

"(2) Before applying to the Secretary of State for consent to the proposed disposal or serving notice under subsection (4) below, the housing action trust shall serve notice in writing on any local housing authority in whose area any houses falling within subsection (1) above are situated—

    (a) informing the authority of the proposed disposal and specifying the houses concerned, and

    (b) requiring the authority within such period, being not less than 28 days, as may be specified in the notice, to serve on the trust a notice under subsection (3) below.

(3) A notice by a local housing authority under this subsection shall inform the housing action trust, with respect to each of the houses specified in the

notice under subsection (2) above which is in the authority's area, of the likely consequences for the tenant if the house were to be acquired by the authority."

(2) In subsection (4) of that section, for paragraphs (d) and (e) there shall be substituted the following paragraphs –

"(d) if the local housing authority in whose area the house of which he is tenant is situated has served notice under subsection (3) above, informing him (in accordance with the information given in the notice) of the likely consequences for him if the house were to be acquired by that authority;

(e) informing him, if he wishes to become a tenant of that authority, of his right to make representations to that effect under paragraph (f) below and of the rights conferred by section 84A below;".

(3) For subsection (5) of that section there shall be substituted the following subsections—

"(5) If, by virtue of any representations made to the housing action trust in accordance with subsection (4)(f) above, section 84A below applies in relation to any house or block of flats, the trust shall—

(a) serve notice of that fact on the Secretary of State, on the local housing authority and on the tenant of the house or each of the tenants of the block, and

(b) so amend its proposals with respect to the disposal as to exclude the house or block;

and in this subsection "house" and "block of flats" have the same meanings as in that section.

(5A) The housing action trust shall consider any other representations so made and, if it considers it appropriate to do so having regard to any of those representations—

(a) may amend (or further amend) its proposals with respect to the disposal, and

(b) in such a case, shall serve a further notice under subsection (4) above (in relation to which this subsection will again apply)."

(4) In subsection (6) of that section, after the words "subsection (5)" there shall be inserted the words "or subsection (5A)".

(5) After that section there shall be inserted the following section—

"84A Transfer by order of certain dwelling-houses let on secure tenancies

(1) This section applies in relation to any house or block of flats specified in a notice under subsection (2) of section 84 above if—

(a) in the case of a house, the tenant makes representations in accordance with paragraph (f) of subsection (4) of that section to the effect that he wishes to become a tenant of the local housing authority in whose area the house is situated; or

(b) in the case of a block of flats, the majority of the tenants who make representations in accordance with that paragraph make representations to the effect that they wish to become tenants of the local housing authority in whose area the block is situated.

(2) The Secretary of State shall by order provide for the transfer of the house or block of flats from the housing action trust to the local housing authority.

(3) The Secretary of State may also by order transfer from the housing action trust to the local housing authority so much as appears to the Secretary of State to be appropriate of any property belonging to or usually enjoyed with the house or, as the case may be, the block or any flat contained in it; and for this purpose "property" includes chattels of any description and rights and liabilities, whether arising by contract or otherwise.

(4) A transfer of any house, block of flats or other property under this section shall be on such terms, including financial terms, as the Secretary of State thinks fit; and an order under this section may provide that, notwithstanding anything in section 141 of the Law of Property Act 1925 (rent and benefit of lessee's covenants to run with the reversion), any rent or other sum which—
>   (a) arises under the tenant's tenancy or any of the tenants' tenancies, and
>   (b) falls due before the date of the transfer,

shall continue to be recoverable by the housing action trust to the exclusion of the authority.

(5) Without prejudice to the generality of subsection (4) above, the financial terms referred to in that subsection may include provision for payments to a local housing authority (as well as or instead of payments by a local housing authority); and the transfer from a housing action trust of any house, block of flats or other property by virtue of this section shall not be taken to give rise to any right to compensation.

(6) In this section—
>   "block of flats" means a building containing two or more flats;
>   "common parts", in relation to a building containing two or more flats, means any parts of the building which the tenants of the flats are entitled under the terms of their tenancies to use in common with each other;
>   "flat" and "house" have the meanings given by section 183 of the Housing Act 1985;

and any reference to a block of flats specified in a notice under section 84(2) above is a reference to a block in the case of which each flat which is let on a secure tenancy is so specified.

(7) For the purposes of subsection (6) above, a building which contains—
>   (a) one or more flats which are let, or available for letting, on secure tenancies by the housing action trust concerned, and
>   (b) one or more flats which are not so let or so available,

shall be treated as if it were two separate buildings, the one containing the flat or flats mentioned in paragraph (a) above and the other containing the flat or flats mentioned in paragraph (b) above and any common parts."

Definitions For "house" and "local housing authority", see the Housing Act 1988, s 92(1); for "block of flats", "flat" and "house" in s 84A of the 1988 Act, as inserted by sub-s (5), see sub-ss (6), (7) thereof, as so inserted.
References See paras 10.16, 10.17 ff.

Housing welfare services

126 Provision of housing welfare services

Part II of the 1985 Act (provision of housing accommodation) shall have effect, and be deemed at all times on and after 1st April 1990 to have had effect, as if after section 11 there were inserted the following section—

"11A Provision of welfare services

(1) A local housing authority may provide in connection with the provision of housing accommodation by them (whether or not under this Part) such welfare services, that is to say, services for promoting the welfare of the persons for whom the accommodation is so provided, as accord with the needs of those persons.

(2) The authority may make reasonable charges for welfare services provided by virtue of this section.

(3) In this section "welfare services" does not include the repair, maintenance, supervision or management of houses or other property.

(4) The powers conferred by this section shall not be regarded as restricting those conferred by section 137 of the Local Government Act 1972 (powers to incur expenditure for purposes not authorised by any other enactment) and accordingly the reference to any other enactment in subsection (1)(a) of that section shall not include a reference to this section."

Definitions For "local housing authority", see the Housing Act 1985, ss 1, 2(2); for "house" and "housing accommodation", see s 56 of that Act.
References See paras 10.18, 10.19 ff.

127 Accounting for housing welfare services

Schedule 4 to the Local Government and Housing Act 1989 (the keeping of the Housing Revenue Account) shall have effect, and be deemed always to have had effect, as if—

(a) at the end of paragraph (b) of item 2 of Part I (credits to the account) there were inserted the words "or income in respect of services provided under section 11A of that Act (power to provide welfare services)"; and

(b) after paragraph 3 of Part III (special cases) there were inserted the following paragraph—

"Provision of welfare services

3A.—(1) This paragraph applies where in any year a local housing authority provide welfare services (within the meaning of section 11A of the Housing Act 1985) for persons housed by them in houses or other property within their Housing Revenue Account.

(2) The authority may carry to the credit of the account—

(a) an amount equal to the whole or any part of the income of the authority for the year from charges in respect of the provision of those services;

(b) any sum from some other revenue account of theirs which represents the whole or any part of that income.

(3) The authority may carry to the debit of the account—

    (a) an amount equal to the whole or any part of the expenditure of the authority for the year in respect of the provision of those services;

    (b) any sum from some other revenue account of theirs which represents the whole or any part of that expenditure."

Definitions For "Housing Revenue Account" and "house", see the Local Government and Housing Act 1989, ss 74, 88(1)(b); as to "revenue account", see ss 41(2), 88(1)(c) of that Act; as to "the account", see the first paragraph of Pt I of Sch 4 to that Act; by virtue of s 88(1)(a) of the 1989 Act, for "local housing authority", see the Housing Act 1985, ss 1, 2(2), and for "year", see s 433 of that Act.
References See para 10.20 ff.

128 Power to repeal provisions made by sections 126 and 127

(1) The Secretary of State may at any time by order made by statutory instrument provide that, on such day or in relation to such periods as may be appointed by the order, the provisions made by sections 126 and 127—

    (a) shall cease to have effect; or

    (b) shall cease to apply for such purposes as may be specified in the order.

(2) An order under this section—

    (a) may appoint different days or periods for different provisions or purposes or for different authorities or descriptions of authority, and

    (b) may contain such incidental, supplementary or transitional provisions as appear to the Secretary of State to be necessary or expedient.

References See para 10.20 ff.

Delegation of housing management

129 Management agreements

(1) At the end of subsection (3) of section 27 of the 1985 Act (management agreements), there shall be inserted the words "and shall contain such provisions as may be prescribed by regulations made by the Secretary of State".

(2) For subsection (5) of that section there shall be substituted the following subsection—

    "(5) The Secretary of State's approval may be given—

        (a) either generally to all local housing authorities or to a particular authority or description of authority, and

        (b) either in relation to a particular case or in relation to a particular description of case,

and may be given unconditionally or subject to conditions."

(3) For subsection (6) of that section there shall be substituted the following subsections—

    "(6) References in this section to the management functions of a local housing authority in relation to houses or land—

        (a) do not include such functions as may be prescribed by regulations made by the Secretary of State, but

        (b) subject to that, include functions conferred by any statutory provision and the powers and duties of the authority as holder of an estate or interest in the houses or land in question.

(7) Regulations under this section—
- (a) may make different provision with respect to different cases or descriptions of case, including different provision for different areas,
- (b) may contain such incidental, supplementary or transitional provisions as appear to the Secretary of State to be necessary or expedient, and
- (c) shall be made by statutory instrument which shall be subject to annulment in pursuance of a resolution of either House of Parliament."

Definitions   For "local housing authority", see the Housing Act 1985, ss 1, 2(2); for "house", see s 56 of that Act; as to "management functions" in s 27 of the 1985 Act, as amended by this section, see sub-s (6) thereof, as substituted by sub-s (3) above.
References   See para 10.21 ff.

---

130 Consultation with respect to management agreements

For section 27A of the 1985 Act there shall be substituted the following section—

"27A Consultation with respect to management agreements

(1) A local housing authority who propose to enter into a management agreement shall make such arrangements as they consider appropriate to enable the tenants of the houses to which the proposal relates—
- (a) to be informed of the following details of the proposal, namely—
  - (i) the terms of the agreement (including in particular the standards of service to be required under the agreement),
  - (ii) the identity of the person who is to be manager under the agreement, and
  - (iii) such other details (if any) as may be prescribed by regulations made by the Secretary of State, and
- (b) to make known to the authority within a specified period their views as to the proposal;

and the authority shall, before making any decision with respect to the proposal, consider any representations made to them in accordance with those arrangements.

(2) A local housing authority who have made a management agreement shall—
- (a) during the continuance of the agreement, maintain such arrangements as they consider appropriate to enable the tenants of the houses to which the agreement relates to make known to the authority their views as to the standards of service for the time being achieved by the manager, and
- (b) before making any decision with respect to the enforcement of the standards of service required by the agreement, consider any representations made to them in accordance with those arrangements.

(3) Arrangements made or maintained under subsection (1) or (2) above shall—
- (a) include provision for securing that the authority's responses to any representations made to them in accordance with the arrangements are made known to the tenants concerned, and

(b) comply with such requirements as may be prescribed by regulations made by the Secretary of State.

(4) Regulations under this section—

(a) may make different provision with respect to different cases or descriptions of case, including different provision for different areas,

(b) may contain such incidental, supplementary or transitional provisions as appear to the Secretary of State to be necessary or expedient, and

(c) shall be made by statutory instrument which shall be subject to annulment in pursuance of a resolution of either House of Parliament.

(5) In the case of secure tenants the provisions of this section apply in place of the provisions of section 105 (consultation on matters of housing management) in relation to the making of a management agreement."

Definitions For "local housing authority", see the Housing Act 1985, ss 1, 2(2); for "management agreement" and "manager", see s 27(2) of that Act; for "house", see s 56 of that Act; for "tenant", see s 621 of that Act.
References See para 10.22 ff.

131 Management agreements and compulsory competitive tendering

After section 27A of the 1985 Act there shall be inserted the following section—

"27AA Management agreements and compulsory competitive tendering

(1) This section shall apply if the Secretary of State makes an order under section 2(3) of the Local Government Act 1988 ("the 1988 Act") providing for the exercise of any management functions to be a defined activity for the purposes of Part I of that Act (compulsory competitive tendering).

(2) The Secretary of State may by regulations provide that in any case where—

(a) a local housing authority propose to make an invitation to carry out any functional work in accordance with the rules set out in subsection (4) of section 7 of the 1988 Act (functional work: conditions), and

(b) the proposal is such that any decision by the authority that the work should be carried out by the person or one of the persons proposed to be invited would necessarily involve their entering into a management agreement with that person,

the provisions of section 27A shall have effect with such modifications as appear to the Secretary of State to be necessary or expedient.

(3) Nothing in section 6 of the 1988 Act (functional work: restrictions) shall apply in relation to any functional work which, in pursuance of a management agreement, is carried out by the manager as agent of the local housing authority.

(4) In this section "functional work" has the same meaning as in Part I of the 1988 Act.

(5) Regulations under this section shall be made by statutory instrument which shall be subject to annulment in pursuance of a resolution of either House of Parliament."

Definitions   For "local housing authority", see the Housing Act 1985, ss 1, 2(2); for "management agreement", see s 27(2) of that Act.
References   See para 10.23 ff.

---

132 Management agreements with tenant management organisations

(1) After section 27AA of the 1985 Act there shall be inserted the following section—

"27AB Management agreements with tenant management organisations

(1) The Secretary of State may make regulations for imposing requirements on a local housing authority in any case where a tenant management organisation serves written notice on the authority proposing that the authority should enter into a management agreement with that organisation.

(2) The regulations may make provision requiring the authority—

    (a) to provide or finance the provision of such office accommodation and facilities, and such training, as the organisation reasonably requires for the purpose of pursuing the proposal;

    (b) to arrange for such feasibility studies with respect to the proposal as may be determined by or under the regulations to be conducted by such persons as may be so determined;

    (c) to arrange for such ballots or polls with respect to the proposal as may be determined by or under the regulations to be conducted of such persons as may be so determined; and

    (d) in such circumstances as may be prescribed by the regulations (which shall include the organisation becoming registered if it has not already done so), to enter into a management agreement with the organisation.

(3) The regulations may make provision with respect to any management agreement which is to be entered into in pursuance of the regulations—

    (a) for determining the houses and land to which the agreement should relate, and the amounts which should be paid under the agreement to the organisation;

    (b) requiring the agreement to be in such form as may be approved by the Secretary of State and to contain such provisions as may be prescribed by the regulations;

    (c) requiring the agreement to take effect immediately after the expiry or other determination of any previous agreement; and

    (d) where any previous agreement contains provisions for its determination by the authority, requiring the authority to determine it as soon as may be after the agreement is entered into.

(4) The regulations may also make such procedural, incidental, supplementary and transitional provisions as may appear to the Secretary of State necessary or expedient, and may in particular make provision—

    (a) for particular questions arising under the regulations to be determined by the authority;

    (b) for other questions so arising to be determined by an arbitrator agreed to by the parties or, in default of agreement, appointed by the Secretary of State;

    (c) requiring any person exercising functions under the regulations to act in accordance with any guidance given by the Secretary of State; and

    (d) for enabling the authority, if invited to do so by the organisation concerned, to nominate one or more persons to be directors or other officers of any tenant management organisation with whom the authority have entered into, or propose to enter into, a management agreement.

(5) Nothing in subsections (2) to (4) above shall be taken as prejudicing the generality of subsection (1).

(6) Regulations under this section—

    (a) may make different provision with respect to different cases or descriptions of case, including different provision for different areas, and

    (b) shall be made by statutory instrument which shall be subject to annulment in pursuance of a resolution of either House of Parliament.

(7) Except as otherwise provided by regulations under this section—

    (a) a local housing authority shall not enter into a management agreement with a tenant management organisation otherwise than in pursuance of the regulations; and

    (b) the provisions of the regulations shall apply in relation to the entering into of such an agreement with such an organisation in place of—

        (i) the provisions of section 27A (consultation with respect to management agreements),

        (ii) in the case of secure tenants, the provisions of section 105 (consultation on matters of housing management), and

        (iii) in the case of an organisation which is associated with the authority, the provisions of section 33 of the Local Government Act 1988 (restrictions on contracts with local authority companies).

(8) In this section—

    "arbitrator" means a member of a panel approved for the purposes of the regulations by the Secretary of State;

    "associated" shall be construed in accordance with section 33 of the Local Government Act 1988;

    "previous agreement", in relation to an agreement entered into in pursuance of the regulations, means a management agreement previously entered into in relation to the same houses and land;

    "registered" means registered under the Industrial and Provident Societies Act 1965 or the Companies Act 1985;

    "tenant management organisation" means a body which satisfies such conditions as may be determined by or under the regulations."

(2) Section 27C of the 1985 Act (which is superseded by this section) shall cease to have effect.

Definitions For "local housing authority", see the Housing Act 1985, ss 1, 2(2); for "management agreement", see s 27(2) of that Act; for "house", see s 56 of that Act; for "tenant", see s 621 of that Act; for "arbitrator", "associated", "previous agreement", "registered" and "tenant management organisation", see s 27AB(8) of the 1985 Act, as inserted by sub-s (1) above.
References See paras 10.24, 10.25 ff.

Priority of charges securing repayment of discount

133 Voluntary disposals by local authorities

(1) For subsection (2) of section 36 of the 1985 Act (liability to repay discount is a charge on the premises) there shall be substituted the following subsections—

"(2) Subject to subsections (2A) and (2B), the charge has priority immediately after any legal charge securing an amount—
    (a) left outstanding by the purchaser, or
    (b) advanced to him by an approved lending institution for the purpose of enabling him to acquire the interest disposed of on the first disposal.

(2A) The following, namely—
    (a) any advance which is made otherwise than for the purpose mentioned in subsection (2)(b) and is secured by a legal charge having priority to the charge taking effect by virtue of this section, and
    (b) any further advance which is so secured,
shall rank in priority to that charge if, and only if, the local authority by written notice served on the institution concerned gives their consent; and the local authority shall so give their consent if the purpose of the advance or further advance is an approved purpose.

(2B) The local authority may at any time by written notice served on an approved lending institution postpone the charge taking effect by virtue of this section to any advance or further advance which—
    (a) is made to the purchaser by that institution, and
    (b) is secured by a legal charge not having priority to that charge;
and the local authority shall serve such a notice if the purpose of the advance or further advance is an approved purpose."

(2) After subsection (4) of that section there shall be inserted the following subsections—

"(5) The approved purposes for the purposes of this section are—
    (a) to enable the purchaser to defray, or to defray on his behalf, any of the following—
        (i) the cost of any works to the house,
        (ii) any service charge payable in respect of the house for works, whether or not to the house, and
        (iii) any service charge or other amount payable in respect of the house for insurance, whether or not of the house, and
    (b) to enable the purchaser to discharge, or to discharge on his behalf, any of the following—

(i) so much as is still outstanding of any advance or further advance which ranks in priority to the charge taking effect by virtue of this section,

(ii) any arrears of interest on such an advance or further advance, and

(iii) any costs and expenses incurred in enforcing payment of any such interest, or repayment (in whole or in part) of any such advance or further advance.

(6) Where different parts of an advance or further advance are made for different purposes, each of those parts shall be regarded as a separate advance or further advance for the purposes of this section."

Definitions   For "local authority", see the Housing Act 1985, s 4(e); for "house", see s 56 of that Act; for "service charge", see s 621A of that Act.
References   See para 10.26 ff.

134 Voluntary disposals by housing associations

(1) For sub-paragraph (2) of paragraph 2 of Schedule 2 to the Housing Associations Act 1985 (liability to repay discount is a charge on the premises) there shall be substituted the following sub-paragraphs—

"(2) Subject to sub-paragraphs (2A) and (2B), the charge has priority immediately after any legal charge securing an amount—

(a) left outstanding by the purchaser, or

(b) advanced to him by an approved lending institution for the purpose of enabling him to acquire the interest disposed of on the first disposal.

(2A) The following, namely—

(a) any advance which is made otherwise than for the purpose mentioned in sub-paragraph (2)(b) and is secured by a legal charge having priority to the charge taking effect by virtue of this paragraph, and

(b) any further advance which is so secured,

shall rank in priority to that charge if, and only if, the housing association by written notice served on the institution concerned gives its consent; and the housing association shall so give its consent if the purpose of the advance or further advance is an approved purpose.

(2B) The housing association may at any time by written notice served on an approved lending institution postpone the charge taking effect by virtue of this paragraph to any advance or further advance which—

(a) is made to the purchaser by that institution, and

(b) is secured by a legal charge not having priority to that charge;

and the housing association shall serve such a notice if the purpose of the advance or further advance is an approved purpose."

(2) After sub-paragraph (4) of that paragraph there shall be inserted the following sub-paragraphs—

"(5) The approved purposes for the purposes of this paragraph are—

(a) to enable the purchaser to defray, or to defray on his behalf, any of the following—

   (i) the cost of any works to the house,

   (ii) any service charge payable in respect of the house for works, whether or not to the house, and

   (iii) any service charge or other amount payable in respect of the house for insurance, whether or not of the house, and

  (b) to enable the purchaser to discharge, or to discharge on his behalf, any of the following—

   (i) so much as is still outstanding of any advance or further advance which ranks in priority to the charge taking effect by virtue of this paragraph,

   (ii) any arrears of interest on such an advance or further advance, and

   (iii) any costs and expenses incurred in enforcing payment of any such interest, or repayment (in whole or in part) of any such advance or further advance;

and in this sub-paragraph "service charge" has the meaning given by section 621A of the Housing Act 1985.

(6) Where different parts of an advance or further advance are made for different purposes, each of those parts shall be regarded as a separate advance or further advance for the purposes of this paragraph."

Definitions For "housing association", see the Housing Associations Act 1985, s 1(1); for "house", see s 106 of that Act; as to "approved purposes" and for "service charge" in Sch 2, para 2 to the 1985 Act, see sub-para (5) thereof, as inserted by sub-s (2) above.
References See para 10.27 ff.

Disposals of dwelling-houses by local authorities

135 Programmes for disposals

(1) For the purposes of this section a disposal of one or more dwelling-houses by a local authority to any person (in this section referred to as a "disposal") is a qualifying disposal if—

 (a) it requires the consent of the Secretary of State under section 32 of the 1985 Act (power to dispose of land held for the purposes of Part II), or section 43 of that Act (consent required for certain disposals not within section 32); and

 (b) the aggregate of the following, namely—

   (i) the number of dwelling-houses included in the disposal; and

   (ii) the number of dwelling-houses which, within the relevant period, have been previously disposed of by the authority to that person, or that person and any associates of his taken together,

  exceeds 499 or, if the Secretary of State by order so provides, such other number as may be specified in the order.

(2) In subsection (1) "the relevant period" means—

 (a) the period of five years ending with the date of the disposal or, if that period begins before the commencement of this section, so much of it as falls after that commencement; or

 (b) if the Secretary of State by order so provides, such other period ending with that date and beginning after that commencement as may be specified in the order.

(3) A local authority shall not make a qualifying disposal in any financial year unless the Secretary of State has included the disposal in a disposals programme prepared by him for that year.

(4) A disposal may be included in a disposals programme for a financial year either—

(a) by specifically including the disposal in the programme; or
(b) by including in the programme a description of disposal which includes the disposal.

(5) An application by a local authority for the inclusion of a disposal in a disposals programme for a financial year—

(a) shall be made in such manner and contain such information; and
(b) shall be made before such date,

as the Secretary of State may from time to time direct.

(6) In preparing a disposals programme for any financial year, the Secretary of State shall secure that the aggregate amount of his estimate of the exchequer costs of each of the disposals included in the programme does not exceed such amount as he may, with the approval of the Treasury, determine.

(7) In deciding whether to include a disposal in a disposals programme for a financial year or, having regard to subsection (6), which disposals to include in such a programme, the Secretary of State may, in relation to the disposal or (as the case may be) each disposal, have regard in particular to—

(a) his estimate of the exchequer costs of the disposal;
(b) whether or not a majority of the secure tenants who would be affected by the disposal are (in his opinion) likely to oppose it; and
(c) the matters mentioned in section 34(4A) or 43(4A) (as the case may be) of the 1985 Act;

and in this subsection "secure tenant" has the same meaning as in Part IV of that Act.

(8) In subsections (6) and (7) "the exchequer costs", in relation to a disposal, means any increase which is or may be attributable to the disposal in the aggregate of any subsidies payable under—

(a) section 135(1) of the Social Security Administration Act 1992 (housing benefit finance); or
(b) section 79 of the 1989 Act (Housing Revenue Account subsidy);

and the Secretary of State's estimate of any such increase shall be based on such assumptions (including assumptions as to the period during which such subsidies may be payable) as he may, with the approval of the Treasury, from time to time determine, regardless of whether those assumptions are or are likely to be borne out by events.

(9) The inclusion of a disposal in a disposals programme for a financial year shall not prejudice the operation of section 32 or 43 of the 1985 Act in relation to the disposal.

(10) The Secretary of State may prepare different disposals programmes under this section for different descriptions of authority; and any disposals programme may be varied or revoked by a subsequent programme.

(11) An order under this section—

(a) shall be made by statutory instrument which shall be subject to annulment in pursuance of a resolution of either House of Parliament;

    (b)   may make different provision for different cases or descriptions of case, or for different authorities or descriptions of authority; and

    (c)   may contain such transitional and supplementary provisions as the Secretary of State considers necessary or expedient.

(12) Any direction or determination under this section—

    (a)   may make different provision for different cases or descriptions of case, or for different authorities or descriptions of authority; and

    (b)   may be varied or revoked by a subsequent direction or determination.

(13) In this section—

"the 1989 Act" means the Local Government and Housing Act 1989;

"dwelling-house" has the same meaning as in Part V of the 1985 Act except that it does not include a hostel (as defined in section 622 of that Act) or any part of a hostel;

"local authority" has the meaning given by section 4 of that Act;

"long lease" means a lease for a term of years certain exceeding 21 years other than a lease which is terminable before the end of that term by notice given by or to the landlord;

"subsidiary" has the same meaning as in section 28(8) of the Housing Associations Act 1985.

(14) For the purposes of this section—

    (a)   a disposal of any dwelling-house shall be disregarded if at the time of the disposal the local authority's interest in the dwelling-house is or was subject to a long lease;

    (b)   two persons are associates of each other if—

        (i)   one of them is a subsidiary of the other;

        (ii) they are both subsidiaries of some other person; or

        (iii) there exists between them such relationship or other connection as may be specified in a determination made by the Secretary of State; and

    (c)   a description of authority may be framed by reference to any circumstances whatever.

References   See paras 10.28, 10.29 ff.

136 Levy on disposals

(1) For the purposes of this section a disposal of one or more dwelling-houses by a local authority to any person is a qualifying disposal if—

    (a)   it requires the consent of the Secretary of State under section 32 of the 1985 Act (power to dispose of land held for the purposes of Part II), or section 43 of that Act (consent required for certain disposals not within section 32); and

    (b)   the aggregate of the following, namely—

        (i)   the number of dwelling-houses included in the disposal; and

        (ii) the number of dwelling-houses which, within any relevant period, have been previously or are subsequently disposed of by the authority to that person, or that person and any associates of his taken together,

exceeds 499 or, if the Secretary of State by order so provides, such other number as may be specified in the order.

(2) In subsection (1) "relevant period" means—

(a) any period of five years beginning after the commencement of this section and including the date of the disposal; or

(b) if the Secretary of State by order so provides, any such other period beginning after that commencement and including that date as may be specified in the order.

(3) A local authority which after the commencement of this section makes a disposal which is or includes, or which subsequently becomes or includes, a qualifying disposal shall be liable to pay to the Secretary of State a levy of an amount calculated in accordance with the formula—

$$L = (CR - D) \times P$$

where—

L   = the amount of the levy;

CR = the aggregate of—

(i) any sums received by the authority in respect of the disposal which are, by virtue of section 58 of the 1989 Act (capital receipts), capital receipts for the purposes of Part IV of that Act and do not fall within a description determined by the Secretary of State; and

(ii) where paragraph (a) or (c) of subsection (1) of section 61 of that Act (capital receipts not wholly in money paid to the authority) applies in relation to the disposal, any notional capital receipts determined in accordance with subsections (2) and (3) of that section;

D   = such amount as may be calculated in accordance with such formula as the Secretary of State may determine;

P   = 20 per cent or, if the Secretary of State by order so provides, such other percentage as may be specified in the order.

(4) A formula determined for the purposes of item D in subsection (3) may include any variable which is included in a determination made for the purposes of section 80 of the 1989 Act (calculation of Housing Revenue Account subsidy).

(5) The administrative arrangements for the payment of any levy under this section shall be such as may be specified in a determination made by the Secretary of State, and such a determination may in particular make provision as to—

(a) the information to be supplied by authorities;

(b) the form and manner in which, and the time within which, the information is to be supplied;

(c) the payment of the levy in stages in such circumstances as may be provided in the determination;

(d) the date on which payment of the levy (or any stage payment of the levy) is to be made;

(e) the adjustment of any levy which has been paid in such circumstances as may be provided in the determination;

(f) the payment of interest in such circumstances as may be provided in the determination; and

(g) the rate or rates (whether fixed or variable, and whether or not calculated by reference to some other rate) at which such interest is to be payable;

and any such administrative arrangements shall be binding on local authorities.

(6) Any amounts by way of levy or interest which are not paid to the Secretary of State as required by the arrangements mentioned in subsection (5) shall be recoverable in a court of competent jurisdiction.

(7) For the purposes of Part IV of the 1989 Act (revenue accounts and capital finance of local authorities) any payment of levy by a local authority under this section shall be treated as expenditure for capital purposes.

(8) Notwithstanding the provisions of section 64 of the 1989 Act (use of amounts set aside to meet credit liabilities) but subject to subsection (9), amounts for the time being set aside by a local authority (whether voluntarily or pursuant to a requirement under Part IV of that Act) as provision to meet credit liabilities may be applied to meet any liability of the authority in respect of any levy payable under this section, other than a liability in respect of interest.

(9) The Secretary of State may by regulations provide that the amounts which may by virtue of subsection (8) be applied as mentioned in that subsection shall not exceed so much of the levy concerned as may be determined in accordance with the regulations.

(10) Any sums received by the Secretary of State under this section shall be paid into the Consolidated Fund; and any sums paid by the Secretary of State by way of adjustment of levies paid under this section shall be paid out of money provided by Parliament.

(11) Before making an order or determination under this section, the Secretary of State shall consult such representatives of local government as appear to him to be appropriate.

(12) An order or regulations under this section—
   (a) shall be made by statutory instrument which shall be subject to annulment in pursuance of a resolution of either House of Parliament;
   (b) may make different provision for different cases or descriptions of case, or for different authorities or descriptions of authority; and
   (c) may contain such transitional and supplementary provisions as the Secretary of State considers necessary or expedient.

(13) Any determination under this section—
   (a) may make different provision for different cases or descriptions of case, or for different authorities or descriptions of authority; and
   (b) may be varied or revoked by a subsequent determination.

(14) Subsections (13) and (14) of section 135 shall apply for the purposes of this section as they apply for the purposes of that section.

Definitions By virtue of sub-s (14), for "dwelling-house" and "local authority", see s 135(13); and as to "authority" and "disposal", see s 135(14).
References See para 10.30 ff.

137 Disposals: transitional provisions

(1) The period beginning with the commencement of section 135 and ending with 31st March 1994 (in this section referred to as "the first financial year") shall be

treated as a financial year for the purposes of that section; but in relation to that period subsection (5) of that section shall not apply.

(2) If before the commencement of section 135 any statement was made by or on behalf of the Secretary of State—

    (a)   that, if that section were then in force, he would prepare under that section such disposals programmes for the first financial year as are set out in the statement, and

    (b)   that, when that section comes into force, he is to be regarded as having prepared under that section the programmes so set out,

those programmes shall have effect as if they had been validly made under that section at the time of the statement.

(3) Any determination or estimate made, or any approval given—

    (a)   before the commencement of section 135,

    (b)   before the making of such a statement as is mentioned in subsection (2), and

    (c)   in connection with the disposals programmes proposed to be set out in the statement,

shall be as effective, in relation to those programmes, as if that section had been in force at the time the determination or estimate was made, or the approval was given.

(4) If before the commencement of section 136 any statement was made by or on behalf of the Secretary of State—

    (a)   that, if that section were then in force, he would make under that section such determinations as are set out in the statement, and

    (b)   that, when that section comes into force, he is to be regarded as having made under that section the determinations set out in the statement,

those determinations shall have effect as if they had been validly made under that section at the time of the statement.

(5) Any consultation undertaken—

    (a)   before the commencement of section 136,

    (b)   before the making of such a statement as is mentioned in subsection (4), and

    (c)   in connection with determinations proposed to be set out in the statement,

shall be as effective, in relation to those determinations, as if that section had been in force at the time the consultation was undertaken.

References   See para 10.31 ff.

Expenses on defective housing

138 Contributions in respect of certain post-March 1989 expenses

(1) In section 157 of the Local Government and Housing Act 1989 (commutation of and interest on periodic payments of grants etc), in subsection (8) (which changes certain contributions under section 569 of the 1985 Act from annual payments to lump sums), for paragraph (b) there shall be substituted the following paragraph –

"(b)   so much of any contributions in respect of an expense incurred on or after 1st April 1989 and before 1st April 1990 as have not been made before 1st April 1990".

(2) This section shall be deemed to have come into force on 1st January 1993.

References   See para 10.32 ff.

139 Contributions in respect of certain pre–April 1989 expenses

(1) Where—
   (a)   before 1st April 1989 a local housing authority incurred any such expense as is referred to in subsection (1) of section 569 of the 1985 Act (assistance by way of reinstatement grant, repurchase or payments for owners of defective housing); and
   (b)   before 1st January 1993, the Secretary of State has not made in respect of that expense any contribution of such a description as is referred to in subsection (2) of that section, as amended by section 157(8) of the Local Government and Housing Act 1989 (single commuted contributions),
any contributions in respect of that expense which are made under section 569 on or after 1st January 1993 shall be annual payments calculated and payable in accordance with the following provisions of this section.

(2) The amount of the annual payment in respect of any relevant financial year shall be a sum equal to the relevant percentage of the annual loan charges referable to the amount of the expense incurred.

(3) Notwithstanding that annual loan charges are calculated by reference to a 20 year period, annual payments made by virtue of this section shall be made only in respect of relevant financial years ending at or before the end of the period of 20 years beginning with the financial year in which, as the case may be—
   (a)   the work in respect of which the reinstatement grant was payable was completed;
   (b)   the acquisition of the interest concerned was completed; or
   (c)   the payment referred to in subsection (1)(c) of section 569 was made.

(4) Subsections (3) and (4) of section 569 (which determine the relevant percentage and the amount of the expense incurred) apply for the purposes of the preceding provisions of this section as they apply for the purposes of that section.

(5) Nothing in this section affects the operation of subsection (6) of section 569 (terms etc for payment of contributions).

(6) In this section—
   "the annual loan charges referable to the amount of the expense incurred" means the annual sum which, in the opinion of the Secretary of State, would fall to be provided by a local housing authority for the payment of interest on, and the repayment of, a loan of that amount repayable over a period of 20 years;
   "relevant financial year" means the financial year beginning on 1st April 1991 and each successive financial year.

(7) This section shall be deemed to have come into force on 1st January 1993.

References   See para 10.33 ff.

Housing Revenue Account subsidy

140 Calculation of Housing Revenue Account subsidy

In subsection (1) of section 80 of the Local Government and Housing Act 1989 (determination of formulae for calculating Housing Revenue Account subsidy), the words "and for any year the first such determination shall be made before the 25th December immediately preceding that year" shall cease to have effect.

References   See para 10.34 ff.

CHAPTER II
SCOTLAND

Rent to loan scheme

141 Eligibility for rent to loan scheme

After section 62 of the Housing (Scotland) Act 1987 (in this Chapter referred to as "the 1987 Act") there shall be inserted the following section—

"62A Eligibility for rent to loan scheme

(1) Subject to subsection (2), a tenant who has the right under section 61 to purchase a house may exercise the right by way of the rent to loan scheme.

(2) Subsection (1) does not apply—
  (a) to the tenant of a house which is designated as defective under Part XIV; or
  (b) to a tenant—
      (i) in respect of whom a determination has been made that he is entitled to housing benefit in respect of any part of the relevant period; or
      (ii) by or on behalf of whom a claim for housing benefit has been made (or is treated as having been made) and has not been determined or withdrawn.

(3) In subsection (2), "the relevant period" means the period—
  (a) beginning twelve months before the date of the application to purchase the house; and
  (b) ending on the day when the contract of sale of the house is constituted under section 66(2)."

Definitions   For "rent to loan scheme" and "tenant", see the Housing (Scotland) Act 1987, s 82, as amended by s 143(5); for "house", see s 338(1) of that Act; for "the relevant period", see s 62A(3) of that Act, as inserted above.
References   See paras 11.4, 11.5 ff.

142 The rent to loan scheme

After section 73 of the 1987 Act there shall be inserted the following sections—

"Rent to loan scheme

73A The rent to loan scheme

(1) Under the rent to loan scheme, the price fixed for a house under section 62 shall be payable in two elements, viz—

    (a) the initial capital payment; and

    (b) the deferred financial commitment.

(2) In the application of subsection (3) of section 62 to the price of a house being purchased by way of the rent to loan scheme, each of the percentage figures specified in that subsection shall be reduced by 15 or such other number as may, with the consent of the Treasury, be prescribed.

(3) The conditions which are, under section 64, to be contained in an offer to sell under section 63(2) shall, in the case of a house which is to be purchased by way of the rent to loan scheme, include a condition providing that the tenant will be entitled to ownership of the house in exchange for the initial capital payment.

(4) The deferred financial commitment shall be secured by a standard security over the house.

73B The initial capital payment

(1) The initial capital payment in respect of a house is a sum determined by the tenant, being of an amount not less than the maximum amount of loan which could be repaid at the statutory rate of interest over the loan period by weekly payments each equal to the adjusted weekly rent for the house.

(2) In this section—

    (a) the "statutory rate of interest" is the rate of interest which would be charged under section 219(4) on the application date by the local authority for the area in which the house is situated;

    (b) the "loan period" is the period beginning on the application date and ending on whichever of the following is the earlier—

        (i) the expiry of a period of 25 years starting on that date; and

        (ii) the date when the applicant will (if he survives) reach pensionable age within the meaning of the Social Security Act 1975 or, in the case of joint applicants, the date when the one who will (if they both or all survive) reach pensionable age later than the other or the others reaches that age,

but if the period arrived at under sub-paragraph (ii) is less than 10 years, then the loan period shall be a period of 10 years beginning on the application date;

    (c) the "adjusted weekly rent" is an amount equal to 90 per cent of the weekly rent for the house payable as at the application date; and

    (d) the "application date" is the date of the application to purchase the house.

73C The deferred financial commitment

(1) The deferred financial commitment in respect of a house is the sum arrived at by—

    (a) finding the difference between—

        (i) the price which was fixed for the purchase of the house under section 62(1); and

        (ii) the initial capital payment;

    (b) expressing that difference as a percentage of the market value which was determined under section 62(2) for the purpose of fixing the price of the house;

    (c) reducing that percentage figure by—

        (i) 7 or such other number as may, with the consent of the Treasury, be prescribed; and

        (ii) in a case where payment has been made under subsection (4), the percentage figure which the amount so paid represents in relation to the market value mentioned in paragraph (b);

    (d) finding the sum which is equal to that resultant percentage of the resale value of the house; and

    (e) in a case to which subsection (5) of section 73D applies, adding to that sum the amount which falls to be added under subsection (6) of that section.

(2) No interest shall accrue on the deferred financial commitment.

(3) Payment of the deferred financial commitment—

    (a) shall, subject to section 73D, be made to the original seller of the house—

        (i) on the sale or other disposal of the house by the rent to loan purchaser; or

        (ii) if the rent to loan purchaser does not sell or dispose of it, on his death; and

    (b) may be so made in whole at any earlier time.

(4) Subject to section 73D(3), payment may be made at any time for the purpose of reducing the deferred financial commitment in accordance with subsection (1)(c)(ii).

(5) Subject to subsection (6), payment of the deferred financial commitment shall be made as soon as may be after the destruction of or damage to the house by fire, tempest, flood or any other cause against the risk of which it is normal practice to insure.

(6) Subsection (5) does not apply where, following the destruction of or damage to a house, it is rebuilt or reinstated.

(7) A standard security granted in security of the deferred financial commitment shall, notwithstanding section 13 of the Conveyancing and Feudal Reform (Scotland) Act 1970, have priority before any standard security securing the liability to make a repayment under section 72(1) but immediately after—

    (a) any standard security granted in security of any amount advanced by a recognised lending institution—

        (i) to enable payment of the initial capital payment or payment under subsection (4);

        (ii) for the improvement of the house; or

        (iii) for any combination of those purposes,

    (together with any interest, expenses and outlays payable thereunder); and

    (b) with the consent of the original seller, a standard security over the house granted in security of any other loan (together with any such interest, expenses and outlays).

In this subsection—

    a "recognised lending institution" is one which is recognised for the purposes of section 222;

references to interest payable under a standard security are references both to present and future interest payable thereunder including interest which has accrued or may accrue; and

references to expenses and outlays include interest thereon.

(8) In this section—

    (a) the "resale value" of a house is, subject to subsections (9) and (10)—

        (i) where it is being sold by the rent to loan purchaser on the open market with vacant possession and a good and marketable title, the price at which it is being so sold;

        (ii) where the rent to loan purchaser has died not having sold or disposed of it, its value for the purpose of confirmation to his estate;

        (iii) in any other case, such amount as is agreed for the purposes of this sub-paragraph between the rent to loan purchaser and the original seller or, failing such agreement, such amount as is determined for those purposes by an independent valuer as the value of the house, assuming it to be available for sale in the circumstances specified in sub-paragraph (i) on a date as near as may be to the date when payment of the deferred financial commitment is to be made; and

    (b) the "original seller" of a house is the body which, as the landlord of the house, sold it in pursuance of this Part to the rent to loan purchaser or, where another body has succeeded to the rights and duties of that body in relation to the house, that other body.

(9) In arriving at the resale value of a house no account shall be taken of—

    (a) anything done by the rent to loan purchaser (or any predecessor of his as secure tenant of the house) which has added to the value of the house; or

    (b) any failure by him (but not by any such predecessor) to keep the house in good repair (including decorative repair).

(10) For the purposes of agreeing or determining the amount of the resale value of a house under subsection (8)(a)(iii) in a case where it has been destroyed or damaged by a cause referred to in subsection (5), that value shall be taken as including the value of any sums paid or falling to be paid to the rent to loan purchaser under a policy insuring against the risk of the cause of destruction of or damage to the house except to the extent that they have been or fall to be applied in meeting the cost of any rebuilding or reinstatement which has been carried out.

73D Deferred financial commitment: further provisions

(1) This subsection applies where—

    (a) the person who has purchased a house by way of the rent to loan scheme sells or otherwise disposes of it to his spouse or any other person with whom he is living as if they were husband and wife and the house is, at the time of the sale or disposal, the spouse's or other person's only or principal home;

    (b) the person who has so purchased the house dies and there succeeds to the house, by operation of the law of succession, a person for whom or persons for whom or for one or more of whom the house was, for the period of 12 months immediately preceding the death, his or their only or principal home; or

(c) in the case of a house which was so purchased jointly, one of the joint purchasers dies and, at the time of the death, the house was the only or principal home of the survivor or the survivors or one or more of them.

(2) Where subsection (1) applies—

(a) the deferred financial commitment shall not be payable on the sale, disposal or death referred to in paragraph (a) of subsection (3) of section 73C but on the sale or other disposal of the house by the person or persons acquiring it, succeeding to it or surviving in the circumstances whereby subsection (1) applies or on the death of such person or of the last of them for whom the house was, both at the time of such acquisition, succession or survival and at the time of his death, his only or principal home; and

(b) paragraph (b) of the said subsection (3) shall have effect accordingly.

(3) A payment made under section 73C(4) shall not—

(a) be less than £1500 or such other sum as may, with the consent of the Treasury, be prescribed;

(b) exceed the statutory maximum; or

(c) be made within the period of one year after any previous such payment in respect of the same transaction.

(4) In subsection (3)(b), the "statutory maximum" is the amount by which the initial capital payment would be required to be augmented so as to produce, by operation of the calculations specified in paragraphs (a) to (c) of section 73C(1), a resultant percentage of 7.5% or such other percentage as may, with the consent of the Treasury, be prescribed.

(5) This subsection applies where—

(a) the subtraction of discount for the purposes of section 62(1) falls to be limited or excluded by operation of subsection (6A) of that section; and

(b) any part of those costs which, in accordance with that subsection, are to be represented by an amount arrived at under that subsection, was incurred in the period commencing with the beginning of the financial year of the landlord which was current 5 years prior to the date of payment in whole of the deferred financial commitment.

(6) Where subsection (5) applies, the amount which is, under section 73C(1)(e), to be added is an amount equal to the difference between the aggregate of the amounts mentioned in paragraph (a) and the amount mentioned in paragraph (b)—

(a) the initial capital payment and the deferred financial commitment (including any payment under section 73C(4)) which would be payable apart from this subsection;

(b) the price which would have been payable under section 62 had the purchase of the house proceeded otherwise than by way of the rent to loan scheme."

Definitions For "offer to sell", "rent to loan scheme", "tenant" and "the rent to loan purchaser", see the Housing (Scotland) Act 1987, s 82, as amended by s 143(5); for "house", "local authority", "prescribed" and "sale", see s 338(1) of that Act; for "the initial capital payment", see s 73B of that Act, as inserted above, and for "adjusted weekly rent", "application date", "loan period" and "statutory rate of interest" in that section, see sub-s (2) thereof; for "the deferred financial payment", see s 73C of that Act, as so inserted, and for "original seller" and "resale value" in that section, see sub-s (8) thereof.
References See paras 11.4, 11.6–11.10 ff.

143 Rent to loan scheme: related amendments

(1) The 1987 Act shall have effect subject to the following amendments (being amendments related to the rent to loan scheme).

(2) In section 63—

    (a) in subsection (1), after paragraph (c) there shall be inserted the following

        "; and

        (d) in the case of a tenant who is entitled to purchase the house by way of the rent to loan scheme, a statement whether he wishes to proceed so to purchase the house.";

    (b) in subsection (2), after paragraph (c), there shall be inserted the following paragraph—

        "(cc) where the application to purchase contains a statement under subsection (1)(d) that the applicant wishes to proceed by way of the rent to loan scheme and the statement has not been withdrawn, the minimum amount of the initial capital payment, a statement that the applicant, if so minded, may make an initial capital payment greater than the minimum and a description of the deferred financial commitment including—

            (i) the amount of the deferred financial commitment calculated as if due to be paid as at the date of the offer to sell;

            (ii) an explanation of why and how the amount of the deferred financial commitment when payable under section 73C(3)(a) can vary from its amount as calculated under sub-paragraph (i); and

            (iii) the procedure for paying the deferred financial commitment."

    (c) at the end there shall be inserted the following subsection—

        "(3) Where, in response to an offer to sell containing the matters referred to in paragraph (cc) of subsection (2), an applicant has informed a landlord in writing of his intention to make an initial capital payment of an amount greater than the minimum, the landlord shall, before the end of the period specified in subsection (2) or, if later, the expiry of one month from the date when the landlord was so informed of the tenant's intention, serve an amended offer to sell in which the calculation of the deferred financial commitment is revised accordingly."

(3) In section 67, there shall be inserted at the end the following subsection—

    "(4) This section does not apply where the tenant is exercising his right to purchase under section 61 by way of the rent to loan scheme."

(4) In section 71—

(a)   in subsection (1)—

    (i)   in paragraph (a), after "offer", in both places where it occurs, there shall be inserted "or amended offer";

    (ii)   in paragraph (d), after "offer" there shall be inserted "or amended offer" and there shall be added at the end "and, in the case of an amended offer, they do not conform with the requirements of section 63(3)"; and

(b)   in subsection (2)—

    (i)   in paragraph (b), after "offer" there shall be inserted "or amended offer"; and

    (ii)   after "63(2)" there shall be inserted "and, in the case of an amended offer, under section 63(3)".

(5)   In section 82—

(a)   after "20" there shall be inserted "214"; and

(b)   the following definitions shall be inserted at the appropriate places—

"the "rent to loan purchaser" of a house is the person who exercised his right to purchase it under section 61 by way of the rent to loan scheme or, where section 73D(1) applies, the person whose selling or otherwise disposing of the house or whose death is, by virtue of subsection (2) of that section, the occasion for payment of the deferred financial commitment, that person;

"rent to loan scheme" means the provisions of sections 62A and 73A to 73D."

(6)   In section 214, there shall be inserted at the end the following subsection—

"(9) This section applies to the deferred financial commitment as it applies to an advance and references in it and in section 215 to the making of advances shall be construed as references to such functions of a local authority under the rent to loan scheme as relate to the creation of the deferred financial commitment, but Schedule 17 shall not so apply."

(7)   In section 216, there shall be inserted at the end the following subsection—

"(10) This section does not apply in the case of the purchase of a house by way of the rent to loan scheme."

Definitions   For "application to purchase", "landlord", "offer to sell", "rent to loan scheme" and "tenant", see the Housing (Scotland) Act 1987, s 82, as amended by sub-s (5) above; for "house", "local authority" and "sell", see s 338(1) of that Act; for "the initial capital payment", see s 73B of that Act, as inserted by s 142; for "the deferred financial payment", see s 73C of that Act, as so inserted.
References   See paras 11.4, 11.12, 11.13 ff.

Right to purchase

144 Abatement of purchase price

After section 66 of the 1987 Act there shall be inserted the following sections—

"66A Abatement of purchase price on landlord's failure before contract of sale

(1) Where a tenant who seeks to exercise a right to purchase a house under section 61 has served an application to purchase on the landlord and the landlord—

    (a) not having served a notice of refusal, has failed to serve an offer to sell on the tenant within 2 months of the application or, where an amended offer to sell falls to be served on the tenant under subsection (3) of section 63, has failed to do so within the time limit specified in that subsection;

    (b) having agreed to serve an amended offer to sell on the tenant in response to a request under section 65(1), has failed to do so within one month of the request;

    (c) following an order by the Lands Tribunal to serve an amended offer to sell on the tenant under section 65(3), has failed to do so within 2 months of the date of the order;

    (d) following a finding by the Lands Tribunal under section 68(4), has failed to serve an offer to sell within 2 months of the date of the finding; or

    (e) following an order by the Lands Tribunal under section 71(2)(b), has failed to serve an offer or amended offer to sell within the time specified in the order,

the tenant may serve on the landlord a notice in writing requiring the landlord to serve on him, within one month of the date of the notice, the offer to sell or (as the case may be) the amended offer to sell which the landlord has failed to serve.

(2) Where the landlord fails to serve the offer to sell or the amended offer to sell within one month of the date of the notice in writing under subsection (1), the price fixed under section 62 shall be reduced by the amount of rent paid by the tenant during the period commencing with the date on which the one month period expired and ending with the date on which the offer is served.

66B Abatement of purchase price on landlord's failure after contract of sale

(1) Where the landlord has failed and continues to fail to deliver a good and marketable title to the tenant in accordance with the contract of sale, the tenant may at any time serve on the landlord a notice (the "initial notice of delay") setting out the landlord's failure and specifying—

    (a) the most recent action of which the tenant is aware which has been taken by the landlord in fulfilment of his duties under this Part;

    (b) a period (the "response period"), of not less than one month beginning on the date of service of the notice, within which the service by the landlord of a counter notice under subsection (2) will have the effect of cancelling the initial notice of delay.

(2) If there is no action under this Part which, at the beginning of the response period it was for the landlord to take in order to grant a good and marketable title to the tenant in implementation of the contract of sale, the landlord may serve on the tenant a counter notice either during or after the response period.

(3) At any time when—

    (a) the response period specified in the initial notice of delay has expired; and

    (b) the landlord has not served a counter notice under subsection (2),

the tenant may serve on the landlord a notice (the "operative notice of delay") that this subsection shall apply to the price fixed under section 62; and thereupon the price fixed under section 62 shall be reduced by the amount of rent paid by the tenant during the period commencing with the date of service of the operative notice of delay and ending with whichever is the earlier of the following dates—

    (i)   the date of service by the landlord of a counter notice; or

    (ii) the date of delivery by the landlord of a good and marketable title in implementation of the contract of sale.

(4) Where the landlord has served a counter notice under subsection (2) the tenant (together with any joint purchaser) may, by serving on the clerk to the Lands Tribunal a copy of the initial notice of delay and of the landlord's counter notice together with a request for the matter to be so referred, refer the matter to the Tribunal for its consideration under subsection (5).

(5) Where the matter has been so referred to the Lands Tribunal it shall consider whether or not in its opinion action which would have enabled a good and marketable title to be delivered in implementation of the contract of sale could have been taken by the landlord and shall find accordingly.

(6) Where the Lands Tribunal finds that action could have been taken by the landlord the tenant shall be entitled to serve an operative notice of delay as if the landlord had not served a counter notice and in that event the commencement date for the purposes of subsection (3) shall be the date on which an operative notice of delay could first have been served if no counter notice had been served.

66C Provisions relating to sections 66A and 66B

(1) Where there is more than one period in respect of which the price fixed under section 62 can be reduced under section 66A(2) or 66B(3), the periods may be aggregated and the price reduced by the total amount of the rent.

(2) If the period in respect of which the price fixed can be so reduced is, or if the periods aggregated under subsection (1) together amount to, more than twelve months, the amount by which the price fixed under section 62 would, apart from this subsection, fall to be reduced shall be increased by 50% or such other percentage as the Secretary of State may by order made by statutory instrument and subject to annulment in pursuance of a resolution of either House of Parliament provide."

Definitions   For "application to purchase", "landlord", "offer to sell" and "tenant", see the Housing (Scotland) Act 1987, s 82; for "house", "Lands Tribunal", and "sell", see s 338(1) of that Act; for "initial notice of delay", "response period" and "operative notice of delay", see s 66B(1), (3) of that Act, as inserted above.
References   See para 11.14 ff.

145 Effect of abatement of purchase price on recovery of discount

In section 72 of the 1987 Act (recovery of discount on early resale), after subsection (1) there shall be inserted the following subsection—

"(1A) Where a tenant has served on the landlord a notice under section 66A(1), the commencement of the period of 3 years referred to in subsection (1) shall be backdated by a period equal to the time (or, where section 66C(1) applies, the aggregate of the times) during which, by virtue of section 66A(2), any payment of rent falls to be taken into account.''

Definitions For "landlord" and "tenant", see the Housing (Scotland) Act 1987, s 82.
References See para 11.14 ff.

Other rights of secure tenants

146 Right to have repairs carried out

For section 60 of the 1987 Act there shall be substituted the following section—

"60 Right to have repairs carried out

(1) The Secretary of State may make regulations for entitling a secure tenant of a landlord prescribed by the Secretary of State, subject to and in accordance with the regulations, to have qualifying repairs carried out to the house which is the subject of the secure tenancy.

(2) Those regulations shall prescribe—
- (a) the maximum amount which will be paid in respect of any single qualifying repair;
- (b) the maximum time within which a qualifying repair is to be completed.

(3) The regulations may also provide that—
- (a) a landlord which has been prescribed under subsection (1) shall—
  - (i) maintain a list of contractors who are prepared to carry out qualifying repairs;
  - (ii) take such steps as may be prescribed to make its secure tenants aware of the provisions of the regulations and of the list of contractors;
  - (iii) where the tenant makes an application to him for a qualifying repair to be carried out, issue a works order to the usual contractor specifying the nature of the repair and the last day of the maximum time prescribed under subsection (2)(b);
- (b) where the usual contractor has not started the repair work by the last day specified in the works order, the tenant shall have the right to instruct one of the other listed contractors to carry out the repair;
- (c) where the repair work is carried out by that other listed contractor, the landlord shall be liable to pay for the work carried out;
- (d) a listed contractor who is instructed by a tenant shall notify the landlord that he has been so instructed as soon as he receives the instruction;
- (e) if the usual contractor fails to carry out the repair within the specified maximum time, the landlord shall pay to the tenant such sum by way of compensation as may be determined by or under the regulations;
- (f) the landlord may set off against any compensation payable under the regulations any sums owed to it by the tenant.

(4) The regulations may—

    (a) make different provision with respect to different cases or descriptions of case, including different provision for different areas;

    (b) make such procedural, incidental, supplementary and transitional provision as appears to the Secretary of State necessary or expedient.

(5) Nothing in subsections (2) to (4) above shall be taken as prejudicing the generality of subsection (1).

(6) Regulations under this section shall be made by statutory instrument.

(7) In this section—

    "listed contractor" means any contractor (including the usual contractor) specified in the landlord's list of contractors;

    "qualifying repair" means a repair prescribed as such in the regulations;

    "usual contractor" means the direct services organisation of the landlord or the contractor to whom the landlord has contracted its repairs."

Definitions For "landlord", "secure tenancy" and "tenant", see the Housing (Scotland) Act 1987, s 82; for "prescribed", see s 338(1) of that Act; for "listed contractor" "qualifying repair" and "usual contractor", see s 60(7) of that Act, as inserted above.
References See paras 11.15, 11.16 ff.

---

147 Right to compensation for improvements

After section 58 of the 1987 Act there shall be inserted the following section—

"58A Right to compensation for improvements

(1) For the purposes of this section—

    (a) "qualifying improvement work" is improvement work which is prescribed as such by the Secretary of State and which is begun not earlier than the commencement of section 147 of the Leasehold Reform, Housing and Urban Development Act 1993;

    (b) "qualifying person" is a person who is, at the time the tenancy comes to an end, the tenant of a landlord named in sub-paragraphs (i) to (iv) of section 61(2)(a); and—

        (i) is the tenant by whom the qualifying work was carried out; or

        (ii) is a tenant of a joint tenancy which existed at the time the improvement work was carried out; or

        (iii) succeeded to the tenancy under section 52 on the death of the tenant who carried out the work and the tenancy did not cease to be a secure tenancy on his succession;

    (c) a tenancy is terminated when—

        (i) any of the circumstances of subsection (1) of section 46 apply and, in a case where the termination is under paragraph (c) or (f) of that subsection, the house which is the subject of the secure tenancy is vacated;

        (ii) there is a change of landlord;

        (iii) it is assigned to a new tenant.

(2) Where the tenant of a landlord specified in sub-paragraphs (i) to (iv) of section 61(2)(a) has carried out qualifying improvement work with the

consent of that landlord under section 57, the qualifying person or persons shall on the termination of the tenancy be entitled to be paid compensation by the landlord in respect of the improvement work.

(3) Compensation shall not be payable if—
   (a) the improvement is not of a prescribed description; or
   (b) the tenancy comes to an end in prescribed circumstances; or
   (c) compensation has been paid under section 58 in respect of the improvement; or
   (d) the amount of any compensation which would otherwise be payable is less than such amount as may be prescribed,

and for the purposes of this subsection a prescribed description may be framed by reference to any circumstances whatever.

(4) Regulations under this section may provide that—
   (a) any compensation payable shall be—
      (i) determined by the landlord in such manner and taking into account such matters as may be prescribed; or
      (ii) calculated in such manner and taking into account such matters as may be prescribed,

and shall not exceed such amount, if any, as may be prescribed; and
   (b) the landlord may set off against any compensation payable under this section any sums owed to it by the qualifying person or persons.

(5) Where, in the case of two or more qualifying persons, one of them ("the missing person") cannot be found—
   (a) a claim for compensation under this section may be made by, and compensation may be paid to, the other qualifying person or persons; but
   (b) the missing person shall be entitled to recover his share of any compensation so paid from that person or those persons.

(6) The Secretary of State may by regulations made under this section make such procedural, incidental, supplementary and transitional provisions as appear to him to be necessary or expedient, and may in particular—
   (a) provide for the manner in which and the period within which claims for compensation under this section are to be made, and for the procedure to be followed in determining such claims;
   (b) prescribe the form of any document required to be used for the purposes of or in connection with such claims; and
   (c) provide for the determination of questions arising under the regulations.

(7) Regulations under this section—
   (a) may make different provision with respect to different cases or descriptions of case, including different provision for different areas;
   (b) shall be made by statutory instrument which (except in the case of regulations which are made only under subsection (6)(b)) shall be subject to annulment in pursuance of a resolution of either House of Parliament."

Definitions For "landlord", "secure tenancy", "tenancy" and "tenant", see the Housing (Scotland) Act 1987, s 82; for "improvement", see s 236(2) of that Act; for "house" and "prescribed", see s 338(1) of that Act; for "qualifying improvement work" and "qualifying person", see s 58A(1) of that Act, as inserted above; for "the missing person", see s 58A(5) thereof, as so inserted.
References See paras 11.17–11.19 ff.

148 Right to information

After section 75 of the 1987 Act there shall be inserted the following section—

"75A Duty of local authority landlord to provide information about right to buy

(1) A landlord which is one of those mentioned in section 61(2)(a)(i) or (ii) shall supply each of its secure tenants at least once every year with information about his right to purchase his house under this Part.

(2) The information supplied under subsection (1) shall be in such form as the landlord considers best suited to explain in simple terms and so far as it considers appropriate the right referred to in that subsection."

Definitions For "landlord", "secure tenant" and "tenant, see the Housing (Scotland) Act 1987, s 82; for "house", see s 338(1) of that Act.
References See para 11.20 ff.

Housing welfare services

149 Provision of housing welfare services

Part I of the 1987 Act shall have effect, and be deemed always to have had effect, as if after section 5 there were inserted the following section—

"5A Power of local authority to provide welfare services

(1) A local authority may provide in connection with housing accommodation provided by them (whether or not under this Part) such welfare services, that is to say services for promoting the welfare of the persons for whom the accommodation is so provided, as accord with the needs of those persons.

(2) The local authority may make reasonable charges for welfare services provided by virtue of this section.

(3) Notwithstanding the provisions of section 203, a local authority may attribute the income from and the expenditure on the welfare services provided under subsection (1) to a revenue account other than their housing revenue account.

(4) In this section "welfare services" does not include the repair, maintenance, supervision or management of houses or other property.

(5) The powers conferred by this section shall not be regarded as restricting those conferred by section 83 of the Local Government (Scotland) Act 1973 (power to incur expenditure for purposes not otherwise authorised) and accordingly the reference in subsection (1) of that section to any other enactment shall not include a reference to this section."

Definitions For "housing revenue account", see the Housing (Scotland) Act 1987, s 203; for "house" and "local authority", see s 338(1) of that Act; for "welfare services", see s 5A(4) of that Act, as inserted above.
References See para 11.21 ff.

150 Accounting for housing welfare services

Schedule 15 to the 1987 Act (the housing revenue account) shall have effect, and be deemed always to have had effect, as if after paragraph 4 there were inserted the following paragraph—

"Provision of welfare services

4A.—Where in any year a local authority provide welfare services under section 5A, they may—

    (a) carry to the credit of the housing revenue account an amount equal to the whole or any part of the income of the authority for the year from charges in respect of the provision of those services;

    (b) carry to the debit of the account an amount equal to the whole or any part of the expenditure of the authority for the year in respect of the provision of those services."

Definitions For "housing revenue account", see the Housing (Scotland) Act 1987, s 203; for "local authority", see s 338(1) of that Act.
References See para 11.21 ff.

151 Power to repeal provisions relating to housing welfare services

After section 5A of the 1987 Act there shall be inserted the following section—

"5B Power to repeal provisions relating to welfare services

(1) The Secretary of State may at any time by order made by statutory instrument provide that, on such day or in relation to such periods as may be appointed by the order, section 5A, this section and paragraph 4A of Schedule 15 shall—

    (a) cease to have effect; or

    (b) cease to apply for such purposes as may be specified in the order.

(2) An order under this section may—

    (a) appoint different days or periods for different provisions or purposes or for different authorities or descriptions of authority; and

    (b) contain such incidental, supplementary or transitional provisions as appear to the Secretary of State to be necessary or expedient."

References See para 11.21 ff.

Miscellaneous

152 Management agreements with housing co-operatives

After section 22 of the 1987 Act there shall be inserted the following section—

"22A Management agreements with housing co-operatives

(1) In this section "housing co-operative" has the meaning given in subsection (1) of section 22 except that the reference in that subsection to the Secretary of State's approval shall be construed as a reference to his approval in relation to the purposes of this section.

(2) On an application by a housing co-operative a local authority shall make an agreement with them for the performance by that housing co-operative, on such terms as may be provided in the agreement, of the local authority's functions under section 17(1) relating to the management of houses which are subject to the agreement.

(3) Before making such an agreement the local authority shall satisfy themselves that the housing co-operative—
    (a) have the approval of the Secretary of State;
    (b) are able to perform the functions competently and efficiently;
    (c) are representative of the tenants of the houses.

(4) Where the local authority refuse to enter into an agreement on the grounds that the housing co-operative do not satisfy paragraph (b) or (c) of subsection (3), the housing co-operative may appeal to the Secretary of State who may confirm or reverse the decision of the local authority.

(5) Where the Secretary of State reverses the decision of the local authority, the authority and the housing co-operative shall make the agreement.

(6) Where the local authority and the housing co-operative are unable to agree on the terms of the agreement, the housing co-operative may appeal to the Secretary of State who may determine the terms of the agreement.

(7) An agreement to which this section applies shall be made only with the approval of the Secretary of State, which may be given either generally or to any local authority or description of local authority or in any particular case, and may be given unconditionally or subject to any conditions."

Definitions   For "house", "local authority" and "tenant", see the Housing (Scotland) Act 1987, s 338(1); for "housing co-operative", see s 22A(1) of that Act, as inserted above.
References   See para 11.22 ff.

153 Standards and performance in housing management

After section 17 of the 1987 Act there shall be inserted the following sections—

"Standards and performance in housing management

17A Publication of information

(1) A local authority shall, in relation to their management of the houses which they hold for housing purposes, publish each year such information as—
    (a) may be prescribed by the Secretary of State about—
        (i) the standard of service of management which the authority undertake to provide;
        (ii) the authority's performance in the past in the achievement of that standard;

      (iii) the authority's intentions for the future in relation to the achievement of that standard;

      (iv) any other matter which he thinks should be included in the information to be published;

  (b) the authority consider it appropriate to publish in relation to the matters mentioned in paragraph (a) above, either as a result of having consulted tenants or otherwise;

  (c) the authority consider it appropriate to publish in relation to any other matter, either as a result of consulting tenants or otherwise.

(2) Before publishing such information, a local authority shall consult their tenants as to the information to be published under subsection (1) and shall take account of the characteristics of the different parts of their districts or areas and of the difference in information which may be appropriate in relation to these parts.

(3) The Secretary of State may direct a local authority to consult tenants or groups of tenants representing less than the whole of their district or area.

17B Power of Secretary of State to direct local authority

At the same time as the information is published, the local authority shall send a copy of the document in which it is published to the Secretary of State who may, if he considers that the publication is unsatisfactory, direct the local authority to publish the information in such manner as he specifies in the direction.

17C Management plan

A local authority shall, if the Secretary of State gives them notice to do so, prepare and submit to him within 3 months after such notice, a plan for the management of the houses which they hold for housing purposes."

Definitions   For "house", "local authority" and "prescribed", see the Housing (Scotland) Act 1987, s 338(1).
References   See paras 11.23–11.25 ff.

154 Further provision as to allocation of housing

In section 20 of the 1987 Act (persons to have priority on housing list and allocation of housing) at the end there shall be added the following subsection—

"(3) A member of a local authority shall be excluded from a decision on the allocation of local authority housing, or of housing in respect of which the local authority may nominate the tenant, where—

  (a) the house in question is situated; or

  (b) the applicant for the house in question resides,

in the electoral division or ward for which that member is elected."

Definitions   For "house" and "local authority", see the Housing (Scotland) Act 1987, s 338(1).
References   See para 11.26 ff.

155 Rules relating to housing list

(1) For subsection (1) of section 21 of the 1987 Act (publication of rules relating to the housing list) there shall be substituted the following subsection—

"(1) It shall be the duty—
- (a) of every local authority to make and to publish in accordance with subsection (4), and again within 6 months of any alteration thereof, rules governing—
  - (i) the admission of applicants to any housing list;
  - (ii) the priority of allocation of houses;
  - (iii) the transfer of tenants from houses owned by the landlord to houses owned by other bodies;
  - (iv) exchanges of houses;
- (b) of Scottish Homes and development corporations (including urban development corporations) to publish in accordance with subsection (4), and again within 6 months of any alteration thereof, any rules they may have governing the matters set out in sub-paragraphs (i) to (iv) of paragraph (a) above."

(2) In subsection (3) of section 19 of that Act (admission to housing list) for the words "Where a local authority has rules which" there shall be substituted the words "Where the rules made by a local authority under section 21(1)".

Definitions   For "development corporation", "house" and "local authority", see the Housing (Scotland) Act 1987, s 338(1).
References   See para 11.27 ff.

156 Defective dwellings: damages for landlord's failure to notify

After subsection (3) of section 299 of the 1987 Act (jurisdiction of sheriff) there shall be added the following subsections—

"(4) Where damages are awarded in proceedings commenced before 1st December 1994 which arise out of a failure on the part of the public sector authority to give a person acquiring a relevant interest in a dwelling notice in writing under section 291, the amount of damages for the purposes of this subsection shall be equal to the difference between—
- (a) the market value of the dwelling assessed as if it were not a defective dwelling and were available for sale on the open market with vacant possession; and
- (b) the market value of the dwelling assessed as a defective dwelling and as if available for sale on the open market with vacant possession.

(5) Subsection (4) applies in relation to proceedings which arise out of a failure by the authority before the coming into force of section 156 of the Leasehold Reform, Housing and Urban Development Act 1993 as it does to proceedings which arise out of a failure by the authority after that date."

Definitions   For "defective dwelling", "public sector authority" and "relevant interest", see the Housing (Scotland) Act 1987, s 303.
References   See para 11.28 ff.

157 Other amendments of 1987 Act

(1) In section 17 of the 1987 Act (management of local authority houses), in subsection (1), the words "and exercised by" shall cease to have effect.

(2) In section 61 of that Act (secure tenant's right to purchase), in subsection (10), subparagraphs (i) and (ii) of paragraph (b) shall cease to have effect.

(3) In section 62 of that Act (price)—

    (a) in subsection (3)(b), the words "continuous" and "immediately" shall cease to have effect;

    (b) after subsection (3) there shall be inserted—

"(3A) There shall be deducted from the discount an amount equal to any previous discount, or the aggregate of any previous discounts, received by the appropriate person on any previous purchase of a house by any of these persons from a landlord who is a person specified in subsection (11) of section 61 or prescribed in an order made under that subsection, reduced by any amount of such previous discount recovered by such a landlord.";

    (c) in subsection (4)—

        (i) for paragraph (a) there shall be substituted—

"(a) the "appropriate person" is whoever of—

        (i) the tenant; or

        (ii) the tenant's spouse if living with him at the date of service of the application to purchase; or

        (iii) a deceased spouse if living with the tenant at the time of death; or

        (iv) any joint tenant who is a joint purchaser of the house,

has the longer or longest such occupation;"

    and

    (ii) at the end there shall be inserted—

"and, for the purposes of subsection (3A), the "appropriate person" is any of the persons mentioned in sub-paragraphs (i) to (iv) of paragraph (a)."

(4) In section 248 of that Act (repairs grants), the proviso to subsection (5) shall be amended as follows—

    (a) after the words "shall not apply" there shall be inserted "(a)"; and

    (b) at the end there shall be added—

"(b) in relation to an application for a repairs grant in respect of works intended to reduce exposure to radon gas."

Definitions For "application to purchase", "landlord" and "tenant", see the Housing (Scotland) Act 1987, s 82; for "house" see s 338(1) of that Act; for "appropriate person", see s 62(4)(a) of that Act, as substituted by sub-s (3) above.
References See para 11.29 ff.

PART III
DEVELOPMENT OF URBAN AND OTHER AREAS

The Urban Regeneration Agency

158 The Agency

(1) There shall be a body corporate to be known as the Urban Regeneration Agency ("the Agency") for the purpose of exercising the functions conferred on it by the following provisions of this Part.

(2) Schedule 17 to this Act shall have effect with respect to the constitution of the Agency and Schedule 18 to this Act shall have effect with respect to the finances of the Agency.

(3) It is hereby declared that, except as provided by section 175, the Agency is not to be regarded as the servant or agent of the Crown or as enjoying any status, immunity or privilege of the Crown and that its property is not to be regarded as the property of, or property held on behalf of, the Crown.

References   See para 12.1 ff for an overview of its functions and para 12.15 ff on the Agency's constitution and finance.

159 Objects of Agency

(1) The main object of the Agency shall be to secure the regeneration of land in England—
- (a) which is land of one or more of the descriptions mentioned in subsection (2); and
- (b) which the Agency (having regard to guidance, and acting in accordance with directions, given by the Secretary of State under section 167) determines to be suitable for regeneration under this Part.

(2) The descriptions of land referred to in subsection (1)(a) are—
- (a) land which is vacant or unused;
- (b) land which is situated in an urban area and which is under-used or ineffectively used;
- (c) land which is contaminated, derelict, neglected or unsightly; and
- (d) land which is likely to become derelict, neglected or unsightly by reason of actual or apprehended collapse of the surface as the result of the carrying out of relevant operations which have ceased to be carried out;

and in this subsection "relevant operations" has the same meaning as in section 1 of the Derelict Land Act 1982.

(3) The Agency shall also have the object of securing the development of land in England which the Agency—
- (a) having regard to guidance given by the Secretary of State under section 167;
- (b) acting in accordance with directions given by the Secretary of State under that section; and
- (c) with the consent of the Secretary of State,

determines to be suitable for development under this Part.

(4) The objects of the Agency are to be achieved in particular by the following means (or by such of them as seem to the Agency to be appropriate in any particular case), namely—
- (a) by securing that land and buildings are brought into effective use;
- (b) by developing, or encouraging the development of, existing and new industry and commerce;
- (c) by creating an attractive and safe environment;
- (d) by facilitating the provision of housing and providing, or facilitating the provision of, social and recreational facilities.

References   For "the main object" of the Agency see para 12.3. For "guidance" and "directions" see para 12.26 ff. For the ancillary object of securing development of land (s 159(3)), see para 12.8. For the "means" of achieving the objects of the Agency, see para 12.9 ff.

160 General powers of Agency

(1) Subject to the following provisions of this Part, for the purpose of achieving its objects the Agency may—

 (a) acquire, hold, manage, reclaim, improve and dispose of land, plant, machinery, equipment and other property;

 (b) carry out the development or redevelopment of land, including the conversion or demolition of existing buildings;

 (c) carry out building and other operations;

 (d) provide means of access, services or other facilities for land;

 (e) seek to ensure the provision of water, electricity, gas, sewerage and other services;

 (f) carry on any business or undertaking for the purposes of its objects;

 (g) with the consent of the Secretary of State, form, or acquire interests in, bodies corporate;

 (h) act with other persons, whether in partnership or otherwise;

 (i) give financial assistance to other persons;

 (j) act as agent for other persons;

 (k) provide advisory or other services and facilities; and

 (l) generally do anything necessary or expedient for the purposes of its objects or for purposes incidental to those purposes.

(2) Nothing in section 159 or this section shall empower the Agency—

 (a) to provide housing otherwise than by acquiring existing housing accommodation and making it available on a temporary basis for purposes incidental to the purposes of its objects;

 (b) to acquire an interest in a body corporate which at the time of the acquisition is carrying on a trade or business, if the effect of the acquisition would be to make the body corporate a subsidiary of the Agency; or

 (c) except with the consent of the Secretary of State, to dispose of any land otherwise than for the best consideration which can reasonably be obtained.

(3) For the avoidance of doubt it is hereby declared that subsection (1) relates only to the capacity of the Agency as a statutory corporation and nothing in section 159 or this section authorises it to disregard any enactment or rule of law.

(4) In this section—

 "improve", in relation to land, includes refurbish, equip and fit out;

 "subsidiary" has the meaning given by section 736 of the Companies Act 1985; and in this section and the following provisions of this Part references to land include land not falling within subsection (1) or (3) of section 159.

Definitions For "the Agency", see s 158; for "improve", "land" and "subsidiary", see sub-s (4) above.

References See para 12.12 ff on the general powers of the Agency.

---

161 Vesting of land by order

(1) Subject to subsections (2) and (3), the Secretary of State may by order provide that land specified in the order which is vested in a local authority, statutory undertakers or other public body, or in a wholly-owned subsidiary of a public body, shall vest in the Agency.

(2) An order under subsection (1) may not specify land vested in statutory undertakers which is used for the purpose of carrying on their statutory undertakings or which is held for that purpose.

(3) In the case of land vested in statutory undertakers, the power to make an order under subsection (1) shall be exercisable by the Secretary of State and the appropriate Minister.

(4) An order under subsection (1) shall have the same effect as a declaration under the Compulsory Purchase (Vesting Declarations) Act 1981 except that, in relation to such an order, the enactments mentioned in Schedule 19 to this Act shall have effect with the modifications specified in that Schedule.

(5) Compensation under the Land Compensation Act 1961, as applied by subsection (4) and Schedule 19 to this Act, shall be assessed by reference to values current on the date the order under subsection (1) comes into force.

(6) No compensation is payable, by virtue of an order under subsection (1), under Part IV of the Land Compensation Act 1961.

(7) In this section—
"the appropriate Minister"—
   (a) in relation to statutory undertakers who are or are deemed to be statutory undertakers for the purposes of any provision of Part XI of the Town and Country Planning Act 1990, shall be construed as if contained in that Part;
   (b) in relation to any other statutory undertakers, shall be construed in accordance with an order made by the Secretary of State;
   and the reference to the Secretary of State and the appropriate Minister shall be similarly construed;
"local authority" means a county council, a district council, a London borough council or the Common Council of the City of London;
"statutory undertakers", except where the context otherwise requires, means—
   (a) persons authorised by any enactment to carry on any railway, light railway, tramway, road transport, water transport, canal, inland navigation, dock, harbour, pier or lighthouse undertaking, or any undertaking for the supply of hydraulic power;
   (b) British Shipbuilders, the Civil Aviation Authority, the British Coal Corporation and the Post Office;
   (c) any other authority, body or undertakers specified in an order made by the Secretary of State;
   (d) any wholly-owned subsidiary of any person, authority or body mentioned in paragraphs (a) and (b) or of any authority, body or undertakers specified in an order made under paragraph (c);
   and "statutory undertaking" shall be construed accordingly;
"wholly-owned subsidiary" has the meaning given by section 736 of the Companies Act 1985.

(8) If any question arises as to which Minister is the appropriate Minister in relation to any statutory undertakers, that question shall be determined by the Treasury.

(9) An order under subsection (1) shall be made by statutory instrument but no such order shall be made unless a draft of the order has been laid before and approved by resolution of each House of Parliament.

(10) An order under subsection (7) shall be made by statutory instrument which shall be subject to annulment in pursuance of a resolution of either House of Parliament.

Definitions For "the Agency", see s 158; for "the appropriate minister", "local authority", "statutory undertakers", "statutory undertaking" and "wholly-owned subsidiary", see sub-s (7) above.
References See para 12.21 on vesting of land by order.

162 Acquisition of land

(1) The Agency may, for the purpose of achieving its objects or for purposes incidental to that purpose, acquire land by agreement or, on being authorised to do so by the Secretary of State, compulsorily.

(2) The Agency may, for those purposes, be authorised by the Secretary of State, by means of a compulsory purchase order, to acquire compulsorily such new rights over land as are specified in the order.

(3) Where the land referred to in subsection (1) or (2) forms part of a common, open space or fuel or field garden allotment, the Agency may acquire (by agreement or, on being authorised to do so by the Secretary of State, compulsorily) land for giving in exchange for the land or, as the case may be, rights acquired.

(4) Subject to section 169, the Acquisition of Land Act 1981 shall apply to the compulsory acquisition of land by virtue of subsection (1) or (3).

(5) Schedule 3 to that Act shall apply to the compulsory acquisition of a right by virtue of subsection (2) but with the modification that the reference in paragraph 4(3) to statutory undertakers includes a reference to the Agency.

(6) The provisions of Part I of the Compulsory Purchase Act 1965 (so far as applicable), other than section 31, shall apply to the acquisition by the Agency of land by agreement; and in that Part as so applied "land" has the meaning given by the Interpretation Act 1978.

(7) In subsection (2)—
"new rights over land" means rights over land which are not in existence when the order specifying them is made;
"compulsory purchase order" has the same meaning as in the Acquisition of Land Act 1981.

Definitions For "the Agency", see s 158; for "compulsory purchase order" and "new rights over land", see sub-s (7) above.
References See paras 12.19 and 12.20.

163 Power to enter and survey land

(1) Any person who is duly authorised in writing by the Agency may at any reasonable time enter any land for the purpose of surveying it, or estimating its value, in connection with—
(a) any proposal to acquire that land or any other land; or
(b) any claim for compensation in respect of any such acquisition.

(2) The power to survey land shall be construed as including power to search and bore for the purpose of ascertaining the nature of the subsoil or the presence of minerals in it.

(3) A person authorised under this section to enter any land—

(a) shall, if so required, produce evidence of his authority before entry, and

(b) shall not demand admission as of right to any land which is occupied unless 28 days' notice of the intended entry has been given to the occupier by the Agency.

(4) Any person who wilfully obstructs a person acting in exercise of his powers under this section shall be guilty of an offence and liable on summary conviction to a fine not exceeding level 2 on the standard scale.

(5) If any person who, in compliance with the provisions of this section, is admitted into a factory, workshop or workplace discloses to any person any information obtained by him in it as to any manufacturing process or trade secret, he shall be guilty of an offence.

(6) Subsection (5) does not apply if the disclosure is made by a person in the course of performing his duty in connection with the purpose for which he was authorised to enter the premises.

(7) A person who is guilty of an offence under subsection (5) shall be liable on summary conviction to a fine not exceeding the statutory maximum or on conviction on indictment to imprisonment for a term not exceeding two years or a fine or both.

(8) Where any land is damaged—

(a) in the exercise of a right of entry under this section, or

(b) in the making of any survey under this section,

compensation in respect of that damage may be recovered by any person interested in the land from the Agency.

(9) The provisions of section 118 of the Town and Country Planning Act 1990 (determination of claims for compensation) shall apply in relation to compensation under subsection (8) as they apply in relation to compensation under Part IV of that Act.

(10) No person shall carry out under this section any works authorised by virtue of subsection (2) unless notice of his intention to do so was included in the notice required by subsection (3).

(11) The authority of the appropriate Minister shall be required for the carrying out of any such works if—

(a) the land in question is held by statutory undertakers; and

(b) they object to the proposed works on the ground that the execution of the works would be seriously detrimental to the carrying on of their undertaking;

and expressions used in this subsection have the same meanings as they have in section 325(9) of the Town and Country Planning Act 1990 (supplementary provisions as to rights of entry).

References   See paras 12.23 and 12.24 on the nature and extent of the power to enter and survey land.

---

164 Financial assistance

(1) The consent of the Secretary of State is required for the exercise of the Agency's power to give financial assistance; and such assistance—

(a) may be given by the Agency only in respect of qualifying expenditure; and

(b) may be so given on such terms and conditions as the Agency, with the consent of the Secretary of State, considers appropriate.

(2) Expenditure incurred in connection with any of the following matters is qualifying expenditure—

(a) the acquisition of land;

(b) the reclamation, improvement or refurbishment of land;

(c) the development or redevelopment of land, including the conversion or demolition of existing buildings;

(d) the equipment or fitting out of land;

(e) the provision of means of access, services or other facilities for land;

(f) environmental improvements.

(3) Financial assistance may be given in any form and may, in particular, be given by way of—

(a) grants;

(b) loans;

(c) guarantees; or

(d) incurring expenditure for the benefit of the person assisted;

but the Agency shall not in giving financial assistance purchase loan or share capital in a company.

(4) A consent under subsection (1) may be given only with the approval of the Treasury.

(5) The terms and conditions on which financial assistance is given may, in particular, include provision as to—

(a) the circumstances in which the assistance must be repaid, or otherwise made good, to the Agency, and the manner in which that is to be done;

(b) the circumstances in which the Agency is entitled to recover the proceeds or part of the proceeds of any disposal of land in respect of which the assistance was provided.

(6) Any person receiving financial assistance shall comply with the terms and conditions on which it is given and compliance may be enforced by the Agency.

Definitions   For "the Agency", see s 158; as to "qualifying expenditure", see sub-s (2) above.
References   See paras 12.13, 12.14.

---

165 Connection of private streets to highway

(1) For the purpose of achieving its objects or for purposes incidental to that purpose, the Agency may serve a notice (a "connection notice") on the local highway authority requiring the authority to connect a private street to an existing highway (whether or not it is a highway which for the purposes of the Highways Act 1980 is a highway maintainable at the public expense).

(2) A connection notice must specify—

(a) the private street and the existing highway;

(b) the works which appear to the Agency to be necessary to make the connection; and

(c) the period within which those works should be carried out.

(3) Before serving a connection notice the Agency shall consult the local highway authority about the proposed contents of the notice.

(4) Within the period of two months beginning with the date on which the connection notice was served, the local highway authority may appeal against the notice to the Secretary of State.

(5) After considering any representations made to him by the Agency and the local highway authority, the Secretary of State shall determine an appeal under subsection (4) by setting aside or confirming the connection notice (with or without modifications).

(6) A connection notice becomes effective—

- (a) where no appeal is made within the period of two months referred to in subsection (4), upon the expiry of that period;
- (b) where an appeal is made within that period but is withdrawn before it has been determined by the Secretary of State, on the date following the expiry of the period of 21 days beginning with the date on which the Secretary of State is notified of the withdrawal;
- (c) where an appeal is made and the connection notice is confirmed by a determination under subsection (5), on such date as the Secretary of State may specify in the determination.

(7) Where a connection notice becomes effective, the local highway authority shall carry out the works specified in the notice within such period as may be so specified and may recover from the Agency the expenses reasonably incurred by them in doing so.

(8) If the local highway authority do not carry out the works specified in the notice within such period as may be so specified, the Agency may itself carry out or complete those works or arrange for another person to do so.

(9) In this section "local highway authority" has the same meaning as in the Highways Act 1980.

Definitions For "the Agency", see s 158; for "highway" and "private street", see s 170; for "connection notice", see sub-s (1) above; for "local highway authority", see sub-s (9) above. For "highway authority" see ss 1, 2 of the Highways Act 1980.
References See para 12.41.

The Agency: supplemental

166 Consents of Secretary of State

A consent of the Secretary of State under the foregoing provisions of this Part—

- (a) may be given unconditionally or subject to conditions;
- (b) may be given in relation to a particular case or in relation to such descriptions of case as may be specified in the consent; and
- (c) except in relation to anything already done or agreed to be done on the authority of the consent, may be varied or revoked by a notice given by the Secretary of State to the Agency.

References See para 12.25.

167 Guidance and directions by Secretary of State

(1) The Agency shall have regard to guidance from time to time given by the Secretary of State in deciding—

    (a) which land is suitable for regeneration or development under this Part; and

    (b) which of its functions under this Part it is to exercise for securing the regeneration or development of any particular land and how it is to exercise those functions.

(2) Without prejudice to any of the foregoing provisions of this Part requiring the consent of the Secretary of State to be obtained for anything to be done by the Agency, he may give directions to the Agency—

    (a) for restricting the exercise by it of any of its functions under this Part; or

    (b) for requiring it to exercise those functions in any manner specified in the directions.

(3) Directions under subsection (2) may be of a general or particular nature and may be varied or revoked by subsequent directions.

References   See para 12.26 ff (guidance) and para 12.28 (directions).

168 Validity of transactions

(1) A transaction between a person and the Agency shall not be invalidated by reason only of any failure by the Agency to observe its objects or the requirement in subsection (1) of section 160 that the Agency shall exercise the powers conferred by that subsection for the purpose of achieving its objects, and such a person shall not be concerned to see or enquire whether there has been any such failure.

(2) A transaction between a person and the Agency acting in purported exercise of its functions under this Part shall not be invalidated by reason only that it was carried out in contravention of any direction given under subsection (2) of section 167, and such a person shall not be concerned to see or enquire whether any directions under that subsection have been given or complied with.

References   See para 12.12.

169 Supplementary provisions as to vesting and acquisition of land

(1) Schedule 20 to this Act shall have effect.

(2) Part I of that Schedule modifies the Acquisition of Land Act 1981 as applied by section 162.

(3) Part II of that Schedule contains supplementary provisions about land vested in or acquired by the Agency under this Part.

(4) Part III of that Schedule contains supplementary provisions about the acquisition by the Agency of rights over land by virtue of section 162(2).

Designation orders and their effect

170 Power to make designation orders

(1) Where, as respects any area in England which is an urban area or which, in the opinion of the Secretary of State, is suitable for urban development, it appears to the Secretary of State—

    (a) that all or any of the provisions authorised by section 171 should be made in relation to the whole or any part of it; or

(b) that either or both of sections 172 and 173 should apply in relation to it, the Secretary of State may by order designate that area and either so make the provision or provisions, or direct that the section or sections shall so apply, or (as the case may require) do both of those things.

(2) In this Part "designation order" means an order under this section and "designated area" means, subject to subsection (5), an area designated by a designation order.

(3) Before making a designation order the Secretary of State shall consult every local authority any part of whose area is intended to be included in the proposed designated area.

(4) A designation order—
   (a) shall be made by statutory instrument which shall be subject to annulment in pursuance of a resolution of either House of Parliament; and
   (b) may contain such savings and transitional and supplementary provisions as may be specified in the order.

(5) The power to amend a designation order conferred by section 14 of the Interpretation Act 1978 includes power to amend the boundaries of the designated area; and where any such amendment is made, any reference in this Part to a designated area is a reference to the designated area as so amended.

(6) In this section "local authority" means a county council, a district council, a London borough council or the Common Council of the City of London.

References   See para 12.29 ff. For consultation under section 170(3) see para 12.32 ff.

---

171 Agency as local planning authority

(1) If a designation order so provides, the Agency shall be the local planning authority for the whole or any part of the designated area—
   (a) for such purposes of Part III of the Town and Country Planning Act 1990 and sections 67 and 73 of the Planning (Listed Buildings and Conservation Areas) Act 1990 as may be specified in the order; and
   (b) in relation to such kinds of development as may be so specified.

(2) A designation order making such provision as is mentioned in subsection (1) may also provide—
   (a) that any enactment relating to local planning authorities shall not apply to the Agency; and
   (b) that any such enactment which applies to the Agency shall apply to it subject to such modifications as may be specified in the order.

(3) If a designation order so provides—
   (a) subject to any modifications specified in the order, the Agency shall have, in the whole or any part of the designated area, such of the functions conferred by the provisions mentioned in subsection (4) as may be so specified; and
   (b) such of the provisions of Part VI and sections 249 to 251 and 258 of the Town and Country Planning Act 1990 and sections 32 to 37 of the Planning (Listed Buildings and Conservation Areas) Act 1990 as are mentioned in the order shall have effect, in relation to the Agency and to land in the designated area, subject to the modifications there specified.

(4) The provisions referred to in subsection (3)(a) are—
- (a) sections 171C, 171D, 172 to 185, 187 to 202, 206 to 222, 224, 225, 231 and 320 to 336 of, and paragraph 11 of Schedule 9 to, the Town and Country Planning Act 1990;
- (b) Chapters I, II and IV of Part I and sections 54 to 56, 59 to 61, 66, 68 to 72, 74 to 76 and 88 of the Planning (Listed Buildings and Conservation Areas) Act 1990; and
- (c) sections 4 to 15, 17 to 21, 23 to 26AA, 36 and 36A of the Planning (Hazardous Substances) Act 1990.

(5) A designation order making such provision as is mentioned in subsection (3) may also provide that, for the purposes of any of the provisions specified in the order, any enactment relating to local planning authorities shall apply to the Agency subject to such modifications as may be so specified.

Definitions For "the Agency", see s 158; for "designated area" and "designation order", see s 170.
References See para 12.35 ff as to the assumption of planning powers by the Agency.

---

172 Adoption of private streets

(1) Where—
- (a) this section applies in relation to a designated area; and
- (b) any street works have been executed on any land in the designated area which was then or has since become a private street (or part of a private street),

the Agency may serve a notice (an "adoption notice") on the street works authority requiring the authority to declare the street (or part) to be a highway which for the purposes of the Highways Act 1980 is a highway maintainable at the public expense.

(2) Within the period of two months beginning with the date on which the adoption notice was served, the street works authority may appeal against the notice to the Secretary of State.

(3) After considering any representations made to him by the Agency and the street works authority, the Secretary of State shall determine an appeal under subsection (2) by setting aside or confirming the adoption notice (with or without modifications).

(4) Where, under subsection (3), the Secretary of State confirms the adoption notice—
- (a) he may at the same time impose conditions (including financial conditions) upon the Agency with which it must comply in order for the notice to take effect; and
- (b) with effect from such date as the Secretary of State may specify, the street (or part) shall become a highway which for the purposes of the Highways Act 1980 is a highway maintainable at the public expense.

(5) Where a street works authority neither complies with the adoption notice, nor appeals under subsection (2), the street (or part) shall become, upon the expiry of the period of two months referred to in subsection (2), a highway which for the purposes of the Highways Act 1980 is a highway maintainable at the public expense.

(6) In this section "street works" and "street works authority" have the same meanings as in Part XI of the Highways Act 1980.

Definitions   For "the Agency", see s 158; for "designated area" and "designation order" see s 170; for "highway" and "private street", see s 185; for "adoption notice", see sub-s (1) above; for "street works" and "street works authority", see sub-s (6) above.
References   See para 12.42 as to the "adoption notice".

173 Traffic regulation orders for private streets

(1) Where—
    (a) this section applies in relation to a designated area;
    (b) the Agency submits to the Secretary of State that an order under this section should be made in relation to any road in the designated area which is a private street; and
    (c) it appears to the Secretary of State that the traffic authority do not intend to make an order under section 1 or, as the case may be, section 6 of the Road Traffic Regulation Act 1984 (orders concerning traffic regulation) in relation to the road,
the Secretary of State may by order under this section make in relation to the road any such provision as he might have made by order under that section if he had been the traffic authority.

(2) The Road Traffic Regulation Act 1984 applies to an order under this section as it applies to an order made by the Secretary of State under section 1 or, as the case may be, section 6 of that Act in relation to a road for which he is the traffic authority.

(3) In this section "road" and "traffic authority" have the same meanings as in the Road Traffic Regulation Act 1984.

Definitions   For "the Agency", see s 158; for "designated area", see s 170; for "private street", see s 185; for "road" and "traffic authority", see sub-s (3) above.
References   See para 12.43 as to traffic regulation orders for private streets.

Other functions of Secretary of State

174 Financial assistance for urban regeneration

For section 27 of the Housing and Planning Act 1986 (power to give financial assistance) there shall be substituted the following section—

"27 Power to give assistance

(1) The Secretary of State may, with the consent of the Treasury, give financial assistance to any person in respect of expenditure incurred in connection with activities contributing to the regeneration of an urban area.

(2) Activities contributing to the regeneration of an urban area include in particular—
    (a) securing that land and buildings are brought into effective use;
    (b) developing, or encouraging the development of, existing and new industry and commerce;
    (c) creating an attractive and safe environment;
    (d) providing housing or social and recreational facilities so as to encourage people to live or work in the area;
    (e) providing employment for people who live in the area;

(f) providing training, educational facilities or health services for people who live in the area."

References   See para 12.44 as to amendments to City Grant powers.

175 Power to appoint Agency as agent

(1) The Secretary of State may, on such terms as he may with the approval of the Treasury specify, appoint the Agency to act as his agent in connection with such of the functions mentioned in subsection (2) as he may specify; and where such an appointment is made, the Agency shall act as such an agent in accordance with the terms of its appointment.

(2) The functions referred to in subsection (1) are—
- (a) functions under section 1 of the Derelict Land Act 1982 or any enactment superseded by that section (grants for reclaiming or improving land or bringing land into use), other than the powers to make orders under subsections (5) and (7) of that section; and
- (b) so far as exercisable in relation to England, functions under sections 27 to 29 of the Housing and Planning Act 1986 (financial assistance for urban regeneration).

(3) In so far as an appointment under subsection (1) relates to functions mentioned in subsection (2)(b), the terms of the appointment shall preclude the Agency from giving financial assistance in respect of expenditure which is not qualifying expenditure within the meaning of section 164.

References   See para 12.43 ff.

176 Power to direct disposal of unused etc land held by public bodies

(1) In subsection (1) of section 98 (disposal of land by public bodies at direction of Secretary of State) of the Local Government, Planning and Land Act 1980 ("the 1980 Act")—
- (a) in paragraph (a), for the words "is for the time being entered on a register maintained by him under section 95 above" there shall be substituted the words "for the time being satisfies the conditions specified in section 95(2) above"; and
- (b) in paragraph (b), for the words "is for the time being entered on such a register" there shall be substituted the words "for the time being satisfies those conditions".

(2) In section 99A of that Act (powers of entry), subsection (2) (which precludes entry on land which is not for the time being entered on a register maintained under section 95) shall cease to have effect.

Urban development corporations

177 Power to act as agents of Agency

(1) The Agency may, with the consent of the Secretary of State, appoint an urban development corporation, on such terms as may be agreed, to act as its agent in connection with such of its functions (other than its power to give financial assistance) as may be specified in the appointment; and where such an appointment

is made, the urban development corporation shall act as such an agent in accordance with the terms of its appointment.

(2) For the purpose of assisting the Agency to carry out any of its functions, an urban development corporation, on being so requested by the Agency, may arrange for any of its property or staff to be made available to the Agency for such period and on such other terms as it thinks fit.

(3) In this section "urban development corporation" means a corporation established by an order under section 135 of the 1980 Act.

Definitions For "the Agency", see s 158; for "urban development corporation", see sub-s (3) above.
References See para 12.46 ff.

---

178 Powers with respect to private streets

For section 157 of the 1980 Act (highways) there shall be substituted the following sections—

"Private streets

157 Adoption of private streets

(1) Where any street works have been executed on any land in an urban development area which was then or has since become a private street (or part of a private street), the urban development corporation may serve a notice (an "adoption notice") on the street works authority requiring the authority to declare the street (or part) to be a highway which for the purposes of the Highways Act 1980 is a highway maintainable at the public expense.

(2) Within the period of two months beginning with the date on which the adoption notice was served, the street works authority may appeal against the notice to the Secretary of State.

(3) After considering any representations made to him by the corporation and the street works authority, the Secretary of State shall determine an appeal under subsection (2) above by setting aside or confirming the adoption notice (with or without modifications).

(4) Where, under subsection (3) above, the Secretary of State confirms the adoption notice—

    (a) he may at the same time impose conditions (including financial conditions) upon the corporation with which it must comply in order for the notice to take effect; and

    (b) with effect from such date as the Secretary of State may specify, the street (or part) shall become a highway which for the purposes of the Highways Act 1980 is a highway maintainable at the public expense.

(5) Where a street works authority neither complies with the adoption notice, nor appeals under subsection (2) above, the street (or part) shall become, upon the expiry of the period of two months referred to in subsection (2) above, a highway which for the purposes of the Highways Act 1980 is a highway maintainable at the public expense.

(6) In this section—

"highway" has the same meaning as in the Highways Act 1980;
"private street", "street works" and "street works authority" have the
same meanings as in Part XI of that Act.

(7) This section does not extend to Scotland.

157A Connection of private streets to highway

(1) An urban development corporation may serve a notice (a "connection
notice") on the local highway authority requiring the authority to connect a
private street in the urban development area to an existing highway (whether
or not it is a highway which for the purposes of the Highways Act 1980 is a
highway maintainable at the public expense).

(2) A connection notice must specify—
  (a) the private street and the existing highway;
  (b) the works which appear to the corporation to be necessary to make
      the connection; and
  (c) the period within which those works should be carried out.

(3) Before serving a connection notice an urban development corporation
shall consult the local highway authority about the proposed contents of the
notice.

(4) Within the period of two months beginning with the date on which
the connection notice was served, the local highway authority may appeal
against the notice to the Secretary of State.

(5) After considering any representations made to him by the corporation
and the local highway authority, the Secretary of State shall determine an
appeal under subsection (4) above by setting aside or confirming the
connection notice (with or without modifications).

(6) A connection notice becomes effective—
  (a) where no appeal is made within the period of two months referred
      to in subsection (4) above, upon the expiry of that period;
  (b) where an appeal is made within that period but is withdrawn
      before it has been determined by the Secretary of State, on the date
      following the expiry of the period of 21 days beginning with the
      date on which the Secretary of State is notified of the withdrawal;
  (c) where an appeal is made and the connection notice is confirmed by
      a determination under subsection (5) above, on such date as the
      Secretary of State may specify in the determination.

(7) Where a connection notice becomes effective, the local highway
authority shall carry out the works specified in the notice within such period
as may be so specified and may recover from the corporation the expenses
reasonably incurred by them in doing so.

(8) If the local highway authority do not carry out the works specified in
the notice within such period as may be so specified, the corporation may
themselves carry out or complete those works or arrange for another person
to do so.

(9) In this section—
  "highway" and "local highway authority" have the same meanings as
      in the Highways Act 1980;

"private street" has the same meaning as in Part XI of that Act.

(10) This section does not extend to Scotland.

157B Traffic regulation orders for private streets

(1) Where—
- (a) an urban development corporation submits to the Secretary of State that an order under this section should be made in relation to any road in the urban development area which is a private street; and
- (b) it appears to the Secretary of State that the traffic authority do not intend to make an order under section 1 or, as the case may be, section 6 of the Road Traffic Regulation Act 1984 (orders concerning traffic regulation) in relation to the road,

the Secretary of State may by order under this section make in relation to the road any such provision as he might have made by order under that section if he had been the traffic authority.

(2) The Road Traffic Regulation Act 1984 applies to an order under this section as it applies to an order made by the Secretary of State under section 1 or, as the case may be, section 6 of that Act in relation to a road for which he is the traffic authority.

(3) In this section—
"private street" has the same meaning as in Part XI of the Highways Act 1980;
"road" and "traffic authority" have the same meanings as in the Road Traffic Regulation Act 1984.

(4) This section does not extend to Scotland."

Definitions For "urban development area" and "urban development corporation", see the Local Government, Planning and Land Act 1980, s 171, as substituted, in the case of the definition "urban development area", by s 179(5); for "adoption notice", see 157(1) of the 1980 Act, as substituted above; for "street works" and "street works authority", see s 157(6) of that Act, as so substituted; for "highway", see ss 157(6), 157A(9) of that Act, as so substituted; for "private street", see ss 157(6), 157A(9), 157B(3) of that Act, as so substituted; for "connection notice", see s 157A(1) of that Act, as so substituted; for "road" and "traffic authority", see s 157B(3) of that Act, as so substituted.
References See para 12.40.

---

179 Adjustment of areas

(1) After subsection (3) of section 134 (urban development areas) of the 1980 Act there shall be inserted the following subsections—

"(3A) The Secretary of State may by order alter the boundaries of any urban development area so as to exclude any area of land.

(3B) Before making an order under subsection (3A) above, the Secretary of State shall consult any local authority the whole or any part of whose area is included in the area of land to be excluded by the order."

(2) In subsection (4) of that section, for the words "this section" there shall be substituted the words "subsection (1) above".

(3) After that subsection there shall be inserted the following subsection—

"(5) The power to make an order under subsection (3A) above—

    (a) shall be exercisable by statutory instrument subject to annulment in pursuance of a resolution of either House of Parliament; and

    (b) shall include power to make such incidental, consequential, transitional or supplementary provision as the Secretary of State thinks fit."

(4) In section 135(2) of that Act (establishment of urban development corporations), for the words "section 134" there shall be substituted the words "section 134(1)".

(5) In section 171 of that Act (interpretation of Part XVI: general), for the definition of "urban development area" there shall be substituted the following definition—

    "urban development area" means so much of an area designated by an order under subsection (1) of section 134 above as is not excluded from it by an order under subsection (3A) of that section;".

References   See para 12.48.

---

180 Transfers of property, rights and liabilities

(1) In subsection (1) of section 165 of the 1980 Act (power to transfer undertaking of urban development corporation), after the words "local authority", in both places where they occur, there shall be inserted the words "or other body".

(2) Subsection (3) of that section (transfer of liabilities by order) shall cease to have effect; and after that section there shall be inserted the following section—

"165A Transfers of property, rights and liabilities by order

(1) Subject to this section, the Secretary of State may at any time by order transfer to himself, upon by such terms as he thinks fit, any property, rights or liabilities which—

    (a) are for the time being vested in an urban development corporation, and

    (b) are not proposed to be transferred under an agreement made under section 165 above and approved by the Secretary of State with the Treasury's concurrence.

(2) An order under this section may terminate—

    (a) any appointment of the corporation under subsection (1) of section 177 of the Leasehold Reform, Housing and Urban Development Act 1993 (power of corporations to act as agents of the Urban Regeneration Agency); and

    (b) any arrangements made by the corporation under subsection (2) of that section.

(3) Before making an order under this section, the Secretary of State shall consult each local authority in whose area all or part of the urban development area is situated.

(4) An order under this section shall be made by statutory instrument which shall be subject to annulment in pursuance of a resolution of either House of Parliament."

(3) In subsection (9) of that section—

    (a) after the words "this section" there shall be inserted the words "and sections 165A and 166 below";

    (b) for the words "the section", in both places where they occur, there shall be substituted the words "the sections".

(4) For subsection (1) of section 166 of that Act (dissolution of urban development corporations) there shall be substituted the following subsection—

    "(1) Where all property, rights and liabilities of an urban development corporation have been transferred under or by one or more relevant instruments, the Secretary of State may make an order by statutory instrument under this section."

(5) For subsection (5) of that section there shall be substituted the following subsection—

    "(5) In this section "relevant instrument" means an agreement made under section 165 above or an order made under section 165A above."

Definitions For "urban development area" and "urban development corporation", see the Local Government, Planning and Land Act 1980, s 171, as substituted, in the case of the definition "urban development area", by s 179(5) ante. Note as to "relevant instrument" in s 166 of the 1980 Act, sub-s (5) thereof, as substituted by sub-s (5) above.
References See para 12.50.

Miscellaneous

181 No compensation where planning decision made after certain acquisitions

(1) Section 23(3) of the Land Compensation Act 1961 (no compensation where planning decision made after certain acquisitions) shall be amended as follows.

(2) After paragraph (a) there shall be inserted the following paragraph—

    "(aa) under section 104 of that Act (acquisition by the Land Authority for Wales);".

(3) After paragraph (c) there shall be inserted the words

    "or

    (d) under Part III of the Leasehold Reform, Housing and Urban Development Act 1993 (acquisition by the Urban Regeneration Agency)."

(4) Subsection (2) above shall apply to an acquisition or sale of an interest in land if the date of completion (within the meaning of Part IV of that Act) falls on or after the day on which this Act is passed.

182 Powers of housing action trusts with respect to private streets

(1) In subsection (1) of section 69 of the Housing Act 1988 (powers of housing action trusts with respect to private streets), for the words "in a private street (or part of a private street) in a designated area" there shall be substituted the words "on any land in a designated area which was then or has since become a private street (or part of a private street)".

(2) In subsection (2) of that section, the words from "on grounds" onwards shall be omitted.

Definitions For "designated area", see the Housing Act 1988, s 60(6); for "private street", by virtue of s 69(6) of that Act, see the Highways Act 1980, s 203(2).

Supplemental

183 Notices

(1) This section has effect in relation to any notice required or authorised by this Part to be given to or served on any person.

(2) Any such notice may be given to or served on the person in question either by delivering it to him, or by leaving it at his proper address, or by sending it by post to him at that address.

(3) Any such notice may—
- (a) in the case of a body corporate, be given to or served on the secretary or clerk of that body; and
- (b) in the case of a partnership, be given to or served on a partner or a person having the control or management of the partnership business.

(4) For the purposes of this section and of section 7 of the Interpretation Act 1978 (service of documents by post) in its application to this section, the proper address of any person to or on whom a notice is to be given or served shall be his last known address, except that—
- (a) in the case of a body corporate or its secretary or clerk, it shall be the address of the registered or principal office of that body; and
- (b) in the case of a partnership, a partner or a person having the control or management of the partnership business, it shall be that of the principal office of the partnership;

and for the purposes of this subsection the principal office of a company registered outside the United Kingdom or of a partnership carrying on business outside the United Kingdom shall be its principal office within the United Kingdom.

(5) If the person to be given or served with any notice mentioned in subsection (1) has specified an address within the United Kingdom other than his proper address within the meaning of subsection (4) as the one at which he or someone on his behalf will accept documents of the same description as that notice, that address shall also be treated for the purposes of this section and section 7 of the Interpretation Act 1978 as his proper address.

(6) If the name or address of any owner, lessee or occupier of land to or on whom any notice mentioned in subsection (1) is to be served cannot after reasonable inquiry be ascertained, the document may be served either by leaving it in the hands of a person who is or appears to be resident or employed on the land or by leaving it conspicuously affixed to some building or object on the land.

References See para 12.51.

184 Dissolution of English Industrial Estates Corporation

(1) The English Industrial Estates Corporation shall cease to exist on the commencement of this section.

(2) All the property, rights and liabilities to which that Corporation was entitled or subject immediately before that commencement shall become by virtue of this section property, rights and liabilities of the Agency.

References   See para 12.7.

185 Interpretation of Part III

In this Part—

"the 1980 Act" means the Local Government, Planning and Land Act 1980;

"the Agency" means the Urban Regeneration Agency;

"designation order" and "designated area" have the meanings given by section 170;

"highway" has the same meaning as in the Highways Act 1980;

"private street" has the same meaning as in Part XI of that Act.

PART IV
SUPPLEMENTAL

186 Financial provisions

(1) There shall be paid out of money provided by Parliament—

(a) any expenses of the Secretary of State incurred in consequence of this Act; and

(b) any increase attributable to this Act in the sums payable out of money so provided under any other enactment.

(2) There shall be paid into the Consolidated Fund any increase attributable to this Act in the sums payable into that Fund under any other enactment.

References   See para 1.30 ff.

187 Amendments and repeals

(1) The enactments mentioned in Schedule 21 to this Act shall have effect subject to the amendments there specified (being minor amendments and amendments consequential on the provisions of this Act).

(2) The enactments mentioned in Schedule 22 to this Act (which include some that are spent or no longer of practical utility) are hereby repealed to the extent specified in the third column of that Schedule.

References   See para 1.30 ff.

188 Short title, commencement and extent

(1) This Act may be cited as the Leasehold Reform, Housing and Urban Development Act 1993.

(2) This Act, except—

(a) this section;

(b) sections 126 and 127, 135 to 140, 149 to 151, 181(1), (2) and (4) and 186; and

(c) the repeal in section 80(1) of the Local Government and Housing Act 1989,

shall come into force on such day as the Secretary of State may by order made by statutory instrument appoint; and different days may be so appointed for different provisions or for different purposes.

(3) An order under subsection (2) may contain such transitional provisions and savings (whether or not involving the modification of any statutory provision) as appear to the Secretary of State necessary or expedient in connection with the provisions thereby brought into force by the order.

(4) The following, namely—
    (a) Part I of this Act;
    (b) Chapter I of Part II of this Act; and
    (c) subject to subsection (6), Part III of this Act,
extend to England and Wales only.

(5) Chapter II of Part II of this Act extends to Scotland only.

(6) In Part III of this Act—
    (a) sections 174, 179 and 180 also extend to Scotland; and
    (b) paragraph 8 of Schedule 17 also extends to Scotland and Northern Ireland.

(7) This Part, except this section, paragraph 3 of Schedule 21 and the repeals in the House of Commons Disqualification Act 1975 and the Northern Ireland Assembly Disqualification Act 1975, does not extend to Northern Ireland.

References   See paras 1.26–1.30 ff.

SCHEDULES

SCHEDULE 1   Section 9
CONDUCT OF PROCEEDINGS BY REVERSIONER ON BEHALF OF OTHER LANDLORDS

PART I
THE REVERSIONER

Freeholder to be reversioner

1 Subject to paragraphs 2 to 4, the reversioner in respect of any premises is the person who owns the freehold of those premises.

Replacement of freeholder by other relevant landlord

2 The court may, on the application of all the relevant landlords of any premises, appoint to be the reversioner in respect of those premises (in place of the person designated by paragraph 1) such person as may have been determined by agreement between them.

3 If it appears to the court, on the application of a relevant landlord of any premises—
    (a) that the respective interests of the relevant landlords of those premises, the absence or incapacity of the person referred to in paragraph 1 or other special circumstances require that some person other than the person there referred to should act as the reversioner in respect of the premises, or

(b)   that the person referred to in that paragraph is unwilling to act as the reversioner,
the court may appoint to be the reversioner in respect of those premises (in place of the
person designated by paragraph 1) such person as it thinks fit.

4 The court may also, on the application of any of the relevant landlords or of the
nominee purchaser, remove the reversioner in respect of any premises and appoint another
person in his place, if it appears to the court proper to do so by reason of any delay or default,
actual or apprehended, on the part of the reversioner.

5 A person appointed by the court under any of paragraphs 2 to 4—
  (a)   must be a relevant landlord; but
  (b)   may be so appointed on such terms and conditions as the court thinks fit.

PART II

CONDUCT OF PROCEEDINGS ON BEHALF OF OTHER LANDLORDS

Acts of reversioner binding on other landlords

6 (1) Without prejudice to the generality of section 9(3)—
  (a)   any notice given by or to the reversioner under this Chapter or section 74(3)
        following the giving of the initial notice shall be given or received by him on
        behalf of all the relevant landlords; and
  (b)   the reversioner may on behalf and in the name of all or (as the case may be) any
        of those landlords—
     (i)   deduce, evidence or verify the title to any property;
     (ii)   negotiate and agree with the nominee purchaser the terms of acquisition;
     (iii) execute any conveyance for the purpose of transferring an interest to the
            nominee purchaser;
     (iv)   receive the price payable for the acquisition of any interest;
     (v)   take or defend any legal proceedings under this Chapter in respect of
            matters arising out of the initial notice.

(2) Subject to paragraph 7—
  (a)   the reversioner's acts in relation to matters within the authority conferred on him
        by section 9(3), and
  (b)   any determination of the court or a leasehold valuation tribunal under this
        Chapter in proceedings between the reversioner and the nominee purchaser,
shall be binding on the other relevant landlords and on their interests in the specified premises
or any other property; but in the event of dispute the reversioner or any of the other relevant
landlords may apply to the court for directions as to the manner in which the reversioner
should act in the dispute.

(3) If any of the other relevant landlords cannot be found, or his identity cannot be
ascertained, the reversioner shall apply to the court for directions and the court may make
such order as it thinks proper with a view to giving effect to the rights of the participating
tenants and protecting the interests of other persons, but subject to any such directions—
  (a)   the reversioner shall proceed as in other cases;
  (b)   any conveyance executed by the reversioner on behalf of that relevant landlord
        which identifies the interest to be conveyed shall have the same effect as if
        executed in his name; and
  (c)   any sum paid as the price for the acquisition of that relevant landlord's interest,
        and any other sum payable to him by virtue of Schedule 6, shall be paid into
        court.

(4) The reversioner, if he acts in good faith and with reasonable care and diligence, shall
not be liable to any of the other relevant landlords for any loss or damage caused by any act
or omission in the exercise or intended exercise of the authority conferred on him by section
9(3).

Other landlords acting independently

7 (1) Notwithstanding anything in section 9(3) or paragraph 6, any of the other relevant landlords shall, at any time after the giving by the reversioner of a counter-notice under section 21 and on giving notice of his intention to do so to both the reversioner and the nominee purchaser, be entitled—

(a) to deal directly with the nominee purchaser in connection with any of the matters mentioned in sub-paragraphs (i) to (iii) of paragraph 6(1)(b) so far as relating to the acquisition of any interest of his;

(b) to be separately represented in any legal proceedings in which his title to any property comes in question, or in any legal proceedings relating to the terms of acquisition so far as relating to the acquisition of any interest of his.

(2) If the nominee purchaser so requires by notice given to the reversioner and any of the other relevant landlords, that landlord shall deal directly with the nominee purchaser for the purpose of deducing, evidencing or verifying the landlord's title to any property.

(3) Any of the other relevant landlords may by notice given to the reversioner require him to apply to a leasehold valuation tribunal for the determination by the tribunal of any of the terms of acquisition so far as relating to the acquisition of any interest of the landlord.

(4) Any of the other relevant landlords may also, on giving notice to the reversioner and the nominee purchaser, require that the price payable for the acquisition of his interest shall be paid by the nominee purchaser to him, or to a person authorised by him to receive it, instead of to the reversioner; but if, after being given proper notice of the time and method of completion with the nominee purchaser, either—

(a) he fails to notify the reversioner of the arrangements made with the nominee purchaser to receive payment, or

(b) having notified the reversioner of those arrangements, the arrangements are not duly implemented,

the reversioner shall be authorised to receive the payment for him, and the reversioner's written receipt for the amount payable shall be a complete discharge to the nominee purchaser.

Obligations of other landlords to reversioner

8 (1) It shall be the duty of each of the other relevant landlords—

(a) (subject to paragraph 7) to give the reversioner all such information and assistance as he may reasonably require; and

(b) after being given proper notice of the time and method of completion with the nominee purchaser, to ensure that all deeds and other documents that ought on his part to be delivered to the nominee purchaser on completion are available for the purpose, including in the case of registered land the land certificate and any other documents necessary to perfect the nominee purchaser's title;

and, if any of the other relevant landlords fails to comply with this sub-paragraph, that relevant landlord shall indemnify the reversioner against any liability incurred by the reversioner in consequence of the failure.

(2) Each of the other relevant landlords shall make such contribution as shall be just to the costs and expenses properly incurred by the reversioner in pursuance of section 9(3) which are not recoverable or not recovered from the nominee purchaser or any other person.

Applications made by other landlords under section 23(1)

9 The authority given to the reversioner by section 9(3) shall not extend to the bringing of proceedings under section 23(1) on behalf of any of the other relevant landlords, or preclude any of those landlords from bringing proceedings under that provision on his own behalf.

SCHEDULE 2   Sections 9 and 40
SPECIAL CATEGORIES OF LANDLORDS

Interpretation

1 (1) In this Schedule—

"Chapter I landlord" means a person who is, in relation to a claim made under Chapter I, the reversioner or any other relevant landlord within the meaning of that Chapter;

"Chapter II landlord" means a person who is, in relation to a claim made under Chapter II, the landlord within the meaning of that Chapter or any of the other landlords (as defined by section 40(4));

"debenture holders' charge" means a charge (whether a floating charge or not) in favour of the holders of a series of debentures issued by a company or other body of persons, or in favour of trustees for such debenture holders;

"mortgage" includes a charge or lien, and related expressions shall be construed accordingly;

"the relevant notice" means—

(a)   in relation to a Chapter I landlord, the notice given under section 13, and

(b)   in relation to a Chapter II landlord, the notice given under section 42.

(2) In paragraphs 5 to 8 any reference to a premium payable on the grant of lease includes a reference to any other amount payable by virtue of Schedule 13 in connection with its grant.

Mortgagee in possession of landlord's interest

2 (1) Where—

(a)   the interest of a Chapter I or Chapter II landlord is subject to mortgage, and

(b)   the mortgagee is in possession,

all such proceedings arising out of the relevant notice as would apart from this sub-paragraph be taken by or in relation to that landlord ("the mortgagor") shall, as regards his interest, be conducted by and through the mortgagee as if he were that landlord; but this sub-paragraph shall not, in its application to a Chapter I landlord, affect the operation in relation to the mortgagee of section 35 or Schedule 8.

(2) Where sub-paragraph (1) above applies to a Chapter I landlord, then (without prejudice to the generality of that sub-paragraph) any application under section 23(1) that would otherwise be made by the mortgagor (whether alone or together with any other person or persons) shall be made by the mortgagee as if he were the mortgagor.

(3) Where—

(a)   the interest of a Chapter I landlord is subject to a mortgage, and

(b)   a receiver appointed by the mortgagee or by order of any court is in receipt of the rents and profits,

the person referred to in paragraph (a) shall not make any application under section 23(1) without the consent of the mortgagee, and the mortgagee may by notice given to that person require that, as regards his interest, this paragraph shall apply, either generally or so far as it relates to section 23, as if the mortgagee were a mortgagee in possession.

(4) Where—

(a) the interest of a Chapter I or Chapter II landlord is subject to a mortgage, and

(b) the mortgagee is in possession or a receiver appointed by the mortgagee or by order of any court is in receipt of the rents and profits,

the relevant notice or a copy of it shall be regarded as duly given to that landlord if it is given to the mortgagee or to any such receiver; but whichever of the landlord, the mortgagee and any such receiver are not the recipient of the notice shall be given a copy of it by the recipient.

(5) Sub-paragraph (4) has effect in relation to a debenture holders' charge as if any reference to the mortgagee were a reference to the trustees for the debenture holders; but, where the relevant notice is given to a Chapter I or Chapter II landlord whose interest is subject to any such charge and there is no trustee for the debenture holders, the landlord shall forthwith send it or a copy of it to any receiver appointed by virtue of the charge.

(6) Where—

(a) a Chapter I or Chapter II landlord is given the relevant notice or a copy of it, and

(b) his interest is subject to a mortgage to secure the payment of money,

then (subject to sub-paragraph (7)), the landlord shall forthwith inform the mortgagee (unless the notice was given to him or a receiver appointed by virtue of the mortgage) that the notice has been given, and shall give him such further information as may from time to time be reasonably required from the landlord by the mortgagee.

(7) Sub-paragraph (6) does not apply to a debenture holders' charge.

Landlord's interest vested in custodian trustee

3 Where the interest of a Chapter I or Chapter II landlord is vested in a person as custodian trustee, then for the purposes of Chapter I or (as the case may be) Chapter II the interest shall be deemed to be vested in the managing trustees or committee of management as owners of that interest, except as regards the execution of any instrument disposing of or otherwise affecting that interest.

Landlord under a disability

4 Where a Chapter I or Chapter II landlord is incapable by reason of mental disorder (within the meaning of the Mental Health Act 1983) of managing and administering his property and affairs, then for the purposes of Chapter I or (as the case may be) Chapter II—

(a) the landlord's receiver appointed under Part VII of that Act or Part VIII of the Mental Health Act 1959, or

(b) (if no such receiver is acting for him) any person authorised in that behalf,

shall, under an order of the authority having jurisdiction under Part VII of the Mental Health Act 1983, take the place of the landlord.

Landlord's interest held on trust for sale

5 (1) Where the interest of a Chapter I landlord is held on trust for sale, any sum payable to the landlord by way of the price payable for the interest on its acquisition in pursuance of Chapter I shall be dealt with as if it were proceeds of sale arising under the trust.

(2) Where the interest of a Chapter II landlord is held on trust for sale—

(a) any sum payable to the landlord by way of a premium on the grant of a new lease under Chapter II or section 93(4) shall be dealt with as if it were proceeds of sale arising under the trust; and

(b) the purposes authorised—

(i) by section 73 of the Settled Land Act 1925, as applied by section 28 of the Law of Property Act 1925, for the application of capital money, and

(ii) by section 71 of the Settled Land Act 1925, as applied aforesaid, as purposes for which money may be raised by mortgage, shall include the payment of compensation by the landlord on the termination of a new lease granted under Chapter II or section 93(4) (whether the payment is made in pursuance of an order under section 61 or in pursuance of an agreement made in conformity with paragraph 5 of Schedule 14 without an application having been made under that section).

Landlord's interest subject to a settlement

6 Where the interest of a Chapter II landlord is subject to a settlement (within the meaning of the Settled Land Act 1925), the purposes authorised—
(a) by section 73 of that Act for the application of capital money, and
(b) by section 71 of that Act as purposes for which money may be raised by mortgage,
shall include the payment of compensation as mentioned in paragraph 5(2)(b) above.

University or college landlords

7 (1) Where a Chapter I landlord is a university or college to which the Universities and College Estates Act 1925 applies, any sum payable to the landlord by way of the price payable for any interest on its acquisition in pursuance of Chapter I shall be dealt with as if it were an amount payable by way of consideration on a sale effected under that Act.

(2) Where a Chapter II landlord is a university or college to which that Act applies—
(a) any sum payable to the landlord by way of a premium on the grant of a new lease under Chapter II or section 93(4) shall be dealt with as if it were an amount payable by way of consideration on a sale effected under that Act; and
(b) the purposes authorised—
   (i) by section 26 of that Act for the application of capital money, and
   (ii) by section 31 of that Act as purposes for which money may be raised by mortgage,
shall include the payment of compensation as mentioned in paragraph 5(2)(b) above.

Ecclesiastical landlords

8 (1) The provisions of this paragraph shall have effect as regards Chapter I or Chapter II landlords who are ecclesiastical landlords; and in this paragraph "ecclesiastical landlord" means—
(a) a capitular body within the meaning of the Cathedrals Measure 1963 having an interest as landlord in property, or
(b) a diocesan board of finance having an interest as landlord in property belonging to the board as diocesan glebe land.

(2) In relation to an interest of an ecclesiastical landlord, the consent of the Church Commissioners shall be required to sanction—
(a) the provisions to be contained in a conveyance in accordance with section 34 and Schedule 7, or in any lease granted under section 56, and the price or premium payable, except as regards matters determined by the court or a leasehold valuation tribunal;
(b) any exercise of the ecclesiastical landlord's rights under section 61, except as aforesaid, and any agreement for the payment of compensation to a tenant in conformity with paragraph 5 of Schedule 14 without an application having been made under that section; and
(c) any grant of a lease in pursuance of section 93(4);
and the Church Commissioners shall be entitled to appear and be heard in any proceedings under this Part to which an ecclesiastical landlord is a party or in which he is entitled to appear and be heard.

(3) Where a capitular body has an interest in property which forms part of the endowment of a cathedral church—

(a) any sum payable to that body by way of—
  (i) the price payable for any interest in the property on its acquisition in pursuance of Chapter I, or
  (ii) a premium on the grant of a new lease under Chapter II or section 93(4),
shall be treated as part of that endowment; and
  (b) the powers conferred by sections 21 and 23 of the Cathedrals Measure 1963 in relation to the investment in the acquisition of land of money forming part of the endowment of a cathedral church shall extend to the application of any such money in the payment of compensation as mentioned in paragraph 5(2)(b) above.

(4) In the case of a diocesan board of finance—
  (a) no consent or concurrence other than that of the Church Commissioners under sub-paragraph (2) above shall be required to a disposition under this Part of the interest of the diocesan board of finance in property (including a grant of a new lease in pursuance of section 93(4));
  (b) any sum payable to the diocesan board of finance by way of—
    (i) the price payable for any interest in property on its acquisition in pursuance of Chapter I, or
    (ii) a premium on the grant of a new lease of property under Chapter II or section 93(4),
shall be paid to the Church Commissioners to be applied for purposes for which the proceeds of any such disposition of property by agreement would be applicable under any enactment or Measure authorising such a disposition or disposing of the proceeds of such a disposition; and
  (c) any sum required for the payment of compensation as mentioned in paragraph 5(2)(b) above may be paid by the Church Commissioners on behalf of the diocesan board of finance out of any money held by them.

(5) In this paragraph "diocesan board of finance" and "diocesan glebe land" have the same meaning as in the Endowments and Glebe Measure 1976.

Definitions For "relevant landlord" and "the reversioner", see s 9; for "the landlord" (in relation to Chapter II), see s 40(1); for "interest", see s 101(1); for "lease" and related expressions (including "landlord"), see s 101(1), (2); for "Chapter I Landlord", "Chapter II landlord", "debenture holders' charge", "mortgage" and "the relevant notice", see para 1(1); for "the mortgagor", see para 2(1); for "ecclesiastical landlord" in para 8, see sub-para (1) thereof; for "diocesan board of finance" and "diocesan glebe land" in para 8 above, see sub-para (5) thereof.
References See paras 2.28–2.32, 2.52, 4.19, 4.20 ff.

SCHEDULE 3 Section 13
The Initial Notice: Supplementary Provisions

Part I
Restrictions on Participation by Individual Tenants, Effect of Claims on other Notices, Forfeitures etc

Prior notice by tenant terminating lease

1 A qualifying tenant of a flat shall not participate in the giving of a relevant notice of claim if the notice is given—
  (a) after the tenant has given notice terminating the lease of the flat (other than a notice that has been superseded by the grant, express or implied, of a new tenancy); or
  (b) during the subsistence of an agreement for the grant to the tenant of a future tenancy of the flat, where the agreement is one to which paragraph 17 of Schedule 10 to the Local Government and Housing Act 1989 applies.

Prior notice by landlord terminating lease

2 (1) A qualifying tenant of a flat shall not participate in the giving of a relevant notice of claim if the notice is given more than four months after a landlord's notice terminating the tenant's lease of the flat has been given under section 4 of the Landlord and Tenant Act 1954 or served under paragraph 4(1) of Schedule 10 to the Local Government and Housing Act 1989 (whether or not the notice has effect to terminate the lease).

(2) Where in the case of any qualifying tenant of a flat—
  (a) any such landlord's notice is given or served as mentioned in sub-paragraph (1), but
  (b) that notice was not given or served more than four months before the date when a relevant notice of claim is given,
the landlord's notice shall cease to have effect on that date.

(3) If—
  (a) any such landlord's notice ceases to have effect by virtue of sub-paragraph (2), but
  (b) the claim made in pursuance of the relevant notice of claim is not effective,
then sub-paragraph (4) shall apply to any landlord's notice terminating the tenant's lease of the flat which—
      (i) is given under section 4 of the Landlord and Tenant Act 1954 or served under paragraph 4(1) of Schedule 10 to the Local Government and Housing Act 1989, and
      (ii) is so given or served within one month after the expiry of the period of currency of that claim.

(4) Where this sub-paragraph applies to a landlord's notice, the earliest date which may be specified in the notice as the date of termination shall be—
  (a) in the case of a notice given under section 4 of that Act of 1954—
      (i) the date of termination specified in the previous notice, or
      (ii) the date of expiry of the period of three months beginning with the date of the giving of the new notice,
whichever is the later; or
  (b) in the case of a notice served under paragraph 4(1) of Schedule 10 to that Act of 1989—
      (i) the date of termination specified in the previous notice, or
      (ii) the date of expiry of the period of four months beginning with the date of service of the new notice,
whichever is the later.

(5) Where—
  (a) by virtue of sub-paragraph (4) a landlord's notice specifies as the date of termination of a lease a date earlier than six months after the date of the giving of the notice, and
  (b) the notice proposes a statutory tenancy,
section 7(2) of the Landlord and Tenant Act 1954 shall apply in relation to the notice with the substitution, for references to the period of two months ending with the date of termination specified in the notice and the beginning of that period, of references to the period of three months beginning with the date of the giving of the notice and the end of that period.

Orders for possession and pending proceedings for forfeiture etc

3 (1) A qualifying tenant of a flat shall not participate in the giving of a relevant notice of claim if at the time when it is given he is obliged to give up possession of his flat in pursuance of an order of a court or will be so obliged at a date specified in such an order.

(2) Except with the leave of the court, a qualifying tenant of a flat shall not participate in the giving of a relevant notice of claim at a time when any proceedings are pending to enforce a right of re-entry or forfeiture terminating his lease of the flat.

(3) Leave shall only be granted under sub-paragraph (2) if the court is satisfied that the tenant does not wish to participate in the giving of such a notice of claim solely or mainly for the purpose of avoiding the consequences of the breach of the terms of his lease in respect of which proceedings are pending.

(4) If—

    (a)   leave is so granted, and

    (b)   a relevant notice of claim is given,

the tenant's lease shall be deemed for the purposes of the claim to be a subsisting lease despite the existence of those proceedings and any order made afterwards in those proceedings; and, if the claim is effective, the court in which those proceedings were brought may set aside or vary any such order to such extent and on such terms as appear to that court to be appropriate.

Institution of compulsory purchase procedures

4 (1) A qualifying tenant of a flat shall not participate in the giving of a relevant notice of claim if on the date when the notice is given—

    (a)   any person or body of persons who has or have been, or could be, authorised to acquire the whole or part of the flat compulsorily for any purpose has or have, with a view to its acquisition for that purpose—

        (i)   served a notice to treat on that tenant, or

        (ii)   entered into a contract for the purchase of his interest in the whole or part of the flat; and

    (b)   the notice to treat or contract remains in force.

(2) Where—

    (a)   a relevant notice of claim is given, and

    (b)   during the currency of the claim any such person or body of persons as is mentioned in sub-paragraph (1)(a) serves or serve, in relation to the flat held by a participating tenant, notice to treat as mentioned in that provision,

the tenant shall cease to be entitled to participate in the making of the claim by virtue of being a qualifying tenant of the flat, and shall accordingly cease to be participating tenant in respect of the flat.

Notice terminating lease given by tenant or landlord during currency of claim

5 Where a relevant notice of claim is given, any notice terminating the lease of any flat held by a participating tenant, whether it is—

    (a)   a notice given by the tenant, or

    (b)   a landlord's notice given under section 4 of the Landlord and Tenant Act 1954 or served under paragraph 4(1) of Schedule 10 to the Local Government and Housing Act 1989,

shall be of no effect if it is given or served during the currency of the claim.

Initial notice operates to prevent termination of tenant's lease by other means

6 (1) Where a relevant notice of claim is given, then during the currency of the claim and for three months thereafter the lease of any flat held by a participating tenant shall not terminate—

    (a)   by effluxion of time, or

    (b)   in pursuance of a notice to quit given by the landlord, or

    (c)   by the termination of a superior lease;

but if the claim is not effective, and but for this sub-paragraph the lease would have so terminated before the end of those three months, the lease shall so terminate at the end of those three months.

(2) Sub-paragraph (1) shall not be taken to prevent an earlier termination of the lease in any manner not mentioned in that sub-paragraph, and shall not affect—

(a) the power under section 146(4) of the Law of Property Act 1925 (relief against forfeiture of leases) to grant a tenant relief against the termination of a superior lease, or

(b) any right of the tenant to relief under section 16(2) of the Landlord and Tenant Act 1954 (relief where landlord proceeding to enforce covenants) or under paragraph 9 of Schedule 5 to that Act (relief in proceedings brought by superior landlord).

(3) The reference in sub-paragraph (2) to section 16(2) of, and paragraph 9 of Schedule 5 to, the Landlord and Tenant Act 1954 includes a reference to those provisions as they apply in relation to Schedule 10 to the Local Government and Housing Act 1989.

Restriction on proceedings against participating tenant to enforce right of re-entry or forfeiture

7 (1) Where a relevant notice of claim is given, then during the currency of the claim—

(a) no proceedings to enforce any right of re-entry or forfeiture terminating the lease of any flat held by a participating tenant shall be brought in any court without the leave of that court; and

(b) leave shall only be granted if the court is satisfied that the tenant is participating in the making of the claim solely or mainly for the purpose of avoiding the consequences of the breach of the terms of his lease in respect of which proceedings are proposed to be brought.

(2) If leave is granted under sub-paragraph (1), the tenant shall cease to be entitled to participate in the making of the claim by virtue of being a qualifying tenant of the flat referred to in that sub-paragraph, and shall accordingly cease to be a participating tenant in respect of the flat.

Restrictions for purposes of s 14(3) on tenant electing to become participating tenant during currency of claim

8 (1) Where a relevant notice of claim is given, a qualifying tenant of a flat may not subsequently make an election under section 14(3)—

(a) if he was prohibited from participating in the giving of the notice by virtue of paragraph 1, 2(1), 3(1) or 4(1) above; or

(b) at a time when he would be so prohibited from participating in the giving of a relevant notice of claim, if such a notice were to be given then.

(2) Where a relevant notice of claim is given, then except with the leave of the court, a qualifying tenant of a flat may not subsequently make an election under section 14(3) at a time when any proceedings are pending to enforce a right of re-entry or forfeiture terminating his lease of the flat.

(3) Leave shall only be granted under sub-paragraph (2) if the court is satisfied that the tenant does not wish to make such an election solely or mainly for the purpose of avoiding the consequences of the breach of the terms of his lease in respect of which proceedings are pending.

(4) If—

(a) leave is so granted, and

(b) the tenant makes such an election,

the tenant's lease shall be deemed for the purposes of the claim to be a subsisting lease despite the existence of those proceedings and any order made afterwards in those proceedings; and, if the claim is effective, the court in which those proceedings were brought may set aside or vary any such order to such extent and on such terms as appear to that court to be appropriate.

(5) References in this paragraph and paragraph 9 below to making an election under section 14(3) are references to making such an election to participate in the making of the claim in respect of which the relevant notice of claim is given.

Effect of tenant's election on certain notices given by landlord

9 (1) This paragraph applies to a qualifying tenant of a flat who, following the giving of a relevant notice of claim, makes an election under section 14(3).

(2) Where in the case of any such tenant—

    (a) a landlord's notice terminating the tenant's lease of the flat has been given or served as mentioned in paragraph 2(1) above (whether or not the notice has effect to terminate the lease), but

    (b) that notice was not given or served more than four months before the date when the tenant makes his election under section 14(3),

the landlord's notice shall cease to have effect on that date.

(3) If—

    (a) any such landlord's notice ceases to have effect by virtue of sub-paragraph (2) above, but

    (b) the claim made in pursuance of the relevant notice of claim is not effective,

then paragraph 2(4) above shall apply to any landlord's notice terminating the tenant's lease of the flat which—

        (i) is given under section 4 of the Landlord and Tenant Act 1954 or served under paragraph 4(1) of Schedule 10 to the Local Government and Housing Act 1989, and

        (ii) is so given or served within one month after the expiry of the period of currency of that claim;

and paragraph 2(5) above shall apply accordingly.

(4) Paragraph 8(5) above applies for the purposes of this paragraph.

Interpretation

10 (1) For the purposes of this Part of this Schedule—

    (a) "relevant notice of claim", in relation to any flat, means a notice under section 13 in the case of which the specified premises contain that flat, and references to participating in the giving of such a notice are references to being one of the persons by whom the notice is given;

    (b) references to a notice under section 13 include, in so far as the context permits, references to a notice purporting to be given under that section (whether by persons who are qualifying tenants or not);

    (c) references to a claim being effective are references to a binding contract being entered into for the acquisition of the freehold and other interests falling to be acquired in pursuance of the claim or to the making of an order under section 24(4)(a) or (b) or 25(6)(a) or (b) which provides for the vesting of those interests; and

    (d) references to the currency of a claim are—

        (i) where the claim is made by a valid notice under section 13, references to the period during which the notice continues in force in accordance with subsection (11) of that section, or

        (ii) where the claim is made by a notice which is not a valid notice under section 13, references to the period beginning with the giving of the notice and ending with the time when the notice is set aside by the court or is withdrawn or when it would (if valid) cease to have effect or be deemed to have been withdrawn.

(2) For the purposes of sub-paragraph (1)(d) the date when a notice is set aside, or would (if valid) cease to have effect, in consequence of an order of a court shall be taken to be the date when the order becomes final.

PART II
PROCEDURE FOR GIVING COPIES TO RELEVANT LANDLORDS

Application of Part II

11 This Part of this Schedule has effect where a notice under section 13 is given in a case to which section 9(2) applies.

Qualifying tenants to give copies of initial notice

12 (1) The qualifying tenants by whom the initial notice is given shall, in addition to giving the initial notice to the reversioner in respect of the specified premises, give a copy of the notice to every other person known or believed by them to be a relevant landlord of those premises.

(2) The initial notice shall state whether copies are being given in accordance with sub-paragraph (1) to anyone other than the recipient and, if so, to whom.

Recipient of notice or copy to give further copies

13 (1) Subject to sub-paragraph (2), a recipient of the initial notice or of a copy of it (including a person receiving a copy under this sub-paragraph) shall forthwith give a copy to any person who—
   (a) is known or believed by him to be a relevant landlord, and
   (b) is not stated in the recipient's copy of the notice, or known by him, to have received a copy.

(2) Sub-paragraph (1) does not apply where the recipient is neither the reversioner nor another relevant landlord.

(3) Where a person gives any copies of the initial notice in accordance with sub-paragraph (1), he shall—
   (a) supplement the statement under paragraph 12(2) by adding any further persons to whom he is giving copies or who are known to him to have received one; and
   (b) notify the qualifying tenants by whom the initial notice is given of the persons added by him to that statement.

Consequences of failure to comply with paragraph 12 or 13

14 (1) Where—
   (a) a relevant landlord of the specified premises does not receive a copy of the initial notice before the end of the period specified in it in pursuance of section 13(3)(g), but
   (b) he was given a notice under section 11 by any of the qualifying tenants by whom the initial notice was given and, in response to the notice under that section, notified the tenant in question of his interest in the specified premises,
the initial notice shall cease to have effect at the end of that period.

(2) Where—
   (a) sub-paragraph (1) does not apply, but
   (b) any person fails without reasonable cause to comply with paragraph 12 or 13 above, or is guilty of any unreasonable delay in complying with either of those paragraphs,
he shall be liable for any loss thereby occasioned to the qualifying tenants by whom the initial notice was given or to the reversioner or any other relevant landlord.

PART III
OTHER PROVISIONS

Inaccuracies or misdescription in initial notice

15 (1) The initial notice shall not be invalidated by any inaccuracy in any of the particulars required by section 13(3) or by any misdescription of any of the property to which the claim extends.

(2) Where the initial notice—

    (a) specifies any property or interest which was not liable to acquisition under or by virtue of section 1 or 2, or

    (b) fails to specify any property or interest which is so liable to acquisition,

the notice may, with the leave of the court and on such terms as the court may think fit, be amended so as to exclude or include the property or interest in question.

(3) Where the initial notice is so amended as to exclude any property or interest, references to the property or interests specified in the notice under any provision of section 13(3) shall be construed accordingly; and, where it is so amended as to include any property or interest, the property or interest shall be treated as if it had been specified under the provision of that section under which it would have fallen to be specified if its acquisition had been proposed at the relevant date.

Effect on initial notice of tenant's lack of qualification to participate

16 (1) It is hereby declared that, where at the relevant date any of the persons by whom the initial notice is given—

    (a) is not a qualifying tenant of a flat contained in the specified premises, or

    (b) is such a qualifying tenant but is prohibited from participating in the giving of the notice by virtue of Part I of this Schedule, or

    (c) (if it is claimed in the notice that he satisfies the residence condition) does not satisfy that condition,

the notice shall not be invalidated on that account, so long as the notice was in fact properly given by a sufficient number of qualifying tenants of flats contained in the premises as at the relevant date, and not less than one-half of the qualifying tenants by whom it was so given then satisfied the residence condition.

(2) For the purposes of sub-paragraph (1) a sufficient number is a number which—

    (a) is not less than two-thirds of the total number of qualifying tenants of flats contained in the specified premises as at the relevant date, and

    (b) is not less than one-half of the total number of flats so contained.

Definitions   For "the relevant date", see s 1(8); for "qualifying tenant", see s 5; for "relevant landlord" and "the reversioner", see s 9; for "the initial notice", see s 13; for "the specified premises", see s 13(12); for "participating tenants", see s 14; for "the court" and "flat", see s 101(1); for "lease" and related expressions (including "landlord" and "tenant"), see s 101(1), (2); as to "an election under section 12(3)" in paras 8, 9, see para 8(5); for "relevant notice of claim", see para 10(1)(a); and as to references to "a notice under section 11", "a claim being effective" and "the currency of a claim", see para 10(1)(b)–(d) above.
References   See paras 3.13, 3.14, 3.20–3.26 ff.

SCHEDULE 4   Section 21

INFORMATION TO BE FURNISHED BY REVERSIONER ABOUT EXERCISE OF
RIGHTS UNDER CHAPTER II

Information to accompany counter-notice

1 (1) This paragraph applies where before the date of the giving of a counter-notice under section 21 the reversioner or any other relevant landlord—

    (a) has received—

        (i) a notice given under section 42 with respect to any flat contained in the specified premises (being a notice to which section 54(1) or (2) applies on that date), or

        (ii) a copy of such a notice, or

    (b) has given any counter-notice under section 45 in response to any such notice.

(2) A copy of every notice which, or a copy of which, has been received as mentioned in sub-paragraph (1)(a), and a copy of every counter-notice which has been given as mentioned in sub-paragraph (1)(b), shall either—

   (a)   accompany any counter-notice given under section 21, or

   (b)   be given to the nominee purchaser by the reversioner as soon as possible after the date of the giving of any such counter-notice.

Continuing duty to furnish information

2 (1) Subject to sub-paragraph (3), this paragraph applies where on or after the date of the giving of a counter-notice under section 21 the reversioner or any other relevant landlord receives—

   (a)   a notice given under section 42 with respect to any flat contained in the specified premises or a copy of such a notice, or

   (b)   any notice of withdrawal given under section 52 and relating to any notice under section 42 of which a copy has already been furnished to the nominee purchaser under this Schedule.

(2) A copy of every notice which, or a copy of which, is received as mentioned in sub-paragraph (1)(a) or (b) shall be given to the nominee purchaser by the reversioner as soon as possible after the time when the notice or copy is received by the reversioner or (as the case may be) the other relevant landlord.

(3) This paragraph does not apply if the notice or copy is received by the reversioner or (as the case may be) the other relevant landlord otherwise than at a time when—

   (a)   the initial notice continues in force, or

   (b)   a binding contract entered into in pursuance of that notice remains in force, or

   (c)   where an order has been made under section 24(4)(a) or (b) or 25(6)(a) or (b) with respect to the specified premises, any interests which by virtue of the order fall to be vested in the nominee purchaser have yet to be so vested.

Duty of other landlords to furnish copies to reversioner

3 (1) Without prejudice to the generality of paragraph 8(1)(a) of Schedule 1, the duty imposed by that provision shall extend to requiring any relevant landlord (other than the reversioner) who—

   (a)   receives a relevant notice or a copy of such a notice, or

   (b)   gives a relevant counter-notice,

to furnish a copy of the notice or counter-notice to the reversioner as soon as possible after the time when the notice or copy is received or (as the case may be) the counter-notice is given by the relevant landlord.

(2) In this paragraph "relevant notice" and "relevant counter-notice" mean respectively any notice of which a copy is required to be given to the nominee purchaser by the reversioner in accordance with this Schedule and any counter-notice of which a copy is required to be so given.

Definitions   For "relevant landlord" and "the reversioner", see s 9; for "the initial notice", see s 13; for "the specified premises", see s 13(12); for "the nominee purchaser", see s 15; for "flat", see s 101(1).
References   See para 3.34 ff.

SCHEDULE 5
VESTING ORDERS UNDER SECTIONS 24 AND 25

Sections 24 and 25

Interpretation

(1) In this Schedule "a vesting order" means an order made by the court under section 24(4)(a) or (b) or section 25(6)(a) or (b)

(2) In this Schedule "the relevant terms of acquisition", in relation to any such order, means the terms of acquisition referred to in section 24(4)(a) or (b) or section 25(6)(a) or (b), as the case may be.

Execution of conveyance

2 (1) Where any interests are to be vested in the nominee purchaser by virtue of a vesting order, then on his paying into court the appropriate sum in respect of each of those interests there shall be executed by such person as the court may designate a conveyance which—

(a) is in a form approved by a leasehold valuation tribunal, and

(b) contains such provisions as may be so approved for the purpose of giving effect to the relevant terms of acquisition.

(2) The conveyance shall be effective to vest in the nominee purchaser the interests expressed to be conveyed, subject to and in accordance with the terms of the conveyance.

The appropriate sum

3 (1) In the case of any vesting order, the appropriate sum which in accordance with paragraph 2(1) is to be paid into court in respect of any interest is the aggregate of—

(a) such amount as is fixed by the relevant terms of acquisition as the price which is payable in accordance with Schedule 6 in respect of that interest; and

(b) any amounts or estimated amounts determined by a leasehold valuation tribunal as being, at the time of execution of the conveyance, due to the transferor from any tenants of his of premises comprised in the premises in which that interest subsists (whether due under or in respect of their leases or under or in respect of agreements collateral thereto).

(2) In this paragraph "the transferor", in relation to any interest, means the person from whom the interest is to be acquired by the nominee purchaser.

Effect of payment of appropriate sum into court

4 Where any interest is vested in the nominee purchaser in accordance with this Schedule, the payment into court of the appropriate sum in respect of that interest shall be taken to have satisfied any claims against the nominee purchaser or the participating tenants, or the personal representatives or assigns of any of them, in respect of the price payable under this Chapter for the acquisition of that interest.

Supplemental

5 (1) In the provisions specified in sub-paragraph (2) references to a binding contract being entered into in pursuance of the initial notice shall be read as including references to the making of a vesting order.

(2) Those provisions are—

(a) section 14(11);

(b) section 15(12) (except so far as it provides for the interpretation of references to the nominee purchaser);

(c) section 16(10);

(d) section 19(5)(b);

(e) section 28(1);

(f) section 30(4); and

(g) section 31(4).

(3) Where, at any time after a vesting order is made but before the interests falling to be vested in the nominee purchaser by virtue of the order have been so vested, any acquiring authority (within the meaning of section 30) serves notice to treat as mentioned in subsection (1)(a) of that section, the vesting order shall cease to have effect.

(4) Where sub-paragraph (3) applies to any vesting order, then on the occasion of the compulsory acquisition in question the compensation payable in respect of any interest in the

specified premises (whether or not the one to which the notice to treat relates) shall be determined on the basis of the value of the interest subject to and with the benefit of the rights and obligations arising from the initial notice and affecting the interest.

(5) In section 38(2) (except so far as it provides for the interpretation of references to the proposed acquisition by the nominee purchaser) the reference to a contract entered into in pursuance of the initial notice shall be read as including a reference to a vesting order.

Definitions   For "the initial notice", see s 13; for "the participating tenants", see s 14; for "the nominee purchaser", see s 15; for "conveyance", see s 38(1); for "the court" and "interest", see s 101(1); for "lease" and related expressions (including "tenant"), see s 101(1), (2); for "a vesting order" and "the relevant terms of acquisition", see para 1 above.
References   See para 3.52 ff.

SCHEDULE 6   Section 32
PURCHASE PRICE PAYABLE BY NOMINEE PURCHASER

PART I
GENERAL

Interpretation and operation of Schedule

1 (1) In this Schedule—
  "the freeholder" means the person who owns the freehold of the specified premises;
  "intermediate leasehold interest" means the interest of the tenant under a lease which is
    superior to the lease held by a qualifying tenant of a flat contained in the specified
    premises, to the extent that—
      (a) any such interest is to be acquired by the nominee purchaser by virtue of
          section 2(1)(a), and
      (b) it is an interest in the specified premises;
  "the valuation date" means the date when the interest in the specified premises
    which is to be acquired by the nominee purchaser from the freeholder is
    determined either by agreement or by a leasehold valuation tribunal under this
    Chapter.

(2) Parts II to IV of this Schedule have effect subject to the provisions of Parts V and VI (which relate to interests with negative values).

PART II
FREEHOLD OF SPECIFIED PREMISES

Price payable for freehold of specified premises

2 (1) Subject to the provisions of this paragraph, the price payable by the nominee purchaser for the freehold of the specified premises shall be the aggregate of—
  (a) the value of the freeholder's interest in the premises as determined in accordance
      with paragraph 3,
  (b) the freeholder's share of the marriage value as determined in accordance with
      paragraph 4, and
  (c) any amount of compensation payable to the freeholder under paragraph 5.

(2) Where the amount arrived at in accordance with sub-paragraph (1) is a negative amount, the price payable by the nominee purchaser for the freehold shall be nil.

Value of freeholder's interest

3 (1) Subject to the provisions of this paragraph, the value of the freeholder's interest in the specified premises is the amount which at the valuation date that interest might be expected to realise if sold on the open market by a willing seller (with neither the nominee purchaser nor any participating tenant buying or seeking to buy) on the following assumptions—

    (a) on the assumption that the vendor is selling for an estate in fee simple—

        (i) subject to any leases subject to which the freeholder's interest in the premises is to be acquired by the nominee purchaser, but

        (ii) subject also to any intermediate or other leasehold interests in the premises which are to be acquired by the nominee purchaser;

    (b) on the assumption that this Chapter and Chapter II confer no right to acquire any interest in the specified premises or to acquire any new lease (except that this shall not preclude the taking into account of a notice given under section 42 with respect to a flat contained in the specified premises where it is given by a person other than a participating tenant);

    (c) on the assumption that any increase in the value of any flat held by a participating tenant which is attributable to an improvement carried out at his own expense by the tenant or by any predecessor in title is to be disregarded; and

    (d) on the assumption that (subject to paragraphs (a) and (b)) the vendor is selling with and subject to the rights and burdens with and subject to which the conveyance to the nominee purchaser of the freeholder's interest is to be made, and in particular with and subject to such permanent or extended rights and burdens as are to be created in order to give effect to Schedule 7.

(2) It is hereby declared that the fact that sub-paragraph (1) requires assumptions to be made as to the matters specified in paragraphs (a) to (d) of that sub-paragraph does not preclude the making of assumptions as to other matters where those assumptions are appropriate for determining the amount which at the valuation date the freeholder's interest in the specified premises might be expected to realise if sold as mentioned in that sub-paragraph.

(3) In determining that amount there shall be made such deduction (if any) in respect of any defect in title as on a sale of the interest on the open market might be expected to be allowed between a willing seller and a willing buyer.

(4) Where a lease of any flat or other unit contained in the specified premises is to be granted to the freeholder in accordance with section 36 and Schedule 9, the value of his interest in those premises at the valuation date so far as relating to that flat or other unit shall be taken to be the difference as at that date between—

    (a) the value of his freehold interest in it, and

    (b) the value of his interest in it under that lease, assuming it to have been granted to him at that date;

and each of those values shall, so far as is appropriate, be determined in like manner as the value of the freeholder's interest in the whole of the specified premises is determined for the purposes of paragraph 2(1)(a).

(5) The value of the freeholder's interest in the specified premises shall not be increased by reason of—

    (a) any transaction which—

        (i) is entered into on or after the date of the passing of this Act (otherwise than in pursuance of a contract entered into before that date), and

        (ii) involves the creation or transfer of an interest superior to (whether or not preceding) any interest held by a qualifying tenant of a flat contained in the specified premises; or

    (b) any alteration on or after that date of the terms on which any such superior interest is held.

(6) Sub-paragraph (5) shall not have the effect of preventing an increase in value of the freeholder's interest in the specified premises in a case where the increase is

attributable to any such leasehold interest with a negative value as is mentioned in paragraph 14(2).

Freeholder's share of marriage value

4 (1) The marriage value is the amount referred to in sub-paragraph (2), and the freeholder's share of the marriage value is—

    (a)   such proportion of that amount as is determined by agreement between the reversioner and the nominee purchaser or, in default of agreement, as is determined by a leasehold valuation tribunal to be the proportion which in its opinion would have been determined by an agreement made at the valuation date between the parties on a sale on the open market by a willing seller, or

    (b)   50 per cent of that amount,

whichever is the greater.

(2) The marriage value is any increase in the aggregate value of the freehold and every intermediate leasehold interest in the specified premises, when regarded as being (in consequence of their being acquired by the nominee purchaser) interests under the control of the participating tenants, as compared with the aggregate value of those interests when held by the persons from whom they are to be so acquired, being an increase in value—

    (a)   which is attributable to the potential ability of the participating tenants, once those interests have been so acquired, to have new leases granted to them without payment of any premium and without restriction as to length of term, and

    (b)   which, if those interests were being sold to the nominee purchaser on the open market by willing sellers, the nominee purchaser would have to agree to share with the sellers in order to reach agreement as to price.

(3) For the purposes of sub-paragraph (2) the value of the freehold or any intermediate leasehold interest in the specified premises when held by the person from whom it is to be acquired by the nominee purchaser and its value when acquired by the nominee purchaser—

    (a)   shall be determined on the same basis as the value of the interest is determined for the purposes of paragraph 2(1)(a) or (as the case may be) paragraph 6(1)(b)(i); and

    (b)   shall be so determined as at the valuation date.

(4) Accordingly, in so determining the value of an interest when acquired by the nominee purchaser—

    (a)   the same assumptions shall be made under paragraph 3(1) (or, as the case may be, under paragraph 3(1) as applied by paragraph 7(1)) as are to be made under that provision in determining the value of the interest when held by the person from whom it is to be acquired by the nominee purchaser; and

    (b)   any merger or other circumstances affecting the interest on its acquisition by the nominee purchaser shall be disregarded.

Compensation for loss resulting from enfranchisement

5 (1) Where the freeholder will suffer any loss or damage to which this paragraph applies, there shall be payable to him such amount as is reasonable to compensate him for that loss or damage.

(2) This paragraph applies to—

    (a)   any diminution in value of any interest of the freeholder in other property resulting from the acquisition of his interest in the specified premises; and

    (b)   any other loss or damage which results therefrom to the extent that it is referable to his ownership of any interest in other property.

(3) Without prejudice to the generality of paragraph (b) of sub-paragraph (2), the kinds of loss falling within that paragraph include loss of development value in relation to the specified premises to the extent that it is referable as mentioned in that paragraph.

(4) In sub-paragraph (3) "development value", in relation to the specified premises, means any increase in the value of the freeholder's interest in the premises which is

attributable to the possibility of demolishing, reconstructing or carrying out substantial works of construction on, the whole or a substantial part of the premises.

(5) Where the freeholder will suffer loss or damage to which this paragraph applies, then in determining the amount of compensation payable to him under this paragraph, it shall not be material that—

(a) the loss or damage could to any extent be avoided or reduced by the grant to him, in accordance with section 36 and Schedule 9, of a lease granted in pursuance of Part III of that Schedule, and

(b) he is not requiring the nominee purchaser to grant any such lease.

Part III
Intermediate Leasehold Interests
Price payable for intermediate leasehold interests

6 (1) Where the nominee purchaser is to acquire one or more intermediate leasehold interests—

(a) a separate price shall be payable for each of those interests, and

(b) (subject to the provisions of this paragraph) that price shall be the aggregate of—

(i) the value of the interest as determined in accordance with paragraph 7, and

(ii) any amount of compensation payable to the owner of that interest in accordance with paragraph 8.

(2) Where in the case of any intermediate leasehold interest the amount arrived at in accordance with sub-paragraph (1)(b) is a negative amount, the price payable by the nominee purchaser for the interest shall be nil.

Value of intermediate leasehold interests

7 (1) Subject to sub-paragraph (2), paragraph 3 shall apply for determining the value of any intermediate leasehold interest for the purposes of paragraph 6(1)(b)(i) with such modifications as are appropriate to relate that paragraph to a sale of the interest in question subject (where applicable) to any leases intermediate between that interest and any lease held by a qualifying tenant of a flat contained in the specified premises.

(2) The value of an intermediate leasehold interest which is the interest of the tenant under a minor intermediate lease shall be calculated by applying the formula set out in sub-paragraph (7) instead of in accordance with subparagraph (1).

(3) "A minor intermediate lease" means a lease complying with the following requirements, namely—

(a) it must have an expectation of possession of not more than one month, and

(b) the profit rent in respect of the lease must be not more than £5 per year;

and, in the case of a lease which is in immediate reversion on two or more leases, those requirements must be complied with in connection with each of the sub-leases.

(4) Where a minor intermediate lease is in immediate reversion on two or more leases—

(a) the formula set out in sub-paragraph (7) shall be applied in relation to each of those sub-leases (and sub-paragraphs (5) and (6) shall also so apply); and

(b) the value of the interest of the tenant under the minor intermediate lease shall accordingly be the aggregate of the amounts calculated by so applying the formula.

(5) "Profit rent" means an amount equal to that of the rent payable under the lease on which the minor intermediate lease is in immediate reversion, less that of the rent payable under the minor intermediate lease.

(6) Where the minor intermediate lease or that on which it is in immediate reversion comprises property other than a flat held by a qualifying tenant, then in sub-paragraph (5)

the reference to the rent payable under it means so much of that rent as is apportioned to any such flat.

(7) The formula is—

$$P = \pounds \frac{R}{Y} - \frac{R}{Y(1 + Y)^n}$$

where—

P = the price payable;
R = the profit rent;
Y = the yield (expressed as a decimal fraction) from 2½ per cent Consolidated Stock;
n = the period, expressed in years (taking any part of a year as a whole year), of the remainder of the term of the minor intermediate lease as at the valuation date.

(8) In calculating the yield from 2½ per cent Consolidated Stock, the price of that stock shall be taken to be the middle market price at the close of business on the last trading day in the week before the valuation date.

(9) For the purposes of this paragraph the expectation of possession carried by a lease in relation to a lease ("the sub-lease") on which it is in immediate reversion is the expectation of possession which it carries at the valuation date after the sub-lease, on the basis that—

(a) (subject to sub-paragraph (10)) where the sub-lease is a lease held by a qualifying tenant of a flat contained in the specified premises, it terminates at the valuation date if its term date fell before then, or else it terminates on its term date; and

(b) in any other case, the sub-lease terminates on its term date.

(10) In a case where before the relevant date for the purposes of this Chapter the landlord of any such qualifying tenant as is mentioned in sub-paragraph (9)(a) had given notice to quit terminating the tenant's sub-lease on a date earlier than that date, the date specified in the notice to quit shall be substituted for the date specified in that provision.

Compensation for loss on acquisition of interest

8 Sub-paragraphs (1) to (4) of paragraph 5 shall apply in relation to the owner of any intermediate leasehold interest as they apply in relation to the freeholder.

Owners of intermediate interests entitled to part of marriage value

9 (1) This paragraph applies where—

(a) the price payable for the freehold of the specified premises includes an amount in respect of the freeholder's share of the marriage value, and

(b) the nominee purchaser is to acquire any intermediate leasehold interests.

(2) The amount payable to the freeholder in respect of his share of the marriage value shall be divided between the freeholder and the owners of the intermediate leasehold interests in proportion to the value of their respective interests in the specified premises (as determined for the purposes of paragraph 2(1)(a) or paragraph 6(1)(b)(i), as the case may be).

(3) Where the owner of an intermediate leasehold interest is entitled in accordance with sub-paragraph (2) to any part of the amount payable to the freeholder in respect of the freeholder's share of the marriage value, the amount to which he is so entitled shall be payable to him by the freeholder.

PART IV
OTHER INTERESTS TO BE ACQUIRED

Price payable for other interests

10 (1) Where the nominee purchaser is to acquire any freehold interest in pursuance of section 1(2)(a) or (4) or section 21(4), then (subject to sub-paragraph (3) below) the price payable for that interest shall be the aggregate of—

    (a)   the value of the interest as determined in accordance with paragraph 11,

    (b)   any share of the marriage value to which the owner of the interest is entitled under paragraph 12, and

    (c)   any amount of compensation payable to the owner of the interest in accordance with paragraph 13.

(2) Where the nominee purchaser is to acquire any leasehold interest by virtue of section 2(1) other than an intermediate leasehold interest, or he is to acquire any leasehold interest in pursuance of section 21(4), then (subject to sub-paragraph (3) below) the price payable for that interest shall be the aggregate of—

    (a)   the value of the interest as determined in accordance with paragraph 11, and

    (b)   any amount of compensation payable to the owner of the interest in accordance with paragraph 13.

(3) Where in the case of any interest the amount arrived at in accordance with sub-paragraph (1) or (2) is a negative amount, the price payable by the nominee purchaser for the interest shall be nil.

Value of other interests

11 (1) In the case of any such freehold interest as is mentioned in paragraph 10(1), paragraph 3 shall apply for determining the value of the interest with such modifications as are appropriate to relate it to a sale of the interest subject (where applicable) to any leases intermediate between that interest and any lease held by a qualifying tenant of a flat contained in the specified premises.

(2) In the case of any such leasehold interest as is mentioned in paragraph 10(2), then—

    (a)   (unless paragraph (b) below applies) paragraph 3 shall apply as mentioned in sub-paragraph (1) above;

    (b)   if it is the interest of the tenant under a minor intermediate lease within the meaning of paragraph 7, sub-paragraphs (2) to (10) of that paragraph shall apply with such modifications as are appropriate for determining the value of the interest.

(3) In its application in accordance with sub-paragraph (1) or (2) above, paragraph 3(6) shall have effect as if the reference to paragraph 14(2) were a reference to paragraph 18(2).

Marriage value

12 (1) Where any such freehold interest as is mentioned in paragraph 10(1) is an interest in any such property as is mentioned in section 1(3)(a)—

    (a)   sub-paragraphs (2) to (4) of paragraph 4 shall apply with such modifications as are appropriate for determining the marriage value in connection with the acquisition by the nominee purchaser of that interest; and

    (b)   sub-paragraph (1) of that paragraph shall apply with such modifications as are appropriate for determining the share of the marriage value to which the owner of that interest is entitled.

(2) Where—

    (a)   the owner of any such freehold interest is entitled to any share of the marriage value in respect of any such property, and

    (b)   the nominee purchaser is to acquire any leasehold interests in that property superior to any lease held by a participating tenant,

the amount payable to the owner of the freehold interest in respect of his share of the marriage value in respect of that property shall be divided between the owner of that interest and the owners of the leasehold interests in proportion to the value of their respective interests in that property (as determined for the purposes of paragraph 10(1) or (2), as the case may be).

(3) Where the owner of any such leasehold interest ("the intermediate landlord") is entitled in accordance with sub-paragraph (2) to any part of the amount payable to the

owner of any freehold interest in respect of his share of the marriage value in respect of any property, the amount to which the intermediate landlord is so entitled shall be payable to him by the owner of that freehold interest.

Compensation for loss on acquisition of interest

13 Sub-paragraphs (1) to (4) of paragraph 5 shall apply in relation to the owner of any such freehold or leasehold interest as is mentioned in paragraph 10(1) or (2) and to the acquisition of that interest as they apply in relation to the freeholder and to the acquisition of his interest in the specified premises (and accordingly any reference in those provisions of paragraph 5 to the specified premises shall be read for this purpose as a reference to the property in which any such freehold or leasehold interest subsists).

PART V

VALUATION ETC OF INTERESTS IN SPECIFIED PREMISES WITH NEGATIVE VALUES

Valuation of freehold and intermediate leasehold interests

14 (1) Where—
  (a) the value of the freeholder's interest in the specified premises (as determined in accordance with paragraph 3), or
  (b) the value of any intermediate leasehold interest (as determined in accordance with paragraph 7),
is a negative amount, the value of the interest for the relevant purposes shall be nil.

(2) Where sub-paragraph (1) applies to any intermediate leasehold interest whose value is a negative amount ("the negative interest"), then for the relevant purposes any interests in the specified premises superior to the negative interest and having a positive value shall be reduced in value—
  (a) beginning with the interest which is immediately superior to the negative interest and continuing (if necessary) with any such other superior interests in order of proximity to the negative interest;
  (b) until the aggregate amount of the reduction is equal to the negative amount in question; and
  (c) without reducing the value of any interest to less than nil.

(3) In a case where sub-paragraph (1) applies to two or more intermediate leasehold interests whose values are negative amounts, sub-paragraph (2) shall apply separately in relation to each of those interests—
  (a) beginning with the interest which is inferior to every other of those interests and then in order of proximity to that interest; and
  (b) with any reduction in the value of any interest for the relevant purposes by virtue of any prior application of sub-paragraph (2) being taken into account.

(4) For the purposes of sub-paragraph (2) an interest has a positive value if (apart from that sub-paragraph) its value for the relevant purposes is a positive amount.

(5) In this Part of this Schedule "the relevant purposes"—
  (a) as respects the freeholder's interest in the specified premises, means the purposes of paragraph 2(l)(a); and
  (b) as respects any intermediate leasehold interest, means the purposes of paragraph 6(1)(b)(i).

Calculation of marriage value

15 (1) Where (as determined in accordance with paragraph 4(3) and (4)) the value of any interest—
  (a) when held by the person from whom it is to be acquired by the nominee purchaser, or

(b)   when acquired by the nominee purchaser,

is a negative amount, then for the purposes of paragraph 4(2) the value of the interest when so held or acquired shall be nil.

(2) Where sub-paragraph (1) above applies to any intermediate leasehold interest whose value when held or acquired as mentioned in paragraph (a) or (b) of that sub-paragraph is a negative amount, paragraph 14(2) to (4) shall apply for determining for the purposes of paragraph 4(2) the value when so held or acquired of other interests in the specified premises, as if—

> (a)   any reference to paragraph 14(1) were a reference to sub-paragraph (1) above; and
>
> (b)   any reference to the relevant purposes were, as respects any interest, a reference to the purposes of paragraph 4(2) as it applies to the interest when so held or acquired.

(3) References in paragraph 16 or 17 to paragraph 14(2) or (3) do not extend to that provision as it applies in accordance with sub-paragraph (2) above.

Apportionment of marriage value

16 (1) Where paragraph 14(1) applies to an interest, the value of the interest for the purposes of paragraph 9(2) shall be nil, unless sub-paragraph (2) below applies.

(2) In a case where paragraph 14(1) applies to the freeholder's interest in the specified premises and to every intermediate leasehold interest—

> (a)   sub-paragraph (1) above shall not apply for the purposes of paragraph 9(2); and
>
> (b)   any division falling to be made on the proportional basis referred to in paragraph 9(2) shall be so made in such a way as to secure that the greater the negativity of an interest's value the smaller the share in respect of the interest.

(3) In a case where—

> (a)   paragraph 14(2) operates to reduce the value of any such superior interest as is there mentioned ("the superior interest"), and
>
> (b)   after the operation of that provision there remains any interest whose value for the relevant purposes is a positive amount,

the value of the superior interest for the purposes of paragraph 9(2) shall be the value which (in accordance with paragraph 14(2)) it has for the relevant purposes.

(4) In a case where—

> (a)   paragraph 14(2) operates to reduce the value of any such superior interest as is there mentioned ("the superior interest"), but
>
> (b)   after the operation of that provision there remains no such interest as is mentioned in sub-paragraph (3)(b) above,

the value of the superior interest for the purposes of paragraph 9(2) shall be the value which it has for the relevant purposes apart from paragraph 14(2).

Adjustment of compensation

17 (1) Where—

> (a)   paragraph 14(2) operates to reduce the value of any such superior interest as is there mentioned ("the superior interest"), and
>
> (b)   apart from this paragraph any amount of compensation is payable under paragraph 8 to the owner of any relevant inferior interest in respect of that interest,

there shall be payable to the owner of the superior interest so much of the amount of compensation as is equal to the amount of the reduction or, if less than that amount, the whole of the amount of compensation.

(2) Where—

> (a)   paragraph 14(2) operates to reduce the value of two or more such superior interests as are there mentioned ("the superior interests"), and

(b)   apart from this paragraph any amount of compensation is payable under paragraph 8 to the owner of any relevant inferior interest in respect of that interest,

sub-paragraph (1) shall apply in the first instance as if the reference to the owner of the superior interest were to the owner of such of the superior interests as is furthest from the negative interest, and then, as respects any remaining amount of compensation, as if that reference were to the owner of such of the superior interests as is next furthest from the negative interest, and so on.

(3) In sub-paragraph (1) or (2) "relevant inferior interest", in relation to any interest whose value is reduced as mentioned in that sub-paragraph ("the superior interest"), means—

(a)   the negative interest on account of which any such reduction is made, or

(b)   any other interest intermediate between that negative interest and the superior interest;

but sub-paragraph (1) shall apply in the first instance in relation to any amount of compensation payable to the owner of that negative interest, and then, for the purpose of offsetting (so far as possible) any reduction remaining to be offset in accordance with sub-paragraph (1) or (2), in relation to any amount of compensation payable to the owner of the interest immediately superior to that negative interest, and so on in order of proximity to it.

(4)   To the extent that an amount of compensation is payable to the owner of any interest by virtue of this paragraph—

(a)   paragraph 2(1)(c) or 6(1)(b)(ii) shall have effect as if it were an amount of compensation payable to him, as owner of that interest, in accordance with paragraph 5 or 8, as the case may be; and

(b)   the person who would otherwise have been entitled to it in accordance with paragraph 8 shall accordingly not be so entitled.

(5) In a case where paragraph 14(2) applies separately in relation to two or more negative interests in accordance with paragraph 14(3), the preceding provisions of this paragraph shall similarly apply separately in relation to the reductions made on account of each of those interests, and shall so apply—

(a)   according to the order determined by paragraph 14(3)(a); and

(b)   with there being taken into account any reduction in the amount of compensation payable to any person under paragraph 8 which results from the prior application of the preceding provisions of this paragraph.

PART VI

VALUATION ETC OF OTHER INTERESTS WITH NEGATIVE VALUES

Valuation of freehold and leasehold interests

18 (1) Where—

(a)   the value of any freehold interest (as determined in accordance with paragraph 11(1)), or

(b)   the value of any leasehold interest (as determined in accordance with paragraph 11(2)),

is a negative amount, the value of the interest for the relevant purposes shall be nil.

(2) Where, in the case of any property, sub-paragraph (1) applies to any leasehold interest in the property whose value is a negative amount ("the negative interest"), then for the relevant purposes any interests in the property superior to the negative interest and having a positive value shall, if they are interests which are to be acquired by the nominee purchaser, be reduced in value—

(a)   beginning with the interest which is nearest to the negative interest and continuing (if necessary) with any such other superior interests in order of proximity to the negative interest;

(b)   until the aggregate amount of the reduction is equal to the negative amount in question; and

(c)   without reducing the value of any interest to less than nil.

(3) In a case where sub-paragraph (1) applies to two or more leasehold interests in any property whose values are negative amounts, sub-paragraph (2) shall apply separately in relation to each of those interests—

(a)   beginning with the interest which is inferior to every other of those interests and then in order of proximity to that interest; and

(b)   with any reduction in the value of any interest for the relevant purposes by virtue of any prior application of sub-paragraph (2) being taken into account.

(4) For the purposes of sub-paragraph (2) an interest has a positive value if (apart from that sub-paragraph) its value for the relevant purposes is a positive amount.

(5) In this Part of this Schedule "the relevant purposes"—

(a)   as respects any freehold interest, means the purposes of paragraph 10(1)(a); and

(b)   as respects any leasehold interest, means the purposes of paragraph 10(2)(a).

Calculation of marriage value

19 (1) Where (as determined in accordance with paragraph 4(3) and (4)) the value of any interest—

(a)   when held by the person from whom it is to be acquired by the nominee purchaser, or

(b)   when acquired by the nominee purchaser,

is a negative amount, then for the purposes of paragraph 4(2) the value of the interest when so held or acquired shall be nil.

(2) Where, in the case of any property, sub-paragraph (1) above applies to any leasehold interest in the property whose value when held or acquired as mentioned in paragraph (a) or (b) of that sub-paragraph is a negative amount, paragraph 18(2) to (4) shall apply for determining for the purposes of paragraph 4(2) the value when so held or acquired of other interests in the property, as if—

(a)   any reference to paragraph 18(1) were a reference to sub-paragraph (1) above; and

(b)   any reference to the relevant purposes were, as respects any interest, a reference to the purposes of paragraph 4(2) as it applies to the interest when so held or acquired.

(3) In this paragraph any reference to any provision of paragraph 4 is a reference to that provision as it applies in accordance with paragraph 12(1).

(4) References in paragraph 20 or 21 to paragraph 18(2) or (3) do not extend to that provision as it applies in accordance with sub-paragraph (2) above.

Apportionment of marriage value

20 (1) Where paragraph 18(1) applies to any interest in any property to which paragraph 12(1) applies, the value of the interest for the purposes of paragraph 12(2) shall be nil, unless sub-paragraph (2) below applies.

(2) Where, in the case of any property, paragraph 18(1) applies to every interest which is to be acquired by the nominee purchaser—

(a)   sub-paragraph (1) above shall not apply for the purposes of paragraph 12(2); and

(b)   any division falling to be made on the proportional basis referred to in paragraph 12(2) shall be so made in such a way as to secure that the greater the negativity of an interest's value the smaller the share in respect of the interest.

(3) Where in the case of any property—

(a)   paragraph 18(2) operates to reduce the value of any such superior interest as is there mentioned ("the superior interest"), and

(b)   after the operation of that provision there remains any interest which is to be acquired by the nominee purchaser and whose value for the relevant purposes is a positive amount, the value of the superior interest for the purposes of paragraph 12(2) shall be the value which (in accordance with paragraph 18(2)) it has for the relevant purposes.

(4) Where in the case of any property—
  (a) paragraph 18(2) operates to reduce the value of any such superior interest as is there mentioned ("the superior interest"), but
  (b) after the operation of that provision there remains no such interest as is mentioned in sub-paragraph (3)(b) above,

the value of the superior interest for the purposes of paragraph 12(2) shall be the value which it has for the relevant purposes apart from paragraph 18(2).

Adjustment of compensation

21 (1) Where in the case of any property—
  (a) paragraph 18(2) operates to reduce the value of any such superior interest as is there mentioned ("the superior interest"), and
  (b) apart from this paragraph any amount of compensation is payable by virtue of paragraph 13 to the owner of any relevant inferior interest in respect of that interest,

there shall be payable to the owner of the superior interest so much of the amount of compensation as is equal to the amount of the reduction or, if less than that amount, the whole of the amount of compensation.

(2) Where in the case of any property—
  (a) paragraph 18(2) operates to reduce the value of two or more such superior interests as are there mentioned ("the superior interests"), and
  (b) apart from this paragraph any amount of compensation is payable by virtue of paragraph 13 to the owner of any relevant inferior interest in respect of that interest,

sub-paragraph (1) shall apply in the first instance as if the reference to the owner of the superior interest were to the owner of such of the superior interests as is furthest from the negative interest, and then, as respects any remaining amount of compensation, as if that reference were to the owner of such of the superior interests as is next furthest from the negative interest, and so on.

(3) In sub-paragraph (1) or (2) "relevant inferior interest", in relation to any interest whose value is reduced as mentioned in that sub-paragraph ("the superior interest"), means—
  (a) the negative interest on account of which any such reduction is made, or
  (b) any other interest in the property in question which is to be acquired by the nominee purchaser and is intermediate between that negative interest and the superior interest;

but sub-paragraph (1) shall apply in the first instance in relation to any amount of compensation payable to the owner of that negative interest, and then, for the purpose of offsetting (so far as possible) any reduction remaining to be offset in accordance with sub-paragraph (1) or (2), in relation to any amount of compensation payable to the owner of such interest falling within paragraph (b) above as is nearest to that negative interest, and so on in order of proximity to it.

(4) To the extent that an amount of compensation is payable to the owner of any interest by virtue of this paragraph—
  (a) paragraph 10(1)(c) or (as the case may be) paragraph 10(2)(b) shall have effect as if it were an amount of compensation payable to him, as owner of that interest, in accordance with paragraph 13; and
  (b) the person who would otherwise have been entitled to it in accordance with paragraph 13 shall accordingly not be so entitled.

(5) In a case where paragraph 18(2) applies separately in relation to two or more negative interests in accordance with paragraph 18(3), the preceding provisions of this paragraph shall similarly apply separately in relation to the reductions made on account of each of those interests, and shall so apply—

    (a) according to the order determined by paragraph 18(3)(a); and

    (b) with there being taken into account any reduction in the amount of compensation payable to any person by virtue of paragraph 13 which results from the prior application of the preceding provisions of this paragraph.

Definitions For "qualifying tenant", see s 5; for "the reversioner", see s 9; for "the specified premises", see s 13(12); for "participating tenants", see s 14; for "the nominee purchaser", see s 15; for "conveyance" and "unit", see s 38(1); for "flat", "interest" and "term date", see s 101(1); for "lease" and related expressions (including "tenant"), see s 101(1), (2); for "the freeholder", "intermediate leasehold interest" and "the valuation date", see Pt I, para 1 above; for "a minor intermediate lease", see Pt I, para 7(3) above; as to "profit rent", see Pt I, para 7(5) above; for "the marriage value", see Pt II, para 4 above; for "the intermediate landlord", see Pt IV, para 12(3) above.

References See paras 3.75, 3.85, 3.93 ff.

SCHEDULE 7   Section 34
Conveyance to Nominee Purchaser on Enfranchisement

Interpretation

1 In this Schedule—

    (a) "the relevant premises" means, in relation to such a conveyance as is mentioned in section 34(1), the premises of which the freehold is to be conveyed by means of the conveyance;

    (b) "the freeholder", in relation to any such conveyance, means the person whose freehold interest in the relevant premises is to be conveyed by means of the conveyance;

    (c) "other property" means property of which the freehold is not to be acquired by the nominee purchaser under this Chapter; and

    (d) "the appropriate time" means the time when the freehold of the relevant premises is to be conveyed to the nominee purchaser.

General

2 (1) The conveyance shall not exclude or restrict the general words implied in conveyances under section 62 of the Law of Property Act 1925, or the all-estate clause implied under section 63 of that Act, unless—

    (a) the exclusion or restriction is made for the purpose of preserving or recognising any existing interest of the freeholder in tenant's incumbrances or any existing right or interest of any other person, or

    (b) the nominee purchaser consents to the exclusion or restriction.

(2) The freeholder shall not be bound—

    (a) to convey to the nominee purchaser any better title than that which he has or could require to be vested in him, or

    (b) to enter into any covenant for title other than such covenant as under section 76(1)(F) of the Law of Property Act 1925 is implied in the case of a person conveying, and expressed to convey, as trustee or mortgagee.

(3) In this paragraph "tenant's incumbrances" includes any interest directly or indirectly derived out of a lease, and any incumbrance on a lease or any such interest (whether or not the same matter is an incumbrance also on any interest reversionary on the lease); and "incumbrances" has the same meaning as it has for the purposes of section 34 of this Act.

Rights of support, passage of water etc

3 (1) This paragraph applies to rights of any of the following descriptions, namely—

    (a) rights of support for a building or part of a building;

    (b) rights to the access of light and air to a building or part of a building;

    (c)   rights to the passage of water or of gas or other piped fuel, or to the drainage or disposal of water, sewage, smoke or fumes, or to the use or maintenance of pipes or other installations for such passage, drainage or disposal;

    (d)   rights to the use or maintenance of cables or other installations for the supply of electricity, for the telephone or for the receipt directly or by landline of visual or other wireless transmissions;

and the provisions required to be included in the conveyance by virtue of sub-paragraph (2) are accordingly provisions relating to any such rights.

(2) The conveyance shall include provisions having the effect of—

    (a)   granting with the relevant premises (so far as the freeholder is capable of granting them—

        (i)   all such easements and rights over other property as are necessary to secure as nearly as may be for the benefit of the relevant premises the same rights as exist for the benefit of those premises immediately before the appropriate time, and

        (ii) such further easements and rights (if any) as are necessary for the reasonable enjoyment of the relevant premises; and

    (b)   making the relevant premises subject to the following easements and rights (so far as they are capable of existing in law), namely—

        (i)   all easements and rights for the benefit of other property to which the relevant premises are subject immediately before the appropriate time, and

        (ii) such further easements and rights (if any) as are necessary for the reasonable enjoyment of other property, being property in which the freeholder has an interest at the relevant date.

Rights of way

4 Any such conveyance shall include—

    (a)   such provisions (if any) as the nominee purchaser may require for the purpose of securing to him and the persons deriving title under him rights of way over other property, so far as the freeholder is capable of granting them, being rights of way that are necessary for the reasonable enjoyment of the relevant premises; and

    (b)   such provisions (if any) as the freeholder may require for the purpose of making the relevant premises subject to rights of way necessary for the reasonable enjoyment of other property, being property in which he is to retain an interest after the acquisition of the relevant premises.

Restrictive covenants

5 (1) As regards restrictive covenants, the conveyance shall include—

    (a)   such provisions (if any) as the freeholder may require to secure that the nominee purchaser is bound by, or to indemnify the freeholder against breaches of, restrictive covenants which—

        (i)   affect the relevant premises otherwise than by virtue of any lease subject to which the relevant premises are to be acquired or any agreement collateral to any such lease, and

        (ii) are immediately before the appropriate time enforceable for the benefit of other property; and

    (b)   such provisions (if any) as the freeholder or the nominee purchaser may require to secure the continuance (with suitable adaptations) of restrictions arising by virtue of any such lease or collateral agreement as is mentioned in paragraph (a)(i), being either—

        (i)   restrictions affecting the relevant premises which are capable of benefiting other property and (if enforceable only by the freeholder) are such as materially to enhance the value of the other property, or

        (ii) restrictions affecting other property which are such as materially to enhance the value of the relevant premises; and

    (c)   such further restrictions as the freeholder may require to restrict the use of the relevant premises in a way which—
        (i)   will not interfere with the reasonable enjoyment of those premises as they have been enjoyed during the currency of the leases subject to which they are to be acquired, but
        (ii)   will materially enhance the value of other property in which the freeholder has an interest at the relevant date.

(2) In this paragraph "restrictive covenant" means a covenant or agreement restrictive of the user of any land or building.

Definitions   For "the relevant date", see s 1(8); for "conveyance", see s 38(1); for "interest", see s 101(1); for "lease", see s 101(1), (2); for "the appropriate time", "the freeholder", "other property" and "the relevant premises, see para 1.
References   See paras 3.94, 3.95 ff.

SCHEDULE 8   Section 35
DISCHARGE OF MORTGAGES ETC: SUPPLEMENTARY PROVISIONS

Construction

1 In this Schedule—
    "the consideration payable" means the consideration payable for the acquisition of the relevant interest;
    "the landlord" means the person from whom the relevant interest is being acquired;
    "the relevant interest" means any such interest as is mentioned in paragraph 2(1).

Duty of nominee purchaser to redeem mortgages

2 (1) Where in accordance with section 35(1) a conveyance will operate to discharge any interest from a mortgage to secure the payment of money, it shall be the duty of the nominee purchaser to apply the consideration payable, in the first instance, in or towards the redemption of any such mortgage (and, if there are more than one, then according to their priorities).

(2) If any amount payable in accordance with sub-paragraph (1) to the person entitled to the benefit of a mortgage is not so paid, nor paid into court in accordance with paragraph 4, the relevant interest shall remain subject to the mortgage as regards the amount in question, and to that extent section 35(1) shall not apply.

(3) Subject to sub-paragraph (4), sub-paragraph (1) shall not apply to a debenture holders' charge, that is to say, a charge (whether a floating charge or not) in favour of the holders of a series of debentures issued by a company or other body of persons, or in favour of trustees for such debenture holders; and any such charge shall be disregarded in determining priorities for the purposes of sub-paragraph (1).

(4) Sub-paragraph (3) shall not have effect in relation to a charge in favour of trustees for debenture holders which, at the date of the conveyance by virtue of which the relevant interest is acquired by the nominee purchaser, is (as regards that interest) a specific and not a floating charge.

Determination of amounts due in respect of mortgages

3 (1) For the purpose of determining the amount payable in respect of any mortgage under paragraph 2(1)—
    (a)   a person entitled to the benefit of a mortgage to which that provision applies shall not be permitted to exercise any right to consolidate that mortgage with a separate mortgage on other property; and

(b) if the landlord or any participating tenant is himself entitled to the benefit of a mortgage to which that provision applies, it shall rank for payment as it would if another person were entitled to it, and the nominee purchaser shall be entitled to retain the appropriate amount in respect of any such mortgage of a participating tenant.

(2) For the purpose of discharging any interest from a mortgage to which paragraph 2(1) applies, a person may be required to accept three months or any longer notice of the intention to pay the whole or part of the principal secured by the mortgage, together with interest to the date of payment, notwithstanding that the terms of the security make other provision or no provision as to the time and manner of payment; but he shall be entitled, if he so requires, to receive such additional payment as is reasonable in the circumstances—

(a) in respect of the costs of re-investment or other incidental costs and expenses; and

(b) in respect of any reduction in the rate of interest obtainable on reinvestment.

Payments into court

4 (1) Where under section 35(1) any interest is to be discharged from a mortgage and, in accordance with paragraph 2(1), a person is or may be entitled in respect of the mortgage to receive the whole or part of the consideration payable, then if—

(a) for any reason difficulty arises in ascertaining how much is payable in respect of the mortgage, or

(b) for any reason mentioned in sub-paragraph (2) below difficulty arises in making a payment in respect of the mortgage,

the nominee purchaser may pay into court on account of the consideration payable the amount, if known, of the payment to be made in respect of the mortgage or, if that amount is not known, the whole of that consideration or such lesser amount as the nominee purchaser thinks right in order to provide for that payment.

(2) Payment may be made into court in accordance with sub-paragraph (1)(b) where the difficulty arises for any of the following reasons, namely—

(a) because a person who is or may be entitled to receive payment cannot be found or his identity cannot be ascertained;

(b) because any such person refuses or fails to make out a title, or to accept payment and give a proper discharge, or to take any steps reasonably required of him to enable the sum payable to be ascertained and paid; or

(c) because a tender of the sum payable cannot, by reason of complications in the title to it or the want of two or more trustees or for other reasons, be effected, or not without incurring or involving unreasonable cost or delay.

(3) Without prejudice to sub-paragraph (1)(a), the whole or part of the consideration payable shall be paid into court by the nominee purchaser if, before execution of the conveyance referred to in paragraph 2(1), notice is given to him—

(a) that the landlord, or a person entitled to the benefit of a mortgage on the relevant interest, requires him to do so for the purpose of protecting the rights of persons so entitled, or for reasons related to the bankruptcy or winding up of the landlord, or

(b) that steps have been taken to enforce any mortgage on the relevant interest by the bringing of proceedings in any court, or by the appointment of a receiver, or otherwise;

and where payment into court is to be made by reason only of a notice under this sub-paragraph, and the notice is given with reference to proceedings in a court specified in the notice other than a county court, payment shall be made into the court so specified.

Savings

5 (1) Where any interest is discharged by section 35(1) from a mortgage (without the obligations secured by the mortgage being satisfied by the receipt of the whole or part of the consideration payable), the discharge of that interest from the mortgage shall not prejudice any right or remedy for the enforcement of those obligations against other property comprised in the same or any other security, nor prejudice any personal liability as principal or otherwise of the landlord or any other person.

(2) Nothing in this Schedule or section 35 shall be construed as preventing a person from joining in the conveyance referred to in paragraph 2(1) for the purpose of discharging the relevant interest from any mortgage without payment or for a lesser payment than that to which he would otherwise be entitled; and, if he does so, the persons to whom the consideration payable ought to be paid shall be determined accordingly.

Definitions For "participating tenants", see s 14; for "the nominee purchaser", see s 15; for "mortgage", see s 35(4); for "conveyance", see s 38(1); for "interest", see s 101(1); for "the consideration payable", "the landlord" and "the relevant interest", see para 1 above.
References See paras 3.96–3.98 ff.

SCHEDULE 9   Section 36

GRANT OF LEASES BACK TO THE FORMER FREEHOLDER

PART I

GENERAL

1 In this Schedule—

"the appropriate time" means the time when the freehold of the specified premises is acquired by the nominee purchaser;

"the demised premises", in relation to a lease granted or to be granted in pursuance of Part II or III of this Schedule, means—

(a) the flat or other unit demised or to be demised under the lease, or

(b) in the case of such a lease under which two or more units are demised, both or all of those units or (if the context so permits) any of them;

"the freeholder" means the person who owns the freehold of the specified premises immediately before the appropriate time;

"housing association" has the meaning given by section 1(1) of the Housing Associations Act 1985;

"intermediate landlord", in relation to a flat or other unit let to a tenant, means a person who holds a leasehold interest in the flat or other unit which is superior to that held by the tenant's immediate landlord;

"other property" means property other than the demised premises.

(2) In this Schedule any reference to a flat or other unit, in the context of the grant of a lease of it, includes any yard, garden, garage, outhouses and appurtenances belonging to or usually enjoyed with it and let with it immediately before the appropriate time.

PART II

MANDATORY LEASEBACK

Flats etc let under secure tenancies

2 (1) This paragraph applies where immediately before the appropriate time any flat contained in the specified premises is let under a secure tenancy and either—

(a) the freeholder is the tenant's immediate landlord, or

(b) the freeholder is a public sector landlord and every intermediate landlord of the flat (as well as the immediate landlord under the secure tenancy) is also a public sector landlord.

(2) Sub-paragraph (1)(b) has effect whether any such intermediate landlord, or the immediate landlord under the secure tenancy, is or is not a qualifying tenant of the flat.

(3) Where this paragraph applies, the nominee purchaser shall grant to the freeholder a lease of the flat in accordance with section 36 and paragraph 4 below.

(4) In this paragraph any reference to a flat includes a reference to a unit (other than a flat) which is used as a dwelling.

Flats etc let by housing associations under tenancies other than secure tenancies

3 (1) This paragraph applies where immediately before the appropriate time any flat contained in the specified premises is let by a housing association under a tenancy other than a secure tenancy and—

    (a)   the housing association is the freeholder, and

    (b)   the tenant is not a qualifying tenant of the flat.

(2) Where this paragraph applies, the nominee purchaser shall grant to the freeholder (that is to say, the housing association) a lease of the flat in accordance with section 36 and paragraph 4 below.

(3) In this paragraph any reference to a flat includes a reference to a unit (other than a flat) which is used as a dwelling.

Provisions as to terms of lease

4 (1) Any lease granted to the freeholder in pursuance of paragraph 2 or 3, and any agreement collateral to it, shall conform with the provisions of Part IV of this Schedule except to the extent that any departure from those provisions is agreed to by the nominee purchaser and the freeholder with the approval of a leasehold valuation tribunal.

(2) A leasehold valuation tribunal shall not approve any such departure from those provisions unless it appears to the tribunal that it is reasonable in the circumstances.

(3) In determining whether any such departure is reasonable in the circumstances, the tribunal shall have particular regard to the interests of the tenant under the secure tenancy referred to in paragraph 2(1) or (as the case may be) under the housing association tenancy referred to in paragraph 3(1).

(4) Subject to the preceding provisions of this paragraph, any such lease or agreement as is mentioned in sub-paragraph (1) may include such terms as are reasonable in the circumstances.

PART III

RIGHT OF FREEHOLDER TO REQUIRE LEASEBACK OF CERTAIN UNITS

Flats without qualifying tenants and other units

5 (1) Subject to sub-paragraph (3), this paragraph applies to any unit contained in the specified premises which is not immediately before the appropriate time a flat let to a person who is a qualifying tenant of it.

(2) Where this paragraph applies, the nominee purchaser shall, if the freeholder by notice requires him to do so, grant to the freeholder a lease of the unit in accordance with section 36 and paragraph 7 below.

(3) This paragraph does not apply to a flat or other unit to which paragraph 2 or 3 applies.

Flat etc occupied by resident landlord

6 (1) This paragraph applies where immediately before the appropriate time—

    (a)   the specified premises are premises with a resident landlord; and

    (b)   the freeholder is the person by virtue of whose occupation of a flat or other unit contained in those premises they are premises with a resident landlord; and

    (c)   the freeholder is a qualifying tenant of that flat or other unit ("the relevant unit").

(2) Where this paragraph applies—

    (a)   the nominee purchaser shall, if the freeholder by notice requires him to do so, grant to him a lease of the relevant unit in accordance with section 36 and paragraph 7 below; and

    (b)   any lease of that unit held by the freeholder immediately before the appropriate time shall be deemed to have been surrendered by him on the grant of the lease referred to in paragraph (a).

(3) Sections 5, 7 and 8 shall apply for the purpose of determining whether, for the purposes of sub-paragraph (1)(c) above, the freeholder is a qualifying tenant of a unit other than a flat as they apply for the purpose of determining whether a person is a qualifying tenant of a flat.

Provisions as to terms of lease

7 (1) Any lease granted to the freeholder in pursuance of paragraph 5 or 6, and any agreement collateral to it, shall conform with the provisions of Part IV of this Schedule except to the extent that any departure from those provisions—

    (a)   is agreed to by the nominee purchaser and the freeholder; or

    (b)   is directed by a leasehold valuation tribunal on an application made by either of those persons.

(2) A leasehold valuation tribunal shall not direct any such departure from those provisions unless it appears to the tribunal that it is reasonable in the circumstances.

(3) In determining whether any such departure is reasonable in the circumstances, the tribunal shall have particular regard to the interests of any person who will be the tenant of the flat or other unit in question under a lease inferior to the lease to be granted to the freeholder.

(4) Subject to the preceding provisions of this paragraph, any such lease or agreement as is mentioned in sub-paragraph (1) may include such terms as are reasonable in the circumstances.

Part IV
Terms of Lease Granted to Freeholder

Duration of lease and rent

8 The lease shall be a lease granted for a term of 999 years at a peppercorn rent.

General rights to be granted

9 The lease shall not exclude or restrict the general words implied under section 62 of the Law of Property Act 1925, unless the exclusion or restriction is made for the purpose of preserving or recognising an existing right or interest of any person.

Rights of support, passage of water etc

10 (1) This paragraph applies to rights of any of the following descriptions, namely—

    (a)   rights of support for a building or part of a building;

    (b)   rights to the access of light and air to a building or part of a building;

    (c)   rights to the passage of water or of gas or other piped fuel, or to the drainage or disposal of water, sewage, smoke or fumes, or to the use or maintenance of pipes or other installations for such passage, drainage or disposal; and

    (d)   rights to the use or maintenance of cables or other installations for the supply of electricity, for the telephone or for the receipt directly or by landline of visual or other wireless transmissions;

and the provisions required to be included in the lease by virtue of sub-paragraph (2) are accordingly provisions relating to any such rights.

(2) The lease shall include provisions having the effect of—

    (a) granting with the demised premises (so far as the lessor is capable of granting them)—

        (i) all such easements and rights over other property as are necessary to secure as nearly as may be for the benefit of the demised premises the same rights as exist for the benefit of those premises immediately before the appropriate time, and

        (ii) such further easements and rights (if any) as are necessary for the reasonable enjoyment of the demised premises; and

    (b) making the demised premises subject to the following easements and rights (so far as they are capable of existing in law), namely—

        (i) all easements and rights for the benefit of other property to which the demised premises are subject immediately before the appropriate time, and

        (ii) such further easements and rights (if any) as are necessary for the reasonable enjoyment of other property, being property in which the lessor acquires an interest at the appropriate time.

Rights of way

11 The lease shall include—

    (a) such provisions (if any) as the lessee may require for the purpose of securing to him, and persons deriving title under him, rights of way over other property (so far as the lessor is capable of granting them), being rights of way that are necessary for the reasonable enjoyment of the demised premises; and

    (b) such provisions (if any) as the lessor may require for the purpose of making the demised premises subject to rights of way necessary for the reasonable enjoyment of other property, being property in which the lessor acquires an interest at the appropriate time.

Common use of premises and facilities

12 The lease shall include, so far as the lessor is capable of granting them, the like rights to use in common with others any premises, facilities or services as are enjoyed immediately before the appropriate time by any tenant of the demised premises.

Covenants affecting demised premises

13 The lease shall include such provisions (if any) as the lessor may require to secure that the lessee is bound by, or to indemnify the lessor against breaches of, restrictive covenants (that is to say, covenants or agreements restrictive of the use of any land or premises) affecting the demised premises immediately before the appropriate time and enforceable for the benefit of other property.

Covenants by lessor

14 (1) The lease shall include covenants by the lessor—

    (a) to keep in repair the structure and exterior of the demised premises and of the specified premises (including drains, gutters and external pipes) and to make good any defect affecting that structure;

    (b) to keep in repair any other property over or in respect of which the lessee has rights by virtue of this Schedule;

    (c) to ensure, so far as practicable, that the services which are to be provided by the lessor and to which the lessee is entitled (whether alone or in common with others) are maintained at a reasonable level, and to keep in repair any installation connected with the provision of any of those services.

(2) The lease shall include a covenant requiring the lessor—

    (a) to insure the specified premises for their full reinstatement value against destruction or damage by fire, tempest, flood or any other cause against the risk of which it is the normal practice to insure;

    (b) to rebuild or reinstate the demised premises or the specified premises in the case of any such destruction or damage.

Covenants by lessee

15 The lease shall include a covenant by the lessee to ensure that the interior of the demised premises is kept in good repair (including decorative repair).

Contributions by lessee

16 (1) The lease may require the lessee to bear a reasonable part of the costs incurred by the lessor in discharging or insuring against the obligations imposed by the covenants required by paragraph 14(1) or in discharging the obligation imposed by the covenant required by paragraph 14(2)(a).

(2) Where a covenant required by paragraph 14(1) or (2)(a) has been modified to any extent in accordance with paragraph 4 or 7, the reference in sub-paragraph (1) above to the obligations or (as the case may be) the obligation imposed by that covenant shall be read as a reference to the obligations or obligation imposed by that covenant as so modified.

Assignment and sub-letting of premises

17 (1) Except where the demised premises consist of or include any unit let or intended for letting on a business lease, the lease shall not include any provision prohibiting or restricting the assignment of the lease or the sub-letting of the whole or part of the demised premises.

(2) Where the demised premises consist of or include any such unit as is mentioned in sub-paragraph (1), the lease shall contain a prohibition against—

    (a) assigning or sub-letting the whole or part of any such unit, or

    (b) altering the user of any such unit,

without the prior written consent of the lessor (such consent not to be unreasonably withheld).

Restriction on terminating lease

18 The lease shall not include any provision for the lease to be terminated otherwise than by forfeiture on breach of any term of the lease by the lessee.

Definitions For "qualifying tenant", see s 5; for "the specified premises", see s 13(12); for "the nominee purchaser", see s 15; for "unit", see s 38(1); for "business lease", see s 101(1); for "disposal", "flat" and "interest", see s 101(1); for "lease" and related expressions (including "landlord" and "tenant"), see s 101(1), (2); for "the appropriate time", "the demised premises", "the freeholder", "housing association", "intermediate landlord" and "other property", see Pt I, para 1 above; for "the relevant flat", see Pt III, para 6(1) above.
References See paras 3.88–3.92 ff.

SCHEDULE 10   Section 37
Acquisition of Interests from Local Authorities etc

Disapplication of provisions relating to disposals by local authorities etc

1 (1) It is hereby declared that nothing in any of the provisions specified in sub-paragraph (2) (which impose requirements as to consent or consultation or other restrictions in relation to disposals falling within those provisions) applies to any disposal of a freehold or leasehold interest in any premises which is made in pursuance of this Chapter.

(2) The provisions referred to in sub-paragraph (1) are—

(a) sections 32 and 43 of the Housing Act 1985 (disposals of land by local authorities) and section 133 of the Housing Act 1988 (certain subsequent disposals);

(b) section 9(1) and (1A) of the Housing Associations Act 1985 (disposals by registered and unregistered housing associations);

(c) section 79(1) and (2) of the Housing Act 1988 (disposals by housing action trusts) and section 81 of that Act (certain subsequent disposals); and

(d) section 105(1) of that Act (disposals subsequent to change of landlord of secure tenants).

Provisions relating to secure tenants following leaseback

2 (1) This paragraph applies where a lease is granted to a public sector landlord in pursuance of paragraph 2 of Schedule 9.

(2) Where—

(a) immediately before the appropriate time the public sector landlord was the immediate landlord under a secure tenancy of a flat contained in the demised premises, and

(b) that tenancy continues in force after the grant of the lease referred to in sub-paragraph (1),

the tenant shall be deemed to have continued without interruption as tenant of the landlord under the secure tenancy, despite the disposal of the landlord's interest which immediately preceded the grant of the lease referred to in that sub-paragraph.

(3) Where—

(a) immediately before the appropriate time a person was a successor in relation to a secure tenancy of a flat contained in the demised premises, and

(b) that person is, in connection with the grant of the lease referred to in sub-paragraph (1), granted a new secure tenancy of that flat which is a tenancy for a term certain,

then for the purposes of sections 87 to 90 of the Housing Act 1985 (succession on death of tenant) that person shall also be a successor in relation to the new tenancy.

(4) Where—

(a) immediately before the appropriate time a person was the tenant under a secure tenancy of a flat contained in the demised premises, and

(b) that person is, in connection with the grant of the lease referred to in sub-paragraph (1), granted a new secure tenancy of that flat,

then, for the purpose of determining whether either of the conditions referred to in sub-paragraph (5) is satisfied, the new tenancy shall not be regarded as a new letting of the flat but shall instead be regarded as a continuation of the secure tenancy referred to in paragraph (a) above.

(5) Those conditions are—

(a) the condition specified in sub-paragraph (1)(b) of paragraph 5 of Schedule 5 to the Housing Act 1985 (exception to the right to buy in case of letting in connection with employment); and

(b) the condition specified in sub-paragraph (1)(b) of paragraph 11 of that Schedule (exception to the right to buy in case of letting for occupation by person of pensionable age etc).

(6) In this paragraph—

(a) any reference to a secure tenancy of a flat is a reference to a secure tenancy of a flat whether with or without any yard, garden, garage, outhouses or appurtenances belonging to or usually enjoyed with it; and

(b) any reference to a flat includes a reference to a unit (other than a flat) which is used as a dwelling.

(7) In this paragraph—
- (a) "the appropriate time" and "the demised premises" have the same meaning as in Schedule 9; and
- (b) "successor" has the same meaning as in section 88 of the Housing Act 1985.

Definitions For "disposal", "flat" and "interest", see s 101(1); for "lease" and related expressions (including "landlord", "tenancy" and "tenant"), see s 101(1), (2).
References See para 3.100 ff.

SCHEDULE 11 Section 40
Procedure where Competent Landlord is not Tenant's Immediate Landlord

PART I
Procedure in Relation to Tenant's Notice

Tenant's notice may be given to any of the other landlords

1 The tenant's notice under section 42 shall be regarded as given to the competent landlord for the purposes of subsection (2)(a) of that section if it is given to any of the other landlords instead; and references in this Chapter to the relevant date shall be construed accordingly.

Tenant to give copies of notice

2 (1) Where the tenant's notice is given to the competent landlord, the tenant shall give a copy of the notice to every person known or believed by him to be one of the other landlords.

(2) Where the tenant's notice is, in accordance with paragraph 1, given to one of the other landlords, the tenant shall give a copy of the notice to every person (apart from the recipient of the notice) known or believed by the tenant to be either the competent landlord or one of the other landlords.

(3) The tenant's notice shall state whether copies are being given in accordance with this paragraph to anyone other than the recipient and, if so, to whom.

Recipient of notice or copy to give further copies

3 (1) Subject to sub-paragraph (2), a recipient of the tenant's notice or of a copy of it (including a person receiving a copy under this sub-paragraph—
- (a) shall forthwith give a copy to any person who—
  - (i) is known or believed by him to be the competent landlord or one of the other landlords, and
  - (ii) is not stated in the recipient's copy of the notice, or known by him, to have received a copy; and
- (b) if he knows who is, or he believes himself to be, the competent landlord, shall—
  - (i) give a notice to the tenant stating who is the person thought by him to be the competent landlord, and
  - (ii) give a copy of it to that person (if not himself) and to every person known or believed by him to be one of the other landlords.

(2) Sub-paragraph (1) does not apply where the recipient is neither the competent landlord nor one of the other landlords.

(3) Where a person gives any copies of the tenant's notice in accordance with sub-paragraph (1)(a), he shall—
- (a) supplement the statement under paragraph 2(3) by adding any further persons to whom he is giving copies or who are known by him to have received one; and

(b) notify the tenant of the persons added by him to that statement.

Consequences of failure to comply with paragraph 2 or 3

4 (1) Where—
   (a) the competent landlord or any of the other landlords does not receive a copy of the tenant's notice before the end of the period specified in it in pursuance of section 42(3)(f), but
   (b) he was given a notice under section 41 by the tenant and, in response to the notice under that section, notified the tenant of his interest in the tenant's flat,
the tenant's notice shall cease to have effect at the end of that period.

(2) Where—
   (a) sub-paragraph (1) does not apply, but
   (b) any person fails without reasonable cause to comply with paragraph 2 or 3 above, or is guilty of any unreasonable delay in complying with either of those paragraphs,
he shall be liable for any loss thereby occasioned to the tenant or to the competent landlord or any of the other landlords.

PART II
CONDUCT OF PROCEEDINGS BY COMPETENT LANDLORD ON BEHALF OF OTHER LANDLORDS

Counter-notice to specify other landlords

5 Any counter-notice given to the tenant by the competent landlord must specify the other landlords on whose behalf he is acting.

Acts of competent landlord binding on other landlords

6 (1) Without prejudice to the generality of section 40(2)—
   (a) any notice given under this Chapter by the competent landlord to the tenant,
   (b) any agreement for the purposes of this Chapter between that landlord and the tenant, and
   (c) any determination of the court or a leasehold valuation tribunal under this Chapter in proceedings between that landlord and the tenant,
shall be binding on the other landlords and on their interests in the property demised by the tenant's lease or any other property; but in the event of dispute the competent landlord or any of the other landlords may apply to the court for directions as to the manner in which the competent landlord should act in the dispute.

(2) Subject to paragraph 7(2), the authority given to the competent landlord by section 40(2) shall extend to receiving on behalf of any other landlord any amount payable to that person by virtue of Schedule 13.

(3) If any of the other landlords cannot be found, or his identity cannot be ascertained, the competent landlord shall apply to the court for directions and the court may make such order as it thinks proper with a view to giving effect to the rights of the tenant and protecting the interests of other persons; but, subject to any such directions, the competent landlord shall proceed as in other cases.

(4) The competent landlord, if he acts in good faith and with reasonable care and diligence, shall not be liable to any of the other landlords for any loss or damage caused by any act or omission in the exercise or intended exercise of the authority given to him by section 40(2).

Other landlords acting independently

7 (1) Notwithstanding anything in section 40(2), any of the other landlords shall, at any time after the giving by the competent landlord of a counter-notice under section 45 and on giving notice to both the competent landlord and the tenant of his intention to be so represented, be entitled to be separately represented—

    (a)   in any legal proceedings in which his title to any property comes in question, or

    (b)   in any legal proceedings relating to the determination of any amount payable to him by virtue of Schedule 13.

(2) Any of the other landlords may also, on giving notice to the competent landlord and the tenant, require that any amount payable to him by virtue of Schedule 13 shall be paid by the tenant to him, or to a person authorised by him to receive it, instead of to the competent landlord; but if, after being given proper notice of the time and method of completion with the tenant, either—

    (a)   he fails to notify the competent landlord of the arrangements made with the tenant to receive payment, or

    (b)   having notified the competent landlord of those arrangements, the arrangements are not duly implemented,

the competent landlord shall be authorised to receive the payment for him, and the competent landlord's written receipt for the amount payable shall be a complete discharge to the tenant.

Obligations of other landlords to competent landlord

8 (1) It shall be the duty of each of the other landlords (subject to paragraph 7) to give the competent landlord all such information and assistance as he may reasonably require; and, if any of the other landlords fails to comply with this sub–paragraph, that landlord shall indemnify the competent landlord against any liability incurred by him in consequence of the failure.

(2) Each of the other landlords shall make such contribution as shall be just to costs and expenses which are properly incurred by the competent landlord in pursuance of section 40(2) but are not recoverable or not recovered from the tenant.

Applications made by other landlords under section 47(1)

9 (1) The authority given to the competent landlord by section 40(2) shall not extend to the bringing of proceedings under section 47(1) on behalf of any of the other landlords, or preclude any of those landlords from bringing proceedings under that provision on his own behalf as if he were the competent landlord.

(2) In section 45(2)(c) any reference to the competent landlord shall include a reference—

    (a)   to any of the other landlords, or

    (b)   to any two or more of the following, namely the competent landlord and the other landlords, acting together;

and in section 47(1) and (2) references to the landlord shall be construed accordingly; but if any of the other landlords intends to make such an application as is mentioned in section 45(2)(c), whether alone or together with any other person or persons, his name shall be stated in the counter-notice.

Deemed surrender and re-grant of leases of other landlords

10 (1) Where a lease is executed under section 56 or 93(4) or in pursuance of any order made under this Chapter, then (subject to sub-paragraph (3)) that instrument shall have effect for the creation of the tenant's new lease of his flat, and for the operation of the rights and obligations conferred and imposed by it, as if there had been a surrender and re-grant of any subsisting lease intermediate between the interest of the competent landlord and the existing lease; and the covenants and other provisions of that instrument shall be framed and take effect accordingly.

(2) Section 57(2) shall apply to the new lease on the basis that account is to be taken of obligations imposed on any of the other landlords by virtue of that or any superior lease; and section 59(3) shall apply on the basis that the reference here to the tenant's landlord includes

the immediate landlord from whom the new lease will be held and all superior landlords, including any superior to the competent landlord.

(3) Where a lease of the tenant's flat superior to the existing lease is vested in the tenant or a trustee for him, the new lease shall include an actual surrender of that superior lease without a re-grant, and it shall accordingly be disregarded for the purposes of the preceding provisions of this paragraph.

Discharge of existing mortgages

11 Where by reason of section 58(2) it is necessary to make any payment to discharge the tenant's flat from a mortgage affecting the interest of any landlord, then if the competent landlord is not the landlord liable or primarily liable in respect of the mortgage, he shall not be required to make that payment otherwise than out of money made available for the purpose by the landlord so liable, and it shall be the duty of that landlord to provide for the mortgage being discharged.

Definitions For "the relevant date", see s 39(8) (and note also Pt I, para 1 above); for "the competent landlord", "other landlord" and "the tenant", see s 40(4); for "the tenant's notice", see s 42; for "mortgage", see s 62(1); for "the court", "flat" and "interest", see s 101(1) (and note also s 62(2)); for "lease" and related expressions, see s 101(1), (2).
References See paras 4.13, 4.86–4.88 ff.

SCHEDULE 12   Section 42
The Tenant's Notice: Supplementary Provisions

PART I
Effect of Tenant's Notice on Other Notices, Forfeitures etc

Prior notice by tenant terminating lease

1 A notice given by a qualifying tenant of a flat under section 42 shall be of no effect if it is given—

(a) after the tenant has given notice terminating the lease of the flat (other than a notice that has been superseded by the grant, express or implied, of a new tenancy); or

(b) during the subsistence of an agreement for the grant to the tenant of a future tenancy of the flat, where the agreement is one to which paragraph 17 of Schedule 10 to the Local Government and Housing Act 1989 applies.

Prior notice by landlord terminating lease

2 (1) Subject to sub-paragraph (2), a notice given by a qualifying tenant of a flat under section 42 shall be of no effect if it is given more than two months after a landlord's notice terminating the tenant's lease of the flat has been given under section 4 of the Landlord and Tenant Act 1954 or served under paragraph (1) of Schedule 10 to the Local Government and Housing Act 1989 (whether or not the notice has effect to terminate the lease).

(2) Sub-paragraph (1) does not apply where the landlord gives his written consent to a notice being given under section 42 after the end of those two months.

(3) Where in the case of a qualifying tenant of a flat who gives a notice under section 42—

(a) any such landlord's notice is given or served as mentioned in sub-paragraph (1), but

(b) that notice was not given or served more than two months before the date on which the notice under section 42 is given to the landlord,

the landlord's notice shall cease to have effect on that date.

(4) If—
- (a) any such landlord's notice ceases to have effect by virtue of sub-paragraph (3), but
- (b) the claim made by the tenant by the giving of his notice under section 42 is not effective,

then sub-paragraph (5) shall apply to any landlord's notice terminating the tenant's lease of the flat which—
- (i) is given under section 4 of the Landlord and Tenant Act 1954 or served under paragraph 4(1) of Schedule 10 to the Local Government and Housing Act 1989, and
- (ii) is so given or served within one month after the expiry of the period of currency of that claim.

(5) Where this sub-paragraph applies to a landlord's notice, the earliest date which may be specified in the notice as the date of termination shall be—
- (a) in the case of a notice given under section 4 of that Act of 1954—
  - (i) the date of termination specified in the previous notice, or
  - (ii) the date of expiry of the period of three months beginning with the date of the giving of the new notice,

whichever is the later; or
- (b) in the case of a notice served under paragraph 4(1) of Schedule 10 to that Act of 1989—
  - (i) the date of termination specified in the previous notice, or
  - (ii) the date of expiry of the period of four months beginning with the date of service of the new notice,

whichever is the later.

(6) Where—
- (a) by virtue of sub-paragraph (5) a landlord's notice specifies as the date of termination of a lease a date earlier than six months after the date of the giving of the notice, and
- (b) the notice proposes a statutory tenancy,

section 7(2) of the Landlord and Tenant Act 1954 shall apply in relation to the notice with the substitution, for references to the period of two months ending with the date of termination specified in the notice and the beginning of that period, of references to the period of three months beginning with the date of the giving of the notice and the end of that period.

Orders for possession and pending proceedings for forfeiture etc

3 (1) A notice given by a qualifying tenant of a flat under section 42 shall be of no effect if at the time when it is given he is obliged to give up possession of his flat in pursuance of an order of a court or will be so obliged at a date specified in such an order.

(2) Except with the leave of the court, a qualifying tenant of a flat shall not give a notice under section 42 at a time when any proceedings are pending to enforce a right of re-entry or forfeiture terminating his lease of the flat.

(3) Leave shall only be granted under sub-paragraph (2) if the court is satisfied that the tenant does not wish to give such a notice solely or mainly for the purpose of avoiding the consequences of the breach of the terms of his lease in respect of which proceedings are pending.

(4) If—
- (a) leave is so granted, and
- (b) the tenant by such a notice makes a claim to acquire a new lease of his flat,

the tenant's lease shall be deemed for the purposes of the claim to be a subsisting lease despite the existence of those proceedings and any order made afterwards in those proceedings; and, if the claim is effective, the court in which those proceedings were brought may set aside or vary any such order to such extent and on such terms as appear to that court to be appropriate.

Notice terminating lease given by tenant or landlord during currency of claim

4 Where by a notice given under section 42 a tenant makes a claim to acquire a new lease of a flat, any notice terminating the tenant's lease of the flat, whether it is—

    (a) a notice given by the tenant, or

    (b) a landlord's notice given under section 4 of the Landlord and Tenant Act 1954 or served under paragraph 4(1) of Schedule 10 to the Local Government and Housing Act 1989,

shall be of no effect if it is given or served during the currency of the claim.

Tenant's notice operates to prevent termination of lease

5 (1) Where by a notice under section 42 a tenant makes a claim to acquire a new lease of a flat, then during the currency of the claim and for three months thereafter the lease of the flat shall not terminate—

    (a) by effluxion of time, or

    (b) in pursuance of a notice to quit given by the immediate landlord of the tenant, or

    (c) by the termination of a superior lease;

but if the claim is not effective, and but for this sub-paragraph the lease would have so terminated before the end of those three months, the lease shall so terminate at the end of those three months.

(2) Sub-paragraph (1) shall not be taken to prevent an earlier termination of the lease in any manner not mentioned in that sub-paragraph, and shall not affect—

    (a) the power under section 146(4) of the Law of Property Act 1925 (relief against forfeiture of leases) to grant a tenant relief against the termination of a superior lease, or

    (b) any right of the tenant to relief under section 16(2) of the Landlord and Tenant Act 1954 (relief where landlord proceeding to enforce covenants) or under paragraph 9 of Schedule 5 to that Act (relief in proceedings brought by superior landlord).

Restriction on proceedings to enforce right of re-entry or forfeiture

6 Where by a notice under section 42 a tenant makes a claim to acquire a new lease of a flat, then during the currency of the claim—

    (a) no proceedings to enforce any right of re-entry or forfeiture terminating the lease of the flat shall be brought in any court without the leave of that court, and

    (b) leave shall only be granted if the court is satisfied that the notice was given solely or mainly for the purpose of avoiding the consequences of the breach of the terms of the tenant's lease in respect of which proceedings are proposed to be brought;

but where leave is granted, the notice shall cease to have effect.

Effect of notice under section 16(2) of Landlord and Tenant Act 1954 on tenant's notice

7 (1) A tenant who, in proceedings to enforce a right of re-entry or forfeiture or a right to damages in respect of a failure to comply with any terms of his lease, applies for relief under section 16 of the Landlord and Tenant Act 1954 is not thereby precluded from making a claim to acquire a new lease under this Chapter; but if he gives notice under section 16(2) of that Act (under which the tenant is relieved from any order for recovery of possession or for payment of damages, but the tenancy is cut short), any notice given by him under section 42 with respect to property comprised in his lease shall be of no effect or, if already given, shall cease to have effect.

(2) Sub-paragraph (1) shall apply in relation to proceedings relating to a superior tenancy with the substitution for the references to section 16 and to section 16(2) of the Landlord and Tenant Act 1954 of references to paragraph 9 and to paragraph 9(2) of Schedule 5 to that Act.

Interpretation

8 (1) For the purposes of this Part of this Schedule—

    (a) references to a notice under section 42 include, in so far as the context permits, references to a notice purporting to be given under that section (whether by a qualifying tenant or not), and references to the tenant by whom a notice is given shall be construed accordingly;

    (b) references to a claim being effective are references to a new lease being acquired in pursuance of the claim; and

    (c) references to the currency of a claim are—

        (i) where the claim is made by a valid notice under section 42, references to the period during which the notice continues in force in accordance with subsection (8) of that section, or

        (ii) where the claim is made by a notice which is not a valid notice under section 42, references to the period beginning with the giving of the notice and ending with the time when the notice is set aside by the court or is withdrawn or when it would (if valid) cease to have effect or be deemed to have been withdrawn.

(2) For the purposes of sub-paragraph (1)(c) the date when a notice is set aside, or would (if valid) cease to have effect, in consequence of an order of a court shall be taken to be the date when the order becomes final.

(3) The references in this Schedule—

    (a) to section 16 of the Landlord and Tenant Act 1954 and subsection (2) of that section, and

    (b) to paragraph 9 of Schedule 5 to that Act and sub-paragraph (2) of that paragraph,

include references to those provisions as they apply in relation to Schedule 10 to the Local Government and Housing Act 1989 (security of tenure on ending of long residential tenancies).

PART II
OTHER PROVISIONS

9 (1) The tenant's notice shall not be invalidated by any inaccuracy in any of the particulars required by section 42(3) or by any misdescription of any of the property to which the claim extends.

(2) Where the tenant's notice—

    (a) specifies any property which he is not entitled to have demised to him under a new lease granted in pursuance of this Chapter, or

    (b) fails to specify any property which he is entitled to have so demised to him,

the notice may, with the leave of the court and on such terms as the court may think fit, be amended so as to exclude or include the property in question.

Definitions   For "qualifying tenant", see s 39(3); for "the tenant's notice", see s 42; for "the court" and "flat", see s 101(1) (and note also as to "flat", s 62(2)); for "lease" and related expressions (including "landlord" and "tenant"), see s 101(1), (2); as to "a notice under section 42", "the tenant by whom a notice is given", "a claim being effective" and "the currency of a claim", see para 8(1), (2) above.
References   See paras 4.25–4.28, 4.32, 4.33 ff.

SCHEDULE 13   Section 56
PREMIUM AND OTHER AMOUNTS PAYABLE BY TENANT ON GRANT OF NEW LEASE

PART I
GENERAL

1 In this Schedule—

"intermediate leasehold interest" means the interest of any person falling within section 40(4)(c), to the extent that it is an interest in the tenant's flat subsisting immediately before the grant of the new lease;

"the valuation date" means the date when all of the terms of acquisition (apart from those relating to the premium and any other amounts payable by virtue of this Schedule in connection with the grant of the new lease) have been determined either by agreement or by a leasehold valuation tribunal under this Chapter.

PART II
Premium Payable in Respect of Grant of New Lease

Premium payable by tenant

2 The premium payable by the tenant in respect of the grant of the new lease shall be the aggregate of—

    (a)   the diminution in value of the landlord's interest in the tenant's flat as determined in accordance with paragraph 3,

    (b)   the landlord's share of the marriage value as determined in accordance with paragraph 4, and

    (c)   any amount of compensation payable to the landlord under paragraph 5.

Diminution in value of landlord's interest

3 (1) The diminution in value of the landlord's interest is the difference between—

    (a)   the value of the landlord's interest in the tenant's flat prior to the grant of the new lease; and

    (b)   the value of his interest in the flat once the new lease is granted.

(2) Subject to the provisions of this paragraph, the value of any such interest of the landlord as is mentioned in sub-paragraph (1)(a) or (b) is the amount which at the valuation date that interest might be expected to realise if sold on the open market by a willing seller (with the tenant not buying or seeking to buy) on the following assumptions—

    (a)   on the assumption that the vendor is selling for an estate in fee simple or (as the case may be) such other interest as is held by the landlord, subject to the relevant lease and any intermediate leasehold interests;

    (b)   on the assumption that Chapter I and this Chapter confer no right to acquire any interest in any premises containing the tenant's flat or to acquire any new lease;

    (c)   on the assumption that any increase in the value of the flat which is attributable to an improvement carried out at his own expense by the tenant or by any predecessor in title is to be disregarded; and

    (d)   on the assumption that (subject to paragraph (b)) the vendor is selling with and subject to the rights and burdens with and subject to which the relevant lease has effect or (as the case may be) is to be granted.

(3) In sub-paragraph (2) "the relevant lease" means either the tenant's existing lease or the new lease, depending on whether the valuation is for the purposes of paragraph (a) or paragraph (b) of sub-paragraph (1).

(4) It is hereby declared that the fact that sub-paragraph (2) requires assumptions to be made as to the matters specified in paragraphs (a) to (d) of that sub-paragraph does not preclude the making of assumptions as to other matters where those assumptions are appropriate for determining the amount which at the valuation date any such interest of the landlord as is mentioned in sub-paragraph (1)(a) or (b) might be expected to realise if sold as mentioned in sub-paragraph (2).

(5) In determining any such amount there shall be made such deduction (if any) in respect of any defect in title as on a sale of that interest on the open market might be expected to be allowed between a willing seller and a willing buyer.

(6) The value of any such interest of the landlord as is mentioned in sub-paragraph (1)(a) or (b) shall not be increased by reason of—

    (a) any transaction which—

        (i) is entered into on or after the date of the passing of this Act (otherwise than in pursuance of a contract entered into before that date), and

        (ii) involves the creation or transfer of an interest superior to (whether or not preceding) any interest held by the tenant; or

    (b) any alteration on or after that date of the terms on which any such superior interest is held.

Landlord's share of marriage value

4 (1) The marriage value is the amount referred to in sub-paragraph (2), and the landlord's share of the marriage value is—

    (a) such proportion of that amount as is determined by agreement between the landlord and the tenant or, in default of agreement, as is determined by a leasehold valuation tribunal to be the proportion which in its opinion would have been determined by an agreement made at the valuation date between the parties on a sale on the open market by a willing seller, or

    (b) 50 per cent of that amount,

whichever is the greater.

(2) The marriage value is the difference between the following amounts, namely—

    (a) the aggregate of—

        (i) the value of the interest of the tenant under his existing lease,

        (ii) the value of the landlord's interest in the tenant's flat prior to the grant of the new lease, and

        (iii) the values prior to the grant of that lease of all intermediate leasehold interests (if any); and

    (b) the aggregate of—

        (i) the value of the interest to be held by the tenant under the new lease,

        (ii) the value of the landlord's interest in the tenant's flat once the new lease is granted, and

        (iii) the values of all intermediate leasehold interests (if any) once that lease is granted.

(3) For the purposes of sub-paragraph (2)—

    (a) the value of any interest of the tenant shall be determined as at the valuation date;

    (b) the value of any such interest of the landlord as is mentioned in paragraph (a) or paragraph (b) of that sub-paragraph is the amount determined for the purposes of paragraph 3(1)(a) or paragraph 3(1)(b) (as the case may be); and

    (c) the value of any intermediate leasehold interest shall be determined in accordance with paragraph 8, and shall be so determined as at the valuation date.

Compensation for loss arising out of grant of new lease

5 (1) Where the landlord will suffer any loss or damage to which this paragraph applies, there shall be payable to him such amount as is reasonable to compensate him for that loss or damage.

(2) This paragraph applies to—

    (a) any diminution in value of any interest of the landlord in any property other than the tenant's flat which results from the grant to the tenant of the new lease; and

    (b) any other loss or damage which results therefrom to the extent that it is referable to the landlord's ownership of any such interest.

(3) Without prejudice to the generality of paragraph (b) of sub-paragraph (2), the kinds of loss falling within that paragraph include loss of development value in relation to the tenant's flat to the extent that it is referable as mentioned in that paragraph.

(4) In sub-paragraph (3) "development value", in relation to the tenant's flat, means any increase in the value of the landlord's interest in the flat which is attributable to the possibility of demolishing, reconstructing, or carrying out substantial works of construction affecting, the flat (whether together with any other premises or otherwise).

PART III
Amounts Payable to Owners of Intermediate Leasehold Interests

Amount payable to owner of intermediate interest

6 In connection with the grant of the new lease to the tenant there shall be payable by the tenant to the owner of any intermediate leasehold interest an amount which is the aggregate of—

    (a)   the diminution in value of that interest as determined in accordance with paragraph 7; and

    (b)   any amount of compensation payable to him under paragraph 9.

Diminution in value of intermediate interest

7 (1) The diminution in value of any intermediate leasehold interest is the difference between—

    (a)   the value of that interest prior to the grant of the new lease; and

    (b)   the value of that interest once the new lease is granted.

(2) Each of those values shall be determined, as at the valuation date, in accordance with paragraph 8.

Value of intermediate interests

8 (1) Subject to sub-paragraph (2), paragraph 3(2) to (6) shall apply for determining the value of any intermediate leasehold interest for the purposes of any provision of this Schedule with such modifications as are appropriate to relate those provisions of paragraph 3 to a sale of the interest in question subject to the tenant's lease for the time being and to any leases intermediate between the interest in question and that lease.

(2) The value of an intermediate leasehold interest which is the interest of the tenant under a minor intermediate lease shall be calculated by applying the formula set out in sub-paragraph (6) instead of in accordance with sub-paragraph (1).

(3) "A minor intermediate lease" means a lease complying with the following requirements, namely—

    (a)   it must have an expectation of possession of not more than one month, and

    (b)   the profit rent in respect of the lease must be not more than £5 per year.

(4) "Profit rent" means an amount equal to that of the rent payable under the lease on which the minor intermediate lease is in immediate reversion, less that of the rent payable under the minor intermediate lease.

(5) Where the minor intermediate lease or that on which it is in immediate reversion comprises property other than the tenant's flat, then in sub-paragraph (4) the reference to the rent payable under it means so much of that rent as is apportioned to that flat.

(6) The formula is—

$$P = £\frac{R}{Y} - \frac{R}{Y(1 + Y)^n}$$

where—

    P = the price payable;

    R = the profit rent;

    Y = the yield (expressed as a decimal fraction) from 2½ per cent Consolidated Stock;

    n = the period, expressed in years (taking any part of a year as a whole year), of the remainder of the term of the minor intermediate lease as at the valuation date.

(7) In calculating the yield from 2õ per cent Consolidated Stock, the price of that stock shall be taken to be the middle market price at the close of business on the last trading day in the week before the valuation date.

(8) For the purposes of this paragraph the expectation of possession carried by a lease is the expectation which it carries at the valuation date of possession after the tenant's lease, on the basis that—

    (a)   (subject to sub-paragraph (9)) the tenant's lease terminates at the valuation date if its term date fell before then, or else it terminates on its term date; and

    (b)   any other lease terminates on its term date.

(9) In a case where before the relevant date for the purposes of this Chapter the immediate landlord of the tenant had given notice to quit terminating the tenant's lease on a date earlier than that date, the date specified in the notice to quit shall be substituted for the date specified in sub-paragraph (8)(a) above.

Compensation for loss arising out of grant of new lease

9 Paragraph 5 shall apply in relation to the owner of any intermediate leasehold interest as it applies in relation to the landlord.

Owners of intermediate interests entitled to part of marriage value

10 (1) This paragraph applies in a case where—

    (a)   the premium payable by the tenant in respect of the grant of the new lease includes an amount in respect of the landlord's share of the marriage value, and

    (b)   there are any intermediate leasehold interests.

(2) The amount payable to the landlord in respect of his share of the marriage value shall be divided between the landlord and the owners of any such intermediate interests in proportion to the amounts by which the values of their respective interests in the flat will be diminished in consequence of the grant of the new lease.

(3) For the purposes of sub-paragraph (2)—

    (a)   the amount by which the value of the landlord's interest in the flat will be so diminished is the diminution in value of that interest as determined for the purposes of paragraph 2(a); and

    (b)   the amount by which the value of any intermediate leasehold interest will be so diminished is the diminution in value of that interest as determined for the purposes of paragraph 6(a).

(4) Where the owner of any intermediate leasehold interest is entitled in accordance with sub-paragraph (2) to any part of the amount payable to the landlord in respect of the landlord's share of the marriage value, the amount to which he is so entitled shall be payable to him by the landlord.

Definitions   For "the landlord", see s 40(1); for "the terms of acquisition", see s 48(7); for "the existing lease", see s 62(1); for "flat" and "interest", see s 101(1) (and note also as to "flat", s 62(2)); for "lease" and related expressions (including "tenant"), see s 101(1), (2); for "intermediate leasehold interest" and "the valuation date", see para 1 above; as to "the marriage value" and "the landlord's share of the marriage value", see para 4 above; for "a minor intermediate lease", see para 8(3) above; for "profit rent", see para 8(4) above.
References   See paras 4.92–4.97 ff.

SCHEDULE 14   Section 61
PROVISIONS SUPPLEMENTARY TO SECTION 61

1 (1) This Schedule has effect where a tenant of a flat is entitled to be paid compensation under section 61, or would be so entitled on the landlord obtaining an order for possession, or where an application for such an order is dismissed or withdrawn.

(2) In this Schedule—

"application for possession" means a landlord's application under section 61;

"the new lease" has the same meaning as in that section; and

"order for possession" means an order made under that section;

and (except in the case of the reference in paragraph 5(1)(b) to the flat as a dwelling) references to the flat held by the tenant under the new lease shall be construed in accordance with subsection (5) of that section.

2 (1) Where an order for possession is made—

(a) the new lease shall determine, and

(b) the compensation payable to the tenant by virtue of the order shall become payable,

on such date as may, when the amount of compensation has been determined either by agreement between the landlord and the tenant or by a leasehold valuation tribunal, be fixed by order of the court made on the application of either the landlord or the tenant.

(2) Where the application for possession was made by virtue of section 61(2)(a), then—

(a) (unless paragraph (b) below applies) an order of the court under this paragraph shall not fix a date earlier than the term date of the lease in relation to which the right to acquire a new lease was exercised;

(b) in a case where section 61(2)(a) applies in accordance with section 61(3), an order of the court under this paragraph shall not fix a date earlier than the term date of the lease in relation to which that right was first exercised.

(3) In fixing the date referred to in sub-paragraph (1) the court shall have regard to the conduct of the parties and to the extent to which the landlord has made reasonable preparations for proceeding with the redevelopment (including the obtaining of, or preparations relating to the obtaining of, any requisite permission or consent, whether from any authority whose permission or consent is required under any enactment or from the owner of an interest in any property).

(4) The court may by order direct that the whole or part of the compensation payable to the tenant shall be paid into court, if the court thinks it expedient to do so for the purpose of ensuring that the sum paid is available for meeting any mortgage on the tenant's interest in the flat in question, or for the purpose of division, or for any other purpose.

3 (1) On the termination of a lease under an order for possession there shall terminate also any immediate or derivative sub-lease, and the tenant shall be bound to give up possession of the flat in question to the landlord except in so far as he is precluded from doing so by the rights of other persons to retain possession under or by virtue of any enactment.

(2) Where a sub-lease of property comprised in the lease has been created after the date of the application for possession, no person shall in respect of that sub-lease be entitled under any of the following provisions (which relate to retaining possession on the termination of a superior tenancy), namely—

(a) subsection (2) of section 137 of the Rent Act 1977, or any enactment (including subsection (5) of that section) applying or extending it,

(b) subsection (2) of section 9 of the Rent (Agriculture) Act 1976 as extended by subsection (5) of that section, or

(c) section 18(1) of the Housing Act 1988,

to retain possession of that property after the termination of the lease under the order for possession.

(3) In exercising its jurisdiction under section 61 or this Schedule the court shall assume that the landlord, having obtained an order for possession, will not be precluded from obtaining possession by the right of any person to retain possession by virtue of—

(a) Part VII of the Rent Act 1977 or any enactment applying or extending that Part of that Act,

(b) the Rent (Agriculture) Act 1976, or

(c) Part I of the Housing Act 1988,

or otherwise.

(4) A person in occupation of any property under a sub-lease liable to terminate under sub-paragraph (1) may, with the leave of the court, appear and be heard on any application for possession or any application under paragraph 2.

4 Where an order has been made by a county court under paragraph 2, that court or another county court shall have jurisdiction to hear and determine any proceedings brought by virtue of the order to recover possession of the property or to recover the compensation.

5 (1) The amount payable to a tenant, by virtue of an order for possession, by way of compensation for loss of his flat shall be the amount which at the valuation date the new lease, if sold on the open market by a willing seller, might be expected to realise on the following assumptions—

    (a)   on the assumption that Chapter I and this Chapter confer no right to acquire any interest in any premises containing the tenant's flat or to acquire any new lease;

    (b)   on the assumption that the vendor is selling—

        (i)   subject to the rights of any person who will on the termination of the lease be entitled to retain possession as against the landlord, but otherwise with vacant possession, and

        (ii)   subject to any restriction that would be required (in addition to any imposed by the terms of the lease) to limit the uses of the flat to those to which it has been put since the commencement of the lease and to preclude the erection of any new dwelling or any other building not ancillary to the flat as a dwelling; and

    (c)   on the assumption that (subject to paragraphs (a) and (b)) the vendor is selling with and subject to the rights and burdens with and subject to which the flat will be held by the landlord on the termination of the lease.

(2) It is hereby declared that the fact that sub-paragraph (1) requires assumptions to be made as to the matters specified in paragraphs (a) to (c) of that sub-paragraph does not preclude the making of assumptions as to other matters where those assumptions are appropriate for determining the amount which at the valuation date the new lease might be expected to realise if sold as mentioned in that sub-paragraph.

(3) In determining any such amount there shall be made such deduction (if any) in respect of any defect in title as on a sale of that interest on the open market might be expected to be allowed between a willing seller and a willing buyer.

(4) In this paragraph "the valuation date" means the date when the amount of the compensation payable to the tenant is determined as mentioned in paragraph 2(1).

6 (1) Part I of the Landlord and Tenant Act 1927 (compensation for improvements on termination of business tenancies) shall not apply on the termination of the new lease or any sub-lease in accordance with this Schedule; and a request for a new tenancy under section 26 of the Landlord and Tenant Act 1954 in respect of the new lease or any sub-lease shall be of no effect if made after the application for possession, or, if already made, shall cease to have effect on the making of that application.

(2) Where a sub-lease terminating with the new lease in accordance with paragraph 3 is one to which Part II of the Landlord and Tenant Act 1954 applies, the compensation payable to the tenant shall be divided between him and the sub-tenant in such proportions as may be just, regard being had to their respective interests in the flat in question and to any loss arising from the termination of those interests and not incurred by imprudence.

(3) Where the amount of the compensation payable to the tenant is agreed between him and the landlord without the consent of a sub-tenant entitled under sub-paragraph (2) to a share in the compensation, and is shown by the sub-tenant to be less than might reasonably have been obtained by the tenant, the sub-tenant shall be entitled under sub-paragraph (2) to recover from the tenant such increased share as may be just.

7 (1) The landlord shall not be concerned with the application of the amount payable to the tenant by way of compensation under an order for possession, but (subject to any statutory requirements as to payment of capital money arising under a settlement or a disposition on trust for sale and to any order under paragraph 2(4) for payment into court) the written receipt of the tenant shall be a complete discharge for the amount payable.

(2) The landlord shall be entitled to deduct from the amount so payable to the tenant—
  (a) the amount of any sum recoverable as rent in respect of the flat up to the termination of the new lease; and
  (b) the amount of any other sums due and payable by the tenant to the landlord under or in respect of the lease or any agreement collateral thereto.

8 (1) Where a landlord makes an application for possession, and it is made to appear to the court that in relation to matters arising out of that application (including the giving up of possession of the flat or the payment of compensation) the landlord or the tenant has been guilty of any unreasonable delay or default, the court may—
  (a) by order revoke or vary, and direct repayment of sums paid under, any provision made by a previous order as to payment of the costs of proceedings taken in the court on or with reference to the application; or
  (b) where costs have not been awarded, award costs.

(2) Where an application for possession is dismissed or withdrawn, and it is made to appear to the court—
  (a) that the application was not made in good faith, or
  (b) that the landlord had attempted in any material respect to support by misrepresentation or the concealment of material facts a request to the tenant to deliver up possession without an application for possession,
the court may order that no further application for possession of the flat made by the landlord shall be entertained if it is made within the period of five years beginning with the date of the order.

9 Where—
  (a) the new lease is held on trust for sale, and
  (b) compensation is paid by the landlord on the termination of the new lease (whether the payment is made in pursuance of an order for possession or in pursuance of an agreement made in conformity with paragraph 5 above without an application having been made under section 61),
the sum received shall be dealt with as if it were proceeds of sale arising under the trust.

10 Where—
  (a) the tenant under the new lease is a university or college to which the Universities and College Estates Act 1925 applies, and
  (b) compensation is paid as mentioned in paragraph 9(b) above,
the sum received shall be dealt with as if it were an amount payable by way of consideration on a sale effected under that Act.

11 Where—
  (a) the tenant under the new lease is a capitular body within the meaning of the Cathedrals Measure 1963 and the lease comprises property which forms part of the endowment of a cathedral church, and
  (b) compensation is paid as mentioned in paragraph 9(b) above,
the sum received shall be treated as part of that endowment.

12 (1) Where—
  (a) the tenant under the new lease is a diocesan board of finance and the lease comprises diocesan glebe land, and
  (b) compensation is paid as mentioned in paragraph 9(b) above,
the sum received shall be paid to the Church Commissioners to be applied for purposes for which the proceeds of any disposition of property by agreement would be applicable under any enactment or Measure authorising such a disposition or disposing of the proceeds of such a disposition.

(2) In this paragraph "diocesan board of finance" and "diocesan glebe land" have the same meaning as in the Endowments and Glebe Measure 1976.

Definitions   For "the landlord", see s 40(1); for "the court", "dwelling", "flat", "interest" and "the term date", see s 101(1) (and note also as to "flat", s 62(2)–(4) and para 1(2)); for "lease" and related expressions (including "landlord" and "tenant"), see s 101(1), (2); as to "commencement of the lease", see s 101(5), (6); for "application for possession", "the new lease" and "order for possession", see para 1(2).
References   See para 4.91 ff.

SCHEDULE 15   Section 66
Section 9 of the Leasehold Reform Act 1967, as Amended

9 Purchase price and costs of enfranchisement and tenant's right to withdraw

(1) Subject to subsection (2) below, the price payable for a house and premises on a conveyance under section 8 above shall be the amount which at the relevant time the house and premises, if sold in the open market by a willing seller (with the tenant and members of his family who reside in the house not buying or seeking to buy), might be expected to realise on the following assumptions:—

  (a) on the assumption that the vendor was selling for an estate in fee simple, subject to the tenancy but on the assumption that this Part of this Act conferred no right to acquire the freehold, and if the tenancy has not been extended under this Part of this Act, on the assumption that (subject to the landlord's rights under section 17 below) it was to be so extended;

  (b) on the assumption that (subject to paragraph (a) above) the vendor was selling subject, in respect of rentcharges to which section 11(2) below applies, to the same annual charge as the conveyance to the tenant is to be subject to, but the purchaser would otherwise be effectively exonerated until the termination of the tenancy from any liability or charge in respect of tenant's incumbrances; and

  (c) on the assumption that (subject to paragraphs (a) and (b) above) the vendor was selling with and subject to the rights and burdens with and subject to which the conveyance to the tenant is to be made, and in particular with and subject to such permanent or extended rights and burdens as are to be created in order to give effect to section 10 below.

The reference in this subsection to members of the tenant's family shall be construed in accordance with section 7(7) of this Act.

(1A) Notwithstanding the foregoing subsection, the price payable for a house and premises,—

  (i) the rateable value of which was above £1,000 in Greater London and £500 elsewhere on 31st March 1990, or,

  (ii) which had no rateable value on that date and R exceeded £16,333 under the formula in section 1(1)(a) above (and section 1(7) above shall apply to that amount as it applies to the amount referred to in subsection (1)(a)(ii) of that section)

shall be the amount which at the relevant time the house and premises, if sold in the open market by a willing seller, might be expected to realise on the following assumptions:—

  (a) on the assumption that the vendor was selling for an estate in fee simple, subject to the tenancy, but on the assumption that this Part of this Act conferred no right to acquire the freehold or an extended lease and, where the tenancy has been extended under this Part of this Act, that the tenancy will terminate on the original term date;

  (b) on the assumption that at the end of the tenancy the tenant has the right to remain in possession of the house and premises—

> (i) if the tenancy is such a tenancy as is mentioned in subsection (2) or subsection (3) of section 186 of the Local Government and Housing Act 1989, or is a tenancy which is a long tenancy at a low rent for the purposes of Part I of the Landlord and Tenant Act 1954 in respect of which the landlord is not able to serve a notice under section 4 of that Act specifying a date of termination earlier than 15th January 1999, under the provisions of Schedule 10 to the Local Government and Housing Act 1989; and
>
> (ii) in any other case under the provisions of Part I of the Landlord and Tenant Act 1954;

(c) on the assumption that the tenant has no liability to carry out any repairs, maintenance or redecorations under the terms of the tenancy or Part I of the Landlord and Tenant Act 1954;

(d) on the assumption that the price be diminished by the extent to which the value of the house and premises has been increased by any improvement carried out by the tenant or his predecessors in title at their own expense;

(e) on the assumption that (subject to paragraph (a) above) the vendor was selling subject, in respect of rentcharges to which section 11(2) below applies, to the same annual charge as the conveyance to the tenant is to be subject to, but the purchaser would otherwise be effectively exonerated until the termination of the tenancy from any liability or charge in respect of tenant's incumbrances; and

(f) on the assumption that (subject to paragraphs (a) and (b) above) the vendor was selling with and subject to the rights and burdens with and subject to which the conveyance to the tenant is to be made, and in particular with and subject to such permanent or extended rights and burdens as are to be created in order to give effect to section 10 below.

(1B) For the purpose of determining whether the rateable value of the house and premises is above £1000 in Greater London, or £500 elsewhere, the rateable value shall be adjusted to take into account any tenant's improvements in accordance with Schedule 8 to the Housing Act 1974.

(1C) Notwithstanding subsection (1) above, the price payable for a house and premises where the right to acquire the freehold arises by virtue of any one or more of the provisions of sections 1A and 1B above shall be determined in accordance with subsection (1A) above; but in any such case—

(a) if in determining the price so payable there falls to be taken into account any marriage value arising by virtue of the coalescence of the freehold and leasehold interests, the share of the marriage value to which the tenant is to be regarded as being entitled shall not exceed one-half of it; and

(b) section 9A below has effect for determining whether any additional amount is payable by way of compensation under that section;

and in a case where the provision (or one of the provisions) by virtue of which the right to acquire the freehold arises is section 1A(1) above, subsection (1A) above shall apply with the omission of the assumption set out in paragraph (b) of that subsection.

(2) The price payable for the house and premises shall be subject to such deduction (if any) in respect of any defect in the title to be conveyed to the tenant as on a sale in the open market might be expected to be allowed between a willing seller and a willing buyer.

(3) On ascertaining the amount payable, or likely to be payable, as the price for a house and premises in accordance with this section (but not more than one month after the amount payable has been determined by agreement or otherwise), the tenant may give written notice to the landlord that he is unable or unwilling to acquire the house and premises at the price he must pay; and thereupon—

(a) the notice under section 8 above of his desire to have the freehold shall cease to have effect, and he shall be liable to make such compensation as may be just to the landlord in respect of the interference (if any) by the notice with the exercise by the landlord of his power to dispose of or deal with the house and premises or any neighbouring property; and

  (b) any further notice given under that section with respect to the house or any part of it (with or without other property) shall be void if given within the following three years.

(4) Where a person gives notice of his desire to have the freehold of a house and premises under this Part of this Act, then unless the notice lapses under any provision of this Act excluding his liability, there shall be borne by him (so far as they are incurred in pursuance of the notice) the reasonable costs of or incidental to any of the following matters:—

  (a) any investigation by the landlord of that person's right to acquire the freehold;

  (b) any conveyance or assurance of the house and premises or any part thereof or of any outstanding estate or interest therein;

  (c) deducing, evidencing and verifying the title to the house and premises or any estate or interest therein;

  (d) making out and furnishing such abstracts and copies as the person giving the notice may require;

  (e) any valuation of the house and premises;

but so that this subsection shall not apply to any costs if on a sale made voluntarily a stipulation that they were to be borne by the purchaser would be void.

(5) The landlord's lien (as vendor) on the house and premises for the price payable shall extend—

  (a) to any sums payable by way of rent or recoverable as rent in respect of the house and premises up to the date of the conveyance; and

  (b) to any sums for which the tenant is liable under subsection (4) above; and

  (c) to any other sums due and payable by him to the landlord under or in respect of the tenancy or any agreement collateral thereto.

References   See para 5.12 ff.

SCHEDULE 16   Section 117(2)

Schedule Inserted After Schedule 6 to the Housing Act 1985

SCHEDULE 6

A Redemption of Landlord's Share

Obligation to redeem landlord's share in certain circumstances

1 (1) The conveyance or grant shall contain a covenant binding on the secure tenant and his successors in title to make to the landlord, immediately after—

  (a) the making of a relevant disposal which is not an excluded disposal, or

  (b) the expiry of the period of one year beginning with a relevant death,

(whichever first occurs), a final payment, that is to say, a payment of the amount required to redeem the landlord's share.

(2) A disposal is an excluded disposal for the purposes of this paragraph if—

  (a) it is a further conveyance of the freehold or an assignment of the lease and the person or each of the persons to whom it is made is, or is the spouse of, the person or one of the persons by whom it is made;

  (b) it is a vesting in a person taking under a will or intestacy; or

  (c) it is a disposal in pursuance of an order under section 24 of the Matrimonial Causes Act 1973 (property adjustment orders in connection with matrimonial proceedings) or section 2 of the Inheritance (Provision for

Family and Dependants) Act 1975 (orders as to financial provision to be made from estate),
and (in any case) an interest to which this paragraph applies subsists immediately after the disposal.

(3) In this paragraph "relevant death" means the death of a person who immediately before his death was the person or, as the case may be, the last remaining person entitled to an interest to which this paragraph applies.

(4) A beneficial interest in the dwelling-house is an interest to which this paragraph applies if the person entitled to it is—

(a)   the secure tenant or, as the case may be, one of the secure tenants, or

(b)   a qualifying person.

Right to redeem landlord's share at any time

2 (1) The conveyance or grant shall include provision entitling the secure tenant and his successors in title to make a final payment at any time.

(2) The right shall be exercisable by written notice served on the landlord claiming to make a final payment.

(3) The notice may be withdrawn at any time by written notice served on the landlord.

(4) If the final payment is not tendered to the landlord before the end of the period of three months beginning with the time when the value of the dwelling-house is agreed or determined in accordance with paragraph 8, the notice claiming to make a final payment shall be deemed to have been withdrawn.

Value of landlord's share and amount of final payment

3 The value of the landlord's share shall be determined by the formula—

$$VS = \frac{V \times S}{100}$$

and the amount required to redeem that share shall be determined by the formula—

$$R = VS - D$$

where—

VS = the value of the landlord's share;

V = the value of the dwelling-house (agreed or determined in accordance with paragraph 8);

S = the landlord's share expressed as a percentage;

R = the amount required to redeem the landlord's share;

D = the amount of the final discount (if any) which is applicable under paragraphs 4 and 5.

Final discount

4 (1) Where a final payment is made by, or by two or more persons who include—

(a)   the secure tenant or, as the case may be, one of the secure tenants, or

(b)   a qualifying person,

the person or persons making the payment are entitled, subject to the following provisions of this paragraph and paragraph 5, to a final discount equal to 20 per cent of the value of the landlord's share.

(2) Sub-paragraph (1) shall not apply if the final payment is made after the end of the protection period, that is to say, the period of two years beginning with the time when there ceases to be an interest to which this sub-paragraph applies.

(3) A beneficial interest in the dwelling-house is an interest to which sub-paragraph (2) applies if the person entitled to it is—

    (a) the secure tenant or, as the case may be, one of the secure tenants, or

    (b) a qualifying spouse.

(4) The Secretary of State may by order made with the consent of the Treasury provide that the percentage discount shall be such percentage as may be specified in the order.

(5) An order under this paragraph—

    (a) may make different provision with respect to different cases or descriptions of case, including different provision for different areas,

    (b) may contain such incidental, supplementary or transitional provisions as appear to the Secretary of State necessary or expedient, and

    (c) shall be made by statutory instrument and shall not be made unless a draft of the order has been laid before and approved by resolution of each House of Parliament.

Restrictions on and deductions from final discount

5 (1) Except where the Secretary of State so determines, a final discount shall not reduce the total purchase price, that is to say, the aggregate of the initial payment, the final payment and any interim payments, below the amount which would be applicable under section 131(1) in respect of the dwelling-house if the relevant time were the time when the value of the dwelling-house is agreed or determined.

(2) The total discount, that is to say, the aggregate of the initial discount, the final discount and any interim discounts, shall not in any case reduce the total purchase price by more than the sum prescribed for the purposes of section 131(2) at the time when the value of the dwelling-house is agreed or determined.

(3) If a final payment is made after the end of the first twelve months of the protection period, there shall be deducted from any final discount given by paragraph 4 and the preceding provisions of this paragraph an amount equal to 50 per cent of that discount.

(4) There shall be deducted from any final discount given by paragraph 4 and the preceding provisions of this paragraph an amount equal to any previous discount qualifying or, the aggregate of any previous discounts qualifying, under the provisions of section 130.

(5) A determination under this paragraph may make different provision for different cases or descriptions of case, including different provision for different areas.

Right to make interim payment at any time

6 (1) The conveyance or grant shall include provision entitling the secure tenant and his successors in title at any time to make to the landlord an interim payment, that is to say, a payment which—

    (a) is less than the amount required to redeem the landlord's share; but

    (b) is not less than 10 per cent of the value of the dwelling-house (agreed or determined in accordance with paragraph 8).

(2) The right shall be exercisable by written notice served on the landlord, claiming to make an interim payment and stating the amount of the interim payment proposed to be made.

(3) The notice may be withdrawn at any time by written notice served on the landlord.

(4) If the interim payment is not tendered to the landlord before the end of the period of three months beginning with the time when the value of the dwelling-house is agreed or determined in accordance with paragraph 8, the notice claiming to make an interim payment shall be deemed to have been withdrawn.

Landlord's reduced share and interim discount

7 The landlord's share after the making of an interim payment shall be determined by the formula—

$$S = \frac{R - IP}{R} \times PS$$

the amount of the interim discount shall be determined by the formula—

$$ID = \frac{PS \times V}{100} - \frac{S \times V}{100} - IP$$

and the amount of any previous discount which will be recovered by virtue of the making of an interim payment shall be determined by the formula—

$$RD = \frac{IP}{R} \times PD$$

where—

S = the landlord's share expressed as a percentage;

R = the amount which would have been required to redeem the landlord's share immediately before the interim payment was made;

IP = the amount of the interim payment;

PS = the landlord's share immediately before the interim payment was made also expressed as a percentage;

ID = the amount of the interim discount;

V = the value of the dwelling-house (agreed or determined in accordance with paragraph 8);

RD = the amount of any previous discount which will be recovered by virtue of the making of the interim payment;

PD = the amount of any previous discount which would be recovered if the tenant were making the final payment.

Value of dwelling-house

8 (1) For the purposes of the final payment or any interim payment, the value of a dwelling-house is the amount which for those purposes—

(a) is agreed at any time between the parties, or

(b) in default of such agreement, is determined at any time by an independent valuer,

as the amount which, in accordance with this paragraph, is to be taken as its value at that time.

(2) Subject to sub-paragraph (6), that value shall be taken to be the price which the interest of the secure tenant in the dwelling-house would realise if sold on the open market by a willing vendor—

(a) on the assumption that the liabilities mentioned in sub-paragraph (3) would be discharged by the vendor, and

(b) disregarding the matters specified in sub-paragraph (4).

(3) The liabilities referred to in sub-paragraph (2)(a) are—

(a) any mortgages of the interest of the secure tenant,

(b) the liability under the covenant required by paragraph I, and

(c) any liability under the covenant required by section 155(3) (repayment of discount on early disposal).

(4) The matters to be disregarded in pursuance of sub-paragraph (2)(b) are—

(a) any interests or rights created over the dwelling-house by the secure tenant,

(b) any improvements made by the secure tenant or any of the persons mentioned in section 127(4) (certain predecessors as secure tenant), and

(c) any failure by the secure tenant or any of those persons—

(i) where the dwelling-house is a house, to keep the dwelling-house in good repair (including decorative repair);

(ii) where the dwelling-house is a flat, to keep the interior of the dwelling-house in such repair.

(5) Sub-paragraph (6) applies where, at the time when the value of the dwelling-house is agreed or determined, the dwelling-house—

(a) has been destroyed or damaged by fire, tempest, flood or any other cause against the risk of which it is normal practice to insure, and

(b) has not been fully rebuilt or reinstated.

(6) That value shall be taken to include the value of such of the following as are applicable, namely—

(a) any sums paid or falling to be paid to the secure tenant under a relevant policy in so far as they exceed the cost of any rebuilding or reinstatement which has been carried out;

(b) any rights of the secure tenant under the covenant implied by paragraph 14(3) of Schedule 6 (covenant to rebuild or reinstate); and

(c) any rights of the secure tenant under the covenant implied by paragraph 15(4) of that Schedule (covenant to use best endeavours to secure rebuilding or reinstatement).

(7) In sub-paragraph (6) "relevant policy" means a policy insuring the secure tenant against the risk of fire, tempest or flood or any other risk against which it is normal practice to insure.

(8) References in this paragraph to the secure tenant include references to his successors in title.

Costs of independent valuation

9 The conveyance or grant shall include provision requiring any sums falling to be paid to an independent valuer (whether by way of fees or expenses or otherwise) to be paid by the secure tenant or his successors in title.

No charges to be made by landlord

10 A provision of the conveyance or grant is void in so far as it purports to enable the landlord to charge the tenant or his successors in title a sum in respect of or in connection with the making of a final or interim payment.

Other covenants and provisions

11 Subject to the provisions of this Schedule, the conveyance or grant may include such covenants and provisions as are reasonable in the circumstances.

Interpretation

12 (1) In this Schedule—

"independent valuer" means an independent valuer appointed in pursuance of provisions in that behalf contained in the conveyance or grant;

"protection period" has the meaning given by paragraph 4(2);

"qualifying person" means a qualifying spouse or a qualifying resident.

(2) A person is a qualifying spouse for the purposes of this Schedule if—

(a) he is entitled to a beneficial interest in the dwelling-house immediately after the time when there ceases to be an interest to which this paragraph applies;

(b) he is occupying the dwelling-house as his only or principal home immediately before that time; and

(c) he is the spouse or surviving spouse of the person who immediately before that time was entitled to the interest to which this paragraph applies or, as the case may be, the last remaining such interest, or is the surviving spouse of a person who immediately before his death was entitled to such an interest;

and any reference in this paragraph to the spouse or surviving spouse of a person includes a reference to a former spouse or surviving former spouse of that person.

(3) A person is a qualifying resident for the purposes of this Schedule if—

    (a) he is entitled to a beneficial interest in the dwelling-house immediately after the time when there ceases to be an interest to which this paragraph applies;

    (b) he is occupying the dwelling-house as his only or principal home immediately before that time;

    (c) he has resided throughout the period of twelve months ending with that time—

        (i) with the person who immediately before that time was entitled to the interest to which this paragraph applies or, as the case may be, the last remaining such interest, or

        (ii) with two or more persons in succession each of whom was throughout the period of residence with him entitled to such an interest; and

    (d) he is not a qualifying spouse.

(4) A beneficial interest in the dwelling-house is an interest to which this paragraph applies if the person entitled to it is the secure tenant or, as the case may be, one of the secure tenants.

(5) References in this Schedule to the secure tenant are references to the secure tenant or tenants to whom the conveyance or grant is made and references to the secure tenant or, as the case may be, one of the secure tenants shall be construed accordingly.

(6) References in this Schedule to the secure tenant's successors in title do not include references to any person entitled to a legal charge having priority to the mortgage required by section 151B (mortgage for securing redemption of landlord's share) or any person whose title derives from such a charge.

Definitions   For "secure tenant", see the Housing Act 1985, ss 79, 185, and note also para 12(5) of Sch 6A to that Act, as inserted by s 117(2) and as set out above; for "relevant time", see s 122(2) of the 1985 Act; for "previous discount", see s 130(2) of that Act, as amended by s 187(1) , Sch 21, para 11; for "initial payment" and "interim payment", see s 143B of that Act, as substituted by s 108, and note also para 6 of Sch 6A to that Act, as inserted by s 117(2) and as set out above; for "the landlord's share", see s 148 of that Act, as substituted by s 113; for "relevant disposal", see ss 159, 163(1) of that Act (and see also s 452(3) thereof); for "flat", see s 183 of that Act; for "dwelling-house", see ss 183, 184 of that Act, as amended, in the case of s 184, by s 187(1), Sch 21, para 24; for "landlord", "lease" and "tenant", see s 621 of that Act; as to "final payment", see the final limb of para 1(1) of Sch 6A to that Act, as inserted by s 117(2) and as set out above; as to "an excluded disposal", see para 1(2) of that Schedule, as so inserted and set out; for "independent valuer", "protection period" and "qualifying person", see para 12(1) of that Schedule, as so inserted and set out; as to "qualifying spouse", see para 12(2) of that Schedule, as so inserted and set out; as to "qualifying resident", see para 12(3) of that Schedule, as so inserted and set out; as to "a beneficial interest in the dwelling-house", see para 12(4) of that Schedule, as so inserted and set out (and note also para 1(4) thereof); as to "the secure tenant's successors in title", see para 12(6) of that Schedule, as so inserted and set out.

References   See paras 9.17–9.20 ff.

SCHEDULE 17   Section 158(2)

CONSTITUTION OF THE AGENCY

Membership

1 (1) The Agency shall consist of such number of members (being not less than six) as the Secretary of State may from time to time appoint.

(2) The Secretary of State shall appoint one of the members to be chairman and may, if he thinks fit, appoint another of them to be deputy chairman.

(3) Subject to the provisions of this paragraph, a member of the Agency shall hold and vacate office in accordance with the terms of his appointment.

(4) A person who ceases to be a member of the Agency shall be eligible for reappointment.

(5) A member of the Agency may resign his office by notice in writing to the Secretary of State.

(6) The Secretary of State may remove a member of the Agency from office if he is satisfied that he—
    (a)   is unable or unfit to carry out the functions of a member;
    (b)   has not complied with the terms of his appointment; or
    (c)   has become bankrupt or made an arrangement with his creditors.

(7) A person shall cease to be chairman or deputy chairman of the Agency—
    (a)   if he resigns as such by notice in writing to the Secretary of State; or
    (b)   if he ceases to be a member of the Agency.

Remuneration, pensions etc

2 (1) The Agency shall pay to its members such remuneration, and such allowances, as the Secretary of State may determine.

(2) The Agency may—
    (a)   pay such pensions, allowances or gratuities to or in respect of any persons who have been or are its members as the Secretary of State may determine;
    (b)   make such payments as the Secretary of State may determine towards provision for the payment of pensions, allowances or gratuities to or in respect of any such persons.

(3) If, when a person ceases to be a member of the Agency, the Secretary of State determines that there are special circumstances which make it right that he should receive compensation, the Agency shall pay to him a sum by way of compensation of such amount as the Secretary of State may determine.

(4) The approval of the Treasury shall be required for any determination of the Secretary of State under this paragraph.

Staff

3 (1) There shall be a chief executive of the Agency who shall be responsible to the Agency for the general exercise of the Agency's functions.

(2) The chief executive shall be appointed by the Agency but no person shall be appointed as chief executive unless the Secretary of State has consented to the appointment.

(3) The Agency may appoint such other number of staff as the Secretary of State may approve.

(4) The terms and conditions of appointment of any person appointed by the Agency under this paragraph shall be determined by the Agency with the consent of the Secretary of State.

(5) The Agency shall pay to members of its staff such remuneration, and such allowances, as it may, with the consent of the Secretary of State, determine.

(6) The Agency may—
    (a)   pay such pensions, allowances or gratuities to or in respect of any persons who have been or are members of its staff;

(b) make such payments towards provision for the payment of pensions, allowances or gratuities to or in respect of any such persons,

as it may, with the consent of the Secretary of State, determine.

(7) Any reference in sub-paragraph (6) to pensions, allowances or gratuities to or in respect of any such persons as are mentioned in that sub-paragraph includes a reference to payments by way of compensation to or in respect of any members of the Agency's staff who suffer loss of office or employment or loss or diminution of emoluments.

(8) The approval of the Treasury shall be required for the giving of any consent under sub-paragraph (4), (5) or (6).

Delegation of powers

4 Anything authorised or required to be done by the Agency under this Part—

(a) may be done by any member of the Agency, or of its staff, who has been authorised for the purpose, whether generally or specially, by the Agency; or

(b) may be done by any committee or sub-committee of the Agency which has been so authorised.

Proceedings

5 (1) Subject to the following provisions of this Schedule, the Agency may regulate both its own procedure (including quorum) and that of any committee or sub-committee.

(2) The Secretary of State may give directions as to the exercise by the Agency of its power under sub-paragraph (1) to regulate procedure; and directions under this sub-paragraph may be of a general or particular nature and may be varied or revoked by subsequent directions.

(3) The validity of any proceedings of the Agency or of any committee or sub-committee of the Agency shall not be affected—

(a) by a vacancy amongst the members of the Agency, committee or sub-committee;

(b) by a defect in the appointment of a member of the Agency, committee or sub-committee; or

(c) by a contravention of directions under sub-paragraph (2) or of paragraph 6.

(4) With the consent of the Secretary of State, persons who are not members of the Agency may be appointed as members of a committee or sub-committee of the Agency, but any such committee or sub-committee may not consist entirely of persons who are neither members of the Agency nor members of its staff

(5) The Agency may pay to any person who is a member of a committee or sub-committee but who is not a member of the Agency such remuneration, and such allowances, as the Secretary of State may, with the approval of the Treasury, determine.

Members' interests

6 (1) A member of the Agency or of any committee or sub-committee who is directly or indirectly interested in any matter brought up for consideration at a meeting of the Agency or of the committee or sub-committee shall disclose the nature of his interest to the meeting.

(2) Where the matter in respect of which such a disclosure is made is a contract or agreement of any description, the member shall not take part in any deliberation or decision of the Agency, committee or sub-committee with respect to the matter.

(3) Where the matter in respect of which such a disclosure is made is one other than a contract or agreement, the member may take part in any deliberation or decision of the Agency, committee or sub-committee with respect to the matter unless the rest of the members decide that the interest disclosed might prejudicially affect the member's consideration of the matter.

Application of seal and proof of instruments

7 (1) The application of the seal of the Agency shall be authenticated by the signature of any member of the Agency, or of its staff, who has been authorised by the Agency, whether generally or specially, for the purpose.

(2) Every document purporting to be an instrument issued by the Agency and to be duly sealed with the seal of the Agency or to be signed on behalf of the Agency shall be received in evidence and, unless the contrary is shown, shall be deemed to be an instrument so issued.

House of Commons disqualification

8 In Schedule 1 to the House of Commons Disqualification Act 1975 (bodies of which all members are disqualified for membership of the House of Commons), in Part II there shall be inserted, at the appropriate place, the following entry—

"The Urban Regeneration Agency.";

and the like insertion shall be made in Part II of Schedule 1 to the Northern Ireland Assembly Disqualification Act 1975.

References   See para 12.15 ff.

SCHEDULE 18   Section 158(2)
FINANCES OF THE AGENCY

Financial year

1 The financial years of the Agency shall be as follows—
   (a)   the period beginning with the commencement of this Schedule and ending with the next following 31st March; and
   (b)   each successive period of twelve months;
and references in this Schedule to a financial year shall be construed accordingly.

Financial duties

2 (1) After consultation with the Agency, the Secretary of State may, with the approval of the Treasury, determine the financial duties of the Agency; and different determinations may be made in relation to different functions of the Agency.

(2) The Secretary of State shall give the Agency notice of every determination, and a determination may—
   (a)   relate to a period beginning before the date on which it is made;
   (b)   contain incidental or supplementary provisions; and
   (c)   be varied or revoked by a subsequent determination.

Government grants

3 (1) The Secretary of State may, out of moneys provided by Parliament and with the approval of the Treasury, pay to the Agency, in respect of the exercise of its functions and in respect of its administrative expenses, such sums as he may, with the approval of the Treasury, determine.

(2) The payment may be made on such terms as the Secretary of State may, with the approval of the Treasury, determine.

Borrowing

4 (1) The Agency may borrow temporarily, by way of overdraft or otherwise, such sums as it may require for meeting its obligations and exercising its functions—
   (a)   in sterling from the Secretary of State; or

    (b)   with the consent of the Secretary of State, or in accordance with any general authority given by the Secretary of State, either in sterling or in a currency other than sterling from a person other than the Secretary of State.

(2) The Agency may borrow otherwise than by way of temporary loan such sums as it may require—

    (a)   in sterling from the Secretary of State; or

    (b)   with the consent of the Secretary of State, in a currency other than sterling from a person other than the Secretary of State.

(3) The Secretary of State may lend to the Agency any sums it has power to borrow from him under sub-paragraph (1) or (2).

(4) The Treasury may issue to the Secretary of State out of the National Loans Fund any sums necessary to enable him to make loans under sub-paragraph (3).

(5) Loans made under sub-paragraph (3) shall be repaid to the Secretary of State at such times and by such methods, and interest on the loans shall be paid to him at such times and at such rates, as he may determine.

(6) All sums received by the Secretary of State under sub-paragraph (5) shall be paid into the National Loans Fund.

(7) The approval of the Treasury shall be required for the giving of any consent or authority under sub-paragraph (1) or (2), the making of any loan under sub-paragraph (3) or the making of any determination under sub-paragraph (5).

Guarantees

5 (1) The Treasury may guarantee, in such manner and on such conditions as they think fit, the repayment of the principal of, and the payment of interest on, any sums which the Agency borrows from a person other than the Secretary of State.

(2) Immediately after a guarantee is given under this paragraph, the Treasury shall lay a statement of the guarantee before each House of Parliament; and, where any sum is issued for fulfilling a guarantee so given, the Treasury shall lay before each House of Parliament a statement relating to that sum, as soon as possible after the end of each financial year—

    (a)   beginning with that in which the sum is issued; and

    (b)   ending with that in which all liability in respect of the principal of the sum and in respect of interest on it is finally discharged.

(3) Any sums required by the Treasury for fulfilling a guarantee under this paragraph shall be charged on and issued out of the Consolidated Fund.

(4) If any sums are issued in fulfilment of a guarantee given under this paragraph, the Agency shall make to the Treasury, at such times and in such manner as the Treasury may from time to time direct, payments of such amounts as the Treasury so direct in or towards repayment of the sums so issued and payments of interest, at such rates as the Treasury so direct, on what is outstanding for the time being in respect of sums so issued.

(5) Any sums received by the Treasury in pursuance of sub-paragraph (4) shall be paid into the Consolidated Fund.

Surplus funds

6 (1) This paragraph applies where it appears to the Secretary of State, after consultation with the Treasury and the Agency, that the Agency has a surplus, whether on capital or on revenue account, after making allowance by way of transfer to reserve or otherwise for its future requirements.

(2) The Agency shall, if the Secretary of State with the approval of the Treasury and after consultation with the Agency so directs, pay to the Secretary of State such sum not exceeding the amount of the surplus as may be specified in the direction.

(3) Any sum received by the Secretary of State under this paragraph shall, subject to sub-paragraph (5), be paid into the Consolidated Fund.

(4) The whole or part of any payment made to the Secretary of State by the Agency under sub-paragraph (2) shall, if the Secretary of State with the approval of the Treasury so determines, be treated as made—

    (a) by way of repayment of such part of the principal of loans under paragraph 4(3); and

    (b) in respect of the repayments due at such times,

as may be so determined.

(5) Any sum treated under sub-paragraph (4) as a repayment of a loan shall be paid by the Secretary of State into the National Loans Fund.

Financial limits

7 (1) The aggregate amount at any time of borrowed sums shall not exceed £200 million or such greater sum not exceeding £300 million as the Secretary of State may by order made by statutory instrument specify.

(2) In sub-paragraph (1) "borrowed sums" means sums borrowed by the Agency under paragraph 4 minus repayments made or treated as made in respect of those sums.

(3) No order shall be made under sub-paragraph (1) unless a draft of the order has been laid before and approved by resolution of the House of Commons.

Grants and loans: accounts

8 (1) The Secretary of State shall prepare in respect of each financial year an account—

    (a) of the sums issued to him under paragraph 4(4) and the sums received by him under paragraph 4(5) and of the disposal by him of those sums; and

    (b) of the sums paid into the Consolidated Fund or National Loans Fund under paragraph 6.

(2) The Secretary of State shall send the account to the Comptroller and Auditor General before the end of the month of November next following the end of that year.

(3) The Comptroller and Auditor General shall examine, certify and report on the account and lay copies of it and of his report before each House of Parliament.

(4) The form of the account and the manner of preparing it shall be such as the Treasury may direct.

Accounts

9 (1) The Agency-shall keep proper accounts and other records in relation to them.

(2) The accounts and records shall show, in respect of the financial year to which they relate, a true and fair view of the Agency's activities.

(3) The Agency shall prepare in respect of each financial year a statement of accounts complying with any requirement which the Secretary of State has, with the approval of the Treasury, notified in writing to the Agency relating to—

    (a) the information to be contained in the statement;

    (b) the manner in which the information is to be presented; and

    (c) the methods and principles according to which the statement is to be prepared.

(4) Subject to any requirement notified to the Agency under sub-paragraph (3), in preparing any statement of accounts in accordance with that sub-paragraph the Agency shall follow, with respect to each of the matters specified in paragraphs (a) to (c) of that sub-paragraph, such course as may for the time being be approved by the Secretary of State with the consent of the Treasury.

Audit

10 (1) The Agency's accounts and statements of accounts shall be audited by an auditor to be appointed annually by the Secretary of State.

(2) A person shall not be qualified for appointment under sub-paragraph (1) unless—

  (a) he is eligible for appointment as a company auditor under Part II of the Companies Act 1989 (eligibility for appointment as company auditor); and

  (b) if the Agency were a body to which section 384 of the Companies Act 1985 (duty to appoint auditors) applies, he would not be ineligible for appointment as company auditor of the Agency by virtue of section 27 of the Companies Act 1989 (ineligibility on ground of lack of independence).

Transmission to Secretary of State

11 As soon as the accounts and statement of accounts of the Agency for any financial year have been audited, it shall send to the Secretary of State a copy of the statement, together with a copy of any report made by the auditor on the statement or on the accounts.

Reports

12 (1) As soon as possible after the end of each financial year, the Agency—

  (a) shall make to the Secretary of State a report dealing generally with its operations during the year; and

  (b) shall include in the report a copy of its audited statement of accounts for that year and such information as the Secretary of State may specify.

(2) The Secretary of State shall lay a copy of the report before each House of Parliament.

Information

13 Without prejudice to paragraph 12, the Agency shall provide the Secretary of State with such information relating to its activities as he may require, and for that purpose—

  (a) shall permit any person authorised by the Secretary of State to inspect and make copies of the accounts, books, documents or papers of the Agency; and

  (b) shall afford such explanation of them as that person or the Secretary of State may reasonably require.

References See para 12.18.

SCHEDULE 19   Section 161(4)

VESTING OF LAND IN THE AGENCY: MODIFICATIONS OF ENACTMENTS

Land Compensation Act 1961 (c 33)

1 The Land Compensation Act 1961 shall have effect in relation to orders under section 161(1) of this Act with the modifications specified in paragraphs 2 to 5.

2 References to the date of service of a notice to treat shall be treated as references to the date on which an order under section 161(1) of this Act comes into force.

3 Section 17(2) (certification of appropriate alternative development) shall be treated as if for the words "the authority proposing to acquire the interest have served a notice to treat in respect thereof, or an agreement has been made for the sale thereof to that authority" there were substituted the words "an order under section 161 of the Leasehold Reform, Housing and Urban Development Act 1993 vesting the land in which the interest subsists in the Urban Regeneration Agency has come into force, or an agreement has been made for the sale of the interest to the Agency".

4 Section 22(2) (interpretation of Part III) shall be treated as if at the end of paragraph (c) there were added the words "or

  (ca) where an order has been made under section 161(1) of the Leasehold Reform, Housing and Urban Development Act 1993 vesting the land in which the interest subsists in the Urban Regeneration Agency".

5 Any reference to a notice to treat in section 39(2) (interpretation) shall be treated as a reference to an order under section 161(1) of this Act.

Compulsory Purchase (Vesting Declarations) Act 1981 (c 66)

6 In section 15 of the Compulsory Purchase (Vesting Declarations) Act 1981 (application to orders under section 141 of Local Government, Planning and Land Act 1980) after the words "vesting declaration)" there shall be inserted the words "or under subsection (1) of section 161 of the Leasehold Reform, Housing and Urban Development Act 1993 (subsection (4) of which makes similar provision)".

7 (1) In Schedule 2 to that Act (vesting of land in urban development corporation), in paragraph 1 after the words "similar provision)" there shall be inserted the words "or under subsection (1) of section 161 of the Leasehold Reform, Housing and Urban Development Act 1993 (subsection (4) of which contains similar provision)".

(2) In paragraph 3(a) of that Schedule for the words "or, as the case may be, the housing action trust" there shall be substituted the words "the housing action trust or the Urban Regeneration Agency (as the case may be)".

SCHEDULE 20   Section 169
THE AGENCY: LAND

PART I
MODIFICATIONS OF ACQUISITION OF LAND ACT 1981

1 The Acquisition of Land Act 1981 (in this Part of this Schedule referred to as "the 1981 Act") shall have effect in relation to the compulsory acquisition of land under this Part of this Act with the modifications specified in paragraphs 2 and 3.

2 (1) Where a compulsory purchase order authorising the acquisition of any land is submitted to the Secretary of State in accordance with section 2(2) of the 1981 Act (procedure for authorisation), then if the Secretary of State—
   (a) is satisfied that the order ought to be confirmed so far as it relates to part of the land comprised in it, but
   (b) has not for the time being determined whether it ought to be confirmed so far as it relates to any other such land,
he may confirm the order so far as it relates to the land mentioned in paragraph (a), and give directions postponing the consideration of the order, so far as it relates to any other land specified in the directions, until such time as may be so specified.

(2) Where the Secretary of State gives directions under sub-paragraph (1), the notices required by section 15 of the 1981 Act (notices after confirmation of order) to be published and served shall include a statement of the effect of the directions.

3 The reference in section 17(3) of the 1981 Act (local authority and statutory undertakers' land) to statutory undertakers includes a reference to the Agency.

PART II
LAND: SUPPLEMENTARY

Extinguishment of rights over land

4 (1) Subject to this paragraph, on an order under section 161(1) of this Act coming into force or the completion by the Agency of a compulsory acquisition of land under this Part of this Act—
   (a) all private rights of way and rights of laying down, erecting, continuing or maintaining any apparatus on, under or over the land shall be extinguished; and
   (b) any such apparatus shall vest in the Agency.

(2) Sub-paragraph (1) does not apply—

    (a)   to any right vested in, or apparatus belonging to, statutory undertakers for the purpose of carrying on their undertaking; or

    (b)   to any right conferred by or in accordance with the telecommunications code on the operator of a telecommunications code system or to any telecommunications apparatus kept installed for the purposes of any such system.

(3) In respect of any right or apparatus not falling within sub-paragraph (2), sub-paragraph (1) shall have effect subject to—

    (a)   any direction given by the Secretary of State before the coming into force of the order or by the Agency before the completion of the acquisition (as the case may be) that sub-paragraph (1) shall not apply to any right or apparatus specified in the direction, and

    (b)   any agreement which may be made (whether before or after the coming into force of the order or completion of the acquisition) between the Secretary of State or the Agency and the person in or to whom the right or apparatus in question is vested or belongs.

(4) Any person who suffers loss by the extinguishment of a right or the vesting of any apparatus under this paragraph shall be entitled to compensation from the Agency.

(5) Any compensation payable under this paragraph shall be determined in accordance with the Land Compensation Act 1961.

Power to override easements

5 (1) The erection, construction, carrying out, or maintenance of any building or work on land which has been vested in or acquired by the Agency under this Part of this Act, whether done by the Agency or by any other person, is authorised by virtue of this paragraph if it is done in accordance with planning permission, notwithstanding that it involves—

    (a)   interference with an interest or right to which this paragraph applies; or

    (b)   a breach of a restriction as to the user of land arising by virtue of a contract.

(2) Nothing in sub-paragraph (1) shall authorise interference with any right of way or right of laying down, erecting, continuing or maintaining apparatus on, under or over land, being—

    (a)   a right vested in or belonging to statutory undertakers for the purpose of the carrying on of their undertaking; or

    (b)   a right conferred by or in accordance with the telecommunications code on the operator of a telecommunications code system.

(3) This paragraph applies to the following interests and rights, that is to say, any easement, liberty, privilege, right or advantage annexed to land and adversely affecting other land, including any natural right to support.

(4) In respect of any interference or breach in pursuance of sub-paragraph (1), compensation shall be payable under section 7 or 10 of the Compulsory Purchase Act 1965, to be assessed in the same manner and subject to the same rules as in the case of other compensation under those sections in respect of injurious affection where the compensation is to be estimated in connection with a purchase by the Agency or the injury arises from the execution of works on land acquired by the Agency.

(5) Where a person other than the Agency—

    (a)   is liable to pay compensation by virtue of sub-paragraph (4); and

    (b)   fails to discharge that liability,

the liability shall (subject to sub-paragraph (6)) be enforceable against the Agency.

(6) Nothing in sub-paragraph (5) shall be construed as affecting any agreement between the Agency and any other person for indemnifying the Agency against any liability under that sub-paragraph.

(7) Nothing in this paragraph shall be construed as authorising any act or omission on the part of any person which is actionable at the suit of any person on any grounds other than such an interference or breach as is mentioned in sub-paragraph (1).

(8) Nothing in this paragraph shall be construed as authorising any act or omission on the part of the Agency or any body corporate in contravention of any limitation imposed by law on its capacity by virtue of its constitution.

Consecrated land and burial grounds

6 (1) Any consecrated land, whether including a building or not, which has been vested in or acquired by the Agency under this Part of this Act may (subject to the following provisions of this paragraph) be used by the Agency, or by any other person, in any manner in accordance with planning permission, notwithstanding any obligation or restriction imposed under ecclesiastical law or otherwise in respect of consecrated land.

(2) Sub-paragraph (1) does not apply to land which consists or forms part of a burial ground.

(3) Any use of consecrated land authorised by sub-paragraph (1), and the use of any land, not being consecrated land, vested or acquired as mentioned in that sub-paragraph which at the time of vesting or acquisition included a church or other building used or formerly used for religious worship or the site thereof, shall be subject to compliance with the prescribed requirements with respect to—

    (a)   the removal and reinterment of any human remains; and

    (b)   the disposal of monuments,

and, in the case of consecrated land, shall be subject to such provisions as may be prescribed for prohibiting or restricting the use of the land, either absolutely or until the prescribed consent has been obtained, so long as any church or other building used or formerly used for religious worship, or any part thereof, remains on the land.

(4) Any regulations made for the purposes of sub-paragraph (3)—

    (a)   shall contain such provisions as appear to the Secretary of State to be requisite for securing that any use of land which is subject to compliance with the regulations shall, as nearly as may be, be subject to the like control as is imposed by law in the case of a similar use authorised by an enactment not contained in this Act or by a Measure, or as it would be proper to impose on a disposal of the land in question otherwise than in pursuance of an enactment or Measure;

    (b)   shall contain requirements relating to the disposal of any such land as is mentioned in sub-paragraph (3) such as appear to the Secretary of State requisite for securing that the provisions of that sub-paragraph shall be complied with in relation to the use of the land; and

    (c)   may contain such incidental and consequential provisions (including provision as to the closing of registers) as appear to the Secretary of State to be expedient for the purposes of the regulations.

(5) Any land consisting of a burial ground or part of a burial ground which has been vested in or acquired by the Agency under this Part of this Act may be used by the Agency in any manner in accordance with planning permission, notwithstanding anything in any enactment relating to burial grounds or any obligation or restriction imposed under ecclesiastical law or otherwise in respect of burial grounds.

(6) Sub-paragraph (5) shall not have effect in respect of any land which has been used for the burial of the dead until the prescribed requirements with respect to the removal and reinterment of human remains and the disposal of monuments in or upon the land have been complied with.

(7) Provision shall be made by any regulations made for the purposes of sub-paragraphs (3) and (6)—

    (a)   for requiring the persons in whom the land is vested to publish notice of their intention to carry out the removal and reinterment of any human remains or the disposal of any monuments;

(b) for enabling the personal representatives or relatives of any deceased person them-selves to undertake the removal and reinterment of the remains of the deceased and the disposal of any monument commemorating the deceased, and for requiring the persons in whom the land is vested to defray the expenses of such removal, reinterment and disposal, not exceeding such amount as may be prescribed;

(c) for requiring compliance with such reasonable conditions (if any) as may be imposed, in the case of consecrated land, by the bishop of the diocese, with respect to the manner of removal and the place and manner of reinterment of any human remains and the disposal of any monuments; and

(d) for requiring compliance with any directions given in any case by the Secretary of State with respect to the removal and reinterment of any human remains.

(8) Subject to the provisions of any such regulations as are referred to in sub-paragraph (7), no faculty shall be required—

(a) for the removal and reinterment in accordance with the regulations of any human remains; or

(b) for the removal or disposal of any monuments;

and the provisions of section 25 of the Burial Act 1857 (which prohibits the removal of human remains without the licence of the Secretary of State except in certain cases) shall not apply to a removal carried out in accordance with the regulations.

(9) Any power conferred by this paragraph to use land in a manner therein mentioned shall be construed as a power so to use the land, whether or not it involves—

(a) the erection, construction or carrying out of any building or work; or

(b) the maintenance of any building or work.

(10) Nothing in this paragraph shall be construed as authorising any act or omission on the part of any person which is actionable at the suit of any person on any grounds other than contravention of any such obligation, restriction or enactment as is mentioned in sub-paragraph (1) or (5).

(11) Sub-paragraph (8) of paragraph 5 shall apply in relation to this paragraph as it applies in relation to that.

(12) In this paragraph—

"burial ground" includes any churchyard, cemetery or other ground, whether consecrated or not, which has at any time been set apart for the purposes of interment; and

"monument" includes a tombstone or other memorial.

(13) In this paragraph "prescribed" means prescribed by regulations made by the Secretary of State.

(14) The power to make regulations under this paragraph shall be exercisable by statutory instrument which shall be subject to annulment in pursuance of a resolution of either House of Parliament.

Open spaces

7 (1) Any land being, or forming part of, a common, open space or fuel or field garden allotment, which has been vested in or acquired by the Agency under this Part of this Act may be used by the Agency, or by any other person, in any manner in accordance with planning permission, notwithstanding anything in any enactment—

(a) relating to land of that kind; or

(b) by which the land is specially regulated.

(2) Nothing in this paragraph shall be construed as authorising any act or omission on the part of any person which is actionable at the suit of any person on any grounds other than contravention of any such enactment as is mentioned in sub-paragraph (1).

(3) Sub-paragraph (8) of paragraph 5 shall apply in relation to this paragraph as it applies in relation to that.

Displacement of persons

8 If the Secretary of State certifies that possession of a house which—

    (a)   has been vested in or acquired by the Agency under this Part of this Act; and

    (b)   is for the time being held by the Agency for the purposes of its objects,

is immediately required for those purposes, nothing in the Rent (Agriculture) Act 1976, the Rent Act 1977 or the Housing Act 1988 shall prevent the Agency from obtaining possession of the house.

Extinguishment of public rights of way

9 (1) Where any land—

    (a)   has been vested in or acquired by the Agency under this Part of this Act; and

    (b)   is for the time being held by the Agency for the purposes of its objects,

the Secretary of State may by order extinguish any public right of way over the land.

(2) Where the Secretary of State proposes to make an order under this paragraph, he shall—

    (a)   publish in such manner as appears to him to be requisite a notice—

        (i)   stating the effect of the order, and

        (ii) specifying the time (not being less than 28 days from the publication of the notice) within which, and the manner in which, objections to the proposal may be made; and

    (b)   serve a like notice—

        (i)   on the local planning authority in whose area the land is situated; and

        (ii) on the relevant highway authority.

(3) In sub-paragraph (2) "the relevant highway authority" means any authority which is a highway authority in relation to the right of way proposed to be extinguished by the order under this paragraph.

(4) Where an objection to a proposal to make an order under this paragraph is duly made and is not withdrawn, the provisions of paragraph 10 shall have effect in relation to the proposal.

(5) For the purposes of this paragraph an objection to such a proposal shall not be treated as duly made unless—

    (a)   it is made within the time and in the manner specified in the notice required by this paragraph; and

    (b)   a statement in writing of the grounds of the objection is comprised in or submitted with the objection.

10 (1) In this paragraph any reference to making a final decision, in relation to an order, is a reference to deciding whether to make the order or what modification, if any, ought to be made.

(2) Unless the Secretary of State decides apart from the objection not to make the order, or decides to make a modification which is agreed to by the objector as meeting the objection, the Secretary of State—

    (a)   shall, before making a final decision, consider the grounds of the objection as set out in the statement comprised in or submitted with the objection; and

    (b)   may, if he thinks fit, require the objector to submit within a specified period a further statement in writing as to any of the matters to which the objection relates.

(3) In so far as the Secretary of State, after considering the grounds of the objection as set out in the original statement and in any such further statement, is satisfied that the objection relates to a matter which can be dealt with in the assessment of compensation, he may treat the objection as irrelevant for the purpose of making a final decision.

(4) In any case where—

    (a)   after considering the grounds of the objection as set out in the original statement and in any such further statement, the Secretary of State is satisfied that, for the purpose of making a final decision, he is sufficiently informed as to the matters to which the objection relates; or

(b)   a further statement has been required but is not submitted within the specified period,

the Secretary of State may make a final decision without further investigation as to the matters to which the objection relates.

(5) Subject to sub-paragraphs (3) and (4), the Secretary of State, before making a final decision, shall afford to the objector an opportunity of appearing before, and being heard by, a person appointed for the purpose by the Secretary of State; and if the objector avails himself of that opportunity, the Secretary of State shall afford an opportunity of appearing and being heard on the same occasion—

(a)   to the Agency; and

(b)   to any other persons to whom it appears to the Secretary of State to be expedient to afford such an opportunity.

(6) Notwithstanding anything in the preceding provisions of this paragraph, if it appears to the Secretary of State that the matters to which the objection relates are such as to require investigation by public local inquiry before he makes a final decision, he shall cause such an inquiry to be held; and where he determines to cause such an inquiry to be held, any of the requirements of those provisions to which effect has not been given at the time of that determination shall be dispensed with.

Telegraphic lines

11 (1) Where an order under paragraph 9 extinguishing a public right of way is made and at the time of the publication of the notice required by sub-paragraph (2) of that paragraph any telecommunication apparatus was kept installed for the purposes of a telecommunications code system under, in, on, over, along or across the land over which the right of way subsisted—

(a)   the power of the operator of the system to remove the apparatus shall, notwithstanding the making of the order, be exercisable at any time not later than the end of the period of three months from the date on which the right of way is extinguished and shall be exercisable in respect of the whole or any part of the apparatus after the end of that period if before the end of that period the operator of the system has given notice to the Agency of his intention to remove the apparatus or that part of it, as the case may be;

(b)   the operator of the system may by notice given in that behalf to the Agency not later than the end of the said period of three months abandon the telecommunication apparatus or any part of it;

(c)   subject to paragraph (b), the operator of the system shall be deemed at the end of that period to have abandoned any part of the apparatus which he has then neither removed nor given notice of his intention to remove;

(d)   the operator of the system shall be entitled to recover from the Agency the expense of providing, in substitution for the apparatus and any other telecommunication apparatus connected with it which is rendered useless in consequence of the removal or abandonment of the first-mentioned apparatus, any telecommunication apparatus in such other place as the operator may require; and

(e)   where under the preceding provisions of this sub-paragraph the operator of the system has abandoned the whole or any part of any telecommunication apparatus, that apparatus or that part of it shall vest in the Agency and shall be deemed, with its abandonment, to cease to be kept installed for the purposes of a telecommunications code system.

(2) As soon as practicable after the making of an order under paragraph 9 extinguishing a public right of way in circumstances in which sub-paragraph (1) applies in relation to the operator of any telecommunications code system, the Secretary of State shall give notice to the operator of the making of the order.

Statutory undertakers

12 (1) Where any land has been vested in or acquired by the Agency under this Part of this Act and—

(a) there subsists over that land a right vested in or belonging to statutory undertakers for the purpose of the carrying on of their undertaking, being a right of way or a right of laying down, erecting, continuing or maintaining apparatus on, under or over that land, or

(b) there is on, under or over the land apparatus vested in or belonging to statutory undertakers for the purpose of the carrying on of their undertaking,

the Agency may serve on the statutory undertakers a notice stating that, at the end of the period of 28 days from the date of service of the notice or such longer period as may be specified therein, the right will be extinguished or requiring that, before the end of that period, the apparatus shall be removed.

(2) The statutory undertakers on whom a notice is served under sub-paragraph (1) may, before the end of the period of 28 days from the service of the notice, serve a counter-notice on the Agency stating that they object to all or any provisions of the notice and specifying the grounds of their objection.

(3) If no counter-notice is served under sub-paragraph (2)—

(a) any right to which the notice relates shall be extinguished at the end of the period specified in that behalf in the notice; and

(b) if, at the end of the period so specified in relation to any apparatus, any requirement of the notice as to the removal of the apparatus has not been complied with, the Agency may remove the apparatus and dispose of it in any way it may think fit.

(4) If a counter-notice is served under sub-paragraph (2) on the Agency, it may either withdraw the notice (without prejudice to the service of a further notice) or apply to the Secretary of State and the appropriate Minister for an order under this paragraph embodying the provisions of the notice with or without modification.

(5) Where by virtue of this paragraph any right vested in or belonging to statutory undertakers is extinguished, or any requirement is imposed on statutory undertakers, those undertakers shall be entitled to compensation from the Agency.

(6) Sections 280 and 282 of the Town and Country Planning Act 1990 (measure of compensation to statutory undertakers) shall apply to compensation under sub-paragraph (5) as they apply to compensation under section 279(4) of that Act.

(7) Except in a case where paragraph 11 applies—

(a) the reference in paragraph (a) of sub-paragraph (1) to a right vested in or belonging to statutory undertakers for the purpose of the carrying on of their undertaking shall include a reference to a right conferred by or in accordance with the telecommunications code on the operator of a telecommunications code system; and

(b) the reference in paragraph (b) of that sub-paragraph to apparatus vested in or belonging to statutory undertakers for the purpose of the carrying on of their undertaking shall include a reference to telecommunication apparatus kept installed for the purposes of any such system.

(8) Where paragraph (a) or (b) of sub-paragraph (1) has effect as mentioned in sub-paragraph (7), in the rest of this paragraph and in paragraph 13—

(a) any reference to statutory undertakers shall have effect as a reference to the operator of any such system as is referred to in sub-paragraph (7); and

(b) any reference to the appropriate Minister shall have effect as a reference to the Secretary of State for Trade and Industry.

13 (1) Before making an order under paragraph 12 the Secretary of State and the appropriate Minister—

(a) shall afford to the statutory undertakers on whom notice was served under paragraph 12(1) an opportunity of objecting to the application for the order; and

(b) if any objection is made, shall consider the objection and afford to those statutory undertakers and to the Agency an opportunity of appearing before and being heard by a person appointed by the Secretary of State and the appropriate Minister for the purpose;

and the Secretary of State and the appropriate Minister may then, if they think fit, make the order in accordance with the application either with or without modification.

(2) Where an order is made under paragraph 12—

(a) any right to which the order relates shall be extinguished at the end of the period specified in that behalf in the order; and

(b) if, at the end of the period so specified in relation to any apparatus, any requirement of the order as to the removal of the apparatus has not been complied with, the Agency may remove the apparatus and dispose of it in any way it may think fit.

14 (1) Subject to this paragraph, where any land has been vested in or acquired by the Agency under this Part of this Act and—

(a) there is on, under or over the land apparatus vested in or belonging to statutory undertakers, and

(b) the undertakers claim that development to be carried out on the land is such as to require, on technical or other grounds connected with the carrying on of their undertaking, the removal or re-siting of the apparatus affected by the development,

the undertakers may serve on the Agency a notice claiming the right to enter on the land and carry out such works for the removal or re-siting of the apparatus or any part of it as may be specified in the notice.

(2) Where, after the land has been vested or acquired as mentioned in sub-paragraph (1), development of the land is begun to be carried out, no notice under this paragraph shall be served later than 21 days after the beginning of the development.

(3) Where a notice is served under this paragraph the Agency may, before the end of the period of 28 days from the date of service, serve on the statutory undertakers a counter-notice stating that it objects to all or any of the provisions of the notice and specifying the grounds of its objection.

(4) If no counter-notice is served under sub-paragraph (3), the statutory undertakers shall, after the end of the said period of 28 days, have the rights claimed in their notice.

(5) If a counter-notice is served under sub-paragraph (3), the statutory undertakers who served the notice under this paragraph may either withdraw it or apply to the Secretary of State and the appropriate Minister for an order under this paragraph conferring on the undertakers—

(a) the rights claimed in the notice; or

(b) such modified rights as the Secretary of State and the appropriate Minister think it expedient to confer on them.

(6) Where by virtue of this paragraph or an order made by the Secretary of State and the appropriate Minister under it, statutory undertakers have the right to execute works for the removal or re-siting of apparatus, they may arrange with the Agency for the works to be carried out by the Agency, under the superintendence of the undertakers, instead of by the undertakers themselves.

(7) Where works are carried out for the removal or re-siting of statutory undertakers' apparatus, being works which the undertakers have the right to carry out by virtue of this paragraph or an order made by the Secretary of State and the appropriate Minister under it, the undertakers shall be entitled to compensation from the Agency.

(8) Sections 280 and 282 of the Town and Country Planning Act 1990 (measure of compensation to statutory undertakers) shall apply to compensation under sub-paragraph (7) as they apply to compensation under section 279(4) of that Act.

(9) In sub-paragraph (1)(a), the reference to apparatus vested in or belonging to statutory undertakers shall include a reference to telecommunication apparatus kept installed for the purposes of a telecommunications code system.

(10) Where sub-paragraph (1)(a) has effect as mentioned in sub-paragraph (9), in the rest of this paragraph—

    (a) any reference to statutory undertakers shall have. effect as a reference to the operator of any such system as is referred to in sub-paragraph (9); and

    (b) any reference to the appropriate Minister shall have effect as a reference to the Secretary of State for Trade and Industry.

15 (1) The powers conferred by this paragraph shall be exercisable where, on a representation made by statutory undertakers, it appears to the Secretary of State and the appropriate Minister to be expedient that the powers and duties of those undertakers should be extended or modified, in order—

    (a) to secure the provision of services which would not otherwise be provided, or which would not otherwise be satisfactorily provided, in relation to relevant land; or

    (b) to facilitate an adjustment of the carrying on of the undertaking necessitated by any of the acts and events mentioned in sub-paragraph (2).

(2) The said acts and events are—

    (a) the vesting in or acquisition by the Agency under this Part of this Act of any land in which an interest was held, or which was used, for the purpose of the carrying on of the undertaking of the statutory undertakers in question; and

    (b) the extinguishment of a right or the imposition of any requirement by virtue of paragraph 12.

(3) The powers conferred by this paragraph shall also be exercisable where, on a representation made by the Agency, it appears to the Secretary of State and the appropriate Minister to be expedient that the powers and duties of statutory undertakers should be extended or modified, in order to secure the provision of new services, or the extension of existing services, in relation to relevant land.

(4) Where the powers conferred by this paragraph are exercisable, the Secretary of State and the appropriate Minister may, if they think fit, by order provide for such extension or modification of the powers and duties of the statutory undertakers as appears to them to be requisite in order to secure—

    (a) the provision of the services in question, as mentioned in sub-paragraph (1)(a) or sub-paragraph (3); or

    (b) the adjustment in question, as mentioned in sub-paragraph (1)(b),

as the case may be.

(5) Without prejudice to the generality of sub-paragraph (4), an order under this paragraph may make provision—

    (a) for empowering the statutory undertakers to acquire (whether compulsorily or by agreement) any land specified in the order, and to erect or construct any buildings or works so specified;

    (b) for applying, in relation to the acquisition of any such land or the construction of any such works, enactments relating to the acquisition of land and the construction of works;

    (c) where it has been represented that the making of the order is expedient for the purposes mentioned in sub-paragraph (1)(a) or (3), for giving effect to such financial arrangements between the Agency and the statutory undertakers as they may agree, or as, in default of agreement, may be determined to be equitable in such manner and by such tribunal as may be specified in the order; and

(d) for such incidental and supplemental matters as appear to the Secretary of State and the appropriate Minister to be expedient for the purposes of the order.

(6) In this paragraph "relevant land" means land in respect of which any of the functions of the Agency under this Part of this Act are being or have been exercised.

16 (1) As soon as may be after making such a representation as is mentioned in sub-paragraph (1) or (3) of paragraph 15—
    (a) the statutory undertakers, in a case falling within sub-paragraph (1), or
    (b) the Agency, in a case falling within sub-paragraph (3),
shall publish, in such form and manner as may be directed by the Secretary of State and the appropriate Minister, a notice giving such particulars as may be so directed of the matters to which the representation relates, and specifying the time within which, and the manner in which, objections to the making of an order on the representation may be made, and shall also, if it is so directed by the Secretary of State and the appropriate Minister, serve a like notice on such persons, or persons of such classes, as may be so directed.

(2) Orders under paragraph 15 shall be subject to special parliamentary procedure.

17 (1) Where, on a representation made by statutory undertakers, the appropriate Minister is satisfied that the fulfilment of any obligations incurred by those undertakers in connection with the carrying on of their undertaking has been rendered impracticable by an act or event to which this sub-paragraph applies, the appropriate Minister may, if he thinks fit, by order direct that the statutory undertakers shall be relieved of the fulfilment of that obligation, either absolutely or to such extent as may be specified in the order.

(2) Sub-paragraph (1) applies to the following acts and events—
    (a) the vesting in or acquisition by the Agency under this Part of this Act of any land in which an interest was held, or which was used, for the purpose of the carrying on of the undertaking of the statutory undertakers; and
    (b) the extinguishment of a right or the imposition of any requirement by virtue of paragraph 12.

(3) As soon as may be after making a representation to the appropriate Minister under sub-paragraph (1), the statutory undertakers shall, as may be directed by the appropriate Minister, do either or both of the following, that is to say—
    (a) publish (in such form and manner as may be so directed) a notice—
        (i) giving such particulars as may be so directed of the matters to which the representation relates; and
        (ii) specifying the time within which, and the manner in which, objections to the making of an order on the representation may be made; and
    (b) serve a like notice on such persons, or persons of such classes, as may be so directed.

(4) If any objection to the making of an order under this paragraph is duly made and is not withdrawn before the order is made, the order shall be subject to special parliamentary procedure.

(5) Immediately after an order is made under this paragraph by the appropriate Minister, he shall publish a notice stating that the order has been made and naming a place where a copy of it may be seen at all reasonable hours, and shall serve a like noticed—
    (a) on any person who duly made an objection to the order and has sent to the appropriate Minister a request in writing to serve him with the notice required by this sub-paragraph, specifying an address for service; and
    (b) on such other persons (if any) as the appropriate Minister thinks fit.

(6) Subject to the following provisions of this paragraph, an order under this paragraph shall become operative on the date on which the notice required by sub-paragraph (5) is first published.

(7) Where in accordance with sub-paragraph (4) the order is subject to special parliamentary procedure, sub-paragraph (6) shall not apply.

(8) If any person aggrieved by an order under this paragraph wishes to question the validity of the order on the ground—

(a) that it is not within the powers conferred by this paragraph, or

(b) that any requirement of this paragraph has not been complied with in relation to the order,

he may, within six weeks from the date on which the notice required by sub-paragraph (5) is first published, make an application to the High Court under this paragraph.

(9) On any application under sub-paragraph (8) the High Court—

(a) may by interim order wholly or in part suspend the operation of the order, either generally or in so far as it affects any property of the applicant, until the final determination of the proceedings; and

(b) if satisfied—

(i) that the order is wholly or to any extent outside the powers conferred by this paragraph; or

(ii) that the interests of the applicant have been substantially prejudiced by the failure to comply with any requirement of this paragraph,

may wholly or in part quash the order, either generally or in so far as it affects any property of the applicant.

(10) Subject to sub-paragraph (8), the validity of an order under this paragraph shall not be questioned in any legal proceedings whatsoever, either before or after the order has been made.

18 (1) For the purposes of paragraphs 15 and 17, an objection to the making of an order thereunder shall not be treated as duly made unless—

(a) the objection is made within the time and in the manner specified in the notice required by paragraph 16 or 17 (as the case may be); and

(b) a statement in writing of the grounds of the objection is comprised in or submitted with the objection.

(2) Where an objection to the making of such an order is duly made in accordance with sub-paragraph (1) and is not withdrawn, the following provisions of this paragraph shall have effect in relation thereto; but, in the application of those provisions to an order under paragraph 15, any reference to the appropriate Minister shall be construed as a reference to the Secretary of State and the appropriate Minister.

(3) Unless the appropriate Minister decides apart from the objection not to make the order, or decides to make a modification which is agreed to by the objector as meeting the objection, the appropriate Minister, before making a final decision—

(a) shall consider the grounds of the objection as set out in the statement; and

(b) may, if he thinks fit, require the objector to submit within a specified period a further statement in writing as to any of the matters to which the objection relates.

(4) In so far as the appropriate Minister after considering the grounds of the objection as set out in the original statement and in any such further statement, is satisfied that the objection relates to a matter which can be dealt with in the assessment of compensation, the appropriate Minister may treat the objection as irrelevant for the purpose of making a final decision.

(5) In any case where—

(a) after considering the grounds of the objection as set out in the original statement and in any such further statement, the appropriate Minister is satisfied that, for the purpose of making a final decision, he is sufficiently informed as to the matters to which the objection relates; or

(b) a further statement has been required but is not submitted within the specified period,

the appropriate Minister may make a final decision without further investigation as to the matters to which the objection relates.

(6) Subject to sub-paragraphs (4) and (5), the appropriate Minister, before making a final decision, shall afford to the objector an opportunity of appearing before, and being heard by, a person appointed for the purpose by the appropriate Minister; and if the objector avails himself of that opportunity, the appropriate Minister shall afford an opportunity of appearing and being heard on the same occasion—

    (a) to the person (being the Agency or the statutory undertakers) on whose representation the order is proposed to be made; and

    (b) to any other persons to whom it appears to the appropriate Minister to be expedient to afford such an opportunity.

(7) Notwithstanding anything in the preceding provisions of this paragraph, if it appears to the appropriate Minister that the matters to which the objection relates are such as to require investigation by public local inquiry before he makes a final decision, he shall cause such an inquiry to be held; and where he determines to cause such an inquiry to be held, any of the requirements of those provisions to which effect has not been given at the time of that determination shall be dispensed with.

(8) In this paragraph any reference to making a final decision, in relation to an order, is a reference to deciding whether to make the order or what modification (if any) ought to be made.

Interpretation

19 (1) Any expression used in this Part of this Schedule to which a meaning is assigned by paragraph 1 of Schedule 4 to the Telecommunications Act 1984 has that meaning in this Part.

(2) In this Part of this Schedule "statutory undertakers" means persons who are or are deemed to be statutory undertakers for the purposes of any provision of Part XI of the Town and Country Planning Act 1990; and "statutory undertaking" shall be construed in accordance with section 262 of that Act (meaning of "statutory undertaker").

(3) In this Part of this Schedule "the appropriate Minister" shall be construed as if contained in Part XI the Town and Country Planning Act 1990; and any reference to the Secretary of State and the appropriate Minister shall be similarly construed.

PART III
Acquisition of Rights

20 (1) The Compulsory Purchase Act 1965 (in this Part of this Schedule referred to as "the 1965 Act") shall have effect with the modifications necessary to make it apply to the compulsory acquisition of rights by virtue of section 162(2) of this Act as it applies to the compulsory purchase of land so that, in appropriate contexts, references in the 1965 Act to land are read as referring, or as including references, to the rights or to land over which the rights are or are to be exercisable, according to the requirements of the particular context.

(2) Without prejudice to the generality of sub-paragraph (1), in relation to the acquisition of rights by virtue of section 162(2) of this Act—

    (a) Part I of the 1965 Act (which relates to compulsory purchases under the Acquisition of Land Act 1981) shall have effect with the modifications specified in paragraphs 21 to 23; and

    (b) the enactments relating to compensation for the compulsory purchase of land shall apply with the necessary modifications as they apply to such compensation.

21 For section 7 of the 1965 Act (which relates to compensation) there shall be substituted the following section—

    "7 (1) In assessing the compensation to be paid by the acquiring authority under this Act regard shall be had not only to the extent, if any, to which the value of the land over which the right is purchased is depreciated by the purchase but also to the damage, if any, to be sustained by the owner of the land by reason of injurious affection of other land of the owner by the exercise of the right.

(2) The modifications subject to which subsection (1) of section 44 of the Land Compensation Act 1973 (compensation for injurious affectation) is to have effect, as applied by subsection (2) of that section to compensation for injurious affection under this section, are that for the words "land is acquired or taken" there shall be substituted the words "a right over land is acquired' and for the words "acquired or taken from him" there shall be substituted the words "over which the right is exercisable"."

22 For section 8 of the 1965 Act (which relates to cases in which a vendor cannot be required to sell part only of a building or garden) there shall be substituted the following section—

"**8** (1) Where in consequence of the service on a person in pursuance of section 5 of this Act of a notice to treat in respect of a right over land consisting of a house, building or manufactory or of a park or garden belonging to a house ("the relevant land")—

    (a) a question of disputed compensation in respect of the purchase of the right would apart from this section fall to be determined by the Lands Tribunal ("the Tribunal"); and

    (b) before the Tribunal has determined that question the person satisfies the Tribunal that he has an interest which he is able and willing to sell in the whole of the relevant land and—

        (i) where that land consists of a house, building or manufactory, that the right cannot be purchased without material detriment to that land, or

        (ii) where that land consists of such a park or garden, that the right cannot be purchased without seriously affecting the amenity or convenience of the house to which that land belongs,

the compulsory purchase order to which the notice to treat relates shall, in relation to that person, cease to authorise the purchase of the right and be deemed to authorise the purchase of that person's interest in the whole of the relevant land including, where the land consists of such a park or garden, the house to which it belongs, and the notice shall be deemed to have been served in respect of that interest on such date as the Tribunal directs.

(2) Any question as to the extent of the land in which a compulsory purchase order is deemed to authorise the purchase of an interest by virtue of the preceding subsection shall be determined by the Tribunal.

(3) Where in consequence of a determination of the Tribunal that it is satisfied as mentioned in subsection (1) of this section a compulsory purchase order is deemed by virtue of that subsection to authorise the purchase of an interest in land, the acquiring authority may, at any time within the period of six weeks beginning with the date of the determination, withdraw the notice to treat in consequence of which the determination was made; but nothing in this subsection prejudices any other power of the authority to withdraw the notice.

(4) The modifications subject to which subsection (1) of section 58 of the Land Compensation Act 1973 (determination of material detriment) is to have effect, as applied by subsection (2) of that section to the duty of the Tribunal in determining whether it is satisfied as mentioned in subsection (1) of this section, are that—

    (a) at the beginning of paragraphs (a) and (b) there shall be inserted the words "a right over";

    (b) for the word "severance" there shall be substituted the words "right on the whole of the house, building or manufactory or of the house and the park or garden"; and

    (c) for the words "part proposed" and "part is" there shall be substituted respectively the words "right proposed" and "right is"."

23 (1) The following provisions of the 1965 Act (which state the effect of a deed poll executed in various circumstances where there is no conveyance by persons with interests in the land), namely—

    (a) section 9(4) (failure of owners to convey);

    (b) paragraph 10(3) of Schedule 1 (owners under incapacity);

    (c) paragraph 2(3) of Schedule 2 (absent and untraced owners); and

    (d) paragraphs 2(3) and 7(2) of Schedule 4 (common land),

shall be so modified as to secure that, as against persons with interests in the land which are expressed to be overridden by the deed, the right which is to be acquired compulsorily is vested absolutely in the acquiring authority.

(2) Section 11 of the 1965 Act (powers of entry) shall be so modified as to secure that, as from the date on which the acquiring authority has served notice to treat in respect of any right, it has power, exercisable in the like circumstances and subject to the like conditions, to enter for the purpose of exercising that right (which shall be deemed for this purpose to have been created on the date of service of the notice); and sections 12 (penalty for unauthorised entry) and 13 (entry on sheriff's warrant in the event of obstruction) of the 1965 Act shall be modified correspondingly.

(3) Section 20 of the 1965 Act (compensation for short-term tenants) shall apply with the modifications necessary to secure that persons with such interests as are mentioned in that section are compensated in a manner corresponding to that in which they would be compensated on a compulsory purchase of the interests but taking into account only the extent (if any) of such interference with such interests as is actually caused, or likely to be caused, by the exercise of the right in question.

(4) Section 22 of the 1965 Act (protection of acquiring authority's possession of land where by inadvertence an interest in the land has not been purchased) shall be so modified as to enable the acquiring authority, in circumstances corresponding to those referred to in that section, to continue to be entitled to exercise the right in question, subject to compliance with that section as respects compensation.

Definitions   For "the Agency", see s 158 ante; for "the operator", "telecommunications apparatus", "telecommunications code" and "telecommunications code system", see, by virtue of para 19(1), the Telecommunications Act 1984, Sch 4, para 1; for "statutory undertakers" and "statutory undertaking", see para 19(2); for "the appropriate minister", see para 19(3); for "compulsory purchase order", see the Compulsory Purchase Act 1965, s 1(1); for "acquiring authority" and "land", see s 1(2) of that Act,; for "owner", see s 1(6) of that Act.

References   See para 12.21.

SCHEDULE 21   Section 187(1)

Minor and Consequential Amendments

Land Registration Act 1925 (c 21)

1 In section 49(1) of the Land Registration Act 1925 (rules to provide for notices of other rights, interests and claims), there shall be added at the end—

> "(k) orders made under section 26(1) or 50(1) of the Leasehold Reform, Housing and Urban Development Act 1993 which in the case of unregistered land may be protected by registration under the Land Charges Act 1972 and which, notwithstanding section 59 of this Act, it may be deemed expedient to protect by notice instead of by caution."

Landlord and Tenant Act 1954 (c 56)

2 In subsection (1) of section 60 of the Landlord and Tenant Act 1954 (special provisions as to premises provided by English Industrial Estates Corporation etc), for the words "the

English Industrial Estates Corporation" there shall be substituted the words "the Urban Regeneration Agency".

Parliamentary Commissioner Act 1967 (c 13)

3 (1) In Schedule 2 to the Parliamentary Commissioner Act 1967 (departments etc subject to investigation), after the entry "Urban development corporations." there shall be inserted the following entry—

"Urban Regeneration Agency."

(2) After Note 10 of that Schedule there shall be inserted the following Note—

"11 In the case of the Urban Regeneration Agency no investigation under this Act shall be conducted in respect of any action in connection with functions in relation to town and country planning."

Leasehold Reform Act 1967 (c 88)

4 In subsection (1A) of section 21 of the Leasehold Reform Act 1967 (jurisdiction of leasehold valuation tribunals), for the words from "be" onwards there shall be substituted the words "comply with any requirements imposed by regulations under subsection (4A)(a) or (b) below".

Land Compensation Act 1973 (c 26)

5 After section 12 of the Land Compensation Act 1973 (tenants entitled to enfranchisement or extension under Leasehold Reform Act 1967) there shall be inserted the following section—

"12A Tenants participating in collective enfranchisement, or entitled to individual lease extension, under Part I of Leasehold Reform, Housing and Urban Development Act 1993

(1) A tenancy to which subsection (2) or (3) below applies ("a qualifying tenancy") shall be treated as an owner's interest as defined in section 2(4) above whether or not the unexpired term on the date of service of the notice of claim is of the length there specified.

(2) This subsection applies to a tenancy if the tenant, on the relevant date—

    (a) is in respect of the tenancy a qualifying tenant for the purposes of Chapter I of Part I of the 1993 Act (collective enfranchisement); and

    (b) by virtue of the tenancy, either—

        (i) is a participating tenant in relation to a claim to exercise the right to collective enfranchisement under that Chapter; or

        (ii) is one of the participating tenants on whose behalf the acquisition by the nominee purchaser has been made in pursuance of such a claim.

(3) This subsection applies to a tenancy if the tenant, on the relevant date and in respect of the tenancy, is a qualifying tenant for the purposes of Chapter II of Part I of the 1993 Act (individual right to acquire new lease) who—

    (a) has on or before that date given notice under section 42 of that Act (notice by qualifying tenant of claim to exercise right); and

    (b) has not acquired a new lease before that date.

(4) If no claim is made in respect of a qualifying tenancy before the claimant has ceased to be entitled to it in consequence of a lease being granted to him by the nominee purchaser or, as the case may be, under Chapter II of Part I of the 1993 Act, the claimant may make a claim in respect of the qualifying tenancy as if he were still entitled to it.

(5) No claim shall be made by virtue of subsection (4) above after the claimant has ceased to be entitled to the lease referred to in that subsection, but such a claim may be made before the first claim day if it is made before the claimant has disposed of that lease and after he has made a contract for disposing of it.

(6) Compensation shall not be payable before the first claim day on any claim made by virtue of subsection (5) above.

(7) Any notice of a claim made by virtue of this section shall contain, in addition to the matters mentioned in section 3 above, a statement that it is made in respect of a qualifying tenancy as defined in this section and, if made by virtue of subsection (4) or (5) above, sufficient particulars to show that it falls within that subsection.

(8) In relation to a claim made by virtue of subsection (4) above, section 4(4)(a) above shall have effect as if the reference to the date of service of notice of the claim were a reference to the relevant date.

(9) In this section—

    (a) "the 1993 Act" means the Leasehold Reform, Housing and Urban Development Act 1993; and

    (b) "participating tenant", "nominee purchaser" and "the acquisition by the nominee purchaser" shall be construed in accordance with sections 14, 15 and 38(2) of that Act respectively."

Local Government Act 1974 (c 7)

6 (1) In subsection (1) of section 25 of the Local Government Act 1974 (authorities subject to investigation), after paragraph (be) there shall be inserted the following paragraph—

    "(bf) the Urban Regeneration Agency;".

(2) In subsection (7) of section 26 of that Act (matters subject to investigation) after paragraph (b) there shall be inserted the following paragraph—

    "(ba) where the complaint relates to the Urban Regeneration Agency, any designated area within the meaning of Part III of the Leasehold Reform, Housing and Urban Development Act 1993;".

(3) In Schedule 5 to that Act (matters not subject to investigation) after paragraph 7 there shall be inserted the following paragraph—

    "8.—Action taken by the Urban Regeneration Agency which is not action in connection with functions in relation to town and country planning."

Rent Act 1977 (c 42)

7 In subsection (1)(b) of section 74 of the Rent Act 1977 (regulations), for the words from "by rent officers" onwards there shall be substituted the words—

    "(i) by rent officers under this Act; and

    (ii) by rent assessment committees whether under this Act or otherwise; and"

Derelict Land Act 1982 (c 42)

8 In subsection (5) of section 1 of the Derelict Land Act 1982 (powers of Secretary of State), in the definition of "the prescribed percentage", for paragraphs (b) and (c) there shall be substituted the following paragraph—

    "(b) in any other case, 80 per cent or such other percentage as may be prescribed by order made by the Secretary of State with the consent of the Treasury."

National Heritage Act 1983 (c 47)

9 After subsection (2A) of section 33 of the National Heritage Act 1983 (general functions of the Historic Buildings and Monuments Commission for England) there shall be inserted the following subsection—

> "(2B) In relation to England, the Commission may make, or join in the making of, applications under section 73(1) of the Leasehold Reform, Housing and Urban Development Act 1993, and may exercise, or participate in the exercise of, any rights or powers conferred by a scheme approved under section 70 of that Act."

Housing Act 1985 (c 68)

10 In subsection (3) of section 101 of the Housing Act 1985 (rent not to be increased on account of tenant's improvements), for paragraph (a) there shall be substituted the following paragraph—

> "(a) a person in whom the tenancy was vested, or to whom the tenancy was disposed of, under section 89 (succession to periodic tenancy) or section 90 (devolution of term certain) on the death of the tenant or in the course of the administration of his estate;".

11 In subsection (2) of section 130 of that Act (reduction of discount where previous discount given), after paragraph (aa) there shall be inserted the following paragraph—

> "(ab) in pursuance of the provision required by paragraphs 3 to 5 or paragraph 7 of Schedule 6A (redemption of landlord's share), or".

12 For subsection (3) of section 140 of that Act (landlord's first notice to complete) there shall be substituted the following subsection—

> "(3) A notice under this section shall not be served earlier than twelve months after—
>
> > (a) the service of the landlord's notice under section 125 (notice of purchase price and other matters), or
> >
> > (b) where a notice has been served under section 146 (landlord's notice admitting or denying right to acquire on rent to mortgage terms), the service of that notice."

13 (1) Immediately before section 153A of that Act (tenant's notices of delay) there shall be inserted the following italic cross heading—

> *"Tenant's sanction for landlord's delays"*.

(2) In subsection (1) of that section—
> (a) in paragraph (e), for the words "right to be granted a shared ownership lease" there shall be substituted the words "right to acquire on rent to mortgage terms"; and
>
> (b) for the words "any of the cases in paragraphs (a) to (d)" there shall be substituted the words "either of the cases in paragraphs (a) and (b)".

(3) In subsection (3) of that section—
> (a) for the words "right to be granted a shared ownership lease" there shall be substituted the words "right to acquire on rent to mortgage terms";
>
> (b) for the words "any of the cases in paragraphs (a) to (d)" there shall be substituted the words "either of the cases in paragraphs (a) and (b)"; and
>
> (c) for the words "section 125, section 146 or section 147" there shall be substituted the words "or section 125".

14 (1) In subsection (1) of section 153B of that Act (payments of rent attributable to purchase price etc), for the words "right to be granted a shared ownership lease" there shall be substituted the words "right to acquire on rent to mortgage terms".

(2) In subsection (2) of that section, for the words "any of paragraphs (c) to (e)" there shall be substituted the words "paragraph (d) or (e)".

(3) In subsection (3) of that section, for the words "the tenant's initial contribution for the grant of a shared ownership lease" there shall be substituted the words "the tenant's initial payment".

15 In subsection (2) of section 158 of that Act (consideration for reconveyance or surrender under section 157), after paragraph (a) there shall be inserted the following paragraph—

> "(aa) any covenant required by paragraph 1 of Schedule 6A (obligation to redeem landlord's share where conveyance or grant executed in pursuance of right to acquire on rent to mortgage terms), and".

16 (1) In subsection (1) of section 164 of that Act (Secretary of State's general power to intervene), for the words "right to be granted a shared ownership lease" there shall be substituted the words "right to acquire on rent to mortgage terms".

(2) In subsection (4) of that section, for the words "the right to a mortgage or the right to be granted a shared ownership lease" there shall be substituted the words "or the right to acquire on rent to mortgage terms".

(3) In subsection (5) of that section, for the words "the right to a mortgage and the right to be granted a shared ownership lease" there shall be substituted the words "and the right to acquire on rent to mortgage terms".

17 In subsection (1) of section 167 of that Act (power to give directions as to covenants and conditions), after paragraph (b) there shall be inserted the words "or

> (c) in the case of conveyances or grants executed in pursuance of the right to acquire on rent to mortgage terms, the conveyances or grants would not conform with Schedule 6A,".

18 In subsection (2) of section 170 of that Act (power to give assistance in connection with legal proceedings), for the words "right to be granted a shared ownership lease" there shall be substituted the words "right to acquire on rent to mortgage terms".

19 In subsection (2) of section 171C of that Act (modifications of Part V in relation to preserved right), for the words "right to be granted a shared ownership lease" there shall be substituted the words "right to acquire on rent to mortgage terms".

20 (1) In subsection (2) of section 177 of that Act (errors and omissions in notices), for the words "right to be granted a shared ownership lease" there shall be substituted the words "right to acquire on rent to mortgage terms".

(2) In subsection (3) of that section, for the entries relating to section 147 and paragraph 1(3) of Schedule 8 there shall be substituted the following entry—

> "section 146 (landlord's notice admitting or denying right to acquire on rent to mortgage terms)."

21 For section 178 of that Act there shall be substituted the following section—

"178 Costs

> An agreement between the landlord and a tenant claiming to exercise—
> (a) the right to buy,
> (b) the right to acquire on rent to mortgage terms, or
> (c) any such right as is mentioned in paragraph 2(1) or 6(1) of Schedule 6A (redemption of landlord's share: right to make final or interim payment),
> is void in so far as it purports to oblige the tenant to bear any part of the costs incurred by the landlord in connection with the tenant's exercise of that right."

22 In subsection (1) of section 179 of that Act (provisions restricting right to buy etc of no effect), for the words "right to be granted a shared ownership lease" there shall be substituted the words "right to acquire on rent to mortgage terms".

23 In subsection (1) of section 181 of that Act (jurisdiction of county court), for the words "a shared ownership lease granted in pursuance of this Part" there shall be substituted the words "a conveyance or grant executed in pursuance of the right to acquire on rent to mortgage terms".

24 (1) In subsection (2) of section 184 of that Act (land let with or used for purposes of dwelling-house), for the words "right to be granted a shared ownership lease" there shall be substituted the words "right to acquire on rent to mortgage terms".

(2) In subsection (3) of that section, for the words "right to be granted a shared ownership lease" there shall be substituted the words "right to acquire on rent to mortgage terms".

25 In section 188 of that Act (index of defined expressions: Part V), at the appropriate places in alphabetical order there shall be inserted the following entries—

"district valuer	section 622"
"final payment	paragraph 1 of Schedule 6A"
"initial payment and interim payment	section 143B and paragraph 6 of Schedule 6A"
"landlord's share	section 148 and paragraph 7 of Schedule 6A"
"minimum initial payment and maximum initial payment	section 143B"
"prescribed	section 614"
"right to acquire on rent to mortgage terms	section 143".

Landlord and Tenant Act 1987 (c 31)

26 In subsection (2) of section 4 of the Landlord and Tenant Act 1987 (relevant disposals), after paragraph (d) there shall be inserted the following paragraph—

"(da) a disposal of any freehold or leasehold interest in pursuance of Chapter I of Part I of the Leasehold Reform, Housing and Urban Development Act 1993;".

27 In subsection (2) of section 13 of that Act (determination by rent assessment committees of questions relating to purchase notices), for the words from "be" to "particulars," there shall be substituted the words "comply with such requirements (if any) as to the form of, or the particulars to be contained in, any such application".

Town and Country Planning Act 1990 (c 8)

28 In subsection (5)(a) of section 1 of the Town and Country Planning Act 1990 (subsections (1) to (4) of that section have effect subject to sections 5 to 8), for "8" there shall be substituted "8A".

29 After section 8 of that Act (local planning authority in housing action area) there shall be inserted the following section—

"8A The Urban Regeneration Agency

(1) Where a designation order under section 170 of the Leasehold Reform, Housing and Urban Development Act 1993 (power to make designation orders) makes such provision as is mentioned in subsection (1) of section 171 of that Act (Agency as local planning authority), the Urban Regeneration Agency shall be the local planning authority for such area as may be specified in the order in place of any authority who would otherwise be the local planning authority for that area for such purposes and in relation to such kinds of development as may be so specified.

(2) Where such an order makes such provision as is mentioned in subsection (3)(a) of section 171 of that Act, the Urban Regeneration Agency shall have the functions

specified in the order for such area as may be so specified in place of any authority (except the Secretary of State) who would otherwise have them in that area."

Planning (Listed Buildings and Conservation Areas) Act 1990 (c 9)

30 (1) In subsection (1) of section 72 of the Planning (Listed Buildings and Conservation Areas) Act 1990 (general duty as respects conservation areas in exercise of planning functions), for the words "powers under" there shall be substituted the words "functions under or by virtue of".

(2) In subsection (2) of that section there shall be added at the end "and sections 70 and 73 of the Leasehold Reform, Housing and Urban Development Act 1993".

31 In paragraphs 2 and 4 of Schedule 4 to that Act (further provisions as to exercise of functions by different authorities), for the words "and 8" there shall be substituted the words "8 and 8A".

Planning (Hazardous Substances) Act 1990 (c 10)

32 After subsection (5) of section 3 of the Planning (Hazardous Substances) Act 1990 (hazardous substances authorities in certain special cases) there shall be inserted the following subsection—

"(5A) If the land is in an area for which the Urban Regeneration Agency is the local planning authority in relation to all kinds of development, the Agency shall be the hazardous substances authority for the land unless subsection (1) or (2) applies."

References   See para 1.30 ff.

SCHEDULE 22   Section 187(2)
REPEALS

Chapter	Short title	Extent of repeal
9 & 10 Eliz. 2. c 33	The Land Compensation Act 1961.	In section 23(3), the word "or" at the end of paragraph (b).
1975 c 24	The House of Commons Disqualification Act 1975.	In Schedule 1, in Part II, the entry relating to the English Industrial Estates Corporation.
1975 c 25	The Northern Ireland Assembly Disqualification Act 1975.	In Schedule 1, in Part II, the entry beginning "The Industrial Estates Corporations".
1980 c 51	The Housing Act 1980.	In section 141, "3,". In Schedule 21, paragraph 3.
1980 c 65	The Local Government, Planning and Land Act 1980.	Section 99A(2). Section 165(3).
1981 c 13	The English Industrial Estates Corporation Act 1981.	The whole Act.
1982 c 52	The Industrial Development Act 1982.	In section 15(1), paragraph (d) and the word "and" immediately preceding it. In Part II of Schedule 2, paragraph 17.

Chapter	Short title	Extent of repeal
1983 c 29	The Miscellaneous Financial Provisions Act 1983.	In Schedule 2, the entry relating to the English Industrial Estates Corporation Act 1981.
1985 c 25	The Industrial Development Act 1985.	Sections 1 to 4.
1985 c 68	The Housing Act 1985.	Section 27C.
		Section 124(3).
		Section 128(6).
		Sections 132 to 135.
		In section 137, in subsection (1), the words "or the right to a mortgage" and, in subsection (2), paragraph (b).
		In section 138(1), the words "and to the amount to be left outstanding or advanced on the security of the dwelling-house".
		Section 139(3).
		In section 140(5), the words "and to the amount to be left outstanding or advanced on the security of the dwelling-house".
		Section 142.
		In section 153A(1), paragraphs (c) and (d).
		In section 153B(1), paragraph (c).
		Section 164(6).
		Section 166(6).
		In section 169(3), paragraph (b) and the word "and" immediately preceding that paragraph.
		In section 171C(2), paragraph (b).
		In section 171H, in subsection (1), the words "or the right to a mortgage" and, in subsection (2), paragraph (b).
		In section 177, in subsection (2)(b) the words "or the Corporation" and in subsection (3), the entries relating to section 135 and paragraph 5 of Schedule 9.

Chapter	Short title	Extent of repeal
1985 c 60–*contd*	The Housing Act 1985–*contd*	In section 180, the words "the Corporation" and "Corporation".
		In section 181(1), the words "and paragraph 11 of Schedule 8".
		In section 182(1), the words "or the right to a mortgage".
		In section 187, the definition of "total share".
		In section 188, the entries beginning "additional share and additional contribution", "effective discount", "full mortgage", "initial share and initial contibution", "prescribed percentage", "right to be granted a shared ownership lease", "right to further advances", "right to a mortgage" and "total share".
		In Schedule 6, in paragraphs 16B(4) and 16C(4), paragraph (c) and the word "and" immediately preceding that paragraph.
		Schedules 7 to 9.
1985 c 71	The Housing (Consequential Provisions) Act 1985.	In section 6(3), "12". In Schedule 2, paragraph 12.
1986 c 63	The Housing and Planning Act 1986.	In Schedule 5, paragraph 5.
1987 c 26	The Housing (Scotland) Act 1987.	In section 17, in subsection (1), the words "and exercised by".
		In section 61, in subsection (10)(b), sub-paragraphs (i) and (ii).
		In section 62, in subsection (3)(b), the words "continuous" and "immediately".
1987 c 31	The Landlord and Tenant Act 1987.	Section 25(3). In section 29(2), the words from "and (c)" onwards.
1988 c 50	The Housing Act 1988.	Section 41(1). In section 69(2), the words from "on grounds" onwards.

Chapter	Short title	Extent of repeal
1985 c 60—*contd*	The Housing Act 1985—*contd*	In section 79(2)(b), the words "in accordance with section 84 below". In Schedule 9, paragraph 12(2).
1989 c 42	The Local Government and Housing Act 1989.	In section 80(1), the words from"and for any year" onwards. Section 164. In Schedule 11, paragraph 51.
1990 c 11	The Planning (Consequential Provisions) Act 1990.	In Schedule 2, paragraph 47.

References   See para 1.30 ff.

Table of defined terms

This table contains references to the various defined terms used in the 1993 Act. Some terms are used in several places with different meanings, so care must be taken to refer to the definition applicable to the provision in question. The table does not contain references to defined terms used in amendments to other legislation.

Defined term	Provisions affected	Place where defined
1965 Act	Sch 20, Pt III	Sch 20, para 20(1)
1967 Act	s 74	s 74(10)
1980 Act	Pt III	s 185
1985 Act	Pt I, Ch V	s 84
1985 Act	Pt II, Ch I	s 104
1989 Act	ss 135, 136	s 135(13)
Acquiring authority	s 30	s 30(7)
Acquisition by nominee purchaser	Pt I, Ch I	s 38(2)
Additional leaseback proposals	s 21	s 21(7)
Agency, the	Pt III	ss 158, 185
Agreement as to terms of acquisition	Pt I, Ch I	s 38(4)
Annual loan charges referable to the amount of the expense incurred, the	s 139	s 139(6)
Application for possession	Sch 14	Sch 14, para 1(2)
Appropriate authority	s 88	s 88(6)
Appropriate authority	s 94	s 94(11)
Appropriate date, the	s 8	s 8(2)
Appropriate date, the	s 23	s 23(7)
Appropriate date, the	s 47	s 47(6)
Appropriate landlord	s 23	s 23(10)
Appropriate Minister, the	s 161	s 161(7)
Appropriate Minister, the	Sch 20, Pt II	Sch 20, para 19(3)
Appropriate period, the	s 24	s 24(6)
Appropriate period, the	s 25	s 25(8)
Appropriate period, the	s 48	s 48(6)
Appropriate period, the	s 49	s 49(7)
Appropriate sum, the	s 51	s 51(5)

Defined term	Provisions affected	Place where defined
Appropriate time	Sch 7	Sch 7, para 1
Appropriate time	Sch 9, Sch 10, para 2	Sch 9, para 1(1)
Appurtenant property	Pt I, Ch V	s 76(3), (6)
Appurtenant property	ss 1, 2, 7	s 1(7)
Associated company	s 5	s 5(6)
Associates	ss 135, 136	s 135(14)
Auditor, the	Pt I, Ch V	ss 78(3), 79(8)
Authorised purpose	s 30	s 30(7)
Becoming final	Pt I	s 101(9)
Board, the	s 31	s 31(8)
Burial ground	Sch 20, para 6	Sch 20, para 6(12)
Business lease	Pt I	s 101(1)
Chapter I landlord	Sch 2	Sch 2, para 1(1)
Chapter II landlord	Sch 2	Sch 2, para 1(1)
Chargeable event	s 31	s 31(8)
Charitable housing trust	s 5	s 5(2)
Commission, the	s 73	s 73(5)
Common parts	Pt I	s 101(1)
Common service charge contributions	s 76	s 76(8)
Competent landlord, the	s 43 and Sch 11	s 40(4)(b)
Compulsory purchase order	s 162	s 162(7)
Connection notice	s 165	s 165(1)
Conservation area	ss 70, 73	s 70(14)
Consideration payable, the	Sch 8	Sch 8, para 1
Constituent dwellings, the	Pt I, Ch V	s 76(2)
Conveyance	Pt I, Ch I	s 38(1)
Counter-notice	Pt I, Ch I	s 21
Counter-notice	Pt I, Ch II	s 45
Court, the	Pt I	s 101(1)
Crown interest	s 88	s 88(6)
Crown interest	s 94	s 94(11)
Current	s 12	s 12(6)
Current	s 41	s 41(5)
Current	s 54	s 54(11)
Date of commencement of lease	Pt I	s 101(5), (6)
Debenture holder's charge	Sch 2	Sch 2, para 1(1)
Demised premises para 2	Sch 9, Sch 10,	Sch 9, para 1(1)
Designated area	Pt III	ss 170, 185
Designation order	Pt III	ss 170, 185
Development value	Sch 6, para 5	Sch 6, para 5(4)
Development value	Sch 13, para 5	Sch 13, para 5(4)
Diocesan board of finance	Sch 2, para 8	Sch 2, para 8(5)

Defined term	Provisions affected	Place where defined
Diocesan board of finance	Sch 14, para 12	Sch 14, para 12(2)
Diocesan glebe land	Sch 2, para 8	Sch 2, para 8(5)
Diocesan glebe land	Sch 14, para 12	Sch 14, para 12(2)
Disposal	Pt I	s 101(1)
Disposal	s 135	s 135(1)
Document	s 11	s 11(9)
Dwelling	Pt I	s 101(1)
Dwelling-house	ss 135, 136	s 135(13)
Ecclesiastical landlord	Sch 2, para 8	Sch 2, para 8(1)
Estate management scheme	Pt I, Ch IV	s 69
Exchequer costs, the	s 135	s 135(8)
Existing lease, the	Pt I, Ch II	s 62(1)
First financial year	s 137	s 137(1)
Flat	Pt I, Ch II	s 62(2)
Flat	Pt I	s 101(1)
Flat	s 61	s 61(5)
Flat	Sch 9	Sch 9, para 1(2)
Flat held by the tenant under the new lease, the	Sch 14	Sch 14, para 1(2)
Freeholder, the	s 1	s 1(7)
Freeholder, the	s 10	s 10(6)
Freeholder, the	Sch 6	Sch 6, para 1(1)
Freeholder, the	Sch 7	Sch 7, para 1
Freeholder, the	Sch 9	Sch 9, para 1(1)
Highway	Pt III	s 185
House, the	Pt I, Ch IV	s 69(1)(a)
Housing association	Sch 9	Sch 9, para 1(1)
Improve	s 160	s 160(4)
Incumbrances	s 34 and Sch 7, para 2	s 34(4)
Initial notice, the	Pt I, Ch I	s 13
Initial notice, the	Pt I, Ch IV	s 74(3)(a)
Initial year, the	s 8	s 8(2)
Interest	Pt I	s 101(1)
Interest of relevant landlord in specified premises	Pt I, Ch I	s 38(3)
Intermediate landlord	Sch 9	Sch 9, para 1(1)
Intermediate landlord, the	Sch 6, para 12	Sch 6, para 12(3)
Intermediate leasehold interest	Sch 6	Sch 6, para 1(1)
Intermediate leasehold interest	Sch 13	Sch 13, para 1
Landlord	Pt I, Ch V	ss 83(3), 84
Landlord	Pt I	s 101(2)
Landlord	s 87	s 87(9)
Landlord for the time being	Pt I, Ch IV	s 69(7)

Defined term	Provisions affected	Place where defined
Landlord, the	Pt I, Ch II	ss 40(1), 43(2)
Landlord, the	Sch 8	Sch 8, para 1
Lease	s 87	s 87(9)
Lease (and related expressions)	Pt I	s 101(1), (2)
Lease at a low rent, as to	Pt I, Ch I, and s 94	s 8
Lease from the Crown	s 88	s 88(6)
Lease from the Crown	s 94	s 94(11)
Lease held by qualifying tenant of flat	Pt I	s 101(3)
Leasehold valuation tribunal	s 75	s 75(5)
Leasehold valuation tribunal	ss 88, 91	s 88(7)
Letting value	s 8	s 8(3)
Local authority	ss 135, 136	s 135(13)
Local authority	s 161	s 161(7)
Local authority	s 170	s 170(6)
Local highway authority	s 165	s 165(9)
Local planning authority, the	ss 70, 73	s 70(14)
Long lease	Pt I, Ch I and ss 59, 94	s 7
Long lease	s 77	s 77(2)
Long lease	ss 135, 136	s 135(13)
Management audit	Pt I, Ch V	s 78(1)
Management functions	Pt I, Ch V	s 84
Minor intermediate lease	Sch 6, para 7	Sch 6, para 7(3)
Minor intermediate lease	Sch 13, para 8	Sch 13, para 8(3)
Monument	Sch 20, para 6	Sch 20, para 6(12)
Mortgage	s 35 and Sch 8	s 35(4)
Mortgage	Pt I, Ch II	s 62(1)
Mortgage	Sch 2	Sch 2, para 1(1)
Negative interest, the	Sch 6, para 14	Sch 6, para 14(2)
Negative interest, the	Sch 6, para 18	Sch 6, para 18(2)
New lease, the	s 61	s 61(1)
New lease, the	Sch 14	Sch 14, para 1(2)
New rights over land	s 162	s 162(7)
Nominee purchaser, the	Pt I, Ch I and ss 74, 91	s 15
Nominee purchaser, the	s 33	s 33(6)
Notice of withdrawal	Pt I, Ch I	s 28(1)
Notice of withdrawal	s 52	s 52(1)
Order for possession	Sch 14	Sch 14, para 1(2)
Other landlord	s 43 and Sch 11	s 40(4)(c)
Other property	Sch 7	Sch 7, para 1
Other property	Sch 9	Sch 9, para 1(1)
Participating tenants	Pt I, Ch I and s 91	s 14
Parties, the	s 24	s 24(7)
Persons interested	s 70	s 70(5)
Planning Acts, the	ss 70, 73	s 70(14)

Defined term	Provisions affected	Place where defined
Premises with a resident landlord	Pt I, Ch I	s 10
Premises, the	Pt I, Ch IV	s 69(1)(b)
Premium payable on the grant of a lease	Sch 2, paras 5–8	Sch 2, para 1(2)
Prescribed	Sch 20, para 6	Sch 20, para 6(13)
Private street	Pt III	s 185
Profit rent	Sch 13, para 8	Sch 13, para 8(4)
Proposed acquisition by nominee purchaser	Pt I, Ch I	s 38(2)
Proposed application, the	s 72	s 72(2)
Public sector landlord	Pt I, Ch I	s 38(1)
Purpose-built block of flats	s 10	s 10(6)
Qualified surveyor	s 13	s 13(7)
Qualified surveyor	s 78	s 78(5)
Qualifying disposal	s 135	s 135(1)
Qualifying property	s 31	s 31(2)
Qualifying tenant	Pt I, Ch I	s 5
Qualifying tenant	Pt I, Ch II	s 39(3)
Qualifying tenant	Pt I, Ch V	s 77(1)
Reference to claim being effective	Sch 3, Pt I	s 8(1)(c)
Reference to currency of claim	Sch 3, Pt I	s 8(1)(d), (2)
Reference to notice under s 11	Sch 3, Pt I	s 8(1)(b)
Relevant claim under Chapter I, the	ss 41, 54	ss 41(5), 54(11)
Relevant claim, the	s 12	s 12(6)
Relevant costs	s 28	s 28(7)
Relevant costs	s 29	s 29(8)
Relevant date, the	Pt I, Ch I	s 1(8)
Relevant date, the	Pt I, Ch II	s 39(8)
Relevant financial year	s 139	s 139(6)
Relevant inferior interest	Sch 6, para 17	Sch 6, para 17(3)
Relevant inferior interest	Sch 6, para 21	Sch 6, para 21(3)
Relevant interest	s 18	s 18(3)
Relevant interest	Sch 8	Sch 8, para 1
Relevant land, the	s 34	s 34(8)
Relevant land, the	Sch 20, para 15	Sch 20, para 15(6)
Relevant landlord	Pt I, Ch I	s 9
Relevant lease	s 36	s 36(3)
Relevant modifications	s 70	s 70(8)
Relevant notice of claim	Sch 3, Pt I	s 8(1)(a)
Relevant notice, the	Sch 2	Sch 2, para 1(1)
Relevant operations	s 159	s 159(2)
Relevant period	s 54	s 54(10)
Relevant period	s 136	s 136(2)

Defined term	Provisions affected	Place where defined
Successor	Sch 10, para 2	Sch 10, para 2(7)
Superior interest, the	Sch 6, para 16	Sch 6, para 16(3), (4)
Superior interest, the	Sch 6, para 17	Sch 6, para 17(1), (2)
Superior interest, the	Sch 6, para 20	Sch 6, para 20(3), (4)
Superior interest, the	Sch 6, para 21	Sch 6, para 21(1), (2)
Suspended contract, the	s 19	s 19(5)
Tenancy (and related expressions)	Pt I	s 101(1), (2)
Tenant	Pt I	s 101(2)
Tenant	Sch 11	s 40(4)(a)
Tenant	Pt I, Ch II	s 43(2)
Tenant	s 87	s 87(9)
Tenant's incumbrances	Sch 7, para 2	Sch 7, para 2(3)
Tenant's notice, the	Pt I, Ch II	s 42
Tenant's notice, the	s 74	s 74(2)
Term date, the	Pt I	ss 101(1), 102
Termination date, the	s 54	s 54(4)
Terms of acquisition, the	Pt I, Ch I	s 24(8)
Terms of acquisition, the	Pt I, Ch II	s 48(7)
Terms of acquisition, the	s 91	s 91(11)
Third party, the	Pt I, Ch II	s 62(1)
Third party, the	s 57	s 57(10)
Total share	s 7	s 7(7)
Traffic authority	s 173	s 173(3)
Unit	Pt I, Ch I	s 38(1)
Unit	Sch 9	Sch 9, para 1(2)
Urban development corporation	s 177	s 177(3)
Valuation date, the	Sch 6	Sch 6, para 1(1)
Valuation date, the	Sch 13	Sch 13, para 1
Valuation date, the	Sch 14, para 5	Sch 14, para 5(4)
Vesting order	Sch 5	Sch 5, para 1(1)
Vesting order under s 26(1)	s 27	s 27(1)
Vesting order under s 50(1)	s 51	s 51(1)
Wholly-owned subsidiary	s 161	s 161(7)

Index

Abbreviations used in the index are as follows:

HA   Housing Act
HSA   Housing (Scotland) Act
LRA   Leasehold Reform Act
SSE   Secretary of State for the Environment
URA   Urban Regeneration Agency

The term 'the 1993 Act' refers to the Leasehold Reform, Housing and Urban Development Act 1993